Inventing Ideas

Inventing Ideas

Patents, Prizes, and the Knowledge Economy

B. ZORINA KHAN

OXFORD
UNIVERSITY PRESS

OXFORD

UNIVERSITY PRESS

Oxford University Press is a department of the University of Oxford. It furthers
the University's objective of excellence in research, scholarship, and education
by publishing worldwide. Oxford is a registered trade mark of Oxford University
Press in the UK and certain other countries.

Published in the United States of America by Oxford University Press
198 Madison Avenue, New York, NY 10016, United States of America.

Library of Congress Cataloging-in-Publication Data
Names: Khan, B. Zorina, author.
Title: Inventing ideas : Patents, Prizes, and the Knowledge
Economy / Khan, B. Zorina, Department of Economics, Bowdoin College and
National Bureau of Economic Research.
Description: New York, NY : Oxford University Press, [2020] | Includes index.
Identifiers: LCCN 2019044713 (print) | LCCN 2019044714 (ebook) |
ISBN 9780190936075 (hardback) | ISBN 9780190936082 (paperback) |
ISBN 9780190936105 (epub) | ISBN 9780190936112 (online)
Subjects: LCSH: Creative ability. | Patents. |
Technological innovations—Awards. | Right of property.
Classification: LCC BF408 .K49 2020 (print) |
LCC BF408 (ebook) | DDC 153.3/5—dc23
LC record available at https://lccn.loc.gov/2019044713
LC ebook record available at https://lccn.loc.gov/2019044714

1 3 5 7 9 8 6 4 2

Paperback printed by Marquis, Canada
Hardback printed by Bridgeport National Bindery, Inc., United States of America

Contents

Tables and Figures

Tables

Figures

Acknowledgments

Like financial obligations, intellectual debts become all the more overwhelming if one defers them over time. After a decade spent in different institutions, different regions, and different countries, I can vividly empathize with the owners of an underwater mortgage. It is impossible to fully credit all of the generous colleagues, students, archivists, and support staff who have aided in this project, and who embody and demonstrate the best advantages of the non-market-oriented system that is academia. Liability for any claims is, of course, limited to the author.

The life of the academic, I have often thought, is analogous to that of a medieval troubadour, who wandered from croft to castle, entertaining and educating the populace, in return for shelter and a place at the table (and no doubt being equally harassed by the bureaucratic complexities of the reimbursement system). It would exhaust my publisher's strict quota on page length to enumerate the dozens of seminars and workshops where different parts of this manuscript were presented or to itemize all of the attendees whose valuable remarks improved the final output. The short list includes Ran Abramitzky, Marcella Alsan, Michael Andrews, Ashish Arora, Jeremy Atack, Pierre Azoulay, Christopher Beauchamp, James Bessen, Dan Bogart, Kevin Bryan, Lee Branstetter, Dan Burk, Diane Burton, Latika Chaudhary, Wesley Cohen, Robert Cooter, Robert Cull, Harold Demsetz, Rochelle Dreyfuss, John Duffy, Richard Epstein, Joseph Ferrie, Alexander Field, Louis Galambos, Alberto Galasso, Alexander Galetovic, Nancy Gallini, Claudia Goldin, Robert Gordon, Wendy Gordon, Stuart Graham, Avner Greif, Kirti Gupta, Stephen Haber, Walker Hanlon, Wes Hartmann, Paul Heald, Deepak Hegde, Philip Hoffman, Adam Jaffe, William Janeway, Jay Kesan, Karim Lakhani, Mark Lemley, Josh Lerner, David Levine, Ross Levine, Keith Maskus, Robert Merges, Michael Meurer, David Mitch, Joel Mokyr, Petra Moser, Adam Mossoff, Neil Netanel, Tom Nicholas, Alan Olmstead, Lisa Ouellette, Yi Qian, James Robinson, Christina Romer, Jean-Laurent Rosenthal, Bhaven Sampat, Frederick Scherer, Mark Schultz, Gonca Senel, Ted Sichelman, Henry Smith, Richard Sousa, Christopher Sprigman, Daniel Spulber, Manuel Tratjenberg, Steven Wilf, Heidi Williams, Brian Wright, Gavin Wright, Joshua Wright, Arvid Ziedonis, and Rosemary Ziedonis.

Today, as in the past, the European administered system makes the generous assistance of insiders invaluable. I spent the 2014–2015 academic year at the London School of Economics, which offered not only a front row seat for the

Brexit initiative but also the rare opportunity to benefit from an entire department dedicated to economic history. I have been exceptionally fortunate to obtain insights from such outstanding colleagues as Robert Allen, Sean Bottomley, Stephen Broadberry, Kristine Bruland, Carsten Burhop, Neil Cummins, Christiane Demeulenaere, Claude Diebolt, Gerard Emptoz, Giovanni Federico, Dominique Foray, Gabriel Galvez-Behar, Leigh Gardner, Graeme Gooday, Leslie Hannah, Liliane Hilaire-Pérez, Per Hjertstrand, Terence Kealey, Alice Kuegler, Debin Ma, Christine MacLeod, Alessandro Nuvolari, Patrick O'Brien, Cormac O'Grada, Mary O'Sullivan, Lars Persson, Gilles Postel-Vinay, Erik Prawitz, Albrecht Ritschl, Patricio Sáiz, Mohamed Saleh, Max Schulze, Leigh Shaw-Taylor, Jochen Streb, Ruth Towse, Felipe Valencia, Stephen van Dulken, Michelangelo Vasta, and Richard Watt, among others.

This book would not have been possible without the contributions of numerous archivists and research librarians, especially those at the Royal Society of Arts in London, U.S. National Archives, U.S. Patent Office, San Francisco Mechanics' Institute, Franklin Institute, Société d'encouragement pour l'industrie nationale, Conservatoire national des arts et métiers, Institut national de la propriété intellectuelle, Bibliotheque nationale de France, Archives nationales de France, Archives de Paris, British Library, and National Archives of the United Kingdom, as well as the libraries of Bowdoin College, University of California (Berkeley and UCLA), Harvard, LSE, Stanford, Boston Public Library, and New York Public Library. Moreover, some of the material in these chapters was published as journal articles and in edited volumes, and I am grateful to the academic publishers who gave permission for their use in this book. Special thanks are due for the efficiency and insights of the editors and assistants at Oxford University Press.

This overall project was made possible by generous funding from the National Science Foundation and from Bowdoin College, over the decade during which the research was completed. Alison Oaxaca of the National Bureau of Economic Research was exceptionally capable and caring throughout the grant management process. A particularly beneficial year at the Hoover Institution of Stanford University was funded by a Hoover National Fellowship. Other awards include the Arch W. Shaw Fellowship, Fletcher Research Award, Engelberg Fellowship, Leonardo da Vinci Fellowship, and Kenan Fellowship. At Bowdoin College, I am indebted to Ginny Hopcroft, Barbara Levergood, Carr Ross, Guy Saldanha, and Elizabeth Weston. During this period, numerous undergraduate research assistants dedicated their rare Maine summers to digitizing all of these data sources, and I cannot thank them enough for their enthusiasm, meticulous care, and proprietary interest in the project.

Among all these exceptional friends and colleagues, three individuals have played a central role as inspiring, altruistic mentors who gave their time and attention without counting the costs in terms of the next best alternative sacrificed. Stanley Engerman's generosity dates back to our meeting in my first year as a graduate student at UCLA, and his repeated requests to send him my manuscripts for detailed comments have not ceased since that day. Naomi Lamoreaux is no doubt a little dismayed by how well I recall her observations from decades ago, but it is a measure of the extent to which I have benefited from her insights about research and "life, the universe and everything." And, it goes without saying, not a day goes by without my thinking about Kenneth Sokoloff (1952–2007) with unending regard and gratitude, and benefiting from his unparalleled example; the best compliment of all would be to know that his continued influence can be detected in these pages.

It is customary to conclude with recognition of the encouragement and support of one's family, who share good times and bad times and make both better. But my obligation to my two sisters is much more significant. Sherry helped with the digitization of the data for extended periods. Esther carefully scrutinized every single sentence and footnote in this book manuscript and ruthlessly eliminated econospeak, and her detailed discussions and insightful critical comments significantly improved the style and content of the final work. This book is therefore dedicated to my sisters, Sherry Richardson and Esther Khan.

1

Introduction

Knowledge, Institutions, and Economic Progress

A page of history is worth a volume of logic.

—Oliver Wendell Holmes (1921)

Economists, regardless of their orientation, are part of a quest to understand the wealth and poverty of nations, and few would dispute that technological change is one of the most significant determinants of societal development. Technology dominates all facets of modern life from corporate enterprise to popular culture. The celebrated opening sequence from the movie *2001: A Space Odyssey* offers a "striking" metaphor for technological progress. A group of primates are engaged in battle, and the victor wields a heavy bone as a weapon to vanquish his opponent. He tosses the bone in the air in triumph, and the jump shot follows its transformation into a modern spaceship. This director's cut of technological advances suggests a continuous transition from the simple manipulation of natural resources to the complex combinations of digital inputs that allow poor farmers with cell phones in remote areas to tap into international grain markets.

However, in New England we do not have to reverse that tracking shot and travel back in time to acquire insights into the world that technology has wrought. Maine in particular endures harsh winters, with frequent snow and ice storms that can down power lines for days or even weeks. When the electricity goes off grid, and cell phones or computers cannot be recharged, we rapidly return to a premodern world. Life is reduced to the primal dilemmas of keeping warm, finding food, and ensuring that the water runs through frozen pipes. Of course, compensatory benefits include a keener appreciation of human interactions unfiltered by distracting or divisive technologies. These wintry storms offer a sobering seasonal reminder that progress is not destiny, and material gains can be reversed as rapidly as they were attained.

Indeed, for much of human experience, the struggle for subsistence and biological replication was accomplished with little leeway for productivity advances or improvements in the quality of life. A time series chart of economic gains per person over the millennia would be indistinguishable from a flatline of "secular stagnation." An era of modest advances initiated in eighteenth-century Europe

Inventing Ideas. B. Zorina Khan, Oxford University Press (2020). © Oxford University Press.
DOI: 10.1093/oso/9780190936075.001.0001

Figure 1.1 Patentees of Progress
The celebrated American inventors in this painting are all patentees, depicted as if they were convened in the U.S. Patent Office building.
Source: *Men of Progress*, by Christian Schussele, 1862. Image provided courtesy of National Portrait Gallery, Smithsonian Institution.

led to gains that have been (contentiously) touted as an industrial revolution in Britain.[1] With greater certainty, we can identify a "second industrial revolution" in the extraordinary arc of sustained growth and technological creativity that began in the United States in the second half of the nineteenth century and heralded the modern knowledge economy. The past two centuries have therefore been unique in world history, and a crucial charge for scholars is to identify the drivers of this exponential surge that has enormously enriched some countries, and the reasons for divergent outcomes in others. The answers are vital for our perspective about the future, leading to a parallel intellectual divergence between the optimists and pessimists, who gloomily predict the demise of economic growth even in wealthy countries like the United States.[2]

Much of the scholarly attention has been directed to the first triumph over subsistence and the start of modern economic growth in Northern Europe. Candidate explanations for European advances range from the specific (deposits of coal, relative wages, demographics, even genetics), to the political (civil wars,

---

[1] For coverage of the debates and contentions, see Mokyr (2018).
[2] Gordon (2017).

subjugation and exploitation of colonial empires, kings, and constitutions), to the general (cultural values, psychology, and the scientific enlightenment). A number of popular accounts propose that differential outcomes today are related to fixed factors or persistent and slowly evolving long-run processes. Jared Diamond attributed thirteen thousand years of social development to geography and the disease environment, a thesis that echoes the writings of the French philosopher Charles-Louis de Secondat (Montesquieu).[3] Philip Hoffman argues that the course of two millennia of economic changes owed to military prowess and gunpowder technology, because elites had an incentive to engage in conflicts from which they benefited, while ensuring that the costs were borne by the masses.[4]

Historical debates about why Britain was the first industrial nation also contrast the differential economic experience in Europe and China.[5] As visitors to the Asia wing in major museums appreciate, that region made lasting contributions to cultural, organizational, and technological innovations, and its achievements equaled those of its Western counterparts at least through 1500. The early Chinese empire was spatially integrated, and the scale of the market allowed for specialization and the division of labor, rural handicraft and manufacturing activities, and flourishing long-distance trading networks. China then experienced an extended era of divergence and stasis (or even decline) from 1800 to 1950. The timing and causes for this retreat from innovation and growth remain disputed. China lost ground and failed to industrialize along European lines for reasons variously identified as cultural, serendipitous lack of access to crucial natural resources, differences in relative prices for inputs, legal institutions, and a lack of political competition. An important contributory factor was a centralized elitist system that ultimately protected its own vested interests at the expense of technological progress and benefits for the masses.[6]

Some of the most captivating (and contentious) narratives about why nations succeed or fail point to the importance of appropriate institutions. Daron Acemoglu and Jim Robinson's magisterial work draws on insights from the Roman empire, medieval Venice, Latin America, Europe, Tunisia, and the U.S. town of Nogales in Arizona to make a compelling case that politics and inclusive political institutions that aligned with notions of distributive justice were responsible for national prosperity.[7] They further highlight the specific role that "state infrastructural capacity" played in providing the conditions that were favorable for the creation of important technological advances in the

---

[3] Diamond (1998).
[4] Hoffman (2015).
[5] These issues are admirably covered in Rosenthal and Bin Wong (2011).
[6] Brandt et al. (2014).
[7] Acemoglu and Robinson (2013).

nineteenth-century United States.[8] Outcomes in the twenty-first century, according to this thesis, can be explained by the persistence of centuries-old political arrangements, which have determined the distribution of power and wealth, and thus the potential for efficiency and growth.

Avner Greif offers a timely reminder that institutions are more complex than simple rule-making structures, examining patterns of medieval trade to show that economic modernity was related to the rise of decentralized merchant guilds and self-governed institutions, rather than the state and collective action.[9] Another important strand of this literature on the state and innovation demonstrates how societies fail to achieve their full potential when rent-seeking coalitions monopolize and limit access to the political and economic system. Rewards that are bestowed on rent-seekers rather than entrepreneurs typically result in a misallocation of talent that can lead to economic stagnation or decline.[10] William Baumol concluded that a major determinant of a nation's economic capacity is the incentive structure that governs and directs entrepreneurial efforts between "productive" and "unproductive" endeavors. He speculated that the misallocation of entrepreneurial efforts, which occurs when unproductive activities receive disproportionate returns, could have a lasting effect on patterns of innovation and on the diffusion of technological information.[11] By contrast, a number of popular accounts are more vociferous about the necessity for intervention by an "entrepreneurial state."[12]

Stanley Engerman and Kenneth Sokoloff amassed an impressive amount of comparative evidence to assess why areas that were initially rich fell behind the North American region. They meticulously trace the ways in which factor endowments (broadly defined to incorporate climate, soils, and natural resources) influenced growth paths, through their effects on inequality and institutional development. In unequal societies, elites maintained their power and redistributed wealth to their own advantage, channeled through self-serving rules about suffrage, access to education, political economic policies, and financial organizations.[13] Engerman and Sokoloff reject the "axiom of indispensability," or the notion that any one specific institution is necessary for growth, because there is substantial variation in the degree of substitutability across different rules and standards. These scholars conclude that a central feature of productive social arrangements lies in whether institutions are sufficiently flexible and responsive to changing circumstances.

---

[8] Acemoglu et al. (2016).
[9] Greif (2006).
[10] Acemoglu (1995); Murphy et al. (1991).
[11] Baumol (1990).
[12] Mazzucato (2015).
[13] Engerman and Sokoloff (2005).

Over the past three decades, Joel Mokyr has produced close to a dozen thought-provoking monographs that directly address the nature of technological change and economic growth, from *The Lever of Riches* (1990) to the *Culture of Growth* (2016). The scope of coverage spans a dizzying number of centuries and societies, but the focus is squarely on Europe, because of the "fundamental unity of the Western world, transcending the superficial differences in national style."[14] This rich tapestry of historical and intellectual insights illustrates the thesis that the modern knowledge economy has its origins in the cultural attitudes and preferences of the European "industrial enlightenment." A forum for ideas flourished during this period, where reputation, rather than expected financial gains, was the most valued currency. Elites and institutions such as the Royal Society of Arts (RSA) helped to lower the costs of access to knowledge and created incentives for productive inventions. A unifying theme across the decades in this body of work is that useful ideas are in scarce supply or exogenous "gifts of Athena," and this scarcity points to the central role of exclusive institutions and great men ("cultural entrepreneurs" like Francis Bacon), great inventions ("macroinventions"), and scientific theories and techniques originating among a small select group of enlightened intellectuals.

Such questions are at the heart of more formal mathematical models of macroeconomists investigating "why the whole world isn't rich," which differ in their treatment of ideas, knowledge, and technology. According to the standard neoclassical models, growth depends on exogenous (external and unexplained) shocks to technology and accumulations in physical capital. Augmented exogenous growth models highlight the role of different sorts of human capital in achieving desired levels of knowledge and technology. Some of these studies are not as concerned about knowledge creation, because of their conviction that poor countries can free ride off the investments of the richer countries.[15]

By contrast, Paul Romer, in a series of influential papers, "endogenized" or tried to explain what determines variation in new ideas.[16] The Nobel Prize in Economic Sciences for 2018 was awarded to Romer and William Nordhaus "for integrating technological innovations into long-run macroeconomic analysis." The committee noted that their research "significantly broadened the scope of economic analysis by constructing models that explain how the market economy interacts with nature and knowledge."[17] Other endogenous growth theorists have similarly explored how institutions and incentives influence innovation and technological progress. However, for many macroeconomists, this "new

---

[14] Mokyr (2002).
[15] Parente and Prescott (2002).
[16] For a sample of these works, see Romer (1990, 1994) and Aghion et al. (1998).
[17] See http://www.nobelprize.org.

growth theory" still remains unpersuasive owing to the mathematical properties of the models and the lack of empirical backing for its predictions. As a result, theoretical macroeconomics seems to have diverged into separate camps, with little prospect for convergence to a consensus about sources of the wealth of nations, unified only by a Platonic perspective that real-world complexities distract from true insights.

In sum, the economic literature on the transformation of human civilization in the very long run offers valuable clues to help resolve the puzzle of the marked variation in material progress that is evident across countries historically, as well as in the twenty-first century. Some of the most stimulating scholarship in economic history has focused on speculations about the European experience, and the answers to the specific question of "Why Britain?" That is, a plethora of publications have examined why the first Industrial Revolution occurred in Britain, and why other European and Asian countries failed to attain equivalent achievements in industrialization and self-sustaining growth. Many economic historians derive lessons of global significance from the "great divergence" of the late eighteenth century, when Britain became the world's foremost industrial economy, and they identify European experiences during that era as the genesis of today's knowledge economy. Despite the importance of such issues, and the extensive scholarly attention, as Joel Mokyr points out, we still "know remarkably little about the kind of institutions that foster and stimulate technological progress and more widely, intellectual innovation."[18]

Inventing Ideas

What contributions does this book make to these debates? The research reported in these chapters bridges the gap between the economics of technological innovation and the analysis of institutions. The current literature reveals a need to empirically identify the institutional sources of technological progress in the modern knowledge economy. To do so, a comparative approach with variation across time and place is required, yet the approach must be conceptualized in a manner that is amenable to empirical testing. Although developments in grand civilizations across the millennia are thought-provoking and informative, it is obviously difficult to control for all relevant factors. Changes in any number of unobservable characteristics might explain key differences, which implies that many of the resulting conclusions must remain largely speculative. As such, I do not attempt to explain the origins of institutions, and instead choose to

---

[18] Mokyr (2016: 6).

analyze the specific economic consequences of variation in institutional rules and standards for individual behavior and technological change.[19]

The countries featured in this study—France, Britain, and the United States— have sequentially dominated the realms of technology and scientific learning over the past four centuries. France was an acknowledged early pioneer in science and technological innovation. England borrowed ideas and techniques from its Continental neighbors and combined favorable resource endowments with domestic ingenuity to become the first industrial nation. However, scholarly assessments that confine themselves to intellectual leveraging of the European experience risk faulty conclusions about the types of knowledge that mattered, about the sorts of individuals who create valuable ideas, about the nature of innovation institutions and incentives, and about their consequences for the present and future wealth of nations.

The story of early modern Britain is compelling, because the first Industrial Revolution allowed for an escape from subsistence and diminishing returns, but the term has been justly derided because economic advances were modest rather than revolutionary. Productivity was concentrated in a few sectors, and economic growth was unbalanced and often owed to extensive additions to resources rather than greater efficiency. And, of course, the British technological and industrial lead proved to be transient. The true revolution in knowledge and industry started in the nineteenth century on a different continent, when the U.S. economy alchemized ideas and inputs to produce an unprecedented and precipitous increase in wealth, consumption, and technical efficiency that spilled over to transform the lives of the general population. As such, if we wish to identify the most relevant sources of modern economic growth, it is necessary to evaluate why *this* time and *this* place led to outcomes that were so remarkably different from the rest of human history.

This book therefore shifts the focus of the debate about the technological foundations of growth to consider "Why America?" How did the United States overtake Europe to become the world's technological and industrial leader, and why was it able to sustain this dominance into the twenty-first century? The twentieth century has popularly been regarded as "the American century," but the foundations for the future were evident since the early Republic. All societies realized that ideas were essential for the attainment of their object- ives, but there was no consensus on the goals, the means, or who should have

---

[19] Technological change spans a sequence of discoveries from the initial conception of a new idea through its invention and improvement (reduction to practical use), innovation (initial commercialization), adoption, and diffusion. Casual discussion tends to incorporate all of these elements into the catch-all term of "innovation." These distinctions matter for measurement and analysis, especially for understanding patented inventions and prize innovations. I have continued this conflation for rhetorical reasons but, when relevant, will specify which particular aspect is being discussed.

access to knowledge, and this measurable variation is valuable for identifying the determinants of technological change and social progress. U.S. incentives for innovation were strikingly different from those in Europe, and this institutional divergence influenced the extraordinary trajectory of this relatively undistinguished colonial outpost that would surge to the forefront of the global economy.[20]

A second contribution of this research project consists of a novel conceptual framework that allows us to bridge the current disconnect between institutional economics and the empirical analysis of technological innovation. Generally, economists regard institutions as the rules and standards that govern human behavior, and the specific design of innovation institutions creates incentives for economic and inventive activity. Institutions are pivotal for economic outcomes, but their complexity has challenged scholars who wish to more precisely gauge their nature and consequences. There is a marked need for systematic empirical research to examine the links between specific rules and standards and innovation, especially in terms of international comparisons of technology policies over the long run. The empirical gap is especially evident in research that addresses the role of such "meta-institutions" as the state in shaping innovation.[21] As a result, many influential studies rely on potentially biased or unrepresentative case studies and qualitative generalizations. This book offers a conceptual and empirical solution to this dilemma, by distinguishing between markets for ideas (discussed later) and administered innovation systems.

Administered systems refer to arrangements where economic decisions about rewards, prices, values, and the allocation of resources are made by administrators or panels. Administered innovation systems range along a spectrum from centralized (state agencies) through decentralized (independent prize-granting bodies) institutions. Decision-making in such institutions often lacks transparency, internal control mechanisms are weak, and there are typically few feedback mechanisms or incentives for adjustments in response to incorrect choices or external changes. Administrators are not subject to a right of appeal from their judgments and typically do not directly bear the consequences of their choices. Stakeholders in such organizations have an interest in publicly projecting overly optimistic assessments of their activities, without adequately acknowledging failures and inefficiencies. I propose to show that decentralized administered institutions are empirically tractable, and their systematic analysis

---

[20] I would like to emphasize that this focus on incentives vested in institutions is intended to complement, rather than replace, other noninstitutional explanations. Moreover, as an empirical microeconomist, I do not propose to speculate about the sources of these national differences.

[21] Studies of state activity to promote technological innovation encounter the problem where so many variables are changing and cannot be controlled for that it is virtually impossible to isolate individual effects.

helps to shed light on empirically-intractable centralized institutions such as the "entrepreneurial state." This approach offers the reader an objective quantitative context for assessing subjective qualitative accounts and case studies that currently prevail in policy discussions.

Conventional economic thinking aligns well with European convictions about the sources of industrial and technical progress but overlooks the dramatic differences in the new approach to growth that were manifested in early U.S. policies. Economic models have an imagined counterfactual standard of comparison to "optimal outcomes" and perfectly competitive markets, which has distracted from the clues that history offers.[22] Their focus tends to underestimate the gains that accrue from improvements that are "just" better than what exists, rather than the best relative to some imagined optimum. The standard analysis of patents, for instance, assumes static inefficiencies from a monopoly grant that harms customers (through "deadweight losses" of higher prices and lower output). These economists assert a greater efficiency of alternative measures such as innovation prizes, which are assumed by default to avoid this loss. Growth models tout the benefits of elites, costly investments in scarce supply factors, and knowledge in the upper tails of the distribution. By contrast, American economic and legal institutions rejected such thinking, and until this is acknowledged and integrated in our analysis, understanding of growth will remain elusive.

Third, *Inventing Ideas* presents an empirical micro-foundation for broader questions about macroeconomic growth processes. As Robert Solow remarked, the growth literature would benefit from more reliable evidence and attention to real-world complexities, since "models of innovation can be constructed out of thin air, but it is surely better to use more durable materials if they are available."[23] Books and articles about economic growth typically make inferences from aggregates at the level of industries, sectors, or sweeping generalizations across countries and cultures. It is useful to remind ourselves that history happens because relatively ordinary individuals make choices and decisions and creatively respond to incentives and constraints. Uniquely, the ideas in this book are grounded in detailed inquiries into the lives and contributions of over one hundred thousand men and women inventors and innovators in Britain, France, and the United States, during the first and second Industrial Revolutions. These original and richly detailed datasets about creative individuals are combined with information about administrators, panels, judges, and other participants and outcomes across different institutions.

---

[22] As Petrarch noted, "Nihil sapientiae odiosius acumine nimio" (nothing is more inimical to understanding than extreme cleverness).

[23] Solow (1994).

Together, they offer consistent individual-level evidence about international and domestic markets in inventive ideas, the way administered systems worked in practice, what sorts of inventions and inventors were likely to emerge as winners or losers from different institutional arrangements, and how alternative approaches affected overall patterns of technological change. Engerman and Sokoloff emphasized that the primary challenge of "new institutional economics" in explaining growth is to devise better means of empirically investigating the relevant mechanisms, and this comprehensive array of new data helps to meet that challenge. The uncovered statistical patterns themselves are a valuable contribution, even if the reader ultimately is unpersuaded that this pointillist method offers a more reliable set of lessons about long-run growth processes.

This comprehensive research project has extended over a decade, and the novel findings shed light on central questions in economics and economic history. They also clarify current debates about the role of ideas and elites in economic development, the efficacy of grand innovation prizes, the function of patent intermediaries ("trolls") and markets in invention, and the costs and benefits of government involvement in science and technology initiatives. The overall empirical patterns further allow us to reliably identify key continuities and discontinuities in the past relative to today's knowledge economy, which differ in important dimensions from the consensus views drawn from early European policies. Ultimately, American institutions and policies rejected the European perspective that attributed progress to the efforts of elites and esoteric knowledge, owing to a fundamental belief in the cumulative effects of the creative ideas of diverse ordinary individuals. As such, analysis of these extensive micro-level data ironically promises to lead to more reliable insights into broad macro-economic processes of economic growth. They suggest that, when institutions are associated with rewards that are misaligned with economic value and productivity, the negative consequences can accumulate and reduce comparative advantage at the level of enterprises and nations alike.

Knowledge and (Alleged) Market Failure

The answers to "the elusive quest for growth" are closely related to the transformation of knowledge and ideas into social and economic goods, and the distribution of the accruing costs and benefits.[24] Debates about the role of knowledge, and questions about who should be allowed access and control over ideas, have been at the forefront of political economy, literature, and philosophy for much

---

[24] The phrase belongs to Easterly (2001).

of recorded history. In Plato's *Republic*, learning and arcane knowledge were limited to an elite governing class, who needed to keep themselves aloof from practical pursuits for fear that participation in the mundane might inhibit their intellectual capacity. Max Weber's monumental work on *Economy and Society* similarly identified control over knowledge as the defining characteristic of bureaucratic administrators, whose power was derived from "domination through knowledge," funneled through ideas vested in specialized technical information.[25] Herman Hesse's finest work, *Magister Ludi*, depicted a society of elite intellectuals in the mythical realm of Castalia who avoided technological and economic pursuits to immerse themselves in an esoteric glass bead game that synthesized all of human knowledge.

The "new philosophy" underlying the discoveries of the scientific revolution in the seventeenth century was new mainly in the sense of a specific awareness of human capacity for molding material progress; but its adherents echoed Plato in the expectation of the identities of the individuals who would make useful contributions to the stock of new ideas. The pre-Enlightenment intellectual Robert Hooke (an experimental scientist, born in 1635, and often regarded as "England's Leonardo") noted in a proposal to the Royal Society that truly productive insights were only to be attained by a small and select "army" of thinkers. Such elite groups, Sir Henry Sumner Maine declared, were also to be credited for important technological discoveries: "All that has made England famous, and all that has made England wealthy, has been the work of minorities, sometimes very small ones. It seems to me quite certain that, if for four centuries there had been a very widely extended franchise . . . the threshing machine, the power loom, the spinning jenny, and possibly the steam-engine, would have been prohibited."[26] These convictions about the sources of useful knowledge were replicated in most European nations and were deeply embedded in their institutions and policies.

Societies that regarded knowledge as the province of a special class, and as a means of social control, were unlikely to create open institutions that would offer equal opportunity for all ideas or all groups in society. Scientists in England or France or Italy certainly shared their ideas with others whom they regarded as their peers. At the same time, the so-called Republic of Letters was something of a misnomer for an exclusive Aristocracy of Letters. As Oliver Goldsmith noted: "The Republic of Letters, is a very common expression among the Europeans and yet, when applied to the learned of Europe, is the most absurd that can be imagined, since nothing is more unlike a republic than the society which goes by that name."[27] European knowledge-elites treated the less eminent

---

[25] Weber (1978: 225).
[26] Maine (1885: 98).
[27] Goldsmith (1834: 269).

with disdain and despised practitioners who were "merely" versed in applied knowledge and practical pursuits. Despite the declared reverence for useful knowledge in the Royal Society, founding member John Evelyn scorned the notion of working on engravings and practical projects because he would be forced to interact with "mechanical and capricious persons." According to this group of alleged republicans, "the mysteries of the universe were beyond the capacities of the vulgar."[28]

Karl Popper regarded Plato as one of the enemies of the "open society," because "if our civilisation is to survive, we must break with the habit of deference to great men" and avoid their initially well-meaning efforts at utopian social engineering that tended to be subverted into mechanisms for the suppression of different or disadvantaged groups.[29] But quite apart from the political aspects of such theories of the knowledge society, the attribution of technological and scientific progress to elites or privileged groups had important economic consequences. In particular, these assumptions influenced policies and incentives that were designed to encourage creativity and promote technological progress. The chapters in this book will examine the effectiveness of institutions that incorporated "the habit of deference to great men," relative to more democratic institutions that celebrated diversity and disruption, and offered incentives to everyone in the population. The specific rules and standards, and their changes over time, were mirrored in patterns of inventive output, productivity, and the capacity for sustained economic advance.

In the United States, the Society for Promoting Useful Knowledge merged with the American Philosophical Society in 1797, and Thomas Jefferson was appointed to the presidency of this conjoined organization the day before he was elected national vice president. Jefferson would certainly have been inducted into Robert Hooke's elite army, as he maintained a vivid curiosity about scientific research and continually exchanged ideas with individual inventors and other societies for the diffusion of knowledge. In a famous letter to Isaac McPherson, he highlighted a key characteristic of ideas and knowledge: "He who receives an idea from me, receives instruction himself without lessening mine; as he who lights his taper at mine, receives light without darkening mine."[30]

Kenneth Arrow, the celebrated economic theorist, formalized this insight about knowledge as a "public good" that is nonrival (consumption by one party does not diminish the amount available for others) and nonexclusive (nonpayers are able to benefit from unauthorized use).[31] If so, inventors might find it difficult

---

[28] Eamon (2006: 223).
[29] Popper (2013: xxxvii).
[30] Washington (1853–1854: 180).
[31] Arrow (1962).

to charge a positive price and secure benefits from their discoveries, leading to the underproduction of knowledge and research, and market failure. If knowledge markets are indeed likely to fail, the standard economic approach suggests a need for state intervention or directed management to prevent the resulting disincentives and misallocation of resources. Government policies include a portfolio of measures such as public provision and oversight, procurement arrangements, grants, subsidies, and credits, along with general taxation to fund or provide the good.

Market failure can also be resolved by finding ways to make markets work better, through strategies that enable creators to receive some form of compensation, and methods to exclude nonpayers. Patents and copyrights with enforcement by the legal system transform the public good into private property in ideas and expression, which can be exchanged in the marketplace through the price mechanism. Alternatively, private solutions to the public good problem of nonexclusivity extend to bilateral or multilateral contracts, retaliatory sanctions within cartels and collectives, and technological barriers such as paywalls and encryption, among others. Inventors and other creative individuals can employ a plethora of appropriation mechanisms such as patronage, tying their ideas to a complementary good that can be sold, pursuing prize awards, crowdsourcing, better job opportunities, and enhanced reputations.

Economists often refer to "knowledge" as if the term covers a homogeneous good. Knowledge, however, is not uniform, and it is important to specify the particular facets that are relevant to the analysis in question. At the most simplistic level, discoveries that are made in a foreign language are effectively exclusive to nonspeakers. George Stigler, for instance, noted that the brilliant work of Léon Walras was ignored in the world of economics until long after his death, owing to his "use of his mother tongue, French, and his depressing array of mathematical formulas."[32] Ideas and information can be effectively rival for creators if their success in the market depends on novelty and on being first, such as academic publications in peer-reviewed journals, a line-up of comedians telling jokes in a club (where success depends on a negative answer to "have you heard the one about . . . ?"), or an investigative journalist with breaking news. Rather than being underproduced, knowledge can be overproduced if inventors or authors are able to "stack" or accumulate rewards from multiple sources for the same discovery.

One of the key features of private property rules is that exchange is consensual and occurs at a price that reflects the subjective valuations of the buyer and seller. According to some, economic markets fail if the creators of knowledge respond to nonfinancial incentives, such as enhanced reputation and better job prospects,

---

[32] Stigler (1994: 228).

as often occurs in the case of open source innovations—or academia for that matter. However, market analysis is still relevant even if information and ideas are consensually shared at a zero monetary price in return for nonpecuniary benefits in terms of utility, valued amenities, or higher future expected income. In the same manner, a firm might choose not to exclude rivals from its invention even if its market share falls as a result, if nonexclusion creates scale effects that increase the company's overall returns. Network effects can create similar incentives for nonprice exchanges owing to greater complementarity among a larger stock of ideas.

On the other hand, "open access" systems are not necessarily nonexclusive and free to all comers. Ostensibly open institutions for knowledge and ideas may include natural and imposed barriers to entry that can function as a means of exclusion. For instance, the human genome database is freely available online, yet very few in the population are able to usefully extract information from this resource. The more specialized the knowledge that is required to contribute to new inventions, the more exclusive the information is likely to be, with a subsequent fall in the likelihood of unauthorized infringement, other things being equal. When Shinichi Mochizuki allegedly solved the "ABC conjecture" in number theory, his work was so abstruse that even fellow mathematicians in his field could not determine its validity. This natural barrier is heightened when tacit knowledge and learning on the job is an important requirement for participation and innovation. Much tends to be made about the potential for outsiders to disrupt industries with novel approaches. My own research on "great inventors" showed that insiders were more likely to make technological discoveries related to bottlenecks in the industry in which they were employed, relative to outsiders to the industry who were effectively excluded from knowledge acquired through learning by doing. A discovery can sometimes be made private simply by shutting the doors to one's factory, as is the case with trade secrets.

The claim of market failure in knowledge provision and exchange can also be challenged in the context of certain types of knowledge, involving "contribution goods" that are nonrival but also excludable.[33] Such goods are characterized by an asymmetry between contributors and noncontributors to a research agenda, because researchers must possess similar levels of cognitive skills and tacit knowledge to benefit from the commons. This asymmetry implies that the costs of copying and commercialization will be higher for noncontributing "outsiders" relative to insiders. Advances in some contribution goods require coordination among potential contributors and depend on the coalescing of a critical mass, or a "visible college." Collaborations and free sharing of knowledge occur in part

---

[33] This paragraph is based on the ideas of Kealey and Ricketts (2014).

through self-interest because they allow participants to gain access to scarcer tacit knowledge. Contribution goods raise questions about the efficacy of policies such as compulsory patent licenses, suggesting that laggards in technological knowledge and countries that fail to invest in know-how or research facilities cannot benefit simply by exercising eminent domain powers over patent rights. This is especially true in the absence of supporting institutions to commercialize and adapt the discovery to suit domestic factor endowments and local market conditions.

When markets are alleged to fail, a fundamental question is, what is the standard of comparison or the viable counterfactual? In economic models, the comparison is generally between a patent monopolist who does not price discriminate and an artificial construct of perfect competition in the market for the existing new invention. That is, the conventional assumption is that the discovery has already been made, and the relevant choice is between allowing exclusive rights to inventors for their own ideas or free access by the public to the inventor's discovery. Nineteenth-century American jurists and legislators, however, regarded this benchmark as unjustifiable, arguing that the relevant counterfactual was a world in which the inventor had not made the discovery.[34] Many new inventions dramatically lowered the production costs and prices, increased output, and even conjured a cornucopia of entirely new products and markets that previous generations could not even have imagined. If prices for a new discovery were higher than for the older substitute, consumers were still free to purchase the cheaper alternative if they wished.[35] Thus, a patent had nothing in common with monopoly, and any supposedly "excess" profits simply reflected the just return to inventive genius. Indeed, far from being odious monopolists who reduced social welfare, patentees were regarded as public benefactors whose efforts and contributions should be universally celebrated. According to

[34] "A monopolist is one who, by the exercise of the sovereign power, takes from the public that which belongs to it, and gives to the grantee and his assigns an exclusive use. On this ground monopolies are justly odious. . . . Under the patent law this can never be done. No exclusive right can be granted for anything which the patentee has not invented or discovered. If he claim anything which was before known, his patent is void, so that the law repudiates a monopoly. The right of the patentee entirely rests on his invention or discovery of that which is useful, and which was not known before. And the law gives him the exclusive use of the thing invented or discovered, for a few years, as a compensation for 'his ingenuity, labor, and expense in producing it.' This, then, in no sense partakes of the character of monopoly." *Allen v. Hunter*, 6 McLean 303 (McLean 1855). "Probably of all species of property, this property in patent rights should be most carefully guarded and protected, because it is so easily assailed. . . . Now, patents are not monopolies . . . a patent is that which brings out from the realm of the mind something that never existed before, and gives it to the country." *Singer v. Walmsley*, 1 Fisher 558 (Md. 1859).

[35] "As to the pretext, that grants of exclusive property . . . tend to enhance the price of the newly-invented manufactures; it may be answered that, as such grants do not compel any one to purchase these new manufactures, the public are left at liberty, at the lower price, to encourage the old: and this they will certainly do, neglecting the new, if their superiority of merit be not adequate to the advance of price." Kenrick, An Address to the Artists and Manufacturers of Great Britain (1774), p. 52.

this perspective, property rights for new inventions were a necessary precondition for effective markets in ideas, rather than a source of monopoly and market failure.

In short, the nature and consequences of market failure in the realm of ideas and technological discoveries is much exaggerated. Both the history and economic theory of technology still remain works in progress and require more attention to variation in the incentives that motivate creative individuals through the market mechanism and through administered systems. This suggests a need to revisit how economics helps to explicate the characteristics of markets and administered innovation systems.

Markets and Administered Systems

The relative efficiency of market-oriented institutions is a founding principle of economic analysis. In competitive markets, consumers are sovereign, and changes in supply and demand are spontaneously coordinated through variation in prices, holding other factors constant. The price system is at the node of market transactions, serving as an index of value, a signal of relative scarcity, and a mechanism to coordinate all transactions. As Friedrich Hayek emphasized, the price system economizes on knowledge and information, leading to the conclusion that "the most significant fact about this system is the economy of knowledge which it operates, or how little the individual participants need to know in order to be able to take the right action."[36] Markets involve decentralized decisions and transactions by individuals who respond to incentives (both price and nonprice) in pursuit of utility or satisfaction, given the existing constraints. In the same way, the market for ideas allows creative individuals, regardless of their background, to benefit from their commercially valuable contributions. Efficiency implies that resources are allocated to their most highly valued use through depersonalized exchange, where the identity of the participants in the trade is irrelevant.

Beyond markets, however, economic insights and understanding tend to falter. In this book, I show how the structure of innovation institutions ranges along a spectrum from free markets to administered systems. Firms illustrate some of the nuances of institutions that incorporate both market and administered characteristics. According to Ronald Coase, firms existed because of fiat, or the authority of the principal, whose dictates were a substitute for the price system.[37] Rather than focusing on the supposed authority of managers, Jensen

---

[36] Hayek (1948: 86).
[37] Coase (2012).

and Meckling view the firm as a "nexus of contracts," or bundles of fungible contractual arrangements that are designed to minimize transactions and agency costs in the marketplace.[38] Others propose a knowledge-based theory of the firm, in which firms coordinate and integrate the specialized knowledge of its participants. While the latter is certainly true, mechanisms to allocate knowledge inputs are hardly unique to firms, since they are an inherent feature of all administered innovation systems. In the final analysis, however, firms are not pure administered organizations, because they are subject to consumer sovereignty and to the price system. Even in supposedly monopolistic industries, there is the potential for competitors to emerge, and enterprises that ignore market signals will be forced to exit in the long run.

The development of open source software and collective invention further comprise arrangements that share characteristics of administered innovation systems but are closer to markets.[39] Here, groups of individuals collaborate on projects "following a diverse cluster of motivational drives and social signals, rather than either market prices or managerial commands."[40] In the world of induced innovation, prices are an important mechanism for coordination, signaling, minimization of informational and other transactions costs, and making necessary adjustments to meet changes in circumstances. However, market activity also comprehends other sorts of nonprice incentives, including amenities and disamenities, that motivate human behavior. Both demand and supply functions include all relevant determinants that influence variation in outcomes. Sharing of knowledge in open source communities, peer-to-peer collaboration, and contributory online networks that use "tokens" as an indicator of value thus all make up informal markets in which participants engage in exchanges that affect their utility and the supply of effort. These informal institutions are never remote from formal markets, and they bargain in the shadow of the price-based system. For instance, many open source participants are employed in large corporations and others expect to leverage their online activities to gain more attractive positions in the labor market.

Economic studies of innovation further assume that the legal monopoly accorded to patented ideas leads to monopoly in the market. Simple textbook models posit that monopolies create higher prices and lower output, which results in net social costs or "deadweight losses." The unexamined assumption that underlies this argument is that the alternative to the monopoly is a more efficient competitive system. This sort of reasoning leads to the conclusion that incentives like innovation prizes are necessarily socially desirable because

---

[38] Jensen and Meckling (1976); Fama (1980).
[39] I am grateful for valuable suggestions from Tom Nicholas on this point.
[40] See, for instance, Benkler (2002).

they avoid deadweight losses. By contrast, this book emphasizes that all institutional arrangements have both costs and benefits that need to be explicitly addressed. Far from being competitive, administered innovation systems typically involve monopsonies, or situations where a single buyer faces numerous potential applicants. Monetary prizes involve fixed returns/prices offered by a sole buyer, where adjustments are limited to one side of the market (variation in the number of applicants for the award). Standard economic analysis of monopsonies suggests the likelihood of a misallocation of resources. Such systems can generate serious efficiency concerns, including the potential for unjust discrimination and rent-seeking, which the historical evidence presented in these pages suggests likely outweigh the costs of market-oriented patents for invention.

Free markets adjust to disequilibria through changes in prices and profits, so firms and their agents internalize the costs and benefits of their decisions. Administered systems, by contrast, generally involve a separation between those who make the decisions and those who suffer the consequences of failure. A crucial feature is that no third-party mechanisms, such as a legal right of appeal, are put in place to ensure that arbitrary or unjust decisions are censured or overturned. The Fields Prize in mathematics, for instance, is overseen by a committee whose decisions are sealed for seventy-five years, and its awards at times reflected the personal agendas of the members of the committees, rather than the objective achievements of the candidates.[41] Thus, unlike market transactions where participants are (directly or indirectly) disciplined by the costs of incorrect choices and of failures, in administered systems there are fewer incentives or impulses to ensure efficient decision-making even in the long term.

Juries, however disinterested or expert, are unlikely to be able to predict the course of future developments or to pick the winners who will prevail through shifting and dynamic conditions. They are typically charged to limit their consideration to the proposals before them rather than to incorporate comprehensive information about the next best alternative on a larger current or intertemporal scale. The standard analysis of decision-making under uncertainty indicates that an option to flexibly defer choices will, holding other things constant, have a greater expected value than a "now or never" decision. Administered systems are likely to exercise options too early, leading to irreversible choices and monolithic path dependence. Markets, by comparison, engender higher-valued options owing to the ability to defer decisions until more information becomes available. For instance, modern patent grants maintain an open option during the life of the patent with a maximum term of twenty years. Markets will thus tend to have more prolific branches on the binomial decision tree than an administered

---

[41] Barany (2015).

process such as a prize system, which perforce will prematurely lop off a greater number of branches at the date when the prize has to be awarded.

Consider a prize system where n ideas are submitted at time t, but only the top three can be selected at time $t + 1$. This implies that $n - 3$ are rejected, even if their value is positive, and those paths are foreclosed and no longer available to the administrator. If market conditions change sufficiently in the future, in such a way that one of the $n - 3$ options is now viable and possibly more valuable, it is unlikely that the administrator will be able to revisit the decision. Administrators further have control over their institutions, and researchers show that the option to defer choices is less likely to be chosen when conflict is low.[42] Planners do not internalize all of the returns from risk-taking, and are thus ill-equipped to confront an innovation process that Bill Janeway wryly characterizes as trial and error and error and error.[43] Administered systems tend to be more closed, with little outside knowledge of the factors that led to the decisions, and once a prize is awarded with great fanfare, it is difficult to trace the subsequent outcome because attention is diverted to other competitions. Planners have an incentive to proclaim their successes and downplay or deny their failures, leading to an asymmetry in the information that is made available. Markets are less likely to have this sort of lock-in and will tend to have access to a greater number of the initial options, as well as more useful information about failures that can benefit all participants.

Similar questions about administered systems—at the national level—were evident in pre–World War II debates about the viability of market socialism, and these have resurfaced in recent years in response to concerns about growing socioeconomic inequality.[44] Léon Walras, the famous French mathematical economist, was an unexpected supporter of the tenets of market socialism, regarding himself as an architect formulating a blueprint for a more just economic system. The most noted model of market socialism supposed that the state could efficiently mimic how prices allocated resources in a market economy.[45] Adherents of market socialism tried to grapple with the question of how to obtain and mobilize disparate forms of knowledge and information in a dynamic process to achieve optimal decisions over time. In particular, they were aware that elite factions were likely to have different visions about what the most desirable ends should be, relative to the majority of participants in the mass market.

Hayek best articulated this "fundamental problem" of how to ensure that scarce resources are distributed to the most valued use when individuals possess

---

[42] Tversky and Shafir (1992).
[43] Janeway (2012).
[44] Bardhan and Roemer (1992).
[45] Lange et al. (1938); Bergson (1967).

private information about costs and benefits and objectives, which are not available to planners. However, he chose to assume that "so far as scientific knowledge is concerned, a body of suitably chosen experts may be in the best position to command all the best knowledge available."[46] This was useful for the purposes of his analysis, but others who adopted such assumptions as self-evident often failed to fully appreciate the differences between technical efficiency (involving decisions based on scientific knowledge) and "the best knowledge available" for the purposes of achieving economic efficiency (based on a combination of technical knowledge and knowledge of prices and value in the market).

For most economists, asymmetries in information between social planners and the participants in markets in inventions were central to the analysis of mechanisms to induce and disseminate inventive ideas and to ensure commercialization of innovations. Theorists agree that, in the presence of such imperfections, patent systems are "obviously superior" incentive systems and have a "peculiar informational advantage" relative to alternatives such as research contracts or prizes.[47] The concerns about strictly economic issues are compounded by problems in political economy, accountability, and the possibilities for corruption and cronyism. Despite the undoubted contributions of mathematical approaches to the economics of incentives and innovation, these abstract discussions highlight the need for more specific studies of the actual implementation of rules and the actual effects of institutional mechanism design.

Markets and Administered Systems in Economic History

All institutional arrangements are associated with both costs and benefits, so the disadvantages of any one system do not necessarily indicate that any other system is "optimal" or even feasible. The philosopher Isaiah Berlin usefully reminds us, in his essays on language, that it is necessary to have a precise and nuanced awareness of the plurality of uses and meanings of what appear to be a single concept, and that is especially true of innovation institutions. Patent systems existed in Britain, France, and the United States, but their motivation and designs differed substantially, in ways that markedly affected the types of both inventors and inventions that flourished in these countries. Some companies chose to obtain returns through trade secrecy or lead time, but this did not imply that patent rights were universally irrelevant to all firms, since industrial knowledge varied in terms of the capacity for rivalry, excludability, and appropriability. Prize systems were the most variable of all, each with unique objectives, widely

---

[46]   Hayek (1945: 521).
[47]   Wright (1983); Gallini and Scotchmer (2002).

varying standards, and inherently subjective decision-making. Thus, specific historical details about rules and their implementation, and comparative institutional analyses, are required in order to grasp exactly how and why and under what circumstances seemingly substitutable social organizations functioned over time.

Patent institutions in the leading industrial countries illustrate the manner in which differences in market orientation affected observed patterns of technological change and economic progress. The specific design of intellectual property and related institutions mattered and had measurable consequences for the production and distribution of useful knowledge. In Europe, administrators assumed that only elites had the mental capacity and access to useful knowledge that would translate into important inventions. Such privileged and well-placed individuals would already possess the financial resources to fund investments and were allegedly also unlikely to be very responsive or concerned about the cost of patent fees. From the perspective of the agents of the British Crown, patents were primarily viewed as a means to raise revenues for the state and to reward incumbents, rather than as an incentive for inventive activity. Consequently, the cost of patents was deliberately set at exorbitant levels that outstripped per capita income. It was regarded as an added advantage that such high fees would exclude the working class from getting property rights for their "small inventions." Despite the democratic rhetoric, French fees and rules had similar effects as the British system.

Thus, in Britain, administrators made rules based on prior assumptions about what should qualify as a valuable invention (those that survived the filter of high fees) and about the identity and social standing of inventors whose interests should be promoted (wealthy and well-connected individuals). A large group of officials obtained significant rents from administering the complicated bureaucracy involved in issuing patent documents, and they had an incentive to block reforms to rationalize the system. Efforts to implement structural changes finally succeeded after two hundred years, but only after heavy compensation was made to the administrative interest groups who had benefited from the byzantine operation of the prior patent system.[48] The judiciary and the legal system operated on the same premises, leading to great ex ante uncertainty about the value of property rights in inventions. Markets in ideas were thin, hampered by legal inhibitions such as limits on the number of parties who could invest in a patent.

---

[48] The patent application procedure required the negotiation of numerous offices, whose employees received their compensation from patent fees and payments that inventors made to expedite the process. As an example, the Irish and Scots Law Officers and clerks who were made obsolete were allocated an annual compensation of £6,000 for the loss of fees that they suffered from the reforms that lowered the cost of filing for patentees.

The conceptual distinction between administered systems and market-oriented institutions, and the extensive new empirical evidence in each chapter of this book promise to shed more light on why France and Britain fell behind, and why the United States succeeded in "inventing ideas." Administered systems were a predominant feature of political-economic policies in Europe during the early industrial era, and indeed, similar beliefs and institutions have persisted to the present day. At their best, according to economic theory, such approaches could function as a means to attenuate the negative consequences of monopolies and to overcome inefficiencies and inequities in the market. In the presence of market failure, administrators could make decisions that internalized externalities, such as finding ways to reduce deforestation and environmental degradation.

A central question is how stated policies were actually implemented and the extent to which the results fulfilled the expectations and public claims of their creators. During the eighteenth and nineteenth centuries, councils and committees drawn from the most influential classes in Europe nominated favored parties who would benefit from special privileges. Courts, elites, and bureaucrats selected winners and determined losers among inventors and other creative applicants and made decisions about the amount of compensation and how returns would be allocated among the coterie of hopeful applicants. In Britain, key institutions such as the RSA assumed that elites would be responsible for the most valuable ideas, and that they would be motivated by honor and prestige rather than by profit. French administrators deliberately funneled resources to elite schools and institutions that maintained the existing structure of privilege, and such activities were so entrenched that they repeatedly survived attempts at drastic reforms. Not only were administered systems a product of undemocratic institutions, but also their rules and implementation perpetuated social and economic inequality.

State and bureaucratic interventions often sought to override the "natural" course of technology and commerce and to pursue alternative channels and outcomes that might have faltered in open markets. A common view among scholars is that Britain advanced because of its retreat from mercantilism and rent-seeking, and this was true in observable areas such as commercial trade policy. However, a detailed examination of the internal records for administrative decisions of elites reveals persistence at the individual level of these discredited policies, in both England and France. Both centralized and decentralized administered groups determined the types of knowledge that should be promoted and the characteristics of innovators whom they deemed to be the most likely to contribute to the objectives they wished to pursue. Administered innovation systems provided a means for the state and insiders to deliberately bypass markets and to instead implement protectionist and mercantilist agendas, beyond the scrutiny of external auditors or a broader audience.

The European approach was also evident in colonial America, but innovation policies permanently altered after the founding of the new Republic. The United States was the first society to conceive of property rights in invention in modern terms, as a means of primarily providing strong incentives for inventive activity and innovation, through flexible market-oriented institutions where consumers would determine success or failure. Elites have always mistrusted markets; wealth and influence often lead to the conviction that the insights of the favored few can outperform spontaneous coordination, and that status and celebrity are a good substitute for specialized knowledge. Instead, significant characteristics of the American approach were its rejection of administered systems and its explicit refutation of the notion that only privileged groups were capable of generating useful knowledge and ideas. Federal government policies toward inventions were largely limited to the classic functions of securing property rights and ensuring their strong enforcement through the legal system. As Robert Gordon noted, "perhaps the most important government activity to stimulate growth was the patent office and the process of patent approval."[49]

As I showed in *The Democratization of Invention*, the United States placed markets in ideas at the center of its technology policies and consciously calibrated property rights in inventions to function as the keystone of a democratic society.[50] According to this thinking, "An invention is property of the highest order."[51] The U.S. Patent Office after 1836 introduced an examination system, which the casual reader might consider to be an administered system. This was decidedly not the case. All novel ideas were by default entitled to property rights, and fees were deliberately kept low to ensure accessibility. The detailed rules and standards governing the operation of the system were set by federal statute, not by the discretion of the patent office administrators. Patent examiners certainly influenced the scope of property rights to novel ideas, but they played no role in determining market value or gauging the usefulness of these ideas (the legal term "utility" simply meant "capable of use"). The award of patent rights was based on the technical contribution of the invention, not on the identity of the inventor or their wealth and connections. Applicants had a right of appeal from the decisions of the Patent Office that could be prosecuted all the way to the U.S. Supreme Court, and this allowed for a valuable stock of legal precedent that helped to reduce uncertainty for all inventors about the nature and boundaries of patent

---

[49] Gordon (2016: 312).

[50] Khan (2005) provides a legal, economic, and empirical comparison across patent and copyright institutions and therefore complements the current work.

[51] *Annual Report of the Commissioner of Patents* (1869).

THE PROGRESS OF THE CENTURY.
THE LIGHTNING STEAM PRESS.   THE ELECTRIC TELEGRAPH.   THE LOCOMOTIVE.   THE STEAMBOAT.

Figure 1.2 A Century of Patented Progress
The steady flow of incremental patented inventions throughout the nineteenth century combined to create great inventions like "the steam press," "the locomotive," and "the electric telegraph." The rapid advances in patented discoveries during the nineteenth and twentieth centuries transformed industry and every facet of everyday life. The optimistic notion of technologically created progress became ingrained in American culture.
Source: Library of Congress.

property. Instead of depending on the ex ante determinations of economic value by administrators, American patentees had to satisfy market demand if they wished to profit from their contributions to useful knowledge.

Douglass North and Robert Thomas argued that the development of patent institutions and intellectual property laws encouraged technological innovation, regardless of the extent of their enforcement. They further proposed a blanket compendium approach that explicitly assumed that all forms of incentives—whether prices, bounties, or subsidies—were equally effective.[52]

---

[52] North and Thomas (1973): "The development of a patent system and other laws protecting intellectual property (however imperfectly enforced) encouraged the growth of innovation. In addition to the patent system (which was always imperfectly enforced) prices, bounties, and subsidies were all used to encourage innovation and produced the same consequences in terms of our model."

Their perspective misses the focal point spelled out in the chapters of this book: innovation incentives and institutions were not all equally effective, and the choice of specific policy instruments had cumulative consequences. Patent systems and related legal enforcement practices varied across countries and time, and that variation affected the types of inventors and the types of inventions that would be created, as well as the likelihood that ideas would be transformed into commercially valuable innovations that would benefit consumers in the marketplace. In the final analysis, the mechanism design of administered systems and of markets in ideas had important implications for the efficient allocation of resources and for dynamic processes of economic growth.

Book Plan: *You Have to Care about the Details*

My research career has been strongly influenced by my training as a graduate student at UCLA, under the supervision of Kenneth Sokoloff, one of the finest economic historians of his generation. Ken's own body of work vividly reflects his conviction that quantitative history is based on a paradox: this method offers insights into grand ideas about "the pursuit of happiness" and the sources of socioeconomic progress, but grand ideas must be grounded in meticulous and minute attention to the strengths and deficiencies inherent in all data. The basic patterns in reliable data should be evident from the summary statistics. Econometric wand-waving, three-stage least-squares regressions, and seductive instrumental variables were useful to bolster confidence in one's results but as often as not served to paper over questionable data inputs that invalidated the central claims. His constant mantra was that "each and every data point matters—you have to care about the details." This fundamental principle seems all the more important today, when many economists employ history merely as anecdotes to support the abstractions in their models.

This book addresses central questions about economic growth and technological change that are of interest to economists, historians, legal scholars, political scientists, entrepreneurs and aficionados of technology, and innovation policymakers. The discussion uniquely draws on original long-run international datasets that allow for the comparative cross-country institutional analysis of technological innovation across time, place, and individuals. The empirical methods provide quantitative backing for all of the principal claims, but my approach in these chapters is to allow the data to speak for themselves, rather than through the medium of opaque statistical massaging. As such, the reader who is averse to econometrics is assured that the reported tables merely employ simple summary statistics to reveal the patterns underlying the experiences of over one hundred thousand creative men and women. The reader who is averse to tables of any sort is further assured that the book can be read and understood without venturing beyond the text. Economists who wish to satisfy their yearning for multivariate regression results are urged to consult my articles and working papers that are cited in the bibliography.

As the title of this book suggests, many of the currently accepted ideas about innovation and growth are based on questionable premises and shaky evidence. In an era of extreme specialization, even (perhaps especially) Nobel Prize–winning economists tend to circulate inaccurate anecdotes about inducement prizes and patent institutions. As a result, the results reported here are deliberately limited to my own research efforts and my own sphere of expertise. I have dedicated more than a decade to acquire, collate, and analyze the underlying data. The matches across different records are not the product of automated data scraping or computer algorithms (not that there is anything wrong with that!). Each of these observations has been entered into digital format by hand, and was meticulously linked by hand, and cross-checked to ensure maximum accuracy. At relevant points, I refer to information about other industrial nations such as Germany and Japan, regions that present valuable opportunities for further comparative research by other scholars. However, my primary focus here is on the archival sources in the three languages I fluently read (English, French, and Spanish), in order to provide first-hand insights into the major topics that are reported in these chapters.

These chapters incorporate information on different sorts of technological prizes and innovation institutions, patentees and innovators, sales of intellectual property rights, women inventors, civil litigation, and political economic factors during two key centuries of the modern era. The panel data (cross-sections that are repeated over place and time) include approximately sixty-five thousand innovation prizes, as well as over one hundred thousand patented inventions in Britain, France, and the United States. Manuscript censuses yielded information on the characteristics of the individuals in these samples, such as their age, occupations, wealth, and propensity to migrate. Citations to inventions, lawsuits, advertisements, congressional and military records, and patent sales helped to shed light on the value of innovations. Account books of prize-granting institutions, membership lists, and detailed reports of their judging committees revealed how and why decisions were made.

The book structure is divided into four parts, and their coverage progresses through time and place. The first section examines the historical context for current controversies in the realm of patents and "inventing prizes." Economists have advocated the use of grand innovation prizes by re-citing largely unsubstantiated historical "facts." My examination of archival records in Britain, France, and the United States reveals information that is inconsistent with common assertions in the literature. Similarly, the prevailing rhetoric about the economic inefficiencies of "patent trolls" and other intermediaries in the market for patented inventions, unparalleled explosions in litigation, and excessive social costs of patent grants does not fit well with the economic evidence over the long term. All social outcomes include extreme cases, but scholarly conclusions should be based on general tendencies rather than unrepresentative outliers.

The second part considers the role of elites, knowledge, and administered innovation systems. Economists and historians alike have raised fundamental questions about the nature of human creativity and the sorts of resources, skills, and knowledge inputs that expand the frontiers of technology. The empirical results reported in this section suggest that some skepticism is warranted about the role that elites and non-market-oriented institutions played in generating technological innovation and long-term economic development. I provide specific measures of different types of knowledge and estimate their role in British industrialization. Even for great inventors and scientists, formal investments in specialized human capital seem to have been less important than appropriate institutional incentives for creativity. The chapters in this section further examine whether innovation prizes served as effective inducements for new inventions and in creating products that were scalable or valuable in the marketplace.

Scholars like Joel Mokyr correctly noted that European innovation strategies were oriented toward nonmarket reward systems, but the empirical data do not support their positive conclusions. The RSA in London was a classic example of an administered system whose elite members formed committees to identify, judge, and award prizes for innovations. The RSA chapter reports on the empirical assessment of a novel dataset, comprising several thousand monetary and honorary prizes, patent records, and detailed archival information about the application and decision-making process between 1750 and 1850. The RSA initially was averse to patents and prohibited the award of prizes for patented inventions, so their experience offers a unique opportunity to assess outcomes when the two mechanisms are substitutes rather than complements.

France was the canonical example of a soi-disant entrepreneurial state, or of a more centralized administered system where public and private agencies attempted to direct the path of industry and invention. This discussion of the French experience identifies the structure and consequences of such technocratic paternalism. The analysis draws on archival documents primarily retrieved from recurring national and international industrial expositions, the Society for the Encouragement of National Industry, the Bureau of Commerce, the National Conservatory for Arts and Trades, the French Academy of Sciences, and records from the patent system. French innovation awards were largely unrelated to productive technologies or sectors. The specific operation of these institutions amply illustrates the political dimension of administered systems, in which discretionary rewards favored well-connected inventors and entrepreneurs and created incentives for rent-seeking and the stacking of awards, rather than commercialization in the marketplace.

The conclusions about administered systems in England and France may possibly have owed to other unobserved features of European society. Americans were skeptical about administered innovation systems, highlighting their transaction costs and the potential for cognitive dissonance or corruption when juries and administrators, rather than markets, determined values and winners. *Scientific American* in 1886 denounced innovation prizes as "special systems, where favors are sought for and obtained by particular parties in a particular manner." However, in major cities prominent mechanics' institutes like the Franklin Institute of Philadelphia flourished in this period, and they regularly hosted industrial and technological fairs for inventors and innovators. The empirical analysis of each of these panel datasets consistently finds that prize awards were largely idiosyncratic and unrelated to factors like inventiveness or the market value of the invention. The evidence from standing committees of the Franklin Institute points to the potential for governance problems like social capture and for prejudice toward "particular parties in a particular manner."

A fundamental question for the economics of innovation is whether and to what extent inventors and inventive activity respond to specific incentives and institutional rules and standards. My first book provided ample evidence to show how responsive creative individuals were to the incentives vested in intellectual property. Those empirical findings were based on cross-sections, times series, the activities of ordinary inventors, great inventors, married women whose benefits from property rights in invention were compromised by state laws that allocated their assets to their husbands, copyright piracy, and the quantitative analysis of intellectual property litigation. The conclusions highlighted the role of private property rights in conveying information and facilitating markets, and their value in reducing risk and uncertainty for relatively disadvantaged inventors with few private resources. Disclosure, mechanisms to publicize patent information, intermediaries, and market transactions all served to enhance the diffusion of new technologies. Patents allowed for the securitization of ideas, and these tradeable assets facilitated market exchange in a process that assigned value, helped to mobilize capital, and improved the allocation of resources.

The third section of this book directly addresses markets in patented inventions, and the new research confirms and extends the conclusions from *The Democratization of Invention*. The lifetime experience of a large sample of inventors shows how the rate and direction of inventive activity responded dramatically to such incentives as the Civil War. The American patent system specifically designed mechanisms to enable the effective diffusion of technical information, and the accumulated stock of knowledge allowed others to build on the revealed knowledge, discover competitive noninfringing substitutes, and come up with their own ideas. Estimates of knowledge spillovers from patents and prize-winning innovations show that patented inventions created knowledge spillovers. By contrast, prize-winning innovations did not generate external benefits for others, owing to a lack of specific mechanisms to reveal and diffuse knowledge and information.

Gender differences provide another perspective on technological creativity. Women are often invisible to the gaze of history, and this is likewise true of studies of their inventive and creative output. My analysis of women's inventions and innovations is based on over twelve thousand patents, prizes, and unpatentable inventions in Britain, France, and the United States. The experience of women inventors illustrates how administered systems might reflect the discriminatory biases of their members. Women's creativity within both the market and the household is best understood by distinguishing between improvements in consumer final goods, changes in designs, and other novel forms of innovations at the boundaries of art and technology. This suggests a need to revisit the question of what is considered useful knowledge, especially in the context of households and nontraded goods.

An extensive global market in patents and innovations developed after the middle of the nineteenth century. The discussion of international markets in ideas considers patterns from the United States, Britain, Germany, Canada, New South Wales, Spain, and Japan during the nineteenth and early twentieth centuries. U.S. knowledge markets were much more extensive relative to its international competitors, and the ability to trade secure inventive assets was especially significant for disadvantaged inventors who did not possess the means or connections to appropriate returns from manufacturing enterprises. The results indicate that the patterns of trade in patent rights varied in accordance with legal and economic factors and also show how markets in ideas were influenced by the specific design of patent institutions.

The final section considers the role of adjacent institutions, including the legal system, in the context of "national innovation systems." As Thomas Jefferson pointed out, too frequent institutional changes can lead to costly uncertainty, but institutions must also keep pace with the times. The flexibility of American legal institutions allowed courts to address the disruptions that technological innovations created. A myopic focus on "explosions" in patent litigation fails to appreciate that disruptive technologies raised new issues and litigation about *all* areas of law—property, contracts, and torts alike. Several thousand civil law disputes show how courts initially responded by stretching existing legal analogies derived from prior rulings but, as these became strained, adopted new legal standards. Such productive institutional responses ultimately accommodated and resolved the transaction costs and conflicts associated with recent innovations. In keeping with the results from decentralized administered systems, government measures to underwrite and manage innovation raised questions about the efficacy of the so-called entrepreneurial state.

The genesis of today's knowledge economy occurred in the "long nineteenth century." This was a time of great experimentation across and within different countries about the most effective way to create knowledge, new ideas, and technological innovations. Europeans were more vested in a top-down technocratic approach that put its faith in the wisdom of elites and their ability to identify the path ahead and implement appropriate policies for progress. The political economy played out differently in France and England, but the contrasts with the decentralized American approach were especially evident in the degree to which ordinary artisans and inventors had an effective voice in the collective process of identifying needs, proposing both modest and ambitious solutions, and benefiting from their successful contributions. As endogenous growth models suggest, the scale and diversity of the population of people and ideas that participated in this process mattered critically and was the major reason that broader markets in ideas prevailed over elite and technocratic approaches.

These results both fit and help to explain the historical parameters. Domestic and international observers credited U.S. markets in ideas and intellectual property institutions for facilitating the unparalleled second Industrial Revolution and the resulting global dominance of American inventors and patented inventions. Regardless of the theoretical allure of promises to improve on market allocations, administered innovation systems eventually encountered intractable problems in their implementation. Prizes to induce innovations dwindled away by the end of the nineteenth century. Other countries—including Britain, Switzerland, Japan, and Germany—emulated American patent and technology policies in an attempt to keep pace with U.S. achievements, and international harmonization of patent laws primarily arose from this voluntary alignment toward the American model. Privileged elites adopted measures that may have resulted in temporary spurts, but such efforts quickly ran into diminishing returns and failed to induce self-sustaining economic growth. As such, the economic history of the past two centuries highlights the central role of market-oriented incentives, in tandem with flexible open-access economic and legal institutions, in promoting sustained technological progress and economic growth in the knowledge economy.

2

Trolls and Other Patent Inventions

The very first official thing I did, in my administration—and it was on the very first day of it too—was to start a patent office.
—Mark Twain (1889) [1]

The patent system is the source of widespread dissatisfaction, many scholars and observers call for multifaceted reforms in its rules and standards, and some even propose the abolition of state-mandated grants of intellectual property. Patents are vilified as unnecessary monopolies that serve to enrich a few corporations and their robber baron executives while harming their competitors and the general public. The popular press is filled with ubiquitous headlines about negative-sum "patent wars" that are waged in boardrooms and courtrooms across the world, culminating in huge litigation and enforcement costs, where the only winners are the lawyers on both sides of the dispute who garner lavish fees regardless of the outcomes. Pervasive copyright piracy of music and other cultural goods leads many to fear the demise of domestic creativity and output. In response to the urging of paid lobbyists, Congress engages in lengthy debates and considers abundant proposals for reforming the patent and copyright system. Prizes and other alternatives are gaining greater favor among a strong antipatent alliance. In general, these acrimonious debates and radical policy proposals are primarily based on rhetoric and self-interest rather than on accurate assessments of empirical evidence.

The previous paragraph refers to discussions and debates that were rife in the nineteenth century about intellectual property systems. Similar claims and counterclaims were prevalent when the British Statute of Monopolies authorized the world's first statutory patent institution in 1624 and have persisted through the centuries with periodic upsurges that replicate the same questions and concerns. In 1950, another period when Congress was paying close attention

---

[1] The author continued that he "knew that a country without a patent office and good patent laws was just a crab and couldn't travel any way but sideways or backways. . . . The first thing you want in a new country, is a patent office; then work up your school system." Twain (1889: 64, 66). The eponymous Connecticut Yankee in the novel was employed as an inventive foreman at a renowned arms manufactory in Hartford (clearly, the Colt patent manufacturing firm), before setting off on his entrepreneurial adventures in Camelot.

Inventing Ideas. B. Zorina Khan, Oxford University Press (2020). © Oxford University Press.
DOI: 10.1093/oso/9780190936075.001.0001

to calls for reform, economists Fritz Machlup and Edith Penrose published an article that described the patent controversy in the nineteenth century, to demonstrate that "despite all the changes in the economic scene, our thinking on the subject has hardly changed over the century."[2] They described the historical evolution of the patent system and its tendency to generate discontent, culminating in a call to abolish patents in the second half of the nineteenth century. Their report effectively illustrated how the same issues and positions have an inveterate tendency to reappear over time, as if nothing had been learned from history.

In the second half of the nineteenth century, the "patent controversy" in Europe included calls for reforms that ranged from changes in the subject matter and scope of patents to the complete abolition of patent systems. Just as today, European economists and politicians who favored the overturn of patent laws declared that patents of invention harmed social welfare. The abolitionists at times justified their position by appealing to the benefits of free trade and competition, and declared that patents belonged to an anticompetitive and protectionist strategy analogous to tariffs on imports. They urged that free and open access to new discoveries would ensure that ideas spread quickly and so benefit all of society. As for incentives, some inventive activity was exogenous and would occur anyway, whereas measures other than monopoly rights could be devised to encourage the rest of the profession. Inventors could be rewarded by alternative policies, such as prizes, stipends or honors from the government, an enhanced reputation, or payments from private industry or associations formed for that purpose. Firms could employ trade secrecy or gain advantages from the lead time that the first inventor acquired over competitors.

Who are the new patent dissidents of the twenty-first century? Just as in the earlier era, interest groups include enterprises that would benefit from royalty-free usage of patented ideas. Objective analysts and academic observers also highlight a range of concerns. Many criticize specific aspects of the administration or consequences of patent rules and standards. Some wish to increase access to essential medicines, and others argue that patents do not function effectively in particular contexts such as gene therapies and software. The most radical critics consist of a coterie of eminent theoretical economists with little or no specialized expertise in intellectual property. They appeal to the sort of analysis that is standard in undergraduate principles of economics classes: patents are intellectual monopolies that drive up prices above cost, create "contrived scarcity," and reduce social welfare owing to "deadweight losses" relative to a perfectly competitive world in which the invention already exists. Nobel Prize economists like Gary Becker argued that property rights should be offered only for goods

---

[2] Machlup and Penrose (1950).

with high research costs, while Joseph Stiglitz declared that prize systems were "an idea whose time has come," because they offered superior alternatives to patents. Other theorists are somewhat less temperate, declaring that patents are an "unnecessary evil"; it is time, they insist, to abolish the entire intellectual property system.[3]

Patents and Monopolies

Intellectual property has a long history as a concept and as a policy instrument, and from its inception has been associated with controversy over the rights of exclusion it confers. Those who regarded patents as state-sanctioned monopolies were more likely to consider them as unproductive or unwarranted, owing to their origins in the exercise of arbitrary royal power. Statutory patent grants were introduced in England as an exception to a ban on monopolies or pervasive privileges that the monarch typically sold to raise revenues. These privileges had raised barriers to entry in guilds and occupations and also created numerous monopolies in a wide variety of markets, ranging from intellectual endeavors to common consumer goods. Parliament finally succeeded in a petition that outlawed all monopolies, with the sole exception of patents for new inventions. The resulting popular antipathy to generic royal privileges carried over to the hostile treatment of exclusive grants for inventions in the form of patent rights. For these historical reasons, patent grants in Britain were grudgingly granted, and their scope and enforcement narrowly construed.

Early European patents were granted through registration systems, which did not attempt to determine the validity of applications.[4] Patents were essentially instruments of taxation whose primary objective was to raise revenues for the state, and anyone who paid the substantial filing fees was granted patent rights. Thus, patentees included wealthy importers who had not invented the devices they patented, as well as employers who chose to file for rights to the innovations their workers had created. Attitudes toward trade in patent rights were imbued with the distaste felt for speculation, and legal provisions to prevent financial bubbles and "stock jobbing" were extended to technology markets, making those markets quite thin and limited. Patent rules and standards in England deliberately limited access to property rights by ordinary working-class inventors. In a reprise of arguments made today, policy was based on the assumption that too many "small" inventions would clutter up the system and create undue problems for the "important" discoveries. These stipulations penalized ordinary inventors

---

[3] Boldrin and Levine (2008).
[4] Khan (2005).

without wealth or influence who wished to obtain protection and benefit financially from their discoveries.

The American patent system was designed to be different from existing
institutions in the rest of the world. For the first time in history, an intellectual
property clause was included in a national constitution. Policies were based
on the presumption that patents for new inventions were not monopolies.
Monopolists diverted public goods to their own selfish ends in a manner that was
"justly odious," whereas offering creative individuals a limited right to their new
ideas did not lead to a monopoly in all related ideas. Moreover, the patentee's right
of exclusion did not preclude competition with substitutes in product markets.
Instead of deprecating patentees as monopolists, policymakers and the courts
regarded them as benefactors whose rights should be strongly defended. If the
patent examination system worked properly, an exclusive right was awarded only
to those who had created a novel invention, because patentees drew on their own
creative abilities to produce something that never existed before and promised
to give it to the world after a limited period. Social welfare coincided with the
individual welfare of patentees, and observers felt "almost lost in wonder at the
vastness of the interests which have been created by the ingenuity of the country
and the immense amount now invested, in this department of property."[5]

As with other types of property, patentees had the full right to determine what
use should be made of their discoveries, or even whether they should lie unused.
Two centuries of U.S. federal patent rules have consistently rejected the argument
that the validity of patent rights or the attendant ability to enforce them should
depend on commercialization or whether patents were "worked" or "practiced."
Working requirements or compulsory licenses were standard policies of colonial legislatures to attenuate monopoly power, but these measures were regarded
as unwarranted infringements of the rights of "meritorious inventors" and incompatible with the philosophy of U.S. patent grants. Besides the adverse effects
on incentives and the expropriation of inventive property rights, compulsory
licensing and working requirements would tend to discriminate in favor of those
with more resources and connections, and disadvantage the ordinary inventor.

In sum, the U.S. Constitution introduced a completely new approach to patents
as accessible and strongly enforced property rights in ideas, providing incentives
for creativity to increase social welfare. Courts were well aware that patent rights
had to be carefully protected and enforced because ideas were far easier to appropriate than other forms of property. The emphasis in the American patent system
was certainly not on the production of goods; in fact, anyone who had previously
commercialized an invention lost the right of exclusion vested in patents. The

---

[5] The citations in this paragraph are from the patent lawsuit, *Singer v. Walmsley*, 1 Fisher 558
(Md. 1859).

decision about how or whether the patent should be exploited remained completely within the discretion of the patentee, in the same way that the owner of physical property is allowed to determine its use or nonuse. Provisions like compulsory licenses were more aligned with coercive legal doctrines of eminent domain and expropriation, which undermined the security of property rights in a free market system. During international patent conventions, the U.S. representatives consistently tried to persuade other nations to follow its example and to abolish these abridgements of inventive property.

Trolls and Patent Inventions

The question of "patent trolls" has recently generated a great deal of public anxiety and proposals for legislative measures to restrict or outlaw their activities. The rhetoric about trolls has been emphatic even though the term remains hazy and disputed. Discussion typically centers on "nonpracticing entities" (whether the inventor or an intermediary) who do not commercialize their discoveries but use licensing to extract profits from (seemingly more meritorious) manufacturers. Trolls, it is argued, reduce market efficiency and social welfare because their activities impose unwarranted costs and create disincentives for true innovators, who fear the prospects of expensive and time-consuming litigation. Other authors focus on "predatory litigation" by patent assertion entities, who accumulate large intellectual property portfolios primarily to hold up other patentees or firms.

According to the Supreme Court in their reported decision for *eBay Inc. v. MercExchange*, "courts should bear in mind that in many instances the nature of the patent being enforced and the economic function of the patent holder present considerations quite unlike earlier cases. An industry has developed in which firms use patents not as a basis for producing and selling goods but, instead, primarily for obtaining licensing fees."[6] This ahistorical view is typical of many influential analysts in this area who, without any inquiry into the actual empirical patterns, contend that the nature of intellectual property has changed in the twenty-first century, and that these new developments require new rules and standards. As such, there is a marked need for more systematic investigation into the nature of markets in ideas since the founding of the early Republic and the innovative American approach to technological creativity.

---

[6] *eBay Inc. v. MercExchange, L.L.C.*, 547 U.S. 388, 396 (2006) (J. Kennedy, concurring).

The repeated claims about the uniqueness of the role of knowledge and innovation in the twenty-first century is somewhat ironic. Rather, current populist attitudes toward "nonpracticing entities" or intermediaries bear a striking resemblance to staunchly held biases from two centuries ago, wherein merit was attached only to the actual production of physical goods or tilling of the soil. Speculation or profiting from trading, in those days, was deemed to be suspect or even unethical. The puritanical regarded financial derivatives and insurance contracts in the same light as gambling and the concocting of moonshine. Markets in futures and options were held to be immoral, because buyers and sellers placed bets on price movements, and nothing "real" was produced. Some state statutes even criminalized these financial "wagers." Such attitudes then and now denied a fundamental premise of all free markets, that value is created through consensual exchange.

The economics of comparative advantage imply that output and productivity increase through specialization, the division of labor and market exchange, in a process through which resources are allocated to their most highly valued use. Intermediaries like publishers, realtors, financial brokers, and venture capitalists generate greater social value because they reduce the costs of search, information, and exchange.[7] Their activities enhance liquidity, improve market depth and breadth, serve as a filter and signal of quality, and increase overall efficiency. Specialized intermediaries are especially valuable in new or emerging markets and in instances where risk, asymmetries of information, and other transaction costs are significant. Relatively disadvantaged individuals, in particular, are likely to benefit from intermediaries and from the ability to obtain returns through markets.

One of the advantages of a system that secures and enforces property rights is that it facilitates contracts and trade, with the attendant benefits of enhanced coordination, capital mobilization, price discovery, and valuation. This is certainly the case in technology markets as well.[8] These standard economic precepts were acknowledged from the inception of the U.S. patent system and integrated into its salient rules and standards. It is therefore hardly surprising that an extensive national network of patent licensing and assignments quickly developed, aided by legal decisions that overturned contracts for fraudulent patents. Intermediation facilitated the ability to divide and subdivide the rights to the

---

[7] This fundamental principle of economic thinking can be traced back to the classical economists. For a more recent exposition, see Ahn et al. (2011).

[8] For an extensive study, see Arora et al. (2004). Howells (2006) concludes that "intermediaries provide a much wider, more varied and holistic role for their clients in the innovation process than has generally been acknowledged."

inventive idea, often with great complexity, across firms, industries, regions, and time. Successful inventors were able to leverage their reputations and underwrite the research and development costs of their inventions by offering shares in future patents. As a result, as Chapter 11 shows, American inventors were able to benefit from markets to a far greater extent than in other jurisdictions. The diffusion of U.S. patent policies to other countries helped to promote trade in patent rights and technological innovations, and numerous American patentees succeeded in establishing multinational enterprises that dominated the global economy.

Adam Smith had highlighted the way in which expanding markets facilitate greater productivity and efficiency through the division of labor and specialization. This mechanism was central to markets in patented ideas. Specialization and the division of labor implied that creators of inventions often differed from the marketers, producers, and commercializers of patented discoveries. Any "troll" who buys up a portfolio of patents is obviously at the same time generating income and benefits for the inventors who find value in transferring their rights to the intermediary. The "great inventors" of the nineteenth century, who were responsible for major disruptive technological innovations, were especially likely to be, or to benefit from, "nonpracticing entities."

This market orientation of the U.S. patent system was highly beneficial to impoverished patentees who did not have the funds to directly exploit their inventions through manufacturing or other business activity. For instance, Elijah McCoy (1844–1929), a black inventor who received his first patent for an automatic lubricating device in 1872, was unable to raise capital to manufacture his improvements in engine lubricators, but he gained returns by selling off the rights to most of his patents. Similarly, John Francis Appleby (1840–1917) licensed and assigned his patents for agricultural binding mechanisms to companies that manufactured the machines. And, of course, according to some definitions, university professors such as Stillman W. Robinson (1838–1910), who sold off the rights to some forty patents in engineering, also exemplify nonpracticing entities.

A remarkably high proportion of the great inventors became wealthy from selling or licensing the rights to their inventive property (Table 2.1).[9] These inventors would not have been able to pursue careers in "high technology" in the absence of the opportunity to engage with intermediaries. The property rights in their discoveries were traded and retraded in secondary and tertiary transactions, including exchanges with speculators who intended to benefit from

---

[9] Khan and Sokoloff (2006).

Table 2.1 Great American Inventors and Technology Markets, 1740–1885

Birth Cohort	Level of Education			
	Primary	Secondary	College	Technical
1740–1794 (row %)	69.5	6.8	12.5	11.3
Sell/license (col. %)	54.9	11.1	84.0	17.7
1795–1819 (row %)	59.1	19.3	5.4	16.2
Sell/license (col. %)	58.2	81.0	42.1	60.4
1820–1845 (row %)	39.2	34.7	16.3	9.7
Sell/license (col. %)	50.7	31.8	37.4	72.8
1846–1865 (row %)	22.2	24.5	20.9	32.4
Sell/license (col. %)	94.5	68.5	46.2	57.1
1866–1885 (row %)	0.2	17.9	21.4	60.5
Sell/license (col. %)	—	1.0	46.3	40.1

Notes and Sources: See the text. "Technical" refers to formal postsecondary education in science or engineering. The percentages are calculated over all patents received by the great inventors in each category. The column percentages for each educational level indicate the share of great inventors' patents that was obtained from selling or licensing their rights in the market.

their specialized knowledge and risk-bearing abilities, rather than from manufacturing. Kenneth Sokoloff and I showed that defining and enforcing a tradable asset in new technological knowledge was vital for fostering a market in technology and for extending and increasing incentives for segments of the population that would otherwise have been unable to directly appropriate returns from their technological creativity. Financially disadvantaged great inventors tended to realize returns from their inventions through sale or licensing, whereas those from more privileged backgrounds were among the least likely to follow that strategy.

As the experience of women inventors suggests (see Chapter 10), these conclusions were even more applicable to less eminent but equally creative individuals who encountered social obstacles that hindered their efforts to benefit from their discoveries. Women in Britain, France, and the United States faced different institutional constraints that enabled or inhibited their inventive activity and commercialization. In France, wealthy women tapped into the resources of family businesses, which offered advantages that were unavailable for inventors without personal connections. American women were better able to support their efforts by exchanging part of their property rights as a means of compensating intermediaries who helped with funding, advice on commercialization, and litigation about property rights and related issues. For instance, Maria Beasley reached an agreement in 1881 to transfer half of the rights in an uncompleted invention to James Henry of Philadelphia in return for an advance of funds to complete the machine.

A series of careful empirical studies by Naomi Lamoreaux and Kenneth Sokoloff confirmed that the experience of the great inventors was typical of the entire market for technology in the nineteenth century.[10] These scholars examined a large random sample of contracts that recorded the transfer of patent rights and found extensive and complex trades in assignments and licensing throughout the country. New markets and institutions always need to respond to problems of asymmetrical information, and networks of intermediaries quickly developed to exchange ideas, signal which discoveries were most likely to lead to commercially valuable innovations, and mobilize funding. "Nonpracticing entities" in this era included celebrated patent attorneys who also took positions in inventions as partners or outright owners.

Patents and the market for technology were closely integrated and related to financial markets, which helped to turn inventions or new ideas into commercially valuable innovations that would transform consumer good markets. The grant of a patent provided a signal that the idea was likely to be technically valid, and this surety helped patentees to mobilize capital that could be used to finalize their research or to interest others in buying or licensing their patent. Ownership of patents facilitated funding for risky new ventures that were unable to interest banks or other conventional financial institutions to underwrite their proposed projects. Their meticulous research reveals that the "venture capital revolution" based on patented inventions that economists identify today was well underway in the nineteenth century.[11]

As markets in invention became more competitive, many patentees and firms cross-licensed their patents to other patent owners to avoid the potential for conflicting rights.[12] The distinction between patentees and licensees was often so blurred as to be meaningless since, once inventors had a foothold in a market, they themselves might become licensees to complete their portfolios of associated patent rights and add to their royalty streams. In some cases, patent rights were allotted to companies that intended to produce the invention or

---

[10] Lamoreaux and Sokoloff (1996, 2001).

[11] Gompers and Lerner (2001).

[12] Nicholas (2011) shows that, between 1921 and 1938, patenting was prevalent among 59% of all firms and 88% of publicly traded firms in his sample of innovative research and development (R&D) firms.

associated final goods. But in many others, "speculators" invested in patents with the sole intention of profiting from the margins of price differentials, without participating in either inventive activity or manufacturing, much as a financial investor might trade in a share in a company in secondary and tertiary markets. In so doing, they added to the liquidity and depth of the market and enabled others to minimize their exposure to risk. These different patterns all characterized a process of securitization that proved to be as fundamental to the development of technology and product markets as it was to the mobilization of financial capital.

In short, intermediaries, who perform central functions in all markets, have been an integral part of social and economic transactions for all of recorded history. "Nonpracticing entities" or patent-rights holders who do not manufacture their inventions or final goods are hardly anomalous and were the norm during the nineteenth century. The historical evidence from technology markets provides ample proof that intermediation benefited creative individuals. Patentees who licensed or assigned their rights to such "trolls" were typically the most specialized and productive inventors. In theory as in practice, the notion that one should draw a sharp distinction between the rights of the first or second or third owner of any asset—intellectual or otherwise—has little economic merit. Overall, the reliance on external sales and licensing was a primary strategy for most patentees, until a noticeable decline in assignments occurred as internal research and development in corporations became more prevalent in the twentieth century. In the concluding chapter, I discuss how technological change has shifted the market in ideas in the twenty-first century back in the direction of the decentralized mediated transactions of the nineteenth century.

Warlike Patentees and Explosive Litigation

Part of the concern about patent trolls relates to their association with costly litigation. Americans from the beginning of the colonial period have always considered themselves to be exceptionally litigious and equally hyperbolic about decrying the negative consequences of legal conflicts. Patent trolls of many denominations are often linked to the proliferation of "patent wars" and held responsible for an "explosion" in patent litigation in recent decades. The prospect of such litigation, according to some economists, implies that patents comprise "probabilistic property rights," analogous to lottery tickets. Many bills have been brought before Congress to provide a solution to this "excessive litigation" and the allegedly attendant "staggering costs."

Costly litigation has always been, and will always be, a feature of patent institutions that protect valuable inventions. Patents provide legal rights to enforce inventive assets and, without the ability to appeal to courts, would be little better than worthless pieces of paper. In the United States, disputes at law increased most rapidly during the periods of the greatest economic and technological progress. Moreover, the vast majority of all disputes are settled out of court, so it is not surprising that the selected sample of higher-valued patents that come before the courts are associated with correspondingly high costs of litigation. In the nineteenth century, as today, specialization and division of labor in technology markets also extended to enforcement of the property rights in invention against infringers or those who wished to overturn the patent rights for their own benefit. Some contracts specified that the purchaser of the partial right would accept the responsibility of funding and bringing lawsuits against potential infringers. The interests of the inventors and these "trolls" were aligned, and star inventors sometimes entered into contractual agreements to make a token appearance in court in the event of litigation to indicate this concordance, even when all of the property rights had been alienated to a third party.

Litigation appears to be socially inefficient relative to a utopian world of zero transaction costs. However, counterfactual analysis based on real-world institutions raises the possibility that litigation might play a productive role and lead to lower social costs relative to actual alternatives.[13] Society has an interest in reducing uncertainty and delineating the boundaries of inventive property rights. Such rights can be determined ex ante, for instance, by allocating enough resources to examination at the patent office to precisely identify the boundaries for each of the millions of patents granted. Given that the vast majority of patents are worthless, the attempt to perfectly define and demarcate each patent right at issue would impose an excessive cost on society. Patent litigation, by contrast, can be regarded as an option in the clarification of property rights that is exercised only for valuable innovations.[14] From this perspective, ex post determination of the boundaries of valuable property through privately funded litigation appears to be more socially beneficial than costly ex ante investments by the patent office.

---

[13] See, for instance, Galasso et al. (2013).

[14] Some types of litigation, such as cases that signal tough strategies by repeat transactors, might help to reduce future disputes. Spillover benefits can also be created when decisions reduce uncertainty for all firms and inventors. The case records provide a stock of knowledge and information for other potential parties and are also invaluable for academics who publish papers denouncing patent trolls.

Today, the contentious discussions about explosive litigation and trollish nonpracticing entities are muddied by a lack of consistency in definitions and imprecision in the use of data. If we define an "explosion" as an increase that is abnormal (in the statistical sense of relative to previous trends), it becomes more feasible to identify the extent to which recent outcomes are anomalous. To do so, this section offers an empirical assessment of patent conflicts and litigation patterns over the past two centuries. Other things being equal, we might expect an increase in litigation if the volume of patents increases, so the rate of litigation relative to patents filed is more informative than the absolute number of cases. The specific basis for comparison is unimportant, since the same conclusions

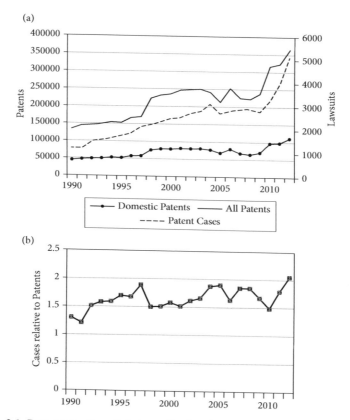

Figure 2.1 Patent Litigation, Relative to Total and Domestic Patent Grants (1990–2015).

(a) Cases and patents. (b) Litigation rate (percentage).

Notes and Sources: Patent cases were retrieved from the Administrative Office of the U.S. Courts, *Annual Reports of the Director: Judicial Business of the United States Courts* (various years). Patent grants were reported by the U.S. Patent and Trademark Office.

hold if another scaling measure is used, such as industrial output or national income.

This exercise shows that the alleged "patent litigation explosion" is much overblown, since the lawsuits merely mirror a parallel "explosion" in patenting (Figure 2.1). Patent applications and grants alike rose sharply, from approximately 270,000 applications and 153,000 grants in 1999 to 543,000 and 253,000, respectively, in 2012, with especially rapid growth between 2009 and 2010. Although the ratio of lawsuits to patents has moderately increased since this period, the litigation rate is still unexceptional. This is especially true because legislative changes in legal rules (ironically intended to reduce litigation) have led to a nominal or administrative increase in the numbers of cases filed.

However, two decades may be insufficient to assess whether patent disputes have reached a pathological level. The period through to 1920 was an extraordinarily creative period in terms of patented innovations, when the numbers of American patents relative to population attained record levels. It is useful to examine the patterns over time of reported patent cases relative to patents filed between 1790 and 2000 (see Figures 2.2 and 2.3). This historical trend in litigation rates relative to patents granted clearly does not support claims that litigation in the past decade has "exploded" above the long-term norm. In fact, the per patent rate of litigation was highest in the era before the Civil War, as well as during the significant market expansion that started in the 1870s and heralded the "second Industrial Revolution" that dramatically improved living standards. If unreported cases are included, these conclusions become all the more evident.[15] Patent litigation rates were moderately rising toward the end of the twentieth century, but this increase still remains well below the long-term norm.

For many commentators today, the nature of modern technologies is sufficiently unique that they are held to raise issues that are different from prior eras. They argue that contributions to information technology, for instance, are so nebulous that it is not possible to readily determine their limits, and this means that it is easy to engage in accidental infringement. Moreover, since any one commercial product is covered by a large number of patents, this creates a plethora of opportunities for frivolous litigation to extract rents from producers. However, these supposed differences are of degree rather than of kind: patents have always belonged to "the metaphysics of the law" (*Folsom v. Marsh*, 9 F. Cas.

---

[15] The published official judicial statistics of patent litigation are not available for this entire period, so they cannot be used to gauge long-run trends and are not directly comparable to the results in Figure 2.1. Moreover, my data include only reported lawsuits, implying that the patterns are even stronger when combined with unreported cases. Beauchamp (2015) has painstakingly traced archival unreported cases and finds that total patent litigation rates in the nineteenth century were significantly higher than in the present. In 1850, for example, New York City and Philadelphia alone had approximately ten times more patent disputes relative to the population of patents than in the entire United States at present.

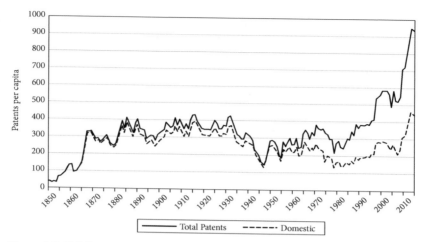

Figure 2.2 U.S. Patenting Rates: Grants Relative to Population, 1850–2015

Notes and Sources: Patent grants data are from the Annual Reports of the U.S. Patent Office, and population data are from the U.S. Census Bureau. Patents are calculated per million of the population.

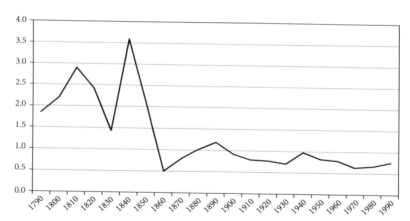

Figure 2.3 Patent Litigation Rates, 1790–2000 (Reported Lawsuits as a Percentage of Total Patents Granted, by Decade)

Notes and Sources: Patent lawsuits were estimated from Lexis and from published volumes of reports of historical patent cases. Patent grants were obtained from annual reports of the U.S. Patent Office.

342, 1841). It is no easier to identify the boundaries of a nineteenth-century electrical discovery; some forms of software have extremely high fixed costs and other nonsoftware inventions also have low costs; most programming is not independent of other discoveries; and inventions such as the sewing machine or automobile similarly contained thousands of patented incremental inventions. As such, information technology does not involve or require dramatically new analysis in the realm of patent rights.

Technological innovations in the twenty-first century have undoubtedly transformed production and consumption; however, their socioeconomic and institutional impacts are arguably not as significant as those of the first century of the U.S. patent system. This was true not just of "great inventions" that significantly expanded production possibilities, but also of the tsunami of supposedly incremental discoveries such as safety pins, aspirin, improved methods of washing clothes, breadmaking machines, and manufactured soap. From the perspective of a world where mail was delivered by stagecoach, the advent of the telegraph in the antebellum era was far more transformative to communications than the change from a landline to a cell phone. The inventive ideas that were being patented were likewise more radical departures from contemporary knowledge, making it difficult for juries and judges of the day to comprehend and distinguish the merits of competing claimants. Electrical inventions, such as the polyphase alternating current system that would exploit the power of Niagara Falls to illuminate regions hundreds of miles away, were based on concepts that were so abstract and novel that these discoveries seemed magical and incomprehensible even to trained observers.[16]

Foreigners, by contrast, found it impressive that in the United States "every good thing deserving a patent was patented."[17] Enormous profits awaited those who were able to successfully commercialize new inventions and satisfy or anticipate market demand, creating wealth for some entrepreneurs on an unprecedented and unmatched scale. Numerous inventors were attempting to resolve similar problems, leading to multiple patent interferences, overlapping claims, and efforts to invent around existing patents. Complex combinations of hundreds of patents often covered any particular device, so it is not surprising that intense competition for these excess returns centered around patent rights.[18] Licensing and litigation were a common strategy by "practicing" and "nonpracticing entities" alike.

---

[16] O'Neill (1944) cites a reporter who marveled that "[Tesla's] accomplishments seem like the dream of an intoxicated god." See also *Edison Electric Co. v. Westinghouse*, 55 F. 490, 514, 516 (1893): "it is exceedingly hazardous for one not an expert to express an opinion on a question so wholly within the domain of scientific exposition. ... It is difficult—impossible, perhaps—to describe what invention is."

[17] Bally and Dubied (1878: 33).

[18] Revision of Statutes Relating to Patents: Hearings Before the S. Comm. on Patents (1922), p. 180.

The more valuable inventions created incentives for infringement and defense against infringers. Austin and Zebulon Parker of Ohio prosecuted claims for licenses against millers across the nation and engaged in countless lawsuits regarding their 1829 patent for an improved waterwheel.[19] George Campbell Carson's smelting patents were held to be worth an estimated $260 million in damages and royalties in 1925. He also floated shares in the Carson Investment Company, which was formed to obtain income from pursuing potential defendants in court. In the railroad industry,

> a ring of patent speculators, who, with plenty of capital, brains, legal talent and impudence, have already succeeded in levying heavy sums upon every considerable railway company in the land. . . . This case is not an isolated one, but there were hundreds of them, and the railway company that made up its mind to insist upon its rights had to keep a large legal force, a corps of mechanical experts, and other expensive accessories, in order to secure that end.[20]

The 1828 Woodworth patent was one of the most contentions examples, attracting public attention and outrage for almost three decades. William Woodworth was a carpenter from Hudson, New York, whose improvement on machines to plane wood dramatically improved productivity in the woodworking industry. Congress was besieged with hundreds of petitions to protest against the Woodworth patent, which one member of the hearing committees deemed "the most onerous burden of taxation for the benefit of a single man which was ever inflicted upon the country." The owners of the Woodworth patent rights were quick to use the legal system to enforce their rights and deter potential infringers. *Scientific American* noted that the widespread demand for the patented invention allowed them to exact "enormous sums from the various kinds of mechanics using such machinery, which they must pay, or incur the hazard of litigation."[21]

Woodworth did not have the resources to pay for the patent or to commercialize his invention, so he initially transferred half of the rights to a backer for $1,500 and used this sum to finance the patent. He ultimately sold off all his rights to members of a wealthy syndicate who intended to subdivide and repackage the patent rights for resale in the national market. These nonpracticing investors obtained several million dollars in annual profits after they assigned

---

[19] In one 1849 case, Zebulon Parker brought charges of infringement of his waterwheel patent against Charles Hoyt, a prosperous mill owner in Aurora, Illinois. Abraham Lincoln represented the defendant and won the case before the federal district court the following summer.

[20] *The American Railway Times*, July 16, 1870, p. 231.

[21] Commissioner on Patents, Woodworth Patent, H.R. Rep. No. 32-156, 1852, p. 179; see also "The Woodworth Patent," *Scientific American*, April 13, 1850, p. 237.

geographic rights to the patent throughout the country and licensed use rights to mills at royalty rates as high as 25%. The relative value of the annual income from the Woodworth patent to the investors in terms of dollars today ranges from $327 million (simple inflation adjustments) to more than $94 billion (in terms of wage equivalents). The network of secondary and tertiary trades was minute and complicated. The complexity of the market for this invention increased after the term of the patent was extended several times, given that investments had been made with the anticipation that the patent was about to expire.

Meanwhile, to add further knots to the already intricate network of transactions, in 1829, Uri Emmons was granted a patent for a similar machine, which he assigned to William Tyack, Daniel H. Toogood, and Daniel Halstead. A patent pool was organized to avoid legal conflicts, and the property rights in question were cross-assigned to all of the parties concerned, in several overlapping geographic regions of the United States. Woodworth died in 1839, but his key patent lived on for another seventeen years because the owners of the patent rights successfully lobbied Congress for an extension in the patent term until 1856. Woodworth had also invented additional improvements, and after his death, these supplementary patents rights belonged to his estate.

In 1843, Woodworth's son made a partial assignment of the seven-year extension to James G. Wilson, "a private speculator" who was a party in the landmark Supreme Court case *Wilson v. Rousseau*, 45 U.S. 646 (1846). The justices in *Wilson* referred with some disdain to these investors who merely "dealt with the patent rights as a matter of business and speculation," but the patent law provided that the benefits of the renewal extended to these early nonpracticing entities. The assignees were involved in countless disputes and a total of seventy-eight reported federal lawsuits, many to suppress competing patent owners, and they typically won significant damages and even permanent injunctions. It is therefore somewhat incongruous that they later petitioned Congress to extend the patent further, arguing that they needed the extra concessions to receive their just returns, because the cost of litigation had dissipated their profits from the invention.

The *Morning Star* newspaper in 1891 wryly noted that, "In reply to the question: 'What is a patent?' the Yankee inventor once said: 'It is the right to sue somebody.'" The complicated tangle of property rights, litigation, and controversy among intermediaries that characterized the Woodworth patent was hardly unique. In a similar case, John C. Birdsell invented in 1858 an improvement on clover threshing machines whose term was extended for another twenty-one years, during which time his rights were infringed upon by a pool of powerful manufacturers of agricultural implements. He appealed to Congress for a further extension on the grounds that, although he had earned over $40 million on the patent, his costs from litigation and other sources had prevented him from profiting over the two decades. In 1878, it was alleged that he had spent $3.2 million dollars in attorney fees.

"Patent wars" were similarly waged in expanding markets in shoemaking, reapers and other agricultural machinery, india rubber products, motion pictures, early aviation, radio, electricity, and telecommunications. The *Oregonian* noted in 1912, "Scarcely any great invention is made in this country without a lawsuit to obstruct its development. This is as true of the telephone as of the aeroplane." The Wrights were so assiduous in enforcing their property rights that the moment the French aviator Louis Paulhan landed in the United States, he was served with a lawsuit alleging that his aircraft infringed on the Wright patents. Disputes and conflicts were associated with controversial exchanges of both ex ante and ex post licensing rights. At the same time, the government exercised fewer constraints on the behavior of industrial and technological rivals than in the modern era, and some of these conflicts over patent rights resulted in outright criminal behavior such as bribes, spying, payoffs, price-fixing and other collusive behavior, and even physical violence. In one amusing report in the *New York Times* in 1888, a clergyman was arrested for physically attacking a patent agent who questioned the validity of his right to a patent for his invention.

My research on great inventors demonstrated that their enterprises often were engaged in legal battles, not just to enforce their rights but also to extend their market power. "Practicing" did not necessarily confer virtue on the relevant party, and neither did patentee status. Many manufacturers obtained the rights to rival patents, to add to their income, to foreclose on competition, or to protect themselves from the prospect of litigation. George Selden, a patent attorney, was never successful as a manufacturer but propelled his 1895 patent for gasoline-powered vehicles through the courts for eight years in an attempt to extract royalties from every car that was produced in the country, until Henry Ford managed to overturn his claims. Charles A. Shaw, patentee of an alleged one hundred inventions, purchased other inventors' patent rights as investments and was continually involved in litigation on account of this large portfolio of combined patents. Shaw and Clark, a famous sewing machine enterprise located in Biddeford, Maine, successfully resisted the combined efforts of Elias Howe, Wheeler & Wilson, Grover & Baker, and Singer & Co. to overturn their patents and ended up with a lucrative stream of income from licenses in the sewing machine market.

The "great india rubber lawsuits" likewise featured intense rivalry among Horace Day, Charles Goodyear, and Nathaniel Hayward and resulted in litigation costs of more than $18 million. Cyrus McCormick, Thomas Edison, King Gillette, George Westinghouse, and Alexander G. Bell were just a few of the patentees who engaged in multiple disputes with prohibitively high litigation costs. A "big radio lawsuit" was litigated all the way to the Supreme Court in 1928, and the De Forest Company was finally awarded the rights in inter-ference over feedback circuit patents, but at a cost of over $10 million in litiga-tion expenses. The sums that were at stake in litigation between these pioneer enterprises were especially impressive when assessed relative to average income or earnings. For instance, the U.S. Steel and Bethlehem Steel 1929 lawsuit over the Grey Beam patent involved claims of $10.6 billion, valued at dollars today rel-ative to the wages of an unskilled worker. Reporters noted that some firms were sufficiently "bumptious" that they did not hesitate to launch threats of lawsuits even against the U.S. government.

Disruptive technologies by definition led to disruptions that require adjudi-cation. The discussion of law and innovation in this book (Chapter 12) points out that "vexatious" and costly litigation regarding *all* areas of law—patents, pro-perty, contracts, and torts alike—were inevitably associated with the advent of important technologies. In 1853, *Scientific American* referred to

> the amount of money used in litigation, and the threats which have been em-ployed by patent capitalists to over-awe the less wealthy or more timorous persons engaged in the same business. . . . Many who would gladly purchase patents and engage in the manufacture of the articles protected by them, have been prevented from doing so by fears of being involved in vexatious lawsuits.

The lesson here is that it was never possible to preassign labels that would predict who would act in a meritorious fashion simply to enforce their legitimate rights and who would engage in unproductive behavior to drive out competitors or to participate in questionable greenmail.

The legal profession certainly benefited financially from these patent confrontations, as they did from all types of disputes in the market. The "mam-moth patent lawsuit" over Henry Burden's 1840 spike patent lasted over a decade and yielded "golden nest eggs" to the attorneys involved. In one lawsuit alone in 1852, Daniel Webster was paid $332,000 in current dollars as lead attorney. Just as today, patent litigation was viewed as prohibitively costly for plaintiffs and defendants, but market solutions were readily available to enable investments in enforcement and to provide countervailing power against wealthier opponents. Multiple defendants at times joined together as a class and pooled resources to counter a plaintiff's litigation threats, to overturn the validity of the patent, or to defeat attempts to extend the term of a valuable patent. Quite early in the nineteenth century, the legal profession in the United States overcame the tradi-tional English disapproval of "barratry," or measures to incite or enable litigation. Contingent fees were conceded as a means to democratize access to U.S. courts and provided another way in which impecunious parties at litigation were able to fund high costs and share the risks of pursuing their claims.

Abraham Lincoln   Daniel Webster

Edwin Stanton   William Seward

Figure 2.4 Patent Attorneys in Antebellum Courts
Patent litigation has attracted some of the most brilliant minds in American history.
Abraham Lincoln, the only U.S. president to file a patent, also acted as a patent
lawyer and his final case before assuming the presidency involved a patent dispute.
He met his secretary of war (Edwin Stanton) and secretary of state (William Seward)
as attorneys in a landmark patent lawsuit. The legendary Daniel Webster (known
at the "Defender of the U.S. Constitution") commanded enormous fees as a patent
lawyer, and a sculpture of Webster (design patent by Thomas Ball in 1853) was one
of the first to be commercialized to a mass market.
Source: Library of Congress.

Abraham Lincoln was the only American president to ever obtain a patent
himself, and he also practiced as a patent lawyer. He was involved in a number
of local patent lawsuits, and Lincoln and his partner William Herndon also
took on cases on behalf of nineteenth-century nonpracticing entities. Their

firm represented Alexander Edmunds, a furniture maker from Mount Pulaski, Illinois, who patented an automated "horological" baby's cradle in 1853, which he marketed as "Mother's Help." This invention was designed to "rock itself until it run down, and so save the continual labor to mother and nurses, of rocking the cradle." Edmunds subdivided the patent by counties and by states and sold the rights for specific geographical areas to other interested parties. The patent right to several states was transferred to McCarty Hildreth and William Turner for a price of $10,000. Turner then resold his share in the patent to John and George Myers for $5,000. The lawsuits about the patent, which were appealed to the state supreme court, dealt with the validity of these assignment contracts.[22]

Lincoln's political campaign was partly underwritten by the payment he received for his silent participation in the high-profile patent lawsuit between Cyrus McCormick and John Manny over the rights to lucrative mechanical reapers.[23] Manufacturers of McCormick's machinery cofunded and launched a large network of lobbyists and lawsuits who colluded to overturn his patent rights:

> If funds are furnished us, we shall surely beat him; but if they are not furnished us, he will as certainly beat us. Please, therefore, take hold and help us to beat the common enemy. The subscriptions have ranged from $100 to $1,000. . . . Send in also to Patent Office hundreds of remonstrances like this: We oppose the extension of C. H. McCormick's patent. He has made money enough off of the farmer.[24]

This landmark case included such legal luminaries as George Harding, who had successfully defended Samuel Morse in the "wireless telegraph wars." Lead counsel in the case, William H. Seward and Edwin Stanton, were later appointed as Lincoln's secretaries of state and war, respectively.

Disputes about commercially valuable inventions were simply part of business amid prosperity in peace time, and (as Chapter 8 on war and technology shows) likewise during military conflict. In a memorandum to Chief of Ordnance George D. Ramsay on March 10, 1864, Lincoln dismissed concerns about patent disputes for improvements in expanding projectiles for rifled cannon. He wrote that he thought

> the Absterdam projectile is too good a thing to be lost to the service, and if offered at the Hotchkiss prices, and not in excessive quantities, nor unreasonable

---

22 *Edmunds v. Myers et al.*, Sup. Ct. Illinois (1854); *Edmunds v. McCarty Hildreth et al.* (1854).
23 *McCormick v. Manny*, 15 F. Cas. 1314 (1856).
24 Casson (1909: 93).

terms in other respects, by either or both parties to the patent controversy, take it, so that the test be fully made. I am for the government having the best articles in spite of patent controversies.[25]

Litigation rates varied by industry and were positively correlated with the advent of the latest technologies that were most profitable in the marketplace. The most prolific disputes occurred in the electricity and telecommunications industry, which accounted for over 40% of all lawsuits that great inventors filed around the time of the second Industrial Revolution. The Brush and U.S. Electric Lighting Companies even threatened their competitors' customers that, owing to their patent rights, purchasing the rival products was tantamount to buying into a lawsuit (Figure 2.5). These legal cases and countersuits proved to be so expensive that the major firms eventually agreed in 1896 to end the "electric patent war" through mutual cross-licenses. However, it was not long before many of the same companies—AT&T, Radio Corporation, Westinghouse, and General Electric—were once again directing resources toward a "battle of the air" over early wireless technology that was equally costly and also ended in pooled interests.[26] Other patent lawsuits wound their way through the courts for years, such as the Knibbs valve patent, which was involved in litigation for twenty-three years. These epic confrontations over the rights to the wealth associated with modern technologies captivated the public imagination and even motivated some scam artists to concoct financial ventures offering shares in patent litigation claims that they offered as golden investment opportunities to the general public.

Summing Up

European systems allowed monopoly patent grants on payment of exorbitant fees that few ordinary inventors could afford. In England, specific measures were put in place to limit the number of outside investors, and courts also undermined markets in patented ideas. At the first exhibition of the Pennsylvania Institute for the Encouragement of Apprentices in 1857, the keynote speaker declared that "travellers in other countries see palaces and grand cathedrals," but in the United

---

[25]   Abraham Lincoln, *Complete Works*, vol. 2 (1920), p. 494.

[26]   "Battle of the Air Developing a Mass of Litigation Which May Bring Congressional Legislation," *Wall Street Journal*, March 12, 1924, p. 10; "The Patent Pool for Radio," *New York Times*, July 12, 1931, "[P]atent pool will bring freedom from the throes of litigation. . . . These conditions have permitted owners of patents to harass the industry, putting its members to millions of dollars of unnecessary litigation expense and extorting from them additional millions for royalties under patents which the courts have ultimately declared invalid."

"BUYING INTO A LAW SUIT"

AN ANNOUNCEMENT OF GREAT IMPORTANCE TO ALL PROSPECTIVE BUYERS OF ELECTRIC PLEASURE CARS

For the information of the general public, dealer and buyer alike, we desire to announce once again that the Ohio Electric Car Company holds basic patents on the following principles of electro-car construction, and the application thereof:

1.   Double drive from both front and rear seat.
2.   Chainless, direct shaft drive without universal joints.
3.   Magnetic control, including magnetic brake.

In this connection we wish to quote a paragraph from an announcement made by us in our publicity on April 29th, 1913, as follows:

"Other manufacturers themselves admit that the double drive makes the single-drive car out of date. Every manufacturer would gladly adopt the double drive were it not for our basic patents. It is safe to say that the next few months will see attempt to get around these patents—for the double drive is the car of the future. It is well to remember, however, that we will defend in the courts of last resort our exclusive right to the double drive principle."

Our attorneys advise us that our patents on all the features named are legally unassailable.

Notice is therefore hereby given to all concerned, whether manufacturer, dealer or buyer, that we shall prosecute to the full extent of the law any infringement of our patents in the manufacture, sale or use of any electric vehicle containing infringing features.

All prospective buyers are advised to familiarize themselves with the features covered by our patents before purchasing any car.

OHIO ELECTRIC CAR CO., Toledo, Ohio.

Los Angeles Distributors: SMITH BROS., 742-748 So. Olive St.

OHIO ELECTRIC

Figure 2.5   Patent Trolling of Prospective Automobile Buyers

This 1913 advertisement by the Ohio Electric Car Company proclaims the strength of its intellectual property rights and warns that purchasers of any competitor's vehicles would have insecure title owing to the firm's "legally unassailable patents."

Source: Los Angeles Times, July 13, 1913, p. II2.

States "he sees none that surpasses in elegance, design and largeness of area, that temple erected to preserve unforgotten the memorials of American genius,— the Patent Office." The central features of the U.S. patent system and adjacent institutions were unique to the world and ensured open access to creative individuals, decentralized decision making, strong legal enforcement of such rights, and extensive markets for technology.

Americans were enthusiastic about the patent system, but the same individuals were often critical of the administration of specific rules and standards that impinged on their own specific interests. As such, it is useful to distinguish the fundamental principles of these property rights from anomalies, and long-run historical patterns allow us to objectively identify the central underlying features of institutions and outcomes. Many have rightly pointed out that current practices in the use and enforcement of patent grants add to the transaction costs of inventive activity and markets in inventions. However, when taken in long-run perspective, today's "patent wars" and "explosion in litigation" are hardly anomalous. New innovations and industries that added significant value have always been associated with extreme competition and upsurges in costly litigation that were resolved through private compromises.

As Thomas Jefferson pointed out, institutions must adjust to the times, but efficient changes need to be consistent with the underlying principles of the system. In the nineteenth century, the vast majority of the flurry of bills and proposals that interest groups produced in response to every new circumstance never resulted in new legislation. The transformative period up to the end of the Civil War featured no more than three major reforms in patent laws. However, numerous new measures have been adopted in the past seventy-five years to confront short-run perceived crises. These changes responded to the ephemeral demands of the most strident interest groups at a single point in time, many were introduced to remedy the negative consequences of the last change, and not a few were inconsistent with the fundamentals of the U.S. system of intellectual property.

It is worth noting that market exchange is most effective when trades are independent of the identities of the parties involved, and remedies that adjust the validity or strength of property rights in patents based on who owns those rights (whether they are a "nonpracticing entity" or "practicing entity") undermine a basic principle of economic efficiency. Such inefficient changes in legal rules and standards create incentives for corresponding changes in business policies that risk the potential misallocation of resources. If courts offer greater protection to producers or patentees, as opposed to intermediaries, the discriminatory treatment serves to subsidize producers and tax nonproducers. Such distortions provide incentives to make nominal investments in production facilities or in the employment of patentees or to further engage in unproductive defenses that would circumvent the rules at higher private and social cost. During the most liti-gious era in the past two centuries, observers pointed out that "the assertion that the patent-system interferes injuriously with intellectual progress by blocking the course of thought is curiously at variance with the evidence of history."[27]

Accounting for Inventions

Technological change has transformed the goods and services at our command, from champagne and laptop computers to one-click shopping baskets and weapons of mass destruction. Markets for technology have encouraged an aston-ishing diversity of options to satisfy the even more diverse tastes and preferences of consumers. Economic theorists have devised ingenious mathematical models that describe this manifest link between useful knowledge and social welfare. However, more precise evidence is needed to reliably understand how specific institutions and incentives affect both inputs and outcomes, and this dilemma still has not been entirely resolved. How can we translate abstract theories about ideas into empirically tractable measures that can capture novel tangible and in-tangible advances?

A classic article by Zvi Griliches carefully spells out the advantages and defi-ciencies of patent data as a measure of inventive activity.[28] Among patentable inventions, inventors may choose not to obtain a patent, for instance, if they can benefit from keeping the idea secret. Other nonpatentees may wish to freely dis-close their ideas to generate network effects and market growth if, despite the lower market share, their profits in absolute terms were likely to exceed the returns from a smaller market. Not all inventions can be patented, but well-known rules specify which categories are patentable and which are unpatentable. U.S. patents require an examination for novelty, relative to the massive stock of accumulated knowledge that examiners consult, and inventors have a right of ap-peal to the decisions of the Patent Office all the way to the Supreme Court. Patent grants represent inventive inputs, whereas inventions that lead to commercially viable products are called innovations. Patented ideas vary in terms of economic and technical value, and many turn out to be worthless and are abandoned.

A major advantage for empirical work is that these features of patent data are well known, and adjustments can be made in the analysis and interpreta-tion to account for their specific characteristics and drawbacks. For instance, researchers have employed proven techniques to identify valuable patented inventions, including renewal data, patent claims and citations, assignments,

[27] Richardson (1878: 103).
[28] Griliches (1998).

litigation, and information from contracts. Kenneth Sokoloff and I assessed the activity of "great inventors" as another means of adjusting the data to gauge how important inventions behaved relative to "ordinary" inventions. As Griliches (1998) concluded:

> In this desert of data, patent statistics loom up as a mirage of wonderful plenitude and objectivity. They are available; they are by definition related to inventiveness, and they are based on what appears to be an objective and only slowly changing standard. No wonder that the idea that something interesting might be learned from such data tends to be rediscovered in each generation.

At the same time, researchers cannot simply download a computer-ready dataset of patent grants and obtain meaningful results the next day. It is particularly important to have a clear understanding of how institutional details and legal enforcement vary across countries and over time. Patent grants are classified into technical categories that bear little relationship to economic industries and as a result must be reordered into industrial classes in which the invention will be used. Accordingly, all patents reported in this project have been reclassified to the sector of final use. For economic purposes, we would also like to know what sorts of inventions and inventors are likely to generate growth and the way in which institutions and incentives affect technological progress. The patent information in this book was further matched to other sources, such as the manuscript census and market transactions, to fully examine inventive activity as well as commercialization and innovations.

Some studies use counts of items displayed at international exhibitions to make sweeping generalizations about the role of patents and the patent system.[29] What do international expositions tell us about technological change and the efficacy of patent institutions? These records include valuable details about efforts to commercialize and publicize products and innovations. Exhibitions gave out awards of all sorts, so they can usefully shed light on how prize systems work. This book shows how idiosyncratic decisions by juries and committees conformed to predictions about administered systems. International exhibitions, by contrast, tell us little about patenting or inventive activity and even less about patent systems in general.

Why did firms and individual exhibitors participate in international exhibitions? Elite inventors who specialized in inventive activity and assigned their discoveries to firms typically did not participate in such spectacles.

---

[29] A sample of such studies is summarized in Moser (2013). Historians of women's contributions, in particular, have made insightful use of records from world's fairs. See Warner (1979) and Darney (1982).

Exhibitors at international events were predominantly export-oriented enterprises and manufacturing firms that traveled around to different exhibitions in hopes of accumulating premiums as a means of differentiating and marketing their products.[30] Inventors like Samuel Colt and Gail Borden turned up because they owned manufacturing companies and were involved in commercialization. Even in the machine halls, the exhibits at the Crystal Palace and other fairs tended to be manufactured goods being displayed by their manufacturers, rather than novel technological contributions on par with patented inventions. Such items did not consist of random draws from the underlying population of either inventions, innovations, or products and were unrepresentative of inventive activity either within or across technologies, industries, firms, or countries.

For instance, the size and content of displays for any country or group of products were biased by distance, language, and political expedience. As Table 2.2 indicates, at the 1851 Crystal Palace, Britain and its dependents accounted for 7,381 or 53% of all exhibitors, in comparison to 1,710 (12.3%) from France, 499 (3.6%) from the United States, and just 12 from the entire continent of South America. At the Paris Universal Exhibition of 1855, on the other hand, France and its dependents made up 50.1% of all 21,779 exhibitors, while Britain and its colonies were a mere 15%, and the number of U.S. exhibitors, at 0.6%, was the same size as the Greek contingent. As such, adding up the number of exhibits in (say) a particular industry in Switzerland or the United States tells us nothing about the nature or degree of inventiveness in either industry or country.

Even if the "home court advantage" is accounted for, there were significant differences in participation within and across industries and countries that were not correlated with technological characteristics or capabilities. For instance, funding for the exhibitions, as well as variation in costs (travel, insurance, and other expenses), influenced the number and composition of displays. The U.S. government was often uninterested in financing these essentially commercial ventures, while in a number of other countries, national governments either paid for or subsidized participation by their citizens. At the Crystal Palace, George Peabody, a wealthy American banker living in London, was so embarrassed by the initial bareness of the U.S. section that he provided funds from his own purse to help decorate the display and transport the exhibits. Many took this private initiative as an indicator of the poverty of centralized state intervention in

---

[30] Prizes at international exhibitions were valued by the manufacturers who assiduously turned up at every fair to tout their products and proclaimed their accumulated stock of medals in brash advertisements. Such displays became less popular toward the end of the nineteenth century, as more effective outlets for advertising products developed, and as consumers turned to alternative entertainment such as radios and movies.

Table 2.2 Exhibitors at World's Fairs in 1851 and 1855, by Country

Country	Number	%
Crystal Palace Exhibition, 1851		
Austria	731	5.2
Belgium	506	3.6
Britain and Colonies	7,381	53.0
China	30	0.2
France	1,710	12.3
Germany	1,536	11.0
Netherlands	113	0.8
South America	12	0.1
Spain	286	2.1
Switzerland	273	1.9
United States	499	3.6
Others	870	6.2
Total	13,947	100
Paris Universal Exposition, 1855		
Austria	1,298	6.0
Belgium	687	3.2
Britain and Colonies	3,269	15.0
China	0	0.0
France and Colonies	10,914	50.1
Germany	2,198	10.1
Greece	131	0.6
Netherlands	411	1.9
Portugal	443	2.0
South America	38	0.2
Spain	569	2.6
Switzerland	408	1.9
United States	131	0.6
Others	1,282	5.9
Total	21,779	100

Source: *Official Catalogue of the Great Exhibition of the Works of Industry of All Nations, 1851* (London, 1852); *Paris Universal Exhibition of 1867: Catalogue of the British Section* (London, 1867); Robert H. Thurston, ed., *Reports of the Commissioners of the United States to the International Exhibition Held at Vienna* (Washington, DC, 1876).

industry and invention, when compared to the strength of decentralized market institutions.[31]

Enormous variation occurred across products and countries at each exhibition, as well as across time, in quite unpredictable ways. At the Paris Universal Exposition of 1855, one observer noted that "the American display cannot teach us anything; the USA is a great nation, as everybody is aware, but it is necessary to know that beforehand, because the Exposition would rather tend to prove the contrary."[32] Instead, Mexico was the sole representative of the New World that had an exhibition of any significance, and the Mexican display "was certainly more complete than that of the United States." The United States was in the middle of a war at the time of the Paris Universal Exhibition of 1862, and Congress allowed only $2,000 to cover expenses, so just 128 Americans participated among the total of 26,348 exhibitors, whereas the U.S. government allocated more than $1.4 million for the Paris exhibition of 1900, which obviously boosted participation. In short, each international fair was a unique cross-section that was not repeated over time and participation in each year and industry varied for idiosyncratic reasons.

Every exposition was assembled according to its own rules and practices, which implies that it is all the more necessary to pay meticulous attention to the institutional details. Patent rules are well defined, and American patent grants must demonstrate inventive novelty. The criteria for awards differed in each international exposition, but it needs to be emphasized that the question of novelty was never at the forefront at any of them. At the London Crystal Palace Exhibition, for instance, three types of awards were distributed: Council Medals, prize medals, and honorable mentions, totaling close to 2,500 premiums.[33] Just 170 Council Medals were bestowed, in part for novelty as perceived by the judges, but also for "peculiarity in the mode of manufacture" and other factors entirely unrelated to technological inventiveness. For instance, Professor A. Kiss won a Council Medal for his rendition in bronze of an Amazon being attacked by a tiger, and 26 Council Medals were given for raw materials and textile fabrics. For all the rest of the prizes, juries were explicitly instructed to consider criteria that had little or nothing to do with novelty, technological inventiveness, or patentability; instead, they rewarded beauty of design and appearance, "adaptability to use, economy in first cost, durability, economy of maintenance, excellency of workmanship, strength."[34] In short, juries at the Crystal Palace and other

---

[31] "No government favouritism raises any branch of manufactures to a preeminence which secures for it the patronage of the wealthy. . . . Everything is entrusted to the ingenuity of individuals, who look for their reward to public demand alone." *New England Farmer*, vol. 4 (1852), p. 59.

[32] Henri Edouard Tresca, *Visite a l'exposition universelle de Paris, en 1855*, p. 167.

[33] More than 40% of total prizes went to British exhibits, and the remainder to the rest of the world.

[34] The interested reader is urged to consult the reports of the juries for the exhibition and the detailed lists of the exhibits. By contrast, some economists have inaccurately claimed that novelty was a requirement for Crystal Palace awards, and that these exhibits of commercialized innovations and manufactured goods can be meaningfully compared to novel patented inventions.

international expositions largely bypassed questions of inventive novelty and indeed were unlikely to have the resources or ability to identify such technical factors.[35]

Ultimately, exhibitions had to stimulate the interest and attendance of the millions of paying visitors, which created a bias toward spectacle rather than toward economically or technically valuable inventions. A gigantic loaf of bread or an outsized church bell was more likely to garner interest than a tiny and visually unattractive widget, even if the widget were a critically important technology that significantly improved productivity. At the Crystal Palace, many visitors ignored the rather plain machinery in the American hall, and such displays were unlikely to include inventions whose appreciation required an understanding of abstract or abstruse principles. Certain types of technologies, such as chemicals or pharmaceuticals, were not amenable to judging on the spot, and others would have required extended testing to determine their technical value.

Any count of exhibits needs to adjust for the fact that many of these items, even within seemingly "technical" industries, had little or nothing to do with patentable technology.[36] Many exhibits were inherently unpatentable because of their subject matter and lack of novelty. Enormous steam engines (displayed because of their gigantic size rather than inventiveness), decorative fountains, minerals, stuffed wild animal specimens, and the Koh-i-Noor diamond were all in evidence at the Crystal Palace. Machines and instruments were often included in the displays because of their attractive design and workmanship, rather than because they were novel inventions. Some exhibits were new products, whereas others had been manufactured many decades before, and juries at the Crystal Palace were explicitly instructed not to pay attention to the age of the entries, which would have been impossible to monitor anyway.

Making economic comparisons between simple counts of these idiosyncratic exhibits and patented inventions is like comparing apples (the fruit) to androids (robots). Some authors have nevertheless argued that "the propensity to patent," or the precise proportion of exhibits that they were able to identify as patented, is a meaningful statistic that suggests inventors were "avoiding patents." A little thought should lead one to realize that it is impossible to determine the

---

[35] U.S. patent examiners were full-time trained specialists who had access to the stock of documented technical information in the centralized Patent Office, the specifications of patent documents from around the world, and the social capital of specialized colleagues. Judges at exhibitions clearly lacked the systematic training of patent examiners—many of the panels at international expositions were appointed as an honor or because of their social status rather than because of their technical expertise. Their decisions often reflected subjective factors and each panel applied its own idiosyncratic interpretation of the quite vague guidelines, leading to frequent charges of bias and scandalous errors in awards. Later chapters confirm that the allocation of awards in such administered systems are almost entirely random, and unrelated to technical or economic value.

[36] See Appendix II for further details.

prevalence of patents and patent systems from counts of exhibits. We can certainly identify some portion of exhibits (say, 11%) that were patented. However, any further claim that this implies "89% of exhibits were unpatented" is manifestly incorrect and misleading. A patented steam press displayed by a manufacturer rather than by its inventor would be identified as unpatented, whereas a single exhibited machine could incorporate hundreds of individual patented components that could never be identified. In short, international exhibitions can offer useful insights into the operation of prize systems; they tell us little or nothing systematic about patent systems.

What about Switzerland?

Patent abolitionists invariably point to the experience of Switzerland and the Netherlands to support their claims that patent laws did not contribute to, or even hindered, innovation. The Netherlands suspended its patent system between 1869 and 1912, and the Swiss did not offer patent protection until 1888. The Netherlands was not concerned about offering incentives for discoveries by domestic inventors, because foreigners completely dominated its patent rosters both before and after their reforms. The Swiss excelled in a narrow range of industries producing artisanal items that typically were not patentable. Both Switzerland and the Netherlands abandoned their former opposition to patent institutions and ultimately decided to protect property rights in invention, so it is useful to examine why these reforms occurred.

How inventive were the Swiss in the era before patents? Some economists point favorably to their performance at the Crystal Palace Exposition in England in 1851. It is therefore surprising to find, on closer inspection, that the Swiss delegation was represented by a mere 273 exhibitors out of a total of almost 14,000 participants. The official reports of the exhibition explicitly recorded that Switzerland was noted for skilled execution and artistic design rather than creativity at new and useful inventions that might qualify for patent protection.[37] These Swiss exhibitors were primarily manufacturers, hawking wares that included a host of miscellaneous items that were inherently unpatentable. Representative entries for Switzerland included instruments and machines of uncertain inventive content, date, or origin, along with numerous embroidered handkerchiefs, "a double American rifle," a table made from 38,000 pieces of 28 different types of wood, fringed shawls, miniature milk tubs, goat skins, cow bells, embossed drinking cups, wood carvings, a watch-stand "made by a

---

[37] See *Official Catalogue of the Great Exhibition of the Works of Industry of All Nations; Reports by the Juries* (1852), p. lxiii.

pupil of the Asylum for the Blind," and a relief model of Strasbourg Cathedral by a bookbinder "who was employed on it incessantly for three years." A count of such items obviously tells us little about whether or how inventive activity is influenced by the presence or absence of patent laws.

An undeniable historical parameter is that Swiss producers were concerned about their loss in competitiveness and became eager to emulate the American model and its patent system. They were soon aware that rates of technical and industrial progress in the United States were far more rapid than in Switzerland, and technological change was rendering Swiss artisanal methods obsolete in products with mass markets. Indeed, before 1890, American inventors had already obtained more than two thousand patents on watches, and the U.S. watch-making industry benefited from patented technological inventions, mechanization, and strong economies of scale that led to rapidly falling prices of output, making them increasingly dominant internationally. As a result, prominent Swiss manufacturers like Edward Bally and Edward Dubied called for "a patent law in Switzerland as a means for perfecting our industries. The author of these lines regards the institution of patents as the first and indispensable measure, without which any other will be utterly useless, for reaching the end that we all have in view."[38] Swiss legislators were urged that "we have but one thing to do, if we will avoid entire decadence of our industry, and that is to imitate the Americans."

Edward Dubied was especially admiring of the ability of specialized technology markets to permit U.S. patentees to become nonpracticing entities and to contribute their inventive capital to new enterprises on the same basis that stockholders could contribute financial capital:

> Secure in the ownership of his invention, he can develop its manufacture so as to render it less costly as well as more valuable; or else, if he does not wish to make the patented article himself, as often happens, he can grant to others the right to make it, reserving to himself a royalty; or his invention leads to an association of capitalists, organized on a great scale, to produce and develop the article invented by the united forces of large capital and perfect mechanism. In this case, a really meritorious invention makes its author a capitalist at one stroke; it is for him the source of a rapid fortune, for it is admitted into the business which is founded on it as a valuable element,—just as much as the capital contributed by the stockholders.[39]

---

[38] Bally and Dubied (1878: 23, 34).
[39] Bally and Dubied (1878: 32).

After examining the American experience of technologically driven economic growth, Switzerland decided to introduce its own patent laws in 1888.
Like his fellow manufacturers, Dubied was one of the beneficiaries of the Swiss
patent reforms, as he subsequently operated one of the largest knitting machine enterprises in the world, with technology based on American patents.[40]
Contemporaries in the United States thought the logic was self-evident:

> It is in this country, where patents are numerous and easily obtained, that
> improved machines and processes are most rapidly introduced, as in textile
> manufactures, in watch-making, and shoe-making; and not in Switzerland,
> where until recently no patents have been granted, or in England and Germany,
> where patents have been hard to get.[41]

In sum, patents are not perfect indicators of inventive activity, but the specific
shortcomings are well known, allowing for meticulous studies of the relationship between incentives and individual effort, technological change, and growth.
Thousands of studies using patent records have significantly advanced our understanding of the sources and nature of technological progress. At the same
time, much of the creativity that falls beyond the boundaries of the patent system
remains unexamined because of the lack of equally reliable and systematic data,
and it is important to attempt to find comparable indices. To increase the utility
of measures that are drawn from unconventional sources, researchers need to
provide full information about the institutional details that affect the interpretation of statistical results and transparently specify what the data can and cannot
convey about technological change.

The empirical methodology in this book is based on the principle that the
most valid sources of measures of inventive activity and innovation are likely
to be associated with institutions that persisted over a significant period and
enforced consistent rules and standards toward identifiable technological discoveries. These include, among others, the Royal Society of Arts in London, the
Society for the Encouragement of National Industry, the Franklin Institute, and
related mechanics' institutes in the major U.S. cities with records spanning over
a century. Such sources demonstrate continuity and at least a minimal degree of
uniformity and regularity in the units of observation in a manner that parallels
the research value of patent records.[42] These quantitative results can then be

---

[40] *American Machinist*, vol. 43 (1915), p. 685, noted that "one does not usually think of Switzerland
as a machine-manufacturing country."

[41] Richardson (1878: 99, 104).

[42] Panel data that combine similar cross-sections at the individual level repeated by year
offer insights into both spatial and temporal elements of inventive activity. Pooling comparable
observations over place and time promises more degrees of freedom, more effective treatment of heterogeneity, and greater efficiency in estimation.

combined with the multifaceted and rich qualitative details from the history of technology to procure reliable general perspectives on the economics of invention and innovation in markets and administered systems.

Many observers today dismiss historical patterns as irrelevant to the twenty-first century and the Brave New World of smartphones, silicon chips, and one-click online shopping baskets. Although technologies obviously vary over time, much of the underlying economic and legal fundamentals remain unchanged, and this chapter has shown that some of the most decried "new" features have proved to be productive characteristics of markets in invention since their inception. Scholars who consider the costs of markets in patented inventions and their enforcement to be excessive often point to the efficacy of such alternatives as innovation prizes. Again, the arguments tend to be based on inaccurate historical anecdotes about administered innovation systems and "myths of invention." This suggests that a systematic empirical analysis of historical patterns and institutional design is necessary to filter out the signal from the noise of the plethora of contradictory claims. The next chapter assesses the validity of commonly cited case studies such as the prize for longitude. Subsequent chapters report on the results from extensive original research into the operation and outcomes associated with markets in ideas and administered innovation systems.

3

Inventing Prizes

Everybody has won and all must have prizes.
—*Alice in Wonderland*, Lewis Carroll (1865)

History, whether it is true or false or forgotten, matters. The twenty-first century is not unique in the realization of the power of knowledge in generating economic and social progress. Current debates reflect and replicate the controversies of earlier eras, ranging from questions about the efficacy of alternative incentives and how (or whether) governments could facilitate enterprise to confrontations about troll-like market intermediaries and "explosions" in patent litigation. Policymakers in the past have already explored the full range of options for promoting ingenuity, including patents, privileges, prizes, subsidies for science, bounties, trade secrecy protection, appointments to desirable jobs, pensions and other types of personal support, cartelization and the protection of monopolies, and government procurement. For many, the technologies of the present are radically different from their precursors and therefore the past has little relevance—"this time is different." For others, the lessons of the first industrial nations have been forgotten, and myths about the past currently circulate as facts that motivate important facets of technology policies across the globe. Such historical amnesia suggests the need to revisit inducements for inventive activity and to systematically examine how they actually worked in practice.

Despite a marked lack of empirical evidence, academics, enterprises, and policymakers today are increasingly enthusiastic about prizes.[1] The National Science Foundation, for instance, organized a committee to investigate the advisability of offering innovation prizes as inducements for technological progress. The panel acknowledged that there was little systematic research on the subject but nevertheless concluded—in a report that uses the term "believe" nineteen times—that "an ambitious program of innovation inducement prize contests will be a sound investment in strengthening the infrastructure for U.S. innovation."[2] One suggestion for part of a prize package was to barter a tour of the U.S. research

---

[1] "Prizes are an idea whose time has come again." See Hendrix (2014: 6).
[2] National Research Council, *Innovation Inducement Prizes at the National Science Foundation* (2007), p. 2.

Inventing Ideas. B. Zorina Khan, Oxford University Press (2020). © Oxford University Press.
DOI: 10.1093/oso/9780190936075.001.0001

facilities in Antarctica, "a rare opportunity that could stimulate a great deal of interest" among the general public. The federal government was urged to "use high-risk, high-reward policy tools such as prizes and challenges to solve tough problems."[3] The America Competes Reauthorization Act of 2010 granted all federal agencies the authority to administer prize competitions to increase innovation. Enormous sums have been diverted to finance prizes to generate new ideas and products, based on the unsubstantiated claim that prizes "have a good track record of spurring innovation." Europeans have not been far behind in rediscovering similar policies. The European Innovation Council, for example, has set aside 2 billion euros for two years of prize competitions, owing to the "growing economic importance of breakthrough and disruptive innovation."[4]

Corporations and wealthy philanthropists have similarly proposed large privately funded prizes throughout the world, for objectives that range from specific targets to solutions for more general problems. The Methuselah Foundation was launched in 2003 to finance research into health and aging, channeling over $4 million to research and development (R&D) in regenerative medicine. The Clay Mathematics Institute offers awards of $1 million for the solution of any of seven identified "Millennium Prize Problems." The Bill and Melinda Gates Foundation has offered numerous awards, such as a prize of $100,000 to a team at the California Institute of Technology, who won first place in the Gates Reinvent the Toilet competition by devising a solar-powered toilet that generated hydrogen and electricity. A prize of $100 million from the MacArthur Foundation's 100&Change goes to "fund a single proposal that promises real and measurable progress in solving a critical problem of our time."[5]

The X-Prize organization, whose motivating principle (according to its website) is "Call us crazy, but we believe," intends to create a "world where everyone has an equal voice in government as well as access to education, shelter, safety and healthcare no matter their gender, race, or economic status." The Ansari X-Prize launched a $10 million competition to build a spaceship that could accommodate three passengers, and in 2014 introduced an Indian offshoot whose directors include members of the wealthy Tata family. The Mahindra Group funded the Rise Prize Challenges, which included a payout of $700,000 to build a driverless car in India, and other discoveries that would "spur breakthrough Indian innovation which captures the mainstream imagination." Similar initiatives have also been introduced in other developing regions, such as the Innovation Prize for Africa.

---

[3] National Economic Council, *A Strategy for American Innovation* (2009).
[4] https://ec.europa.eu/commission/news/european-innovation-council-2019-mar-18_en.
[5] https://www.macfound.org/programs/100change/.

The generously funded Breakthrough Initiatives address the question "Are we alone? Now is the time to find out."[6] Their prime directive would be familiar to any fan of *Star Trek*, to seek out and make contact with extraterrestrial life forms. The Breakthrough Listen Initiative offers $100 million over ten years to search for signals from alien civilizations. The mission of the Watch Initiative is to identify the biosignatures of planets that can sustain life. Breakthrough Starshot also boasts a $100 million budget, for proof of the concept of a spacecraft fleet capable of reaching Alpha Centauri that could, within twenty years after their launch, capture images and other information about planets in this star system. Individual annual prizes of $3 million are allocated to researchers in the life sciences, physics, and mathematics. Breakthrough Message offers an annual prize of $1 million for digital communications to extraterrestrial civilizations on behalf of humankind—a species of intergalactic Twitter dispatches.[7]

James English points to "the peculiar resistance prizes seem to have mounted against any real scrutiny of their functions and effects."[8] This chapter therefore directs "real scrutiny" to the specific institutional details of how innovation prizes have worked in practice. As a starting point, it is useful to distinguish between *ex ante* awards to induce innovation, *targeted* prizes that relate to a specific and well-defined problem, *ex post* prizes such as payouts to the winners of competitions, and *recognition* prizes for nonspecific achievements such as lifetime-career awards. These categories overlap and are not mutually exclusive. More expansive definitions of innovation awards include research grants, subsidies for inputs into technology, tax credits, job offers and procurement contracts, and fellowships, among other policy instruments. However, since the objective here is to present an in-depth analysis of institutions and incentives for inventive activity, the primary focus is on patents and prizes for technological achievements.

---

[6] https://breakthroughprize.org and https://breakthroughinitiatives.org/. The Breakthrough Initiatives are "a program of scientific and technological exploration, probing the big questions of life in the Universe: Are we alone? Are there habitable worlds in our galactic neighborhood? Can we make the great leap to the stars? And can we think and act together—as one world in the cosmos?" The funders include Sergey Brin, Priscilla Chan, Yuri Milner, Anne Wojcicki, and Mark Zuckerberg. Specific information is somewhat scanty, as is typical of most of these grand prizes; the committees are drawn from previous winners of the awards, and the process of selection from nominations is publicly unknown.

[7] *Punch*, the satirical London paper, similarly offered £30,000 in prize money in 1906 for achievements that were manifestly "delayed by lack of encouragement," including an award for the first astronaut to make a round trip to Mars within a week. The rules specified that "it will be obligatory upon the winner of the first award to bring back from Mars some tangible Martian trophy—the tail feathers of a Martian, supposing the inhabitants of the planet to have any . . . or the prospectus of a Martian book club, supposing them to have enterprise. A live Martian would of course be best." November 28, 1906, p. 380.

[8] English (2005: 25).

Many economists lobby for these non-market-oriented policies as complements or superior alternatives to intellectual property rights.[9] Their rationale for promoting innovation prizes is largely based on the attractive properties of abstract theoretical economic models.[10] Both technological discovery and the transformation of an invention into a commercially useful innovation are difficult to predict, so it is important to understand the role of information, valuation, and incentives in policy alternatives. A pioneering article concluded that the optimal choice between intellectual property and other mechanisms will mainly depend on the degree of informational asymmetry between inventors and prize-granting agencies. If value and cost can be accurately determined by grantors, then prizes will dominate other incentive mechanisms.[11] Obviously, this crucial "if" is something of a blue-sky proposition that assumes away both the central benefit of market transactions and the inherent inability of administrators to accurately gauge the commercial value of a discovery.

Potential solutions would need to overcome problems of asymmetric information, where applicants know more about the value of the discovery than the administrating panel. Alternative patent buyout models propose an ingenious hybrid system. The patent is transformed into a prize that is auctioned to the highest bidder in a competitive process that reveals the underlying value of the invention; the government could then engage in patent buyouts of high-valued inventions and turn them over to the public domain. No mechanisms are specified for how the information about the donated discovery should be made accessible and usable by members of the public.

Prizes could be optimal if the probability of success is moderately high, the supply elasticity of inventions is low, and awards can be adjusted ex post. Expected awards (the probability of winning times the amount of the prize) would need to at least match the market value of the invention. Since the size of the award is fixed upfront, this suggests that the expected benefit to the winner would decrease with the number of entrants in the competition, so the amount of the prize would have to be excessive relative to the market value, holding other things constant. The probability of winning is not necessarily a straightforward inverse proportion of the number of participants, however. Economic models fail to take into account other determinants of the probability, such as bias toward/against specific groups or characteristics or simple cognitive dissonance among judges, which imply that probabilities are a function of largely unpredictable factors that vary at the individual level. If probabilities are unknowable, manageable risk shifts into the realm of unmanageable uncertainty. Even if an

---

[9] Joseph Stiglitz, "Give Prizes Not Patents," *New Scientist*, 2006, p. 21.
[10] Hall et al. (2014).
[11] Wright (1983).

administrator could perfectly replicate the dynamic market mechanism, the credibility or efficiency of bureaucrats in holding to contracted promises might be questioned, leading to a diminution in the expected return from a prize.

The theoretical and practical problems with prizes have not been adequately examined or recognized. A multitude of factors affect supply and demand, and changes in prices serve as a signal and an incentive for adjustments toward equilibrium. Even if these static models of prizes were correct, administered arrangements face potentially intractable challenges in mimicking the functions of markets in a stochastic environment, requiring the determination of appropriate prices, knowledge of changes in supply and demand, and the allocation of resources across time and place. Other complexities arise, such as how to disentangle the interdependent benefits arising from sequential innovations; if only the prize winner gets returns from cumulative efforts, this amounts to an expropriation of the rights of prior contributors. Prize races involve a misallocation of resources (many invest in competing, but only one person can win the award) that is even greater than patent races (where participants can still obtain different patents in the same field).

Moreover, as the first chapter discussed, part of the value chain of uncertain technological processes is associated with the ability to defer decisions. Success or failure at different points in time also provides valuable information to other participants in the industry. Administered innovation decisions often imply that the early exercise of one option forecloses on other potential choices and outcomes. By contrast, markets involve more "live" branches on decision trees and the possibility of later exercise of innovation options, leading to the possibility of greater varieties of products, information, and solutions. This diversity of ideas, inputs, and outcomes is a central virtue of a spontaneously coordinated, decentralized, market system.

Administered innovation systems—situations where panels or juries make decisions about rewards for inventions—can be characterized as *monopsonies*, involving a market in which a single buyer selects among various sellers of the particular product.[12] A serious oversight in the economic literature is the lack of attention paid to the monopsonistic features of prize systems. Theorists usually assume that prize systems follow an idealized model of perfect competition, offering lower prices and greater output relative to the alleged monopolies of patents. The assumption that the alternative to imperfect competition is some form of perfect competition is often incorrect in practice. Instead, one form of imperfect competition historically tends to be replaced by another form of

---

[12] To my knowledge, no other economists have identified or assessed the monopsony element in technological prizes. For a more conventional (and equally rare) analysis of monopsony in labor markets, see Manning (2003).

imperfect competition. When the United States engaged in widespread international copyright piracy in the nineteenth century, the publishing industry was not competitively organized, since firms engaged in cartelization. Monopsony creates inefficiencies such as unfair discrimination and arbitrary decisions by the sole buyer among the multiple sellers, and this is a particular concern in administered systems without legal or other third-party mechanisms for appeal.

The empirical analysis in this book considers real alternative institutions and how they actually worked. The results uniformly show that prize-granting monopsonies involved choices or allocations that were based on the identity of the parties in question, rather than on the productivity of the invention. Personalized exchange was exacerbated by the inability of administrators to distinguish value at the margin. Prize awards were not independent of each other, and cascade effects were a constant feature of decision making in prize systems. Information cascades are especially likely to occur when panels do not have the ability or knowledge to distinguish among competing claims. As a result, choices are instead based on extrinsic factors such as the reputation of the sponsoring institution, the identity of mentors, social background, and connections. Some of these "markers" might be positively correlated with value or productivity, but if not, the costs of errors are magnified over time. Such problems of innovation prizes were compounded because a single discovery often garnered multiple payouts; this stacking of awards created an incentive for winners to devote their attention to simply accumulating nonmarket rewards for the same idea, rather than investing in commercialization and returns in the market through benefits to consumers.

Innovation prizes create different incentives and outcomes for all parties involved—grantors, judges, recipients, and society in general. The costs and benefits vary depending on the level of administration, whether the prize system is sponsored by the state (the closest substitute to national patents) or by individuals or private institutions. When social benefits exceed private benefits, the standard argument is that government involvement could help to "internalize" these spillovers. However, funding from general taxation of the public redistributes income from all of society to select beneficiaries, which creates the potential for distortions and reductions in social welfare. Social costs are exacerbated because of the wasted investments and efforts of the crowd of losers in the competition. Even if the prize is supported by wealthy private individuals, there is an implicit cost in terms of the alternatives that are sacrificed when (say) scientists turn away from economizing on data transmission capacity toward seeking out signals from extraterrestrial lifeforms. Such "moonshot" endeavors might benefit the Next Generation, but in economic terms the present value is quite low relative to more current concerns.

San Francisco Mechanics Institute (USA)   Society for Encouragement of National Industry
(France)

Royal Society of Arts (Britain)

Figure 3.1 Records of Prize-Granting Institutions
The discussion in this book is based on extensive original archival research that
draws on thousands of unpublished records and documents in Britain, France, and
the United States.
Source: Images of nineteenth-century documents, author's photographs.

The *Alice in Wonderland* quote illustrates an interesting facet of prizes, which is especially evident in the case of nonmonetary awards. Patents ensure that rewards will accrue to every inventor who produces an innovation that is valued by the market. However, prizes are positional goods, whose worth lies in their relative scarcity, which creates a dilemma. In prize systems "there will be only one" first-place winner, perhaps along with second- and third-place spots, and the ranking of the other losing participants is irrelevant. The scarcer the award and the more value that is attached to winning, the greater the controversies about errors and outcomes, which creates an incentive for administered systems with low-cost awards to offer more prizes over time. In some international exhibitions, as many as two-thirds of participants received some form of recognition. Since the signal function of prizes depends on relative scarcity, when almost everyone receives a medal or certificate, the value of the prize is dissipated or eliminated. If everyone gets a gold star, then the star wars are lost for everyone. As Fred Hirsch pointed out in his discussion of positional goods, when everybody stands on tiptoes, then no one sees.[13]

The economic theory of innovation incentives is clearly still undeveloped. At the same time, the theories are justified by widely circulated and often repeated fables rather than systematic empirical analysis. The discussion in both the academic literature and policy circles tends to be limited to unverified secondary sources. These cited reports typically were generated by the prize-granting institutions themselves, which had a self-interest in producing overly optimistic (or even misleading) information for their sponsors and for the public. Prizes were usually announced with great fanfare and grand promises, but one looks in vain for follow-up details about the actual operation and outcomes of these efforts. Evidence about the manifest failure of any current initiative was often countered with untestable claims about potential long-run future benefits that had not yet been detected.

Longitude and Other Myths of Inventions

The most popular and influential example of an inducement prize is the significant sum that was offered for an accurate method of gauging longitude at sea, so it is worth reexamining this case study. Specialists with a detailed knowledge of this award tend to be somewhat skeptical about the effectiveness of the Longitude Prize, which nobody ever officially won.[14] This failure has not

---

[13] Hirsch (2005).
[14] Landes (1983); Sobel (1995).

deterred researchers and policymakers from persistently highlighting the search for a means to measure longitude as solid proof for the benefits of "grand innovation prizes."

The British Parliament passed a bill in July 1714 "for providing a public reward for such person or persons as shall discover the longitude at sea."[15] The board that managed the awards included twenty-four eminent personages, many of whom lacked any technological capabilities. Interim payments were made to a number of individuals such as £3,700 to Thomas Earnshaw, for improvements on the marine chronometer, and £1,700 to John Arnold, even though neither had produced a successful method of gauging longitude. There was also a sort of "mission creep," in which the board paid out sums for miscellaneous reasons that were only tangentially connected to the problem of longitude, such as £100 to Mrs. Catharine Price "as a Reward for having delivered to the Public the Manuscript papers of her late Father Doctor Halley." The Longitude Board spent a total of £157,000 (unadjusted for inflation) during its existence. These expenditures included £53,000 that was allocated for interim awards, but a similar amount of £52,477 was devoted to salaries and other expenses.[16] In short, half of the total amount expended was funneled to cover overhead costs of the administration of the prize.

John Harrison (1693–1776), a poor, uneducated clockmaker who is now credited with solving the problem of calculating longitude at sea, encountered numerous obstacles in his dealings with the board that administered the prize, including competition from some of its members who were also attempting to win the money on their own account. The entire sum that was advertised for the Longitude Prize was never actually awarded. Interim payouts were made that helped to support research efforts, including those by Harrison. However, forty-seven years elapsed before Harrison actually received full compensation, although this was from another source than the Longitude Board. It is possible that the information about interim discoveries or about the winning technology generated spillovers that benefited the industry.[17] However, the incentives were quite different for losers who bore the risk of revealing their inventive ideas without obtaining a return—for instance, after Thomas Earnshaw demonstrated his improvement on escapements, another competitor patented this design in his own name in 1782.

---

[15] Statute 12 Anne 2 c.14 (1714).

[16] Howse (1998).

[17] Burton and Nicholas (2017) suggest that the prize generated spillovers in part through patent disclosures of competitors who filed patents. This point might be relevant for patents today, but patent specifications in England during the longitude era remained unpublished and difficult to locate, and, in the absence of any examination system, many were deliberately vague and uninformative.

The board's criteria for success in its trials continually changed over time, leading to confusion and concerns about how impartially the judging was conducted. Harrison protested against the moving target:

> I cannot help thinking but I am extremely ill used by Gentlemen who I might have expected a different treatment from; for if the Act of the 12th of Queen Anne be deficient why have I so long been encouraged under it, in order to bring my invention to perfection? and, after the completion, why was my Son sent twice to the West Indies? Had it been said to my son, when he received the last Instructions, there will, in case you succeed, be a new Act at your return in order to lay you under new Restrictions which were not thought of in the Act of the 12th of Queen Anne; I say, had this been the Case, I might have expected some such Treatment as I now meet with.

The board ultimately stipulated that it was not sufficient just to create an accurate chronometer, but it was further necessary to make sure that the submissions could be produced at a low cost, and with an adequate supply that could serve the needs of the navy.[18] These were not unreasonable rules, but the point is that they were not specified upfront.

The positive assessment of the role of prizes in generating a solution to long-standing problems at times risks faulty logic involving *post hoc ergo propter hoc* (after this, therefore because of this) fallacies. David Landes points out that, while it is true that the British prize was associated with numerous attempts to resolve the problem, the issue had been publicized for more than a century prior to the passage of the Longitude Bill in 1714.[19] Enormous sums had been offered throughout Europe for the discovery of a means of measuring longitude, long before the British introduced their own prize, and those had all failed to produce a positive outcome. Despite the outlay of significant resources toward assessing and aiding applicants, Spain, Venice, and Holland had eventually given up. Claims that this case offers positive proof of the efficacy of inducement prizes therefore deliberately ignore decades of failure for Longitude awards. Markets may have failed because of third-party benefits that could not be privately captured by the inventor, but it is also possible that, even in the absence of the British Longitude Prize, another substitute would have been developed, because of the

---

[18] "It must be owned my Case is very hard, but I hope I am the first, and, for my Country's sake, shall be the last that suffers by pinning my faith on an English Act of Parliament. . . . And I must sit myself down in Old Age & thank God I can be more easy in that I have made the Conquest & though I have no Reward than if I had come short of the matter & by some delusion had the Reward. I am Lords & Gentlemen Your humble Servant John Harrison. May 30th. 1765." Board of Longitude, Confirmed minutes of the Board of Longitude, 1737–1779 (RGO 14/5), p. 98.

[19] Landes (1983).

significant profits in the market that awaited anyone who resolved the problem at the right time.

In Europe, an extensive array of targeted prizes was conferred on inventors who directed their efforts to specific discoveries, such as the premium offered for margarine and food preservation and the process to make soda from sodium chloride. In a related example, the French Academy of Sciences in 1775 offered a cash prize for the discovery of a process to create sodium carbonate from the cheaper sodium chloride. Nicolas Leblanc succeeded in finding a viable manufacturing solution, but he never received the prize, and his factory was further expropriated by the revolutionary government. Similarly, the French Ministry of the Interior under Napoleon proposed a contest for flax-spinning machines in a decree of 1810, which declared that the winner would be decided at the end of a three-year period. The prize was the considerable sum of 1 million francs, and entries came from France and from numerous other countries. However, this prize was never awarded. In short, the failure of innovation prizes is usually not included in popular accounts, leading to a selection process because greater attention is directed to the introduction of prizes, and little or none to failed outcomes. It is clearly illogical to conclude that prize systems are effective by cherry-picking the successes and ignoring the failures.

From one perspective, such prizes succeeded if—despite the failure of Harrison or Leblanc to win the award—the offers did induce inventors to turn to the issue in need of a resolution. However, even if unawarded prizes provided an effective one-period inducement, this argument fails to take into account the deterrent effect owing to a fall in the credibility of the granting agency or mechanism. That is, the process of invention is a repeated game, and when a prize is not granted even though the conditions are satisfied, this occurrence reduces the perceived probability of future awards and thus the expected benefits from prizes.

Other prominent examples of innovation prizes reveal additional complexities, including the overcompensation of inventors through multiple overlapping awards. Premiums from the state or any prize-granting institution did not preclude inventors from also pursuing profits through other means, including patent protection. For instance, Napoleon III offered a monetary prize for the invention of a cheap substitute for butter that may have induced Hippolyte Mège-Mouriès to make significant improvements in margarine production. In assessing the efficacy of this prize, it should be noted that many inventors worldwide were already pursuing the idea of a cheap and longer-lasting substitute both for butter and for the use of such fats in candles and soap. Mège-Mouriès not only collected the prize money but also obtained patent protection for fifteen years in France in 1869. He further patented the original invention and several improvements in England, Austria, Bavaria, and the United States. After he sold the patent rights in Holland and the United States, his assignees made the improvements that transformed the patented product into a commercially viable good. In the absence of these follow-on patent rights, it is not clear that Mège-Mouriès himself would have had the incentive to invest in efforts to turn the discovery into a marketable product.

The award for billiard balls and the experience of the inventor John Wesley Hyatt is also often cited as an example of a successful inducement prize that was administered by a private American company. The billiard table producers Michael Phelan and Hugh Collender offered a prize of $10,000 in 1863 for a material to replace the costly and increasingly scarce ivory. This New York company continually introduced patented innovations, and both owners were successful multiple patentees. The partners were flamboyant promoters, and the prize may have been offered as a means of gaining free publicity. Billiards was a popular pastime that was many enjoyed, including George Washington and Alexander Hamilton. Billiard balls were made from the imported ivory of elephant tusks, and the balls had to be finished in a drying room for several years before being ready for use. The quest for a substitute for costly ivory was not a new area of inquiry, as witnessed by the accomplishments of British inventors Alexander Parkes and Daniel Spill, as well as the roster of prior American patents.

The billiard ball prize was never paid out, but the publicity still benefited the sponsors (whose names live on in articles by economic theorists today). It is possible that Hyatt himself chose not to accept the award in exchange for the rights to his invention, which had a much greater market value than the promised compensation. Hyatt was born in 1837 in Starkey, New York, and was a journeyman printer without any formal technical education. The son of a blacksmith, early on he displayed an inventive mind, and his first patent in 1861 was for a knife grinder. Instead of the prize, Hyatt sustained an independent patent claim on his contribution and then formed an enterprise to produce the balls.[20] Hyatt's Billiard Ball Company proved to be successful in the marketplace, with a retail price that was half that of ivory balls. He filed over two hundred patents on a wide variety of inventions over his career and was honored as one of the exceptional entrepreneurs of the century. His business ventures (including the prosperous Celluloid Manufacturing Company) allowed him to obtain benefits as a multiple patentee and entrepreneur. This example illustrates problems of adverse selection (where only "lemons" are awarded the payoff) and also indicates the difficulties of arriving at an accurate inducement "price" when part of the benefit to the winner includes immeasurable gains such as reputation and market power.

---

[20] *Celluloid Manuf'g Co. v. American Zylonite Co.*, 26 F. 692 (1886).

The French award for food preservation is another case study that is commonly cited as evidence of the success of inducement prizes, with grandiose claims that this prize created the canning industry. The award was actually an ex post award—not an ex ante inducement—for a process to provision an army while it was on the move. In 1810, Nicolas-François Appert received a payout of 10,000 francs for improvements in food preservation, although his method of employing heated glass bottles was not entirely novel and proved to be limited in usage because of its unpracticality. Appert had long been experimenting on the job to discover ways to improve on the flavor of preserved foods, and this work drew the attention of influential officials. He was a former gourmet chef, and the samples he offered the test panel included luxuries like preserved truffles, cherries, raspberries, and cream, made by a very labor-intensive process. As might be expected, this array of delicacies won enthusiastic testimonials from the elite panelists.

However, it should not be surprising that Appert's approach and glass bottles were not ideal for provisioning an army on the march. Instead, the patented English method of canning (with American improvements) proved to be more efficient and scalable for the mass market, and it was this form of preservation that proved to be successful and persisted over time. In France, "Appertized" establishments remained small artisanal shops, the price of these preserved foods was too expensive for large-scale usage, soldiers detested the taste of the mass-produced version, cases of massive food poisoning led to wariness, and these goods remained a niche product until the end of the nineteenth century.[21] A lack of coordination across prize-granting societies allowed Appert to garner cash awards and prizes for the same discovery from several different sources, including a silver medal in 1816, followed by a gold medal in 1820.[22] In short, the inventor of a known process was able to benefit by accumulating multiple prize awards for a method that largely failed in the market.

In view of current advocacy in favor of prizes for medical discoveries, it is relevant to note that several prizes were offered in nineteenth-century France, and in other countries, for cures, preventive measures, and medical solutions to public health problems such as cholera.[23] The French Academy of Sciences bestowed a prize of 5,000 francs on Léon Doyère for his experiments on cholera victims, whereas specialists disparaged his efforts, saying that some points were

---

[21] See Bruegel (1997).

[22] Similarly, James Douglas, an English engineer from Manchester, was able to obtain the support of influential officials, including Jean-Antoine Chaptal, which he was able to parlay into a portfolio of benefits, including a large loan from the Conservatoire des Arts et Métiers, patents for his machines, as well as funds from the Society for the Encouragement of National Industry and from the Ministry of the Interior.

[23] An example is Medical Innovation Prize Fund Act, S. 627, 113th Congress (2013).

already known and others incorrect. The Russian government offered 25,000 rubles for the best treatise on this subject and made investments in examining 125 entries, none of which was practicable.[24] A well-known and often cited prize of 100,000 francs, the Bréant award, was offered for a means of curing cholera, or for prevention of epidemics. The Bréant fund made a minor payout but remained largely intact and unclaimed well into the twentieth century, despite numerous submissions that proved to be largely ineffective or even irrelevant. Clearly, "money left on the table" in this way created an opportunity cost in terms of more viable or productive alternatives that could have been funded or investigated.

Patent Buyouts?

In an influential series of articles, Michael Kremer argues in favor of a "patent buyout" policy, citing the example of the "Daguerreotype patent." The French government allegedly purchased the rights to a patent of great social value and allowed everyone free access to the technology, thus turning the private property right into a sort of prize award. According to Kremer's account, "In 1839 the French government purchased the Daguerreotype patent and placed it in the public domain. Such patent buyouts could potentially eliminate the monopoly price distortions and incentives for rent-stealing duplicative research created by patents, while increasing incentives for original research."[25] The actual facts are somewhat different, however. A comprehensive search of nineteenth-century patent records reveals that Daguerre never obtained a patent in France at any point in his life for this or any other invention. As such, there was no patent for the French government to buy out. The case study instead highlights the incentives for unproductive "rent stealing" that arises when returns can be negotiated through a political process that bypasses the market.

In popular accounts, Daguerre typically receives sole credit for the discovery of a method of reproducing photographic images. However, work in photography had been in progress for over a century, and the most significant advances up to that date had been made by Joseph-Nicéphore Niépce. Daguerre entered into a partnership with Niépce, who died in 1833. The heir of the inventor, Isidore Niépce, agreed that for marketing purposes Daguerre should have the sole attribution rights to the discovery.[26] The political economy

[24] See Kotar and Gessler (2014).
[25] Kremer (1998). All theoretical papers on this subject invariably also cite the Daguerre example as supporting evidence for their mathematical models.
[26] Isidore Niépce, Historique de la découverte improprement nommée Daguerréotype, précédée d'une notice sur son véritable inventeur M. Joseph-Nicéphore Niépce de Chalon-sur-Saône; par son fils (1841).

behind Daguerre's prize of August 1839 was typical of the stratagems and manipulations that French inventors often adopted to get support and payouts from the authorities. Instead of paying the extremely high fees for a patent and then trying to interest licensees or assignees, Daguerre was able to secure the patronage of François Arago. Arago, a politician and influential member of the Académie des Sciences, lobbied strongly on Daguerre's behalf in favor of a government grant. When the inventor turned over to the Ministry of the Interior a packet with the information on the discovery, Arago was also involved in the process of examining and verifying its validity on behalf of the French government. (In a fitting congruity, Rue Daguerre is quite close to the Boulevard Arago in present-day Paris.)

In view of the "patent buyout" argument, it is ironic that Daguerre's main plea to the French legislature was that he was unable to apply for a patent to gain benefits from the process:

> Unfortunately for the authors of this great discovery, it is impossible for them to commercialize it and thereby obtain compensation for the sacrifices they have endured as a result of their long and hitherto fruitless trials. *Their invention is not susceptible to patent protection.* . . . It is therefore necessarily the case that this process must belong to everyone or else it must remain unknown.[27]

Daguerre thus argued that his idea was an unpatentable trade secret and, once it was revealed, the whole world would have free access to his ideas and he would be unable to appropriate any returns. As such, the choice before the legislature was for his secret to die with him and be lost to the world or for the state to award him compensation and so benefit the public. An appeal was further cannily made to the essentially mercantilist nature of the French authorities; Daguerre hinted that, otherwise, foreigners might make him an offer he could not refuse. The request was initially for a large upfront award of 200,000 francs, but an annual lifetime payment seemed more politically expedient. The measure was quickly approved, and an annuity of 10,000 francs was paid out for the discovery.

At the same time, Daguerre proceeded to file for a patent in England under the name of Miles Berry (a British patent agent), giving the lie to the notion that the invention was unpatentable, and reneging on the bargain that the French government was acquiring the discovery on behalf of the entire world. Daguerre and Berry then placed a true patent buyout prospectus before the British government,

---

[27] Louis-Jacques-Mandé Daguerre, Historique et description des procédés du daguerréotype et du diorama (1839).

on the grounds that the inventor was "obliged to ask so large a sum to Individuals for Licenses that few can afford to take them."[28] As a result of this alleged myopic failure of the market to recognize the true value of the invention, the inventor wished "to solicit Her Majesty or the Government of England to purchase the said Patent right for the purpose of throwing it open in England for the benefit of the Public and preventing this important Discovery being fettered or limited by individual interest or exertion."[29] Daguerre's British patent buyout proposal was made on March 30, 1840; the government representative politely and tersely declined the opportunity on March 31, 1840.

Patent buyouts are often proposed because they would allow ideas to circulate freely, and because such access enables cumulative inventions to flourish without the transaction costs and deadweight loss that a monopolistic right of exclusion might impose. The Daguerre-Niépce method did indeed spread quickly, an undoubted benefit of the French policy, but this approach to photographic reproduction was also short-lived as the dominant process in the marketplace. Instead, the English inventor William Fox Talbot independently patented a new technique in 1841 through which photographic prints could be developed from negatives, and it was this method that ultimately prevailed throughout the nineteenth and twentieth centuries.

The state annuity to Daguerre also created its own problem of cumulative invention by putting in the public domain all of the efforts of prior inventors that were incorporated in the Daguerreotype, without their permission and without offering them any compensation. This is an inherent problem of "grand innovation prizes" that ignore the incremental nature of all inventive activity. Additional questions remain about whether the public monetary award accurately gauged the true value of the invention, given the availability of substitutes that were not taken into account in the public accounting; the net social loss of taxation and redistributive effects of using public funds to benefit one group in society (photographers); and, ultimately, the incentives that such a policy creates for inefficient rent seeking and patronage on the part of inventors and their influential connections. As the Daguerre example shows, even if one prize was accurately calibrated in value, the inventor was incentivized to pursue further handouts that could increase his returns beyond its social valuation. Under such a regime, it is hardly unexpected that, as Liliane Hilaire-Pérez succinctly notes, "in France, to invent meant to go into politics."[30]

---

[28] Wood (1980).
[29] Ibid.
[30] Hilaire-Pérez (1991).

British Great Inventors

When many may be equally deserving, the question arises of why the one winner is selected, and observers identify numerous instances when awards, medals, and prestigious appointments were associated with nepotism, bias, and even corruption.[31] Between 1731 and 1839, the vast majority of the prestigious Copley awards (90%) went to higher-status gentlemen and professionals, with only 10% given to artisans or tradesmen, and scholars note a certain degree of "internal favoritism" in the selection process.[32] As a number of economists have reminded us, elites and talented innovators can engender social benefits and growth; however, rent-seekers in privileged positions might not only redistribute wealth but also have the potential to reduce growth. If potential inventors were aware that prize winners would be drawn from the more privileged classes, such awards were unlikely to induce inventors from disadvantaged groups to make contributions to new technologies. In short, the biases of elite or socially exclusive institutions could become self-perpetuating if excluded parties anticipated rejection and never tried to apply in the first place.

Systematic insights into the relationship between incentives and innovation can be gleaned from a large sample of British inventors who were responsible for the great inventions of the period before World War II.[33] Sherard Cowper-Coles stands out with a portfolio of some nine hundred patents, and inventors such as Sir Henry Bessemer, Samuel Lister, and Robert Mushet were also prolific patentees, but they were the exception. George Stephenson, Henry Fourdrinier, and Henry Shrapnel each barely mustered half a dozen patented inventions, and some forty-seven of the British patentees failed to obtain patent protection for their discoveries (compared to thirteen of the American great inventors). American great inventors contributed to technologies in a wide range of industries that included varying degrees of capital intensity, engaged in more experimentation, and were quick to switch to emerging and riskier fields of invention. British inventors, however, were heavily specialized in a narrow range of already leading capital-intensive industries such as textiles, heavy metals, engines, and machinery. Among the great inventors born between 1820 and 1845, over 40% of those in Britain had fathers who were in elite or professional occupations, whereas just 18% of those in the United States came from such privileged backgrounds.

---

[31] Great Britain, *Report of the Committee Appointed by the Board of Trade to Make Enquiries with Reference to the Participation of Great Britain in Great International Exhibitions* (1907).

[32] Bektas and Crosland (1992). Just 12% of the Copley Medals were bestowed in the area of mechanics.

[33] Khan (2011b).

The biographies of the British great inventors include information about honors and awards they earned. Almost 40% of the sample received such recognition, ranging from the recipients of gifts of silver plate from the Crown to two winners of the Nobel Prize (Sir Edward Appleton and Guglielmo Marconi). It is impossible to fully trace all the awards that any inventor received, but the majority of these creative technological innovators never received any prizes. Other things being equal, statistical analysis of the factors that influenced the probability of an inventor receiving a prize shows that patentees were more likely to get prizes, so any incremental incentive effects of an additional prize were likely quite low. Rather than ex ante inducements, most prizes for great inventions functioned as windfall recognition awards, to acknowledge a striking achievement or given out toward the end of the inventor's career.

The empirical results highlight the potential inefficiencies of administered awards, which were susceptible to the possibility of discrimination, personal prejudices, cronyism, and corruption. Objective factors—such as specialized education in science and engineering, patentee status, employment in science or technology, experience in the field—had little or no impact on the probability of getting a prize. Awards were somewhat linked to affiliations with "learned societies," which resembled gentlemen's social clubs where membership simply depended on personal connections and payment of substantial dues. However, the most significant variable affecting whether or not a British inventor received a prize was elite education at Oxford or Cambridge, which substantially increased the odds of getting an award, despite the traditional hostility of such institutions to pragmatic technical or scientific instruction. In short, the grants of prizes to British great inventors were primarily connected to elite status itself and not to factors that might have enhanced inventive productivity.

An interesting facet of the relationship between privilege, science, and technological achievement in Britain is reflected in the experience of the ninety great inventors who were also Fellows of the Royal Society. The likelihood that an inventor received prizes and medals was higher for men who had gained recognition as famous scientists or Fellows of the Royal Society. The Royal Society itself was the target of persistent criticism throughout this period, including scathing assessments by its own members. Many were disillusioned with these award systems, attributing outcomes to arbitrary factors such as personal influence, the persistence of one's recommenders, or the self-interest of the institution making the award. Sir William Grove, a great inventor who belonged to the society, was only one of the many contemporary observers who attacked the nepotism and corruption of the Royal Society and other elite scientific institutions. Such findings help to explain the growing disillusionment in Europe with prizes as an incentive mechanism for generating innovation over the course of the nineteenth century.

Montyon Prizes

The Montyon Prizes are often referred to as an Enlightenment precursor to the Nobel Prizes. Jean-Baptiste de Montyon (1733–1820) was a benevolent French aristocrat whose legacy endowed financial awards for science and technology. Montyon designated premiums for contributions to such areas as experimental physiology and mechanics, the salubriousness of industry, and medicine and surgery. He further established a foundation to help poor debtors to retrieve property that they had been obliged to pawn, and others to buy pensions for the indigent and to reward ordinary individuals for acts of virtue and heroism. His philanthropic efforts culminated in a legacy of about 25,000 francs for prizes that were administered by the Académie Française, the Académie des Sciences, and the Académie Nationale de Médecine.

Montyon had specified which areas were to be awarded prizes, and this led to a surplus of funding for those subjects relative to other topics that were not eligible for the award. The generous supply of funds for a few fields implied that it was sometimes difficult for the committees to find deserving candidates on whom to bestow the annual awards in medicine and surgery or industrial and public health. As the size of the endowment compounded, there was increasing pressure for the administrators of the awards to spend the money, regardless of whether there were any worthy prospects. Crosland examined the financial accounts for the society from 1824 to 1833, and these reveal that the academy was actually spending significant amounts of the legacy for purposes that were not in accordance with the intent of the bequest.

Over time, measures were undertaken that markedly deviated from the objectives set out by the donor. A royal ordinance in 1829 decreed that only half of the Montyon legacy had to be actually spent on the prizes he had stipulated. After 1845, the money going to each of the prizes was limited to 2,500 francs, which increased the discretionary funds at the disposal of the academy. The committees often concluded that none of the entries was worthy of the entire sum available for the award and instead gave out smaller amounts as "encouragements." Many of the prizes were not distributed year after year; for instance, the award for mechanics was not bestowed on any candidates during much of the 1850s.

The paucity of payouts allowed for greater discretionary spending by administrators, and increasing amounts of the Montyon endowment were diverted for salaries and honoraria and to pay for the expenses of running the academy. Large sums covered expenditures that the committee members argued were necessary to test the merit of submitted projects, to buy books and journals for the library of the academy, and fund its own publishing enterprise. After the 1830s, the interpretation of the term "prizes" was broadened to include unrestricted "grants." Applicants were able to get funding for travel, for speculative experiments, to defray expenses of equipment, and to subsidize publications.[34] Academics with more stringent grant oversight will envy the applicant who was permitted to expend 2,400 francs on travel to an exotic volcanic island in the Mediterranean. The accounts expose significant honoraria paid out from the Montyon endowment to members of the academy themselves.

The Montyon Prizes reflected a general tendency for administrators to shift from inducement prizes to less-restrictive grants for funding research. On the other side of the Atlantic, Count Rumford's endowment for a prize to reward studies of heat and light was not bestowed for a significant period, resulting in a large surplus that the American Academy of Arts similarly decided to use to provide research support. From one vantage point, the move to broader investments in research enabled individuals without private resources to undertake more costly studies and experiments, and thus expanded the number of projects beyond those that would have qualified for a prize. At the same time, the process weakened the constraints of committees, and the greater scope for discretionary expenditures created perverse incentives that resulted in larger and increasing fractions of the awards being directed toward "overheads" and administrative expenses.

Noble Awards?

Of the many thousands of accolades that are bestowed in science and technology, the most renowned prize system is, of course, administered by the Alfred Nobel Foundation. The Nobel Prizes for six designated fields are limited in scope and number, but the announcements generate global publicity for particular fields that arguably serves as an incentive for some to direct their attention and efforts toward these specialties. Between 1901 and 2018, a total of 590 Nobel Prizes were awarded to 935 Laureates. These awards include 112 in Physics, 110 in Chemistry, 109 in Medicine, 110 in Literature, 99 for promoting Peace, and 50 in Economic Sciences.[35] Nobel's original intention was to encourage young scholars by offering prizes for outstanding recent work, but this led to awards for discredited results and high variance in decision making, mainly owing to the inability of panels to recognize quality unaccompanied by other signals. As a result, the prize system evolved toward an ex post recognition of the lifetime achievement of senior scholars.

As in the case of most important prizes, Nobel awards have always been controversial, and their record underlines some of the general difficulties with

---

[34] Crosland (1979).
[35] All data are from http://www.nobelprize.org.

administered innovation systems. The allocation of Nobel Prizes is highly secretive and opaque, and the administration and methods through which the committees reach decisions cannot be disclosed to outsiders. The rules of the foundation require that differences of opinions should not be recorded in the minutes of the proceedings, and the public is not allowed access to these documents until fifty years later. Moreover, the governing charter specifies that there is to be no possibility of appeal regarding the committee's decisions about the awards. This lack of transparency and accountability, the absence of third-party oversight, and the inability to dispute manifestly unjust outcomes are inherent characteristics of such institutions.

Between 1901 and 1966, the Nobel Prize winners were selected from a total of over twenty-two thousand nominations. The physicist Arnold Sommerfeld was nominated over seventy times but failed to receive a single prize. This leads to the question of what determines who will be singled out from the thousands of nominees who have been considered by their peers to be worthy of a prize. For many who have studied this and related questions, decisions often reveal more about the panel of judges than about the candidates. Indeed, the determination of the type of research that was worthy of a prize was significantly related to the research specialties of the committee members.[36] The politics of the Nobel awards are repeatedly deprecated in studies of the committee deliberations, ranging from problems of ignorance to petty feuding to selfish manipulation of outcomes.[37] For instance, one of the selection committee blocked awards to potential winners such as Henri Poincaré who had criticized the panelist's work. The prize has not been made on dozens of occasions, and some have claimed that the administrative rules create incentives to delay or avoid giving an award because this allows committee members to divert the interest income to support their own research agenda.

Alfred Nobel's will in 1895 specified that it was his "express wish that in awarding the prizes no consideration be given to the nationality of the candidates, but that the most worthy shall receive the prize." Nevertheless, nominees have always been most likely to come from Europe and North America, exhibiting a bias against scientists from other regions, especially those whose publications were in a non-European language. Part of this skew may owe to observed "nomination nepotism," where members of specific networks or "research families" tend to nominate other members belonging to their particular group.[38] The perceived regional bias caused some countries to set up their own parallel awards

---

[36] Crawford et al. (1987); Crawford (1990); Dardo (2004).
[37] Friedman (2001).
[38] Kantha (1991).

system, such as the Japan Prize for science (50 million yen) and the Kyoto Prize for basic science and advanced technology (45 million yen).

The degree of gender imbalance at all levels of the review process has raised questions about discrimination against women. The members of the committee in the past were overwhelmingly male, and today approximately 75% of nominators are men. About 10% of the nominees are female, and just fifty-one women received Nobel Prizes between 1901 and 2018. The first woman to be nominated for an award was Marie Curie in 1902, and she received the Nobel Prize in Physics in 1903, as well as a second Nobel Prize in Chemistry in 1911. Marie Curie's daughter Irène Joliot-Curie, her husband, and her son-in-law also received recognition from the Nobel committee, for a family total of five prizes. Supporters of the discrimination thesis point to the lack of recognition for other deserving women such as Lise Meitner in chemistry and Jocelyn Bell in physics. As is common for all grand innovation prizes, the Nobel Prize gives credit to the lead researcher but ignores other team members whose contributions might have been essential for arriving at the final breakthrough.

Hargittai's thought-provoking analysis of the Nobel Prizes highlights his misgivings about the limitations of administered awards and related peer-review systems.[39] He compares scientists who won the prize to those of similar standing who failed to be recognized and suggests that winners may have prevailed because of personality and marketing, rather than because of their superior human capital or objective scientific achievements. These endowed awards cover a limited area of contributions to knowledge prevalent at the time of the legacy, with a bias against more modern approaches such as medical psychiatry. In the deliberations about novel contributions, the process is inherently constrained by the knowledge of the administrators of the prize, and the committee members are likely to be overly conservative about areas in which their expertise is limited. After posing the question "Could science history be compiled on the basis of the Nobel Prizes?," he concludes, "I think not."

As for the winners of the lottery for such grand prizes, the consequences for their reputations and purses are strongly positive, and the attendant benefits spill over to their institutions. For the general public, the prize seems to confer universal authority, and this encourages narrow specialists to make pronouncements and policy recommendations that extend well beyond their individual expertise. At the same time, even after controlling for age, the scientific productivity of awardees typically declines after the receipt of prestigious honors. Nobel Prize winners changed their orientation and the way they conducted research and were less likely to engage in teamwork and collaborations. This decline in

---

[39] Hargittai (2002).

productivity was more drastic for scientists whose prestige had been boosted to a greater extent by the prize, relative to scholars who had already attained a stellar reputation.[40] A study of the Fields Medal in Mathematics compared the achievements of the winners after the prize to their peers of similar abilities and publications records and likewise found that the productivity and focus of the Fields medalists subsequently suffered.[41] In short, many researchers are induced by these awards to become celebrities rather than innovative scientists.

Longitude Redux

Private and public prizes for innovations are currently experiencing a renaissance, following their marked decline during the nineteenth century. Debates about such incentive mechanisms tend to employ canonical historical anecdotes to motivate and support theoretical analyses and current policy proposals. In one notable instance, a contemporary prize has set out to replicate the 1714 Longitude Act, three centuries after the original statute. The Nesta "Innovation Foundation" has been funded by the UK Lottery to "back new ideas to tackle the big challenges of our time." Antibiotic-resistant infections have increased rapidly throughout the world, leading to a need for diagnostic tests that would quickly identify microbial pathogens and prevent the unnecessary use of antibiotics. The new Longitude Award is intended to induce medical innovation, rather than maritime devices.

The specific objective has not been defined, since the judges wish to elicit "truly novel and unforeseen" responses. Instead, the parameters of the challenge were open ended: "The Longitude Prize is a £10m prize fund that will reward a competitor that can develop a point-of-care diagnostic test that will conserve antibiotics for future generations and revolutionise the delivery of global healthcare. The test must be accurate, rapid, affordable and easy to use anywhere in the world."[42] More than 250 teams from different countries were involved in the competition. Interim awards to aid in the research process were provided from a variety of sources, including private enterprises such as Merck, and a public-sector corporation of the Government of India, which offered funding only to teams from India. The challenge is somewhat vague on a number of key issues;

---

[40] Zuckerman (1967).

[41] Borjas and Doran (2015). The Fields Medal was first awarded in 1936 and is regarded as the mathematics analog to the Nobel Prize. The records for the Fields Medal are even more unbalanced in terms of the gender of recipients: the only woman to ever win this prize was Maryam Mirzakhani, who received the award in 2014 for her work in the area of dynamics and geometry of Riemann surfaces.

[42] https://longitudeprize.org.

for instance, it has not specified whether the winning device could be patented, pricing strategies, or how or whether the product would reach the consumer. Initially designated as a five-year competition that would lead to an award in 2019, the deadline was extended "until a winner is chosen," because (as the organization stated) the challenge was proving to be challenging to accomplish.[43] Meanwhile, commercial enterprises are pursuing the same objectives, induced by profit incentives in the market.

Another targeted award, the Netflix Prize, is often cited to demonstrate the use of crowdsourced solutions to problems that are costly to resolve in-house, which allow the sponsor to avoid the probabilistic nature of research investments. Netflix, a movie rental company that was established in 1997 by Reed Hastings (a Bowdoin graduate) and Marc Randolph, stockpiled information about the preferences and characteristics of its millions of customers. Many of these viewers rated movies they had watched and also maintained a queue or list of films they wished to order from Netflix. The database had accumulated to almost two billion observations, providing an invaluable source of information that could be used to identify and predict consumer choices. The firm's computerized recommendation system, Cinematch, used past ratings and decisions to assess which other movies the viewer might appreciate. Recommendation systems are not unique to Netflix, since these algorithms are central to online providers such as Amazon, Pandora, and Google.

In 2006, Netflix announced a prize of $1 million for an algorithm that would improve the firm's ability to predict the choices of its clients by a margin of 10%.[44] The contest was scheduled to run for five years, or until the criteria had been attained, at which point the grand prize would be awarded. The competition attracted more than forty thousand entrants from numerous countries, many of whom collaborated and worked as teams. The contest was open to everyone, including entries from "Just a guy in a garage" (who turned out to be a retired management consultant, aided by his teenage daughter). However, despite this apparent diversity, the frontrunners were all professionals in the fields of computer science, machine learning, and "big data" statisticians. BellKor's Pragmatic Chaos, a consortium of seven researchers, illustrated the "crowdsourcing within crowdsourcing" model. (Apparently, BellKor's Pragmatic Chaos had considered the alternative name of Resistance Is Futile but rejected it as a "bit too aggressive.") Their supra-team included members of the former BellKor group (employees from the Statistics Research group in AT&T

labs), BigChaos (Austrian consultants), and Pragmatic Theory (Canadian computer engineers).

The final result in 2009 was essentially a tie, but the grand prize was given to the BellKor's Pragmatic Chaos consortium. Their team filed its submission twenty-four minutes before the Ensemble, a competitor who had also attained the required margin of improvement. Interim payouts or "progress prizes" had been presented for improving on the prior year's achievements in 2007 and 2008. BellKor members belonged to the teams that won both of the $50,000 progress prizes, and during the first year they spent more than two thousand hours on finding the solution. The team that won in the second year, BellKor in BigChaos, had combined with their closest competitors BigChaos. The latter group formed a consulting company to create and deliver customized recommender systems, building on the enhanced reputation they gained as participants in the competition. As a result of their receiving the Netflix Prize, the Austrian government in 2009 bestowed the Federal State Award on this firm, which likely boosted their consulting business.

The Netflix case offers several lessons regarding the benefits to the providers and contestants in prizes. The publicity proved to be the most valuable return for Netflix. The firm later reported that the tangible benefits it derived from the prize-winning code were limited. The proposed methods were not cost-effective to implement, indicating the usual discrepancy between technical value and commercial value in solutions elicited in such contests. Moreover, technological change had improved the viability of online streaming, and the findings from the competition were less relevant to the changed and changing market environment. Even if the outcome had been commercially useful to Netflix, one might question the net social costs of the enormous allocation of time and computing resources by the thousands of nonwinner participants.[45] This is a standard criticism of "patent races," but patent contests are continuous and ongoing; moreover, runners-up in patent races can typically use the acquired information for subsequent patents for related inventions.

What were the benefits to the participants in the competition for the Netflix Prize, especially the vast majority who received no monetary payout? The participants—even the winners—likely lost out in terms of the attributed wage value of their time. However, those who expended the most time and effort (as proxied by their ranking) seemed to have been salaried employees, whose efforts were (knowingly or unknowingly) effectively subsidized by their home

---

[45] Netflix had identified a single well-defined task, but one that had broad applicability to other online recommendation systems. For sponsors, well-defined tasks that are entirely specific to their needs provide them with greater benefits; however, the social costs are much higher in that case, since losers cannot recoup their investments from related activities.

institutions. According to a member of the winning team, "We got a big prize by learning and interacting with other teams. This is the real prize for us."[46] Prizewinners had to publicize their approaches so that everyone could build on their findings, and an informal open source community developed. In addition to formal collaborations, interested parties shared data, code, and hypotheses on the Netflix Prize Forum, and the winning entry combined more than a hundred different models. The Netflix Prize competition therefore functioned as a coordinating mechanism that created knowledge spillovers that had general implications for many online markets and services.

A further question of interest relates to the database that Netflix made freely available for the simulations. In the modern knowledge economy, "big data" hold extraordinary value. The Netflix sample included over 100 million ratings from 480,000 subscribers on approximately 18,000 movie titles, for the period between 1998 and 2005.[47] The simple description of the prize contest by employees of the company has received over 1,100 citations by academic and technical articles that have used these data to generate publishable research. It is therefore difficult to identify the incremental value of the Netflix Prize itself relative to a scenario in which only the database was distributed to all interested parties at a zero price. In a final irony, these data were used to successfully "de-anonymize" the allegedly unidentifiable Netflix subscribers in the sample, leading to private lawsuits and an investigation by the Federal Trade Commission into the firm's alleged violation of individual rights of privacy.[48]

Crowdsourcing and open source and collective invention have generated a great deal of interest as models that illustrate the democratizing nature of the information economy.[49] As in most well-developed markets, several firms now perform as specialized intermediaries in this arena for ideas. Kaggle.com was founded in 2010 to host competitions for data modeling and analysis, moderating bids for challenges such as a $1 million prize to improve the classification of potentially cancerous lesions in the lungs. Another leading hosting platform, Innocentive.com, has mediated over 2,000 challenges, for which more than 62,000 potential solutions were submitted by a community of over 380,000 participants, leading to total awards of over $50 million.[50] Innocentive serves as an intermediary between seekers (demanders who wish to find a solution to a specific problem) and solvers (suppliers who apply to solve the problem). The losing parties get no payment for their submissions and are likely to encounter

---

[46] https://www.wired.com/2008/02/mf-netflix/.
[47] Feuerverger et al. (2012).
[48] As a result of their settlement with the Federal Trade Commission, Netflix canceled a second contest that it had planned to launch.
[49] See Garrigos-Simon et al. (2015).
[50] https://www.innocentive.com/about-us/.

difficulties in monitoring the justice of outcomes. Both Innocentive and the seeker (who can remain anonymous) have access to the proposed solutions, and the solver must agree to cede all rights when the payment is made by Innocentive on behalf of the client.

The CEO of Innocentive, Alpheus Bingham, referred to the recent advent of "an open innovation marketplace" and noted that this represented the "democratization of science: What happens when you open your company to thousands and thousands of minds, each of them with a totally different set of life experiences?"[51] For those who regard an open innovation marketplace and the operation of patent intermediaries as purely an outgrowth of the modern information economy, it is useful to juxtapose Bingham's remarks with a speculation, from the nineteenth century, when open innovation markets in patents similarly flourished. In his 1829 speech to the Boston Mechanics' Institute, Supreme Court Justice Joseph Story, one of the formative influences on the development of the American intellectual property law system, posed an almost identical question regarding the patent system: "Ask yourselves, what would be the result of one hundred thousand minds . . . urged on by the daily motives of interest, to acquire new skill, or invent new improvements?"

In the United States, the statutes from the earliest years of the Republic ensured that the progress of science and useful arts was to be achieved through a complementary relationship between law and the market in the form of a patent system. Notable Americans such as Benjamin Franklin and Alexander Hamilton advocated the award of prizes and subsidies for invention and innovation, but despite their support, the premium system in the United States has always been sporadic and limited in scope. For instance, the New York Society for Promoting Arts, Agriculture, and Economy was founded in 1764 and offered £600 in premiums for innovations in spinning flax, manufactures, and agricultural products but was dissolved a decade later. New York State provided premiums in 1808 for textile goods but similarly ceased after a few years, whereas the Pennsylvania Society for the Encouragement of Manufactures and the Useful Arts occasionally offered gold medals and cash premia. In general, the granting of premia was far more prevalent in agriculture than in manufacturing, because many agricultural innovations were not patentable. Little success met the proposals that were repeatedly submitted to Congress throughout the nineteenth century to replace the patent system with more centralized systems of national prizes, awards, or subsidies by the government.

Individual benefactors also offered prizes for advances in American technology. As Chapter 7 discusses, the most significant included the Franklin

---

[51] Bingham and Spradlin (2011).

Institute Awards, including those funded by Elliott Cresson's 1848 endowment, the Longstreth Medal, and the John Scott Medal and Premium. Other prizes were designed to address specific problems, such as "Ray Premiums" offered by F. M. Ray for innovations "to improve the conveniences and safety of railroad travel."[52] Nevertheless, more extensive proposals to enhance the premium system ultimately failed to persuade, because it was argued that the process of rapid technological change was most likely to be attained through decentralized decision making by inventors themselves, impersonal filtering of value by the market, and legal enforcement by judges confronting individual conflicts on a case-by-case basis.

Just 30% of the great inventors in the United States received prizes, primarily bestowed by foreign nations and institutions, as well as the Franklin Institute. Contributors to electricity innovations such as Elihu Thomson, Thomas Edison, and George Westinghouse, in particular, were overwhelmed with numerous medals, accolades, and titles. Edison was appointed a Chevalier of the French Legion of Honour; the Royal Society of Arts bestowed the Albert Medal for his career achievements; and Congress presented him with a gold medal in recognition of his "development and application of inventions that have revolutionized civilization in the last century." The inventors of military implements in particular were accorded accolades throughout the world: Samuel Colt received a Telford Medal, Hiram Maxim was the first American to be knighted in England, while John M. Browning was appointed a Chevalier by order of the king of Belgium for his improvements to armaments. However, the majority of awards were acquired by manufacturers. Amasa Marks and Thaddeus Fairbanks, who manufactured and assiduously sought medals for their products, won over thirty medals for their patented prosthetics and improvements to scales, respectively.

The general conclusion is that Americans tended to be far more skeptical about premiums for inventions than their European counterparts. For instance, Charles B. Lore of Delaware submitted H.R. 5,925 in 1886 to set up an alternative system of rewards for inventors, to be administered by an "Expert Committee." The editors of Scientific American were scathing about the proposal and pointed out:

> The Expert Committee would have a very delicate duty to perform in fixing the cash valuations, and they would constantly be subjected to risks and

---

[52] The 1853 awards included $1,500 for the best invention that saved lives in railroad accidents, $800 for the best way to prevent dust from entering the cars, $400 for improvements in brakes, and $300 for sleeping seats in railroad cars. The committee reported that "although there were many very ingenious and highly creditable inventions offered, yet from doubts of their utility in actual service . . . we do not feel prepared to recommend any" for the first two prizes. *Annual Report of the American Institute of New York* (1854), p. 78.

probabilities of making egregious errors. For instance, if they were to allow $10,000 as the value of the patent for the thread placed in the crease of an envelope to facilitate opening the same, how much ought they to allow for the second patent, that was granted for the little knot that was tied on the end of the thread, so that the finger nail could easily hold the thread? Then, again, how much ought the committee allow for a simple device like the patent umbrella thimble slide, a single bit of brass tubing that costs a cent and a quarter to make? Probably the committee would think that one thousand dollars would be a most generous allowance, while two hundred thousand dollars—the limit of the bill—would, of course, be regarded as a monstrous and dishonest valuation. But the real truth is, the patent for this device is actually worth nearer one million dollars than two hundred thousand.[53]

A battle of dueling case studies, however, quickly runs into diminishing returns and adds little to our knowledge about the nature and consequences of institutional incentives for technological creativity. Instead, the following chapters examine the activities of over one hundred thousand innovative men and women, drawn from different countries and institutions, across two centuries of the most rapid economic transformation in all of human history. This systematic individual-level analysis of comparative institutions in Britain, France, and the United States sheds light on the sources of technological progress and the nature of administered innovation systems and markets for ideas in the knowledge economy.

---

[53] *Scientific American* 54, no. 14 (1886): 208.

4

Elites and Useful Knowledge in Britain

> All that has made England famous, and all that has made England
> wealthy, has been the work of minorities, sometimes very small ones.
> —Sir Henry Sumner Maine (1885)

Elites, Knowledge, and Economic Growth

Growth theorists have developed mathematical models based on the premise
that knowledge and ideas are a significant source of economic progress. This
approach raises fundamental questions about the nature of human creativity;
what sorts of resources, skills, and other personal characteristics are condu-
cive to extraordinary achievements; and how those factors vary over time
and with the field of endeavor. They imply it is necessary to determine the
types of knowledge inputs that were in elastic supply and the extent to which
they were responsive to economic incentives and to institutional rules and
standards.

Such concerns are longstanding but are still being debated today. Walt Rostow
and Nathan Rosenberg, for instance, contended that a precondition for economic and social advance was progress in scientific knowledge and technical
applications, inputs that typically are scarce in many developing countries.[1]
Some scholars regard such discoveries as "gifts from Athena," impervious to
incentives and largely beyond social control.[2] Scientists are often depicted as disinterested individuals who are motivated by intangible rewards such as enhanced
reputations and honor, the desire to benefit mankind, and pursuit of timeless
truths rather than material benefits. These issues bear on the general question of
whether creativity can be induced by incentives and market demand or depends
on investments in costly human capital. If highly specialized skills and scientific
knowledge are prerequisites for generating productivity gains but such inputs are

---

[1] Rostow (1960). Rosenberg (1974: 97) emphasized that if we wish to understand economic progress, "we must pay close attention to a special supply-side variable: the growing stock of useful knowledge," and further claimed that "a large part of the economic history of the past 200 years" was due to
science and specialized knowledge. See also Jacob (1997).

[2] Mokyr (2002).

Inventing Ideas. B. Zorina Khan, Oxford University Press (2020). © Oxford University Press.
DOI: 10.1093/oso/9780190936075.001.0001

in scarce or inelastic supply, this has important implications for innovation policies and prospects for growth.

The relevance of different types of knowledge to economic development has been especially contentious in the context of industrialization in Britain.[3] The literature on the economic history of the British Industrial Revolution is exhaustive and ranges from whether there was indeed a "revolution," through the factors that caused industrial advances, to the consequences of such changes. Some studies propose that observed patterns owed to factor prices and, in particular, relative wages, whereas others highlight endowments of coal and raw materials. Researchers have examined the role of collective invention or general access to knowledge and debate the nature and consequences of literacy, numeracy, and different forms of education in the growth process during British industrialization. British universities, others point out, did not engage in the study of practical science and engineering until late in the nineteenth century, well after the achievements of the Industrial Revolution.[4]

Little consensus has emerged from the plethora of research on this topic, in part because of a lack of systematic evidence about knowledge inputs. For the most part, anecdotes and case studies are cited to support the notion that science and scarce knowledge helped to produce productivity advances. According to some historians, the biases of the European scientific establishment toward abstract theory help to explain why Britain and not (say) France was the first industrial nation. They point to formal and informal links between scientific discoveries and technological change in the former country and conclude that Britain's industrial lead depended on its scientific standing.[5] In a variant of this theme, Joel Mokyr highlights the impact of the rational scientific revolution in the seventeenth century, although his emphasis is on the general and untestable influence of the intellectual contributions of a select few such as Bacon, Hooke, and Newton rather than on specific applications of their scientific results to industry.

Similarly, other writers point to the effects of social clubs whose membership included inventors and scientists. The eighteenth-century Lunar Society, for instance, held monthly dinners in the Midlands that were attended by Erasmus Darwin, Matthew Boulton, Josiah Wedgwood, James Keir, Joseph Priestley, and James Watt, among others. This social interaction is cited as proof by association

---

[3] For a survey, see Ó Gráda (2016).

[4] See, for instance, Allen (2009); Broadberry et al. (2015); Sanderson (1999).

[5] Musson and Robinson (1969: 7) declared that the Industrial Revolution "was not simply a product of illiterate practical craftsmen, devoid of scientific training. In the development of steam power, in the growth of the chemical industry, . . . and in various other industries, scientists made important contributions and industrialists with scientifically trained minds also utilized applied science in their manufactures."

of the thesis that natural philosophy and practical discoveries increased industrial and technological growth. Related institutions in the nineteenth century
included the "X-Club," whose eminent members included notable scientists
like Sir Joseph Hooker, Thomas Huxley, Sir Edward Frankland, John Tyndall,
Herbert Spencer, and Thomas Hirst, among others, and presidents of the Royal
Society. More general enthusiasm for scientific studies was manifested in the
rapid growth of less eminent scientific and natural philosophy societies, whose
number increased from fewer than 50 at the end of the eighteenth century to
some 1,500 by the 1850s. Extreme versions of the "science matters" thesis go
so far as to propose that almost all inventors in Britain during the Industrial
Revolution were influenced by scientific advances.

Empirical analysis of the thesis that scientific knowledge played an important role during industrialization in Europe has been limited to noncausal
correlations between the presence of elites and proxies for innovation in particular regions. Baten and van Zanden used book titles as a proxy for human capital
and access to scarce knowledge and conclude that such variables were associated
with early economic growth. Another study contends that total subscriptions to
the *Encyclopédie* by city in mid-eighteenth-century France captures "upper tail
knowledge." The tallies of subscribers occurred in the same locales as various
proxies for technological innovation, and this coincidence is regarded as proof
that scientifically oriented elites increased productivity in industrial technology
and promoted economic progress.[6] These authors acknowledge that geographical correlations between such aggregated variables might not indicate a causal
relationship, but their conclusions implicitly or explicitly tend to be based on
causal inferences.

By contrast, many prominent scholars decidedly reject the argument that the
stock of scientists and scientific knowledge influenced early British advances
in technology.[7] British innovations toward the end of the eighteenth century
and at the start of the nineteenth century were produced by artisans with little
formal education, who benefited from apprenticeships and on-the-job learning.
Significant problems such as the measurement of longitude at sea were resolved by relatively uneducated artisans, through trial-and-error experimentation, rather than by means of abstract or formal scientific observation. Until the
middle of the nineteenth century, even the frontier of science and engineering
was closer to organized intuition. Scientific endeavors of the day owed to skit-
tish dons or aristocratic amateurs, whose efforts were directed to impractical
pursuits and general principles in astronomy, magnetism, mathematics, botany,
and chemistry, rather than to useful applied knowledge that could enhance

---

[6] Baten and van Zanden (2008); Squicciarini and Voigtländer (2015).
[7] Landes (1969).

technological productivity. Chapter 5 on the Royal Society of Arts likewise indicates that the activities of the primary elite learned society in Britain between 1750 and 1850 had little or no impact on the course of technological innovation and industrialization. A comprehensive survey of the question concludes that elite "societies lent scientific knowledge respectability, [but] their role in spreading it was limited."[8]

As these diverse propositions suggest, significant aspects of the relationship between knowledge, science, and technology in the Industrial Revolution still remain untested and unresolved. This chapter offers a systematic estimation of different types of knowledge in British industrialization. The analysis is based on a sample of "great inventors" who were included in biographical dictionaries because of their notable contributions to technological progress. Instead of using indirect and potentially inaccurate proxies, I define scientific inputs specifically in terms of demonstrable scientific credentials, such as formal training in science and engineering, as well as wider dimensions of achievement such as membership in the Royal Society, scientific eminence, publications, and the receipt of prizes and nonmonetary rewards. The sample further includes information on the numbers of patents filed and the length of inventors' careers, the industry and region in which they were active, and the degree of specialization at invention.

This approach allows us to examine the backgrounds, education, and inventive activity of the major contributors to technological advances in Britain during the crucial period between 1750 and 1930 and to determine the extent to which such advances owed to specialized human capital and knowledge. More generally, the results shed light on the sources of outward shifts in the frontier of technology during early economic development.

Great Inventors and Inventions

This chapter analyzes the cohort of British inventors who made significant technological discoveries during the first and second Industrial Revolutions, from 1750 through 1930. The "great inventors" dataset was compiled from biographical dictionaries, including the *Oxford Dictionary of National Biography* (DNB), the *Biographical Dictionary of the History of Technology* (BD), other biographical compilations, and numerous accounts of the lives of specific inventors. A few of these entries would undoubtedly be debatable, but this triangulation of sources minimizes the possibility of egregious error, and it should be remembered that the objective is to obtain a representative sample rather than the entire

<hr>

[8] Ó Gráda (2016).

population of inventors.[9] This personal information was matched with all patented and unpatented inventions that the inventors obtained between 1750 and 1930. Although patents vary in their technical and commercial value, it might be expected that this portfolio of discoveries belonging to the great inventors would have a higher average value than those of their peers.

The resulting sample of British great inventors includes 438 men and one woman who made significant contributions to technological innovations and productivity change between 1790 and 1930. These eminent inventors include such well-known icons as Sir Humphry Davy, Sherard Osborn Cowper-Coles, John Dunlop, Charles Macintosh, Charles Babbage, Edmund Cartwright, Lord Kelvin, Guglielmo Marconi, and George Stephenson. The lone woman inventor, Henrietta Vansittart (1833–1883), is referenced in the DNB as an engineer whose educational background is unknown.[10] She improved upon her father's screw propeller invention, for which she obtained two British patents and awards from a number of countries.

As Table 4.1 shows, the majority of great inventors were born in the South of England, and London stands out as the birthplace of a high and fairly constant share of the scientist-inventors who were born in the nineteenth century. The birth cohort before 1780 contributed to the onset of industrialization, and it is striking that almost a quarter of the great inventors during this critical period originated from Scotland and other locations outside of England. For instance, Sir Isaac Holden, a prominent contributor to wool-combing technology, was born in 1807 near Glasgow, Scotland. Other noted inventors who were born in other areas outside England include Lord Kelvin (Ireland), Richard Roberts (Wales), and Warren de la Rue (Guernsey). The renowned Marc Isambard Brunel was born in Normandy, France, and such foreign-born inventors increased among the birth cohorts after 1820, including Gugliemo Marconi, Gisbert Johann Kapp, and Sir John Gustav Jarmay. It is noticeable

---

[9] While it is true that any individual compilation will be based on somewhat subjective determinations about who should be included and who should be excluded as an important inventor, the use of numerous such sources reduces the probability of significant bias. One way to determine the extent of systematic sample bias is to estimate the probability that an inventor drawn from a particular biographical source (e.g., the DNB) was selected on different criteria relative to inventors from other sources. The overall results underline the representativeness of the great inventors' sample. We can further reject the hypothesis of bias for almost all variables of interest, including time of first invention, educational status, science background, and occupation. Moreover, the data on the "great inventors" were significantly related to other measures of both economic and technical value, including patent assignments, litigation about inventions, and long-term patent citations.

[10] Another potential candidate is Eleanor Coade (1733–1821), the owner of an innovative stone-making factory. However, her status as an inventor is completely speculative: there is no evidence that she was responsible for the innovations her factory produced, and they might well have been the product of her employees.

Table 4.1 Birthplace of British Great Inventors: by Birth Cohort and Technical Orientation (Percentages)

| | Birth Cohort | | | | | | | | | | |
| | Before 1780 | | 1781–1820 | | 1821–1845 | | After 1845 | | All Cohorts | | |
Birthplace	S&T	None	S&T	None	S&T	None	S&T	None	S&T	None	Total
London	12.5	5.6	18.2	9.5	19.2	20.6	22.6	12.2	19.1	11.5	13.7
South	12.5	18.3	25	23.8	15.4	19.1	20.4	24.5	20.4	21.5	21.6
Midlands	12.5	11.3	6.8	13.3	3.9	15.9	7.5	2	7.5	11.5	10.1
North	12.5	22.5	15.9	22.9	19.2	19.1	15.7	30.6	15.7	23.3	20.7
Other Britain	41.7	31	31.8	18.1	26.9	12.7	28.6	18.4	28.6	20.1	23
Overseas	4.2	5.6	2.3	4.8	15.4	6.4	11.3	10.2	8.2	6.3	6.9
Number	24	71	44	105	26	63	53	49	147	288	435

Notes: "S&T" indicates postsecondary training in science and engineering or listing in a dictionary of scientific biography; "None" indicates inventors who did not have such training and were not listed. The home counties are included in the South; London includes Middlesex; "Other Britain" refers to Cornwall, Scotland, Ireland, Wales, the Isle of Wight, and the Isle of Man. The "unknown" category is not reported, so percentages will not total to 100.

that inventors who were born outside of England tended to be disproportionately trained in science, as indicated by the fraction of scientists (approximately 37%) relative to nonscientists (26%).

There are different facets to science, so the analysis considers three alternative measures of scientific orientation. These include formal postsecondary education, including university education; eminence as gauged by listing in biographical dictionaries of scientists; and membership in the Royal Society. Approximately 20% of the great inventors were educated at the postsecondary level in the sciences, mathematics, or medicine. Similarly, 16.6% could be considered as eminent scientists. A significant number (20.7% of all inventors) were Fellows of the Royal Society. We might expect that the role of formal education and specialized knowledge would vary over time. The distribution of inventors in terms of their science background indeed changed over the course of industrialization (Table 4.2).

The nature of important technological innovations changed for the generation of inventors who were born after 1870, since scientists accounted for a significantly higher proportion of the later cohorts. For instance, the percentage of inventors with scientific training in universities increased from

Table 4.2 Science and Engineering Backgrounds of Great Inventors

Year	Science Training		Listed Scientist		Engineering Training	
	N	%	N	%	N	%
Before 1820	10	10.0	18	16.8	1	1.0
1821–1851	21	18.8	24	19.5	3	2.7
1852–1870	14	20.0	8	9.6	7	10.0
1871–1890	21	33.3	14	18.2	16	25.4
After 1890	11	23.4	8	17.0	17	34.7
Total	78	19.8	75	16.6	44	11.1

Notes: "Science training" refers to postsecondary school education in the sciences, mathematics, or medicine. A great inventor who is included in biographical dictionaries of scientists is denoted as a "listed scientist." "Engineering training" indicates formal postsecondary school training in engineering. The time periods refer to year of first invention.

20% between 1852 and 1870 to 33.3% between 1871 and 1890. These patterns are even more marked for great inventors with technical training (as gauged by formal postsecondary school education in engineering), who made up 11.1% of all inventors. Inventors with such formal engineering qualifications increased from a mere 1% before 1820 to 25.4% of all great inventors from 1871 to 1890. Since part of our concern is with the contribution of this sort of specialized knowledge to innovation, the following section further explores the extent of formal training among the great inventors and the role of education in science and engineering over the course of industrialization.

Characteristics of the Great Inventors

Economic studies have shown the importance of appropriate institutions in promoting self-sustaining growth. Britain long remained an oligarchic society whose governing premise was based on the conviction that merit was causally related to inherited social class. Compulsory education was introduced in 1880, and limited free public education was not made available until 1891. The British educational system failed to match up to institutes of higher learning in Germany and the United States, and access was restricted at all levels until late in the nineteenth century. However, the costs of such policies are a function of the degree to which productive economic activities depended on the acquisition of these sorts of scarce human capital.

The educational background of British great inventors by birth cohort shows that they were more educated than the general population (Figure 4.1). At the same time, it is clear that formal training in an educational institution was not a prerequisite for important technological inventions during the early period of industrialization. The majority of great inventors had no formal education beyond the primary or secondary school levels. This was the case even as late as the 1821–1845 birth cohort, many of whom contributed to the "second Industrial Revolution" that started in the 1870s. Thus, the claim that "virtually all of the inventors" had exposure to scientific training is questionable. Instead, the experience of these creative inventors suggests that the Industrial Revolution drew on traditional informal institutions, such as apprenticeships and on-the-job training, that enhanced creative abilities through learning by doing.

The route of craft-apprenticeship was taken by an impressive roster of great inventors, including some who came from quite privileged backgrounds. Apprenticeship was a flexible source of human capital acquisition, which did not preclude social mobility or further education. The skills that the inventor obtained by apprenticeships could be combined with informal attendance at lectures offered by mechanics' institutes, and could even provide a route toward a university degree later in life. A prominent example, Sir Joseph Wilson Swan, was apprenticed at age fourteen to a pharmacy store but attended lectures at the Athenaeum in Sunderland, which helped him to become an internationally renowned chemist and electrical inventor. Both the Fairbairn brothers (Sir Peter Fairbairn [1799–1861] and Sir William Fairbairn [1789–1874]) were apprenticed

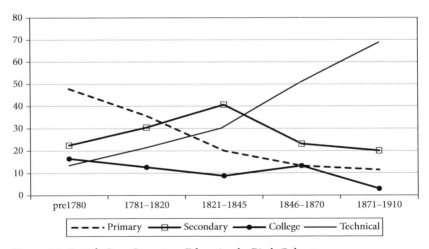

Figure 4.1 British Great Inventors: Education by Birth Cohort

Notes: For information about the sample of "great inventors," see the text.

as millwrights in a colliery at an early age but were able to achieve distinction in a number of fields. William Fairbairn, in particular, although he was self-taught, was appointed a member of the Academy of Science in France, a Fellow of the Royal Society, and president of the British Association. The military academies also allowed inventors to combine apprenticeships with more formal but some-what diffuse training.

Over time, the importance of higher education in science steadily increased. Engineering proficiency was more discontinuous and was associated with a jump in the technical orientation of the 1821–1845 birth cohort. More than half of all twenty-seven inventors who received higher education in engineering first produced inventions between 1871 and 1890. This is consistent with the finding that scientific and technical invention became more prevalent after 1870. By the beginning of the twentieth century, a college degree in science or technical ed-ucational was typical of the majority of great inventors, and many even received advanced doctoral degrees in science. Degrees in science and engineering may have enhanced the ability of these inventors to make useful inventions. However, college degrees were also correlated with such other arbitrary factors as family income and connections that gave these individuals preferment.

Cardwell claimed that there were few institutional obstacles to innovation in England in the nineteenth century, for it was "a remarkably open society," and many of the inventive "heroes" in both science and technology were from humble origins.[11] The facts suggest otherwise (Table 4.3). The common percep-tion that the heroes of the British Industrial Revolution were primarily from modest backgrounds is somewhat overstated. Instead, an examination of the family backgrounds of the great inventors indicates that, in the area of tech-nological achievement, elites were overrepresented relative to the population. A third of the inventors did indeed come from farming, low-skilled, or undis-tinguished (likely most of the unknown category) backgrounds. However, the majority of the British great inventors were born to families headed by master artisans, manufacturers, white-collar workers, or well-off families in the elite and professional classes. It is quite striking that inventors with education in science were twice as likely to belong to these elite and professional families, and this pat-tern is invariant over the entire period.

An increasing fraction of inventors were educated at elite schools such as Oxford or Cambridge, which were unlikely to offer much in the way of direct knowledge or skills that would add to either scientific or technological produc-tivity. Advancement at these institutions primarily depended on excellence in divinity and classical subjects, and the engineer John Perry even declared that

---

[11] These specific claims are made in Cardwell et al. (2003).

Table 4.3 Social Background of the Great Inventors, by Birth Cohort and Technical Orientation (Percentages)

Year	Family Connections		Elite Education		Fellows of the Royal Society	
	N	%	N	%	N	%
Before 1820	31	29.0	11	10.3	21	19.6
1821–1851	27	22.0	13	10.6	25	20.3
1852–1870	15	18.3	14	16.9	17	20.5
1871–1890	19	26.0	18	24.7	20	27.4
After 1890	6	12.8	9	19.2	7	14.9
Total	99	22.8	65	14.9	90	20.7

Notes: The percentages are within-period proportions, based on a total of 435 inventors. "Family connections" imply an elite family background or other family members being listed in the Oxford DNB. "Elite education" indicates that the great inventor attended Oxford, Cambridge, Durham, or one of the Royal Colleges or obtained a postgraduate degree overseas (mainly Germany).

"Oxford fears and hates natural science." Cambridge had offered the Natural Science Tripos (NST) since 1848, but for much of the nineteenth century the impact was nominal; as late as 1880 only 4% of Cambridge undergraduates read for the NST.[12] The antipragmatism of Oxbridge was ironically also reflected in the "red-brick" institutions that were established toward the end of the nineteenth century to remedy the lapses in the scientific and technical curricula of the elite schools. Even at the Scottish universities, which were widely regarded as leaders in science education in Britain, few nonmedical students had the opportunity to participate in laboratories or research.[13] It is not surprising that serious British students of science and technology chose to pursue graduate studies in the German academies, which were acknowledged as the world leaders in higher education in such fields as chemistry, physics, and engineering. However,

[12] For an illuminating analysis, see MacLeod and Moseley (1980). Most Cambridge graduates were destined for conventional upper-tier occupations such as the clergy. There was a general disdain among the Dons for the notion that science should be directed toward professional training, and they eschewed practical laboratory work; so it is not surprising that only 4% of the NST graduates entered industry. Students who did take the NSTs tended to perform poorly because of improper preparation and indifferent teaching. The first chaired position in engineering was created in Oxford in 1907. The contrast to the United States is striking: Harvard and Brown established their first engineering schools in 1847, and Yale closely followed in 1852. MIT alone had seven engineering professors in 1891.

[13] See *Report of the Royal Commissioners Appointed to Enquire into the Universities of Scotland: Returns and Documents, Parliamentary Papers* xxxv (1878).

opportunities for a foreign education were reserved for students from a secure social and financial background.

Some might contend that programs at elite universities like Cambridge and Oxford, while not directly addressing technological matters, nevertheless enhanced rational methods of thinking that facilitated innovation. This proposition is, of course, inherently untestable, but we can obtain some insights by comparing the social backgrounds of great inventors who attended college across the two leading industrial nations of Britain and America. If it were true that elites prevailed because their privileged background and subsequent advantages in obtaining a college degree gave them an objective edge in technological creativity, we might expect similar patterns across countries. In the period before 1820, college attendees in both Britain and the United States predominantly belonged to elite families. However, after 1820, the share of elites shrinks noticeably in the United States, and the vast majority of graduates come from nonelite backgrounds, whereas the pattern in Britain remains for the most part unchanged. Other researchers have also shown that the benefits of tertiary education in Britain owed more to its association with elite status than to the ability to acquire or apply useful knowledge.

The rather privileged background of many of the British great inventors is reflected in other dimensions of elite standing. Twenty-nine percent of the inventors who were active before 1820 had families who were connected to those in power or who were otherwise distinguished. An interesting facet of the relationship between privilege, science, and technological achievement in Britain is reflected in the ninety great inventors who were also appointed as Fellows of the Royal Society. The Royal Society was founded in 1660 as an "invisible college" of natural philosophers who included Isaac Newton, Christopher Wren, Robert Hooke, and Robert Boyle. Fellows of the society were elected and many of the members consisted of individuals who were not professional scientists but who were wealthy or well connected. The Royal Society was widely criticized for its elitist and unmeritocratic policies.[14] Great inventors William Sturgeon and William Robert Grove were representative of those who publicly assailed the nepotism and corruption of scientific institutions in the nineteenth century, and Babbage attributed a large part of the failure of British science to features typified by the Royal Society. The society long retained the character of a gentleman's club and, despite a series of reforms, did not become a genuine professional scientific

---

[14] Babbage (1830: 52) noted that "those who are ambitious of scientific distinction, may, according to their fancy, render their name a kind of comet, carrying with it a tail of upwards of forty letters, at the average cost of 10£. 9s. 9d. per letter. It should be observed, that all members contribute equally, and that the sum now required is fifty pounds. . . . The amount of this subscription is so large, that it is calculated to prevent many men of real science from entering the Society, and is a very severe tax on those who do so."

organization until after the 1870s. Even in 1860, more than 66% of its membership consisted of nonscientists and medical practitioners, whose inclusion was not altogether merited on the basis of their scientific contributions. Accordingly, many of its projects were so absurd and fantastical that Jonathan Swift satirized the Royal Society as the "Grand Academy of Projectors" in his novel *Gulliver's Travels*. In short, scarce human capital was not a significant factor in important inventive activity during the period of early industrialization. The prevalence of elite education among British inventors at the start of the twentieth century primarily reflected their privileged backgrounds rather than the need for specialized knowledge to generate technological innovation.

Patents, Productivity, and Market Incentives

Numerous scholars have contended that prospects for early growth depended on specialized knowledge inputs such as formal scientific training. The experience of the greatest inventors in Britain and America instead shows that science and knowledge in the "upper tails of the distribution" were only weakly related to technology during the era of industrialization. It has further been claimed that, especially during the early stages of industrialization, scientists were not sensitive to market factors, which would imply that they would tend to respond inelastically to economic inducements. This section uses patent records to compare productivity at invention among scientists and nonscientists and to gauge the extent to which scientist-inventors were responsive to market incentives.

American patent institutions were extremely favorable to inventors of all classes, and virtually all U.S. great inventors chose to obtain patent protection for their inventions. The figure was lower for British great inventors. Charles Wheatstone observed that "some thought it not quite consistent with the habits of a scientific man to be concerned in a patent," but it is still the case that around 87% of the British sample of great inventors were patentees (Table 4.4). It is noticeable that the proportion of patentees is similar across all science classes, whether proxied by educational background, scientific eminence, or membership in the premier Royal Society.[15] Although the British great inventors overall exhibited a lower propensity to patent than their American counterparts, this was more related to institutional factors rather than to scientific disdain for material returns.

In particular, the per capita patenting rates significantly increase after 1851. This period stands out because in 1852 the British patent laws were reformed in the

---

[15] See Cooke (1857).

Table 4.4 Propensity to Patent among British Great Inventors, by Year of First Invention

	Before 1820	1821–1851	1852–1870	1871–1890	All Years
All Great Inventors					
N	89	105	78	65	337
%	83.2	85.4	94.0	89.0	86.9
All Science (FRS, Science Education, Eminence)					
N	28	37	23	28	116
%	80.0	82.2	95.8	90.3	85.3
Fellows of the Royal Society					
N	17	21	16	19	73
%	81.0	84.0	94.1	95.0	88.0
Science Education					
N	7	17	13	19	56
%	70.0	81.0	92.9	90.5	83.6
Eminent Scientists					
N	14	19	8	14	55
%	77.8	91.2	100.0	100.0	85.9

Notes: The figures indicate the number of inventors who had obtained at least one patent by the year 1890. "FRS" is a Fellow of the Royal Society. For descriptions of the various categories, see the text and notes to prior tables.

direction of the American system in ways that increased access to patent institutions and strengthened the security of property rights in patents. Significant aspects of the institutional overhaul included lower patent fees, the administration was rationalized, and measures were undertaken to enhance the provision and dissemination of information. In 1883, further improvements in the rules and standards were introduced and the fees fell again. The high monetary and transaction costs of patenting in England served as a disproportionate constraint on inventors with lower wealth and significantly reduced the efficiency of the allocation of resources by creative individuals. When the fees were reduced in line with the "cheap patent" model of the United States, the number of credit-constrained inventors increased and the long-run result was a doubling of higher-quality patents.[16]

The reforms provide a well-defined natural experiment to determine the extent of responsiveness of great inventions and their variation across knowledge

[16] Kuegler (2018).

inputs.[17] If great inventors in general, and scientists in particular, differed from ordinary patentees in terms of their responsiveness or commercial orientation, then we would expect their patterns of patenting to be largely unaffected by these institutional changes. Instead, the great inventors responded to the decrease in monetary and transactions costs (and potential rise in net expected returns) by increasing their investments in patented invention (Figure 4.2). This responsiveness was exhibited by scientists and nonscientists alike, undermining the notion that the former were immune to economic motivations (Figure 4.3).

The patent records also enable us to examine whether a science background increased productivity at invention (Table 4.5). Again, the patterns suggest that a background in science did not add a great deal to inventive productivity during the early industrial era through 1870. If scientific knowledge gave inventors a marked advantage, it might be expected that they would demonstrate greater creativity at an earlier age than those without such human capital. Inventor scientists were marginally younger than nonscientists, but both classes of inventors were primarily close to middle age by the time they obtained their first invention (note that this variable tracks inventions rather than patents). This suggests that important inventive insights were the result of experience and learning by doing, rather than scarce formal knowledge in science or related subjects. Productivity in terms of average patents filed and career length are also similar among all great inventors irrespective of their scientific orientation. In short, the kind of knowledge and ideas that produced significant technological contributions during British industrialization seem to have been rather general and available to all creative individuals.

Total career patents offer another measure of human capital in inventive activity, since inventors with greater numbers of patents would be more likely to have accumulated larger stocks of useful knowledge and know-how. Career patents were higher in the South of England, where markets (as gauged by income and population) were more extensive. As for the patentees' science and technology knowledge, the patterns are consistent with all the findings reported in this chapter. Elite education, science degrees, and even involvement in formal research and development

---

[17] Widespread dissatisfaction with the British patent system had existed more than a century before the reforms of 1852. The motivation for making changes in the patent rules came when the Crystal Palace Exhibition in 1851 revealed that Britain was in danger of losing its industrial competitiveness to the United States. It was argued that part of the growing American advantage owed to its favorable patent institutions. As a result, the British patent laws were explicitly revised in the direction of the U.S. system (Khan 2005). The motivation for the change therefore was exogenously driven by the perceived rise of American industrial superiority, and not to accommodate an increased propensity to patent in Britain.

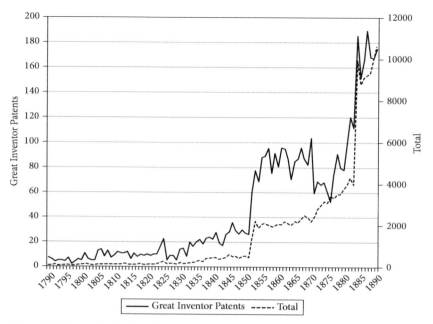

Figure 4.2 Patenting by British Great Inventors and by All Patentees, 1790–1890

Notes: The patent information was obtained from the *Reports of the Commissioners of Patents*, various years. For the "great inventors" sample, see the text.

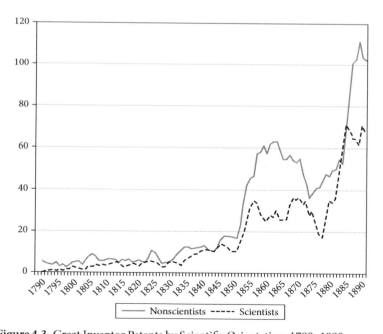

Figure 4.3 Great Inventor Patents by Scientific Orientation, 1790–1890

Notes: The patent information was obtained from the *Reports of the Commissioners of Patents*, various years. For the "great inventors" sample, see the text. *Scientists* include great inventors who were listed in a dictionary of scientific biography; received college training in medicine, mathematics, or the natural sciences; or were Fellows of the Royal Society.

Figure 4.4 Prometheus Unbound, or Science on Olympus
"Prometheus unbound" is a common metaphor for human creativity. This 1879 sketch by the British satirical artist John Tenniel shows an array of Olympian deities who are astonished by scientific advances and the display of such technological marvels as the power press, telephone, electricity, and weapons. Ironically, the most significant of these inventions had actually been invented by patentees in the United States, few of whom at that time had any scientific training, and none of whom were elites who were likely to be consorting in Olympus.
Source: Library of Congress.

laboratories did not lead to higher patenting over an inventor's career. Career patents were higher for inventors who had engineering degrees, but, as the descriptive statistics indicated, engineering qualifications were prevalent only later in the century.

We can also examine the relationship between inventive activity and different proxies for specialized human capital. For instance, one such measure relates to the extent of industrial specialization, or the fraction of an inventor's patents that were filed in a particular industry. Industries like agriculture and construction were less likely to be specialized, whereas patents for textiles and the electrical industries went to inventors who were more specialized. As might be expected, formal technical education in engineering and technology was associated with higher sectoral specialization. However, elite degrees from Oxford or Cambridge, degrees in science, and publications of books and articles all indicated lower tendencies for specialization. None of these measures of formal science backgrounds adds much explanatory power in statistical models of technical specialization.

Table 4.5 Patents and Productivity among Scientists and Nonscientists, by Year of First Invention

	Before 1820	1821–1851	1852–1870	1871–1890	All Years
Nonscientists					
Age of first invention	35.1	35.2	33.9	29.5	33.6
Average patents	4.2	14.1	17.2	13.1	10.7
Career length	18.0	20.3	25.7	30.1	23.2
No. of inventors	72	78	59	42	286
Industrial specialization					
% of patents by specialized inventors	57.5	45.4	69.3	73.9	60.3
Total no. of patents	180	497	678	390	1,776
Industrial distribution (select industries, % of patents by nonscientists)					
Engines	17.9	11.7	11.2	26.9	13.6
Electric-telecoms	2.2	2.6	13.9	9.5	7.5
Textiles	25.6	19.7	6.2	11.0	14.1
Manufacturing	25.4	31.4	36.1	28.6	31.5
Total no. of patents	313	1,094	978	528	2,945
All Science (FRS, Science Education, Eminence)					
Age of first invention	32.4	32.9	29.8	29.0	31.2
Average patents	4.9	16.2	17.2	16.8	12.8
Career length	21.2	25.6	24.5	34.2	26.9
No. of inventors	35	45	24	31	153
Industrial specialization					
% of patents by specialized inventors	63.5	31.0	48.7	85.4	54.0
Total no. of patents	113	228	202	452	1,012
Industrial distribution (select industries, % of patents by scientists)					
Engines	16.3	10.6	3.6	14.4	11.0
Electric-telecoms	1.1	16.6	28.0	54.6	28.2
Textiles	15.2	3.7	4.8	1.1	4.3
Manufacturing	41.0	43.8	40.0	18.2	35.0
Total no. of patents	178	736	415	529	1,875

Notes: The patent information was obtained from the Reports of the Commissioners of Patents, and patents were categorized according to sector of final use. "Career" refers to lifetime career, defined as the difference between the first and last invention. "FRS" is a Fellow of the Royal Society. See notes to prior tables and text.

In the third quarter of the nineteenth century, elite education was becoming moderately more specialized than earlier on, but the orientation of science graduates from elite schools did not differ significantly from individuals without any formal training. Similarly, the technological contributions of scientists remained diffuse and unspecialized throughout the entire period. The inventive activity of those with formal technical education in such subjects as electrical and civil engineering did not become significantly more specialized until the last decade of the nineteenth century. By the beginning of the twentieth century, inventive productivity was drawing on scarcer human capital that was enhanced by investments in technical skills, and this process was associated with greater specialization.

All of these empirical findings together suggest that, by focusing their efforts in a particular industry, relatively uneducated inventors were able to acquire specific knowledge that allowed them to make valuable additions to the available technology set. After 1820, as the market expanded and created incentives to move out of traditional industries such as textiles and engines, both scientists and nonscientists responded by decreasing their specialization. The patent reforms in 1852 in part encouraged the non-science-oriented inventors to increase their investments in sectoral specialization, but even so, industrial specialization among the scientists lagged significantly. As such, any comparative advantage from familiarity with science may have been based on broad unfocused capabilities such as rational methods of analysis that applied across all industries.

The time path of specialization is especially informative in terms of electrical and telecommunications technology, which required more technical knowledge inputs than traditional areas such as textiles. Electrical innovation was also heavily specialized across regions, and two-thirds of all related patented inventions were filed by residents of London. The expansion in this industry after the 1870s led to higher marginal returns for those with formal education, and this likely induced the substantive specialization in this industry among scientist-inventors, as well as among college-educated engineers.[18]

The experience of the British great inventors also shed light on the reward systems that are frequently recommended as substitutes for patents. Prizes and medals, in particular, might be more effective inducements than patents

---

[18] The Society of Telegraph Engineers (later the Institution of Electrical Engineers) was founded in London in 1871 by eight men and rapidly became one of the largest societies in Britain. Its membership rose from 352 in 1871 (8.5% of all enrollment in engineering institutions) to 2,100 (14.0%) in 1890 and to 4,000 (17.2%) in 1910. Even these professional institutions resisted formal education, and apprenticeships remained the favored mode of human capital acquisition among the engineering class examinations throughout the nineteenth century.

if scientists were uninterested in financial returns and were simply motivated by the desire to serve the common good or by the recognition of their peers. Between 1826 and 1914, the Royal Society (not to be confused with the Royal Society of Arts) awarded 173 medals, 67 of which were given for work in mathematics, astronomy, and experimental physics, and only 2 to engineers. The majority of premia were made later in life to those who had already attained eminence, or as ex post "recognition awards."

The likelihood that an inventor would receive prizes and medals was higher for unspecialized scientific men, and even more so for those who had already gained recognition as famous scientists, and for those who had influential connections. Prizes and medals tended to be awarded to the same individuals who had already received patents, and indeed, prizes were associated with higher numbers of patents. The incremental value of these administered awards was therefore likely to be somewhat low—not because scientists were unresponsive to incentives, but because their response was higher for financial motivations including the returns vested in patents. It is not surprising that, early in the twentieth century, the Council of the Royal Society decided to change its emphasis from the allocation of medals to the financing of research, concluding that these awards served neither science nor society.

Conclusions

What was the role of science, specialized knowledge, and knowledge-generating institutions in the creation of important technological inventions during British industrialization? During this era the evidence regarding technical knowledge of all kinds comported more with James Nasmyth's definition of engineering as "common sense applied to the use of materials." The biographies, backgrounds, and patenting experience of the great inventors in Britain suggest that the formal acquisition of human capital did not play a central role in the generation of new inventive activity, even in the second Industrial Revolution. Indeed, British science entered its golden age long after the advent of industrialization, and, even as late as 1884, Francis Galton concluded that "an exhaustive list" of scientists in the British Isles "would amount to 300, but not to more." Alexander Parkes (1813–1890), the creator of the first synthetic plastic, was trained as an apprentice to a firm of brass founders in Birmingham and initially described his occupation as a decorative artist, only later declaring himself as a chemist.

These patterns may have owed in part to the character of the British educational system, which largely restricted access to higher education to the privileged classes, in the nineteenth century and beyond.[19] The evidence on educational institutions is particularly striking when one contrasts the British experience to the United States. College graduates from elite universities, especially those in science and technical fields, were generally better represented among great inventors in Britain than in the United States. There were stark differences in the distribution of education attainments, as well as in the social class of those who were able to go to college, between the two countries. College education was not so prevalent among the U.S. inventors until quite late in the nineteenth century, but, judging from the occupations of fathers, even those graduates were drawn from a much broader range of social classes. The proportion of great inventors who were scientists in Britain actually overstates the importance of a science education for making a significant contribution to technological knowledge. Despite all the advantages accruing to elites, scientists were not well represented among the great British inventors nor among patentees during the height of industrial achievements. This is perhaps unsurprising since scientific efforts of the time were fairly abstruse without many practical applications. Instead, many of the most productive inventors, such as Charles Tennant, were able to acquire or enhance their inventive capabilities through apprenticeships and informal learning, honed through trial-and-error experimentation.[20]

Economic historians of Britain have pointed out that its early economic growth was unbalanced and productivity advances were evident in only a few key sectors. Moreover, significant increases in total factor productivity growth were not experienced until the middle of the nineteenth century. The reasons for these patterns have not been fully elaborated on. This chapter highlighted constraints on the generation of knowledge inputs and the elitist institutions that hampered their full attainment during the critical period of industrialization.

The oligarchic nature of British society likely limited the size of the market, suppressed the widespread acquisition of human capital through educational institutions, and encouraged rules and standards that discriminated against the efforts of disadvantaged members of society. According to the *London Times*, "it is evident that technical education is not needed for the mass of the workpeople.

---

[19] Reports from a number of Royal Commissions—including the Samuelson (1868 and 1882) and Devonshire (1878) Commissions—outlined the inadequacy of British science and its institutions of scientific and technical training. Enrollments in science classes at the secondary school level were regarded as "negligible," and university science was "seriously deficient in quantity and quality." Despite the frequent investigations by commissions of this sort, reform was slow and sporadic. The government was involved in the establishment of the National Physical Laboratory, the Imperial College of Science and Technology, and the Medical Research Committee, but a significant role for state funding awaited World War I.

[20] Charles Tennant (1768–1838), the son of a Scottish weaver, developed such inventions in chemistry as bleaching powder and founded a firm that was the precursor of Imperial Chemical Industries.

Indeed, they are better without it, since it is usually imperfect when done, and only teaches the workman to think that he is as good as his master or overseer."[21] Technological innovation and related activities responded to incentives and were likely inhibited by such factors. Whatever the underlying reasons, the transformations that made science and technical backgrounds crucial to the creation of important inventions were not achieved until after the end of the nineteenth century.

More generally, the experience of the first industrial nation indicates that additions to advanced science and technical knowledge is somewhat different from creativity that actually enhances economic efficiency through successful improvements in products and productivity in the market. The sort of inventiveness that led to spurts in economic and social progress consisted of insights that were motivated by perceived need and institutional incentives and could be achieved by drawing on practical abilities or informal education and skills. The acquisition of useful knowledge also depended on informal transmission mechanisms within households, from fathers to children, and within crafts and guilds, from masters to apprentices. These informal mechanisms were crucial for women, in particular. Apprenticeships offered a particularly effective and flexible means of acquiring training and skills for creative individuals to engage in inventive activity and innovation. Elites and their "upper-tail knowledge" were neither necessary nor sufficient for technological productivity and economic progress in the first or the second Industrial Revolutions.

The claim that highly specialized knowledge and capital were fundamental for growth also seems inconsistent with much of the twentieth-century experience. The "great transformation" of human capital in the second Industrial Revolution was not the increase of engineering graduates or scientists, but the spread of fairly basic educational inputs in the secondary school movement. Even so, less than 10% of the eligible U.S. population had completed secondary schooling in 1910, and a bare majority had done so up to World War II. When Claudia Goldin and Larry Katz characterized the twentieth century as the "human capital century" and pointed to the central role that human capital played in the rise of the U.S. economy, they were mainly referring to American leadership in improving literacy and broad-based skills through decentralized investments in primary and secondary education.[22] Europe and Latin America lagged in economic achievements owing to their elitist orientation and a "closed, unforgiving" system of learning that undervalued mass education, and instead funneled resources to tertiary education that mainly benefited the already privileged classes.

---

[21] *The Times* (London, England), January 20, 1897, p. 9.
[22] Examples of this extensive literature include Goldin and Katz (2008) and Goldin (2001). Engerman and Sokoloff (2012) consider schooling throughout the Americas.

In the twenty-first century, specialized human capital and scientific knowledge undoubtedly make valuable contributions to economic growth in the developed economies. However, for developing countries with scarce resources, such inputs at the frontier of "high technology" might be less relevant than the ability to make incremental adjustments that can transform existing technologies into inventions and innovations that are appropriate for general domestic conditions. And, just as in the Industrial Revolution, improvements in informal training and institutions are quite likely to have significant returns at the margin that exceed those from costly inputs into tertiary institutions that typically subsidize elites at the expense of the general population. As Thomas Jefferson pointed out, a small innovation that can improve the lives of the mass of the population might be more economically important than a technically advanced discovery that benefits only the few.[23]

---

[23] Thomas Jefferson noted that a smaller invention, "applicable to our daily concerns, is infinitely more valuable than the greatest which can be used only for great objects. For these interest the few alone, the former the many." From a letter Jefferson sent to George Fleming in 1815.

5

Prestige and Profit

The Royal Society of Arts

Knowledge . . . be worth all the merchandize in the kingdom.
—Gabriel Plattes (1641)

Utopian tracts of the early seventeenth century suggested proposals for reforms that highlighted the need to draw on the skills and ideas of ordinary artisans, as well as scientists and inventors. A noteworthy example, the "Kingdome of Macaria," is framed as a dialogue between a traveler and a scholar whose objective was to "trade in Knowledge."[1] Macaria is an economic utopia, administered by enlightened governing councils that encourage agriculture, commerce, and colonization; impose taxes for infrastructure; and offer rewards for improvements. Improving institutions such as a "College of Experience" would busy itself with the creation and dissemination of knowledge and policies to improve "the health or wealth of men." Similarly, the author of "Nova Solyma" (1648) proclaimed that "a good stock of really useful knowledge" was the best endowment for economic success, and material incentives such as prizes were necessary to promote knowledge and industry.[2]

These utopian visions of enlightened administered systems inducing useful knowledge might have become hazy over time, but to some extent they are reflected in European policies that featured a wide array of state-sponsored and private incentives for improvements, innovation, and economic growth. Despite ongoing debates about the timing and nature of an industrial revolution, a consensus acknowledges that the pattern of technological change and total productivity growth toward the end of the eighteenth century was significantly different from the previous era. Some scholars attribute these advances in Europe to an "industrial enlightenment" that melded together a fortuitous and diverse array of beliefs, most notably that social and economic progress could be attained through methodical approaches to nature, science, and technology.[3] Numerous

---

[1] Gabriel Plattes, "A Description of the Famous Kingdome of Macaria" (1641).
[2] Samuel Gott, *Nova Solyma, the Ideal City* (1648), p. 128. An entire chapter of this work was devoted to the benefits of prize giving.
[3] See, for instance, Mokyr (2002).

Inventing Ideas. B. Zorina Khan, Oxford University Press (2020). © Oxford University Press.
DOI: 10.1093/oso/9780190936075.001.0001

institutions for the promotion of science and useful knowledge were founded after the middle of the eighteenth century. Early antecedents included the Royal Society, which coalesced in the 1660s as an "invisible college" for the improvement of "natural knowledge" through observation and experimentation. Such communities of intellectuals and entrepreneurs as the Birmingham Lunar Society, the Dublin Society, and the Society for the Encouragement of National Industry in France typify the incentives and institutions that are credited with cultural and industrial progress in Europe.

Although many of the utopian tracts of the seventeenth century had conceived of open institutions that would educate and encourage the industry and creativity of ordinary artisans, in practice this democratic orientation was hardly typical of improving societies in Europe. Indeed, current scholars of European economic development often celebrate the claim that elites played a central role in the process. Economists have correlated subscriptions to the French *Encyclopédie* to various measures of technological achievements and drawn the causal conclusion that "upper-tail knowledge" generated French industrialization and growth.[4] Another thesis compares the location of membership in scientific societies with exhibits at the Crystal Palace Exhibition and argues that the match indicates that such elites should be credited with increased technological innovation during the Industrial Revolution.[5] Other European scholars such as Joel Mokyr have identified the Royal Society of Arts in London as the canonical knowledge institution of this era. This chapter therefore assesses detailed archival evidence from the society's own records to determine the way this classic administered system actually functioned in practice.

The Royal Society of Arts

The London Society for the Encouragement of Arts, Manufactures, and Commerce, most often known as the Royal Society of Arts (RSA), embodied the improving spirit of the age. This institution was established in 1754 to "embolden enterprise, enlarge science, refine art, improve our manufacturers and extend our commerce." The imposing façade of the (still-existing) headquarters in London features the slogan "Arts and Commerce Promoted." The RSA was influential both because of its own status and because it became a model for other institutions that wished to contribute to social welfare through the promotion of technological progress, in Europe and beyond. The RSA bestowed many thousands of cash and honorary prizes on applicants, and even today is often

---

[4] Squicciarini and Voigtländer (2015).
[5] Dowey (2017).

Figure 5.1 Royal Society of Arts: Arts and Commerce Promoted?
The Royal Society of Arts (RSA) published lists of cash and honorary inducement prizes ("premiums offered") in its house journal. The facing self-portrait in the 1804 issue shows James Barry, an artist who painted six murals in the Great Room of the RSA building in the Adelphi. The series of paintings traced the arc of human knowledge and culture, and flatteringly depicted the distribution of prizes at the RSA as contributing to such progress.
Source: Photographs by author.

cited as an institution that should serve as a model for the adoption of "induce-ment prizes."[6]

The RSA initially was convinced that its efforts were crucial for the process of industrial and cultural development in the eighteenth century. The institution was not hesitant in issuing self-congratulatory proclamations:

> Whoever attentively considers the benefits which have arisen to the Publick since the institution of this Society . . . will readily allow, no money was ever more usefully expended; nor has any nation received more real advantage from any public body whatever than has been derived to this country from the rewards bestowed by this Society.[7]

The wealth and prominence of the membership, their personal influence, and the glittering social events contributed to the façade of an organization that was essential for economic progress. Both then and now, the correlation between the operation of the RSA and the "takeoff" of industrialization in Britain led casual observers to make a causal inference between its policy of granting prizes and the pace of technological change.

RSA membership expanded rapidly, attracting wealthy patrons from the pres-tigious Royal Society, as well as subscriptions from influential political and so-cial groups. In 1755, its total membership amounted to just over a hundred, but exponential growth occurred in numbers of both subscribers and subscriptions. At its peak in the 1760s, over two thousand individuals belonged to the society, and annual subscriptions and income exceeded £4,000. Among the subscribers were eminent figures of the day such as Adam Smith, Edmund Burke, Jeremy Bentham, Josiah Wedgwood, Horace Walpole, and Samuel Johnson. The nobility and landed gentry increased from 10% of the membership roster in the 1760s to 20% in the 1780s and included the Earl of Radnor and the Dukes of Buccleugh and Northumberland. Victoria's consort, Prince Albert, would later serve as president of the RSA for almost two decades. Merchants made up only 7% of the members in 1764, while artisans, manufacturers, and tradesmen accounted for a further 11%, but even these belonged to the upper ranks of their occupations. The subscription fee of two guineas per annum (£20 for a lifetime membership) provided the largest source of income for its activities and was sufficiently high relative to average earn-ings (approximately £14) that persons of lesser rank were necessarily excluded.[8]

---

[6] For instance, Joseph Stiglitz, "Give Prizes Not Patents," *New Scientist*, September 16, 2006, p. 21. He proclaims that "the alternative of awarding prizes would be more efficient and more equitable. It would provide strong incentives for research but without the inefficiencies associated with monopol-isation. This is not a new idea—in the UK for instance, the Royal Society of Arts has long advocated the use of prizes. But it is, perhaps, an idea whose time has come."

[7] *Gentleman's Magazine* 83 (1798): 333.

[8] Allan (1979).

The RSA engaged in many worthwhile activities, including offering educational lectures, conducting experiments and diffusing information, and
maintaining a repository of mechanic inventions and other items of interest to
technology and culture. Starting in 1761, the society held regular exhibitions and
also employed knowledgeable artisans to explain the models and displays for
the benefit of visitors. However, in keeping with its founding objectives, it was
primarily known for policies that were designed to encourage inventions. These
measures were based on the conviction that "Profit and Honour are two sharp
Spurs, which quicken Invention, and animate Application."[9] The twin incentives
of prestige and profit were therefore employed as ex ante inducements to attract
applications for the provision of new products and processes.

The administration of inducement prizes was one of the central mandates
of the RSA. As such, its extensive archival records offer researchers a valuable
opportunity to fully analyze the costs and benefits of administered innovation
awards. Members of the society volunteered, or were appointed to, standing
committees with oversight over concerns relating to the Polite Arts, Mechanics,
Agriculture, Chemistry, Manufactures, and Colonies and Trade.[10] The chairman
had to be selected from among the members whose professions were different
from the focus of the particular committee; for example, a professional chemist
could not chair the committee dealing with chemistry. This rule prevented
conflicts of interest, and the possibility of "capture," but also meant that the chair
was unlikely to have relevant specialized knowledge regarding the proceedings.

The society published lists of inventions or activities that the members deemed
deserving of rewards to encourage potential inventors across the kingdom to
turn their attention to meeting these advertised needs. In 1798, for example, over
240 premiums were offered for a wide array of potential inventions (broadly defined), ranging from methods for preserving cabbages to textile machines. The
promised awards consisted of cash payments or premiums, along with honorary
prizes that included gold and silver medals and palettes. Medals had a monetary
value that varied according to the price of its metal components and the size of
the medal. A gold medal was worth about £15 and a silver medal around £1 in the
1780s, whereas in 1840 a large gold medal was valued at £13, a small gold medal
a little over £6, and a silver medal £1. Applicants for an award could turn up in
person at the RSA headquarters in London to explain their invention and plead
their cause before the committees but would have to do so at their own expense,
reducing the net expected payout.

---

[9] *Gray's Inn Journal* (1753), p. 75.
[10] See the Rules and Order, in the *Transactions of the Society Instituted at London for the
Encouragement of Arts, Manufactures, and Commerce*, various years. However, this rule did not per-
tain to the ordinary membership of the relevant committee.

The policy objectives and administration of the society were the target of persistent criticism throughout the era of industrialization, including scathing assessments by its own members.[11] Samuel Sidney, a Birmingham lawyer who had served as an assistant commissioner at the Crystal Palace Exhibition, made a presentation at the RSA in 1862, in which he launched a scathing indictment of the efficacy of prizes for inducing innovation and manufacturing. He dismissively referred to such incentives as based on "a theory which is much in favour with a large and increasing class in modern society, composed of gentlemen of wealth and position, with a slight knowledge of divers practical pursuits, some enthusiasm, a great love of patronage, and nothing to do." Sidney had spent an entire decade examining the operation and effects of innovation prizes. The grand claims of success that enthusiasts advertised, he noted, were refuted by the evidence: "We turn over page after page, year after year, of awards, without finding an instance of remarkable inventions brought to light, or of obscure merit discovered and rewarded."

Sidney was not unique in his skepticism—the society was continually accused of a lack of good judgment, poor governance, and even corruption.[12] Critics attributed the outcome of prize deliberations to arbitrary factors such as personal influence, the persistence of one's recommenders, the self-interest of committees, and sympathy or simple friendship. Panels of judges were deemed to have applied idiosyncratic criteria to the selection among applications, and many of the awards may have been motivated by reasons other than the quality of the invention. It was inevitable that controversies would surround the administration of payouts of money and medals, and it does seem that for the most part members had good intentions and attempted to establish and revise rules for effective governance. For instance, reforms stipulated that members of the society could be awarded honorary medals, but they were not entitled to apply for or obtain monetary premiums. Those who had a stake in a particular issue were not allowed to participate in the vetting of related applications and were also prohibited from voting on matters that concerned their own relatives. Nevertheless, the perception of bias and unfair decisions, whether or not true, has implications for expected returns and for the type of groups that are likely to respond to such incentives.

Several prominent RSA members and administrators admitted to anxiety about whether their activities had been ultimately ineffective or redundant. Their concerns have implications that are broader than the assessment of this particular organization and are relevant to the understanding of administered systems in general. A central issue was whether members of committees had the

---

[11] "Of the petty premiums presented by the Societies for the Encouragement of Arts and Manufactures, supported by popular subscription, I shall say but little, as indeed but little is to be said. Instituted on public-spirited principles, but perverted by private cabals, the laudable purposes of their institution have been seldom attained." Kenrick (1774).

[12] Sidney (1862), Paskins (2014).

ability to identify or predict the path for important new technologies. Sir Henry Trueman Wood, a long-time secretary of the RSA, became disillusioned with the general and specific operation of prize incentives. He ultimately acknowledged that the attempt to guide the course of technological change had been "futile," because "a committee which could anticipate the direction in which industry or science would progress would have to be composed of men with prescience beyond their fellows."[13] Others concluded that the profits associated with economic and market expansion "made obsolete the whole idea of encouraging industrial progress by the award of prizes."[14]

Even those who regarded the institution from a more sanguine perspective nevertheless acknowledged that

> the Society of Arts can take no credit for the development of the iron industry in Britain, or that of the steam-engine, and little for the creation of the Lancashire textile industry. It may even be doubted whether the awards of prizes and medals would have had the least effect in strengthening enormous economic forces.[15]

Rather, it seemed that the truly valuable contributions were made by inventive individuals who "preferred to trust themselves to the market economy rather than to a paternalistic reward system."[16] The real experience of the RSA can shed more light on the nature and consequences of incentives for creativity and offers a valuable opportunity to systematically investigate the functions of an influential administered innovation system.

Patterns of Prize Awards

The fortunes of the RSA in this era were reflected through the prism of its stated objective of granting prizes to promote enterprise and encourage innovation. As mentioned before, the membership drew up lists of inventions that they considered to be valuable for social and economic progress of the nation. These lists were advertised and also later printed in the *Transactions* of the society, which was sold at the substantial price of 5 shillings in 1790, and over 10 shillings in 1815. The reports mentioned both the items that were currently open

---

[13] See Wood (1913: 241, 260). He added that "various prizes were offered, and certain small improvements were duly rewarded. None of them, however, were of any great value, and, as we fully recognize now, the efforts of the Society were quite futile, and its energy was entirely misdirected."

[14] Hudson and Luckhurst (1954: 177).

[15] Hall (1974: 644).

[16] Golinski (1999: 56). Another study concurs that "It was ambitious and flexible individuals, not bureaucratic institutions such as the Society of Arts, who helped to initiate the Industrial Revolution." Kent (2007: 214).

for applications, as well as those that had already been bestowed in the prior year. The RSA Housekeeper maintained a handwritten Register of the Premiums and Bounties that were offered and bestowed. Entrance to the RSA was not open to the general public, but paid-up members could sponsor interested parties who wished to visit the building in London to inspect some of the prize-winning models and machines. This restricted accessibility obviously limited the diffusion of ideas and information, especially for ordinary inventors without any connections.

Between 1754 and 1782, approximately 6,000 (5,932) premiums were proposed, and this number has often been cited as an indicator of the important work of the society during that period. However, when one carefully goes through the unpublished account books, it becomes clear that significantly fewer awards were actually paid out, amounting to just a third of the listed offers. As a sardonic contemporary noted:

> The annual list of premiums proposed form a most amusing contrast to the subjects claiming them, and the rewards actually bestowed. Judge the Society by the one, and we shall place it high in the number of the useful institutions of Europe; by the other, and it will sink to a level with the most insignificant.[17]

The RSA inducement prize system peaked quite early in its existence (Figure 5.2). The first half of the decade of the 1760s was the high point in terms of both amounts offered and paid out. In 1763, the various committees offered 375 cash awards, for a total value of more than £18,000, along with 64 gold and silver medals. The following year 147 awards were distributed, with £2,200 in cash payments. The value of proposed payouts quickly fell, and by 1770 the number of offers had fallen to 178, for a total value of less than £3,500. The gap between the amounts offered and the actual grants made widened significantly over time. Indeed, the society likely expected that a large number of its premiums would never be paid out, since the total revenues in its account typically would have been substantially insufficient to cover the full value of the premiums on its list. For instance, in the period between 1760 and 1764, the average annual receipts of the society amounted to £4,083, compared to a premium list with a value of £12,862 per annum.[18]

The majority of the proposed prizes were never claimed and failed to attract any attention from inventors or even importers of inventions. Robert Dossie,

---

[17] *London Journal of Arts and Sciences* (1825), p. 362. The author of the commentary attributes this pattern in part to "the trouble and expence of dancing attendance upon their long and protracted deliberations."

[18] These data were calculated from manuscript account ledgers in the RSA archives in London.

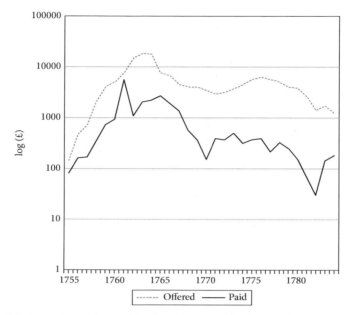

Figure 5.2 Annual Premiums Offered and Bestowed by the Royal Society of Arts, 1754–1784

Notes: The cash value of gold and silver medals offered was inferred from the average values for the eighteenth century.

Source: Summary Abstracts of the Rewards Bestowed by the Society, 1754–1782, London: Royal Society of Arts, 1806; *Annual Transactions of the Royal Society of Arts*, London, various years; *Manuscript Accounts Ledgers of the Royal Society of Arts.*

an enthusiastic supporter and booster of the society, acknowledged numerous instances in which the call for applicants failed to obtain a response.[19] It was invariably the case that the number and value of awards made was disproportionately small relative to the offers, and payouts were often entirely unrelated to the items listed. Many of the proposed projects were not economically feasible; for example, saltpeter was impossible to effectively produce in England because of prohibitively high costs of inputs and the inappropriate climate. The premium inventions could be idiosyncratic and even nonsensical, such as the 1777 gold medal offered for establishing a standard for the degree of sweetness in saccharine substances. Some items on the list had been discovered long before and were

[19] As with other members of the society, Robert Dossie (1768–1782) repeatedly documented the failure of the premiums to induce useful results but then proceeded to disregard these facts in favor of falsely optimistic conclusions about the overall effectiveness of their policies.

already in common use. For instance, in 1782, a gold medal was offered for a cheap and portable instrument that could be used to time the transit of celestial bodies, although such devices had long been available in the market.

In other cases, the amount of the monetary award was regarded as inadequate relative to the expected or actual market value of the innovation. A premium for ironmaking was unsuccessful because "none but the proprietors of considerable works could possibly perform what was required to be done; and they have infinitely greater inducements than the sum offered, to possess themselves of the means, if they were within their reach."[20] The society offered £10 for the production of a sufficient quantity of marbled paper in 1760 but increased the sum to £100 after potential applicants complained that the amount of the reward was negligible compared to the commercial value.[21] Moreover, possessors of an important trade secret would be unlikely to reveal their methods to competitors unless the present value of the award exceeded expected future revenues from their specialized knowledge—a price that was unlikely to be accurately determined by a committee.[22] Potential applicants who did not have influential connections to increase the likelihood of a positive outcome could be deterred by the bureaucratic procedures, time and expense, and anticipation of biased decisions.

The difference between "inducements" and "bestowals" varied significantly across broad categories of inventions. Table 5.1 shows the total value of sums offered and disbursed to prize winners by the major committees of the society between 1754 and 1782. During this key period of emerging British industrialization, the largest sums of prizes on offer were proposed for colonial projects, essentially as a means of indirectly benefiting Britain. The primary inducements for domestic enterprise were in agriculture, in terms of the gross amount as well as the percentage of cash awards and medals. Manufacturing and mechanics together merely accounted for a minor fraction (10.8%) of all proposed awards.

The second part of the table displays the amounts that were actually paid out as cash prizes and medals, consisting of gold and silver medals and palettes. Over this entire period, £26,704 was distributed as financial incentives, and £1,510 in medals, for a total of £28,214. The amount spent on awards accumulated to some £40,000 by 1801. Less than half of these expenditures on prizes was allocated to inventions and discoveries in agriculture, chemistry, manufacturing, and

---

[20]   Dossie (1768–1782: 220).

[21]   Several payments were made, including one in 1763 to Henry Houseman, who had already obtained a patent for this method. Attempts to produce marbled paper predated the premium, and patents had been granted as early as 1724. Nevertheless, the society proclaimed that its efforts had succeeded in encouraging the diffusion of marbling and the development of the paper industry.

[22]   A 1760 premium to catch rats attracted several applicants but no premium was awarded because the information that they provided was too inadequate, since "the sum offered is not a sufficient consideration for a man to lay open the secret of a business, by which he gets his livelihood." Dossie (1768–1782: 215).

Table 5.1 Royal Society of Arts: Premiums Offered and Bestowed by Sector,
1754–1782

a) Premiums Offered (£)					
Sector	Cash Prizes	Medals	Total	% Medals	% Total
Agriculture	32,739	12,122.0	44,861	27.0	29.8
Chemistry	15,125	1,045.0	16,170	6.5	10.8
Colonies	53,480	1,668.0	55,148	3.0	36.7
Manufacturing	10,045	585.0	10,630	5.5	7.1
Mechanics	5,191	333.0	5,524	6.0	3.7
Polite Arts	16,863	1,133	17,996	11.3	**12.0**
TOTAL	133,443	16,886	150,329	11.2	100.0
b) Premiums Paid Out (£)					
Sector	Cash Prizes	Medals	Total	% Medals	% Total
Agriculture	3,281	598	3,879	15.4	13.7
Chemistry	1,391	25	1,416	1.8	5.0
Colonies	2,786	102	2,888	3.5	10.2
Manufacturing	2,058	11	2,069	0.5	7.3
Mechanics	2,453	80	2,533	3.2	9.0
Polite Arts	14,735	694	15,429	8.2	**54.7**
TOTAL	26,704	1,510	28,214	5.4	100.0

Notes and Sources: The sectoral categories correspond to the titles of the committees that administered the awards. "Polite Arts" includes musical instruments, painting, sculptures, and related items.
The cash value of the gold and silver medals offered was inferred from the average values for the
eighteenth century. The column "% Medals" indicates the value of gold and silver medals as a fraction of prizes in the sector. *Summary Abstracts of the Rewards Bestowed by the Society, 1754–1782*
(London: Royal Society of Arts, 1806); *Annual Transactions of the Royal Society of Arts* (London, various years); *Manuscript Accounts Ledgers of the Royal Society of Arts*.

mechanics, areas that might be expected to have a direct impact on the course of
industrialization. Similarly, medals were more prevalent in agriculture, making
up 15.4% of the value of awards, relative to less than 1% in manufacturing.
Funding for manufacturing and mechanics amounted to just £4,602, or 16.3% of
the total awarded, whereas agriculture received 13.7%.

A useful comparison can be made between the proposed offers and the premiums
that were actually bestowed in the different sectors. Over half (52%) of proposed

payments in the polite arts were actually made, relative to 46% in mechanics and just 20% in manufacturing. By way of contrast, the fractions for agriculture, chemistry, and the colonies were significantly lower. It is not possible to determine whether this discrepancy was due to variation in the demand for premiums, the quality of proposals, or differential screening of applicants by the various committees. However, the information on aggregate offers does seem to suggest that the attention of the RSA was largely focused on the concerns of landowners and other elites, who formed a significant fraction of the society's membership. Many of the prizes in agriculture were given to scions of the nobility, and the awards in the pure arts also catered to the upper classes, even though they were deemed to have the meritorious benefit of educating the working class in the higher realms of culture.

To investigate these patterns at a more disaggregated level, I compiled a random sample of approximately 2,500 RSA awards that were given out over the course of the century between 1754 and 1850. Table 5.2 shows the mean and standard deviation for cash awards in the eighteenth and nineteenth centuries. Table 5.3 presents the proportion of prizes awarded by sector in each decade and illustrates how their relative importance changed over time. The patterns revealed in these data do not support the claim that the award of prizes by the society succeeded in generating technological innovation during the British Industrial Revolution. Inconsistencies are evident in the allocation of awards across and within sectors and also in terms of the timing of the prizes in relation to the timing of industrial and productivity growth. The overall results suggest that the difference between the prizes offered and those that were allocated occurred because of a selection effect. Inventors or creators of items that were valued in the marketplace had an incentive to try to profit through other channels than the grant of prizes, whereas those with "lemons," or innovations of low market value, tended to pursue RSA awards.

Initially, the prize-granting committees had the mercantilist objective of aiding British industry, and this was especially true of the awards to the colonies and in the polite arts. The intent of grants to the arts was to facilitate improvements in the design of manufactured goods such as pottery and textiles and to make the country competitive with the elegant and higher-quality luxury products that were imported at high cost from the Continent. The 1758 premium list included several invitations for submissions to improve industrial designs, including "the best drawings fit for cabinetmakers, coach makers, manufacturers of iron, brass, china, or earthen ware, or any other mechanic trade that requires taste."[23] Very few inventors responded to this appeal, perhaps because these

---

[23] In addition, the premiums for improving the arts were justified by the fact that good taste and drawing skills were "absolutely necessary to all persons concerned in building, furniture, dress, toys, or any other matters where elegance and ornament are required." See premium list of 1758.

Table 5.2 Value of Cash Premiums Bestowed, 1754–1840

	Eighteenth Century		Nineteenth Century	
	Mean	**S.D.**	**Mean**	**S.D.**
Industry				
Agriculture	23.7	35.3	27	28.8
Chemistry	36.1	27.9	16.3	13.1
Colonies	77.4	78.5	38.5	23
Manufactures	20.1	16.9	8.3	5.6
Mechanics	21.6	16.9	15.1	12.2
Polite Arts	11.5	17.2	27.5	14.1
Patentability				
Patentable	25.7	30.4	14.7	11.6
Not Patentable	15.3	24.2	17.7	18
Gender				
Men	17.7	26.1	16.7	14.8
Women	5.2	4	4.4	3.3
TOTAL	16.8	25.4	16	14.7

Notes: S.D. indicates standard deviation. The industrial categories were assigned by the names of the committees that adjudicated the applications and bestowed the awards. Patentability was determined by whether the item fell under the subject matter that could be eligible for a patent, and by searches in the patent records.

higher-end artisans already had a ready demand for their products, and the society did not yet have much of a reputation. In any event, most members of the RSA considered industrial design as a "lower branch" of the tree of knowledge, and they were more inclined toward the "purer" and more elevated arts such as paintings and sculpture. Their proselytizing bent was based on the conviction that "after the eyes of the public are familiarized with specimens of the best decorative art, they will prefer them to subjects which are vulgar and gaudy."[24] As a result, the policies rapidly shifted away from applied or industrial design, and the

---

[24] *Official Directory*, The International Exhibition of 1862, vol. 1, p. 10.

Table 5.3 Distribution of Awards by Industry, 1754–1840

	1750s	1760s	1770s	1780s	1790s	1800s	1810s	1820s	1830s	Total
Agriculture										
Row %	3.4	52.8	11.1	2.7	12.3	7.9	5.9	3.2	0.7	100%
Col %	6.7	22.5	17.8	22.0	40.3	26.7	11.5	3.6	1.6	16.5%
Chemistry										
Row %	12.5	30.6	11.1	0.0	4.2	2.8	13.9	19.4	5.6	100%
Col %	4.3	2.3	3.2	0.0	2.4	1.7	4.8	3.9	2.2	2.9%
Colonies										
Row %	9.2	52.3	12.3	0.0	4.6	7.7	4.6	9.2	0.0	100%
Col %	2.9	3.6	3.2	0.0	2.4	4.2	1.4	1.7	0.0	2.6%
Manufactures										
Row %	9.9	44.7	10.6	1.2	3.1	2.5	3.1	17.4	7.5	100%
Col %	7.7	7.5	6.7	4.0	4.0	3.3	2.4	7.7	6.6	6.5%
Mechanics										
Row %	3.2	16.3	9.2	3.2	9.7	6.6	15.8	24.6	11.5	100%
Col %	5.3	6.0	12.7	22.0	27.4	19.2	26.4	23.7	21.9	14.2%
Polite Arts										
Row %	10.7	39.5	9.8	1.9	2.1	3.9	7.9	15.4	8.8	100%
Col %	71.8	58.0	54.6	52.0	23.4	45.0	53.4	59.5	67.8	56.9%
Total (N)	209	956	253	50	124	120	208	363	183	2466
Row %	8.5	38.8	10.3	2.0	5.0	4.9	8.4	14.7	7.4	100.0%

Notes and Sources: The data consist of a random sample of awards bestowed between 1754 and 1840. *Annual Transactions of the Royal Society of Arts* (London, various years).

premiums were overwhelmingly awarded to painters, sculptors, and drawings "to encourage a love of the polite arts, and excite an emulation among persons of rank and condition," without any further rhetoric about benefiting industry.[25]

---

[25] The citation is from the premium list of 1758. This emphasis on fine art persisted until Prince Albert became president of the society in 1843 and reminded members of its original objectives. He advised that public welfare would be better served by promoting applied arts that enhanced the nation's manufacturing sector (Wood 1913).

A second deviation away from the original aims of the Society for the Encouragement of Arts, Manufactures, and Commerce is evident in the patterns of offers and awards for agriculture, a pursuit that also dominated the awards to the colonies. In the eighteenth century, the major subscribers to the RSA were gentlemen and landowners, so it is not surprising that during that period almost half the number of proposed premiums were in agriculture. A significant fraction of the actual awards was given out for planting trees and similar agricultural improvements of interest to the wealthy owners of landed estates. Successes included the many tests and experiments that the society sponsored for horticulture, and the RSA also enhanced the diffusion of many minor agricultural implements. A number of these "extension" policies in the agriculture sector likely had beneficial spillover effects that are hard to measure. At the same time, economic historians have remarked that in the second half of the eighteenth century, British agriculture was "remarkable for its stagnation."[26] The timing is also off for the nineteenth century, since agricultural output and productivity increased significantly through 1850, whereas RSA awards in agriculture dwindled markedly in number and total value over the same period.

The movement for the encouragement of British industry was essentially protectionist in nature, and import substitution was promoted in many forms. Contemporary institutions with the same aims also included the Anti-Gallican Society (that roundly denounced French imports and offered minor prizes for domestic substitutes), along with the Sublime Society of Beef Steaks (founded to counter the obviously pernicious effects of French cuisine). The RSA often referred to the customs list of imported goods to identify areas in which premiums should be offered. The mercantilist doctrines that informed the premium choices meant that a great deal of time and funds were devoted to attempts to replicate items and inputs that already existed and were being produced more efficiently in foreign countries. The highest average payouts in the entire period were given to "Premiums for the Advantage of the British Colonies," with the ultimate aim of securing cheap products for the advantage of Britain at the expense of the colonies.

In the seventeenth century, notable Americans like John Winthrop and William Penn had agreed with Enlightenment thinkers that it was vital to encourage "useful knowledge" but felt that the objective should be the advancement of their own territories. Benjamin Franklin, who had written an early paper on the subject, was appointed a corresponding member of the RSA, and he even donated 20 guineas toward the RSA premium fund. The RSA wrote that "Their desire is to make Great Britain and her Colonies mutually dear and

---

[26] Allen (1999).

serviceable to each other: They know their Interests are the same." After he traveled to England, Franklin actively participated in meetings of the society, and in 1761 he co-chaired the Committee for the Colonies and Trade. However, Franklin ultimately concluded that the goal of the RSA premiums and awards was to benefit Britain rather than its overseas constituents, and their efforts had a net negative impact on the American economy. He noted dryly in 1770, "What you call Bounties given by Parliament and the Society are nothing more than inducements offered us . . . to quit a Business profitable to ourselves and engage in one that shall be profitable to you; this is the true Spirit of all your Bounties."[27]

The RSA did occasionally provide beneficial aid for the colonies, such as funding a trip to send the artisan James Stewart to Maryland, to help with the development of the American potash industry. Colonial premiums were available for the production of such goods as the making of silk, Turkey red dyes, and marbled paper that was of similar quality to the items imported from Europe. However, it was certainly the case that the RSA was more interested in obtaining raw materials and natural resources from their dependencies and decidedly less enthused about encouraging self-sustaining manufacturing in the colonies, which might compete with British goods. The discrepancy between prizes offered and those that were bestowed in part reflected the differences in the objectives of the RSA and those of the colonists. Between 1760 and 1766, for instance, the society continually offered premiums of several hundred pounds for the cultivation of hemp in the American colonies, which failed to elicit any applications, despite changes that made the terms increasingly more favorable.

After the "present and unhappy disputes" resulted in independence for the American colonies, the society shifted its attention to less rebellious regions, such as Australia and the West Indies, although their taste for colonial improvements had suffered a permanent setback. John M'Arthur received two gold medals in 1822 for the largest quantity and the best quality of wool imported into England from New South Wales.[28] In the same session, John Raine was given a large silver Ceres Medal for his business transactions in selling merino rams and importing wool from Tasmania, and a second medal for his imports of several tons of elephant seal oil. RSA medals were neither necessary nor sufficient inducements for the completion of such transactions. Wool was fetching high prices in the market,

---

[27] Goodwin (2016). An acquaintance of Franklin's, Thomas Godfrey, had submitted his invention of a quadrant to the Royal Society (not the RSA), which made him a present of furniture, but Hadley, the vice president of the Royal Society, allegedly pirated the invention, which became known as Hadley's quadrant.

[28] M'Arthur, a sheep farmer in New South Wales, was adept at acquiring advantages from various sources. After he testified before the Privy Council, he received land grants in the colony to encourage his sheep farming, and was also allowed to buy stock from the King's estates.

and even the RSA *Transactions* explicitly recognized that such prices served as the most effective incentive for exports from New South Wales to England.

Other sectors offer a number of important general insights into the operations of the innovation prize system. Committees encountered difficulties in verifying quality, there were recurring problems about finding the right inducement price, and there was utter failure in the commercialization of prize-winning methods that often were not scalable. Awards for chemistry, for instance, absorbed a low but fairly steady proportion of the funding over time. Europeans expended a great deal of effort to try to replicate Turkey red dyes, which the French, Swiss, and Indians had already succeeded in reverse-engineering. The RSA offered a premium in 1760 and gave out an award for a suggested method of making the dye. However, the process turned out to be ineffective, so the premium was renewed. The second award in 1764 still did not achieve the desired effect. The cost of inputs and the high price of the dye, as well as the poor quality, limited the usage and commercial success of the prize-winning methods. The English attempts continually failed, until artisans from France decided to share their own trade secret about how to make the dyes. In 1781, Louis and Abraham Borell, dyers from Rouen, approached interested parties in England about their willingness to reveal the secret. They received £2,500 from Parliament in 1786 for revealing the information, a sum that was significantly greater than the £100 the RSA offered as an inducement.[29]

Unusually for its era, the RSA adopted progressive policies toward women and was the first such institution in Britain to be open to female members. The original 1753 prospectus for the society noted that "Ladies as well as Gentlemen are invited into this Subscription, as there is no Reason to imagine they will be behind Hand in a generous and sincere Regard for the Good of their Country." Their confidence in the generosity of women was not in vain, and eminent patrons of the society included the wealthy "bluestocking" Elizabeth Montagu, the Countess of Denbigh, and the Duchess of Northumberland. At the other end of the social spectrum, Ann Birch Cockings, the female Housekeeper from 1802 to 1844, kept the books, attended committee meetings, and wielded a great deal of influence that went well beyond her mundane job description.

The "ingenious of both sexes" were invited to apply for premiums, and some 10% of the awards were given out for contributions by women.[30] A number of women received accolades because of excellence in producing handmade goods, such as spinning, knitting threads for lace, and the making of starch. In 1824, numerous awards were given to Mary Marshall of Ireland, the Dyer sisters of Hampshire, and other women from various parts of the United Kingdom who

---

[29] Dossie (1768–1782).
[30] *Transactions of the Society of Arts*, vol. 16 (1798).

had made bonnets using local materials. More atypical feminine inventions included a waterwheel and a lever that could be used for raising earth in building. The Committee for Chemistry in 1773 bestowed £10 10s upon Mrs. Johanna Khruelle for her method of cleaning ivory carvings. However, the majority of the female recipients obtained awards from the Committee for Polite Arts, including the fine arts, sculpture, and designs. Mary Pingo, whose family had a long and close connection with the society, won four prizes between 1758 and 1762, including a cash award of £5 while she was still a teenager. The Pingo family were engravers and medalists who supplied the society, and collectively they received the greatest number of awards in the history of the institution.

The society itself was initially self-congratulatory and complacent about its contributions, but specialists have dismissed its "highly coloured view of its own usefulness" and rejected the claim that the awards had an effect on such key technologies as textile machinery.[31] The average value of prizes in the significant industries was relatively low in the earlier period and fell further in the nineteenth century. Total factor productivity growth during British industrialization was most evident in capital-intensive industries such as textiles and iron manufactures and in improvements to motive power and transportation.[32] Over time the numbers of RSA awards in manufactures and mechanics increased, but even so they amounted to just 20% of all prizes.

Closer examination of the individual awards also reduces one's confidence in the economic and technological significance of the inventions associated with the prizes. For instance, premiums were offered in 1795 for spinning wheels, decades after this process had been mechanized. Less than 3% of the total awards were in transportation, and these were offered for esoteric or trivial improvements in ways of examining the bottom of ships, anchors, revolving lights for boats, braces for coaches, and adjustments to carriage wheels. An assessment of actual inventions, the biographical details regarding the prize winners, and the absence of the majority of recognized inventors and their canonical inventions on the list of prize winners all support the argument that the contributions of the RSA prize system to economic advances were relatively minor.

Profit or Prestige?

Economists have long considered how different rules and institutions provide incentives for human behavior. Many theorists contend that prizes offer more

---

[31] Wadsworth and Mann (1965: 476). Wood (1913: 241) acknowledges that few of the canonical inventors or inventions of the Industrial Revolution appear on the society's list of prize winners.
[32] Crafts and Harley (1992).

effective and less distorted incentives that are likely to provide greater benefits for society than allegedly inferior alternatives such as exclusive property rights to ideas. The focus on pecuniary incentives, according to other scholars, is myopic; economic approaches will necessarily be limited to a very narrow range of behavior unless efforts are made to understand nonmonetary incentives based on prestige and social norms. This schism between "profit and prestige" is reflected in empirical studies of prizes, which tend to use data based on honorary awards such as medals at exhibitions, whereas current policy discussions typically center around monetary awards. The experience of the RSA, which included both monetary payments and medals, offers a uniquely valuable opportunity to assess both profit and prestige. This section therefore examines the factors that were associated with honorary awards as well as cash payouts for prizes.

The rationale for the founding of the society was the belief that creative individuals of all sorts responded positively to incentives, but RSA subscribers were somewhat divided on whether the most effective motivation was provided by monetary awards or through appeals to honor and prestige. Adam Smith, briefly a member of the society, felt that pecuniary rewards were ineffective because they could not be calibrated to reflect the value of the invention, but he speculated that premiums given to artists might serve to increase the quality of their output at a modest cost. Many RSA members were convinced that true artists and members of the elite would disdain financial inducements. Henry Baker, for instance, contrasted the effectiveness of "the Desire of Gain" and "the Desire of Esteem" and felt that cash prizes would serve to encourage ordinary artisans, whereas the approbation of one's peers was the most effective incentive among ingenious minds, scholars, and gentlemen of high estate.

The descriptive statistics of premiums proposed and disbursed showed that the nature of the awards of the RSA varied significantly in terms of number and value. The account books of the society allow us to estimate the monetary value of the honorary medals, which varied in size and material composition (bronze, silver, and gold). Figures 5.3 and 5.4 illustrate the different types of prizes, including cash payments, gold medals, and other nonmonetary awards, over the period when the RSA focused its attention on such policies. The number of cheaper gold and silver medals increased to 117 in 1770, and to over 250 a decade later. At the same time, the cash value of both honorary medals and financial premiums exhibited a longitudinal decline, but with significant variation around the falling trend. The "prestige and profit" incentives were also unevenly distributed across different industries in the same time period. The awards for the arts shifted markedly from cash payments in the eighteenth century toward honorary medals of lesser value (silver) in the nineteenth century (Table 5.4). Gold medals were given disproportionately to individuals in the area of agriculture and the colonies. These differences provide a useful means of distinguishing the factors that were associated with the allocation of the awards.

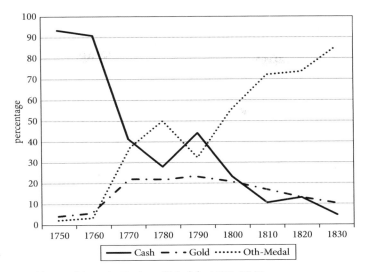

Figure 5.3 Types of Awards: Cash and Medals, 1754–1840

Notes: The graph is based on a random sample of 2,466 awards bestowed between 1754 and 1840. The percentages indicate the number of awards in each category, as a fraction of the total number in that decade.

Source: Annual Transactions of the Royal Society of Arts, London, various years.

Another dimension of the prize data is revealed through an examination of the extent to which the subject matter of the awards was patentable. Patentability was determined by conformity to the patent laws and by searches in the patent records to establish whether a patent had ever been granted for that type of invention. It is noticeable that the proportion of patentable prizes increased somewhat over time, but just 14.8% of the awards over the entire period were patentable (Table 5.5). As might be expected, very few of the contributions to the arts were patentable. Entries in mechanics exhibited a high degree of patentability, but these inventions accounted for a small fraction of all the prizes. Very low patentability characterized innovations in agriculture (5.4%) and chemistry (12.5%). Patentability was atypical even in manufacturing (37.3%), and the fraction of patentable manufacturing awards fell over time from 40.2% to 30.6%. These patterns suggest that inventors with patentable discoveries largely bypassed the prize system—an issue that will be explored in the following section.

Which variables influenced the likelihood that a specific type of inducement was awarded?[33] The decision about how to allocate prizes seems to have been

[33] Statistical analysis (multivariate logistic regressions) in Khan (2017b) allows us to better understand the determinants of cash payouts relative to medals, as well as what led to the award of gold and silver medals.

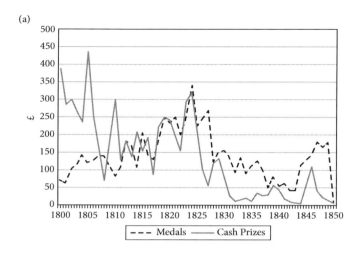

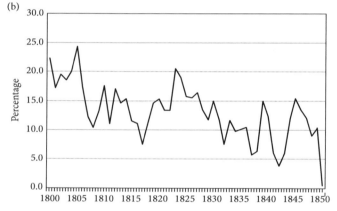

Figure 5.4 Royal Society of Arts: Financial and Honorary Incentives, 1800–1850

Notes and Sources: RSA Accounts Ledgers (Manuscript). Figure (a) shows the nominal monetary value of all awards (medals and cash) made in each fiscal year. Figure (b) indicates the value of awards made, as a percentage of total receipts of the Royal Society of Arts in that fiscal year.

quite idiosyncratic and, from the perspective of the invention itself, prize systems are essentially lotteries. In all estimations of the factors that determine prize awards, whether in the RSA or in other prize-granting institutions in France and the United States, any ability to explain variation in gold and silver medals is quite low. When one compares the RSA prizes across the various sectors, gold medals tended to be given out in agriculture and mechanics, but such honorary awards were made more frequently to the polite arts. The probability of financial payments for textile and chemistry inventions was significantly higher than

Table 5.4 Types of Awards by Industry, 1754–1840

		Eighteenth Century		Nineteenth Century		Total		
		Cash	Gold	Cash	Gold	Cash	Gold	Other Medal
Agriculture	row %	62.7	25.7	11.1	40.3	53.6	28.6	18.2
	% all	13.2	5.4	0.9	3.3	8.8	4.7	3
Chemistry	row %	85.7	7.1	26.7	30	61.1	16.7	22.2
	% all	2.3	0.2	0.9	1	1.8	0.5	0.7
Colonies	row %	70.6	27.5	35.7	21.4	63.1	26.2	10.8
	% all	2.3	0.9	0.6	0.3	1.7	0.7	0.3
Manufactures	row %	93.8	1.8	49	4.1	80.1	2.5	17.4
	% all	6.6	0.1	2.8	0.2	5.2	0.2	1.1
Mechanics	row %	85.5	4.1	27	18.1	51.3	12.3	36.4
	% all	7.8	0.4	6.3	4.2	7.3	1.7	5.2
Polite Arts	row %	81.1	4.2	1.4	9.5	52.4	6.1	41.5
	% all	45.7	2.4	0.8	5.5	29.8	3.5	23.6
TOTAL	%	77.8	10	12.2	14.7	54.5	11.6	33.8
	N	N = 1,592		N = 874		N = 2,466		

Notes: The data consist of a random sample of the number of awards bestowed between 1754 and 1840. The types of awards include cash, gold medals, and other medals (which is the excluded category for the row percentages in the first two periods). The industrial categories were assigned by the names of the committees that adjudicated the applications and bestowed the awards.

for other sectors. The RSA outcomes differed significantly by gender, holding other factors such as industry constant. Women were significantly less likely to receive cash awards. Moreover, few women obtained the mostly highly valued gold medals; instead, they tended to earn minor recognition in the form of silver or bronze medals or testimonials.

The empirical results revealed two further aspects of patents and prizes. The first was the independent impact of patentability on the award of prizes, holding other factors constant. Multivariate quantitative analysis confirmed that the RSA was implementing its policy based on the principle that ordinary mechanics were likely to care about monetary rewards to a greater extent than elite artists. Patentable inventions, or those that were characterized by the same subject matter that was eligible for a patent award, had a higher probability of getting a financial prize rather than an honorary award. Unpatentable inventions were

Table 5.5   Patentability of Prizes Awarded by Industry, 1754–1840

		Pct Patentable		
		Eighteenth Century	Nineteenth Century	Total
Agriculture	row %	4.5	9.7	5.4
	% all	0.9	0.8	0.9
Chemistry	row %	14.3	10	12.5
	% all	0.4	0.3	0.4
Colonies	row %	21.6	0	16.9
	% all	0.7	0	0.4
Manufactures	row %	40.2	30.6	37.3
	% all	2.8	1.7	2.4
Mechanics	row %	78.6	72.6	75.1
	% all	7.2	16.9	10.6
Polite Arts	row %	0.1	0.2	0.1
	% all	0.1	0.1	0.1
TOTAL	%	12.1	19.9	14.8
	N	1,592	874	2,466

Notes: The industrial categories were assigned by the names of the committees that adjudicated the applications and bestowed the awards. Patentability was determined by whether the item fell under the subject matter that could be eligible for a patent and by searches of patent records during the entire period. The row percentage indicates the proportion of all awards in that sector that was patentable. The "% all" figure indicates the percentage of all awards in that period that was patentable.

more likely to get the highest honorary prizes, but there was no difference in the patentability of the inventions that were given less prestigious medals. Similarly, the probability of acquiring gold and silver medals was unrelated to higher-valued inventions in technological areas that garnered large numbers of patents through to the end of the nineteenth century. These findings are consistent with the operation of a process of adverse selection, in which high-valued ideas were submitted for patents and primarily low-valued patentable items were entered in the prize competitions.

Another way of considering the RSA policies is to examine variation in the monetary value of cash awards as well as prizes and to determine the factors that influenced how much an inventor received. Frequent prize winners tended to receive higher-valued prizes, perhaps because of a reputation effect or because they were encouraged by positive outcomes to either create or submit more important discoveries. Patentability was significantly associated with higher cash payments, suggesting that the awards were greater for the inventions with higher technical value. Despite this positive variation of awards with patentability, inventors with greater numbers of patents before application for the prize, and with large stocks of lifetime career patents overall, received significantly lower cash payments. In short, patentees participated in the RSA prize competitions to obtain payouts for their inventions that were not eligible for patent protection and for inventions that were not as valuable in the marketplace.

Of Patents and Prizes

Studies of honorary awards such as silver medals at agricultural fairs have contended that these awards provided effective incentives for inventive activity. However, exhibitions did not examine entries for novelty, and they did not verify whether the exhibitor had invented the device, so it is impossible to accurately determine such issues. Even if the applicant were the first and true inventor, it was still possible to obtain prizes, patents, and other forms of compensation for the same invention, implying that the type of incentive was not a choice variable. When the inventor is able to obtain multiple forms of compensation simultaneously, it becomes impossible to identify the effects of any particular incentive, and also raises the question of whether inventors are being overcompensated for their discovery. This is especially likely because awards were not independent, and prior winners of a prize were more likely to get subsequent payments because of a reputation effect. Inventors today who wish to obtain patents are required to avoid prior use of their discovery and would need to choose between intellectual property rights and a prize.

All of these considerations suggest that it would be analytically useful to identify a situation where specific types of rewards were available as substitutes rather than complements. The RSA Rules and Orders stipulated that patented items were not eligible for prizes, prize winners were not permitted to obtain patents for their inventions, and patented inventions were not even included in the displays in the RSA repositories. Notably:

> Every person who shall receive any premium or bounty from the Society, shall relinquish all pretensions to a patent for any matter for which he has obtained such premium or bounty. No model or machine, for which a patent has been

obtained, or is proposed to be obtained, shall be admitted into the repository of the Society.[34]

Members who had obtained patents for inventions were barred from participating in discussions on the subject at meetings and from taking part in decisions by committees about prizes that were related to their field of discovery. The RSA therefore provides a unique opportunity to examine innovation incentives that were actually substitutes.

In January 1780, John Mitchell sent an application to the society, but his dossier was not considered because he disclosed his intention of applying for a patent. Mitchell instead chose to obtain patent no. 1250, 3/30/1780, for an invention to treat "spent lees from which soap has been made, rendering it again fit for use." John Morris, a carpenter from Greenwich, submitted an invention for improvements in window shutters, for which the committee voted to award him 20 guineas. However, when he was informed about the terms on which the grant was made, he preferred to take out a patent and forfeit the prize.[35] As one contemporary observer pointed out:

Of the importance of these discoveries the Society is by no means ignorant; but as, in connection with the majority of the industries which grew out of these discoveries, patents were obtained, the Society refused to take cognizance of them, having effectually closed its doors against all patented inventions; the necessary result, as coal, iron, and the steam engine extended their influence, was that the Society lost power and position till at length it practically died out.[36]

Adam Scott of Guildford, Surrey, submitted an application for a prize that was announced for an improvement in ploughs. The committee made several experiments, and Scott was given a bounty of 30 guineas in exchange for a model and information about the invention. The society later discovered that Scott was selling his award-winning plough under a patent filed in another person's name, a practice that was possible under the British patent rules. The award had stipulated that the plough should be sold for a competitive price of 2½ guineas, but the market price the inventor set for the patented plough was four times that amount. The society issued a public warning in 1798:

The Public are requested to guard against imposition, from persons advertising or pretending to have patents, for articles rewarded by the Society. It is a

---

[34] *Transactions of the Society* (1812).
[35] *Transactions of the Society* (1783), p. 239.
[36] The quote is from an address of the financial officer of the society, Samuel Thomas Davenport, in 1868.

stipulated condition, that all persons who receive premiums, or bounties, from the Society, shall relinquish all pretensions to a patent for articles so rewarded, and shall allow them to be made by any person whatever.[37]

Scott was blacklisted from receiving any future awards, and interested parties were invited to freely inspect the specification of the invention and make their own copies at the RSA offices. The matter was widely reported in the press, and the inventor was denounced for his immoral behavior.

Despite the institutional hostility to patents, a number of the members of the RSA were themselves patentees, and they illustrate the decision-making process behind the choice of whether to obtain returns via patent protection or through the prize award system. Bryan Donkin (1768–1855), a vice president of the society and chairman of the Committee on Mechanics, received two gold medals for minor machines (a tachometer and counting machine) that he submitted to the society for awards. However, his major discoveries in printing and textiles were patented, and he not only obtained numerous patents for his own inventions but also purchased the rights to other inventors' patents. Jacob Perkins, a famous American patentee, accumulated a large portfolio of valuable patents from many countries. After moving to England to set up a printing enterprise that used his own patented method of engraving that was less susceptible to counterfeiting, he became a member of the RSA, probably as a way of acquiring influential connections. Perkins received three medals from the society in 1820 for submitting inventions for which he had already obtained patents and profits in the United States.

As a result of such policies, it was widely recognized that the annals of the RSA prizes were largely devoted to undistinguished contributions, and the truly significant innovations were to be found in the roster of patentees rather than in the society's records.[38] The inventor Samuel Clegg patented a highly profitable gas meter in 1815, and the RSA gold medal was instead given for an incremental improvement on Clegg's patent. The successes of the RSA were typically in subject areas that were unpatentable, such as the 1802 medal and cash award to Henry Greathead, who also received numerous other awards from Parliament and from other institutions.[39] The *Journal of the Royal Society of Arts* notes prizes that never received worthy applications over the course of decades and other prizes

---

[37] *Transactions* (1798), p. xiv.

[38] Wood (1912) censures some of the decisions that were motivated by "lamentable ignorance" but looks on the bright side, musing that "while a great many undeserving inventions were rewarded, there are not a great many which were rejected and which afterwards proved themselves of any value."

[39] Greathead received 50 guineas and a gold medal from the Royal Humane Society, 100 guineas from Trinity House of London, and another 100 guineas from Lloyds of London, and Parliament gave him an award of £1,200. He was also the subject of an ode composed by a naval surgeon.

that had been listed for problems that had already been patented. The empirical results support the claim that such policies toward patents led to an adverse selection effect, because the owners of important inventions obtained patents and bypassed the RSA, whereas the owners of minor discoveries had an incentive to try to get a prize award that was likely to be in excess of the market value of their invention.

Another way to consider the consequences of such policies is in terms of their impact on the future stock of inventions. These data can be used to estimate whether prize awards had a significant influence on the cumulative stock of patented inventions that had been filed in the specific technology field of the prize award. Thus, a positive relationship would be expected if the prize were given for an influential area of technological discovery, after holding other potentially causal factors constant. Instead, one finds that both gold and silver medals were negatively and significantly related to the cumulative stock of future innovations. Similarly, frequent winners of awards were less likely to contribute to these technologically fruitful areas, whereas a positive relationship existed in the case of prize winners who had acquired patent-specific human capital in the form of prior patents. Thus, both the qualitative and quantitative evidence support the interpretation that inventors chose market returns over administered awards.

Many observers and key personnel in the RSA ultimately recognized that "the exclusion of patented inventions had been extremely detrimental to the interests of the Society."[40] The more pragmatic groups advocated the abandonment of the premium-granting system, but influential elite members of the society were initially able to block reforms in that direction. However, in the early decades of the nineteenth century, the society faced bankruptcy and irrelevance and was forced to change or become extinct. The result was a dramatic turnaround in its attitude toward patents for invention. By the time of the Crystal Palace Exhibition in 1851, the RSA had fully recognized the value of the patent system and became active in lobbying for improvements in the problematic British patent laws along the lines of the U.S. model. Contemporaries, both insiders and outsiders, noted that the drastic shift in its attitude toward patents was primarily responsible for a rapid improvement in the fortunes and influence of the society. They concluded that "the barriers to progress were thrown down; the restrictions which had kept patented inventions and their inventors from its doors were removed," and that by so doing, the Society "set free invention."

---

[40] Wood (1913: 347).

6

Administered Invention in France

Mais pourquoi charger le gouvernement d'un soin que le négociant
peut bien prendre lui-même. . . .

—Isaac de Bacalan (1768)[1]

In Voltaire's *Candide*, the hero arrives in Bordeaux on his way to the grand city
of Paris. He decides to entrust his brilliant red sheep to the care of the regional
Academy of Sciences, which promptly introduces a prize competition to prove
why the wool of the animal was so unusually colored. The award is given to a
scientist from the North who "demonstrated by A plus B, minus C, divided by
Z, that the sheep must necessarily be red." The satirical jibe was likely incited
by the author's experience in a prize competition in 1714, where the judges
rejected his poem in favor of an inferior work by the well-connected M. l'abbé
du Jarry. The practice where the state and quasi-governmental institutions ran
prize competitions was pervasive in all realms of endeavor in France, and these
measures persisted throughout the nineteenth century. Indeed, France presents
a classic model of a large-scale administered system, whose mercantilist and na-
tionalist policies were directed toward attempts to promote manufacturing, enterprise, and innovation.

Institutional economists characterize the ideal state as an essentially neutral
entity that engages in a mutually advantageous exchange with its citizens, in
which the government sells protection and justice in return for the payment of
taxes.[2] From this classic liberalist perspective, the appropriate role of the state is
active (to secure and enforce property rights, to facilitate private initiative) and
passive (to avoid active intervention in the allocation of resources, including involvement in picking and compensating winners). Both active and passive roles
are designed to facilitate market efficiency. Careful empirical studies of present-
day "bureaucrats in business" have cautioned about the negative outcomes when

---

[1] "Why make the state responsible for tasks that businessmen can very well undertake themselves?" Bacalan, who belonged to a wealthy and influential family from Bordeaux, was appointed as
professor of law at the university and died in 1769 at the age of thirty-three. A brilliant thinker, he can
be regarded as one of the first French liberalist economists, who favored competitive markets and free
trade and rejected the nationalism and mercantilism of his contemporaries.

[2] North and Thomas (1973).

Inventing Ideas. B. Zorina Khan, Oxford University Press (2020). © Oxford University Press.
DOI: 10.1093/oso/9780190936075.001.0001

states overreach in the attempt to generate entrepreneurship and development.[3] Many have proposed that if market functions are replaced by administrators and government officials, this is likely to create an inverse relationship between state involvement and the potential for long-run economic growth.[4] Other studies have shown the productivity gains owing to state withdrawal from key areas of the economy and found that a reduction in the dominance of bureaucratic elites can create improvements in the extent of entrepreneurship and innovation in the knowledge economy.[5] Nevertheless (as Chapter 13 will discuss in further detail), in recent years there has been a resurgence of scholarship with a far more glowing view of government intervention, promoting "national innovation systems" and an "entrepreneurial state." These claims tend to be supported with lists of alleged successes and little or no attention to failures or foregone alternatives. The resulting selection bias implies the need for more extensive consideration of large-scale administered innovation systems.

France in the early industrial period offers a classic example of a national administered system for science and innovation. The French approach involved a routinization of earlier privileges, administered through a plethora of agencies and institutions that affected and regulated key areas of enterprise and technology. Despite the continual changes in overall political arrangements over time, one detects a continuity in the orientation of innovation institutions that persisted even after the revolution. Elites were at the forefront of the administration of eighteenth-century privileges and also in the decisions of the quasi-governmental institutions in the modern era. This elite orientation was evident in the mercantilist visions of such influential figures as Jean Baptiste Colbert in the seventeenth century and the interventionist strategies of Jean-Antoine Chaptal in the early nineteenth century. In a world where only a very narrow segment of the population had access to specialized formal education, the realm of privileges was replicated in discriminatory allocations made by technocrats.

Some revisionists contend that these discriminatory grants by administrators provided positive results. They are convinced of the "dynamism" of the French mercantilist state and point to the use of privileges as an innovative mechanism to promote economic development. "Privileges of liberty," according to this perspective, allowed favored interests to benefit from the asymmetrical removal of regulations and taxes, and thus offered the "most effective means of encouraging more capitalistic entrepreneurial practice."[6] Closer examination of the evidence

---

[3] Shirley (1995); Lerner (2009).

[4] An early paper on the "entrepreneurial state" concluded "there is no reason to believe that the state's activities are an effective means of achieving national control over industrialization." Freeman and Duvall (1984: 391).

[5] Trumbull (2004).

[6] Horn (2015: 19).

suggests otherwise. In nineteenth-century France, elitist privilege was not eradicated; it merely adopted a different dress. Special interests were clothed in a false objectivity, which appealed to science and specialization, but functioned in a manner that was analogous to privileges that were derived from hereditary rights. Such political-economic strategies were likely to lead to greater uncertainty, incorrect relative prices, and lower incentives for investments in inventive activity. A society based on special privileges for the few provided disproportionate benefits for elites and those with personal connections, disadvantaged creativity that was radically new or ideas that threatened existing interests, and all too often promoted rent-seeking rather than productivity and innovation.

Privileged Pursuits

The French historical experience is intriguing and informative because it offers insight into the entire portfolio of incentives and institutions that could be directed to promote industrial change and innovation. Technology policies were based on an extensive array of publicly administered rewards and incentives that were designed to increase the nation's standing relative to England and other industrial competitors.[7] Inventors and importers or introducers of inventions could profit from appointment to the nobility, lifetime pensions, assistance to spouses and offspring, interest-free loans, lump-sum grants, bounties or subsidies, tax exemptions, gifts of land and other assets, royal employment, and a host of other pecuniary and nonmonetary benefits. In the eighteenth century, large numbers of exclusive privileges were allocated to petitioners, especially those who were well connected and could find favor with influential members of the court.[8] The government even paid salaries to scientists such as Joseph Louis Gay-Lussac. Some of these initiatives were linked to specific outcomes and could be annulled if the beneficiary did not comply with his promises. Moreover, a number of important technologies were introduced that benefited French industry. To balance the success stories, many sponsored enterprises failed despite substantial public funding, and projectors received payouts for blue-sky propositions that were manifestly of questionable value.

---

[7] See, for instance, Hilaire-Pérez (2000).

[8] "The government was eager to develop the nation's economic life, and to this end made heavy subsidies. . . . Unfortunately the government had no uniform policy for all inventors. Some it aided financially; others it did not. More flagrantly inconsistent was its policy of granting monopolistic rights in many lines to court favorites, so that the greater number enjoying exclusive privileges were not inventors." McCloy (2015: 171). See also Archives Nationales, F/12/2424: "Encouragement donné aux artistes et aux inventeurs de 1786 à 1793."

Monopoly privileges were available for manufacturing and innovation, as well as for the introduction of foreign discoveries that were new to France. An early example of one such privilege was made in 1551 to Abel Foullon, director of the Mint under Henry II and attendant to the king. Foullon was allowed a ten-year monopoly on his holomètre, a geometrical instrument. In the same year, the Italian artisan Theseo Mutio obtained a ten-year privilege for the exclusive right to produce Venetian-style glass work, and at its expiration he was also elevated to the French nobility. Under royal patronage, Mutio and his partner Louis Delbertin established a glassmaking enterprise in Saint-Germain-en-Laye, which created luxury pieces for the Crown and the nobility, but this enterprise ultimately failed.[9] Other lavish privileges were offered to entice glassworkers from Venice, where harsh penalties were imposed on artisans (and their families) who revealed the secrets of the Murano trade.[10]

Privileges were based on arbitrary decisions about who would benefit from state-sanctioned monopolies. These grants raised questions about whether just compensation would be received by the inventor and how other competitors and the public would be affected. Uncertainty about such measures was high, most especially for innovators without any political or social influence. Numerous examples, such as the experience of Nicolas l'Empereur, illustrate the potential costs to the knowledge economy when critical decisions were made by individuals and panels who, instead of engaging in objective impersonal assessments, chose to pursue their own agendas or personal biases. Despite his name, Nicolas l'Empereur was an undistinguished employee of the French East India Company, who devoted much of his life and personal income to meticulous research on the botanical species in the Indian state of Orissa, which he documented in fourteen volumes that included many useful pharmaceutical remedies. He submitted this extraordinary work to the Academy of Sciences where, despite its undisputed value, the resident expert in the field refused to recognize this work because of his personal disdain for the lack of formal qualifications of the author.[11]

Privileges were supplemented with other policy instruments, such as subsidies and benefits to royally sponsored manufacturing enterprises in textiles, tapestries, porcelain, and other luxury items. Daniel Charles Trudaine offered financing for John Holker, the Jacobite émigré, to establish factories for spinning, weaving, and cloth finishing, and Holker was also elevated to the nobility.

---

[9] Vanriest (2015).

[10] According to the Venetian laws, absconding workers and artists risked the imprisonment of their families and assassination. Apparently, the death threats were not entirely idle, and many defecting workers allegedly died under suspicious circumstances. After a significant number of failures and missteps, in 1688 a thirty-year French privilege was granted for a method of making large panes of glass by casting. This secretive process may have helped the Saint Gobain establishment maintain its century-long dominance over this trade.

[11] Raj (2007).

Jean-Claude Flachat obtained generous funding, exemptions, and privileges, including a government-financed trip to the Levant to collect information on dyeing methods, and assistance to import Ottoman artisans who could aid in textile production at his newly established factory near Lyon. Overlapping grants, including exemptions from military service, were made to innovators who claimed to have solved the secrets of the sought-after Turkey red dye. However, it is important to note that many privileges did not function as incentives for inventive activity, and some (such as those that might have unpopular employment effects) were even designed to inhibit certain technological innovations. Markets in privileges were limited because, if the owner wished to transfer or sell these rights, it was necessary to first secure official permission or the transaction would be invalidated.

This elaborate network of privileges was based on decisions by panels of administrators, who were marshaled in Paris and around the country to assess thousands of petitions from hopeful applicants, in an ever-changing institutional context. For instance, in 1791, the state-appointed members of the Bureau of Consultation of Arts and the Trades included thirty appointees, and only six years later this bureau was dissolved and replaced by the National Institute of the Sciences and Arts. National institutions were replicated by, and overlapped with, regional and local analogs, and often it was necessary for a petitioner to negotiate with several different committees and organizations in different locations to achieve a single objective.

Members of these boards deliberated about the submitted inventions and recommended whether or not rewards should be bestowed on the petitioners, the amount that should be given, and the terms of the grant. In some cases, the examination was thorough and the financing strategy cautious, offering awards in stages that were contingent on success in the prior tasks. For instance, the inventor of a windmill was given part of the sum that he requested and was told that he would secure the rest when the invention had been shown to be actually useful. Indeed, France can be viewed as having introduced the examination system for processing technological innovations, which would later be viewed as a uniquely American institution.

However, despite the seemingly rational rule-based procedures, the privilege system was essentially arbitrary, and the technical or economic value of the submission was often the least relevant criterion in reaching the final outcome. One advantage of a bureaucratic allocation system is that it creates a paper trail, and the archives in Paris and in the provinces are the repository for massive ledgers and files stuffed with letters, formal petitions, complaints, pathetic pleas, and testimonials. This tsunami of handwritten records in fading brown ink reveals the hopes and frustrations of French inventors and introducers in dealing with an overwhelmed and overwhelming bureaucracy. They highlight the nontrivial

administrative and personal costs when rewards to creative individuals are derived from appeals to panels and demonstrate the likelihood of idiosyncratic
decisions. The potential for cognitive dissonance and even corruption was especially likely in cases where the panel members had vested interests to protect.

French innovation policies transmuted a potential market for inventions into
a political market for favors to special interests and an administered system of
pleas and negotiations. As a result, for innovators of even the most valuable discoveries, outcomes were decidedly probabilistic in a manner that differed greatly
from transactions in the market. Even for those assured of assistance, "winners"
could not rely on politically motivated promises. Mechanisms to enforce such
implied contracts were limited, and participants did not have the right of appeal
to legal rules based on a stock of analogous precedents. Obviously, the risk of
hold-ups or outright expropriation was heightened if the inventor had already
made large fixed investments with low resale value. Other things being equal,
expected rewards were positively associated with influential patrons who could
not only convince committee members that it would be worthwhile to accept a
particular project but also signal that it would be costly for the decision makers if
the petition were rejected or if bargains were not honored.

Political backing gave innovators the leverage to negotiate more beneficial terms relative to applicants without such advantages. In 1788, Philemon
Pickford, an English machinist who was sponsored by Jean François Tolozan,
the influential Intendant of Commerce, arrived in France. The mule jenny and
other machinery he proposed could be used to make muslins, bonnets, and expensive fabrics. Pickford demanded that the state provide him with income to
the tune of 12,000 pounds, along with accommodations and a workshop. He was
accorded the housing and workshop, but his emolument was scaled down to a
grant of 6,000 pounds, and royalties of 300 pounds per machine built. The establishment was set up two years later with textile machinery that completed its
tasks "with all the perfection possible" in Brive-la-Gaillarde and later in Paris. He
had been promised a "gratification" in vague terms that would be offered when
his work was accomplished, but he was able to secure upfront payment even before he publicized the information or made the machinery to meet the market
demand.[12]

The extensive files for John Kay, the famous Lancashire textile machinery
inventor, indicate the asymmetries in bargains between petitioners and state
authorities.[13] Kay, like many other foreign artisans and innovators, had also
been enticed by the French authorities to leave his native land because of lavish
pledges, which included the promise of an annual pension, funding for the

---

[12] Procès-verbaux des Comités d'agriculture et de commerce de la Constituante (septembre 1792).
[13] See file F12/992 in the National Archives in Paris, France.

construction of textile machines, and other subsidies. Kay lived up to his end of the arrangement, training local employees, providing knowledge and know-how, and continuing to devise valuable inventions well into his seventies. However, he only received part of the promised support, and a continual series of letters over several decades documents his frustrations and despair with the failures of the French administration to fully honor its pledges to him. The worn-out inventor's later attempts to appeal to English authorities for aid were equally unsuccessful, as he was reviled as an economic traitor, and he died in poverty in France.

Although foreign immigrants were more likely to be vulnerable to uncertain contractual rights in dealing with the state, French citizens were not immune to the effects of political risk. A decree of Napoleon I in 1810 promised the imperial sum of 1 million francs to the creator of the best flax-spinning machine. Philippe de Girard, an inventor from Avignon, decided to compete for the prize and partnered with his brothers to raise the capital to realize the project. Girard was confident that his investments would be amply repaid through the prize money and, like many others in such situations, was induced to overspend on the basis of his great expectations. The machine he invented fully satisfied the terms of the competition, but the prize was never awarded.[14] Girard and both his brothers were financially ruined, and Girard had to leave the country. When Louis Napoleon later visited Vaucluse, Girard's birthplace, the town flew a flag demanding "Justice for Philippe de Girard." Several years after Girard's death in 1845, his contributions to the textile industry were finally officially acknowledged, when a pension of 6,000 francs was given to his brother Joseph and a similar sum awarded to his niece.[15]

As George Stigler noted, "Economic relationships are never perfectly competitive if they involve any personal relationships between economic units."[16] In France, individual-level details reveal a deeply personalized institutional context that differed markedly from the impersonal economic structures and transactions that theoretically typify an advanced market economy. A key feature of entrepreneurship and innovation is the ability to manage uncertainty and to exploit the attendant risks to attain higher returns. Nineteenth-century France was subject to great political and economic turmoil, creating a precarious business environment for all, but particularly so for creative entrepreneurs who could

---

[14] Gabriel Desclosières, *Vie et inventions de Philippe de Girard* (1881).

[15] "Récompense nationale accordée aux héritiers de Philippe de Girard," *Le Génie industriel* 5 (1853): 297. Girard was active in pursuing the rights and rewards for his own inventions and for the commercialization of others, and further filed for patents in France and England. He was given the English rights to an invention credited to Nicolas Appert and assigned that patent for £1,000. Like many eminent inventors, he was quick to migrate to more promising markets and promoted his machinery in several countries. He exhibited and received a gold medal for an improved steam engine at the National Exposition of 1806 and obtained more accolades at the National Exposition of 1844.

[16] George Stigler, *The Theory of Price* (1946), p. 24.

be outmatched by less innovative competitors with greater access to patrons who might intercede on their behalf in dealing with the state-sponsored institutions. The following sections illustrate the private and social costs and benefits associated with such policies, through a closer examination of the experiences of specific agencies in the French-administered innovation system.

Councils of Commerce and the Administration of Innovation

The Councils of Commerce and Manufactures, in various iterations and reincarnations, were at the center of innovation policy in France. First created in 1700, they had the declared objective of conducting economic and commercial policy on an inclusive democratic basis. Administrators' decisions would be informed by views from a wide cross-section of stakeholders, including guilds, merchants, workers, and specialists from all the major industries, such as silk, wool, cotton, and leather. The earliest Council of Commerce encouraged the twelve major city centers to send representatives to sit on the council, and these elected deputies were typically the most prominent citizens from their towns. Intendants of Commerce served as the chairs for deliberations that related to the specific region they supervised. Other key functionaries included provincial intendants and inspector generals who were responsible for reporting to the council on developments in commerce, innovation, and manufacturing. The payments to inventors and entrepreneurs who introduced foreign technologies to the French economy were underwritten by import taxes, signaling the mercantilist orientation of these policies.

Two registers, the procès-verbaux and the plumitifs, provide insights into the operation and decisions of the Council of Commerce (later renamed the Bureau of Commerce) in the eighteenth century.[17] The registers include numerous petitions and exchanges with inventors, manufacturers, nobles, and other interested parties. Applicants for funding would first approach the Academy of Sciences for professional approval and references, then submit their plea to the Bureau of Commerce. These two institutions often conflicted in their assessments and objectives, leading to frustration on the part of the petitioner. The bureau solicited the advice of intendants, or local administrators, from the township in which inventor originated, and these held their own potentially self-interested views about the extent to which inventors should be indulged. Toward the end of the eighteenth century it became more difficult for inventors to receive financial

---

[17] Pierre Bonassieux and Eugène Lelong, *Conseil de Commerce et Bureau du Commerce, 1700–1791, Inventaire analytique des procès-verbaux* (1900).

awards from the state. The shift away from funding inventors and manufacturers, however, did not imply that the state and its representatives in Paris were becoming less involved in the allocation of resources for innovation. Instead, the change signaled a growing lack of flexibility on the part of the administrators.

The democratic founding rhetoric in France has led some commentators to assume that such institutions functioned essentially as pioneering rational Weberian bureaucracies. However, closer inspection of the empirical evidence instead suggests a routinization of privilege, rather than of rational rules. The councils that oversaw commerce and manufacturing embodied a form of patronage, where favors were dispensed through both official and covert mechanisms. Even if the decisions were justified through appeals to social welfare, this did not imply that outcomes were necessarily motivated by impersonal considerations. As Tocqueville pointed out, in such organizations one "sees a man above himself whose patronage is necessary to him, and below himself another man whose co-operation he may claim." Influence flowed through liens with elites, and merchants and local guilds implored aristocrats, statesmen, and religious officials to intercede on their behalf, along the lines of traditional patron–client relationships. A class of paid lobbyists and agents in Paris could be retained to obtain inside information and to plead the causes of moneyed petitioners who lacked their own personal connections. Informal side payments (bribes) were not uncommon. Such strategies reduced uncertainty for some but increased the financial and transaction costs of an inherently arbitrary administrative system.

The Conseil général des manufactures in the early nineteenth century exhibited similar characteristics to its eighteenth-century counterparts.[18] This Council for Manufactures met weekly in Paris. The minister of the interior appointed its members, along with representatives from industry, which accorded with the impression of "social inclusiveness" that some scholars have identified in the Bureau of Commerce.[19] In practice, these Parisian institutions disadvantaged representatives from the provinces, owing to the location, leading to high rates of absenteeism. As a result, since only a few businessmen from Paris and nearby areas attended regularly, this meant that their particular industries and interests had a disproportionate representation in decision making. In particular, the textile manufacturers had a disproportionately strong presence in these negotiations, whereas the concerns among provincial industrialists, such as the need to reform the patent system of 1791, remained unaddressed in the files of the council for more than fifty years.

---

[18] Gille (1961); Parker (1965); Barker (1969).
[19] Smith (2002).

As might be expected, political factors influenced the appointment of council members and whose voices would be heard. Adherents of Napoleonic strategies wished to pursue strongly protectionist policy, with high tariff barriers to encourage domestic production and limit revenues to competing nations. Some influential entrepreneurs were able to successfully petition the council to secure large loans and compensation for the losses they suffered under protectionism, compounding the redistributive effects and social costs of import substitution policies. Representatives on the council who wished to promote an export-oriented strategy based on competitive enterprises at the forefront of innovation were less likely to influence outcomes, and not surprisingly, these members became resentful and disinterested in participation, adding to the high rate of absenteeism. Thus, despite the inclusiveness of French innovation policies on paper, protectionist Parisian interest groups disproportionately influenced the national agenda and outcomes in their own favor, at the expense of overall social welfare.

Society for the Encouragement of National Industry

Discussions with prominent French economic historians reveal that few would dispute the characterization of innovation policy (or, indeed, of most institutions in France) as one where special favors are directed to special interests. Most shrug and consider this political infiltration of economic issues as an inherent and ingrained part of French culture. However, one way to avoid the bias that can arise from case studies, or informal surveys of one's colleagues, is to systematically consider patterns from a large representative sample.

The Société d'encouragement pour l'industrie nationale (SEIN) was founded in 1801 to provide state sponsorship of technological and industrial developments throughout France.[20] The brilliant opening ceremony at L'Hôtel de Ville de Paris was attended by Napoleon himself, along with other consuls, prefects, and officials. The keynote speech loftily declared that "This Society is not an Academy, it is an association of good citizens. . . . The institution you are founding completes the work of the Government, far from contradicting or competing with it. . . . [Y]ou answer its call in the name of the whole nation; Happy union, sublime alliance of an enlightened administration, and of the national spirit!"

---

[20] This section is largely based on archival data, including several thousand pages of handwritten committee reports, stored in the attic of the society's headquarters in Saint-Germain des Prés, Paris. I am exceedingly grateful to everyone who aided in my research visits, especially Serge Benoit, Anne Chanteux, Christiane Demeulenaere, Gérard Emptoz, and Liliane Hilaire-Perez. As they correctly warned me: *Il y a là un gros travail à faire!*

This organization, in practice, proved to be the canonical administered innovation system. The objectives of the society included the assessment of new inventions, support for inventors, the publication of a bulletin, and other means to disseminate information about discoveries. The initial focus of the society was on employing honorary and pecuniary awards as the central policy instrument for encouraging technological innovations. The operations were funded through a combination of subscription fees, personal donations, and financing from the Ministry of the Interior. In 1818, M. le Comte Jean-Baptiste-Moïse Jollivet bequeathed some 300,000 francs to increase the endowment of the society; he stipulated that half of the income was to be directed toward prizes for innovations, in the fond expectation that (as he stated) before long such policies would lead to the triumph of French industry over its foreign competitors. Later in the nineteenth century, however, innovation prizes lost favor, and the society became more involved in providing support and funding for laboratories and research and development.

As in other French institutions, within the bureaucratic structure of the society, individual administrators wielded a marked degree of personal patronage and influence. Jean-Antoine Chaptal, Comte de Chanteloup, chemist, and minister of the interior, was one of the most formidable administrators and served as the first president of the society. Chaptal was inspired by the popular myth of the central contributions that the Royal Society of Arts in London had made to British industrial progress. The SEIN circulated its own "founding myth" claiming that the institution was organized purely through private initiatives.[21] Instead, it was essentially a state-run entity, created by representatives primarily from the Ministry of the Interior and other government departments. Almost all of the early members were associates of Chaptal and other state officials, and establishment figures from the Council of Agriculture, Arts et Commerce, and the Bureau of Arts and Manufactures.

M. le Baron Joseph-Marie De Gérando, the secretary of the SEIN for over four decades, drew up the initial charter, made key decisions about the award of prizes, and organized all of the reports and meetings. Members who subsequently joined the board included his own father and many of his personal acquaintances. Lucien Bonaparte also appointed Gérando to the Bureau consultatif des arts et du commerce, and he was involved in the administration of several other influential committees and societies. SEIN membership changed somewhat in orientation in the 1850s, when participation shifted from bureaucrats and elites to manufacturers, inventors, scientists, and engineers. However, throughout its first century, most of the administrators, committees, and members were drawn

---

[21] Butrica (1998).

from the elite circles of aristocrats, scientists, politicians, professors, bankers, and wealthy manufacturers.[22] Artisans, machinists and technicians, and ordinary businessmen were not well represented in the society. Jury or committee membership was in part offered as an honor, rather than as a means of obtaining the most technologically qualified personnel; such individuals may have been successful in their own spheres but typically were not qualified to gauge novel inventive merit.

In accordance with its charter, the society's primary objective was to promote economic development by furthering technological innovation and manufacturing. The award of prizes to induce inventiveness was considered to be a central part of achieving this mission during the nineteenth century. The SEIN published an annual list of proposed areas to which it sought to attract applicants for cash prizes, medals, and "encouragements" or other forms of support for projects. The premium list identified the problem, in specific terms in some cases and quite broad and vague phrases in others, along with the monetary value of the prize at stake. Foreigners, as well as French inventors, were allowed to apply for awards, although the former were required to cede the property rights to their ideas to the society.

The transition from the ancien régime system of privileges to the allegedly objective innovation policies of the nineteenth century was personified by the Marquise d'Argence, who was adroit in exploiting all available political avenues to gain support for her endeavors. As an appointed lacemaker to the royal court, she devised (or claimed credit for) a machine that could spin flax into very fine thread that was useful for making delicate lace for the garments of the nobility. She employed a number of poor young women in a factory setting, ostensibly as a charitable project, to produce small amounts of thread that were then exhibited at expositions. The influential M. Molard, her advocate before a committee of the Society for the Encouragement of National Industry, drew attention to her philanthropy, physical disabilities and advanced age, and the recent death of her husband. Attempts to elicit information from the marquise about the technical process itself, however, received the terse rejoinder, "It is my secret."[23] The investigating committee understandably noted that it was not clear whether hers was a new or economical method but still proceeded to include a notice on her behalf in the SEIN bulletin, a prestigious achievement

---

[22] For a listing of the members of the board of directors since the society's inception, see the *Bulletin de la Société d'Encouragement pour l'Industrie Nationale* (1893), pp. 813–840.

[23] *Bulletin* (1819), pp. 139–141. The marquise paid the substantial fees to obtain a patent for her invention in 1818, and also patented an improvement the following year, but her charitable intentions did not extend to diffusion of the information, and she again stipulated that the patent office should keep the specifications secret.

that undoubtedly boosted the market value of any discovery that received this honor.

The society at times was associated with systematic research and development, such as in the case of Marguerite-Marie Degrand of Marseille. The combination of female scientific expertise and successful entrepreneurial acumen is uncommon in any era, but she provides a prominent example of an entrepreneur who made valuable contributions to scientific and industrial advances in France.[24] Mme Degrand née Gurgey had apprenticed with her father, Nicolas Gurgey, and inherited his cutlery workshop in Marseille. She married Elzéard Degrand, an innovative machinist and multiple patentee, in 1815. In 1819, the society awarded her an honorable mention, reporting in its bulletin that "Mme Degrand knows how to make a type of Damascus steel which the Turks might take for a product made in their own country. It is a veritable conquest over the East which enriches our industry." The English declared that they had triumphed in the international quest to replicate crucible steel from Damascus when the renowned chemists Stoddart and Faraday published their findings on steel alloys in 1820. But, owing to the achievements of Mme Degrand, their claim to priority was contested by the French. The society later bestowed its Grand Medal on Marguerite-Marie Degrand, and in 1824 she was one of its rare female members.

The society offered valuable funding for heavy industry and metals, including forges, locomotives, machine tools, and steam engines. Scholars typically point to the Jacquard loom for silks and improvements in turbines to support overall favorable assessments of the institution. Table 6.1 provides a more representative perspective on the work of the society. The first part of the table analyzes the subject matter for the total amount of prizes granted during the first half century of the SEIN's existence. The percentage distribution by value indicates the relative importance of the awards during this critical period, and these patterns show that the prizes were not wholly aligned with the economic value of innovations for the individual industry. Awards for the domestic cultivation of sugar beets and sugar production accounted for 9.3% of prizes, compared to a mere 1.2% for locomotives, and it is not clear why sugar should have been viewed as more meritorious than improvements in transportation. The ceramics industry obtained a surprising 12.7% of funding, while fine arts and music received a further 11% of the prizes and encouragements. The criteria for some grants were associated with inventive novelty and higher productivity, but most were unrelated to technological excellence. Reasons for the awards ranged

---

[24] Later accolades by the society rated her work as superior to other nations, enthusing that she had made "une lame de sabre beaucoup plus belle et plus parfaite que celles qui se fabriquent en Syrie, attirait les regards de tous les connaisseurs." On her death, she passed on the Gurgey business to her niece, suggesting a female-oriented family enterprise.

Table 6.1(a) Awards of the Society for the Encouragement of National Industry, 1802–1851

| Category | (French Francs) | | | | | |
	Prizes	%	Medals and Other	%	Total	%
Agriculture	28,600	12.3	21,980	8.3	50,580	10.1
Fine arts	16,100	6.9	32,040	12.1	48,140	9.7
Boats	11,000	4.7	8,935	3.4	19,935	4.0
Ceramics	34,700	14.9	28,810	10.8	63,510	12.7
Chemical products	6,600	2.8	2,480	0.9	9,080	1.8
Clocks and opticals	0	0.0	8,575	3.2	8,575	1.7
Domestic economy	1,200	0.5	1,000	0.4	2,200	0.4
Dyes	0	0.0	3,990	1.5	3,990	0.8
Foods	8,500	3.6	9,150	3.4	17,650	3.5
Forges	0	0.0	11,050	4.2	11,050	2.2
Hats and shoes	4,000	1.7	3,930	1.5	7,930	1.6
Heat and light	9,000	3.9	9,670	3.6	18,670	3.7
Legacies	0	0.0	16,613	6.3	16,613	3.3
Locomotives	0	0.0	6,185	2.3	6,185	1.2
Machine tools	8,500	3.6	23,350	8.8	31,850	6.4
Metals	22,000	9.4	11,180	4.2	33,180	6.7
Music	2,000	0.9	4,495	1.7	6,495	1.3
Orthopedics	1,000	0.4	5,315	2.0	6,315	1.3
Paper	5,000	2.1	3,030	1.1	8,030	1.6
Political economy	0	0.0	1,500	0.6	1,500	0.3
Prize Argenteuil	24,000	10.3	0	0.0	24,000	4.8
Steam engines	17,500	7.5	15,900	6.0	33,400	6.7
Sugar	21,700	9.3	6,620	2.5	28,320	5.7
Weapons	0	0.0	795	0.3	795	0.2
Weaving	11,800	5.1	27,665	10.4	39,465	7.9
Wines	0	0.0	1,280	0.5	1,280	0.3
Total	233,200	100	265,538	100	498,738	100

Table 6.1(b) Awards of the French Society for the Encouragement of National
Industry, 1852–1914

	Bronze Medals	Silver Medals	Platinum Medals	Gold Medals	Cash Awards (No.)	Cash Awards (Value)	Total Awards (No.)
1852–1854	28	23	10	9	3	0	73
1855–1859	31	50	12	19	34	46,100	146
1860–1864	43	66	21	16	1	12,000	147
1865–1869	30	19	12	15	0	0	76
1870–1874	37	51	15	16	18	46,100	137
1875–1879	23	28	20	29	11	11,850	111
1880–1884	24	32	26	44	21	45,900	147
1885–1889	29	45	18	31	25	41,700	148
1890–1894	17	59	7	56	68	122,000	207
1895–1899	15	53	3	52	56	103,300	179
1900–1904	27	37	0	39	35	55,700	138
1905–1909	23	32	0	30	6	6,200	91
1910–1914	35	56	0	60	15	19,000	166
Total	362	551	144	416	293	509,850	1,766
Percent	20.5	31.2	8.2	23.6	16.6		

Source: *Annuaire de la Société d'Encouragement pour L'industrie Nationale* (Paris, various years).

from close imitation of foreign goods to good workmanship and the beauty of an item, and even references to the moral character of the applicants and their household. As the second part of the table shows, the majority of awards were honorary prizes that aided in commercialization rather than offering effective inducements for inventiveness.

Part of the disconnect between the decisions of the society and the needs of practical artisans or manufacturing enterprises lay in the tendency for the elaborate to attract favorable notice from panelists, even if a simple outcome might be more efficient and profitable. An example is the prize of 3,000 francs, which the society in 1818 offered for the best means of producing artesian wells. Just three entries were received and the winner, M. Garnier, an engineer at the elite Royal Corps of Mines, provided detailed specifications of his convoluted proposed solution. The

American Quarterly Review declared that this work was extremely impressive in offering a wealth of propositions for achieving the desired ends, but "whether all the minutiae that he has laid down in his work be essential to the boring of these Artesian wells, is left for the consideration of the French." The reviewer added blandly that in the United States "the case is different; we adopt a more simple process."[25] Garnier's report had been printed up and distributed among a large number of government committee members, at the expense of the state.

In other cases, juries made awards based on questionable judgments about the marketability of the inventions that were presented. They selected devices that were deemed to be uneconomical, but good substitutes for foreign imports, and were overly optimistic about the extent to which the submissions for prizes were likely to succeed as commercial products. In one instance, the SEIN offered an award of 500 francs for improvements in the art of lithographic printing. M. Tudot had submitted a plan to use rollers made with soft calf skin that distributed ink evenly over paper. His rollers were far more expensive than the existing seamed models, but he received the prize because the judges "confidently" expected that once it went into manufacture, the excessively high price of the rollers would eventually fall to a more economical level.

Accounts of such administered innovation institutions frequently emphasize successes but omit consideration of failures or nonresponses. The society's bulletin for 1820 showed that 184,000 francs had been offered as prizes since the founding of the institution, whereas only 41.6% of this sum actually was granted. In some instances, the prize was withdrawn because the problem had already been resolved elsewhere or because no applicants were deemed worthy. Such decisions provide positive indications that attention was being paid to the progress of the specific technology and that standards were being maintained. However, in many other areas, the award remained unclaimed throughout its history because of a lack of entries, indicating that nobody had been "induced" by the offer, perhaps because the award was too low or the problem was insoluble or uninteresting. Such failures obviously need to be taken into account to avoid a selection bias in the assessment of inducement prizes. The overall patterns for the SEIN in France therefore replicate the results that were discussed in connection with the Royal Society of Arts in London.

Administering Science and Technology Institutions

Europeans, like Americans, were well aware that ideas were essential for social and economic advances. In France, knowledge was regarded as a pyramid,

[25] *American Quarterly Review* 22 (1837): 331.

in which theoretical science and esoteric mathematics were at the apex, and acolytes in these subjects were regarded as the most fit to supervise and oversee the applied fields, including mechanics, which were relegated to the base. Thus, elites who privileged the study of the classics and theory and remained hostile and dismissive of technical problem solving were endowed with the power to administer and make key decisions that would shape the course of technological discoveries.

The Royal Academy of Sciences was founded in 1666 and still survives as one of the most prestigious scientific institutions in France. The academy was an agent of the state, and Napoleon Bonaparte himself was its president in 1800. The government funded the budget, almost all of which was spent on overhead salaries and administrative expenses. The membership was limited to the upper classes, and women were entirely excluded until the second half of the twentieth century. Affiliation with the institution ensured a great deal of influence, including the power of patronage in appointments at the most prestigious universities. The Royal Academy of Sciences and the equally elitist "corps savants" (Corps d'Artillerie, Corps de Génie Militaire, Corps des Mines, and Corps des Ponts et Chaussées) dominated the creation, administration, and public consumption of knowledge in accordance with the goals of the political regime. During the early industrial era, the committees from the academy were tasked with making judgments about matters relating to both science and technology. The academy and its prestigious participants contributed to the professionalization of science, but in the realm of technology their record was decidedly mixed. It is perhaps unsurprising that their overall perspective and practice emerged as rigid and undemocratic, and the filters they applied imposed undue constraints on technological innovation. In particular, the structure focused attention on Paris and discriminated against talented scientists in the provinces, a theme that constantly recurs in French history.

As was true in all other echelons of the government supervision of knowledge in France, the academy enthusiastically promoted and administered a flurry of prize competitions. Ample allowances were available for generous prizes in very specific areas of inquiry, whereas funding in other areas of science was pinched and inadequate. A large endowment provided income just for prizes in celestial mechanics and in naval science, for example. As the study and practice of science and technology became more professional and less the province of amateurs, the cost of research and development increased. This implied that well-off applicants for prizes could afford the necessary start-up expenditures and were better able to participate in competitions, whereas poor inventors were less likely to compete or to prevail. Small grants to younger researchers clearly would have been more effective than large cash awards to already prosperous scientists who could have engaged in the research even without the prizes.[26] Like its counterparts in other countries, the Paris Academy ultimately acknowledged these problems and decided to shift from inducement prizes and ex post awards to offering grants to help underwrite research and development inputs.

Questions might be raised about the governance of the academy in the prize endowments and their expenditures. The funds were supposed to be disbursed subject to the approval of the Ministry of the Interior; nevertheless, the academy independently made decisions, sometimes in ways that conflicted with the mandate for the award. The organization spent significant amounts of the funds for purposes that were not in accordance with their original intent. As the size of the available endowments increased, pressure to spend the money grew, regardless of whether there were worthy applications. The academy finagled the accounts to shift flows of funds toward its own administrative expenses. The accounts reveal significant honoraria to members of the academy and salaries for its affiliates. Applicants obtained funding for travel to conduct speculative experiments in exotic locations.

The overall contributions of the academy to technological innovation were minor. However, even in the realm of science, some scholars have been critical of the effectiveness of the academy's activities and orientation. According to Robert Fox, the personal and institutional biases of the centralized Parisian administration led to long-term stagnation in French science. This institution underestimated and neglected the creativity of researchers in the provinces and the contributions of other independent thinkers. In France, throughout the nineteenth century, "governmental patronage of science was rarely enlightened and only intermittently generous."[27] French scientific achievements occurred despite government actions, and its most evident successes owed to individual efforts by such scholars as Pierre-Simon Laplace and Claude-Louis Berthollet, who used their own funds and initiative to pursue new and original problems outside the mainstream. The reports of the academy required committee members to present a coherent and unique conclusion, in the course of which all dissent was eradicated. The insistence on consensus narrowed the range of useful knowledge, because suppressed minority opinions offered insights that could have helped in fashioning more precise policies or in presenting alternative options that might have become more valuable when circumstances changed.

The Academy of Sciences in Paris was often the initial arbiter of the value of applications for compensation to inventors from across the country. Since the membership was biased toward pure theory and abstract mathematics, this led

---

[26] Crosland (1979).
[27] Fox (1973); Gillispie (2004).

to frequent conflicts with technological inventors and innovators whose discoveries typically emerged through an experimental process of trial and error. These methodological differences were especially prevalent when the committees made pronouncements regarding the commercial value of the proposals. When the Abbé de Mandre invented a motor that could pull a train of thirty boats on the river, the Academy of Sciences found the motor to be "new and ingenious" but opined that the value was not large enough to warrant a significant reward. Despite their ruling, the motor proved to be a commercially useful invention. By contrast, they enthusiastically approved a cannonball invention created by the Marquis de Bellegard, which failed to be adopted or put into general use. Indeed, as in most administered innovation systems, follow-on commercialization or practical application was not a primary concern at the academy.

Members of the elite and landed gentry were more likely to have the savoir-faire to maneuver and arbitrage among the plethora of professional bodies, encouragement societies, and governmental bureaucracies. Cora Elisabeth Millet was adept at enhancing her standing in these influential groups by participating in exhibitions, submitting papers, and circulating free copies of her books. An experimental agronomist and expert on household management, she was a corresponding member of the Société centrale d'agriculture de France and the Société d'agriculture, sciences et arts de Poitiers, and affiliated with several other regional bodies. She and the members of her family received numerous accolades and medals for their research in agriculture. Her communications on innovations and improved methods of farming, and the cultivation of silkworms and silk production, were reprinted overseas in influential journals. Mme Millet's magisterial handbook, *Maison rustique des dames*, was first published in 1849 and ran into over twenty editions, with a new English translation in 2017. In 1884, she was one of the first two women appointed Chevalière de l'Ordre du mérite agricole, to recognize her outstanding contributions to agriculture.[28]

The network of overlapping innovation institutions in France could and did lead to frequent conflicts among the different interest groups. Elisabeth Gervais, from a prominent landowning family in Montpellier, was renowned in the world of winemaking because of her research and development into oenology. Her findings resulted in the award of two valuable patents in 1818 and 1820 for apparatuses to condense the vapors in the process of making alcohol. Her invention was designed to conserve approximately 10% to 15% of the losses from condensation and to improve the bouquet and quality of the final product. Contemporary

---

[28] The first award in 1883 was bestowed on Louis Pasteur. The minister of agriculture wished to offer the agricultural sector "a new testimonial of the regard of the government of the Republic, and an inducement to redouble efforts to maintain the rank that it must occupy in a country that depends on farming for its wealth and security." See https://agriculture.gouv.fr/histoire/3_merite_agr/index_merite_agricole.htm.

scientists were dismissive about the originality of her innovation and disparaged the technical and commercial value of her contributions. The Bordeaux Royal Academy in particular awarded a prize in 1822 to another researcher for work that allegedly refuted the claims of the novelty and superiority of the Gervais approach.[29] Despite their quibbling, Mlle Gervais sold her discovery to practicing winemakers and earned "considerable profits."[30] She established an enterprise in Paris to market the patent rights divided up by geographical districts. Her company in Montpellier was managed by her brother, Jean-Antoine Gervais, who was a member of the SEIN. It was likely because of this link to SEIN that the ubiquitous Chaptal, himself a chemist with interests in oenology, provided her with a letter of recommendation and also served on the board of directors for her Paris company.

The French scientific elites at times clashed with the technical and industrial bureaucracy. The example of the gas industry illustrates how private interests could be pursued behind a façade of nationalism and supposedly objective knowledge and expertise. Chaptal and his associates objected to the development of gas lighting, which depended on nonrenewable coal reserves, because they wished to retain the coal stocks to supply steam engines and the production of iron, which were more central to industrialization. By contrast, the academy relied on the recommendations and analysis of a small group of chemists, who had financial stakes in the gas industry.[31] The academic scientific elites could also be conservative and reluctant to support measures that did not rely on their own particular expertise. This was evident in environmental issues, where concerns were raised by an inchoate lobby including members of the general population, hygienists, naturalists, and technocrats.[32] The Ministry of the Interior took the initiative to collect survey data from a wide variety of sources dealing with meteorology, temperatures, agriculture, and natural disasters to engage in assessments of the relationship between deforestation, climate changes, and flooding. The academy, however, undermined these efforts because the survey reports did not meet their standards of mathematical rigor.

The quasi-monopolies that the state established over the knowledge economy in France hindered the coevolution of scientific interactions with technology in a number of key areas. For contemporaries, the members of these bureaucracies were often incompetent in practical matters and in conflict with broader social

---

[29] The debate is covered at length in B. A. Lenoir, *Traité de la culture de la vigne et de la vinification* (1830).

[30] See the *Bulletin of the Société royale d'agriculture, arts et commerce des Pyrénées Orientales* (1820), p. 207.

[31] Fressoz (2007).

[32] Ford (2016).

interests. Similar concerns were evident after the Ministry of the Interior was given the power to regulate the pharmaceutical industry in 1810. The legislation was intended to reverse-engineer the trade secrets of medicines, with the stated objective of protecting the public from shoddy nostrums and noxious substances. An advisory commission was formed that included members of the Academy of Medicine. Their statutory mandate was to study the composition of the medications, ascertain their efficacy, determine whether the government should purchase the remedy on behalf of the public, and stipulate the fair price for compensating the inventor of the drug. Their deliberations, however, proved to be unworkable and ineffective, and only a miniscule number of remedies were actually assessed. The lack of productive and disinterested results from the state-sponsored administered system led to private initiatives, such as the formation of the Société générale de contrôle et de garantie alimentaires, which hired its own chemists to verify the safety of foods.

French Patents and Innovations

The patent system in France reflected the tendency toward institutional path dependence that was observed in the prize systems. French revolutionaries intended to sweep away the privileges of the former regime and were concerned about the possibility that patents would recreate the potential for arbitrary monopolies. In the debates before the National Assembly, Chevalier Stanislas de Boufflers played a key role in calming their apprehensions about adopting an incentive system with an English provenance.[33] In his address, he pointed to the way in which patents served as an instrument that promoted democracy in the United States: "The proud and wise Americans have not had such futile misgivings. Instead, in their new constitution those worthy friends of complete liberty have adopted the English [patent] legislation as the most effective means of securing both the emancipation and the prosperity of their own industry." This rhetoric carried the day, and the assembly failed to appreciate that the American institutions explicitly rejected key features of the British practices as undemocratic.

---

[33] The chevalier himself had been a valued member of the prerevolutionary aristocracy, who characterized Napoleon as "the nightmare of the Universe." De Boufflers was popular at Versailles for his florid poetry and romantic affairs, his military record as Maréchal de Camp, many eclectic contributions to art and literature, airy bons mots, and witty conversational skills. One of his "jolis vers" included his own epitaph: "Ci-gît un chevalier qui sans cesse courut, Qui sur les grands chemins, naquit, vécut, mourut. Pour prouver ce que dit le sage, Que notre vie est un voyage." See Nesta Webster, *The Chevalier De Boufflers* (1916).

The fundamental principles of the French patent system were introduced in the early legislation and survived until modern times.[34] Instead of a special favor from the Crown, the statute of 1791 declared that every person had a natural right to the products of their own creativity, and that "every discovery or invention, in every type of industry, is the property of its creator; the law therefore guarantees him its full and entire enjoyment."[35] The government was not involved beyond the initial grant and did not "in any manner guarantee either the priority, merit or success of an invention." In keeping with this principle, no panel of examiners was charged with deciding whether or not the right should be granted. Instead, like the English, France introduced a registration system, where the sole filter was the ability to pay costly fees. The patentees could make the decision themselves about the term of legal protection, over a period of five, ten, or fifteen years.[36] After 1844, the fees amounted to 500 francs ($100) for a five-year patent, 1,000 francs for a ten-year patent, and 1,500 francs for a patent of fifteen years, payable in annual installments. As in Britain, anyone who wished to consult the roster of patent grants had to pay for access to the information, and the registers were not readily available for consultation.

It is ironic that the intention to create an institution that was not tainted with privileges for the wealthy instead had the opposite effect. Members of the nobility and manufacturers obtained a disproportionate number of patents in the first half of the nineteenth century, some initially for financial speculation.[37] Artisans and workers, who accounted for a much larger share of the population, obtained 18.8% of patents (Table 6.2). Key contributory factors for the bias against the poor included the high price of patent protection, the ability to obtain property rights without necessarily being the original creator, the lack of government assurance regarding the validity of the grant, working requirements that necessitated setting up a manufacturing establishment, and the uncertainty of legal enforcement. Importers of overseas inventions and patents were accorded the same "natural rights" as the original inventors, which were more

---

[34] Perpigna (1852); Khan (2005); Galvez-Behar (2008).

[35] See the Decret du 30 Decembre 1790, in the Code des Pensions, 30 Decembre 1790, p. 45. Many inventor lobby groups in France correctly argued that patent rights should be perpetual under a natural rights system.

[36] Extensions were rarely allowed: only twenty of the five thousand patents obtained in the first forty years of the system were extended. "What makes the government so averse to prolongations, is that they are never demanded but for successful inventions, and such as society at large is most anxious to enjoy. They are detrimental to trade and damp the spirit of enterprise." See Perpigna (1852: 32).

[37] William Westoby, *The Legal Guide for Residents in France* (1858), notes that "After the passing of the laws of 1791, speculators began to patent financial schemes of all kinds. The first of such patents was for a tontine; this was followed by patents for banks of all kinds, tables for different kinds of assurance, exchange offices, etc.; when the National Assembly, fearing that such schemes would further increase the then financial embarrassments, passed a law, declaring void all patents granted for such schemes, and prohibiting the government from granting any more for like purposes."

Table 6.2 Characteristics of Patenting in France, 1791–1855

	Patents	Percent
Industry		
Agriculture	19	1.5
Apparel	90	7.3
Chemicals/medical	95	7.7
Engines/machines/transport	286	23.1
Food	90	7.3
Household/building	191	15.4
Iron/metals	137	11.1
Printing/arts	128	10.4
Textiles	191	15.5
Miscellaneous	8	0.6
Total	1235	100.0
Patent Term		
5 years	549	44.5
10 years	232	18.8
15 years	352	28.5
Addition	102	8.2
Total	1235	100.0
Occupation		
Professional	205	24.1
Businessman	87	10.3
Manufacturer	238	28.0
Teacher	17	2.0
Artisan/worker	160	18.8
Engineer/machinist	142	16.7
Total	849	100.0
Residence		
Paris	641	53.6
Provinces	454	38.0
Foreign	101	8.4
Total	1196	100.0

Notes and Sources: Patents were categorized into the industry of final use. Each patent was assigned to a single inventor, even if the rights were shared with collaborators. Sample of patents from Ministère de l'agriculture, *Catalogue des brevets d'invention, d'importation et de perfectionnement* (various years).

likely to be granted if plaintiffs could show that they had traveled abroad at "great expense and loss of time." Employers could appropriate the rights to workers' improvements and file for a patent in their own name, since there was no examination and no rationale for rejecting any application. Working requirements could be avoided with a little exercise of legal ingenuity, but the need to justify a "nonpracticing" strategy was an added transaction cost. Moreover, the uncertainty of the property right increased the difficulties for inventors who wished to leverage their patent to mobilize capital through the marketplace.

The patent laws included further provisions that encouraged rent-seeking rather than commercialization through individual initiative. The decree of 1790 allowed that "when the inventor prefers to deal directly with the government, he is free to petition either the administrative assemblies or the legislature, if appropriate, to turn over his discovery, after demonstrating its merits and soliciting a reward."[38] In other words, the inventor of a discovery could choose between a patent or conveying the invention to the nation in exchange for an award from funds that were set aside for the encouragement of industry. Through this policy, the award of assistance and pensions to inventors and their families continued well into the nineteenth century. Instead of efforts to engage in commercialization and private enterprise, patentees and inventors had an incentive to lobby the state to pay upfront for patent fees, to fund extensions of their property rights, and to give out lump-sum payments for their discoveries, which (they invariably contended) were guaranteed to revolutionize the industry and assure the French of global leadership.

One of the administrative dossiers covered the case of a master locksmith with influential patrons who was able to call in favors, as well as letters of recommendation from members of the nobility. The Bureau of Arts and Manufactures paid the patent fees for his invention, on the grounds that locks were necessary for ensuring national security and increased social well-being. Shoes, however, were evidently less meritorious than locks, as a Parisian shoemaker without such connections found out when he urged the state to purchase his invention. Instead, he received a response with the stricture that he should bear in mind that "It is your own responsibility to manage the exploitation of your invention, or else you should interest a few investors in advancing you the necessary capital."[39] The rebuke seems to have suitably chastened its recipient, who abandoned his petitioning for government funding and succeeded in selling the patent rights in the following year to a Parisian entrepreneur. At the end of the nineteenth

---

[38] Code des Pensions, 30 Decembre 1790.
[39] National Archives, F/12/1025 (1816).

century, the French government was still persisting in offering subsidies to incentivize technological improvements . . . in sailing ships.

One notable achievement of the state innovation system was its leadership in publicizing the development and accomplishments of French manufacturing and industrial innovation through a series of influential expositions in the nineteenth century. Table 6.3 illustrates how the French Exhibitions of National Industry expanded in scope and objectives between 1798 and 1849. The first exposition in 1798 had the modest objective of reassuring French industrialists that they could successfully match the British attainments in technologies and products that seemed to be far superior to their own domestic manufactures. Exhibitions provided advertising for the efforts of producers and firms, and attracted custom from other tradesmen as well as from consumers. The grandeur, spectacle, and popularity of the events rapidly grew over time, and by 1844 the displays of almost four thousand exhibitors were showcased in specially designed structures in a grand expanse that covered the entire Champs-Élysées. The numbers of exhibitors, size of the display space, degree of technological sophistication, and amount of prizes also increased steadily over this period. As is typical in prize systems, "grade inflation" in the number of awards per exhibitor is evident, and by the end of the period over 80% of the entries would receive a medal or honorable mention.

These data offer unique insights into the experience of entrepreneurs, who demonstrated exceptional initiative and business acumen. Many of these participants belonged to a privileged class of the wealthy or influential upper echelons of the commercial world. The exhibitions also shed light on a group of particular interest, namely, entrepreneurial women who headed prosperous and innovative enterprises (Table 6.4). One of these, Mary Louise Sensitive Armfield (1793–1871), was the daughter of Thomas Armfield, a manufacturer who immigrated to France from Birmingham and established a textile spinning factory in the Indre-Loire region in 1806. Mary married her father's business partner in 1814 and participated in the running of the business. Some sources claim that she did so only after being widowed; however, the exhibition evidence clearly identifies her as the responsible party during his lifetime. On the death of her husband in 1828, she took sole control of the company and managed it for over four decades.

The enterprise, Toiles de Mayenne, grew rapidly. The strategies were innovative, including the early introduction of mechanical steam-driven processes, and they produced high-quality products in large quantities, at competitive prices. Their silver medals at the Exposition of French Industry in 1823 and 1827, according to the judges, were "distinctions that were well deserved." These merits were sustained, and thirty years later accolades were still being bestowed on the firm. Toiles de Mayenne also illustrates the importance of nontechnological

Figure 6.1   Paris Universal Exhibition

The *Expositions Universelles* took place between 1855 and 1937, with the most spectacular events in 1889 to mark the centennial of the French Revolution. As with all international exhibitions, their objectives ranged from patriotism, to publicity for industrial achievements, to entertainment for the hordes of paying spectators who flocked through the crowded halls to sample the manufactured goods and marvel at the innovations on display. In this instance, the spectators are trying out Edison's phonograph.

Source: Livre d'Or de l'Exposition, 1889.

innovations in the success of business enterprises, and in particular the introduction of "family-friendly" management practices that improved the conditions of the labor force. A contemporary guide to the district noted that Mme Armfield's factory was "a source of good, not only for the owner, but for the entire population."[40]

[40]   Heinrich Reichard, *Guide classique du voyageur en France* (1827), p. 168.

Table 6.3 Exhibitors and Awards at the French Expositions, 1798–1855

Year	Exhibitors	Medals	All Awards	% Winners
1798	110	3	23	20.9
1801	220	34	80	36.4
1802	540	42	254	47.0
1806	1,422	131	610	42.9
1819	1,662	308	869	52.3
1823	1,648	475	1,091	66.2
1827	1,795	425	1,254	69.9
1834	2,447	708	1,785	72.9
1839	3,381	868	2,305	68.2
1844	3,958	1,277	3,253	82.2
1849	4,650	1,652	3,738	80.4
Total	21,833	5,923	15,262	69.9
1855*	10,731	6,564	10,564	—

* The total number of exhibitors for the 1855 Universal Exposition was 21,779, of which 10,731 were from France and its colonies.

Notes and Sources: Total awards consist of medals (gold, silver, and bronze) and citations or honorable mentions. Rapport du jury central, *Catalogues des Expositions des produits de l'industrie française* (Paris, various years through 1849); *Catalogue de l'Exposition Universelle a Paris, 1855* (Paris, 1856).

Conclusion

In the early industrial era, France faced evident constraints, including less favorable natural resource endowments than England, as well as the drawback of continual military engagements and political turmoil. Still, French economic history has puzzled foreign and local observers alike, with cycles of interpretations that have been revised by subsequent revisionists. Traditional views about the course of French economic development tend to be phrased in terms that range from "creditable" to "modest," or even "retarded." Growth was characterized by regional and industrial imbalances, with a greater weight on traditional lagging industries, and lower rates of structural transformation from rural activities to more modernized pursuits. Some scholars hypothesized that the upper classes in France were too conservative and inimical to industrialization and manufacturing, and this static approach required an activist state to overcome the social inertia. Instead of faulting elite groups for their reluctance to engage in risk-taking and commercialization, more charitable historians propose that

Table 6.4 Women's Participation in Industrial Expositions by Marital Status, 1791–1855

	Single (%)	Widow (%)	Married (%)	Total (%)
Industry				
Apparel	28.2	11.9	29.9	20.5
Arts	16.4	16.3	14.5	14.5
Corsets	4.5	1.1	12.2	5.4
Food	2.7	4.7	1.8	3.3
Household	19.1	12.6	15.8	14.1
Nontraditional	3.6	18.1	9.5	11.6
Textiles	25.5	33.2	14.5	28.7
Miscellaneous	1	2.3	1.8	1.6
Occupation				
Artisan	17.4	7.7	16.7	12.2
Businesswoman	2.2	7.1	8.8	6.9
Corset maker	6.5	0.6	9.6	5
Manufacturer	73.9	78.9	57.9	70.5
Other	0	5.8	7	3.5
Time				
1791–1834	34.6	30	31.2	29.5
1835–1844	13.6	17.3	14	14.6
1845–1850	20	14.8	22.6	17.5
1851–1855	31.8	37.9	32.1	38.4
Awards				
None	34.6	32.5	35.3	37.4
One	38.2	29.6	40.3	33.3
Two	15.4	19.9	17.6	17.2
More than two	11.8	18.1	6.8	12.1
Collaborators	27.3	31.8	11.3	22.3
Patentee	17.3	20.1	22.7	19.3
Paris residency	59.1	51	67.2	54.8
Total	17.1%	43.0%	34.3%	N = 645

Notes and Sources: The table shows column percentages for 645 observations; totals may not sum to 100 because of missing values. The data include all women who obtained at least a citation by the juries for the expositions. "Nontraditional" fields for women include engines, transportation, chemicals, and heavy industries. Patent holders were determined by matching the names of exhibitors to the records of the Institut national de propriété industrielle. Rapport du jury central, *Catalogues des expositions des produits de l'industrie française* (Paris, various years through 1849); *Catalogue de l'Exposition Universelle à Paris, 1855* (Paris, 1856).

French entrepreneurs followed their own path to industrialization, focusing on new product designs and fashions, and not on "hard" mechanized technological innovations.

The French experienced institutional persistence, whereby special interests and entrenched bureaucracies were able to coopt attempts at reforms behind a façade of market-oriented rhetoric. This chapter on innovations in France emphasizes the need to closely investigate how institutions are designed and, even more important, the specific details about the way in which the proclaimed rules and standards are implemented. Rules and standards are merely symbols on paper unless they are well enforced and protected by checks and balances, including the right of appeal to neutral third parties. The declared "liberal democratic" principles of the French Republic differed markedly from the prevailing elitist administered innovation system, and that discrepancy had negative consequences for the population of inventors and inventions, and for economic development in general.

In France, the rhetoric of competition and freedom of trade was used as a cloak for continued efforts to ensure that administered institutions redistributed resources toward particular groups.[41] The unpredictable changes in the mandates, organization, and membership of public institutions created uncertainty for innovators and opportunities for arbitrage and rent-seeking across different systems. Regulatory policies were touted as necessary to prevent fraud, protect free enterprise, and ensure continued economic progress for all, while functioning as a tool of exclusion. Longstanding regulations were not removed, merely incorporated into populist decrees about freedom of enterprise, in the guise of numerous and pervasive "exceptions." Personalized interactions could be as important as—if not more important than—prices in allocating resources, and influential elite families and merchants engaged in collusive and predatory practices that allowed them to maintain industrial dominance and benefit from unearned economic rents that persisted over the long term.[42]

Protectionism, nationalism, and mercantilism were openly advocated in the eighteenth century. However, even when liberal economic policies were espoused, at best they superimposed a veneer of market democracy on a directed system. François Crouzet deprecated "the statist tradition and the fact that, even in the nineteenth century, intervention by government—and bureaucracy—in the economy was more widespread in France than, say, in Britain or the US."[43] In the realm of innovation policies, nineteenth-century France offers a prime

---

[41] Hirsch (1991).
[42] Gille (1959).
[43] Crouzet (2003).

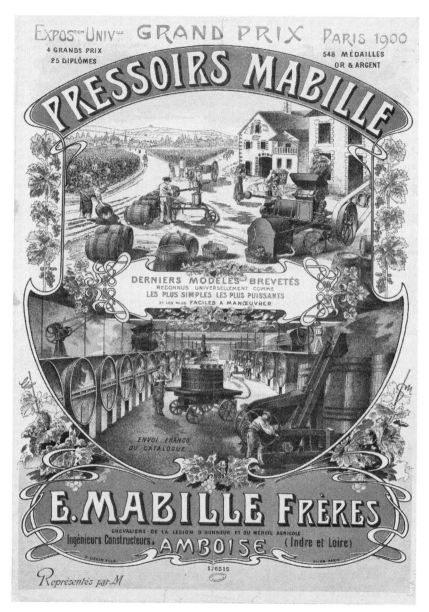

Figure 6.2 Prizes and Commercialization

This company patented commercially successful agricultural presses to make wine, cider, and olive oils. Like many other enterprises, the Mabille brothers were regular exhibitors over the course of several decades who accumulated numerous prizes to advertise and commercialize their patented inventions. By the time of the Universal Exposition of 1900, they had received 548 gold and silver medals, four Grand Prizes, and twenty-five diplomas.

Source: Bibliotheque Nationale, France.

example of a moral economy, where outcomes were related to norms and relationships rather than spontaneous coordination based on price incentives, where returns were aligned with productive risk-taking. The network of administered systems operated under the rubric of encouraging inventors and aiding economic advance; in practice, outcomes favored elites and special interests, created distortions, and skewed resources away from potentially dynamic sectors. The historical record demonstrates the essential inability of bureaucrats to replicate the market mechanism; nevertheless, the conviction that entrepreneurial efforts by administered agencies could improve on economic outcomes has persisted until the present day in modern France.[44]

[44] Casanova and Lévy-Leboyer (1991).

7

Going for Gold

Prizing Innovation

The further consideration of whether prizes are wisely given or not is
one we prefer to leave to our successors.
—*Exhibition Report* (Boston, 1874)

The nineteenth century was an era of marvels that truly qualify for the term
of technological disruption, arguably to a greater extent than today. Unlike in
Europe, growth in the United States was far more balanced, affecting all sectors
and industries in the economy, and transforming all facets of everyday life for
ordinary people and elites alike. As the manufacturing sector grew in economic
importance and innovations increasingly captivated the public, mechanics'
institutes quickly emerged throughout the country. Mechanics' institutes engaged in activities that combined technological innovation, education, and
entertainment. Their broad mandate was to facilitate an industrial enlightenment among the artisanal yeomen who were building the factories, machines,
and products that would generate output and efficiency advances in the coming
decades.

Industrialization in the United States first gained momentum during the
critical period between 1820 and 1840. Those decades were also notable for
the establishment of prominent mechanics' organizations such as the Franklin
Institute of Philadelphia (1824), the Maryland Institute for the Promotion of the
Mechanics' Art (1826), the Ohio Mechanics' Institute of Cincinnati (1828), and
the American Institute of New York (1828). These institutes regularly arranged
specialized exhibitions to display technological inventions and the output
from innovative industries and awarded premiums for the best products and
inventions.[1] As was the case at all exhibitions, whether national or international,

[1] Long before the advent of large-scale international expositions, hundreds of county and state
fairs were held throughout the United States. One of the first significant county fairs was organized
in 1807 in Berkshire, Massachusetts. The New York Agricultural Society and the state of New York
authorized $8,000 annually to promote agriculture and domestic manufactures in an early example
of a recurring state fair. These gatherings were initially devoted to showcasing livestock, fruit and
vegetables, handicrafts, and other farm-related commodities. Local fairs often highlighted domestic (in the sense of household) industry and new machinery that would interest farmers and the

Inventing Ideas. B. Zorina Khan, Oxford University Press (2020). © Oxford University Press.
DOI: 10.1093/oso/9780190936075.001.0001

the vast crowds who attended these exhibitions expected to be astonished and engaged by the wonders that were on display.

Mechanics' institutes quickly diffused beyond the Northeast and Midwest to the Pacific Coast. The Mechanics' Institute of San Francisco (SFMI) was established in 1855 and closely followed the model of its East Coast counterparts. It introduced technical education in California and offered paying members access to a library and to scientific apparatus, as well as night classes and public lectures. Similarly, its annual exhibitions privately benefited the organization by adding to its revenues and reputation. Understandably, they chose instead to publicly highlight how the fairs served "particularly for the business benefit of the exhibitors, and to add to the reputation of their wares." The SFMI was somewhat protectionist in its aims and reserved the most prestigious gold medals for local manufacturers and for West Coast inventions and innovations that had never received any prior recognition. Toward the end of the century, the managers modestly noted that "the past Exhibitions held by the Institute have done more than all other means combined to illustrate the advance in inventions and mechanic arts upon this Coast." The self-interest of any organization that depends on outside donations for its funding dictates an exaggerated and unreliable public self-evaluation, upon which scholars should hesitate to rely. Their internal records, by contrast, offer valuable sources for the objective assessment of the operations of specialized prize-granting panels.

The research in this book uses a triangulation methodology, where comparable criteria for the selection of the data and identical questions and methods are applied to well-defined samples across time and place. The chapters on European policies empirically assessed the role of key institutions that encouraged inventions and how specific incentives worked in practice. The conclusion was that administered innovation systems were elitist, were non–market oriented, and failed to successfully induce useful inventive activity and the diffusion of information. However, it is always possible that these conjectures were affected by unobserved factors that were unique to Europe. We can be more confident about the general conclusions if they were replicated in a completely different context. When compared to the findings from other prize systems in Europe, this chapter provides insights that allow us to draw general inferences about the nature and consequences of administered systems.

---

fair-going public, but technological discoveries were a minor part of the show. State fairs of varying scale sporadically raised funds to reward the best improvements in the diverse categories among the exhibits, including Ohio (1846), Michigan and New Hampshire (1849), Indiana and Wisconsin (1851), Massachusetts and Connecticut (1852), Maine (1856), and Iowa (1857).

The Franklin Institute of Pennsylvania

The Franklin Institute for the Promotion of the Mechanic Arts (FI) was established in 1824 in Philadelphia. This society was the first truly national innovation
organization and is typically regarded as having significantly and successfully
helped the United States on its path to global leadership in technological ingenuity and industrial development. The idea for the institute was realized when
Samuel Vaughan Merrick (1801–1870) wished to acquire knowledge that would
help him to run the foundry he had inherited. He recruited William H. Keating, a
European-trained academic scientist; Alexander Dallas Bache, professor of natural philosophy; and other prominent residents of the city to form the FI. The
historical accounts typically portray the members as "philosopher mechanics,"
whose policies offered effective inducements for technological and scientific discoveries. The *Journal of the Franklin Institute* is acknowledged as an unparalleled
source of scientific and technical information for ordinary inventors throughout
the nation. Scholars highlight its pioneering role as a precursor of government-
funded research and standards setting, as well as facilitating the diffusion of
useful knowledge and the elevation of the working class.

The FI can be compared to European institutions such as the Royal Society of
Arts (RSA), and the assessment across countries is invaluable for determining
the extent to which the individual results owed to local idiosyncrasies or whether
they were endemic to administered systems. Just like the RSA, an image of energetic vibrancy and national importance was assiduously disseminated by the
FI itself, even when the organization was experiencing periodic crises of identity and funding that threatened its existence.[2] Closer examination of the evidence reveals the discrepancies between the public declarations and the actual
outcomes. The declared democratic spirit and boosterism of the humble artisan
actually quickly dissipated, and the FI primarily functioned as a society administered by elites and for elites.

Like its European counterparts, the membership of the FI embodied the
perspective that social and technical elites were responsible for progress.
Membership lists, as well as the records of awards and prizes bestowed, refute
the notion that ordinary artisans were deeply involved in its operations. The first
cadre of officials even referred to themselves with satisfaction as "the Franklin
Institute Clique," and appointments to the executive management positions were
often continued across generations. Potential members had to be proposed by

---

[2] These crises occurred throughout the nineteenth century. The report for 1887 despaired about
the situation at that time and noted the need to clarify its future goals and the possibility of having
to close its doors. The author seemed perplexed that the institute was "doing invaluable work for the
City of Philadelphia and for the world. Yet it is embarrassed in every direction."

an existing member and formally approved by the board of managers. Annual dues ranged from $5 to a lifetime membership fee of $100, at a time when an ordinary laborer would earn about 50 cents for a day's work. It is therefore not surprising that the distribution of occupations of members was quite undemocratic and unrepresentative of the population of innovators. Only 10% of the membership were artisans or workers, and even among these, many were quite well-off. Less than a quarter of the members were employed as mechanics, engineers, or scientists, and they accounted for just 15% of the roster of life members (a proxy for commitment). Instead, the typical member belonged to the elite class of wealthy or aspiring professionals and industrialists.

The proliferation of elite families on the roster indicates the extent to which prize-granting institutions functioned as social clubs for the wealthy and well connected. The social dimension to the FI does not imply that members had no demonstrated connection or interests in technological innovation. For those who did have such interests, however, their attention tended toward abstract questions of science and technology, rather than the concerns of ordinary mechanics and artisans.[3] One of its presidents dismissed the notion that the FI was similar to the mechanics' institutes that were replicating throughout the country "like mushrooms," because it was "constructed on a higher plane." The academic and professional scientists, influential engineers, and wealthy industrialists who made up the administration considered science to be superior to pragmatic technical topics.[4] They evinced some pride in the observation that, whereas the first issue of the house journal had focused on prizes for "such practical purposes as the best stove or grate for burning anthracite," later issues would address weightier topics such as "Spectroscopy and Bohr's Theory of Atomic Structure."

This perceived hierarchy of knowledge affected the orientation of the institute and the efficacy of the administering committees. For instance, FI officials rejected Zebulon Parker's pathbreaking paper on the theory of reaction wheels in turbines, a "disastrous" decision that resulted in "a great loss to millwrights and inventors." The patentee of Parker's waterwheel was untutored in the rhetoric of formal science, and the more established scientists at the FI did not look beyond their disdain for his "vernacular science."[5] In 1850, *Scientific American* published Parker's work, noting that he was the foremost authority on the subject of turbines and hydraulics, and celebrated his unparalleled expertise that was derived from decades of experimentation and landmark patented discoveries.

---

[3] Sinclair (1974) notes that "The Institute was always directed by men who by circumstances of birth or natural endowments had different interests from the majority of those the society presumed to aid."

[4] From another perspective, as late as 1910, only 6% of eminent scientists were occupied in jobs that applied their knowledge for practical ends such as engineering or industry.

[5] Layton (1990).

Some scholars today point to the irony of that era, when practical inventors like Parker, disdained by "true" scientists, were able to make contributions that subsequently led to the most significant scientific discoveries in their field. More systematic insights, however, can be gained from the records of the innovation prize system of the institute.

Franklin Institute Prize System

The University of Pennsylvania library guide to the FI describes its prize system as "America's oldest and most prestigious recognition of achievement in science and technology." The FI was not the first to offer prizes for technological discoveries, either in the colonies or the early Republic, but its awards were certainly greatly valued. As such, it is worthwhile to further investigate the nature and efficacy of this administered innovation system. The records of the FI exhibitions highlight the role of prizes as a means of marketing rather than as incentives or inducement mechanisms, while the decisions of the specialized Committee on Science and the Arts (CSA) illustrate the potential for "social capture" among administrators in repeat interactions.

The FI sponsored a series of exhibitions in the antebellum period, which offered competitive premiums for items on display. The exhibition in April of 1824 was deemed the "first of its kind to be undertaken in this country" (it was not), and the organization's centenary retrospective grandly concluded that "for the encouragement of invention and discovery no method is more efficacious" (it was not). An entrance fee was charged for admission to these events, which was designed to raise revenues and to exclude "indolent and useless persons." Between 1824 and 1858, twenty-six exhibitions were held, but the practice then lapsed, as was generally the case with such events elsewhere in the United States and Europe. After the Civil War, just three expositions were held: a fair to commemorate the semicentennial in 1874, the International Electrical Exhibition of 1884, and the Novelties Exhibition in the following year.

On the occasion of the fiftieth anniversary of the FI, the board of managers effusively declared that it "cannot be denied that much of the general progress of the Mechanic Arts may fairly be attributed" to such exhibitions.[6] Initially, the FI tried to induce inventions by offering premiums for discoveries that the principals in the organization regarded as desirable, but this inducement model quickly failed. For instance, in 1830, thirty-seven premiums were proposed for

---

[6] *Journal of the Franklin Institute* 97 (1874): 438.

Figure 7.1 Franklin Institute Exhibitions
Like the majority of prize-granting institutions, the Franklin Institute lost its
enthusiasm for innovation awards over the course of the nineteenth century. This
electrical exhibition was one of the last such events that they organized.
Source: Library of Congress.

specified inventions, but only three of these were successfully awarded, and the
following year only fifteen of the proposed eighty-nine ex ante premiums were
awarded. After 1838, the institute completely abandoned the notion of directing
the path of inventive activity and simply offered ex post prizes for the items that
inventors and manufacturers submitted for consideration.[7] Despite the failure of
the inducement strategy, the institute still remained confident that "the honor of
possessing these tokens of achievement without doubt has been a strong incentive to useful research, and the cause of many notable and useful discoveries and
inventions."

The practice of holding exhibitions faltered in part because of numerous
problems with the administration of the prize system. Internal controversies continually surfaced, and early questions were raised about the utility of such awards

---

[7] "In the earlier Exhibitions held by the Franklin Institute, a list of premiums offered was published
beforehand, but experience proved that many of the Medals were neither earned nor awarded, while
the acknowledged excellence or novelty of other articles exhibited, compelled the award of Medals
which had not been proposed. The plan was therefore definitely abandoned in 1838," *Journal of the
Franklin Institute* 97 (1874): 439.

and whether it was efficient to divert the organization's resources to efforts that often fell short of the aim to promote valuable technological discoveries. The report of the board of managers in 1838 speculated whether "the energies of the institute have become too valuable to be expended in getting up a mere idle pageant." At the same time, observers and participants were critical about the objectivity and capacity of the judges, and unsuccessful competitors protested vociferously. In response, the institute boosted the proportion of submissions to which prizes were awarded, reducing the effectiveness of the signal. Again, this inflation over time in prizes is consistent with patterns in other domestic exhibitions, as well as in Britain and France.

The criteria for the allocation of prizes at the FI exhibitions differed significantly from those for the grant of patents (Table 7.1). Patent systems are based on transparent legal rules that determine whether or not a patent will issue, examiners are professionals who specialize in the issuing of patents, and the examiner's decision is subject to internal and external review. By contrast, in administered systems, decentralized and secretive decision making by different

Table 7.1 Franklin Institute Exhibitions, 1840–1874 (Percentages)

	Antebellum	Postbellum	All
Resident of Pennsylvania	79.3	50.0	77.7
Female	3.6	1.2	2.9
Firms	25.6	60.0	34.9
Award granted	48.7	68.1	55.3
Judging (reasons for decision)			
Appearance/workmanship	82.9	71.4	80.1
Utility	6.8	10.1	7.6
Novelty/improvement	8.4	20.9	11.5
Cheapness	1.0	2.1	1.2
Comparable to imports	4.0	0.8	3.2
Total number of observations	2,298	868	3,166

Notes and Sources: *Records of the Committee of Science and Arts, Franklin Institute, 1824–1900; Reports of the Annual Exhibitions of the Franklin Institute* (various years). The data on applicants were matched to the federal manuscript population censuses to obtain information on residence, occupation, wealth, birthplace, and age. Patent matches were obtained from the files of the U.S. Patent Office. The percentages are calculated relative to total nonmissing observations for each variable. Unsuccessful entries refer to exhibits that did not win any prizes. Exhibition prizes include cash awards, medals (gold, silver, bronze), and certificates of merit. The reasons for decisions (granting or not granting a prize) are not mutually exclusive.

groups of judges was likely to lead to inconsistencies, especially if there was no right of appeal. Judges primarily considered the aesthetic characteristics of the entries, giving out more than 80% of the awards because of superior workmanship or beauty. Only 11% of premiums were evaluated in terms of novelty or because they were regarded as an improvement over the existing standard. The focus on visual aspects of exhibits occurred because—as they candidly admitted—the committees often were incapable of adequately evaluating the technical or substantive merits of the exhibits. At the twenty-seventh exhibition of the FI, G. Boyd of Philadelphia was awarded a medal, even though the committee confessed they did not "think themselves competent to judge of the machinery." Some judges declined to make any determination of the relative merits and all of the exhibits were given equal recognition, while some deferred the decision to the CSA.

Committee on Science and the Arts

The CSA was the most influential group at the Franklin Institute. The panel's main mandate was to administer the innovation prize system. An FI public retrospective boldly declared that "it is no exaggeration to claim that there exists nowhere—either at home or abroad— . . . any organization more directly useful in its aims and more actively helpful in its work, than this committee." The institute's internal records, however, noted that "when we consider the prolific genius of America, and read a list of the patented and other inventions for any one year, your Committee feel surprise that this fund should be so little known, or that so few persons should claim from it an honorary or pecuniary reward."[8] Between 1825 and 1900, the CSA examined 2,200 case files from applicants (in some instances, there were several files for the same discovery) and distributed approximately 850 prizes. By way of comparison, about 700,000 patents had been issued over the same period.

The FI administered a number of prestigious annual cash prizes and medals that were conceived and financed through private philanthropy. The John Scott Legacy Award was established in 1816 by a mysterious $4,000 bequest from an Edinburgh chemist (who had never visited the United States), "to be distributed among ingenious men or women, who make useful inventions." However, even the Scott Award was "usually for devices of limited application and simple basic principles rather than for work which involved fundamental discoveries."[9] The Elliott Cresson Medal, funded by an endowment of $1,000 in 1848, recognized

---

[8] *Report of the Committee*, April 27, 1837.
[9] Fox (1968).

original research or inventions, including products embodying excellence in workmanship. The Longstreth Award offered medals and cash payments that were donated by a former employee of the Baldwin Locomotive Company and was bestowed for a wide range of activities including journal articles and scientific or artistic works. The most esteemed medals were not inducements for future work but recognized already well-known celebrities like Ernest Rutherford, Emile Berliner, Nikola Tesla, Elihu Thomson, and Gugliemo Marconi.

The Boyden Prize illustrates the idiosyncrasies that can emerge when rewards are dictated by the concerns of wealthy philanthropists rather than by more decentralized and demand-driven sources. The famous patentee Uriah Boyden (1804–1879) donated $1,000 in 1859 for the specific objective of rewarding meritorious experiments to discover the velocity of infrared rays and other types of invisible light rays, a subject that he personally regarded as highly important.[10] Boyden expected that the award would immediately prompt research that would result in the prize being awarded within the year. However, more than half a century had elapsed before it was bestowed for the first time. Just two dozen entries were submitted over this entire period, and they were all regarded to be of too poor quality to merit any award.

During the first century of its existence, both the membership and prize system of the FI were predominantly local rather than national in scope, and the majority of the participants lived in, or close to, Philadelphia (Table 7.2). The organization proclaimed the "democratic character which has always been its distinguishing mark," but participants in the prize system were primarily drawn from the wealthy or privileged classes, as gauged by financial resources and occupations. Scientists, technically trained engineers and machinists, prosperous industrialists, and wealthy professionals dominated the roster of recipients. The personal and real estate wealth of these individuals was far in excess of the norm, and the average rose over time. The number of artisans or workers who were ever considered for prizes was nominal and increased from a mere 8.3% to just over 14%.

The Scott Legacy Award was explicitly intended to benefit "ingenious men or women," but prize winners were overwhelmingly male, and no woman was recognized with an award of any sort in the antebellum period.[11] The website

---

[10] Boyden was a successful inventor whose patents were assigned to numerous mills and manufacturing enterprises, including the Lowell Machine Shop, Great Falls Manufacturing Company, Amoskeag Manufacturing Company, and Merrimack Manufacturing Company. He possessed a practical, imaginative, and curious mind; read widely in English, French, and German; and investigated a breathtaking range of interests in meteorology, chemistry, physics, and social questions.

[11] Women provided large bequests that made up a significant source of funding for the institute over the years. Apart from their role as generous donors, they were noticeably absent in all other spheres, at a time when patent records showed that innovative women were surging into markets for entrepreneurship and invention. In 1875, just six women were members—four decades later the number had surged to a grand total of ten—as part of privileged family groups who all belonged to

Table 7.2 Membership in the Franklin Institute

	Number	Percent
Occupation		
Artisans and workers	159	10.5
Engineers	143	9.5
Machinists	170	11.3
Scientists	46	3.1
Manufacturers	370	24.5
Merchants/commerce	164	10.9
White collar/professional	454	30.1
Women	6	0.5
Life member	526	28.8
Pennsylvania resident	1,765	96.8

Notes and Sources: Membership information was determined from records of the Franklin Institute in 1875.

of the FI currently prominently profiles Catherine Louise Gibbon (1852–1893), who received a Scott medal in 1892, for her improvements in the construction of street railway tracks. Catherine Gibbon obtained two patents on railway tracks in 1890 and was a coinventor on two additional patents with her husband in 1891. Thomas H. Gibbon, a civil engineer who emigrated from England, had obtained several related patents in the previous decade. His boltless rail fastener was regarded as a marked advance in this technology, reducing operating costs by as much as 50%, and his firm, the Gibbon Boltless Rail Joint Company, produced this patented innovation in Albany, New York. Thomas Gibbon's rail fastener was awarded a silver medal at a Chicago exhibition in 1885, but his submission to the FI in the same year was unsuccessful.

Catherine Gibbon was one of just five women inventors who received awards from the CSA over the entire nineteenth century, and it is not clear that any of

the FI. Jane Reuben Haines (1832–1911), who came from one of the oldest families in Philadelphia, was an extremely wealthy single woman without any profession. Lydia Holman, another wealthy woman, was related to D. Shepherd Holman, actuary of the institute. Harriet Judd Sartain (1830–1923), a trained homeopathic physician, belonged to the socially prominent Sartain clan, which included her husband, Samuel; his brothers; and their father, John Sartain, all of whom were lifetime members of the institute.

them benefited greatly from the honor. Elizabeth White Stiles, a Vermont-born inventor with three patents, was the most well known of these female laureates largely because of her own business acumen. *Arthur's Illustrated Home Magazine* declared in its 1877 full-length feature that "Mrs. Stiles's success in a business way has been most remarkable of all." She patented her 1875 "improvement in reading and writing desks" and promptly sent it off to the exhibition of the American Institute of New York, where it was heartily commended and awarded a silver medal. She then participated in the 1876 Centennial Exhibition in Philadelphia, using innovative marketing techniques, and her combination desk was singled out as one of the most ingenious designs at the event. Her inkstand invention won a silver medal at the fourteenth exhibition of the Massachusetts Mechanics' Institute in 1881, and the judges expansively noted that "these inkstands seem to be well adapted for use on shipboard, on railway trains, in offices, in the school-room, and in fact wherever the use of ink is required." Stiles was flooded with investment offers and was able to launch her own firm, E. W. Stiles and Co., in Hartford, Connecticut. She was one of the few women to obtain a government contract to furnish federal offices in Washington, DC with her patented desks. An assiduous promoter and clever entrepreneur, Stiles would have succeeded even without the 1876 commendation from the FI, which was just one of the many accolades she secured.

The CSA kept records that explained the reasons for its decisions about the bestowal of awards (Table 7.3). Most reports by the judges cited novelty or improvements over the existing arts as grounds for rejecting or accepting an application, although this criterion was neither necessary nor sufficient for success. Since there was no formal process for examination of the prior arts, the determination of novelty was largely a function of the opinions of the relevant panel, who were not necessarily specialists in the subject. Fifteen percent of medals were bestowed because of appearance ("conspicuous beauty") and workmanship, and a further 11% were granted because it was estimated that the item would be economical to make or cheaper to sell in the market. More than a third of the assessments were based on the utility or usefulness of the innovation, as perceived by the members of the committee.

As might be expected, judges encountered greater difficulty in accurately determining the merits of new processes. When Victor Gustave Bloede submitted his new method to treat dyed fabric, the CSA subcommittee reported in 1896 that they regarded "his process in no respect superior to that already in use." Bloede was outraged and contacted William Wahl, the president of the FI. He complained that he would not object to adverse comments from intelligent and conscientious critics, but the CSA judges had "failed to grasp the essential features of the invention." Although this might be dismissed as the rantings of a disgruntled applicant, Bloede was one of the leading manufacturing chemists in the country, with

Table 7.3 Administration of Innovation Prizes at the Franklin Institute, 1824–1900

Committee on Science and the Arts		
	1824–1864	1865–1900
Award granted (percent)	51.6	65.6
Applicants for Awards		
Female (percent)	0	1.2
Foreign born (percent)	10.3	29.7
Age (average)	43.2	43.7
Real estate wealth (average)	$16,304	$12,785
Personal wealth (average)	$4,307	$13,838
Occupation of Applicants (percent)		
Scientists, engineers, machinists	41.1	45.3
White collar, professional	22.8	17.5
Manufacturers, merchants	25.5	18.9
Artisans and workers	8.3	14.6
None, other	2.3	3.7
Residence of Applicants (percent)		
Pennsylvania	68.0	52.1
Other Mid-Atlantic	14.5	20.5
New England	7.3	8.0
Midwest	3.8	8.0
South (incl. DC)	5.8	4.51
Foreign	0.4	5.8
Judging (reasons for decision, percent)		
Appearance/workmanship	15.0	16.9
Utility	38.0	31.0
Novelty/improvement	54.1	71.0
Cheapness	11.2	11.5

(*Continued*)

Table 7.3 *Continued*

	1824–1864	1865–1900
Patenting		
Patentees (percent)	16.8	37.8
Number of patents (average)	1.7	6.4
Assignments of patent (percent)	5.3	42.8
Attorney assisted (percent)	7.7	85.0
Coinventors (percent)	12.9	20.5
Citations (average)	1.6	3.2
Subject Matter of Patents (percent)		
Engines, energy and power	18.5	28.2
Household articles	16.6	15.1
Manufacturing	15.2	12.2
Chemistry and science	5.5	5.5
Tools and instruments	13.3	14.0
Transportation	25.4	17.0
Miscellaneous	5.4	8.0
Total cases	793	1,377

Notes and Sources: See notes to Table 7.2.

a quarter of a century of experience. His innovative methods were recognized by dozens of commercially successful patents (his first patented invention was sold at age eighteen) and numerous medals from international expositions; in fact, just two years before, he had been the recipient of the institute's Longstreth Medal.

Possession of a patent did not disqualify the inventor from obtaining awards from the institute, and many of the inventions submitted had previously been patented. Among FI candidates, the inventors who could be identified as patentees held more than 3,800 patents. The subject matter of patented inventions before the CSA was markedly narrower than that of the general population of patents or that of valuable inventions. More than half of the patented entries submitted for prizes related to capital-intensive innovations in transportation, power, and engines. In the antebellum period, few of these patents were assigned (a proxy for success in the marketplace), and the likelihood of citations from later patents (a proxy for technical value) was similarly low. The prize system of the FI therefore mirrors its counterparts in other countries; it failed to induce important discoveries and mainly offered marketing benefits for manufacturers and publicity for inventors.

Governance and Administered Systems

Administered systems like the prize-granting FI incurred time and monetary costs. It is worth noting that, as in many such institutions, the costs of administering the awards typically exceeded the amount that was actually given out to prize winners. As mentioned before, members paid a subscription fee, and some even owned shares in the FI corporation. Part of the return to membership was in the form of reputation and networking. The CSA initially included forty volunteers, and consideration of particular applications was delegated to subcommittees. The groups that examined each submission ranged from one to a dozen members, but the average was approximately three judges. The whole CSA met once a month except during the summer, and they socialized and enjoyed a fine dinner before settling down to business. Questions were increasingly raised about the competency of volunteers to assess specialized technologies, and as a result, after 1886 members were elected to the judging committee.

The case files and deliberations of the committee were confidential, and all records were sealed until fifty years after the decision. Empirical analysis of the identities of CSA judges, members of the institute, and prize winners raises questions about governance, especially when there is no formal right of appeal or other feedback mechanisms (Table 7.4). The CSA could not bestow an award on one of its sitting members, but there was no prohibition on applying for a prize once the individual had rotated off the panel. The information collected was limited to the first two judges on each committee and the roster of members in 1875 and 1880, so it is not possible to determine the insider status of all of the prize applicants. However, even this truncated information shows a significant relationship between prize awards and affiliation with the FI. Over 22% of prizes were secured by insiders, and over a fifth of award winners were members of the FI. Statistical estimations of the likelihood of getting an award and a positive decision show that insiders had a marked advantage over outsiders. For members of the FI, insider status translated into a higher probability of securing an award for themselves, holding other factors constant.

Numerous presidents and members of the executive board of managers were in-house recipients of accolades awarded by the FI. Cyprien Chabot (1824–1889), for instance, was one of the FI's "most energetic and capable members," who served on the management board and was also very actively involved on

Table 7.4 Franklin Institute: Governance and Allocation of Prizes, 1824–1900

Applicants	TOTAL		PRIZE WINNERS		REJECTIONS	
	Number	%	Number	%	Number	%
Total cases	1,416	100	861	60.8	555	39.2
Affiliates of Institute	259	18.3	190	22.1	69	12.4
Franklin Institute member	239	16.9	175	20.3	64	11.6
Lifetime member	52	3.7	40	4.7	12	2.2
Executive	77	5.4	59	6.9	18	3.2
Member of judging panel	159	11.2	116	13.5	43	7.8
Occupation						
Scientists, engineers, machinists	252	43.1	177	46.2	75	47.3
White collar, professional	100	17.1	60	15.7	40	19.9
Manufacturers, merchants	153	26.2	100	26.1	53	23.7
Artisans and workers	64	11	37	9.7	27	13.4
None, other	15	2.6	9	2.4	6	3
Patentees	458	32.4	310	36	148	26.7

Notes and Sources: See notes to Table 7.2. Membership was determined by records for 1875 and 1880. "Member of judging panel" includes the first two judges on each prize committee.

the CSA. Membership allowed him entrée into an influential network, and he was also able to benefit from the society's awards. He received numerous prizes from the FI for his patented watchmaking and shoe-sewing machine inventions, including both the Scott Medal and the Cresson Premium in 1885. Among the multiple prize winners were William Wahl (secretary of the FI), Matthias Baldwin (president of the FI and founder of the Baldwin Company), and Samuel Vauclain (president of the Baldwin Company and a member of the FI).

Families and corporate associates also benefited through connections with influential members of the institute. The Tatham Brothers Company was founded as a partnership among five brothers, and the firm became a successful and innovative manufacturer of lead pipe in Philadelphia and New York. William Penn

Tatham (1820–1899) joined the FI in 1850 and served almost continuously as an executive administrator, including president of the institute from 1879 to 1886 and vice president from 1888 to 1897. William Tatham received the Cresson Premium in 1875 while he was on the FI governing board of managers. In the same year, his brother Benjamin Tatham, who ran the New York branch of the firm, received an award from the institute for his patented elevator safety catch invention. The Women's School of Design, which was initially affiliated with the institute, was administered for over three generations by lifetime FI member John Sartain, followed by his daughter, and then by his granddaughter.

The Boyden Premium to determine the velocity of light rays was not given out until 1907 and, over the subsequent fifty years, the prize was awarded to just two more recipients. The first winner was Paul Renno Heyl, a high school teacher whose study did not entirely satisfy the stated criteria of the award. Paul Heyl was the son of a revered member of the FI, Henry Renno Heyl (1842–1919). Heyl Sr. had served as vice president of the institute, and was also appointed as the chair of the CSA. Henry Heyl himself also received two awards, including the prestigious Scott Prize, during his tenure at the institute. As leaders of Philadelphia's industrial and social elite, it is not wholly surprising that insiders at the FI should have deemed their own families worthy of such recognition.

A central part of any administered system is the process that leads to key decisions and outcomes. Subcommittees on the CSA were not allowed to blatantly give themselves a premium, and the preferential outcomes might have owed more to cognitive dissonance than to outright corruption. Moreover, insiders had access to privileged information about implicit norms and practices that would lead to more favorable reviews of their applications. More troubling is the operation of what may be regarded as "social capture." Social capture occurs when a panel's current decisions are unduly influenced by the expectation that individuals who are under consideration today will likely be in the position in the future to make decisions that will affect the welfare of members of the present panel. None of this necessarily implies that such individuals were undeserving, but it does point to the fact that nonmembers who were equally (or perhaps even more) deserving were relatively disadvantaged in any such system.

The Franklin Institute: Beyond Prizes

Like its counterparts elsewhere, the FI proved unable, and acknowledged its inability, to successfully induce inventive activity. As such, the most significant contributions of the institute were not its attempts to influence the path of technological innovation but rather its policies to enhance learning and the dissemination of useful knowledge. Committees prepared treatises and policy proposals regarding water power, the strength of materials, uniformity in weights and measures, meteorological observations, standardization in screw threads, and electrical products. They received an award of $2,000 to investigate the explosion of steam boilers from the Treasury Department, an early example of government funding for research. This meticulous and balanced inquiry was widely cited, even though it did not immediately influence government policy. The pedagogical efforts of the organization contributed to practical and technical education, and between 1824 and 1908, over fourteen thousand individuals benefited from lectures and classes offered by the FI.

The colonial and antebellum eras were rife with curiosity about the natural world and about the underlying principles behind the discoveries that were transforming daily life. This burgeoning interest in technical topics was met by exponential growth in coverage by general and specialized newspapers, magazines, books, and lectures, in Europe and in the United States.[12] The *Journal of the Franklin Institute* was first launched in 1826, and annual subscription to this monthly publication cost $5, a price that was significantly out of reach of any ordinary worker. Subscriptions were typically paid by libraries and other learned organizations and by wealthier or privileged individuals. Indeed, only about 6% of the members of the FI actually subscribed to the journal, and the total number of subscribers was between one and two thousand. By way of contrast, *Scientific American* was published every week at an annual price of just $2, and the topics were (despite the name) more germane to the needs of the pragmatic mechanic and patentee. So it is not surprising that the total number of subscriptions to *Scientific American* rapidly grew to fourteen thousand in 1850, and this magazine played an unparalleled role in the dissemination of technological information.

The Massachusetts Mechanics' Association

Like the FI in Philadelphia, the Massachusetts Mechanics' Association (MMA) of Boston sponsored innovation prizes that firms and entrepreneurs competed to accumulate. "Who has been? or mayhap the question may be more properly put, Who has not been? during the past month, to the Exhibition of

---

[12] In the United States more than 10,000 weekly and 1,350 monthly publications about science and technology were being published. Early publications include the *American Review* (1801), *American Medical and Philosophical Register* (1810), *Repository of Useful Knowledge* (1816), *North American Review* (1815), and Benjamin Silliman's popular *American Journal of Science* (1818). Medical journals included the *New England Journal of Medicine* (1828), as well as hundreds of specialized publications for a range of subjects from pharmacy to insanity to phrenology. Similarly, trade magazines were devoted to the concerns of millers, manufacturers, machinists, railroad workers, and other professions and industries, and over seventy agricultural journals were in circulation before the 1850s. Cantor and Shuttleworth (2004).

the Massachusetts Charitable Mechanic Association," gushed a reporter in nineteenth-century Boston.[13] The MMA was founded in 1795 as an initiative of prominent local artisans, and Paul Revere was its first president. The first of the regularly recurring exhibitions had taken place in the autumn of 1837, and the eminent statesman Edward Everett delivered the keynote opening speech. Everett had notably presented a two-hour marathon oration that preceded Abraham Lincoln's two-minute Gettysburg Address, and his performance on this occasion was equally impressive (the "hastily thrown together" speech ran to some twenty-four pages). He praised the thousands of articles displayed, which reflected credit on the improvers and inventors of the region, and testified to the vast importance of the mechanical arts. Other human faculties "sink to nothing compared with . . . the necromancy of the creative machinist." Among such a wealth of inventive talent, it would be a difficult task to decide how to award the prizes for the best exhibits. Everett ended on a rousingly optimistic note, exhorting his audience to recall that "however vast the space measured behind, the space before is immeasurable; and though the mind may estimate the progress it has made, the boldest stretch of its powers is inadequate to measure the progress of which it is capable."

According to its organizers, MMA industrial fairs were noted for offering

> the best specimens of American ingenuity and skill, in every branch of mechanics, rare and valuable productions natural and artificial, labor-saving machines, implements of husbandry, and models of machinery in all their variety, and for superior workmanship in all useful and ornamental branches of the arts, including the beautiful and delicate handiwork of females.

Gold medals were granted "only for very valuable and meritorious inventions or improvements," and silver medals for entries that showed excellence in workmanship, new applications, or significant improvements. In addition, bronze medals and diplomas were bestowed on other articles deserving notice.

As in all exhibitions, the MMA wished to recoup its outlays on the exhibition by boosting attendance, an objective that necessarily had implications for the selection of exhibits and their evaluation by the admission committees and juries. The first exhibition in 1837 proved to be enormously popular and, what is more, profitable, encouraging the organizers to hold them on a regular basis. Figure 7.3 itemizes the total receipts, expenditures, and profits for each of these events. The earliest exhibitions were held in Faneuil and Quincy Halls in Boston, but the association later acquired its own dedicated building on Huntington

---

[13] *The Repository* 51 (1874): 396.

Figure 7.2 Massachusetts Exhibition and Prize Medals

New England was the center of early manufacturing and inventive activity, and that technological vibrancy was reflected in the industrial fairs of this prominent mechanics' institute.

Source: Annual Report of the Association.

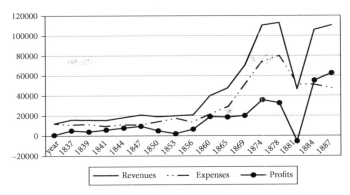

Figure 7.3 Net Income from the Massachusetts Exhibitions, 1837–1890

Source: Massachusetts Charitable Mechanic Association, *Annals of the Massachusetts Charitable Mechanics Association, 1795–1892*, 1892.

Avenue, conveniently close to major transportation arteries. At the second exhibition in 1839, the two-week event attracted some 70,000 visitors, at a time when the population of Boston was approximately 93,000 residents. This fair included 1,196 exhibits, which were awarded 25 gold medals, 133 silver medals, and 254 diplomas. By 1890, the halls displayed the efforts of 1,300 exhibitors, and the medals included 55 of gold, 175 of silver, and 144 of bronze, along with 235 diplomas. The 1890 fair ran for two months, and total attendance was estimated at 500,000, about the same as the population of the town. The organizers discouraged itinerant traders to ensure that the exhibition represented the "latest and best in our industrial life, and not a bazaar for the sale of merchandise."[14]

As discussed before, a system that offers greater accolades to elites has different implications for economic prospects than one that promises rewards will accrue to the most productive. The increase in inventive activity during the antebellum era was generated by an influx of individuals with little prior experience at technological innovation. Patent rights accrued to artisans (approximately one-third) and manufacturers (21%), whereas the elite social class of merchants, professionals, and white-collar workers decreased over time. The importance of more technically qualified machinists and engineers grew substantially after the middle of the nineteenth century, but such skills were hardly necessary even for significant discoveries, as studies of the "great inventors" show. The most valuable inventions of the time, such as Thomas Blanchard's woodworking lathe or Cyrus McCormick's reaper, were typically based on commonly available information

[14] *Annual Report, MMA* (1892), p. 11.

applied to a bottleneck or specific practical problem that the inventor encountered on the job. Great inventors who made significant contributions to productivity growth and economic progress also came from a diverse range of occupations and socioeconomic backgrounds.

Unlike the patent system, the participants in the FI's prize system belonged to the wealthy or well-connected classes, and this pattern was repeated in the MMA. A key mandate of the association was to assist innovative workers and artisans, and diplomas of the exhibition featured an illustration of "a procession of artisans" presenting their inventions as candidates for prizes. Nevertheless, Figure 7.4 shows that participants in the fairs were drawn from more prominent occupations than the general population of patentees. Indeed, even though the exhibition estimates exclude the category of firms from the analysis, prize

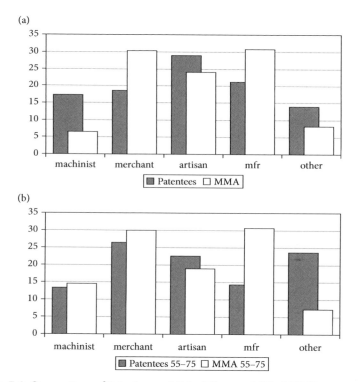

Figure 7.4 Occupations of Patentees and Prize Winners, 1835–1875 (Percentages) (a) Occupations 1835–1850. (b) Occupations 1855–1875.

Notes and Sources: Occupations were obtained from census matches. The Massachusetts Mechanics' Association sample of prize winners was matched with the manuscript population census that was closest to the date of the exhibition.

winners were less likely than patentees to be artisans and ordinary laborers. The participation of artisans at the exhibitions also declined over time: over 24% of those who participated at the fairs before 1855 were artisans, compared to 18.5% after this period. It was, of course, likely that the innovations firms displayed were created by artisans in their employment. However, the point is that, when appropriating returns on their own account, inventors without social backing were more likely to turn to the patent system than to try for prizes. At the same time, it is true that occupational class does not directly translate into economic or social status or influence, as witnessed by the institute's founder, Paul Revere. For this, we turn to the records on wealth holding in the federal population censuses of 1850, 1860, and 1870.

The information on wealth allows us to more directly assess the economic status of exhibitors relative to patentees in general. The white male population owned an average of $2,230 and $2,140 in real estate in 1860 and 1870, respectively, and approximately $1,550 and $970 in personal property over the same period. About 57% of white men in 1860 possessed no real estate wealth, and 43% owned no personal estate, a pattern that was maintained in 1870.[15] My own estimates indicate that, on the eve of the outbreak of war, poor patentees were on average rather like the general population, and over half of all such inventors held no real estate, while over a third recorded no personal wealth. Poor inventors were more likely to sell off the rights to their patents, so it is not surprising that the assets of many of these formerly impecunious patent inventors increased over the decade. Patentees in general experienced greater upward economic mobility than the American population.

Like their FI counterparts, the participants in the Massachusetts exhibitions were substantially wealthier than the general population. Recall that these data do not include information on corporations and companies whose owners could not be identified, which is likely to significantly bias the estimates of property holding downward. Forty-six percent of the exhibitors owned no real estate, and 32% had no personal property. A number of patentees were exceptionally wealthy for this era, owing to the success of their innovations in the market. Edward H. Ashcroft, who possessed $150,000 in real estate and $20,000 in personal property in 1870, was the inventor of twelve technically and commercially valuable steam engine patents, which are still cited in patent applications today. Nevertheless, Figure 7.5 illustrates how the assets of the exhibitors significantly exceeded that of the sample of general patentees. In 1860, the MMA sample owned twice more average personal property than the patentees, and more than double their average real estate holdings.

---

[15] Soltow (1975).

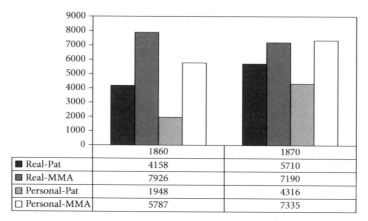

	1860	1870
■ Real-Pat	4158	5710
▨ Real-MMA	7926	7190
▨ Personal-Pat	1948	4316
□ Personal-MMA	5787	7335

Figure 7.5 Real and Personal Wealth of Patentees and Prize Winners, 1860 and 1870

Notes and Sources: The Massachusetts Mechanics' Association sample was matched with the
manuscript census that was closest to the date of the exhibition. This resulted in 404 matches for
1860 and 329 matches for 1870, over which these averages for real estate and personal wealth were
estimated. Missing values are treated as zero. Wealth is expressed in terms of real 1860 dollars.

What were the factors that influenced patenting and prizes in Massachusetts?
A significant fraction of the variation in patenting activity in the general population owed to economic factors including access to markets and expected profit
opportunities; in fact, we can identify the reasons for over two-thirds of the total
variation in patenting. However, the results are dramatically different when one
tries to ascertain whether an exhibit would receive a gold or silver medal. At the
exhibitions of the MMA, statistical analysis of factors influencing the award of
gold medals alone had zero explanatory power. Similarly, most of the variation in
the silver or gold awards together also remains unexplained.

Amid this welter of null results, two findings stand out. The first is that women
were less likely to receive the highest accolades at the exhibitions. The second
is striking: exhibitors with greater personal wealth experienced a greater probability of winning gold and silver medals. However, the mechanism through
which wealthier exhibitors gained an edge over their competition is unclear.
The finding could be due to greater expenditures on their presentation at the
fairs, or to a noncausal correlation whereby more innovative and deserving
entrepreneurs also tended to be richer. A more speculative interpretation is that
judges were unable to accurately distinguish the quality of entries and used the
standing or reputation of the applicant as a signal.

The use of such proxies was not always effective in identifying worthy entries.
The 1860 portfolio of iron-founder Amos Chafee Barstow (1813–1894) included
$288,500 in real estate and $151,500 in personal goods, and he employed four

servants in his home. Barstow was a stove manufacturer and proprietor of the Barstow Stove Company on Point Street in Providence, Rhode Island, and he was appointed as mayor of the city in 1852 and Speaker of the House in 1870. A capable inventor who specialized in cooking appliances, Barstow devised and patented some eight successful inventions. The improvement in stoves that he patented in 1873 was awarded the Grand Medal of Merit at the 1873 Vienna World's Fair, but at the MMA exhibition of 1874 this innovation only received a bronze medal. Such discrepancies in the allocation of prizes leads to speculation about the determinants of technological awards.

The allocation of prizes for the most part consists of what statisticians term "noise," or random variance. Such variables as occupation and industrial classification had little influence on the award of the MMA medals. We might expect that machinists and engineers would be responsible for more technologically advanced discoveries, but in fact their technical abilities did not give them any advantage over unskilled exhibitors. Patent assignments are a proxy for commercially successful inventions, but they were similarly unrelated to the likelihood of a medal. Urbanization is associated with higher productivity at invention, but adding cities does not offer any additional explanatory power. As the summary statistics showed, medals were awarded uniformly across technology and industry classes, and similarly, industry effects are minimal. Since it is quite unlikely that (say) handmade furniture was as technologically creative as communications or transportation inventions, it is clear that medals did not accurately reflect inventiveness, industrial productivity, or technological innovation.

The idiosyncrasies of such administered awards are reflected in the experiences of talented inventors like Isaac W. Lamb. Lamb obtained his first patent at age nineteen, and several of his important patented improvements are still incorporated into knitting machines today. At the Paris World's Fair of 1867, his invention was awarded the silver medal, and he later established knitting factories in Europe that employed his internationally patented technology. However, at the 1869 exhibition of the MMA, his knitting machine only received a common bronze medal. On the other hand, John O'Neil's 1852 patent application was rejected for want of novelty, but the churn he exhibited at the MMA still received a prize. Judges bestowed awards on the New York Safety Steam Power Co.'s vertical engines ("we know of no distinctive feature in this engine that calls for particular mention"), Charles Wardwell's Wood Planing Machines and Blind Slat Planer ("there is nothing new or novel in their construction"), and George Cavanagh's machines ("neatly made" but "we think it would be very liable to get out of order").

The judging committees stated their objective was to reward novelty and inventive ingenuity, but in practice they bestowed medals for an array of other reasons besides inventiveness, ranging from good workmanship and cheapness of the item to neatness and aesthetic factors. Sympathetic juries also allocated prizes to craftsmen who had overcome personal adversity and other deserving cases based on personal characteristics, in an echo of the French handouts to inventors with large families, neat households, and well-brought-up children. In one amusing example, Mrs. Rebecca H. Christians, domiciled at 10 Tyler Street, Boston, Massachusetts, received a bronze medal for "One Quilt, one Baby Quilt.—Made by a lady one hundred and two years old, without glasses." The prize committee then added a demurrer: "Crazy quilts and patchwork, when made by elderly women or invalids, should receive just commendation; in all other cases, the occupation is an entire waste of time, and should be discouraged."

The juries that awarded prizes included "gentlemen of character and standing, and as far as is practicable of thorough technical knowledge of their respective subjects . . . who will in no case be competitors for premiums."[16] Although they did not compete in the particular exhibition for which they were appointed as judges, many of the judges and trustees of the MMA did participate in exhibitions in other years, so there was a repeated-game element that had the potential for unconscious or explicit bias in the awards. The lack of transparency and private nature of their decision-making process and the absence of appeal from their rulings encouraged idiosyncratic and inconsistent decisions, echoing the findings from the FI. In addition, just as in Europe, a mercantilist orientation was evident in awards for American products that equaled foreign innovations. It is therefore not surprising that observers continually (and sometimes bitterly) criticized the lack of "a methodical, systematic, and intelligent basis" for the awards.

The managers of the 1874 exhibition pointed to

> the necessity of a uniform standard of merit for rewards should prizes continue to be given. . . . In the past, each set of Judges has fixed its own standard of awards, and as a consequence some have been rigidly exacting in the qualities of usefulness and originality, while others have been profuse and generous, touched by sympathy or good-fellowship; others, again, have asked the question whether their Department was receiving its full share of the higher awards, as though the bestowal, not the merit, was the consideration influencing them.[17]

The analysis in this chapter is likewise consistent with the notion that "the bestowal, not the merit," was indeed the consideration. Almost two decades later, the same criticisms were still being repeated:

---

[16] Massachusetts Charitable Mechanic Association, *The Exhibition and Fair in the City of Boston*, September 18, 1837.
[17] *Report of the MMA Exhibition* (1874), p. vii.

If any radical change is needed in connection with our exhibitions, I think it should be in the method of bestowing the medals. Each committee is now almost the sole judges of awards. They establish their own standard of excellence for goods, and bestow medals accordingly. Some are conservative in their estimate of merit, while others are found to be generous. The result is a great disparity in the significance of the award.[18]

The 1874 MMA report declared "there is no doubt" that awards at the exhibitions provided "an incentive and stimulus to the best effort." This chapter has shown that, even in a regularly occurring series of events overseen by one institution, the allocation of prizes was idiosyncratic and related to attempts to commercialize innovations. In none of these institutions did technological prizes serve as effective incentives for inventive activity. Despite their grandiose public claims, both the FI and the MMA abandoned their fruitless attempts to induce particular inventions. To assuage conflicts and controversies about the justice of decisions, more awards were distributed, reducing their effectiveness as a signal. Administered systems depend on judges, whose decisions are often secretive and not subject to appeal, and the arbitrary nature of judging is a theme that recurs in all prize systems, whether domestic or international. In all cases, prize awards typically reflected the identity of the applicant rather than the merits of the invention, and wealthier applicants had a significant advantage in gaining the attention of the judges, regardless of the technological merits of their contributions.[19] These administered innovation systems were fundamentally undemocratic, promoting ideas that elites or privileged groups regarded as interesting or useful.

In 1873, the Missouri Board of Agriculture published an assessment of innovation prize systems, noting that

the dissatisfaction with the award of these premiums seems to grow worse, and although the number of entries may increase, their intrinsic value, and the estimation of the award of premiums to them, decrease . . . most, if not all, exhibit more for the purpose of advertising themselves to the public and less with a view to obtain the paltry reward or doubtful distinction of the "premiums." . . . To go

---

[18] *Annals of the Massachusetts Charitable Mechanic Association, 1795–1892* (1892), p. 327.

[19] For a contemporary assessment, see "Awards at Exhibitions" in the *Electrical Review* of August 22, 1885, p. 172: "The cynic will say that medals, like kissing, go pretty much by favour. . . . Gold medals are limited in number; and while two hundred firms may deserve them, two hundred cannot receive them. . . . [W]hile a gold medal indicates the reputation of a firm, the lack of a gold medal does not necessarily indicate an inferior reputation. . . . The majority of gold medals call for no comment, but when we come to the silver medals the process of selection seems more invidious. It is very difficult to see why certain names should be selected as being more worthy than some of those in the 'bronze' class."

into details to illustrate the above remarks, to point out some of the many errors and superfluities of the premium list, to name instances where unjust and disreputable awards have been made, and just ones persistently denied, would extend this article beyond its scope, and become odious.[20]

In short, as with all administered systems, the objectives of competitors were different from those of grantors, and awards and decisions tended to be misaligned with productivity and market value.

[20] *Missouri Yearbook of Agriculture*, vol. 8 (1873), p. 490.

8

"Creative Destruction"

War and Technology

War . . . is a contest of Science and Wealth.

—New York Times (1862)

Large-scale world wars in the twentieth century ratcheted up the incursion of administered systems in civilian activities as well as in the military realm. Research and development expenditures were increasingly funded from government budgets, and many researchers have argued that government sponsorship was indispensable for the conception and growth of crucial sectors such as telecommunications, computing, and internet technologies. Advocates of an "entrepreneurial state" tend to highlight case studies of government administration of innovation during wartime initiatives and military expenditures on defense. The exclusive focus on World War II and its aftermath fails to take into account the possibility of a counterfactual approach, in which other sources of funding and lower levels of top-down government direction might lead to equally effective developments. In other words, state intervention might have crowded out private initiatives.

Robert Fogel usefully warns against the "axiom of indispensability," or the notion that there are no feasible alternatives to prevailing observed outcomes. This chapter provides a counterexample that suggests the need for more nuanced thinking about the necessity for administered systems even in connection with military technologies. The American Civil War, in particular, illustrates how rapid technological innovation occurred through market intermediation rather than centralized government initiatives. This was the first modern technologically oriented war, and the final outcome was in large part determined by divergence in the technical capabilities of the North and South. Both inventive activity and military decision making about technology procurement were decentralized. The variation in patented inventive activity during the American Civil War shows at the most granular level how quickly and precisely patentees and patenting responded to the incentives created by this major conflict.

The concept of "creative destruction" originated with Werner Sombart, who argued that wars have a positive impact on industrialization and technological

Inventing Ideas. B. Zorina Khan, Oxford University Press (2020). © Oxford University Press.
DOI: 10.1093/oso/9780190936075.001.0001

change.[1] More recently, the "triumph of the West" itself has been attributed to its aggressive and technologically innovative military traditions.[2] Wars lead to explicit human costs of mortality and injuries, and implicit costs in terms of the output that is sacrificed when labor and other resources are diverted into the military. For some, significant negative consequences include the effects on inventive ideas. John Nef, for instance, felt that armed conflict was detrimental to invention and innovation. He contended that wartime technologies were merely based on already existing ideas, which diverted the attention of inventors and innovators from more productive endeavors. He even speculated that military conflict had the capacity to destroy the potential for inventiveness, new ideas, and progress.[3]

Charles and Mary Beard later posited their own version of the "creative destruction" thesis, when they suggested that the American Civil War promoted the economic prosperity of the Northern economy.[4] The newspaper of record linked the progress of the North in war and peace to the common factor of technological ingenuity:

> The iron gunboats are merely an exponent of those qualities which have gained the victory—the ingenuity, mechanical skill, perseverance and calm courage of a Northern free people. . . . [T]he genius which has won such successes in the arts of peace is now applied constantly to the formation of implements of destruction, or to the combinations of strategy. . . . [N]ew weapons will be invented, and all the energy of our untiring and ingenious national improvement will be turned to the shortest, and most terrible methods of destruction.[5]

A vast array of books and articles have exhaustively explored even esoteric aspects of the American Civil War, such as a proposal for an "airforce" of aerial balloonists. Surprisingly, none provides a systematic analysis of inventive ideas and technological change during this period. After all, few would question that, in the "Republic of Technology" that flourished during the nineteenth century, Americans approached militarization in the same spirit as they did industrialization.

The American Civil War was a watershed in military technique and technology, a transition from the (literally) more regimented European precedent toward modern strategies that placed a premium on the tools of warfare. The Civil War heralded the advent of a more capital-intensive approach to armed conflict

---

[1] Sombart's opus, *Krieg Und Capitalismus*, remains untranslated into English.
[2] Parker (1995).
[3] Nef (1950).
[4] Beard and Beard (1927)
[5] *New York Times*, February 17, 1862, p. 4.

and a quest for superior innovations to quickly transform untutored recruits into formidable adversaries. Historians have produced extensive case studies of specific strategies and technological innovations that were introduced during the war, encompassing repeating firearms, breech-loading rifles, explosives, hand grenades and underwater torpedoes, aeronautics and aerial reconnaissance, pontoon bridges, ironclad battleships, manned submarines, trench warfare, and the military use of telegraphy, encryption, and rail transportation.

Key players in military strategy were patentees, from President Lincoln (a sometime patent lawyer) to members of his cabinet and many of the generals. John Ericsson (one of the "men of progress" portrayed in Chapter 1) advised President Lincoln that the Union's

> cause will have to be sustained, not by numbers, but by superior weapons. By a proper application of mechanical devices alone will you be able with absolute certainty to destroy the enemies of the Union. . . . [I]f you apply our mechanical resources to the fullest extent, you can destroy the enemy without enlisting another man.

Ericsson himself, one of the most widely known and celebrated patentees of the period, designed the ironclad *Monitor,* which incorporated other important patented inventions such as Theodore Timby's revolving gun turrets. The *Monitor* was involved in the crucial encounter with the *Merrimac* early in 1862, and the emphasis on ironclads radically altered naval technology.

The North and the South obviously diverged dramatically on many grounds, but they remained united in the belief that property rights in inventive ideas were the most effective means of ensuring technological and military progress. The *Annual Report of the Secretary of War for 1860* requested an appropriation of $50,000 to fund experiments to improve military supplies and protested a provision inhibiting the purchase of patented weapons. Senator Jefferson Davis of Mississippi had inserted a clause into the U.S. appropriations bill for that year: "No arms nor military supplies whatever, which are of a patented invention, shall be purchased, nor the right of using or applying any patented invention, unless the same shall be authorized by law and the appropriation therefore explicitly set forth that it is for such patented invention." Cynics would point to Davis's decamping for the Confederacy shortly afterward as consistent with an attempt at technological destabilization through patent policy. Davis's antipatent measure was quickly repealed.

Meanwhile, back in the South, one of the first acts of the Confederate Congress was to introduce a patent system. Jefferson Davis was now revealed as a pro-patent advocate, and he advised the Congress of the Confederate States in April 1861 that "I refer you to the report of the Attorney General, and concur in his recommendation for immediate legislation, *especially on the subject of patent rights*" (my emphasis). The intellectual property clause of the U.S. Constitution was replicated verbatim in the Confederate Constitution: "To promote the progress of science and useful arts, by securing for limited times to authors and inventors the exclusive right to their respective writings and discoveries."[6] Nevertheless, the Confederacy was technologically unprepared for the advent of modern warfare. In an 1895 retrospective, Josiah Gorgas, the confederate chief of ordnance, noted: "In the winter of 1861-'62, while McClellan was preparing his great army near Alexandria, we resorted to the making of pikes for the infantry and lances for the cavalry. . . . No access of enthusiasm could induce our people to rush to the field armed with pikes."[7]

In economic terms, the Civil War was a large exogenous shock that affected markets for land, labor and capital, aggregate demand, the distribution of expenditures, and the level and growth of national income. The war also altered the set of profit opportunities, creating incentives for entrepreneurs to take advantage of the potential for supranormal returns. Such indirect microeconomic effects of large-scale armed conflict are not simple to measure or interpret, but they warrant examination if we seek a better understanding of the more subtle costs and consequences of wars. For instance, some scholars have approached the study of war in terms of its "totality," defined as the degree of centralization, large-scale mobilization, and federal control. Yet, such organizational factors are neither necessary nor sufficient to explain the impact of war on a society as a whole. When enough private individuals respond to new incentives during a war, substantial changes in the allocation of resources could occur even within a decentralized structure with little federal control and low labor participation in the military.[8]

The existing body of research leaves many questions unexplored. How did the Civil War affect patterns of patenting and comparative advantage in inventive activity across regions? Which individuals, or types of individuals, were most likely to take advantage of the opportunities that the American Civil War afforded? Were contributions to the war made primarily by individual entrepreneurs who radically changed their orientation, or did the major response emanate from

---

[6] *Scientific American* 4, no. 20 (1861): 307. The writer, however, was dismissive of the notion that "inventive talent has suddenly sprung up among the Southern people." Sec. 50 of the Confederate patent statute maintained the U.S. provision that only the first and true inventor should be recognized. However, they amended the terms to provide that if the inventor were a slave "the master of such slave may take an oath that the said slave was the original inventor; and on complying with the requisites of the law, shall receive a patent for said discovery or invention and have all the rights to which a patentee is entitled by law."

[7] Cited in Fuller and Steuart (1944: 117).

[8] Engerman and Gallman (1997) define total war by the degree of a population's economic mobilization for war and the amount of centralized direction imposed by the state. By this measure, they find that the claim for total war was greater in the South than in the North.

those who were already specialized in weaponry during the antebellum period? As Nef pointed out, it is important to consider whether wars created new technologies or simply diverted existing inventive resources into the military sector, since technological creation tends to have greater reallocative effects than does technological diversion. Finally, a linking of military innovation to returns on entrepreneurial activity can reveal whether war-responsive inventors enjoyed disproportionate changes in their wealth relative to inventors in other sectors or to the overall population.

Patenting during the Civil War

Richard Jordan Gatling (1818–1903) illustrates the responsiveness of inventors and markets for ideas that helped the North to prevail in the Civil War. Gatling was a prolific inventor of patented agricultural machinery, including a wheat drill, a steam tractor, and a machine to sow rice. When the Civil War broke out he immediately turned his attention from farming machinery to meeting the demand for more efficient firearm inventions. He was motivated, he later related, by the conviction that mechanization would reduce the need for large numbers of soldiers to risk their lives in military conflicts. This humanitarian bent did not hinder his efforts to profit from his patented military inventions. The Gatling Gun, a multibarreled machine gun, was patented in 1862, and later models of this weapon could fire as many as 1,200 rounds per minute. Mark Twain had the opportunity to test one of these guns in 1868 at the Colt factory near his home in Hartford, Connecticut, and two decades later, his fictional Connecticut Yankee (a foreman at Colt's Patent Firearms Company) would be able to subjugate King Arthur's world with the aid of thirteen "gatlings."[9] Benjamin "Beast" Butler was the first Civil War general to purchase these guns (for the enormous price of $12,000), but its most widespread adoption came later. The Gatling Gun was central to victories in many international conflicts and was the basis for automatic weapons developed in the twentieth century.

Gatling was just one of thousands of patentees who besieged Washington, DC and directly contacted military officers touting their devices and discoveries. The *New York Times* in 1861 reported that

---

[9] Twain described the weapon he tried out: "It feeds itself with cartridges, and you work it with a crank like a hand organ: you can fire it faster than four men can count. When fired rapidly, the reports blend together like the clattering of a watchman's rattle. It can be discharged four hundred times in a minute! I liked it very much, and went on grinding it as long as they could afford cartridges for the amusement—which was not very long." *Daily Alta California* 20, no. 6562 (1868): 3.

the war has so stimulated the inventive Yankee brain that the Office at Washington fairly groans (we believe that is the figure) under the weight of instruments of destruction, and Gen. McClellan has but to adopt any one out of ten thousand patent kill-alls to utterly annihilate the rebels' "grand army of the Potomac."

Patents for improvements to cannon, projectiles, small arms, cartridges, and tents increased by more than 300% within the space of a few short years. However, the greatest relative increase was in improvements to firearms and cartridges, which were the most "scalable" in promising the largest market. As the Commissioner of Patents noted, "whatever improvements tend to the perfecting of the weapons of the private soldier must have a great value in warfare, where, as is usually the case, masses of men are marshaled to oppose collected masses."[10]

This section examines the lifetime experience of a large sample of inventors to determine how the incentives of the conflict affected the rate and direction of inventive activity. Patterns for "war-related" inventions such as weaponry and explosives, and changes in benefits to veterans, allow us to clearly identify the effects of the war on markets in technology. Nineteenth-century inventors were especially anxious to secure their rights through patenting. It is not a mere co-incidence that President Lincoln was a patentee and former patent lawyer, his secretary of war a patent lawyer, his secretary of the Treasury a commissioner of the Patent Office, and his chiefs of navy ordnance and military engineering eminent inventors. President Lincoln's State of the Union Address in 1861, soon after the outbreak of the war, made a point of mentioning the condition of the Patent Office, and a landmark revision in the statutes was approved that year. Moreover, even with all the pressures of a bitter and divisive conflict, Lincoln was involved daily in personal communications with inventors and in tests of their military innovations. Patent rights became even more valuable during the war, because patent portfolios could serve as a signal of reputation and reliability that gave an advantage to bidders for military contracts. For example, in 1866, more than 80% of those on the Surgeon General's list of approved suppliers of prosthetic devices that the federal government funded had secured patents on these products. Patents were also beneficial because they differentiated products and signaled quality, at a time when shoddy goods could literally have explosive negative consequences.

Changes in the patterns of patenting during this period were representative of inventive activity in general, and of military inventions in particular.[11]

---

[10] *New York Times,* December 6 1861, p. 4; *Annual Report of the Commissioner of Patents for 1863,* p. 33.

[11] Bruce (1989) estimates that Lincoln read three times as many letters from inventors as from other sources.

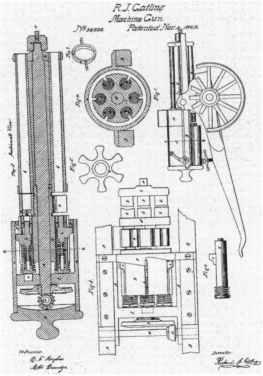

Figure 8.1 Civil War Weaponry: The Gatling Gun
Richard Gatling was a former inventor of agricultural machinery who responded
to the incentives of the Civil War. The in/famous Gatling Gun was patented in 1862,
with the intention of reducing the human costs of military conflicts.
Sources: U.S. Patent Office; Library of Congress.

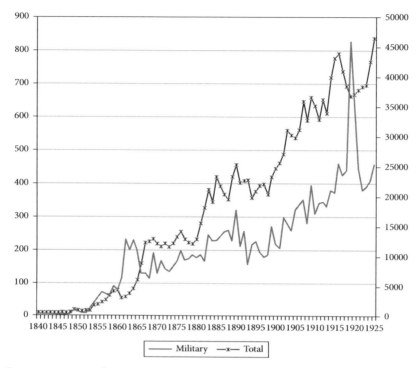

Figure 8.2 Patents for Weapons and Total Patents Granted, 1840–1925

Notes and Sources: Weaponry is defined as an invention falling within patent classes 42 (firearms); 86, 102, and 149 (ammunition and explosives); 89 (ordnance); and 124 (mechanical guns), according to the U.S. Patent Office Annual Reports.

At the most aggregate level, the patenting rates support those who contend that wars retard inventive activity. On the eve of the Civil War, the United States was poised for rapid growth in innovation and industrialization, and patenting was increasing at an annual average rate of 19%, well in excess of population growth. As Figure 8.2 shows, the immediate after-effect of the Civil War was a fall in patent grants, from 4,363 in 1860 to 3,040 in 1861 and 3,781 in 1863. Patenting recovered to some extent in the following two years, then jumped significantly at the end of the war, and more than 12,300 patents were recorded in 1867. This decline in patent grants was not due to a lag in processing applications, since the patent application series follows the patents granted closely. The tremendous surge in patenting that occurred everywhere immediately after the war suggests that the conflict likely retarded the emergence of certain new technologies.

The Civil War did not significantly alter regional comparative advantages, and per capita patenting was notably resilient in all localities. Table 8.1 shows the

Table 8.1 Patenting and Population in War and Peace, 1830–1900

	Pre-1861	Eve of War	Civil War	Postwar	1870s	1880s	1890s
New England							
Patents per capita	102.1	260.1	308.1 (484.4)	746.3	725.3	820.2	698.4
Total patents (%)	28.0	23.8	22.8	22.5	19.8	17.8	15.8
Total pop. (%)	10.0		9.5		8.8	8.2	7.9
Middle Atlantic							
Patents per capita	70.4	212.4	236.5 (346.7)	506.5	561.3	626.4	547.0
Total patents (%)	45.9	41.1	42.3	37.4	38.9	35.7	33.3
Total pop. (%)	23.7		23.4		22.3	21.6	21.3
East North Central							
Patents per capita	19.9	114.6	124.0 (212.7)	340.3	317.0	417.3	409.4
Total patents (%)	12.0	17.9	21.2	24.5	22.5	24.7	25.8
Total pop. (%)	22.0		22.9		22.8	22.5	22.1
West North Central							
Patents per capita	6.1	72.7	53.6 (102.6)	171.9	204.0	277.9	269.2
Total patents (%)	1.2	2.4	3.0	4.4	6.2	8.4	9.5
Total pop. (%)	6.9		8.3		9.8	11.4	12.3
West							
Patents per capita	5.0	83.3	90.9 (175.8)	193.6	367.7	464.2	504.6
Total patents (%)	0.3	1.0	1.9	1.8	3.0	4.1	5.6
Total pop. (%)	2.0		2.2		2.6	3.3	3.9
South							
Patents per capita	3.0	46.5	18.5 (41.9)	65.0	91.5	107.0	107.6
Total patents (%)	12.7	12.2	4.4	6.2	9.5	9.3	10.0
Total pop. (%)	35.4		33.7		33.6	32.9	32.5
United States	36.4	130.6	129.5 (202.4)	316.2	322.1	379.1	349.8

Notes and Sources: The data around the Civil War period derive from a random sample of 1,074 patents filed on the eve of the war (1855, 1857, 1859, and 1860), 2,070 patents filed each year between 1861 and 1865 (inclusive), and 1,990 patents filed in the immediate postwar period (1866 and 1867). Data for total patents during the other years were computed from the *Annual Report of the Commissioner of Patents for 1891*. Population data are from the Census of the United States, computed at the decadal midpoint by exponential interpolation. Patents per capita are per million residents; the entries are inflated to the decadal total. Hence, the italicized per capita figures for the Civil War period refer to the total if the war pattern had lasted for the entire decade, whereas the figures in parentheses show the actual per capita figures for the 1860s.

broad geographical patterns in patenting before, during, and after the war. The South and the Confederate states experienced a sharp decline in patenting during the war for which filings in the Confederate Patent Office could not compensate. The Northern states saw minor variation in relative positions over the war years from 1861 through 1865. For instance, Pennsylvania lost ground, and New York marginally increased its share. The share of patents in the frontier regions of the Midwest and West likewise increased, and patenting in Illinois grew from 3% to almost 7%. However, none of these developments were markedly different from the trends in technological change during the entire nineteenth century.

Within the expected general stagnation in total patents, inventors responded immediately and disproportionately to the stimulus that the war provided. Broad changes in the distribution of patents across sectors were minor, but within sectors a sharp and marked increase in military inventions occurred. At the start of the war, the "belligerent arts" were underdeveloped. Combatants received muzzle-loading muskets with minimal range and accuracy, unreliable fuses, paper cartridges that dissolved in the rain, cannon that exploded after several rounds, and projectiles with unpredictable trajectories. Patentees quickly turned their attention to remedying these routine defects and also contrived new disruptive technologies, which would have implications for military strategies around the globe.

For those who argue that World Wars I and II are typical of armed conflict, it should be noted that the propensity for inventors to patent weaponry was twice as high during the Civil War. This pattern is evident in Figure 8.3, which presents a time series involving the ratio of weaponry to total patents filed between 1790 and 2000. Patentees were also responsive to other demands besides the need for weapons and other overt military technologies. A significant number of them turned their attention to improving war-related accessories, including knapsacks, tents, groundsheets, ambulances, and military flares. William B. Johns, an army captain from Georgetown in Washington, DC, obtained patents in 1861 for several military-related inventions. These included saddle leggings that were "very well adapted to army use, not only for mounted officers, but for general cavalry use" and improved military equipment that could be converted from a sheet into a knapsack, tent, or military cloak. He also patented a portable fireplace whose specification noted that it would "take up but little of the most valuable room, while the property of retaining the heat thus gained renders it peculiarly desirable for keeping the tent comfortable during the great part of cold nights, so that it thereby becomes very useful for an army in winter quarters."

Prosthetics were an especially poignant category of war-related inventions that clearly demonstrate the sensitivity of inventors to potential market returns. Patents for prosthetic inventions jumped by over 400% during the 1860s, relative to the previous decade (Figure 8.4). Approximately 20,560 (over 8%) wounded

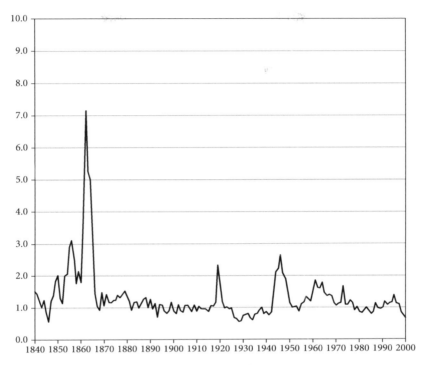

Figure 8.3 Weaponry as a Percentage of U.S. Total Patents, 1840–2000

Notes: See notes to Figure 8.3.

Civil War soldiers suffered amputation, the incidence of which was higher during this war partly because of the devastating effects of heavy lead bullets and the increased range of rifles and artillery, while more effective usage of anesthetics also helped to increase soldiers' survival rates. As a result, an immense number of soldiers and veterans required artificial limbs.

In 1865, Commissioner of Patents Thomas C. Theaker recorded a fall in "warlike implements," while patents for "numerous improvements in hospital beds, ambulances, stretchers, apparatus for treating fractured and bruised limbs . . . all bear melancholy testimony to the horrors of the war."[12] Patents for improvements in prosthetics initially declined toward the end of the war. When Congress decided in 1866 and in 1870 to continue underwriting the cost of artificial limbs provided to disabled soldiers, there was a sharp upturn in the number of patents

---

[12] *Annual Report of the Commissioner of Patents* (1866), p. 40.

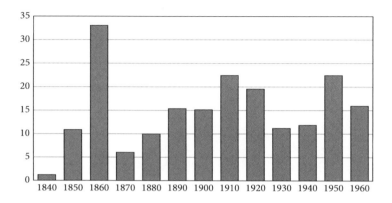

Figure 8.4

Figure 8.4 Prosthetic Patents Relative to Population, 1840–1960

Notes and Sources: U.S. Census, and Patent Office Annual Reports. Decadal counts. *Hartford Daily Courant*, September 30, 1865, p. 3.

in this category. By the middle of 1866, the government had funded prosthetics for 6,075 amputees, at a cost of approximately $358,000 (some $6 million in current dollars). The Salem Leg Company, one of the federally approved suppliers, was deemed to be "regularly organized and in possession of all the patents of the inventor," and its inventions were touted as so superior "that the company can have no lack of orders, especially from those who have suffered amputation in the army, as this invention has the sanction and recommendation of the government, which pays the expense of furnishing the limbs."[13]

---

[13] *South Danvers Wizard*, June 1, 1864.

This rapid responsiveness in patented medical instruments and devices was all the more remarkable because the Code of Ethics of the American Medical Association was decidedly antipatent and disdainful of professional participation in the marketplace for ideas. Adopted in 1847, it declared that "equally derogatory to professional character is it, for a physician to hold a patent for any surgical instrument or medicine; or to dispense a secret nostrum, whether it be the composition or exclusive property of himself or of others." Knowledge should be free and open to society, rather than exclusive or traded like any common commodity. Doctors who offered testimonials in advertisements and other forms of commercial certification were deemed to be "reprehensible." Since the patent records include countless examples of medical doctors claiming the exclusive rights to their ideas, and their advertisements even in professional journals were typically accompanied by extensive positive endorsements from their colleagues, it is clear that in practice this code was generally regarded as an irrelevant "nullity."[14]

An article in the journal of the association, entitled "Do We Obey the Code of Ethics?," addressed the reasons for this dismissal of the notion that patents were unethical. The article argued that it was the duty of medical practitioners to participate in competitive markets, to ensure the survival of the fittest ideas, and to direct the course of medical discovery in the most effective direction. The author concluded:

> The test of the ethicality of any measure is its being in accord with social good. Is the granting of patents a benefit or an injury to society? Every patent by virtue of being a patent, is not a secret. Its character is fully known. It becomes public property in a few years. Does it pay society to grant patents? Surely no one will deny the fact that the patent office is the greatest stimulant of discovery and invention in the world. Patents granted on anything stimulate discoveries in the direction of that thing. . . . These men never could devote their time, talent and capital to such work if they did not hope to get it back with interest. Stop the taking out of medical patents on goods of this kind and you will stop medical progress.[15]

[14] The president of the American Medical Association acknowledged in his inaugural address of 1875 that "the Code of Ethics was violated every day, either wilfully or ignorantly, not only by the rank and file, but by men high in the profession; men who were considered leaders, advanced thinkers and workers."

[15] R. G. Eccles, "Do We Obey the Code of Ethics?," *Journal of the American Medical Association* 33 (1899): 1648. An editorial in *Medical Brief*, vol. 36 (1908), similarly dismissed this aspect of the code, opining that "The position of the profession on this point is out of tune with modern progress. The position of the medical profession in supporting and maintaining that part of the code of ethics relating to the patenting of medical and surgical appliances is illogical, not altruistic and is operating in a manner detrimental to the public welfare."

Entrepreneurship and the Market for Inventions

The patterns of patenting during the Civil War offer insights into the relationship between war and technology, and markets for inventions. The analysis is based on a stratified random sample of almost 1,400 inventors who filed at least one patent between 1855 and 1870, along with information on over 8,500 patented inventions.[16] The experience of inventors of weaponry and war-related patents can be compared to that of the population at large and to patentees of other kinds of invention. Some of the inventors who filed patents for military inventions during the Civil War may have had purely patriotic motives, but most were also attempting to exploit the opportunity for financial gain. Both ordinary and "great inventors" dramatically changed the rate and direction of their activities toward military technologies, as well as toward other areas where demand was expanding, such as in the market for cotton substitutes.

The occupational distribution of inventors before and after the war provides useful information about reallocation during the war (Table 8.2). As might be expected, a number of the inventors of weaponry and war-related devices were eminent military men, such as Henry M. Naglee, a West Point graduate and brigadier-general in the Union Army, who in 1863 devised an apparatus for locating and exploding submarine torpedoes. For the most part, however, inventors were artisans, farmers, laborers, and professionals without particular technical skills. Among the relatively undistinguished Civil War patentees was John Oliphant, a laborer from Uniontown, Pennsylvania, who obtained a patent in January 1863 for a safety catch on firearms. As the celebrated musical about Alexander Hamilton at the Battle of Yorktown illustrates, soldiers on the move were ordered to take the bullets out of their guns. Oliphant's patent specification attributed the inventor's motivation to "the custom in the army, for the purpose of preventing accidents of this nature, to require the soldiers to march with empty guns, they not being permitted to load until they are in the immediate presence or neighborhood of the enemy, thus constantly running the risk of being suddenly surprised by an ambuscade with empty guns in their hands."

---

[16] The sample includes 720 patentees of general inventions and 639 patentees of military inventions. From 1855 to the Civil War, 255 of the inventors filed patents—673 from the Civil War period and 431 from the postbellum period through 1870. The full patenting record amounts to a total of 8,542 patents. The patentees were matched across manuscript censuses in 1860 and 1870 to capture changes that occurred in their individual circumstances before and after the war. The linkage to manuscript censuses yields information about age, place of birth, residence, migration, occupation, real estate wealth, personal wealth, and military status (veteran or not).

Table 8.2 Characteristics of Inventors

	Age at Time of First Invention (percentage)							
	General Inventions		Weaponry		War-Related Inventions		All	
Age	All	Civil War	All	Civil War	All	Civil War	All	Civil War
Less than 20 years	0.6	0.7	0.7	1.0	0.0	0.0	0.6	0.8
20–29 years	19.5	14.9	21.2	19.9	13.0	10.8	19.7	16.8
30–39 years	38.9	43.3	36.1	37.8	42.0	43.2	38.0	40.7
40–49 years	25.1	22.7	23.6	25.6	26.0	27.0	24.6	24.6
50–59 years	13.3	14.2	13.4	13.5	14.0	13.5	13.4	13.8
60 years and over	2.3	3.9	1.1	0.3	3.0	4.5	1.9	2.3
Average age	38.7	39.5	37.9	37.8	40.0	40.2	38.5	38.8
Number	710	281	517	301	98	73	1,325	655

	Occupations in 1860 and 1870 (percentage)							
	General Inventions		Weaponry		War-Related Inventions		All	
	1860	1870	1860	1870	1860	1870	1860	1870
Artisans	20.3	16.3	17.7	12.8	17.8	16.8	19.1	15.0
Blacksmiths	2.8	2.4	1.9	1.1	1.0	0.0	2.3	1.7
Engineers	2.4	1.5	3.9	3.9	0.0	1.0	2.8	2.4
Inventors	1.0	5.4	1.7	4.3	1.0	0.0	1.3	4.6
Machinists	9.4	9.2	10.8	6.5	7.9	3.0	9.9	7.7
Farmers	11.9	12.6	5.8	4.8	6.9	4.0	9.1	8.9
Medical	2.8	1.5	5.2	3.5	12.9	6.9	4.5	2.7
Merchants	2.6	1.7	3.9	3.4	4.0	3.0	3.2	2.4
Manufacturers	8.5	15.8	9.9	11.9	10.9	25.7	9.2	15.0
Military	0.1	0.1	5.2	4.8	1.0	2.0	2.2	2.1
Professionals	5.6	5.7	5.9	5.2	7.0	7.0	5.8	5.6
Laborers	10.1	9.6	6.5	3.9	5.0	2.0	8.3	6.8
Traders	5.1	6.5	4.8	3.2	6.9	6.0	5.2	5.2
None	5.7	2.8	2.2	2.0	0.0	1.0	3.9	2.4
Unknown	11.7	9.0	14.7	28.6	17.8	22.8	13.3	17.7
Number	720	720	538	538	101	101	1,359	1,359

(Continued)

Table 8.2 *Continued*

Inventors by Total Number of Patents Filed over Lifetime (percentage)			
	General Inventions	Weaponry	War-Related Inventions	All
1 patent	31.3	28.6	46.5	31.4
2–4 patents	32.0	27.9	29.7	30.2
5–9 patents	21.8	21.4	11.9	20.9
10–19 patents	9.5	12.8	9.9	10.8
20 patents and above	5.4	9.3	2.0	6.7
Average patents	6.0	7.2	3.9	6.3
Total inventors	720	538	101	1,359
Inventors by Length of Patenting Career (percentage)				
1 year	32.9	31.1	49.5	33.4
2–4 years	11.4	7.3	3.0	9.1
5–9 years	10.4	13.2	18.8	12.2
10–19 years	22.9	20.5	15.8	21.4
20 years and above	22.4	27.9	12.9	23.9
Average career	11.3	12.8	7.6	11.6

Notes: The data consist of a stratified random sample of 1,359 inventors who filed at least one patent between 1855 and 1870, and who could be traced in the 1860 and/or the 1870 manuscript censuses. The patents for all of the individuals in the sample were traced throughout their entire lifetime. The inventors in the sample filed a total of 1,842 military patents and 8,542 total patents during their lifetimes. "General inventions" refer to patents that are unrelated to war or the military. "Weaponry" includes patents for firearms, cannon, ordnance, and explosives. "War-related inventions" include miscellaneous patents, other than weapons, that mentioned war and the military in the specifications or that were incidental to the war (such as uniforms, knapsacks, tents, canteens, shields for warships, artificial limbs, and military signals). The length of an inventor's patenting career was measured by the difference between the first and last patent filed plus one year. Of the inventors in the sample, 1,177 were traced in the 1860 census, 1,120 in the 1870 census, and 974 in both censuses. The sample includes 147 inventors who were identified as veterans of the Civil War, 745 who did not appear in war records, and 467 whose status as veterans could not be determined.

Although farmers accounted for the single largest occupational category in the general population, the majority of inventors fell into three basic classes: workers and artisans, consisting of farm laborers, bakers, carpenters, and jewelers; a more elite group of professionals, including such technical and white-collar inventors as bookkeepers, engineers, and physicians; and market-oriented manufacturers and traders, including merchants, salesmen, and retail and wholesale dealers. A substantial number of patentees attempted to capitalize on their invention by manufacturing the product themselves. An increase in the commercial orientation of inventors was especially evident in the production of war-related patents, where the share of manufacturers increased from 11% to over 25%. For instance, the linkage of patent records and manuscript censuses reveals that George B. Jewett—who had been a clergyman in Salem, Massachusetts, before the war—filed six patents for an improvement in artificial limbs during the war and, by 1870, he was a successful manufacturer of prosthetics.

If there is support for the claim that the war enabled technological creation rather than diversion, it would appear among the almost 50% of inventors during the Civil War who were first-time patentees. Women, in particular, increased their patenting markedly during this period, from just seventy-two patented inventions in the entire period before the war to eighty-six during the war years alone. Many of their inventions were related to the war effort and to women's participation in production outside the home. For instance, in 1864, Mary Jane Montgomery of New York, who would later acquire an "enviable reputation as an inventor," obtained a patent for an improved war vessel, with "parts applying to other structures for defense." Sarah J. A. Hussey, an inventive Quaker from Cornwall, New York, was buried in 1898 with military honors in her hometown. She noted in her 1865 patent specification that her invention was inspired by her "long experience as a nurse in the United States army hospitals." Many of these patents were widely marketed—a notable example being the $20,000 that Martha J. Coston received by authority of Congress on June 5, 1862, granting the U.S. Navy the rights to her chemical flares. Coston founded a company and manufactured the signals at cost for the military during the war. According to a testimonial by the Bureau of Navigation of the Navy, "No lights or other symbols for making night signals in fleets or squadrons have been found . . . *in any degree comparable to those known as Coston Night Signals.*"[17]

Whether or not there was a war, we would expect some entry from new inventors. However, the patterns of new entrants differed significantly

---

[17] *Report of the Committee of Patents*, May (1880), p. 2 (emphasis in original).

according to their military orientation. Approximately 40% of general inventors were new entrants during the Civil War, whereas 58.2% of the creators of improvements in weapons and 74.5% of war-related inventors were first-time filers. Hence, inventors of military innovations appear to have been significantly more responsive than general patentees to the prospects that the war offered. The average age of inventors at the time of first patenting was an experienced forty. However, those who entered this field for the first time during the Civil War tended to be older than the average inventor, and certainly older than the average age of the general population. Only 10.8% of these war-related first-timers were younger than thirty, in comparison to the 20.3% of all inventors who were in that age group, suggesting that the predominantly middle-aged inventors who were contributing to military technology were responding to the specific incentives for innovation that the war presented.

Telling information about the identities of those who were making contributions to technological change during the war comes from data about career patents (Table 8.3). The inventors of weaponry differed from those who created miscellaneous devices that were incidental to the war. Almost one-half of the war-related inventors produced a single patent and had brief careers; only 12.9% had careers of twenty years or more. By way of contrast, the 538 patentees of weapons tended to have longer careers and to hold more patents; more than 22% of them filed ten or more patents—a profile consistent with the greater specialization of weapon inventors. The war undoubtedly attracted new entrants into the area of miscellaneous war-related inventions (technological creation), but the invention of new weaponry per se was more likely to come from existing patentees who had changed their orientation (technological diversion) because of the prospects that the war offered.

Another way to assess this elastic response is through patterns for average patenting per inventor and patents granted throughout inventors' entire lifetime, across regions and occupations (Table 8.3). Foreign-born immigrants were especially responsive to the technological exigencies of the conflict. Career patenting was highest in the well-developed markets of the Northeast, and otherwise uniformly distributed across regions. Although they lagged in terms of average patents per inventor, the West and West North Central frontiers accounted for large surges in wartime patenting, indicating a widespread response to the anticipated growth in the market for military inventions. As might be expected, war veterans, who were responsible for fewer lifetime patents than the average inventor, were disproportionately likely to produce military inventions. However, among general inventors, the commitment to patenting fell markedly among

Table 8.3 Inventive Careers: Lifetime Patents and Average Number of Patents

	Number	Military Inventions		General inventions		Lifetime Inventions
		Before War	Civil War	Before War	Civil War	
Veterans	147	0.20	0.66	0.61	1.09	5.40
Nonveterans	745	0.18	0.38	3.48	1.17	6.23
Occupation						
Artisan	290	0.16	0.40	7.01	1.06	4.33
Farmer	124	0.16	0.19	0.53	0.73	3.07
Technical	172	0.24	0.49	1.62	1.52	9.12
Manufacturer	125	0.62	1.02	1.90	1.93	11.62
Professional	187	0.31	0.95	1.27	1.74	6.67
Trader/merchant	114	0.06	0.69	0.98	1.44	6.54
Laborer	113	0.10	0.40	0.54	0.88	4.39
None	53	0.02	0.26	0.40	0.96	6.19
Unknown	181	0.23	0.45	0.59	0.77	5.91
Region of Birth						
New England	468	0.32	0.61	5.30	1.43	7.21
Middle Atlantic	408	0.19	0.60	0.89	1.31	6.04
East North Central	84	0.04	0.41	0.58	0.95	5.92
West North Central	7	0.43	0.43	0.43	0.71	3.86
South	101	0.21	0.41	0.73	0.73	4.64
Foreign	274	0.16	0.50	0.63	1.11	5.76
Unknown	17	0.24	0.35	0.71	0.59	8.12
Region of Patenting						
New England	415	0.30	0.60	5.67	1.41	6.62
Middle Atlantic	458	0.21	0.67	1.11	1.38	6.61
East North Central	256	0.12	0.31	0.62	0.98	4.73
West North Central	50	0.02	0.34	0.12	0.76	3.80
South	115	0.32	0.60	0.91	1.02	5.09
West	28	0.03	0.29	0.14	0.71	5.21
Other	17	0.06	0.30	0.06	0.42	2.76
Unknown	20	0.65	1.10	0.75	1.50	6.25
All inventors	1,359	0.22	0.55	2.32	1.27	6.29
Total patents		304	749	3,147	1,677	8,542

Notes: The table defines migration conservatively to enable comparison with the general population. Lifetime migration through 1870 simply indicates any change that occurred across birthplace, location in the 1860 census, and location in the 1870 census. Since the U.S. population sample is restricted to native-born residents, the last row in the table presents the results for native-born inventors.

artisans and New England residents, groups that may have suffered disproportionately from the war.

As Alexis de Tocqueville noted, Americans remained "restless in the midst of their prosperity," and migration—both international and internal—has long been part of the U.S. experience. Geographical mobility is a key indicator of resource reallocation, signaling the flexibility necessary for entrepreneurial success. Since investments in human capital are usually associated with higher mobility, holding other things constant, patentees might be expected to exhibit greater mobility than their less inventive counterparts. Inventors from other countries were disproportionately attracted by the opportunities that this country offered. In 1860, more than 20% of patentees were immigrants to the United States; 7.6% of those in the sample were from Britain and 5.3% from Germany. Native-born inventors were clustered in states where per capita patenting was especially high—New York, Massachusetts, and Connecticut accounting for 18.7%, 12.3%, and 8.6% of the inventors in the sample, respectively.

The records note the residence of patentees at each point of patenting; a measure of migration that takes into account these changes in residence yields rates of interstate migration that are exceedingly high for all inventors, military or otherwise. Table 8.4 defines migration more conservatively, however, to enable comparison with the general population. Lifetime migration through 1870 simply indicates any change that occurred across birthplace, location in the 1860 census, and location in the 1870 census. The middle of the 1850s saw a rapid increase in the rate of international immigration into the United States. The 1850 census recorded that less than 10% of the population were immigrants, but by 1860, 13.2% of the population was foreign born, and in 1870 the proportion of foreign-born residents was 14.4%.

Individuals who possessed inventive capital exhibited significantly greater movement across states, by any measure of geographical mobility, relative to the general population. By 1870, 42.3% of the U.S. population had moved from their birthplace to another state, but both military inventors and total inventors experienced higher mobility (53.4% and 52.8%, respectively). Their destinations tended to be places with greater commercial opportunities. Although inventors exhibited higher rates of mobility during their careers than did the general population, the war retarded the likelihood that they would switch locations. Between 1860 and 1870, their rates of geographical mobility, and the distance between old and new locations, were approximately the same as that of the resident white male population. The war may have lowered expected benefits or increased the risks and costs

Table 8.4 Geographical Mobility of Inventors and the U.S. Population

	Migration between 1860 and 1870									Lifetime Migration through 1870			
	U.S. Population			Military Inventors			All Inventors			Military Inventors		All Inventors	
	All	Migrant		All	Migrant		All	Migrant		Migrant		Migrant	
Residence in 1860		Row %	Col %		Row %	Col %		Row %	Col %	Row %	Col %	Row %	Col %
East North Central	25.1% N=430	19.8	32.2	12.4% 48	22.9	18.0	19.7% 191	13.6	18.4	93.8	18.5	82.7	26.9
Middle Atlantic	25.2% N=432	11.4	18.6	35.5% 137	11.0	24.6	31.7% 307	11.4	24.8	56.2	31.7	51.8	27.0
New England	14.4% N=246	13.4	12.5	36.5% 141	14.2	32.8	34.0% 329	14.9	34.8	49.7	28.8	48.6	27.2
South	25.5% N=436	13.4	22.2	10.4% 40	25.0	16.4	9.2% 89	21.4	13.5	77.5	12.8	66.3	10.0
West	2.0% N=35	27.9	3.7	2.3% 9	33.3	4.9	1.9% 18	22.2	2.8	100.0	3.7	100.0	3.1
West North Central	7.8% N=133	21.6	10.9	2.8% 11	18.2	3.3	3.6% 35	22.9	5.7	100.0	4.5	97.1	5.8
Total %	100%	—	15.4%	100%	—	15.8%	100%	—	14.6%	—	63.0	—	60.7%
Total N	1,711	—	264	386	—	61	969	—	141	386	243	969	588
Native born only													
Total %	100%	—	15.4%	100%	—	16.6%	100%	—	14.9%	—	53.4%	—	52.8%
Total N	1,711	—	264	307	—	51	790	—	118	307	164	790	409

Notes: The table defines migration conservatively to enable comparison with the general population. Lifetime migration through 1870 simply indicates any change that occurred across birthplace, location in the 1860 census, and location in the 1870 census. Since the U.S. population sample is restricted to native-born residents, the last row in the table presents the results for native-born inventors.

of migration disproportionately for those with higher investments in inventive capital.

Individuals often move for personal reasons, but in many instances, migration was tied to job search. Geographical and occupational mobility are often a function of similar individual characteristics—age, inherent ability, the accumulation of investments in human capital, and access to information over time. Responses to an exogenous shock like the Civil War would have varied depending on these individual characteristics. Although labor-market theory does not offer a basis for predicting the direction of change, it suggests that the share of individuals at risk for change might be negatively related to investments in human capital, because of a fall in the set of occupations that might lead to greater returns as education and skill increase.

Inventive capital was positively related to social advance, since such creativity helped to avoid downward mobility and facilitated upward mobility. Further insights can be obtained from changes in the distribution of occupations between 1860 and 1870 for a sample drawn from the general population, as well as all inventors and inventors of military patents (Table 8.5). Inventors in higher-status skilled and white-collar occupations experienced greater persistence relative to the population. In the general population, about one-half of all men in market-oriented occupations (the commercial class) remained there after the war. Patentees were not only significantly more likely to remain in commercial occupations but also demonstrated greater entrepreneurial abilities in terms of the propensity to switch to such occupations after the war. Similarly, inventors were able to move up from unskilled workers to skilled or white-collar occupations to a greater extent than their peers. Workers in the general population who made the transition to another occupational class were more likely to become farmers (33.5% of all laborers in the general population, compared to 7% of war-related inventors) rather than progress to skilled or commercial pursuits. Moreover, farmers in the general population were twice as likely as inventor-farmers to fall into the laborer category.

To what extent did inventors who responded to the war differ from inventors without a military orientation? Although some might suppose that highly specialized machinists and engineers would have an advantage at military innovation, strictly technical expertise did not yield greater numbers of military inventions. Other things being equal, the poorer segments of the population who owned less than $100 in total wealth in 1860 filed the bulk of military patents, but this pattern changed somewhat during the Civil War. Instead, manufacturers and the professional class of physicians, lawyers, and other white-collar workers filed the greatest number of military inventions.

Table 8.5 Occupational Mobility of Inventors and U.S. Population, 1860–1870

Occupations (1860,1870)	U.S. Population	All Inventors	Military Inventors
Commercial, commercial	49.8	72.4	76.5
Commercial, farmer	17.8	3.8	6.2
Commercial, skilled	6.8	10.8	6.2
Commercial, white collar	19.6	10.8	11.1
Commercial, worker	6.0	2.2	0.0
N (1860, 1870)	(105, 171)	(185, 257)	(81, 110)
Farmer, commercial	4.9	19.8	20.8
Farmer, farmer	76.6	60.4	58.3
Farmer, skilled	3.8	9.4	8.3
Farmer, white collar	2.3	3.8	8.3
Farmer, worker	12.4	6.6	4.2
N (1860, 1870)	(656, 682)	(106, 104)	(24, 27)
Skilled, commercial	13.2	19.6	18.2
Skilled, farmer	18.0	4.2	2.6
Skilled, skilled	48.8	61.9	68.2
Skilled, white collar	7.5	9.3	8.4
Skilled, worker	12.5	5.0	2.6
N (1860, 1870)	(256, 195)	(378, 299)	(154, 124)
White collar, commercial	19.1	11.1	9.9
White collar, farmer	13.7	2.2	2.5
White collar, skilled	4.1	9.6	8.6
White collar, white collar	58.5	73.3	77.8
White collar, worker	4.7	3.7	1.2
N (1860, 1870)	(101, 125)	(135, 165)	(81, 89)
Worker, commercial	11.0	14.4	24.2
Worker, farmer	33.5	15.6	6.9
Worker, skilled	11.3	24.4	17.2
Worker, white collar	3.9	7.8	6.9
Worker, worker	40.3	37.8	44.8
N (1860, 1870)	(306, 247)	(90, 69)	(29, 19)
Total	1,421	894	369

Notes and Sources: The percentages refer to the first-mentioned occupational class (commercial, farmers, skilled, white collar, and workers) in 1860 that fell within the adjacent class in 1870. The repeated categories (e.g. worker, worker) in boldface indicate no occupational mobility. Commercial occupations include traders, merchants, and manufacturers; skilled occupations include machinists, engineers, artisans, and mechanics; white-collar occupations include such professionals as physicians and bookkeepers; workers include farm laborers and unskilled individuals. The dataset includes only those individuals for whom occupational information was available in both years and excludes those who had no occupation or who were not located in one of the years.

In general, military inventions were more numerous in New England and the South, but inventors who responded to the war came from all regions of the country.

In sum, when markets first expanded during the antebellum period, the new inventors were more often than not ordinary people without much technical training, who responded to perceived needs by filing job-related patents. Similarly, the change in market demand during the Civil War attracted a number of general inventors. Inventors who first patented during the war held significantly fewer patents throughout their lifetimes than did more experienced patentees, and they had shorter careers. Even though we cannot know whether they would have invented anything in the absence of the war, weapons patentees who were active for the first time during the war were less likely to have done so. Newcomers to weapons invention were usually newcomers to invention per se and not much interested in patenting after the war. At the same time, those who filed larger numbers of military patents during the war were already specialists in military invention. Although the war temporarily diverted a number of individuals with considerable human and financial capital from other activities into military production, the greatest numbers of patents came from manufacturers and professionals who had already committed to this type of activity. The social returns to such reallocation are debatable, but we can be more specific about the *private* returns by examining whether a military orientation was associated with greater additions to personal wealth by the end of the 1860s.

Military Innovation and Returns to Inventors

For many in the population, war was associated with pain, displacement, and death; for others, however, war was a business that promised financial prosperity. Profits signal the most highly valued allocation of resources; in the absence of data about profits, changes in wealth can serve as a rough estimate of the reallocation in resources that the conflict permitted. For instance, Daniel B. Wesson, the manufacturer of the Springfield rifle and inventor of the legendary Smith & Wesson revolver, experienced an increase in wealth from $1,000 in 1860 to $350,000 in 1870. The Smith and Wesson factory in Springfield was located close to the federal armory in Springfield, the largest in the country. The business grew rapidly from 700 employees in June 1861 to 2,600 employees by January 1865 and produced more than 800,000 rifles during the war. Wesson's was undoubtedly an extreme case, and the degree to which other military patentees could emulate him depended in part on the market for new innovations.[18]

The patent records indicate a rapid increase in inventive activity directed toward military improvements, but it is also important to know whether new technologies were actually adopted during the Civil War. Historians debate the extent to which innovation was pervasive during this period, and their disputes reflect similar disagreements among military leaders during the war. Some generals were enthusiastic about new technology, whereas others pointed to the need for standardization and centralization in times of large-scale mobilization. Among the skeptics was James W. Ripley, chief of army ordnance, who in June 1861 referred to the "vast variety of the new inventions . . . each having its own advocates," as a "great evil." He recommended that it "be stopped by positively refusing to answer any requisitions for or propositions to sell new and untried arms and steadily adhering to the rule of uniformity of arms for all troops of the same kind."[19] The procurement of new equipment was undoubtedly costly and risky at both ends of the supply and demand chain. It not only led to the possibility of hold-ups by either party but also created the potential for corruption in the requisitions process. Innovations in manufacturing inputs or final products might reduce the future cost of production and increase military productivity, but some officials were more concerned that they might divert funds away from current production.

Nonetheless, George McClellan, J. E. B. Stuart, Ambrose Burnside, and a substantial number of other military leaders were successful patentees. Others, like the notorious Benjamin Butler, were enthusiastic about new technologies and quick to adopt promising patent innovations. Stephen Benet, chief of ordnance, refers (in a letter of March 6, 1875, to the secretary of war) to the statute of 1854, appropriating $90,000 for the purchase of breech-loading rifles:

> The effect of this measure was to stimulate the ingenuity of inventors in devising and perfecting methods of operating arms at the breech; and the records of the Patent Office show, in the number of patents issued for breech-loading arms about this time, that it is here properly that the era of breechloaders in this country begins.

However, not much of the money was actually spent because the army selected only carbines for the cavalry. Initially, Burnside's patented rifle was chosen

---

[18] Wartime demand for Smith & Wesson revolvers far exceeded the firm's ability to supply them. The firm earned more than $1 million in gross income between 1862 and 1868.

[19] Congressional series of United States public documents (1862), pp. 30–31.

because it used metallic cartridges, but the order was later canceled. The money was spent instead on carbines from Benjamin Joslyn and on rifles by the more established patentees Samuel Colt, Edward Maynard, and Christian Sharps. Suppliers had substantial leeway in fulfilling their obligations, because contracts were so vague that their terms could be variously interpreted.

Scattered evidence suggests that patentees did not labor entirely in vain, even in the South. The Confederate Congress offered subsidies as high as 50% to firms that established factories to support the war effort. Scattered armories were set up in towns like Richmond and Fayetteville, and at least some of the new patented inventions filed in the Confederacy went into production. Nathan T. Read manufactured his patented firearm at Keen, Walker & Co.'s establishment in his hometown of Danville, Virginia. Thomas Cofer's Confederate patent of August 12, 1861, was granted for a revolver that was manufactured in Portsmouth, Virginia. Despite the outbreak of hostilities, on May 14, 1861, the U.S. Patent Office granted Virginian Lorenzo Sibert a patent for his magazine rifle, which was produced in the Confederacy. Nevertheless, the government largesse proved insufficient to overcome nonfinancial obstacles, and the majority of Confederate firearms were not produced in the South but were purchased elsewhere. The Confederates sent agents to Cuba and Mexico, and to Europe, to procure weapons. Jean Alexander LeMat of Louisiana received an order for five thousand of his patented revolvers, but they were manufactured in France. The Confederacy even smuggled arms from the North. Gorgas, the Confederate chief of ordnance, reported in 1864 that they encountered little difficulty in acquiring arms through imports, bypassing the naval blockades.

In the North, a number of the most commercially successful military inventors were career officers—Thomas Rodman, Robert Parrott, John Dahlgren (inventors of guns, projectiles, and ordnance), and Henry Sibley (the patentee of Sibley's conical tent, which saw extensive use in the army). Others were experienced patentee/manufacturers, including Edward Maynard, Samuel Colt, Christopher Spencer, Oliver Winchester, Christian Sharp, Eli Remington, and Simeon North. But the outside-contracting method meant that even small-scale producers were able to benefit from the military market. For instance, George W. Morse obtained orders for his patented breech-loading arms, which he manufactured during the war. As noted before, military commanders had significant discretion in placing orders for equipment with promising innovations, thus bypassing the formal requisitions process. According to Stanley Engerman and Robert Gallman, "the wartime procurement system left the Northern economy largely in the hands of small entrepreneurs who responded to market incentives rather than to government

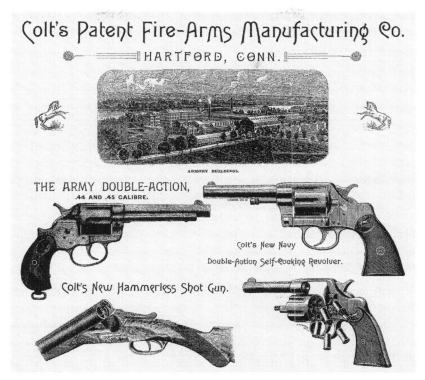

Figure 8.5 Weaponry in Civil War: Colt Revolvers
Samuel Colt's company was able to successfully make the transition from the Civil War by taking advantage of the growing demand in the American West. The firm actively traded in patent rights, lobbied for numerous prizes and accolades, and engaged in innovative commercialization in foreign markets.
Source: Frank Leslie's Illustrated Newspaper, October 5, 1889, p. 161.

incentives."[20] Procurement of military equipment and provisions involved a mixed supply system with centralized government production but with considerable outsourcing to private firms.[21]

One way to gauge the extensive markets in inventions is by the percentage of patents that were assigned (sold) when granted, calculated relative to the

---

[20] Engerman and Galman (1997, p. 243).

[21] Further evidence that a remarkably diverse array of patented items were in widespread use during the war can be gleaned from archaeological findings at prominent battlefields. The most comprehensive account of military procurement and expenditures is Wilson (2006).

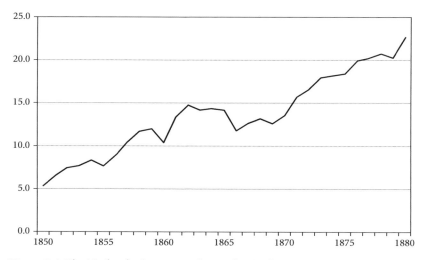

Figure 8.6 The Market for Inventions during the Civil War, 1850–1880

Notes and Source: U.S. Patent Office Annual Reports. The figure shows the percentage of patents that were assigned at time of issue. These data do not account for patents that were licensed, nor do they include patents that were assigned after the date of granting.

total record of patents filed in the United States. However, it should be noted that these assignments at issue seriously underestimate overall market activity in inventions, because patents could be sold and resold anytime during their term (in 1861 the life of a patent was extended from fourteen years from date of issue to a single seventeen-year term). The general trend in sales between 1850 and 1880 is positive; the proportion of patent assignments grew from 5.3% in 1850 to 22.6% in 1880. The Civil War boosted the sale at issue of new patent rights, from 10% in 1860 to more than 14% during the war (Figure 8.6). What sorts of improvement were being sold at the time of patenting during the war? Between 1861 and 1865, almost half of these assigned new patents were for military inventions. The market for inventions was thus thriving in the middle of a devastating conflict and enhancing the allocation of inventive resources toward the war effort.

Patented inventions may have been sold, and successful patentees like Wesson amassed great riches, but a key question is whether contributions to the war effort made a significant difference in the returns to the average inventor. If technological improvements served to increase military productivity, greater returns and financial mobility for military inventors might be expected, holding other things constant. Both the 1860 and 1870 censuses include entries on real estate and personal wealth, which allow an examination of wealth directly before and after the war. In 1860, 57% of white men possessed no real estate wealth and 43% owned no personal estate, which was also true ten years later. The implications from Table 8.6 regarding the distribution of inventors' wealth by asset level are that on the eve before the outbreak of war, more than one-half of all inventors, like the rest of the white male population, held no real estate and that more than one-third recorded no personal wealth.

Well-enforced patent rights increased the effectiveness of markets in invention by creating tradable assets that helped relatively disadvantaged inventors to gain returns by selling their rights, rather than by trying to raise capital through personal sources or through financial markets.[22] Because poor inventors were more likely to assign their inventions, it is not surprising that many of them, unlike the general population, succeeded in accumulating assets within this critical decade. Inventors without property were more likely to file patents for military technology, perhaps because a military orientation was associated with significantly higher wealth on average. However, the evidence concerning the rewards for switching to military inventions is less clear-cut. The average real estate wealth for inventors with first-time military patents fell by $287 between 1860 and 1870, and the change in their personal wealth was below the average for all inventors. Thus, for new entrants, a focus on war-related inventions did not typically lead to higher returns relative to other types of inventions.

Occupation played a significant role in explaining additions to wealth, and job persistence was associated with higher returns. Within the overall general population, manufacturers and artisans suffered a greater decline in prosperity during this period than did all other classes. However, among inventors, patentees with a commercial orientation (traders and manufacturers) and those in more developed urban markets benefited the most throughout this decade. As the experience of the "great inventors" showed, additions to personal wealth during the decade were associated with entrepreneurial responses to changes in the market. New entrants to invention during the war, regardless of their military orientation, did not benefit much from their efforts. Instead, more committed inventors (those who filed greater numbers of patents) and manufacturers of patented discoveries were rewarded with higher returns. As might be expected, the accumulation of wealth was positively related to age and to prior stocks of assets. The wealth of inventors varied little in terms of the geographical location of their patenting, suggesting a broader market-oriented explanation for outcomes.

---

[22] See Khan (2005); Lamoreaux and Sokoloff (2001).

Table 8.6 Distribution of Inventors' Wealth by Military Orientation (Percentage)

	General Inventors		Military Inventors		All Inventors	
	1860	1870	1860	1870	1860	1870
Real estate						
None	51.6	40.9	57.1	45.3	54.0	42.7
$1–$499	3.1	3.4	3.4	2.1	3.2	2.8
$500–$999	5.2	6.2	2.5	3.7	4.0	5.2
$1,000–$1,999	11.9	10.2	9.9	9.2	11.0	9.8
$2,000–$4,999	13.5	18.1	7.8	13.8	11.0	16.4
$5,000–$9,999	8.0	8.8	8.4	9.7	8.2	9.2
$10,000 and above	6.8	12.3	10.9	16.3	8.6	13.9
Average	4,158	5,710	7,552	8,716	5,641	6,908
Median	0	993	0	709	0	922
Std. dev.	40,000	22,501	31,195	28,249	36,438	24,980
N	616	657	493	435	1,012	1,092
Personal Wealth						
None	32.9	26.2	40.1	31.3	36.0	28.3
$1–$499	31.3	25.5	22.4	18.2	27.5	28.3
$500–$999	5.4	13.4	6.2	12.7	5.7	13.1
$1,000–$1,999	12.5	8.8	12.0	10.6	12.3	9.5
$2,000–$4,999	8.0	12.7	7.1	11.7	7.6	12.3
$5,000–$9,999	6.2	4.1	3.0	3.5	4.8	3.9
$10,000 and above	3.8	9.3	9.2	12.0	6.1	10.4
Average	1,948	4,316	4,063	6,246	2,873	5,019
Median	300	426	300	567	300	447
Std. dev.	6,558	20,215	16,276	22,268	11,871	21,067
N	578	656	493	434	1,012	1,090

	Average Wealth Before and After War					
	Real Estate Wealth			Personal Wealth		
	1860	1870	Change	1860	1870	Change
Inventors responsive to war						
First military invention filed during war	8,859	8,508	−287	4,071	5,954	1,630
First invention filed during war	4,112	5,490	2,850	2,576	3,595	1,558
U.S. pop. (Soltow)	2,231	2,141	—	1,549	966	—
U.S. pop. sample	1,521	1,712	734	892	880	−13
Median	0	709	0	200	355	55
Std. dev.	3,768	6,864	6,605	2,844	2,796	3,414

Notes and Sources: The computations exclude observations with missing values in either year. Wealth in 1870 is adjusted for inflation to obtain real values. The wealth statistics for the U.S. population are from Lee Soltow, *Men and Wealth in the United States, 1850–1870* (1975).

The American Civil War was a landmark event in the history of military technology. Large numbers of individuals reoriented their attention to the expanding market for improved methods of destruction and to satisfy the needs of the military. The patent records show a distinct response to the advent of conflict that was uniform across every region, except the South. New entrants into nonmilitary invention during the war tended to be impoverished and so less likely to possess the resources or the reputation to commercialize their product. The war reduced the tendency to migrate that was a feature of successful entrepreneurship and innovation during the antebellum and post-bellum periods. Technological innovation yielded higher average returns to inventors prior to the war but not during the war, possibly because the exaggerated increase in military innovation drove down the marginal return. The plight of patentees who shifted into the market for military technology while the conflict was ongoing exemplifies the war's misallocation of resources. These people tended to be professionals, a class with arguably higher opportunities that had been sacrificed. Moreover, their attention to military invention did not carry over into the postwar period for good reason since, unlike other inventors, they experienced a fall in personal wealth.

An interesting question is why the South failed to keep pace with Northern achievements in military technologies. After all, the South had established their own patent institutions to secure and protect the inventive discoveries of their own inventors. Moreover, they did not recognize the property rights in Northern inventions that were patented outside of their jurisdiction and could freely copy the technologies created by their military rivals. Any response must necessarily be speculative, and no doubt would be subject to endless debates. Possible reasons include barriers such as the absence of tacit knowledge, the inability to benefit from learning by doing, or scarcity of human inventive capital. Perhaps the Southern leadership failed to understand that the world had changed and military victory would now be secured through technological advances, rather than esoteric knowledge about classical maneuvers and strategies. Rather than causal factors, these all seem to be outcomes that still need explaining. Nevertheless, an important part of the answer must be the absence of effective markets in ideas that characterized this region before, during, and after the war. Government transfers and subsidies, however generous, could not compensate for this institutional deficiency.

Sheridan, evidently an optimist regarding the role of weapons technology, thought that "the improvement in the material of war was so great that nations could not make war, such would be the destruction of human life." Sombart similarly contended that the net outcome of wars on the economy and technology was positive. These observers were not correct, but fortunately, pessimists like Nef were equally incorrect in their view that wars destroyed the capacity for future technological progress. The most telling indicator of how military conflicts affect the potential for improvements in material well-being comes not from the Civil War but from the resilient and dramatic surge in inventive activity at its close. The outbreak of peace, not war, propelled the United States toward the permanently higher trajectory of technological achievement that was to establish it as the foremost industrial nation of the twentieth century.

9

Of Apples and Ideas

Knowledge Spillovers in Patents and Prizes

> On the improvement of society by the diffusion of knowledge.
> —Thomas Dick (1840)[1]

Private goods like apples are said to be "rival," because consumption by one person reduces the amount that is available for others, and "if you have an apple and I have an apple and if we exchange these apples then you and I will still each have one apple."[2] However, public goods like ideas are "nonrival," because ideas can be shared without reducing the knowledge of the original creator. "If, however, you have one idea and I have one idea, and we exchange these ideas, then you will have two ideas and I will have two ideas. We will both profit by the interchange."[3]

Unlike a crate of apples, if knowledge can be readily acquired by nonpayers, suppliers of novel ideas must consider how to obtain returns from their efforts and investments, including ways to exclude unauthorized users. Exclusion can be created by property rights that are enforced by the state (patents and copyrights) or by private methods (such as contract or technological barriers to use). As discussed in Chapter 1, scholars in this area tend to overlook natural barriers to the replication of ideas, such as the complexity of the discovery. Jan Matzeliger's shoe-lasting machinery was so novel and intricate that even the Patent Office examiners found it difficult to understand the specifications. Today, all of the data from the Human Genome Project are available online, but very few have the knowledge and expertise to use them. "Contribution goods" are a subset of public goods that involve knowledge, whether tacit or explicit, that requires

---

[1] "The general diffusion of knowledge among all ranks is an object much to be desired," Thomas Dick, *On the Improvement of Society by the Diffusion of Knowledge* (Philadelphia: E. C. Biddle, 1840).

[2] The Royal Society of Arts, many intellectual property professors, and Kanye West, among others, have attributed to George Bernard Shaw this quote of unknown origin. Tempted by the apple, an academic work has confidently cited Shaw's *The Apple Cart*. With equal confidence, I can confirm that this statement does not appear in *The Apple Cart*. A bona fide quote from that work is "Our present way of giving votes to ignorance and calling it democracy will upset any plan."

[3] From "a writer" associated with the *Maritime Farmer and Co-operative Dairyman*, vol. 24 (1918), p. 40.

Inventing Ideas. B. Zorina Khan, Oxford University Press (2020). © Oxford University Press.
DOI: 10.1093/oso/9780190936075.001.0001

active participation and prior experience in the arts before they can be of value to the user.[4] As study of the great inventors showed, knowledge with the characteristics of contribution goods implies that insiders would have an advantage over outsiders in detecting profitable areas for investments in new ideas.

New information, whether a pure public good or ideas that are protected by rights of exclusion, can create advantages for society in the form of externalities, or spillover benefits that are in excess of the private benefits to their producer. Theories of endogenous economic growth highlight the importance of knowledge spillovers in promoting economic progress.[5] Knowledge spillovers have important implications for the dynamic distribution of income within and across regions, since the ability to benefit from externalities likely plays a role in the longitudinal tendency toward convergence and divergence in wealth and standards of living. As such, the extent to which knowledge diffuses over time and space is a question of paramount importance.[6] An extensive literature empirically analyzes the nature and determinants of knowledge spillovers and the patterns of diffusion in information, using a variety of methods, data, and levels of aggregation.[7] These studies agree that externalities in ideas are to a large extent bounded by such factors as language and distance, and inventive spillovers are primarily local rather than global.[8] Part of this discussion relates to the ways in which institutions can enhance or inhibit the flow of ideas and technological knowledge. To date, a great deal of research attention has been directed to the role of property rights and institutions in agriculture and their relation to informational spillovers in farming and the nonfarm sectors.

From a static theoretical perspective, social welfare might be improved by ensuring open access to ideas and inventions. However, if inventors of productive discoveries cannot appropriate the returns from their efforts, or if innovation markets do not function effectively, underinvestment in innovation is likely to occur. The common justification for offering patent protection proposes a bargain or a social contract by means of which inventors obtain a temporary exclusive right to their own discoveries, in return for disclosing their ideas in sufficient detail that the invention can be recreated by someone who is skilled in the arts. By contrast, alternative methods of appropriation include the use of lead

---

[4] Kealey and Ricketts (2014).

[5] Romer (1990).

[6] Regional scientists have long shown that geographical factors were an integral part of social and technological patterns. Researchers have considered whether the spatial transmission of knowledge becomes more difficult the greater is the degree of knowledge intensity. Others argue that economic progress is a function of "weightless" innovations, which defy boundaries of time and space: once created, these discoveries spontaneously diffuse without geographical or locational limits.

[7] Döring and Schnellenbach (2006); Hornbeck and Keskin (2015).

[8] Keller (2002).

time, private methods of exclusion, trade secrecy, bundling with complementary goods, and prizes. Although these mechanisms might benefit the owners of new technologies, at the same time they could impose a social cost if the information were not available to others despite its low incremental cost. Today a number of economists support inducements for innovation through prizes rather than exclusive property rights in patented inventions, because they implicitly assume that the prize-winning ideas will automatically be freely accessible and usable for everyone in society. In practice, it is not clear whether prize systems with unpatented ideas would tend to promote knowledge spillovers or inhibit them. The assumption that prize systems are better at diffusing information needs to be empirically examined.

Geography and location have always played a central role in the historical approach to technological change. This historical perspective exploits information from temporal variations, which allows us to better understand the relationship between geographical location and knowledge spillovers. For instance, if we observe external benefits in the innovations of the first and second Industrial Revolutions, then spillovers are less likely to be a function of specific technologies. In a pioneering study, Kenneth Sokoloff showed that the expansion of transportation networks that allowed access to markets was important in promoting inventive activity in the antebellum period, and this was especially true in rural locales.[9] Among the great inventors in the United States, the majority migrated across regions and countries, and tended to cluster in areas with expanding markets where they were able to tap into knowledge networks and markets in patented ideas. All the evidence we have collected shows that productive inventors paid close attention to the patenting records, and intermediaries like patent agents and attorneys facilitated access to such information. In this and other respects, technologically and economically important contributions exhibited similar patterns to those of less eminent patentees.

Access to markets varied over the course of the nineteenth century and so did innovation institutions, and this variation offers richer insights into the nature and causes of the diffusion of information. A number of effective economic history studies have addressed the locational dimension of innovation in terms of the external effects from technological creativity outside the United States. Patented inventions in Germany, for instance, provided evidence of technological and geographical knowledge spillovers.[10] Patents, of course, offer their owners a right of exclusion, whereas most prizes, at least officially, do not. Prefectures in

---

[9] Sokoloff (1988).
[10] Richter and Streb (2011).

Meiji Japan offered large numbers of prizes, and a study of the patterns in this region argues that prizes created large spillovers of technical knowledge, although these findings could be due to variables that were omitted from the analysis.[11] Such projects add to our understanding of the nature of technological change but still leave open the question of the impact of different rules and standards and, in particular, whether patented inventions tended to generate greater spillovers than prizes that were not subject to legal rights of exclusion.

The previous chapter analyzed annual industrial exhibitions of prominent mechanics' institutes in the United States. Some studies of mechanics' institutes in Britain have suggested that these organizations served as a means of socialization and social control by the moneyed manufacturing class that was intended to quell any tendency to rebel against new technologies that might threaten to displace the artisanal crafts.[12] That was decidedly not the case for these organizations across the United States. American mechanics' institutions primarily focused on ensuring that artisans and working-class inventors had access to the latest advances in practical fields that would benefit them in their occupations and allow them to acquire more human capital and social standing. The exhibitions that these institutes sponsored similarly had the objectives of promoting the transmission of useful knowledge and technical training, stimulating new inventions through prize and cash incentives, and sparking a spirit of emulation among the skilled artisans and machinists. Thus, mechanics' institutions offer a valuable opportunity for examining the social spillovers derived from different sorts of property rights in technological inventions.

This chapter examines spatial patterns in prizes and patented innovations in the United States to discover what they reveal about how different sorts of property rights in inventive activity affected the rest of society. In particular, the discussion addresses whether knowledge spillovers varied according to the nature of institutions that promoted inventive activity and innovation during the period of early industrialization. The first section discusses the dataset, including utility patents and a sample of technological prizes awarded at the annual fairs of the American Institute of New York. The descriptive statistics identify the characteristics of the patentees, exhibitors, and innovations and the patterns of inventive activity across industrial and sectoral categories. The analysis compares the effects of geographical proximity across patenting and prizes at the county level. This comparison leads to the conclusion that patent rules and standards were more effective than prizes in generating knowledge spillovers.

---

[11] Nicholas (2013).
[12] See Berg (1982).

Patents, Prizes, and Technological Change

The early industrial period in the United States amounted to an age of patented ideas, where inventors who devised patentable inventions were quick to secure property rights in their discoveries, and many exchanged patent rights in extensive markets in invention. At the same time, more decentralized institutions were founded to offer encouragement to inventors and to promote all the different stages of science and technology, from knowledge creation to the diffusion and commercialization of inventive ideas. As the manufacturing sector grew in economic importance and new discoveries captured (indeed, often captivated) popular interest, specialized industrial exhibitions developed to display mechanical inventions and the output from factories.

The American Institute of New York was one of the most significant "encouragement" institutions of the day. The institute was founded in 1828, with the objective of "encouraging and promoting domestic industry in this State, and the United States, in Agriculture, Commerce, Manufacturing and the Arts, and any improvements made therein, by bestowing rewards and other benefits on those who shall make such improvements, or excel in any of the said branches."[13] The institute was acknowledged to be successful in promoting both local and national economic development, and the New York state legislature voted in 1841 to award an annual sum to subsidize the efforts of the organization. Artisans, engineers, scientists, manufacturers, and honorary members such as Henry Clay and Daniel Webster joined with others motivated by the common goal of boosting American innovation and output. The organization also represented the interests of inventors and manufacturing firms in the political arena, lobbying for tariff protection, internal improvements like the Erie Canal, and patent reforms.

A major stated objective of all participants was to enhance economic development through the diffusion of technical knowledge and other "useful information":

> The American Institute, located as it is in the metropolis of the Union, and embracing the great objects contained in its charter, we believe affords greater facilities for observation, enquiry, comparison, and the diffusion of important facts, pertaining to the industrial pursuits of men, than any similar association within our knowledge. It was the pioneer in the great movement of association for disseminating useful information, and practically illustrating the productions of agriculture, manufactures, and the handicraft of the mechanic.[14]

[13] Lucius Eugene Chittenden, *The Value of Instruction in the Mechanic Arts* (New York: American Institute, 1889), p. 13.

[14] *Transactions* (1850), p. 8.

James Tallmadge, the president from 1831 to 1850, was also a cofounder of New York University at the same time. The institute compiled an extensive library of statistical and scientific reference books, sponsored lectures and classes, and further published its own journal with reports on experiments and notices of inventions, as well as detailed information on activities such as their industrial fairs. Standing committees continually attended to questions affecting technological innovations in manufactures, arts and sciences, commerce, and agriculture.

Over the course of the nineteenth century, the institute showcased American industry and enterprise in annual fairs that initially catered to entrants primarily from New York State and the surrounding Mid-Atlantic area. However, the success of these exhibitions soon attracted participants from more distant regions. The organizers of the American Institute paid for the transportation costs of all exhibits, which implies that variation in such costs did not influence the observed outcomes. The competition among entries was managed by technically qualified judges, who awarded premiums primarily in the form of cash, certificates, and medals. The classes of exhibits at the annual fairs included fine arts and education, dwellings, dress and handicraft, chemistry and mineralogy, engines and machinery, communications, and agriculture and horticulture. The statesman James Pendleton Kennedy was impressed by the

> dazzling display of the rich and rare creations of mechanical skill . . . an array of the products of art, of which it is not too much to affirm that, for excellence in the workmanship, beauty in the design, genius in the invention, or variety in the kind, may challenge competition with the works of any equal number of artisans in the most elaborately trained and dexterous community upon the face of the globe.[15]

Industrial fairs may have had the stated objective of promoting inventive activity and innovation, but their organizers were well aware of the potential tradeoffs that existed with their joint objective of attracting attendance and participation by firms. As Table 9.1 illustrates, the incentives of exhibitors and the institute were aligned: exhibitions that were popular among the general public would prove to be profitable for the sponsors. Similarly, the greater the likelihood of receiving accolades for their products and the more numerous the viewers of their displays, the more the exhibitors would be inclined to make the investments to attend. At the annual fair of 1850, over 2,800 exhibitors offered

---

[15] John P. Kennedy, *An Address Delivered Before the American Institute* (New York: George F. Hopkins & Son, 1833).

Table 9.1 Finances of the American Institute Exhibitions, 1840–1870

Year	Exhibitors (Number)	Receipts ($)	Costs ($)	Returns (%)	Awards ($)	Cash Awards (%)
1840	1,600	6,581	5,128	28.3	—	—
1845	1,985	12,600	8,683	45.1	2,250	7.6
1850	2,830	22,419	14,694	52.6	4,000	7.7
1855	2,254	27,705	19,505	42.0	3,527	8.6
1859	1,293	16,241	23,360	–30.5	4,038	5.1
1865	1,271	29,201	24,014	21.6	3,000	0.3
1870	1,678	72,074	51,031	41.2	1,793	0

Notes and Sources: Annual Reports of the Board of Managers for the American Institute of New York (Albany, NY, various years). Fairs were held in the city of New York, including the New York Crystal Palace building. Returns indicate the difference between revenues from the ticket sales at the fair, less the expenditures, as a percentage of the latter. Winners could choose the cash equivalent of their award instead of the actual prize. "Cash awards" show the value of prizes that were given out in cash, relative to the dollar value of total "Awards." The cash value of awards in an average year was over $1.2 million in current 2019 dollars.

thousands of items on display, largely in the category of manufacturing, and the organizers distributed some $4,000 worth of medals, silver cups, cash, and other awards. The finance committee reported earnings of $22,419 with $14,694 in expenditures, for a return of 52.6% over outlays. To put these figures into perspective, note that 4,800 exhibitors, half of them American, participated in the International New York Crystal Palace industrial fair in 1853. Participants who displayed their inventions were keenly interested in the patent system and, during the 1850 American Institute fair, a plenary lecture on the patent laws was delivered by George Gifford, a celebrated patent lawyer who had been involved in landmark disputes regarding such inventions as the telegraph and sewing machine.

Over time, the scope and scale of the exhibition expanded. The American Institute claimed, with good reason, that its annual exhibitions were more representative of domestic ingenuity than the items transported and displayed in the U.S. pavilion at the sporadic world's fairs held in foreign countries. At the American Institute exhibition in 1870, the items on display occupied over a hundred thousand square feet. Among the invited speakers were Horace Greeley (president of the institute at that time) and Benjamin Silliman, the celebrated Yale chemist. Approximately six hundred thousand visitors attended the fair, generating revenues of $72,000, along with expenditures of $51,000, and the event yielded a return of 41.2%. Some 140 judges deliberated before awarding

$1,800 in premiums, although they decided that none of the exhibits in that year was worthy of the coveted Grand Medal of Honor.[16]

The reports of the institute included an account of all the exhibits that were entered in competition for prizes that year. These volumes offered information about the names of exhibitors, their city and state of residence, a description of the invention, and the type of prize allocated to exhibits that received awards. Some of the committee records mentioned the reasons for their decisions, such as the degree of novelty in the exhibit (a patentable characteristic) or their admiration of the attractiveness, fine finish, and superior workmanship associated with the item (unpatentable characteristics). These records on the exhibits were matched to patent documents to identify a sample of patented inventions on display, and to the manuscript population censuses to acquire further data on all of the inventions and inventors or exhibitors.

As was typically the case for such technological prize awards, most exhibitors did not seek prizes as a source of revenue, but as a means of product differentiation. Recipients could opt for the equivalent cash value of an award, but few winners chose money over medals, and nonmonetary prizes prevailed (see Table 9.1). Rather, these gold and silver medals were "prized" as a means of signaling value to consumers or investors and as a way to promote, advertise, and commercialize exhibited innovations in the marketplace. Such objectives are a central feature of ex post prizes that add to the difficulty of optimally "pricing" such awards and in part explain why participants in prize competitions generally have an incentive to engage in expenditures in excess of the expected reward. Highly successful with visitors during much of the nineteenth century, by 1897 the institute's *Annual Report* conceded that "the era of the fair as an advertising medium, as well as a popular resort, must be recorded as an amusement and business venture of the past." The decline of both international and national industrial fairs and competition for prizes in general coincided with the advent of the age of professional advertising for mass markets.

Participants at the New York Fair

The participants at the fairs of the American Institute of New York included inventors, manufacturers, and commercializers. Great inventors like Cyrus McCormick, Richard Gatling, and Charles Goodyear who manufactured their patented inventions participated, like all manufacturers of innovations, to advertise their products. But, as was the case at all industrial fairs, the inventors who

---

[16] These details are taken from the *Annual Reports* of the American Institute for the relevant years.

specialized in inventive activity had no incentive to turn up at exhibitions. Since most of the great inventors were just such specialized professional inventors, the majority of the exhibitors were less eminent inventors and manufacturers.

A more representative example, Gardner Chilson of Boston, Massachusetts, had been born in Connecticut in 1804; worked as an apprentice in pattern and cabinet making in Sterling, Connecticut; moved to Providence; and then set up shop in Boston. In 1850, his occupation was listed as a trader, and he did not report any wealth. His foundry in Massachusetts initially manufactured stoves invented by other patentees. Subsequently, like most other creative artisans, he was inspired while learning on the job and obtained his own patents to protect both novel inventions and new designs for stoves and furnaces. At the 1852 exhibition in New York, he displayed a portable hot air furnace that he had patented in 1850 and manufactured in his factory. The patent records reveal that Chilson was a multiple patentee in the United States, England, and France, and he ultimately owned an estate that was valued in excess of $300,000.

The exhibits at the American Institute allow us to compare the patterns from federal patents to the items that received technological prizes given to innovations outside the patent system. The panel dataset for the analysis in this chapter consists of random samples of 6,500 observations drawn from patent records and 5,700 technological innovations from the annual exhibitions at the American Institute, between 1835 and 1870. Patent rights are filtered through an examination process that screens for novelty, whereas access for exhibitors was for the most part unrestricted, although the fairs excluded peddlers and hawkers from the standing exhibits. It is interesting to note that, whereas some observers have suggested that the patent system was (and is) biased against women inventors because few have obtained patent protection, inventions by women were even scarcer at all the industrial exhibitions, even though they were encouraged to participate. Women did feature prominently in areas such as sewing and paintings and displays of food items, but only thirty-one appear in the roster of technological inventions and innovations. Thus, the evidence suggests that reasons for their relatively low contributions to conventional inventive creativity owed to factors beyond the nature of technological institutions.

Prize exhibits in world fairs and domestic exhibitions primarily consisted of manufactured final products such as guns, watches, and rubber goods (Table 9.2). Industries differ in terms of their technical inputs and capital intensity, and their capacity for effective trade secrecy or for generating spillovers also varies. For instance, in the absence of distinct measures for transmitting information, it might be expected that manufacturing processes or inputs into manufacturing are less susceptible to unauthorized copying than a change in final goods such as the wheel of a carriage or the barrel of a gun. The second column of data in Table 9.2 denotes whether the exhibit fell under the subject matter that was patentable

Table 9.2 Industrial Distribution of Prizes and Patents

Industry	Total	Patentable	Patents	Gold Medal	Silver Medal	Bronze Medal
Agriculture (*n*)	456	284	53	38	120	35
Col %	8.4	11.5	10.1	7.2	9.3	5.9
Row %		80.0		10.7	33.7	9.8
Arts (*n*)	271	156	14	37	41	21
Col %	5.0	3.5	2.7	7.6	3.2	3.6
Row %		55.1		23.7	26.3	13.5
Construction (*n*)	523	185	63	40	127	69
Col %	9.7	7.7	12.0	8.2	9.9	11.8
Row %		48.9		10.2	32.5	17.6
Furniture (*n*)	326	234	22	20	64	38
Col %	6.0	2.2	4.2	4.2	5.0	6.5
Row %		23.1		8.3	26.7	15.8
Heat and power (*n*)	674	500	90	68	183	103
Col %	12.5	20.2	17.2	14.0	14.2	17.6
Row %		92.1		12.5	33.6	18.9
Medical (*n*)	128	101	16	19	30	8
Col %	2.4	2.2	3.1	3.9	2.3	1.4
Row %		53.5		18.6	29.4	7.8
Machines (*n*)	698	448	76	57	183	91
Col %	12.0	18.1	14.5	11.7	14.2	15.6
Row %		83.1		10.6	34.0	16.9
Manuf. goods (*n*)	1,367	523	97	108	296	141
Col %	25.3	21.1	18.5	22.2	22.9	24.1
Row %		51.3		10.6	28.9	13.8
Textiles (*n*)	418	308	38	49	114	24
Col %	7.7	5.7	7.3	10.1	8.8	4.1
Row %		45.8		15.9	36.9	7.8
Transportation (*n*)	523	188	51	49	124	51
Col %	9.7	7.6	9.7	10.1	9.6	8.7
Row %		45.3		11.8	29.7	12.2
Total (*n*)	5410	2475	524	486	1288	585
%	100	60.6	39.8	11.9	31.4	14.2

Notes and Sources: See Table 9.1. The percentages in the table include the undisplayed calculations for 1,740 honorary diplomas, given to 42% of the 4,100 exhibits that received awards. "Patents" refer to exhibits that were patented.

(note that this is a very minimal criterion, since patentability further required substantive novelty in terms of both time and place, which cannot be determined from any exhibition data).[17] The exhibits varied significantly in terms of their patentable subject matter, ranging from over 90% of heat and power innovations to below a quarter in the furniture industry.

Discussions of such exhibits often speculate about the "propensity to patent" among displayed items. However, as discussed in the case of the Massachusetts Mechanics' Institute in Chapter 7, this concept is not meaningful, and the patterns here support those findings. Over 35% of the exhibits belonged to firms that (according to U.S. patent law) could not obtain patents in their own name, and other items were likewise submitted by agents and other individuals who were not the original inventors. Hence, it is impossible to systematically trace whether all exhibitors held patents on the innovations they displayed. Of the total 3,100 innovations that were credited to individuals, 524, or 16%, were traced in the patent records. About 1,521 of exhibits fell within patentable subject matter. A third of such patentable innovations were actually patented, but it is impossible to determine the key category of novelty, which is the primary qualification of the U.S. patent grant.

Another interesting characteristic is the types of industries that were represented in these exhibitions. Table 9.2 reports on the distribution of medals by industrial category, which were allocated based on the final use of the invention. If medals were awarded based on technological contributions, we would expect that the proportions would vary by industry. But, similar to the findings for other regional and international exhibitions, prizes seem to have been allotted on a fixed ratio, with a quota allocated to each type of industrial class, rather than on the basis of overall productivity. As in the other administered systems such as the Royal Society of Arts, it is noticeable that the most evident deviation from this finding is in the category for the arts, such as musical instruments and the printing of elaborate blank books. This is consistent with the exhibition reports, which frequently praised items for their visual attractiveness, finish, or workmanship, and to a lesser extent for such criteria as novelty or technological improvements that could lead to patents being granted.

The sample from the expositions at the institute can also be examined in terms of their industrial and geographical distributions (Table 9.3). The exhibits and the general population of patents are fairly similar in sectoral coverage, apart from the lower percentage of agricultural innovations being shown at the fairs. Specific types of technologies, such as engines and manufacturing machinery, featured in the patent records as well as at the exhibitions. However, in keeping

---

[17] Patentability was determined by subject matter and by searches in the patent records for the entire nineteenth century. See the discussion in Appendix II.

Table 9.3 Patents and Prizes in New York

| | PATENTS ($N = 6,490$) | | | | | | | |
| | Before 1855 | | 1855–1859 | | 1860–1864 | | 1865–1869 | |
	N	%	N	%	N	%	N	%
Sector								
Agriculture	58	15.7	175	19.9	236	16.2	646	17.1
Construction	36	9.7	69	7.9	81	5.6	339	9.0
Engines	47	12.7	102	11.6	109	7.5	355	9.4
Manufacturing	207	56.0	496	56.5	930	63.9	2219	58.7
Transportation	18	4.9	30	3.4	78	5.4	183	4.8
Other	4	1.1	6	0.7	21	1.4	39	1.0
	Before 1855		1855–1859		1860–1864		1865–1869	
	N	%	N	%	N	%	N	%
Region								
New York	110	29.7	219	24.9	414	28.5	950	25.1
Mid-Atlantic	84	22.7	162	18.4	227	15.6	574	15.2
New England	91	24.6	222	25.3	339	23.3	814	21.5
Other	84	22.7	274	31.2	474	32.6	1445	38.2
	PRIZES ($N = 5,700$)							
	Before 1855		1855–1859		1860–1864		1865–1870	
	N	%	N	%	N	%	N	%
Sector								
Agriculture	233	9.1	126	7.6	51	10.4	64	6.5
Construction	227	8.9	198	11.9	34	7.0	102	10.3
Engines	129	5.0	148	8.9	43	8.8	96	9.7
Manufacturing	1672	65.3	983	59.1	323	66.1	641	64.8
Transportation	248	9.7	194	11.7	27	5.5	77	7.8
Other	52	2.0	15	0.9	11	2.3	9	0.9
	Before 1855		1855–1859		1860–1864		1865–1870	
	N	%	N	%	N	%	N	%
Region								
New York	1,879	73.4	1,254	75.4	381	77.9	709	71.7
Mid-Atlantic	263	10.3	147	8.8	26	5.3	95	9.6
New England	363	14.2	215	12.9	80	16.4	162	16.4
Other	56	2.2	48	2.9	2	0.4	23	2.3

Sources: See text. Innovations are allocated to industry and sector of final use. The Mid-Atlantic region includes New Jersey, Pennsylvania, Maryland, and Delaware; the New England region includes Connecticut, Maine, Massachusetts, New Hampshire, Rhode Island, and Vermont.

with the patterns at all industrial exhibitions and world's fairs, more manufacturing firms and their products are included in these data than among the patent records. Thus, patents were more representative of the entire population of new technologies (novel inventions), whereas the prizes showcased draws from the population of innovations (commercialized items).

As one might expect, the patent data are more broadly distributed across regions. The annual exhibitions of the American Institute were located in New York and, although innovators from surrounding regions were quick to take advantage of the opportunity to display their products, the representation of the majority of exhibitors does not extend beyond the Mid-Atlantic and New England. The New York exhibits fail to track the increasing importance of the Midwest and West in technological innovation after the Civil War. However, it is important to note that the scope of regional coverage is not significant for our purposes. First, the Mid-Atlantic and New England regions were the locus of the majority of patents filed in this early period, accounting for two-thirds of all patents. Second, in the period before the 1880s, the effective geographic range of knowledge spillovers would likely be fairly restricted, due to the substantial information costs and other transaction costs that prevailed before the spread of low-cost, high-speed transportation and telecommunications. Moreover, the emphasis here is on the relative performance of patent institutions and prize systems in generating local spillovers, and this can be determined more effectively if we reduce sources of unobserved variation by restricting the comparative analysis to the representative Mid-Atlantic region.

Patents and prize-winning innovations differed in many regards, apart from geography and location. Statistical analysis of patents in New York and the other regions in the United States can explain two-thirds of the variation in patenting rates, suggesting that inventive activity that is protected by intellectual property rights is quite systematic. By way of contrast, the award of prizes uniformly consists of largely unexplained variation. The signal-to-noise ratio is similarly low in all national and international exhibitions, in the United States and overseas. The grant of gold medals is almost totally random, and the precision is not much improved with both gold and silver awards.

Thus, like the allocation of prizes in general, the awards at the New York exhibitions can be viewed as unsystematic lotteries. Firms were somewhat more likely to win the better class of medals, especially if they filed exhibits that fell under patentable subject matter. However, professional inventors who had larger numbers of patents in their portfolios did not glean any special advantage for their exhibits, even if their inventions were valued in the marketplace and assigned to a second party. Similarly, machinists and engineers, who typically possessed the highest amount of specialized knowledge and inventive human capital, did not show any higher propensity to win in competitions for prizes.

Unlike patented inventions, location and spatial factors such as cities, urbanization, and estimates of longitude and latitude add virtually nothing to explain prize awards. If prizes also had a lower likelihood of being associated with location and geography, then such awards would fail the necessary precondition for the prevalence of geographical and technological spillovers. The next section therefore specifically considers the geographical relationships among patents and exhibits. (Appendix III includes spatial econometric estimates that support, but are not necessary for understanding, the discussion.)

Correlations across Time and Space

To what extent do institutional differences influence knowledge spillovers? Positive spillovers exist when benefits freely accrue to third parties (those who are not directly involved in a transaction), such as a passerby who listens to the information provided by a tour guide to his paying customers. This chapter estimates the extent to which patent institutions generate spillovers for all inventors relative to prize institutions, which are generally held to promote inventive activity more effectively because prize-winning ideas are not subject to a right of exclusion.

Knowledge spillovers can be measured by the relationship between clusters of inventions in defined geographical areas, and a vast amount of academic work has employed similar methods. However, no other study of knowledge spillovers has considered whether patents and prize innovations differ in their spatial relationships. Research about spatially distributed patenting in the modern period examines geographical links at a fairly high level of aggregation, including countries and states, and shows that inventiveness is boosted by proximity to high patenting areas. However, spillovers, productivity, and output in the nineteenth century were confined to more disaggregated units, so the analysis in this chapter is based on location of the patentees and prize winners at the county level.

To estimate the prevalence of spillovers, it is necessary to identify a measure of "spatial proximity," or the geographic adjacency of innovations. We might expect that influence is inversely related to distance, and closeness can be determined by the distance of the location of the invention from other counties, using specific locations described in degrees of latitudes and longitudes. This distance instrument does not incorporate transaction costs, nor does it include barriers like inhospitable topography or facilitating factors such as major transportation networks. Another way to analyze distance is based on a contiguous counties approach, which calculates the effects of patenting or innovations in a specific county on adjacent counties that share a common border ("queen contiguity" in Figure 9.1).

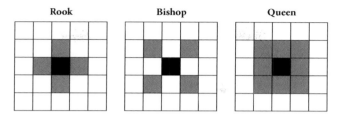

Figure 9.1 Knowledge Spillovers: Measures of Geographical Contiguity

Sources and Notes: The figure shows common measures of geographical proximity. Each square represents a county: the black indicates the central or primary county of interest; the shaded areas show the space over which spillovers are estimated. The analysis in this chapter is based on "queen" contiguity, in which interactions are not directionally constrained.

Spatial autocorrelation exists when the values of a variable are affected by others in a nearby location. In this measure, spillovers would be detected if inventive activity in nearby counties increases after an invention occurs in a specific location, controlling for other factors. Moran's statistic allows us to test for the existence of spatial autocorrelation. A value that significantly exceeds zero indicates that similar values are closely located (positive spatial autocorrelation), and a value that is less than zero implies that dissimilar values are closely located (negative autocorrelation).[18]

The results for total patents per capita are highly significant, indicating the existence of geographical spillover effects. For purposes of comparison with the exhibitions data, it is noticeable that New York displayed a statistically significant pattern of correlation, both in the antebellum period and after. New England and the entrants into technological markets in the West and Midwest also experienced high benefits from closeness to innovative counties. This might be expected, owing to the smaller geographical area of the New England region and to the abundance of modes of transportation over water and land that prevailed even in the early years of settlement of these counties. It is noticeable and plausible that in the postbellum period the degree of spatial correlation falls somewhat in other areas (even becoming indistinguishable from zero in the Mid-Atlantic) but experiences a moderate increase in the frontier regions. As followers or latecomers, the frontier areas were likely beneficiaries from the investments that the Northeast had made in technological inputs.

The evidence for patented inventions thus indicates the presence of geographical knowledge spillovers. However, the results are very different for the prize-winning innovations from the American Institute exhibitions that had not

[18] Tables in Appendix III present the results of testing whether there is a spatial relationship between patented inventions and prize-winning inventions.

been identified as patented inventions. The region of interest here is New York, which was the place of residence for most of the innovators, and it is striking that the correlations are essentially not different from zero. These differences in outcome across patents and prize-winning innovations within New York suggest that state-specific factors were unlikely to account for the variation in geographical spillovers. Instead, patent institutions offered greater potential for spillover benefits to the general population of inventors, including patentees and those who did not themselves obtain patents.

Patenting in adjacent counties was positively affected by higher inventive activity at the county level. This is consistent with the bargain or contract view of patents, in which society offers a temporary property right to inventors in exchange for knowledge about the discovery that increases future social welfare. The American patent grant requires a specification that is sufficiently detailed to enable a person who is skilled in the arts to recreate the patented invention. From the earliest years of the patent system, policymakers engaged in discussions about how to ensure that the accumulated stock of knowledge was available to the broader public. The benefits from uniformity in rules and standards were a major reason that a federal patent law replaced the state-level intellectual property rules that had prevailed in colonial America. Patent legislation and the patent system included measures to distribute information about patents that were granted.

Inventors were able to quickly retrieve published information from both private and public sources. Newspapers across the country listed patents that were granted and those that had expired. The report of the Commissioner of Patents was distributed throughout the country, and cumulative indices were periodically published. Inventors and visitors to Washington noted how useful they found the precisely constructed models of the prior art that were displayed in the Patent Office (Figure 9.2). They could also consult extensive registers of patent sales and contracts that dated to the beginning of the patent system. Regardless of their place of residence, interested parties could also readily obtain copies of drawings and full specifications of specific inventions, and it is impressive to note how often inventors—even those who prosecuted their own applications unassisted—made references to recently acquired patents in their own patent applications. And, of course, a key function of patent intermediaries and attorneys was to reduce such informational costs for their clients.

My own career in patent research started with the serendipitous discovery in the UCLA University Research Library of a compendium of all patents granted through 1846, authorized by Edmund Burke, the Commissioner of Patents at that time, and a later subject matter index in three volumes through 1873, which was compiled by Mortimer Leggett. I dedicated months of work to painstakingly transcribing these Patent Office records into digital format on the computer.

MUSEUM OF UNITED STATES PATENT OFFICE.

Figure 9.2 Patent Office as a Repository of Useful Knowledge
The U.S. patent system from its inception established detailed rules to enable open
and free access to information and specific mechanisms to enhance the diffusion
of information. The grand Patent Office building, one of the most elegant in
Washington, DC, attracted numerous visitors and inventors who wished to examine
the intricate patent models and records that were displayed in this perceived "temple
to technology."
Source: Library of Congress.

Subsequently, as a professor in New England, I often spent entire days in the
Patent Office depository at the Boston Public Library, paging through precarious
stacks of the annual reports of the Commissioner. These enormous tomes had to
be shared with patent lawyers who were still finding it useful to consult the hard-
copy drawings and specifications in these historical records.

An especially thought-provoking discovery included a full set of nineteenth-
century Patent Office reports that was located in the Shakers' library in the village

of Sabbathday Lake, Maine. The Shakers, a communitarian religious society, lived in small villages scattered through New England and New York.[19] They were typically described as "otherworldly" and "unmaterialistic" pacifists who retreated into economically self-sufficient enclaves. Members of Shaker communities were noted for the craftsmanship and creativity of their products and for their mechanical and inventive abilities. A common notion is that Shakers were opposed to the idea of acquiring property rights to their inventions and commercialization. Although this was true in some cases, many had actually been meticulous in protecting their inventions, and the patent records reveal that the "unmaterialistic" Shakers had obtained several hundred patents. A number of the most successful Shaker inventors even left the sect to pursue the opportunity to financially benefit from their discoveries. Such isolated communities provide an extreme example of the benefits that creative inventors derived from the diffusion initiatives and outreach of the U.S. Patent Office.

In the internet era, it is easy to dismiss the importance of such low-tech mechanisms as physical availability of books. Nevertheless, recent research underlines the role of patent depository libraries in generating spillovers, well into the twentieth century.[20] Access to patent volumes lowered the cost to potential inventors of acquiring technical information, including details about geographically distant inventive claims and an expanded scope of technical fields. The opening of patent libraries increased local patenting by some 17%, after controlling for other variables. More remote effects likely included ancillary gains in new business ventures and employment. As such, although some patentees and firms might have an incentive to "game the system" in attempts to circumvent disclosure rules, the U.S. patent system nevertheless functioned effectively in creating knowledge spillovers that benefited potential inventors and follow-on inventions.

By contrast, the evidence here shows that supposedly open access to ideas that were granted prizes did not generate as much diffusion as in the case of inventions that were protected by patent grants. Exhibits at the American Institute might have been open to the public, and some inventors were able to copy from the displays, but there was likely a selection effect that influenced the owners of inventions that were readily duplicable not to display them at fairs or submit them for prizes. Other machinery might be sufficiently abstruse or complex that their composition offered a natural exclusivity. Moreover, even if inventors had access to knowledge about innovations because they were able to turn up

---

[19] Andrews and Andrews (1982).
[20] Furman et al. (2018). Hegde and Luo (2017) note that this "credible, standardized, and centralized repository" for useful knowledge lowered information costs and encouraged transactions in the market for ideas.

in person at fairs, there were few or no mechanisms that might have led to the further spread of information. This was of course a function of the decentralized nature of the prize system in the United States, but even in European countries that offered centralized institutions such as the Royal Society of Arts, access to prize-winning inventions and to information about them was quite limited.

Reports for individual inventions—whether for the Royal Society of Arts in London, the Society for the Encouragement of National Industry in Paris, or national and international exhibitions—varied significantly in terms of the amount of knowledge that was made available to the public and the utility of that information. Some panels published detailed reports on tests and experiments, whereas others prepared descriptions that were technically useless, and were terse to the point of providing no information about the invention and the rationale for their decisions. Many prize-granting processes were deliberately shrouded in secrecy. In Europe, institutions to encourage technological innovations switched away from prize systems to supporting patent reforms. They further decided to offer grants for research and directly provided technical information and support for artisanal education, because they found that the award of prizes did not contribute to the advancement of knowledge and social welfare. In the case of the Royal Society of Arts, the administration "clearly perceived about halfway through this period that a more valuable function for the Society would be the communication of knowledge of technical or commercial matters, and the discussion of papers, rather than prize awards."[21]

Patents, unlike prize-winning innovations, created external benefits for third parties such as other potential patentees. Another interesting question is whether spillovers from patents influenced general rates of creativity. This can be gauged by examining the effects of geographical clustering of patents in counties adjacent to areas of prize-winning innovations that were not associated with patents, after adjusting for population (see Table A.4). Recall that prize exhibits of the American Institute were more heterogeneous than patents, and the award of prizes was quite random and idiosyncratic. Nevertheless, the inclusion of spatial effects increases our ability to explain variation in unpatentable innovations as well as those that could not be identified as patented. Moreover, proximity to high-patenting counties had a significantly positive effect on the frequency of this class of exhibits.

In general, a 10% increase in patenting activity in neighboring counties increased the amount of nonpatented and unpatentable innovations per capita in a county by as much as 3%. Such an impact could have been due to the possible influence of manufacturing industries, available capital funding, or urban

---

[21] Hall (1974: 648).

amenities. However, controlling for manufacturing labor force and urbanization does not materially alter the results. Other locational factors are only marginally significant. Following other authors, the analysis also tests the impact of location in terms of latitude and longitude on the changes in unpatentable innovations. It is interesting to observe that distance has an effect through latitude, but not in terms of longitude, possibly owing to the influence of the Erie Canal. In sum, this analysis of patented inventions and prizes at a key series of industrial exhibitions shows that prize-winning inventions created private benefits for their owners but provided few additional external benefits for the rest of society. However, patents were associated with knowledge spillovers that also benefited other innovators, including those who had not themselves filed for property rights in their inventions or created patentable inventions.

A Summing Up

Useful ideas are different from apples and other rival goods, because certain kinds of knowledge can be replicated and reused at low or zero cost. This chapter shows marked differences in knowledge spillovers across prizes and patented inventions, which in part derive from the design of U.S. patent institutions. More than any other country in history, from its inception the U.S. patent system was designed to facilitate the diffusion of useful knowledge. Patents required detailed disclosure of information, and U.S. patent documents provide an unparalleled stock of accumulated knowledge about technological advances over the course of more than two centuries. The patent system—unlike prize institutions— explicitly incorporated mechanisms for systematic recording, access, and dispersion of technical information across place and time. For both isolated inventors and those who resided among the thriving clusters of patentees in large cities, the information disclosed in patent documents offered invaluable ideas and insights into the state of the art and aided the formulation of their own novel incremental contributions.

Today, many economists have become disenchanted with patents as a policy to promote technological and economic progress and have lobbied for prizes as a substitute. Their focus is on the theoretical deadweight loss that monopolies engender, which is assumed to be absent in the case of prizes. However, this literature has largely ignored other facets of the tradeoff between patents and prizes, including the role of inventive spillovers and the diffusion of information. In recent decades, economists have begun to pay more attention to the role of geography and distance in enhancing and inhibiting technological change. A plethora of studies in the modern period attest to the existence of significant spatial externalities that are due to knowledge spillovers. Even so, the research on knowledge spillovers is typically limited to identifying its existence rather than to determining the specific mechanisms through which spillovers operate. By comparing patented inventions and innovations that were entered in competition for prizes, we can gain valuable insights into the institutional mechanisms that influence technological externalities.

International exhibitions provided an effective means of fulfilling political agendas and of advertising and commercializing innovations by export-oriented firms, but were unrepresentative of novel contributions at the frontier of technology. The primary goals of mechanics' institutes were to promote technical training and the advancement of inventive abilities, and their annual exhibitions permit a systematic approach that avoids the most serious analytical drawbacks of international expositions. For instance, the exhibitions of the American Institute avoid the significant selection biases created by variable costs and distance traveled. Their frequency, consistent location, and continuity in sponsorship and rules add a time-series component to cross-sections that avoids the idiosyncratic nature of individual international exhibitions in different countries.

The analysis of technological spillovers in this chapter was based on econometric measures that are commonly used to measure externalities that are a function of geographical location and spatial distribution. The first section tested the hypothesis of spatial autocorrelation in patenting and in the innovations that were exhibited at the annual fairs of the American Institute in New York. In keeping with the contract theory of patents, the procedure identified high and statistically significant spatial autocorrelation, indicating the prevalence of geographical spillovers in the sample of inventions that were patented. At the same time, prize innovations were much less likely to be spatially dependent, especially in the key area of New York State. These results demonstrate that inventions that garner prizes and commercial innovations were less effective in generating external benefits from knowledge spillovers. The second part of the analysis showed that patents provided significant positive externalities, not just for other patentees, but also for all creative individuals, regardless of whether or not they themselves were patent inventors or engaged in the commercialization of unpatentable innovations. By way of contrast, prizes may have offered private benefits to the competitors involved but were less likely to create externalities in useful knowledge that could enhance social welfare in general.

These results about the diffusion of information through patent disclosure and policy initiatives help to explain why patenting of useful ideas did not necessarily lead to monopolies in product markets. Even if patentees had acquired exclusive rights to their idea for (at that time) fourteen to seventeen years, access to detailed information about the discovery facilitated substitute inventions that worked around the initial patent or led to ideas for follow-on inventions. Interference records document how numerous inventors were inspired by the accomplishments of prior patentees. Instead of a single sewing machine or stove, the patent records were rife with hundreds and thousands of variants of key inventions, even during the life of the initial property right. Dominance of product markets often owed to related but different factors, such as entrepreneurship, reputation, economies of scale, and perceived quality.

The "paradox of patenting" holds that patents limit the diffusion of inventions in the short run but facilitate the diffusion of inventions in the long run. Economists have tended to focus narrowly on the short-run right of exclusion that patents enable, which they have linked to inefficiencies that arise from monopolistic tendencies to increase product prices above the competitive level and to create "artificial scarcity." This analysis is rooted in the zero-sum world of apples, where one person's ownership necessarily implies another person's lack of access. More significantly, this perspective overlooks the fact that, while the patentee's specific discovery is protected, the patented idea can give rise to a potentially unlimited supply of related but noninfringing ideas and inventions. In the world of ideas, exclusive rights benefited their owners and, when coupled with a duty to disclose, generated spillover benefits for other inventors and innovations. The founders of American industrial policies were therefore prescient in their decisions regarding the appropriate role of patents and prizes in promoting the progress of science and useful arts in the knowledge economy.

10

Designing Women

Gender and Innovation

A newe way by her invented.

—Amy Everard (1637)

According to Voltaire, "women have been scientists and warriors, but there have never been any female inventors."[1] The underrepresentation of women inventors has never been as stark as Voltaire claimed, but it is perplexing that a technology gender gap still persists even in the most developed countries in the twenty-first century. An assessment of women's inventions raises fundamental questions about conventional perspectives regarding the scope and nature of knowledge and innovation. Some critics contend that the gap exists because patent institutions have actively excluded women as inventors. Whether this is true can be gauged by considering women's creativity in different institutional settings, both within and beyond the patent system, and across different nations, during the first and second Industrial Revolutions.

This chapter presents a new perspective on women and technology by combining patent records with innovation prizes that included unpatentable inventions and innovations. Most empirical studies of women in technology are limited to small samples in a single country. The discussion here, by contrast, draws on the experience of women in Britain, France, and the United States, who were responsible for over 12,200 inventions. Women in all jurisdictions employed entrepreneurial abilities to overcome institutional and cultural constraints and to ensure their inventions were valued in the marketplace. Bolstered by a democratic patent system and markets for technology, American women inventors of all backgrounds primarily demonstrated their comparative advantage in household and domestic innovations. European women, who confronted barriers such as costly patent fees and the biases of panels in administered systems, exploited links with family firms and other socioeconomic advantages that were not available to all their peers. The overall patterns of inventive activity and innovation

---

[1] "On a vu des femmes très savantes comme il en fut de guerrières; mais il n'y en a jamais eu d'inventrices." Voltaire, *Dictionnaire philosophique* (Paris, 1829), p. 354.

Inventing Ideas. B. Zorina Khan, Oxford University Press (2020). © Oxford University Press.
DOI: 10.1093/oso/9780190936075.001.0001

highlight the effects of specific rules and standards in intellectual property rights systems, as well as the role of adjacent institutions such as the legal system and more informal networks and connections.

The study of women's inventions at the individual level draws attention to certain features of the economic analysis of inventive activity and innovation that inhibit a fuller understanding of technological advances. A serious shortfall is the failure, in both theory and quantitative estimations, to capture improvements in consumer final goods and designs. The tendency to simply count up and aggregate women's inventions by industry, without carefully scrutinizing their qualitative descriptions, frequently misses subtle changes in consumer final goods, especially in the case of product designs that extend beyond alterations in the visual appearance of the item. Moreover, a general lacuna exists in empirical scholarship regarding creativity that lies at the borders of aesthetics and utility, and of art and technology narrowly defined. As this study shows, women tended to make disproportionately greater contributions in just such areas, and part of the "gender gap" arguably is due to the analytical gap regarding the sort of knowledge and ideas that are conventionally considered as technological innovation.

The Scope of Technological Creativity

The conventional approach to the economics of technology centers on advances in producer goods and inputs that lead to an expansion in production possibilities. More recently, a number of theorists have incorporated consumer goods in their models of economic growth and have discussed the central and mutually reinforcing roles of demand, consumption, and human learning in attaining growth. Allocative efficiency, on the other hand, refers to changes in the composition of output that improve consumer welfare without increasing productive possibilities, holding other things constant. Although it is acknowledged that improvements in the nature and quality of consumer products and design innovations might have a direct impact on household satisfaction, such innovations are difficult to measure and quantify. As a result, both theoretical and empirical economic studies have tended to underestimate these sorts of incremental changes, and it is likely that such drawbacks are replicated when male judges or committee members confront women's contributions.

During the past decade, significant advances have been made in the economic analysis of new goods. At the same time, many of these studies evince a bias toward the "grand innovation" model of technological change, which characterizes inventions in terms of sharp discontinuities and economy-wide disruption and ignores or dismisses the incremental nature of all inventive activity. Prominent economists contend that fundamental differences exist between "new goods which open up whole new product categories and other new goods which increase quality or variety within product categories.... [N]ew goods that establish entire new categories (like the automobile) will be economically more important than improvements that occur within categories."[2] This heuristic of approaching technological innovation in terms of overly broad discrete categories—"the" jet plane, telephone, radio, automobile, or computer—does not merely mischaracterize the inventive process. Just as important, it has negative implications for the analysis and valuation of women's technological contributions, which tend to be located well within such expansive categories.

Ironically, a similar orientation was evident among nineteenth-century feminists, who wished to prove male–female equivalence. Their political rhetoric demanded heroines of invention and idealized women who patented "great inventions" or technical machinery. They were determined "to make no note of the inventions of women unless it is something quite distinguished and brilliant. We must not call attention to anything that would cause us to lose ground."[3] This branch of the women's movement increasingly denigrated traditionally female activities such as housework and attempted to downplay the importance of incremental "feminine technologies." As an official Women's Bureau Bulletin declared: "If the steady increase in the numbers of patents granted women is accounted for merely by the increase in the number of patented hairpins, hair curlers, and such trifles in feminine equipment, it is without large significance either to civilization or as an indication of women's inventive abilities." The organizers of the Women's Pavilion at the World's Columbian Exposition in 1893 were deeply concerned to find that potential entries mainly included ordinary household products such as kitchen utensils and apparel.

Traditional economic theory has additional shortcomings when applied in historical context. For instance, the positive effects on social welfare of free trade based on comparative advantage implies that mercantilism and nationalism are characterized as a deviation from efficiency. The United States was the first country to offer patent protection that was contingent on a global definition of novelty; that is, the invention had to be new to the world. However, mercantilism was a central approach of European societies in the nineteenth century, a bent that was also evident in their technology policies. As such, their definition of novelty in technological innovation was restricted to national boundaries, and the objective was often to recreate, or offer patents of importation for, foreign technologies that could have been obtained more cheaply through free trade.

The Maryland Institute noted in 1850 that "there is in woman's mind and hand full capacity for excellence in the art of Design, and that the practice of

---

[2] Bresnahan and Gordon (2008: 12).
[3] Cited in Weimann (1981: 429).

them is congenial to her sphere." Within the context of a closed economy, the re-creation of foreign goods increased domestic consumption possibilities. This form of import substitution was especially directed toward designs, dyes, colors, the decorative arts, and luxury goods, where women's innovations were dispro-portionately represented. At the Royal Society of Arts, early awards were offered for the domestic production of verdigris, Turkey red dyes, madder, and marbled paper that was of similar quality to the items imported from Europe. In France, Mlle Manceau received awards from the National Industrial Expositions and from the Conservatory for Arts and Trades, because her firm recreated a type of bonnet that was original to Italy. She was able to export the bonnets to other cities in Europe, the United States, and "remarkably" Naples and Florence as well, possibly because of the lower price of her products.

Scholars in the history of technology and gender studies have directed a great deal of attention to the question of how to adequately capture these contributions of women. Judith McGaw, for example, calls for an extension of the scope of tech-nology beyond masculine hardware to incorporate the skills and knowledge that typically belong to women. However, her discussion of "feminine technologies" seems equally narrowly focused, highlighting innovations related to women's bi-ological and social differences.[4] The feminist perspective has only recently re-vised their conception of what constitutes technology to also incorporate design studies. This can be combined with research in marketing and consumer goods, which confirms the significant market value of artistic and aesthetic components of products.[5] As such, from both an economic and a social perspective, it is useful to investigate the activities of women inventors in conventional technologies, as well as consumer and design-related innovations.

Women Inventors and Innovation Institutions

Institutions, or the rules and standards that frame human interaction, create opportunities and boundaries for women that have varied by place and time, but our knowledge about women's activities through history is limited. Patent records are especially valuable because they enable women to become visible once again. Patents offer an admittedly narrow window on inventive activity by women, but even this limited glimpse reveals significant systematic details that cannot be replicated elsewhere. At the same time, patent protection is limited to inventions that satisfy the rules for patentability, which implies that certain types of creativity are not represented. In the absence of analogous information

[4] McGaw (1997).
[5] Postrel (2004).

about technological discovery and commercialization outside the patent system, historians have used entries and awards from industrial exhibitions as a means of gauging other dimensions of women's contribution to innovation.[6]

Early examples of women pioneers of invention include English patentee Sara Jerom, who filed in 1635 for legal protection for a machine to slice wood into thin pieces to make items such as bandboxes. Two years later, the patent specification (description) of Amy Everard, a widow, declared her intention "to use and exercise within England and Wales the mistery, skill, and invention of making, ordering, or contriving of saffron into a manner or forme which shall dissolve into tincture and of divers other vegetables (as of roses, gilliflowers, and the like), into an essence, after a newe way by her invented." The British records also notably include the patents granted to Thomas Masters of Philadelphia in 1715 and 1716, for a means of curing Indian corn and for making straw bonnets; the patents were actually obtained on behalf of his wife, Sybilla, who was thus the first American colonist to obtain a patent in England.

The British patent system did not examine whether the applicant was the true inventor, and patents were often bestowed on individuals who simply acquired an invention, such as importers of foreign discoveries. As noted before, procedures for obtaining a patent were extremely costly in terms of time and money. Patent agents and lawyers could help to negotiate the bureaucracy and legal pitfalls, but at an additional cost. The system also inhibited the diffusion of information and made it difficult for inventors outside of London to conduct patent searches, increasing the likelihood that their property rights would later be subject to adverse judicial rulings. After two centuries of dissatisfaction, reforms in the system occurred in 1852 and in 1884.[7] The time series (Figure 10.1a) show that these changes had a significant impact on all British inventors, including women patentees. The cheaper patents after 1884 disproportionately benefited women, who typically would have had lower financial resources and access to capital markets. Conversely, the conclusion is that the pre-reform institutions disproportionately inhibited women.

The central features of the French patent system were similar to the British. Access to property rights in invention was also hampered by fees that were several multiples of average income, and the registration system left the sorting of claims about priority, novelty, and general validity to the costly arena of the

---

[6] Examples include Cordato (1989) and Warner (1979).

[7] The patent application process was rationalized in one patent office, and the patent term varied according to willingness to pay for extensions to the life of the property right. The initial grant was contingent on a payment of £25, an extra £50 was due after three years, and after seven years patentees were required to pay £100 to maintain the patent to full term. The costs fell further after 1883, when only £4 was charged for the initial term of four years, and the remaining £150 could be paid in annual increments.

courts. In short, in both Britain and France, wealthy inventors had a greater ability to file for patent protection, to commercialize their inventions, and to enforce their rights at law, and the system disadvantaged the creators of incremental inventions. French women were nevertheless relatively more successful

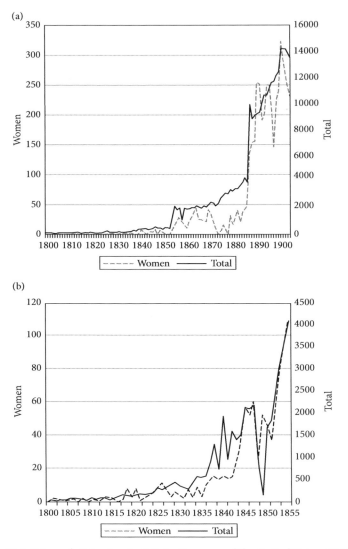

Figure 10.1 Women's Patenting in Britain, France, and the United States, 1800–1900 (a) Britain: Women and Total Patenting. (b) France: Women and Total Patenting, 1791–1855.

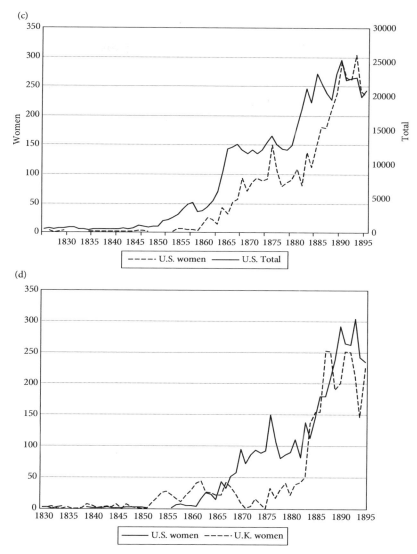

Figure 10.1 (c) United States: Women and Total Patenting, 1830–1900.
(d) Patenting by Women in Britain and the United States, 1830–1900.

Notes and Sources: National patent offices. The data for women patentees from France and the United States consist of all patents granted. The estimate of women patentees in the United Kingdom was drawn from a random sample and adjusted for the total population.

than their British counterparts at negotiating the process of obtaining patent rights and appropriating returns from their efforts. The proportion of patents that was issued to women in France increased after legal reforms in 1844, rising from 1.6% to 3.0% of total grants. Filers could choose the term of the patent life, and, despite the significantly higher fees for long-term protection, French women were noticeably more likely than men to file for these higher-valued patents. I have shown elsewhere that part of the reason for women's innovativeness in France arose from their association with family firms, suggesting that these female inventors were wealthier than their counterparts without such connections.[8] As such, these rules and standards disadvantaged ordinary women, but those with an elite standing were able to circumvent or reduce the attendant obstacles.

As discussed in other chapters, the American patent system offered strong incentives for inventive activity, regardless of the wealth or identity of the inventor. At a time when women faced barriers in most contexts, the first U.S. Patent Act of 1790 specifically allowed "That upon the petition of any person or persons that *he, she, or they*, hath invented of discovered any useful art, . . . it shall be lawful . . . to cause letters patent to be made out in the name of the United States" (my emphasis). As a result, in the federal patent system, creative women had the same standing as their male counterparts. Female inventors also benefited because patent fees were deliberately kept low, so that the sole filter was technical creativity rather than financial standing.[9]

The Patent Office was progressive in its hiring of women and in the use of competitive examinations for technically skilled positions, before such practices became standard. Notably, Clara Barton was likely the first woman to secure full-time employment in the federal civil service, hired in 1854 as a secretary and copyist at the same salary offered to men.[10] Coveted positions in the patent examination division were achieved by technical knowledge and proficiency, rather than political connections. In 1872, the pioneering Anna Nichols of Melrose, Massachusetts, successfully sat for the required test and was appointed as the first female patent examiner in the United States (and

---

[8] See Khan (2005, 2016). The 1791 French statute stipulated patent fees from 300 livres through 1,500 livres, based on the declared term of the patent. After the reforms of 1844, fees fell but were still out of reach of the working class, ranging from 500 francs ($100) for a five-year patent to 1,000 francs for a ten-year patent to 1,500 for a patent of fifteen years, payable in annual installments.

[9] Patentees in the nineteenth century paid a fee of $30 to $35 to the Patent Office (average per capita income nationally was approximately $130 at this time, and $180 in the inventive Northeast region).

[10] According to Barton, this equal-pay policy attracted "no little denunciation on the part of those who foresaw dangerous precedents." At the outbreak of the Civil War, Barton was again working as a copyist for the Patent Office, before embarking on her legendary humanitarian career. Percy Epler, *The Life of Clara Barton* (1915), p. 26.

likely the world). She entered as third assistant examiner, with equal pay to her male colleagues, and just two years later was promoted to the position of second assistant examiner. The following year, Sarah J. Noyes, who had apprenticed with a patent lawyer in Connecticut, joined the Electrical Division as a clerk. Several newspapers announced in July 1874 that she had passed the civil service examination and been elevated from the ranks of clerical employees to third assistant examiner, at a salary of $1,400. Noyes had a long career that spanned over two decades in the "complex and exacting" area of burgeoning electrical inventions, owing to a deep knowledge of the subject matter that won the respect of her peers. Later appointees included Frances R. Lybrand, second assistant examiner of civil engineering, who specialized in railroads and conveyers, and Amelia Tyler, second assistant examiner ("there is not a person in the world today with a broader or more minute technical knowledge of railroad gate construction than Miss Tyler"). These rational gender-neutral employment rules for patent examiners would have underlined that the vetting of women's patent applications was far from the arbitrary practices of administered innovation systems.

In a key departure from patent rules in Britain and France, in the United States only the first and true inventor was permitted to apply for patent protection. As a result, American patent records offer more accurate indexes of inventive activity by women. For instance, Ella E. Boland's 1897 invention for a curtain pole bracket was designed "to avoid the necessity of climbing upon chairs, tables, and step ladders which are dangerous and inconvenient for any one and especially for ladies." The British patent for the curtain pole bracket included Joseph Boland, her husband, as a coinventor. However, to avoid invalidity, the U.S. patent was issued in her name alone. Ella Boland was involved in both sides of the market for invention, selling half of the rights to her U.S. patent to a merchant tailor in Pittsburgh, and purchasing another curtain pole patent belonging to Otto E. Wagener.

Patent records provide invaluable information about women's inventive activity, but all inventions are not patentable, and not all inventors apply for patents. If intellectual property rules and standards exclude women, as some have claimed, then we should observe different patterns outside the patent system. One way to supplement patent information is to consider prize-granting institutions.[11] Industrial fairs, for instance, typically did not require potential exhibitors to pay entry fees, and there was no technical examination, so

---

[11] The nonpatent sources used in this chapter include prizes and exhibits from the Royal Society of Arts in England, the Exhibitions of National Industry in France, the Paris Universal Exhibition of 1855, the 1876 Centennial Exhibition, and the 1893 World's Columbian Exposition. Mechanics' institutes in the United States sponsored industrial fairs in most large American cities, on a roughly annual or biennial basis, and these were sampled to construct a panel dataset of prizes

they should represent a larger and more diverse population of innovations. As discussed in other chapters, panels of judges in decentralized committees granted prizes, based on a wide array of criteria that ranged from novelty to aesthetics, as well as idiosyncratic characteristics of the entrants.[12] The organizers of many industrial exhibitions directly encouraged women to submit entries, expecting that their "taste and delicacy" would lead to visually appealing displays that would attract more visitors to the events. Special gallery spaces were often set aside for a "Woman's Department," to boost female participation.[13] The unpatentable innovations on display illustrate the considerable and diverse creativity that was occurring outside the formal patent system.

In all three countries, women's patenting is significantly below the number of patents that men filed, over the entire period (Figure 10.1). However, the overall variation in women's patenting is similar to the general population of patentees, suggesting that women responded to many of the same factors. This is not to say that the experience of male and female inventors was identical, since they were affected by different rules and standards. One notable adjacent institution was the legal system, where legal rules and their enforcement could either constrain or enable inventive activity and innovation. During much of the nineteenth century, while single women had the same legal rights as men, married women in all three countries were subject to the rules of coverture, which vested legal rights in their husband. Coverture affected women's economic activities negatively: legal reforms that removed such laws altered the economic costs and benefits associated with women's involvement in commercial activity and significantly increased inventive activity by female patentees.[14] Similarly, women's entrepreneurship was constrained by their legal disability under the law, and this uncertainty about enforcement created greater capital imperfections for women relative to men.

Women and Inventive Activity

During the early industrial period, middle-class women, in particular, have often been characterized as populating a "separate sphere," allegedly retreating from

and technological innovations from major cities—including Boston, New York, Philadelphia, San Francisco, Chicago, Cincinnati, and St. Louis—over the course of the nineteenth century.

[12] The Centennial rules, for example, provided that "awards should be based upon inherent and comparative merit; the elements of merit being held to include considerations relating to originality, invention, discovery, utility, quality, skill, workmanship, fitness for the purposes intended, adaptation to public wants, economy and cost." *Report of the United States Centennial Commission* (J. B. Lippincott, 1877), p. 15.

[13] See the *Report of the Exhibition* (1887), p. 16.

[14] Khan (1996, 2005, 2016).

activity in the market economy in accordance with social norms. As one journalist observed in the nineteenth century, "they talk about a woman's sphere,
as though it had a limit." As economic actors, women had a visible presence
largely as unskilled workers in factories, as sole proprietors, petty producers,
and investors in low-risk bank shares.[15] The records for patents and innovation
prizes reveal a much more complex reality, in which women of all backgrounds
and marital status were directly and actively engaged in creative endeavors that
encompassed the entire range of technological discovery, from conception
through commercialization in the market.

Summary statistics for women's patenting reveals a striking similarity in the
central tendencies across the three countries (Table 10.1). As contemporary
feminists highlighted, a number of women's inventions were technically sophis-
ticated and made lasting contributions to industrial machines and production
innovations. However, the majority of women's patented inventions exploited
their comparative advantage in household activities and consumer-oriented
technologies. It is significant that the exhibitions data also mirror these general
patterns. The records for women inventors underline the difference between
technical value and economic value, since many of the commercially profitable
items were hardly complex technologies. The *New York World* newspaper in 1889
featured an article about a U.S. woman patentee who manufactured little bags
to hold powder puffs that "filled a long felt want," and "now advises women who
toil at fancy work for the shops for a pittance to 'go invent something, for it pays
much better.'"

Rather than retreating to a "separate sphere," inventive women productively
combined household and nonhousehold activities.[16] Regardless of whether
they worked outside the home or not, women were engaged in devising creative improvements that benefited society. Families often provided resources
and a social context that had the potential to increase women's inventive activities. French women inventors demonstrated greater productivity at both invention and commercialization, in part because they were able to exploit family
connections, as well as the tangible and intangible assets of relatives and of family
businesses. This was especially true because married women could circumvent legal constraints by operating within the ambit of family businesses. The
experience of women inventors emphasizes that institutions were not fixed and

---

[15] Khan (2019b) shows that many women in antebellum New England were far from passive
investors and were frequently involved in funding risky start-ups in manufacturing and transportation, to a greater extent than previously estimated.

[16] "All questions relating to 'woman's sphere' are so far as the writer's position is affected set aside
as settled. It is accepted that any honest remunerative work a woman can do well is proper work for a
woman to do." Etta M. Taylor, *How: A Practical Business Guide for American Women of All Conditions
and Ages, Who Want to Make Money, But Do Not Know How* (Minneapolis, 1893), preface.

Table 10.1 Women Patentees in Britain, France, and the United States

	U.S.		U.K.		France	
	Patents	Percent	Patents	Percent	Patents	Percent
Multiple Patenting						
1 patent filed	2,683	66.6	2,133	69	368	36.8
2 or 3	874	21.7	659	21.3	346	34.6
4–9	324	8	285	9.2	227	22.7
10 or more	149	3.7	14	0.5	60	6.0
Coinventors						
Female, related	19	6	45	5.8	20	7.8
Male, related	115	36.3	214	27.6	99	38.8
Female, unrelated	35	11	84	10.8	36	14.1
Male, unrelated	148	46.7	432	55.7	100	39.2
No coinventors	3,857	92.4	2,526	81.7	746	74.5
Marital Status						
Single	127	21.2	—	—	296	29.6
Married	240	40	—	—	414	41.4
Widowed	233	38.8	—	—	290	29
Foreign Patents						
Women	167	4	565	18.3	45	4.5

Notes and Sources: Coinventors' relationships were determined by whether the individuals had the same surname, which will tend to be an underestimate. Marital status in the United States was determined by matching names of patentees to manuscript population censuses.

nonintersecting; rather, they adjusted and compensated for deficiencies in existing rules and standards in other areas.

Families often functioned as quasi-apprenticeship institutions, allowing knowledge and know-how to be transferred across generations for daughters as well as sons. Similarly, wives often served as active and coequal business partners. For women who were restricted to the household, family training offered an especially important mechanism for the acquisition and transmission of technical and inventive capital. In France, Madame Houel and her daughter provide insights into the relationship between entrepreneurial inventor-mothers and their children. Mme Houel received a favorable citation from the jury at the 1823 exposition in Paris for a type of paint that dried quickly without a strong smell, which could be used on wood and metal alike. Her daughter later made her own improvements on this paint and was accorded a bronze medal at the 1839 Paris exhibition. Similarly, the 1881 U.K. census shows that the thirty-year-old housewife Caroline Newman Bintcliffe was married to a builder, and she lived in the same London house as her brother-in-law, a manufacturer of stationery. In 1897, she obtained a patent for envelopes and recorded her occupation as a stationer. By the census of 1911, a family business had developed, where Caroline was now herself operating as a "manufacturing stationer," assisted by her adult son.

The information on coinventors reflects some of the mechanisms that promoted inventive activity by women. The majority of U.S. women patentees (92.4%) had no coinventors, indicating the independent nature of female inventive activity, and this was also true to a lesser extent for the French and British inventors (74.5% and 81.7%, respectively). The Prest siblings—Thomas, James, and Mary—of Blackburn, Lancaster, were all joint applicants for an 1898 patent to protect their improvements in bicycle tires. Another example is the long-term family collaboration between sisters Eva and Cecilia MacKenzie of Inverness, who together obtained six patents between 1895 and 1913, including two for improvements in hairpins with their mother, Mrs. Georgina MacKenzie. By 1911, when they applied for another patent for improvements in apparel for women and children, the sisters listed their occupation as manufacturers. A significant fraction of multiple-inventor patents included unrelated males, typically from the same geographical location. Many of the coinventor listings in the United States testified to women's collaborations with machinists, engineers, pattern makers, toolmakers, manufacturers, and artisans, who, according to patent law, were required to have made a substantive contribution to the invention to be granted coinventor status.

Patentees in need of the services of lawyers to help with such transactions as foreign patent filing were able to pay upfront by assigning part of their patent rights. The attempt to file for patent rights in foreign countries may be regarded as an index of higher-valued inventions, so it is worth noting that approximately one in five of the U.K. women's patents came from overseas, primarily from the United States. Foreign women who entered the competitive American market often filed patents for inventions that were especially valuable. Alberta Caspar of London, England, declared herself to be an "inventor of easy artistic processes." She devised a popular way of decorating surfaces with an ornate metallic luster in brilliant tints and founded her own company to market do-it-yourself projects to amateur home decorators. She further obtained an 1884 patent for improvements in imitation stained glass. When she proceeded to file for a U.S. patent not long after, she assigned half of her rights in the invention to Eugene Pearl, a patent lawyer in New York, as compensation for his services. The American patent received two citations from inventors in the late twentieth century, indicating that it was an influential technology. Caspar successfully engaged in litigation to prevent unauthorized use of her intellectual property.

The number of patents per person indicates the magnitude of investments in inventive capital and professionalism in patenting activity. The patterns for multiple inventions (as gauged by both patents and prize awards) were significantly different in France, relative to the other two countries. In Britain and the United States, two-thirds of women's patents were issued to inventors who never filed a second patent, whereas almost three-quarters of French patents (including improvements) were for multiple patents. For instance, Sophie-Geneviève Mercier obtained fifteen patents between 1842 and 1855, the majority for various inventions to treat laundry, and two for cleaning cutlery, which all required some familiarity with chemical processing. In France, professional patenting was closely associated with ownership of enterprises in related lines of business.

Women inventors who wished to obtain financial returns from their efforts benefited significantly from markets in patents.[17] The ability to assign part of their property rights provided a means of compensating intermediaries who helped with funding, advice on commercialization, and litigation about property rights and related issues. Intermediaries helped women inventors to mobilize venture capital and to exploit their inventions in other ways, and some also took positions in inventions as business partners or outright purchasers of the patent rights. For instance, Maria Beasley transferred part of the rights in an invention to James Henry of Philadelphia in exchange for advance financing to complete her machine. Lloyd Wiegand, a mechanical engineer and draughtsman, joined her in coinventing a shoe-lasting machine. Beasley, who had no formal mechanical training, also collaborated with many other patentees, including Emil Hugentobler, a New York engineer.

Maria Elizabeth Beasley (1836–1913), a middle-aged housewife, achieved extraordinary commercial and financial success as a professional inventor and multiple patentee.[18] Although atypical, her career illustrates how entrepreneurial women were able to readily manage and commercialize their ideas through the patent system. Beasley was born in North Carolina to a well-off family. As a young girl she played around her father's mill and obtained materials and tools to conduct experiments in making waterwheels and boats to transport herself and her pets. Her grandfather, Jacob Hauser, owned a distillery in Kentucky, and during visits she observed the coopers working in his shop and accompanied him on trips to identify better ways of making

---

[17] *Daily Tribune of Bismarck, North Dakota*, October 31, 1889.
[18] The sources of biographical information include censuses, city directories, trade journals, and contemporary newspaper records.

barrels. After the Civil War her family's fortunes declined, and she worked as a milliner to supplement her husband's income. In 1876, she moved with her husband and two sons to Philadelphia, where she was fascinated by the inventions on display at the Centennial Exhibition. By the time of the World's Columbian Exposition in 1893, she had become one of the leading women inventors in the world, and her patented machines were prominently displayed. Her husband, John Q. Beasley, a doctor, changed his profession to patent agent to market her inventions, and her son Walter was employed in running her factory.

Maria Beasley's first attempts at invention included a foot warmer and roasting pan, which were patented in 1878 and 1879. She then started thinking again about the problem that had occupied her grandfather and soon devised a machine that automated the process of making hoops, which markedly increased output to 1,700 barrels per day. The rights to her invention were sold outright to two intermediaries, who licensed the patent to the Standard Oil Corporation for royalties of $175 per month. This success encouraged her to specialize in inventions to mechanize the production of barrels. Engineering journals deemed her barrel-making machinery "the most remarkable inventions of labor-saving machines of recent date." Beasley's discoveries transformed the industry, which had previously been largely labor intensive, and enormously increased productivity and lowered operating costs. A skilled artisan could complete a maximum of eight barrels per day, whereas her machinery required just three unskilled operators to daily produce eight hundred barrels of uniform and reliable quality.

Beasley was quickly able to secure enthusiastic financial backers, which allowed her to establish her own enterprise in 1884 to make and sell barrels. The Beasley Standard Barrel Manufacturing Company, in which she was the majority shareholder, was acquired in 1891 by the American Barrel and Stave Company of New Jersey for $1.4 million in equity. She continued to closely supervise the operations of the machine shop in Philadelphia that produced her inventions. Her reputation in barrel-making machines allowed her to leverage her expertise to technologies in unrelated industries. After patenting a means of increasing the safety of railways, she became one of the founders and directors of the Wabash Avenue Subway Transportation Company of Chicago, with an initial capitalization of $10 million.

Entrepreneurship requires flexibility to meet new opportunities, and this characteristic can be observed in many other women in this sample—indeed, one might argue that all individuals who participated in patenting or exhibitions had to some extent demonstrated entrepreneurial abilities. Table 10.2 suggests that participation in business and in the labor market provided obvious advantages for women that furthered their ability to obtain returns from their creativity.

Table 10.2 Occupations of Women Patentees and Prize Winners in Britain, France, and the United States (Percentages)

Occupations	U.S.		U.K.	FRANCE	
	Patents	Prizes	Patents	Patents	Prizes
Artisan/worker	26.9	11.7	8.8	10.6	8.8
Artist/designer	6.4	32.9	7	0	5.7
Businesswoman	18.4	2.5	5.3	9	7.6
Corset maker	9.7	3.2	7	9.8	5
Manufacturer	19.3	28.6	24.6	47.4	62.6
Mechanical	3.5	3.9	5.3	0	4.1
Professional/elite	11.1	7.8	35.1	17.9	6
Teacher	4.7	9.5	7	5.3	0.3
Percentage who did not work outside the home	33.7	41.1	45.7	38.0	50.5

Notes and Sources: The percentages for jobs outside the home are based on all women with listed occupations, exclusive of those who did not work outside the home (keeping house, at home, none). Occupations in the United States were obtained from city directories and from the population census. British occupations were included in patent documents and in the population census. French occupations were drawn from the patent documents and from the reports of the exhibitions.

Still, in an era when official labor force participation rates were low, it is illuminating to find abundant evidence in these records for previously undocumented entrepreneurial and commercial activities. This is especially evident in the French context, where manufacturers accounted for a disproportionate number of occupations (47.4% of patentees and 62.6% of exhibitors). For instance, the Joly sisters obtained a full-term patent on corsets and listed themselves as corset makers in 1848; however, by 1853, the sisters were manufacturing envelopes that were secure enough to use for confidential business transactions, for which they had obtained another patent.

The exhibitions data are also valuable for revealing women's activities in commercialization and innovation. Mme Désirée Debuchy inherited a large-scale and prosperous textile-making enterprise in Tourcoing (Nord), which, under the ownership of her husband, had won medals each year from 1827 up to the time of his death. Under her management, the juries at the 1849 and 1855 exhibitions rewarded the products with prizes for their good taste, low prices, success in the marketplace, and competitiveness with English goods. Other women, such as Mme Gevelot, were explicitly commended for improving on the products of their family businesses. Gevelot devised a new form of fuses for cartridges, which became greatly sought after in the market. The reports on her enterprise in 1844 noted that, while her husband was in charge, the business was well run, but under her management, the factory operated all the better.

The much higher fees for patents in Britain and France reduced the representation of working-class women among European women patentees, in marked contrast to the United States (Table 10.2). The democratic nature of the American patent system is evident in the higher percentage of patentees from the artisan and worker classes (26.9%), as compared to Britain (8.8%) and France (10.6%). These patterns are reinforced by the difference in the occupations of women who obtained patents and those who participated in exhibitions, which were much less costly and therefore associated with lower financial barriers. The proportion of teachers and professional women was roughly the same for patents and exhibitions in the United States but varied markedly in France, where this category accounted for 23.2% of known occupations for patentees and just 6.3% for exhibitors. Of course, not all innovative women had formal occupations. In the United States, 33.7% of female patentees who could be traced were listed as keeping house or without occupations, relative to 45.7% in the United Kingdom and 38.0% in France.

The industrial distribution of patents filed by working women shows that, like the "great inventors," the majority of women inventors were "insiders" who tended to produce job-related inventions. This correlation between inventiveness and occupation suggests that tacit knowledge and learning on the job contributed to their creativity. Elizabeth Barnston Parnell of Sydney, Australia, a professional metallurgist, obtained several British patents for her improved methods of processing ores and furnaces, which met a need in the production of complex minerals with sulfides of copper, lead, zinc, silver, and antimony. The E. B. Parnell Sulphur process and an improved furnace were successful in trial experiments and created a great deal of interest among investors, who formed a syndicate (in which she retained a majority interest) to prosecute her inventive claims in a large number of countries and colonies. Lizzie H. Goggs, an art dealer in Liverpool, obtained a patent for making metallic paints, along with T. T. Irvine, her partner in the Fine Art Company. A more esoteric example is offered by Elizabeth French, a medium and practitioner of "galvanic medicine," who obtained an 1875 U.S. patent for an electrotherapeutic device that influenced future innovations in this area.

Manufacturers were also likely to be responsible for inventions that were related to their enterprises. For instance, Martha Kerr, a manufacturer of washing machines in Liverpool, filed a patent claim for a spring-lever washing machine. French widows who inherited businesses that had been founded or managed by their husbands, in particular, were the least likely to enter exhibits in traditionally female industries such as apparel and household items; instead, 18.1% of their awards were in technical fields, and one-third were in the textile industry. Similarly, Eliza Rippingille became the head of a flourishing lamp and stove manufacturing company when her husband and father-in-law both died on the same day. She obtained a patent along with her foreman in the Aston Brook Lamp Works, the Birmingham branch of her enterprise producing "world renowned patent oil cooking & warming stoves, lamps." Of course, the causality was sometimes reversed, when inventors established manufacturing enterprises to appropriate returns from their inventive activity, either on their own accord or along with partners and investors who provided financial or physical capital to float the business.

Nevertheless, since all women participated in household activity, it is not surprising that, regardless of their formal occupations, a significant fraction of their contributions owed to personal experience and to their role in the home and the family. Victoria Isabella Heliodora Bundsen, an internationally famous opera singer and prima donna alto, obtained a British patent in 1898 for a folding umbrella. Lydia Huntley Sigourney, a notable American "poetess" from Hartford, Connecticut, exhibited an improved silk stocking at the Massachusetts Mechanics' Institute in 1853. Sophronia Dodge, a resident of the state of Iowa, which suffers from cold winters, patented an appliance in 1872 for raising dough that "does the work thoroughly and perfectly in the coldest weather." Eliza Scofield Wood, an American farmer's wife, invented a wring mop bucket, for which she submitted two patents, in 1889 and 1891.

This household orientation was especially evident in the case of exhibitions, where women of all backgrounds tended to display unique works of arts and craft, clothing, and household and domestic enterprise. When Margaret P. Colvin of Battle Creek, Michigan, exhibited the Triumph rotary washing machine at the Philadelphia Centennial Exhibition, she noted that her invention was "the successful result of years of experiment by a practical woman, to accomplish the perfect cleansing of all fabrics, from carpets to laces, without rubbing. With this machine, a child of twelve years can do more work, and do it better, than two women by ordinary methods."[19] Maria Beasley's last patent, at the age of sixty-seven, was for "a kneading-machine which shall be so thorough and uniform in its action that the maximum amount of dough shall be produced from any given amount of flour."

Consumer Technologies and Design Innovations

According to some historians, a specialization by gender was evident in the nineteenth century, in which men concerned themselves with "production,

---

[19] *Official Catalogue of the Philadelphia Centennial Exhibition* (1876), p. 87.

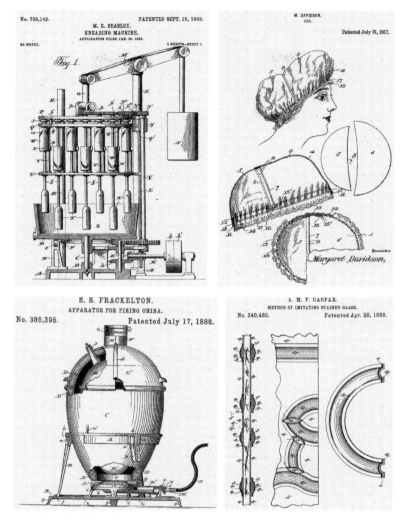

Figure 10.2 Feminine Creativity

Maria Beasley, the patentee of extremely technical machinery, was atypical of women inventors. More representative of feminine ingenuity were Margaret Davidson, Susan Frackleton, and Alberta Caspar, whose inventions created improvements in consumer final goods and designs at the boundaries of art and technology.

Source: U.S. Patent Office.

competition, and material gain," whereas women belonged to a sphere that encompassed "ideal virtues, beauty, and consumption."[20] Such dichotomies fail to capture the interactions between production and consumption, and the similarities between material incentives and the desire (at times overly competitive) to improve household welfare through innovations. It is well recognized that "it is need in the market that causes industrial progress," and "when a need manifests itself, everyone starts working to develop a solution."[21] However, it is important to stress that both need in the market and need in the household can cause social progress. For instance, my own research showed that women on the American frontier disproportionately devised improvements to remedy their lack of access to household help.

Women's contributions to technology—especially their unpatentable innovations—varied significantly from those of male inventors. The category of arts and education (Table 10.3) reveals a stark distinction between the industrial allocation of women's patents and exhibited inventions. This difference was most evident in the 86.7% of the entries attributed to women who applied for awards at the Royal Society of Arts in London. Among the inventors who worked outside the home, a third of the women exhibitors in the United States were identified in official records as professional artists and designers. Many of these artists, who were responsible for the patenting of such items as corsets, tapestries, and apparel inventions, were devising improvements at the intersection of design, art, and technology. The descriptive statistics suggest that an understanding of "feminine ingenuity" requires a broader perspective than the conventional focus on production technologies, machinery, and industrial inventions that dominates the patent records and empirical research in the history of technology.

This section therefore considers women's innovations in consumer final goods and improvements in designs. Some of these inventors' contributions could have been protected by copyrights or design patents, especially because the boundaries of these types of rights was somewhat blurred during this period. The U.S. statute of 1842 allowed for the protection of industrial designs, but early patent examiners found it difficult to distinguish between functional utility and aesthetics.[22] The 1862 case in the circuit court of New York, between plaintiffs

---

[20] Owen (2001: 16).

[21] *Rapport sur l'exposition universelle de 1855 présenté à l'Empereur* (Paris, 1856), p. 148.

[22] French protection of the work of silkworker guilds in 1711 evolved into the pioneering design law of 1806, but some items could still be copyrighted. In England, designs were first covered by the copyright protection laws of 1787. Utility patents are granted for new and useful functional improvements. U.S. statistics for design patents are similar to utility patents, since women accounted for just 3% of designs granted in 1900. The law of product designs and commercial art required a precarious balance on the borders of patent, copyright, and trademark laws. Several hundred design patents actually covered trademarks, and there was also overlap with utility patents: "The Patent Office, until of late, held that new shapes, patterns, etc., whose object and purpose is utility, were

Table 10.3 Industrial Distribution of Patents and Prizes for Women (Percentages)

Industry	U.S.		U.K.		France	
	Patents	Prizes	Patents	Prizes	Patents	Prizes
Agriculture	2.1	1.8	1.8	1.1	1.7	0.3
Apparel	17.3	20.3	20.7	6.5	19	25
Chemicals/medical	8.3	3.6	7.8	0.0	12	5.0
Machines, engines, and transport	21.3	1.2	17.2	1.5	7.6	1.7
Food	0.7	2.7	4.7	0.0	10.3	3.1
Household/building	32.1	31.7	23.0	0.0	17.8	9
Industrial	4.2	2.4	13.6	1.5	8.6	11.9
Arts and education	5.4	32.7	5.4	86.7	5.0	14.6
Textiles	5.8	1.1	3.6	2.7	15.3	28.9
Miscellaneous	2.8	2.6	2.3	0.0	2.7	0.5

Notes: Entries were allocated to industry of final use.

Jonas and Lavinia Drury, against John and Sarah Ewing, shows that some design innovations were also covered by copyright. Lavinia Drury had copyrighted a "system of taking measures for, and cutting ladies' dresses, with instructions for its practical use," which the defendants had infringed, and an injunction was issued. In the 1880 census, Lavinia Drury's occupation was listed as an "inventor of scale for cutting garments," and she entered her inventions at exhibitions and county fairs in Ohio.

The patent records and the exhibitions both included improvements to consumer goods and design-related inventions that had been granted utility patents. About 46.1% of the patented inventions in France were consumer final goods, a figure that did not diverge greatly from the 43.4% for the United Kingdom. American patents by women were significantly less likely to be consumer oriented, but this category still made up almost one-third of all inventions. As might be expected, the proportion of utility patents that were related to changes in designs was lower than was the case for consumer final goods, and the patterns

patentable as designs; but it now, and correctly, holds that only those things,— mentioned in section 71 of the Act of July 8, 1870, as patentable subjects,—whose object and purpose is aesthetic or ornamental, are properly patentable as designs." Simonds (1874: 166). Possibly the most iconic design patent is U.S. Patent D11,023, granted in 1879 to the French sculptor Auguste Bartholdi to protect the Statue of Liberty.

were more similar across countries. Some of these grants were for machinery and producer inventions. However, the majority of the improvements in clothing typify the sort of consumer final goods that were difficult to distinguish from designs, and patents for corsets, bonnets, skirts, shoes, and other forms of apparel accounted for a fifth of the patents filed in all three countries (Table 10.3).[23]

Women inventors were especially concerned with the look and feel of improvements. Such concerns were central to market demand for many of their creations, since attractive appearance was a valuable form of perceived quality and product differentiation in areas such as women's clothing. Digital text analysis of early patent specifications for high-frequency adjectives regarding aspects of beauty or appearance results disproportionately in patents by female inventors. Mrs. Margaret Davidson of Philadelphia noted in her 1917 patent that her invention would "provide an attractive and useful head covering chiefly designed for feminine wear," and the specification included nine phrases relating to un/attractiveness. She also noted that "Of course, the quality and beauty of the cap will be entirely governed in direct ratio to its economic cost, for instance, when the cap is employed for morning wear it will be relatively plain, but when a cap of the above character is utilized as a dress garment it may be more or less elaborate in its aspect."

When Beatrice McMaster of Surrey, England, obtained a patent in 1916 for a glove for waiters, she noted that "cloths or serviettes rapidly become dirty and are unsightly in appearance" and employed the word "elegant" four times to describe her invention, adding that she preferred to add an edging of lace when the item was used by a woman. Other women's patents similarly frequently conflated the item's attractiveness in appearance with its functional utility. Ethel Eva Levien's 1900 application was quickly processed within a month, and she was granted a British patent for "improved women's cycling knickers" that were "more graceful in appearance and more convenient in every way from a hygienic point." Moreover, because the potential market was large, such "feminine technologies" as appealing corset innovations could prove to be extremely profitable, encouraging several professional women inventors to specialize in this product.[24] In France, Mlle Caroline-Françoise Lukkow assigned the rights to her orthopedic

---

[23] Observers in all three countries made disparaging remarks about this (factually true) tendency of women to contrive improvements in clothing. "There is no need to make mention here of patents for mechanical inventions, taken on behalf of the woman when she runs a trading house or factory or workshop. It is easy to see, in this case, the idea is due to a manager, a worker. . . . Now, where we find the hand and mind of the woman herself is in the patented manufacturing of new corsets." A. de Neuville, "Le génie de l'invention chez les femmes," La Revue mondiale 32, no. 1 (1900): 184–191.

[24] Corset-related inventions made up 5.4% of female patenting in France and 5.8% in the United States. However, although women filed corset improvements disproportionately, it should be noted that men obtained approximately 90% of the total patents for corsets that were issued during the nineteenth century.

corset invention even before the patent was granted, to Auguste Daubian, a medical doctor, signaling the commercial value of the improvement.

A significant number of the patentees of consumer final goods and design-related innovations were associated with the American arts and crafts movement. Indeed, invention and technological innovation were central to the arts and crafts ideal.[25] Diffusion of technical information at exhibitions was more likely in the case of changes of appearance that were evident on their face, such as innovations in decorated ceramics. French potters had created an underglaze technique that was on display at the 1876 exhibition in Philadelphia, and after viewing the pieces, Mary Louise McLaughlin, of Cincinnati, Ohio, was able to replicate it. McLaughlin became an iconic American ceramic painter and potter, who influenced numerous artists and potters throughout the country. This reinvention was not patented, probably because the technique was not sufficiently different from the French precedents, but the method quickly spread among artists and artisans, and the products were known throughout the United States as "Cincinnati faïence." However, her expertise in this method suggested other areas for improvement. In 1894, she obtained a patent for a novel ceramics process involving "the application of decorations of clay or of clay mixed with mineral colors to the inner surface of the mold."

McLaughlin was a professional rival of Maria Longworth Nichols, who established the influential Rookwood Pottery in Cincinnati in 1880. Longworth herself obtained a patent in 1887 for "the chromatic ornamentation of pottery," noting that this allowed the artist to "obtain greater depth and richness of color and more delicate blending of color with color, and transition from shade to shade, than by any admixture of colors before application." The Rookwood establishment was careful to get patent protection for all of its innovations and also acquired related patent assignments from outside inventors. At its peak, Rookwood Pottery employed several hundred men and women, who were trained in the firm's methods, and many also devised their own innovations. Some of these artisans moved to other companies and even opened their own establishments, and this labor mobility created the possibility for conflict over the ownership and use of intellectual property rights.

Laura Anne Fry, a Rookwood employee, designed a method of creating subtle gradations of color using an atomizer, which she patented in 1889. Several newspapers publicized her discoveries, reporting that "Miss Laura A. Fry of Chicago is a bright young artist who has discovered a secret which has puzzled many a learned chemist. She has taken out a patent for applying color to pottery

---

[25] Zipf (2007: 60) points out that "women inventors involved in the Arts and Crafts production were better equipped to develop their ideas into useful and marketable products."

and china. . . . [H]er invention is remarkable for its extreme simplicity and ease of application."[26] The device sprayed wet clay to the ceramic item:

> As the coloring-matter is blown from the tube of the atomizer and carried therefrom in a cloud of line, almost imperceptible, particles, it may be readily directed upon the article in such manner as may be found best adapted to produce the desired effect, the application being freely made where the color is to be intense, and more delicately made in proportion as the color effect is to be delicate, or otherwise varied as the taste, skill, or ingenuity of the operator may dictate.

After Fry moved from Rookwood Pottery to work for a competing firm, she filed a lawsuit against her former employers claiming that their usage illegally infringed on her patent. The court was instructed to consider "whether the step she took in the art required the exercise of the inventive faculty," and the case was dismissed on the grounds of want of invention, despite the widespread use and commercial profitability of the Fry method.[27]

Many of these inventions were related to pursuits in which women specialized, and the (predominantly male) patent examiners may have found it difficult to distinguish the degree of novelty in such applications.[28] For instance, Mary Tillinghast applied in 1881 for a patent to protect an invention for "a new article of manufacture of artistic character, which may be termed Needle-Woven Tapestry, . . . for purposes of decoration or for any artistic use it presents an extremely rich appearance and is of great value." Tillinghast, a notable artist in her own right, had been a former associate and employee of Candace Wheeler, a leading pioneer in the field of interior and textile designs. Wheeler also applied for a patent for an invention regarding the "art of embroidering tapestries" in July 1881. This led the Patent Office to declare an interference, which occurs when it seems that two individuals have made the same invention. However, ultimately each woman was granted her own patent in 1882, implying that further investigation had revealed the differences in their techniques.

The ceramics industry and the arts and crafts movement highlight the close relationship between many female-intensive creative pursuits and improvements in designs and consumer final goods. Thousands of women throughout the nation

---

[26] *The Daily Evening Bulletin of San Francisco*, March 7, 1891.

[27] *Fry v. Rookwood Pottery Co.*, S. D. Ohio, No. 4,531 (1898), was initiated in 1892. Fry had used the resources of the pottery over the course of several years to experiment and perfect her method. Judge William H. Taft's decision noted that, even if Fry's patent were upheld, her dealings with Rookwood Pottery implied a license for them to freely use her invention.

[28] However, as noted before, the Patent Office was a leader in progressive policies to encourage women as inventors and examiners.

Figure 10.3 Women in the Patent Office
The U.S. Patent Office was a pioneer in the employment of women in the nineteenth century. The portraits show Clara Barton, the first woman hired as a full-time employee in the federal civil service; Sarah J. Noyes, patent examiner in the electrical division; and Frances Lybrand, another examiner and specialist in civil engineering. In 2019, the U.S. Patent and Trademark Office honored women's contributions to technological creativity by naming its public meeting space the Clara Barton Auditorium.
Source: Library of Congress; *Sunday Oregonian*, July 2, 1893.

joined formal and informal clubs and increasingly attended schools of art and design, gaining technical knowledge and learning by doing that contributed to their inventive capital. A specialization by gender was initially evident in the pottery and glass industry, where women worked as painters or decorators, whereas men dominated the more technical aspect of firing the items in professional kilns. Women's participation in the entire process from shaping to firing the end-product received a substantive boost when inventors such as Susan S. Frackelton and Ellen M. Ford obtained patents for small portable kilns to finish decorated items. As Ford's 1882 patent description noted: "it is no small advantage to an artist anywhere to have the means of acquiring practice in firing, thus being able to accomplish the entire work of decorating from beginning to end, and increasing his own abilities and talents by the additional knowledge which such experience affords."

Fair Women

These examples show that women were participating in patents for consumer good inventions, but their creativity also extended well beyond the boundaries circumscribed by formal intellectual property and conventional conceptions of technology. The information from industrial fairs and prize-granting institutions testifies to their creativity regarding items that were largely unpatentable. Institutions like the Massachusetts Mechanics' Institute and the San Francisco Mechanics' Institute were eager to highlight women's inventions and commercialization. Their efforts included allocating space for women at the annual exhibitions, education in art and design, vocational training, and the provision of facilities so women could practice their craft. In the case of the Maryland Mechanics' Institute, influential women members helped to ultimately change its orientation from mechanics to a school of art and design. Many of the participants in annual exhibitions were elite or middle-class women who had no intention of engaging in the marketplace and had no further interest in pursuing financial returns from their creativity. Nevertheless, their recorded activities offer valuable evidence regarding the nature of women's innovativeness within the household.

The Royal Society of Arts in England adopted progressive policies toward women and was the first such institution in the country to include women as members. The society also actively encouraged the participation of women as potential prize winners:

The ingenious, of both sexes, are invited to submit their works and their inventions to the inspection of the Society, . . . and thereby secure to themselves not only honour and profit, in the present instance, but have also the pleasing consciousness that their names will stand recorded to posterity, among those who have contributed to the increase of the Arts, the Manufactures, and the Commerce of their Country.[29]

Despite this equal opportunity approach, the items displayed at exhibitions reflected a marked difference by gender (Table 10.4). The majority of entries featured some degree of consumer orientation. Approximately half of the innovations for which men received awards were in the consumer good- and design-related categories, whereas almost all of the items females submitted were consumer final products that included some aspect of improvements in design. Over 10% of the premiums were given for contributions by women, and many received favorable notice for excellence in such consumer goods as improvements in starch. In 1824, prizes were given to women from various parts of the United Kingdom who had made bonnets using local materials. However, the majority of these female recipients obtained awards in the "polite arts," among which a typical example is Hannah Chambers's design for a candelabra. Mary Pingo, who won four design-related prizes between 1758 and 1762, was a member of the noted Pingo family of engravers and medalists, who were associated with the Royal Society of Arts. Many of these changes in materials or designs or new colors would not have met the rules for patentability, but the reports of the juries testify to the degree of creativity evinced by the women who received premiums for such improvements. These patterns were reflected in other countries. In France, the notable entrepreneur Madame Amélie de Dietrich was credited with being the first to introduce decorative designs into industrial products made from cast iron in her innovative business enterprise.

The contrast by gender in inventive activity at exhibitions is even more evident among the participants in the major American cities, as the lower quadrant of Table 10.4 shows. Only 19% of men's exhibits consisted of consumer final products, and even fewer of them were changes in the design of products. By way of contrast, three-quarters of the women's exhibits were consumer goods, and designs constituted an even larger proportion. The variance in the technical inputs of items that women offered was extremely high, ranging from embroidered rugs, pleating, and varieties of lace, featherwork, and artificial flowers (made from wax, paper, silk, feathers, and other materials) to commercially successful dishwashers and sewing machine components.[30]

---

[29] *Transactions of the Society of Arts*, vol. 16 (1798), p. xvii.

[30] This commercial diversity is sometimes evident in the backgrounds of individuals, as evidenced by exhibitor Mme Minnetta Mourgeanna, who was listed in city directories as an artist, photographer, hairdresser, and maker of hair restorers and toiletries. Similarly, Mrs. A. O. Cook of San Francisco participated in numerous fairs, winning cash prizes and medals for her innovations in preserved flowers, wax shells, statuary, hair jewelry, and other decorative devices.

Table 10.4 Patents and Prizes: Consumer Final Goods and Design Innovations

	U.S.		U.K.		France	
	Number	Percent	Number	Percent	Number	Percent
Patents						
Women						
Consumer final products	704	30.7	1340	43.4	461	46.1
Design innovations	458	19.9	480	15.5	222	22.2
Prizes						
Women						
Consumer final products	2,250	74.4	243	92.4	394	61.1
Design innovations	2,468	81.6	246	93.5	195	30.2
Men						
Consumer final products	593	19.1	1,210	54.9	—	—
Design innovations	380	12.2	1,190	54.3	—	—

Notes: Consumer final goods exclude furniture and appliances. Design innovations relate to all entries, including capital goods. Percent refers to the percentage of total observations for patents and prize-winning exhibits by gender (women's patents, women's exhibits, men's exhibits).

The participants at expositions are more representative of the general population of creative women. Overall, the efforts of these exhibitors varied in terms of market and technical value to a greater extent than for patentees. For the most successful in terms of awards, the fraction of women exhibitors that earned medals was closer to the patenting rates: only 25 (0.5%) obtained a gold medal, 157 (3.1%) silver medals, and 86 (1.7%) bronze medals.[31] Relative to male exhibitors and to female patentees, women at exhibitions were significantly less likely to receive the top financial awards and gold medals. These systematic differences were in part due to the type and quality of their inventions. Outcomes were also influenced by gender biases among judging panels and committees against the nontechnical and interdisciplinary orientation of much of women's innovations.

At a national level, some of these exhibited inventions were responsible for increases in market demand and supply, export industries, and employment for

---

[31] The 1850 exhibition of the Maryland Institute for the Promotion of Mechanic Arts rewarded creativity by gender: they presented men with gold and silver medals, whereas women received butter knives, ladles, teaspoons, pencils, and thimbles.

children, men, and women. Most notably, professional patentees like Helen Augusta Blanchard earned large fortunes from royalties and assignments in several countries and from the establishment of their own manufacturing enterprises. Helen Blanchard was one of the principals in the Blanchard Overseaming Company of Philadelphia and the Blanchard Hosiery Machine Company. She obtained twenty-one U.S. sewing machine patents through 1895, and her patenting career (which included patents in Britain) continued until the year before her death in 1916.

A more typical example is the industry for hats and bonnets in the United States, which in 1830 amounted to $10 million with exports of about half that value. *Scientific American* in 1859 published the first-hand account of twelve-year-old Betsy Metcalf, who independently devised a method to make hats from braided straw that she and her aunt had bleached with the smoke from "brimstone." She earned as much as $1.50 per day for several years and instructed residents in nearby towns, leading to a flourishing women's bonnet industry in the region. Sophia Woodhouse of Connecticut similarly obtained a large silver medal and 20 guineas from the Royal Society of Arts for information about another type of bleached straw material that could be used to make bonnets, and she also obtained an American patent for the process. Numerous other women obtained premiums and cash awards for unpatentable changes in materials associated with new or improved products that were valued in the household and in the marketplace.

For professional women who participated in fairs, such recognition provided valuable advertisement and publicity that could enhance their reputations and lead to more profits for traders. For instance, Dr. Carrie Wolfsbruck, a young and attractive dentist, gained an international reputation (probably the first and only celebrity dentist!) after she exhibited her work on artificial teeth, fillings, and dentures at the World's Columbian Exposition. The *British Journal of Dental Science* featured her in an article on "Women Who Pull Teeth," noting that "this lady has received a medal for artificial work." Newspaper articles across the country published features about her, reporting how she won a large sum at roulette in Monte Carlo and "created a sensation" during her European travels. Wolfsbruck progressed from having a practice in an unfashionable part of New York City to an office on Madison Avenue.[32]

---

[32] *British Journal of Dental Science* 40 (January–December 1897). She was likely born in 1863, as shown in the 1900 census, although she was cavalier in the declaration of her date of birth on her several passport applications. In 1889, Wolfsbruck was the first woman to graduate from New York State Dental School. She had learned the trade between 1880 and 1886 as an assistant to Gardner Colton, the notable dental surgeon who introduced the use of nitrous oxide during extractions. She was then employed by Henry Deane, the defendant in a trademark infringement lawsuit that Colton brought to prevent her new employer from free-riding off of Colton's reputation, with a claim of $10,000 in damages. Colton disparaged her abilities, claiming that even a child could perform her duties, and an injunction was granted.

Conclusions

According to some scholars, "in the Western nations which pioneered industrialization . . . technology is firmly coded male."[33] Many reject implicit or explicit assumptions that women feature exclusively as consumers of technology. They argue that an accurate assessment of women as innovators requires a redefinition that expands the scope of technology research beyond hardware, to incorporate the skills and knowledge that are characteristic of women's contributions.[34] The Women's Rights Convention in New York declared in 1852 that "the economy of the household is generally as much the source of family wealth as the labor and enterprise of man." Such concerns are reflected in the dissatisfaction of economists with the current state of theoretical and empirical approaches to technology, especially in the effort to measure and account for innovations that transform or adapt characteristics of existing products and new goods.

This chapter contributes to the existing literature by offering the first large-scale empirical study of women inventors in Britain, France, and the United States during the period of the first and second Industrial Revolutions, from 1750 through 1930. The panel dataset includes patent records, prizes, and exhibits, as well as biographical information from city directories and population censuses. Although it is inherently impossible to determine the representativeness of such a sample relative to the entire population of innovators, these combined data offer broader and more reliable insights than existing studies based on rather limited numbers. The overall patterns reveal different facets of inventive activity by capturing discoveries that were likely to be protected by patents, as well as the unpatentable inventions and innovations that women were making. Moreover, the analysis allows for the systematic assessment of women's creativity within the nonmarket household sector.

Economists have investigated the "gender gap" in many contexts, including that of patenting. Contemporary differences in the organization of work settings affect the likelihood of women's involvement in scientific patenting. Similarly, this study shows that patent systems were associated with differences in the inventive activity of women relative to institutions with less exclusive rules. Patent rules in Britain and France served as a filter that excluded or deterred women without financial backing or connections and further led to significantly lower

---

[33] Francesca Bray, "Gender and Technology," *Annual Review of Anthropology* 36 (2007): 37–53.

[34] Judy Wajcman, "Reflections on Gender and Technology Studies: In What State Is the Art?," *Social Studies of Science* 30, no. 3 (2000): 447–464, notes that in conventional approaches "technology tends to be thought of in terms of industrial machinery and military weapons, the tools of work and war, overlooking other technologies that affect most aspects of everyday life. The very definition of technology, in other words, is cast in terms of male activities."

proportions of patents for incremental household inventions in these countries. Exhibitions, on the other hand, were administered by committees and judges, who imposed their own arbitrary standards on prizes, in part accounting for the lower propensity of women to gain the highest awards. Women may have internalized the expectation that male-dominated institutions like the Franklin Institute were unlikely to regard their contributions from an impartial perspective (Chapter 7). Only five women were given prizes at the Franklin Institute over the entire nineteenth century in part because women expected that few of their inventions would be recognized as worthy by these administered innovation systems.

The results in Britain, France, and the United States together challenge standard conclusions about the nature of women's economic and social involvement in the nineteenth century and their role in industrialization. Adjacent institutions such as the legal system and cultural norms may have inhibited female activities, but middle-class women did not choose to retreat away from the marketplace and from participation outside the domestic sphere, as many have claimed. The experience of female innovators in France, in particular, highlights the hidden nature of their extensive participation in business, entrepreneurship, and management oversight of sole proprietorships, as well as large-scale corporations. It is worth emphasizing that their inventive and commercial endeavors ranged over the entire life cycle and were typically not interrupted by marriage. Indeed, many female discoveries were motivated by the challenges they encountered in the course of their duties as mothers, wives, and managers of households.

One of the major difficulties in accounting for the role of women in technological progress arises because their contributions defy unique categorizations and lie at the intersection of well-defined conventional boundaries. The distinction between consumption and production becomes blurred when the process of consuming creates insights that allow users to alter the set of available goods. In particular, the experience of women inventors who did not work outside the home illustrates the skills and creativity that can be derived from learning by using. Perhaps the most valuable result of the empirical analysis of women's patenting and creativity is that it highlights the prevalence of their innovations in consumer goods and designs. These extensive quantitative records, which allow us to trace so many thousands of examples of female ingenuity within the home and market, support the conclusion that women in general tended to specialize in technological change that is embedded in new varieties of standard goods. Their innovations consisted of subtle changes in function and perceived value that accompanied design improvements at the interstices of art and technology. Such feminine creativity was valued in the market and in the household alike; their divergence from male technological achievements failed to overcome the biases of men involved in the governance of administered innovation institutions. A more optimistic conclusion is that these findings suggest that economic research underestimates the extent of technological progress and advances in consumer welfare attained within households and the market economy.

11

Selling Ideas

Global Markets for Patented Inventions

> There is no patron to be compared with the public. . . . The natural
> reward of inventions . . . is the profit to be derived from them in the
> way of trade.
>
> —Jeremy Bentham (1825)[1]

Early economists explored the links between the expansion of competitive markets to economic growth and the relationship between new ideas and
advances in productivity. If administrators offered rewards for inventions,
they noted, inevitable errors in judgment would result in the misallocation of
resources. In free markets, by contrast, ideas that added value to consumers
and producers would garner rewards, whereas useless proposals would simply
be ignored and their creators would bear the cost themselves. As Adam Smith
pointed out, "if the invention be good and such as is profitable to mankind, he
will probably make a fortune by it; but if it be of no value he will also reap no
benefit."[2] American patent rules were based on the same precept that market
demand, rather than courts or administrators, was the most effective arbiter of
value. Supreme Court Justice Joseph Story and other members of the judiciary
echoed the Smithian perspective when they ruled that the utility of the invention
"is a circumstance very material to the interest of the patentee, but of no importance to the public. If it is not extensively useful, it will silently sink into contempt
and disregard."[3]

Patents provided property rights in inventions and enforcement that facilitated
markets in ideas. Many of the great inventors exploited personal connections
that allowed them to readily tap into capital markets.[4] However, the majority of
innovative patentees lacked either the desire or ready access to the means to directly commercialize their inventions, and technology markets allowed them to

---

[1] Bentham (1825: 68, 321).
[2] *Lectures on Jurisprudence* (1982 ed.), p. 103.
[3] *Lowell v. Lewis*, 15 F. Cas. 1018 (1817). "The popular demand for an article is, in the long run, the
best test of utility," *Turrel v. Spalth*, 14 O.G. 377 (1878).
[4] Khan and Sokoloff (2006).

Inventing Ideas. B. Zorina Khan, Oxford University Press (2020). © Oxford University Press.
DOI: 10.1093/oso/9780190936075.001.0001

specialize in inventive activity and obtain returns from the sale or licensing of their rights. Well-enforced property rights in invention facilitated the securitization of ideas, which allowed inventors to benefit by selling their ideas to third parties. In short, defining and enforcing a tradable asset in new technological knowledge was central to the evolution of open markets in technology, in part because such incentives for investment in inventive activity were especially important to relatively disadvantaged groups who would otherwise have found it difficult to benefit from their technological creativity.[5]

For instance, Francis Strong and Thomas Ross were two young New England mechanics "of limited means and compelled to rely upon their daily labor for their support" who would go on to devise six valuable patented inventions for platform scales. Strong was a journeyman at an iron foundry, and Ross was an immigrant apprentice in a small town in Vermont. The two collaborated on ingenious improvements that resulted in extremely sensitive platform scales, several tons in size, that could allegedly detect the weight of a penny. The patented scales were durable and impervious to the harsh cold and heat, operated equally well on a steep incline, and could be constructed by unskilled workers. However, "large capital was necessary to enable the inventors to compete successfully with the wealthy manufacturing establishment which . . . had a practical monopoly of the business. This they did not possess."[6]

The inventors were able to tap into the market for patents to finance their inventive activity. John Howe Jr., a very wealthy manufacturer of iron wheels, was impressed with their demonstration. He advanced a payment of $2,000 out of future royalties on the patent to allow the partners to meet their debts. His firm also retained Strong and Ross on a five-year employment contract, which included royalties on all scales sold. After six years, Howe bought the initial 1856 patent outright for $15,000 and paid $75,000 for the rest of the patents.[7] John Howe Jr. joined with his brother Frank in 1864 to open the Howe Scale Company, which became of one of Vermont's most important businesses. The manufacturers and their agents displayed the scales at numerous exhibitions and widely advertised all the premiums that the innovation had accumulated ("seven within sixty days"), highlighting the awards from the Franklin Institute exhibition. The

---

[5] Khan and Sokoloff (2004).

[6] Statement in *Decisions of the Commissioner of Patents*, granting the extension of the patent, January 6, 1871, notice of which was reported overseas. According to the *Encyclopedia of Vermont Biography* (1912), p. 328, "This scale, which had its inception in the little iron foundry of Vergennes, is accepted by all civilized nations as a standard of weights." The scales were demanded as far afield as Russia and Asia, and throughout South America. Litigation in 1879 provides details on the numerous assignments and subassignments that still characterized the market for the Strong and Ross patents. *Brandon Mfg Company v. David W. Prime*, 16 Blatchf. 453 (1879).

[7] In 1870, at the age of forty, Francis Strong held a portfolio of $70,000 in personal and real estate assets.

business was later acquired by the Brandon Manufacturing Company, largely because of the valuable patent rights, which firmly established the town of Brandon as a major producer of scales for the global market.

Globalization of Markets in Ideas

Observed changes over time in international comparative advantage in technological innovation and industry support the claim that intellectual property rights mattered. Crucial advances in global technology increasingly originated in the United States, and its position as a leading industrial nation had become evident by the so-called second Industrial Revolution that started around the 1870s. American patentees who were benefiting from the well-articulated domestic market for ideas extended the scope of their patenting and licensing activities to other countries. Foreign observers were convinced that American success at economic growth and innovation was related to its institutions to protect intellectual property, and this encouraged the harmonization of intellectual property laws across nations in the direction of the U.S. patent system.[8] American participation in global technology markets gathered momentum and consolidated early in the twentieth century.[9] In the process, innovative U.S. enterprises began to flourish and dominate both national and foreign markets.

The Singer Manufacturing Company offers an early example of the many American patentees who secured a prominent position in the global market for innovations and patented products.[10] Singer's claims as the inventor of key sewing machine improvements are debatable, but he was undoubtedly an exceptional innovator and entrepreneur (Figure 11.1). His enterprise was one of the largest in the United States and utilized modern techniques of product placement and marketing. Singer was an important player in the market for patent rights, building up a large portfolio of overlapping intellectual property rights. The company further secured their own patents in France and England and subsequently expanded their factory operations throughout Europe. Other corporations, such as Wheeler & Wilson, followed similar measures to retain their relative advantage in the industry. The sewing machine oligopoly became notorious for its pooling of patents and cross-licensing, and in the process large-scale U.S. enterprises began to flourish in both national and foreign markets.

---

[8] Penrose (1951).

[9] Wilkins (1974, 1988).

[10] Adam Mossoff (2011) provides an insightful analysis of the "sewing machine wars" at the middle of the nineteenth century. See also Davies (1969).

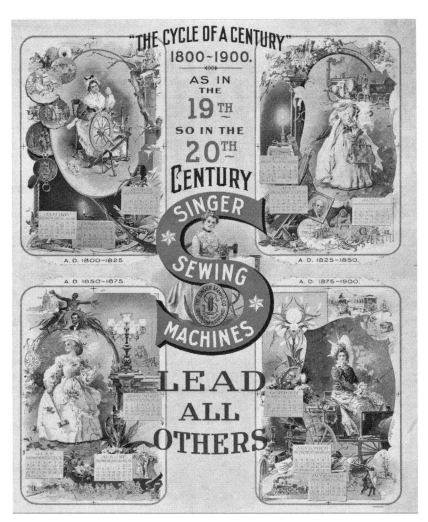

Figure 11.1 Singer Manufacturing Company in Global Markets
Isaac Singer was able to leverage his patents for improvements in sewing machines
into dominance of "universal markets" (as the company claimed) through
commercialization and the adept use of marketing techniques. In the battle for
medals and other awards, Singer claimed to have amassed over two hundred prizes
by the 1880s.
Source: Library of Congress.

Theoretical models in international economics suggest that exchange across countries creates the potential for greater access to a portfolio of higher-quality innovations. International trade in technology also tends to lower prices and increase output and variety in the marketplace, resulting in net gains from trade, and growth in national income for both sides of the market. Analyses of the relationship between relative market size and productivity at inventive activity indicate that strongly enforced intellectual property rights and patents were more effective in relatively larger markets, whereas less innovative countries initially benefited from furthering the interests of consumers rather than producers. Patenting and technology transfers in U.S. multinational enterprises typically increase when intellectual property rights are strengthened.[11] However, links between technological exchanges across countries and economic progress are complex and would benefit from further empirical investigation.

This chapter presents a comparative analysis of markets for inventions and patents across a diverse sample of countries over time. Patent assignments, or the sale of patent rights, provide an index of trade within national markets in technology over time. Further, foreign patenting, or the propensity of inventors to obtain property rights in other countries, is a proxy for transfers of important technologies across global markets. Foreign patentees seek to obtain rights in other countries for a number of reasons, ranging from the intent to appropriate returns from valuable inventions with a global market demand to the wish to protect a manufacturing enterprise producing the patented product in the foreign locale. Such patentees may have also filed for protection overseas to forestall on potential competition by employing their patent monopolies to block imitators or inhibit cumulative invention. Thus, assignments and foreign patenting offer different but complementary perspectives on markets in invention across countries.

Inventive activity and innovation markets were affected by institutional differences in the United States, Britain, Canada, New South Wales, Spain, Germany, and Japan during the nineteenth and early twentieth centuries. The discussion in this chapter first identifies salient features of patent rights and legal institutions in these different jurisdictions. The second part assesses the nature of technology markets and reports the results from quantitative analyses of factors that affected changes in patent assignments and foreign patenting. The final part highlights a case study of the market for technology in the chemical industry and further sheds light on foreign patenting and innovation markets in the United States. The overall findings confirm that the design of U.S. patent institutions enhanced the scope and efficiency of markets in ideas.

---

[11] Branstetter et al. (2006).

International Patent Institutions

Over the course of the first Industrial Revolution, evidence accumulated that technological progress was capable of altering the fate of nations, and appreciation of the potential importance of national technology policies grew over this era. As the chapters on France and Britain showed, an extensive variety of schemes were considered and implemented at one time or another, including grants, subsidies, procurement and investments by the government, cash prizes and honorary awards, and permanent monopoly privileges. However, by the end of the nineteenth century, non-market-oriented administered systems had lost favor, and patent systems emerged as the dominant method by which national governments attempted to promote the progress of new ideas, inventiveness, and economic growth. Despite the international consensus about the importance of patent laws and their enforcement, important differences existed across countries in how intellectual property institutions were structured (Table 11.1). Such differences persisted even after a series of international conventions over the 1870s and 1880s pursued uniformity in patent rules and standards.

Britain's early lead in industrialization and in new technological information was waning by the middle of the nineteenth century, and many attributed the loss of their competitive advantage to defects in the structure and management of British patent institutions. Jeremy Bentham was disparaging of the British system, in which an inventor

> goes with a joyful heart, to the public office to ask for his patent. But what does he encounter? Clerks, lawyers, and officers of state, who reap beforehand the fruits of his industry. This privilege is not given, but is, in fact, sold for from 100*l.* to 200*l.*: sums greater perhaps than he ever possessed in his life. He finds himself caught in a snare, which the law, or rather extortion, which has obtained the force of law, has spread for the industrious inventor. It is a tax levied upon ingenuity, and no man can set bounds to the value of the services it may have lost to the nation.[12]

British patent laws, administration, and enforcement disadvantaged the granting of property rights to inventors of smaller inventions and individuals with fewer financial resources, and they did little to encourage effective trade in technological information. Patent rights involved high monetary and transaction costs, and patent fees were deliberately set as a filter that selected inventors and inventions by the wealth of the applicant and rejected poor inventors and

---

[12] Bentham (1825: 73).

Table 11.1 International Patent Systems

	Examination System	Restrictions on Patent	Equal Treatment for Foreign Inventors	Cost
Canada				
1850	N	Y	N	Expensive
1870	Y	Y	Y	Cheap
1900	Y	Y	Y	Cheap
1920	Y	Y	Y	Cheap
Germany				
1900	Y	Y	Y	Expensive
1920	Y	Y	Y	Expensive
Japan				
1900	Y	Y	N	Moderate
1920	Y	Y	N	Moderate
New South Wales				
1870	N	N	Y	Expensive
1900	N	N	Y	Cheap
1920	Y	Y	Y	Cheap
Spain				
1850	N	Y	Y	Costly
1870	N	Y	Y	Costly
1900	N	Y	Y	Moderate
1920	N	Y	Y	Moderate
United Kingdom				
1850	N	N	Y	Expensive
1870	N	Y	Y	Expensive
1900	N	Y	Y	Expensive
1920	Y	Y	Y	Expensive
United States				
1850	Y	N	N	Cheap
1870	Y	N	Y	Cheap

Continued

Table 11.1 *Continued*

	Examination System	Restrictions on Patent	Equal Treatment for Foreign Inventors	Cost
United States				
1900	Y	N	Y	Cheap
1920	Y	N	Y	Cheap

Notes:

Cost: The code for cost indicates the estimated cost in current U.S. dollars for a patent taken to its full term; Cheap: Below $100; Moderate: $100–$250; Costly: $250–$400; Expensive: above $400.

Examination: The U.S. examination was the most stringent, consisting of a worldwide search for novelty. Britain's searches extended just to British patents filed in the previous fifty years and did not include foreign specifications. Spanish rules did not require novelty; patents were granted as long as they had not been previously practiced in Spain.

Restrictions: Primarily working requirements and/or compulsory licenses.

Treatment of foreign inventors: Before 1869, inventors who were not subjects of the queen could not obtain patents in British Canada. In Japan, foreigners could obtain patents only if their country had entered into a treaty with Japan; nonresidents had to be represented by a registered Japanese patent attorney or the patent right would be revoked. The earliest U.S. statutes restricted rights in patent property to citizens or to residents who declared their intention to become citizens. The first patent statute of April 1790 made no distinction regarding citizenship, but in 1793 patents were limited to citizens of the United States. In 1800 patent rights were extended to foreigners living in the United States for two years who swore that the invention was new to the world. The 1832 Patent Act allowed patents to resident aliens who intended to become citizens, provided that they introduced the invention into public use within one year, a period that was changed to eighteen months with the 1836 reforms. In 1836, the stipulations on citizenship or residency were removed but were replaced with discriminatory patent fees that retaliated for the significantly higher fees charged in other countries: nonresident foreigners could obtain a patent in the United States for a fee of $300, or $500 if they were British. The patent laws that stipulated discriminatory treatment of foreign nonresidents were repealed in 1861, and utility patent rights were available to all applicants on the same basis without regard to nationality. After 1904, New South Wales patents were granted as part of the federal system of the Commonwealth of Australia.

Sources: John Kingsley and Joseph Piesson, *Laws and Practice of All Nations and Governments Relating to Patents of Inventions* (New York, 1848); Fitch and Co., *United States and International Patent Office Manual* (New York, 1871); British and European Patent Agency, *Epitome of the World's Patent Laws and Statistics* (New York, 1891); Arthur Greeley, *Foreign Patent and Trademark Laws* (Washington, DC, 1899); W. P. Thompson, *Handbook of Patent Law of All Countries* (London, 1920).

"small inventions." Legal enforcement initially was questionable, with arbitrary judicial decisions that overturned even patents that had proven to be valuable in the marketplace. The law did not offer any relief to the purchaser of an invalid or worthless patent, so potential buyers in the market for ideas had to engage in costly searches before entering into contracts.

At the same time, ineffective provisions for public disclosure of the full specification (technical description) of patented inventions resulted in asymmetrical information between buyers and sellers that further hindered the market in technology. Policymakers were suspicious of "stock jobbing" and vigilant to protect an unsuspecting public from fraudulent financial schemes on the scale of the South Sea Bubble, so ownership of patent rights was limited to five investors (later extended to twelve). The uncertainty that was inherent in the registration system added to the demand for specialized professionals who interceded on behalf of the applicant for a fee. Potential conflicts of interest arose when clerks employed at the Patent Office acted as agents, and a number of patent agents followed their self-interest and lobbied against reforms that would reduce the inefficiencies in the law. In short, despite its "firstcomer" status, the network of innovation and legal institutions in Britain hampered the potential for sustained growth in inventive activity and markets in patents.

Large numbers of interested parties, such as the renowned metallurgist and patentee Sir Robert Abbott Hadfield (1858–1940), voiced dissatisfaction with the pace and nature of institutional change in Britain. Hadfield was echoing complaints like Bentham's in the nineteenth century when he observed that "invention is discouraged by excessive fees, by inadequate preliminary search of the patent records, and by the complexity of the rules." In the early twentieth century, he advocated "a radical revision of the whole system after the American model, and he gives point to his suggestion by comparing the number of patents taken out in Great Britain and the United States. This suggestion, coming from a man who has taken out several hundred patents in England and abroad, is worthy of attention, but there are no indications that it is likely to be adopted."[13] Despite the inflexibility in its domestic institutions, patent systems in the British overseas jurisdictions were allowed some degree of autonomy, as the examples of New South Wales and its sister colonies in Australia indicate.

Institutions that allow for widespread democratic access were disproportionately associated with advances in economic and social welfare, as Stanley Engerman and Kenneth Sokoloff have demonstrated.[14] So it is not coincidental that patent institutions in the United States were based on the notion that, regardless of their identities, all inventors should have the opportunity to obtain and exploit rights to their creativity. Observers in other countries acknowledged that the American system was the most favorable in the world to all patentees, and its markets in patent rights were the most developed. A nineteenth-century English treatise on the law and practice of patents was merely echoing a common perspective when it stated that "in no country in the world are the rights of inventors more cherished than in the United States, and the number of patents issued there annually far exceeds that granted in any other country."[15] Large numbers of differentiated versions of a product could be protected, leading to a rapid expansion of available choices in the market for final goods. "The protection afforded by the

---

[13] U.S. Bureau of Foreign and Domestic Commerce, *Special Agents Series* (1920), p. 50.
[14] Engerman and Sokoloff (2012).
[15] Johnson and Johnson (1890: 422).

patent and the hope of reward have proved the incentives to invention, and the public, enabled to choose from many devices, obtains the best thing."[16]

From the beginning, policymakers in the United States had the objective of promoting extensive markets in patent rights.[17] Both the patent system and legal institutions were market oriented and likewise encouraged extensive trade in patented technologies. The first statute of 1790 included a special provision for keeping a national registry of all assignments (sales of patent rights), which made it easy to trace ownership and transactions in patented inventions. The patent agency of Munn & Company smugly noted:

> From January 1, 1865 to the 1st of December, the whole number of applications for patents to the British Patent Office will not have exceeded three thousand. Within the same period the applications made by Munn & Co. to the United States Patent Office number at least three thousand five hundred; thus showing that our professional business considerably exceeds the entire business of the British Patent Office.[18]

Patent agents in the United States acknowledged that the application process was so straightforward that inventors could prosecute a claim by themselves, and the primary role of intermediaries was in commercialization and market placement.[19]

American patent policy was exceptional in its insistence on affordable fees. The legislature debated the question of appropriate fees, and the first patent law in 1790 set the rate at the minimal sum of $3.70 plus copy costs. The 1869 *Report of the Commissioner of Patents* compared the $35 fee for a U.S. patent to the significantly higher charges in European countries such as Britain ($875), France ($300), Russia ($450), Belgium ($420), and Austria ($350). The commissioner pointed out that in the United States the fees were not intended to exact a price for the patent privilege or to raise revenues for the state—the disclosure of information was the price of the patent property right; rather, they were imposed merely to cover the administrative expenses of the Patent Office.[20]

Samuel Fisher, Commissioner of Patents, presented an insightful synopsis of the functions of the American patent system. It was impossible for society to offer inventors ample compensation for their contributions through some form

[16] *Annual Report of the Commissioner of Patents* (1869), p. 8.
[17] Khan (2005).
[18] *Scientific American* 13 (1865): 415.
[19] *Scientific American*, which was associated with the patent agency of Munn & Co., noted, "we advise every inventor who is able, to make application for himself, and thereby save some expense. There are forms and rules that will require study, but you can soon master them."
[20] *Report* (1869), pp. 4–9.

of administered process. Instead, he noted, the recompense is made in terms of time, by carving out a period during which inventors themselves can obtain financial rewards by taking advantage of market demand. The primary feature of the American patent system since 1836 was that all applications were subject to an examination for conformity with the laws and for novelty. The financial cost of an examination by the Patent Office was just $15, and Fisher was certain that both the private and social cost of patenting were lower in a system of impartial specialized examiners than under a system where similar services were performed on a fee-per-service basis by private solicitors on behalf of clients. The Patent Office was one of the few agencies that was consistently self-supporting financially throughout the century, but this was due to economies of scale in administration rather than to overly high fees.

The examination process, the central feature of the "American system," enabled early reviews of the technical validity of the patent grant. This certification helped to reduce uncertainty about inventive property, facilitated enforcement of rights, and furthered trade in patented technologies. As Chapter 9 discussed, American legislators from the very beginning realized that the diffusion of information would benefit both private and social welfare. They took particular care to ensure that details about the stock of patented knowledge was accessible, usable, and rapidly transmitted at low cost to interested members of the public.

Another fundamental principle of the American system, as Table 11.1 shows, is that the property right was unconditional. Once a patent was issued to the inventor, the validity was assured, and fraud constituted the only reason that courts accepted for overturning a patent grant. Property rights in new ideas wholly belonged to their creators, perhaps more securely than for the holders of titles in land, since there was no doctrine of eminent domain to expropriate owners of inventions. The United States universally rejected efforts to curtail the rights of patentees and did not distinguish between "practicing inventors" and non-practicing entities. Working requirements or compulsory licenses were regarded as unwarranted infringements of the rights of meritorious inventors. In short, American patent laws provided strong protection for citizens of the United States and, after 1861, such rights were available to all applicants on the same basis without regard to nationality or residence.[21]

---

[21] See Khan (2005). The earliest statutes restricted patent property to citizens or to residents who declared their intention to become citizens. However, these provisions were not strictly enforced, and numerous foreign inventors were able to obtain patent rights by petitioning the legislature. In 1836, the stipulations on citizenship or residency were removed, but in retaliation for the high patent fees that Americans were charged overseas, foreigners could obtain a patent in the United States for a fee of $300, or $500 if they were British. The sole exception to this equal treatment was in times of war, when different policies were implemented against enemy combatants, but even they were later able to claim compensation.

Figure 11.2 Patent Examiners at the U.S. Patent Office
Patent examiners in the nineteenth century, as today, were highly specialized in
specific technological areas and identified the technical novelty of applications in
accordance with the law. The patent examination process never attempted to gauge
usefulness or commercial value, and it was up to the patentee to obtain returns in
the marketplace. The examination system helped to secure property rights and
facilitated markets in ideas.
Source: Library of Congress.

In the international sphere, lobbying by U.S. interest groups succeeded in
overcoming controversies about patents, and intellectual property systems proliferated among the newly developing countries that followed the American lead.
Their patent policies, however, were not entirely aligned with the orientation or
objectives that motivated American intellectual property rights. When follower
countries decided to establish or revise their patent rules, they modified existing
institutions to fit their own particular needs. As might be expected, countries like
Spain adopted patent systems that were very much focused on securing flows of
technology from abroad, especially technological knowledge that was embodied
in actual production. Patents of introduction were granted to any entrepreneur
who wished to produce foreign technologies that were new to Spain, even if they
were not the inventor. Patentees were required to work the patent or else the

Table 11.2 Patent Grants in Select Countries, 1800–1930

	1800–1870	1871–1900	1901–1930	1800–1930
Canada	87	2,241	7,662	2,815
Population	1.2	4.7	8.2	3.6
Germany	—	4,975	14,534	8,802
Population	—	47.3	67.0	56.4
Japan	—	262	2,390	1,650
Population	31.5	38.6	53.8	33.8
New South Wales	34	220	357	220
Population	0.07	1.0	1.9	0.41
Spain	62	938	3,020	1,176
Population	13.5	17.4	20.6	15.9
United Kingdom	706	7910	15,327	5,704
Population	25.4	36.3	46.5	30.1
United States	1,692	18,453	37,380	13,703
Population	15.3	58.2	102.5	30.0
US patents as % of total	65.6	61.5	56.5	—

Notes and Sources: The table shows annual average patents granted in each subperiod and population (in millions) at the midpoint of each period. Patent statistics are from P. J. Federico, "Historical Patent Statistics 1791–1961," *Journal of the Patent Office Society* 46 (February 1964): 89–171, and from annual reports of patent offices in each country. The data for New South Wales ranges from 1854 to 1920; for Germany from 1871 to 1930, excluding 1914–1919; and for Japan from 1885. Population data are from B. R. Mitchell, *International Historical Statistics, 1750–2005* (London, 2007).

invention would revert to the public domain.[22] Since patents of introduction had a brief term, they encouraged the production of items with immediate profits and a quick payback period.

Shortly after the end of the Civil War, American patentees expanded to international markets, and many began to attain dominant positions throughout the world economy (Table 11.2). In response, other countries implemented policies to protect and to moderate the potential negative impact on influential domestic interest groups. Britain introduced compulsory licenses in 1883 for fear that foreign inventors might injure British industry by refusing to grant other

[22] The most authoritative work on this topic is Sáiz González (1999).

local manufacturers the right to use their patent rights. Concerns also arose that patents by foreigners might be used to block production in Britain, so patentees who manufactured abroad were required to make the patented product in Britain or risk losing their property rights. Among today's leading economies, Japan and Germany stand out in terms of the extent to which they were influenced by the American example. Nevertheless, both still moderated the U.S. model to satisfy their own needs and priorities.[23] As might be expected, many developing countries imposed stronger restrictions than in Europe, with even higher fees and more attention to working requirements and compulsory licenses.

Harmonization of patent laws was motivated by the need to reduce the transaction costs of international trade in ideas. The United States was the acknowledged global leader in innovation and industry, and its self-interest dictated freer trade and open markets. American representatives coordinated with other developed countries and pursued the overarching goal of uniform international patent laws, although, even among these countries, there was little agreement about the specific rules and standards.[24] Ironically, owing to its already liberal patent rules, the United States found itself in a weaker bargaining position than nations that could make concessions by changing their restrictive provisions. Negotiations were further complicated because it soon became clear that the goals of nations with net demand often diverged from those of the regions that were net providers of innovations. Two issues that persisted concerned the rights of foreign patentees and protectionist trade policies. Countries resisted offering equal protection to foreigners because they feared that American patentees would overwhelm their domestic markets, and even the United States continued to use tariffs as a counterpoint to their liberal intellectual property laws. As a result, differences in international markets in invention persisted despite the publicly lauded international treaties for the harmonization of intellectual property laws.

Global Markets in Patents and Inventions

For researchers, the persistent variation in global innovation markets and institutions offers a valuable opportunity to explore significant facets of international markets in invention. This section investigates differences in patent rules and standards, in relation to two important features of global markets in ideas.

---

[23] Nishimura (2011).

[24] Meetings included the International Union for the Protection of Industrial Property in 1884. Other conferences were held in 1878, 1880, and 1883; Rome (1886); Madrid (1890–1891); Brussels (1897–1900); Washington (1911); The Hague (1925); and London (1934). See Khan (2005) and Penrose (1951).

First, patenting activity in foreign countries offers an index of inventive ideas that were likely to be of higher value. Second, the exchange of patent assignments and licenses provides another useful perspective on commercially valuable transfers of technology.

The propensity to file patents overseas varied significantly across nations, as Table 11.3 shows. Among all of these countries, the American experience in the realm of technological innovation was exceptional. U.S. laws were the most liberal to foreign inventors in the world, allowing them equal rights to patent protection by the 1830s, and the domestic market for inventions and innovations was rapidly expanding, creating the potential for abnormal profits. Nevertheless, during the early industrial period, the fraction of foreign patentees obtaining protection in the U.S. market was extremely low, averaging less than 7% between 1840 and 1920. George Richards Elkington, an inventor from Birmingham, England, was one of the foreign residents who obtained patents for his electroplate inventions in the United States. In 1838, he was granted a U.S. patent for an improvement in gilding metals, and in 1843, he also acquired the rights to Ernst Werner Siemen's German patent for electroplating. However, as a foreign patentee who was able to prevail in the highly competitive U.S. market, Elkington was anomalous.

American inventors and their inventions were renowned and admired throughout the world. But when they tried to obtain patents in other countries, they encountered a bewildering kaleidoscope of laws on the books and idiosyncratic practices that inhibited market efficiency for both buyers and sellers of ideas. This was true even of the colonies under British jurisdiction. One of the Fellows of the Chartered Institute of Patent Agents in England pointed out that "the American can place his invention more easily on the market than a British inventor can." However, he wryly continued, the patentee who wished to match the size of the U.S. market by selling the rights to his invention throughout the British empire "has to apply for thirty-nine different Patents; that is to say, he has thirty-nine different holes in his purse through which his money leaks if he wishes to take the fullest commercial advantage of his Majesty's Empire."[25]

Aspiring participants in global markets for ideas could refer to the proliferation of manuals containing advice and information that were increasingly published for their benefit. The handbook by Philip E. Edelman, an electrical engineer and patentee from New York, warned American inventors that foreign patent procedures were "full of pitfalls for the unwary."[26] Still, the profit incentives of going global were significant, and the American inventors who

---

[25] *Transactions*, Chartered Institute of Patent Agents (1902), pp. 211 and 212.
[26] Philip E. Edelman, *Inventions and Patents* (1915), p. 176.

Table 11.3 Markets in Technology, 1840–1920

	1840–1870	1871–1900	1901–1920	Total
Canada				
Foreign patents (%)	70.1	74.2	84.9	77.7
Assignments (%)	70.5	87.4	46.4	54.7
Germany				
Foreign patents (%)	—	34.6	33.6	34.0
Assignments (%)	—	5.5	10.1	8.1
Japan				
Foreign patents (%)	—	20.4	28.8	27.7
Assignments (%)	—	—	—	—
New South Wales				
Foreign patents (%)	—	30.1	37.8	—
Assignments (%)	16.1	26.6	31.4	27.0
Spain				
Foreign patents (%)	49.5	62.8	57.7	59.2
Assignments and licenses (%)	6.8	4.5	4.9	4.8
United Kingdom				
Foreign patents (%)	14.4	19.4	36.8	22.1
Assignments and licenses (%)	—	22.2	15.0	19.4
United States				
Foreign patents (%)	2.6	7.6	10.8	6.5
Assignments at issue (%)	12.0	23.1	28.1	25.2
Average for all countries				
Foreign patents (%)	27.8	57.0	45.6	45.4
Assignments (%)	13.5	26.4	22.4	22.3

Notes and Sources: Annual patent statistics are from P. J. Federico, "Historical Patent Statistics 1791–1961," *Journal of the Patent Office Society* 46 (February 1964): 89–171; and the World Intellectual Property Rights Organization. Patent assignments and foreign patents are from reports of the relevant patent offices, with the exception of the United States, Spain, Germany, and the United Kingdom. The U.S. foreign and assignments data were estimated from a sample of patent grants. Foreign patenting in the United Kingdom was calculated from a sample of some 15,000 patent grants, in which Ireland, Scotland, and Wales were included as domestic counts. I am grateful to Patricio Sáiz who provided the data for Spain, and to Carsten Burhop for the German assignments data. Percentages are expressed as a fraction of total patents granted. U.K. and Spanish data include both assignments and licenses, whereas the numbers for all other countries refer to assignments alone. The German time series extends from 1877 through 1913 for assignments, and from 1883 to 1920 for foreign patents. New South Wales became part of the Australian federal patent system in 1904.

achieved marked success in penetrating foreign markets provided encouraging examples.[27] As one publication optimistically declared:

> American inventors having valuable inventions, who do not secure such foreign patents as would seem to be of value, simply throw away their chances of realizing large profits, and in many cases large fortunes. Ordinarily it may be said that when an invention is valuable in this country that it is equally so in foreign countries. Indeed, American ingenuity is now so well known and appreciated that the foreign patents can frequently be sold to better advantage and in shorter time than the United States patent.[28]

Growth theories propose a positive relationship between trade, increasing returns to innovation, and the size of the market, and these models are supported by the historical patterns. In the antebellum United States, when transportation networks improved and contributed to expansions in market demand, inventive activity surged in response, especially in formerly isolated areas that had just gained access to markets.[29] Relatively ordinary individuals, such as artisans or workers without skills, were especially likely to turn to inventions that provided solutions to perceived bottlenecks and problems. Empirical analysis indicates that a similar process can be detected in international markets, for both inventions and sales of patent rights.[30] Foreign patenting and assignments were higher in regions with more profitable markets, as gauged by per capita gross domestic product. The same relationships between sales and foreign patents were observed when changes in market access were measured in terms of the spread of railroad networks. Foreign markets for patents may not have been as hospitable or transparent as in the United States, but American patentees and supporting intermediaries were entrepreneurial in their strategies to overcome market frictions.

David Meade Randolph, a Virginia merchant and relative of Thomas Jefferson, exploited his personal connections and persuaded an English friend to process his application for a patent in England in 1809 to protect his improvement in shoe-making.[31] Others had recourse to more professional intermediaries, including patent agencies with international representatives, who reduced

---

[27] Foreign patenting in registration systems is underestimated, since patents were often taken out in the name of the foreign patent agent or representative. For instance, Daniel Treadwell obtained a patent for improvements in ordnance carriages in 1845, under the name of the U.S. consul in London, Thomas Aspinwall (English Patent No. 10728 of December 23, 1845).

[28] E. L. Richards & Co., *The Inventors' Handbook* (1882), p. 18.

[29] Sokoloff (1988); Sokoloff and Khan (1990).

[30] For the supporting multivariate regression analysis, see Khan (2013a).

[31] David Meade Randolph was also the author of the 1810 *Treatise on Wheel Carriages*.

transaction costs for inventors who wished to participate in global markets.[32] The roster of the Chartered Institute of Patent Agents in England, which was founded in 1882, included 212 members in 1898, 82 of whom were domiciled overseas; in 1902, membership included 151 domestic agents and 101 foreign affiliates.[33] By the second half of the nineteenth century many American agents were skilled in negotiating international transactions in patent rights and patented technologies, either in person or through alliances. The *International Directory of Patent Agents* for 1897 included information on some 2,500 agents throughout the world, while the third edition in 1901 listed more than 4,000 professional intermediaries in this global market. The vast majority of entries on these international lists were American patent agents or foreign associates concerned with U.S. trade.

Geographical proximity was another factor that explained the distribution of foreign patenting for some countries. Canadians obtained 371 patents in the United States in 1890, relative to 178 by French inventors. At the same time, French patentees dominated the early market for invention in neighboring Spain, accounting for fully 75% of foreign patents filed in Spain prior to 1879.[34] In Japan, foreign patentees originated primarily from the leading industrial nations of the United States, Britain, and Germany, but rates of foreign participation in domestic patenting were nevertheless strikingly low.[35] We might speculate that the low rates of foreign patenting in Japan and New South Wales in the early twentieth century owed in part to the "tyranny of distance" and to the extent of the market. Low foreign patenting was also affected by concerns about the security of property rights, if not for patents themselves, then for other forms of assets. For instance, in Japan, the state could expropriate patents that were deemed

[32] "We (E. L. Richards & Co.) have agents in all the principal foreign countries, and have every facility for giving thorough work and securing the patents in the shortest possible time. The most desirable foreign patents for American inventors to secure are those of Canada, England, France, Germany, Spain, and Belgium. These six patents secure the exclusive monopoly among about One Hundred and Fifty Millions of the most intelligent people in the world." See also Swanson (2009).

[33] See the *Transactions of the Chartered Institute of Patent Agents* (various years). William Phillips Thompson (founder in 1873 of W. P. Thompson & Co., an agency that is still in existence) had also become a certified U.S. patent attorney, and the firm maintained links and formal alliances with other patent representatives throughout the world.

[34] According to Patricio Sáiz González, French dominance fell rapidly during the second Industrial Revolution, and the foreign roster for corporate patenting during the 1820–1939 period consisted of Germany (29.7%), France (19.7%), the United States (14.5%), and the United Kingdom (13.7%).

[35] It might be expected that the newly established Japanese patent office would lack the materials to conduct thorough searches, especially where leading technologies were described in a foreign language. Thompson (1920: 108) claimed that the Japanese patent procedures were somewhat arbitrary, and "the office are very apt to reject inventions which they consider closely resemble in appearance others known, and they frequently reject an invention as 'publicly known' without citing any specific proof." In 1903, Americans accounted for 52.6% of foreign patent applications in Japan, followed by Britain (21.0%) and Germany (14.2%).

in the public interest, whereas perceived infringement was punishable by harsh criminal penalties, including fines and imprisonment.

The early cross-border firms like the notable and notorious East India Company obtained profits in the traditional areas of trade in raw materials and natural resource extraction. More modern American multinational enterprises were characterized by trade based on technological innovations, and they typically exploited large portfolios of patents from different countries that leveraged their expertise in the domestic market. Transaction costs in the external markets for technology across national boundaries often led American firms to avoid arm's-length deals by setting up their own overseas subsidiaries. One of the first examples was Samuel Colt, a leading firearms patentee and founder of the Colt Patent Fire-Arms Manufacturing Company in Hartford, Connecticut. The inventor had been careful to secure patents from France and Britain, but he was still concerned about the potential for British firms to pirate his technology, given the lack of information and shaky legal enforcement by the courts. Accordingly, Colt traveled to England, where he established an English subsidiary, which began production at the start of 1853. This direct foreign investment allowed him to maintain quality control and to foreclose on potential competition. Colt carefully cultivated influential personal connections in Europe and was directly involved in commercialization. For instance, he attended the exhibition at the Crystal Palace and was honored with a large silver Telford Medal from the London Institution of Civil Engineers (apparently the most cherished of the twenty-four medals he received).

American patentees Richard Hoe and George Pullman also leveraged their inventions through early multinational enterprises. Hoe's patented rotary press revolutionized the printing of newspapers, and he initially expanded his New York custom to England to build the presses on contract. Demand proved to be so extensive that in 1857 he founded a London branch, which was managed by William Conquest, one of his main machinists. This direct investment strategy was in part motivated by nationalistic concerns of the *London Times* and other leading British newspapers, which did not wish to be viewed as patronizing a foreign American firm. Like Richard Hoe and Company, George Pullman (patentee of more than fifty inventions between 1860 and 1900) first went to Europe to satisfy bespoke orders, using parts that initially were made in Michigan and shipped for assembly overseas. Demand for the output of Pullman's Palace Cars Company proved to be so voluminous that it was deemed necessary to build factories not just in England but also in Italy, Belgium, and other countries.[36]

[36] Southard (1931).

In countries that did not honor patent rights to the same extent as in the United States, some American companies strategized to retain full control over their foreign subsidiaries, even to the extent of bringing over their own American employees. These alternative means of exclusion were especially important in protectionist jurisdictions where courts were biased against alien companies that were attempting to enforce their patent rights against domestic infringers. Indeed, one of the reasons that firms like Singer chose to set up shop themselves was to avoid the difficulty of monitoring and securing returns from arm's-length agreements with foreign entities. Singer in particular had learned this lesson when a French partner reneged on a contract in which the patentee would transfer the property rights and know-how for manufacturing his sewing machines in return for a fixed payment and per unit royalties on the units produced. This sort of market failure, of course, was precisely the reason that enforceable intellectual property rights were all the more important as firms entered into international markets and that U.S. representatives were lobbying for uniformity in laws and policies.

Foreign subsidiaries were not entirely immune to the array of transaction costs that arose from unfamiliar inputs, environments, institutions, and language. These difficulties created incentives for some companies to enter into joint ventures with local firms, a development that masked the extent of foreign participation in patenting and innovation markets. For instance, General Electric (GE) was affiliated with Tokyo Electric Company and Shibaura Engineering Works (the two companies merged in 1939 and are now known as Toshiba). GE entered into contractual agreements that allowed these affiliates in Japan to apply under their own names for patents that wholly belonged to GE.[37] GE was responsible for about three thousand patents that were filed in Japan under the name of their local affiliates in the interwar period. By allowing their patents to be filed as domestic inventions, GE was able to avoid significant bureaucratic hurdles and other transaction costs, including the costs of negotiation with their affiliates, and they also avoided the need to acquire information about the local markets. In effect, GE minimized the costs of participation in international patent markets by specializing in the creation of technology and outsourcing the management of its patent portfolios to local Japanese firms.

What were the factors that influenced the transfer of technology across countries? Statistical techniques that control for other variables show that technological capability in the receiving economy played a significant role.[38] Lower rates of

---

[37] Nishimura (2011).
[38] The multivariate regressions that support the general conclusions in this chapter are reported in Khan (2013a).

foreign patenting were related to greater indigenous innovation, whereas higher rates signaled a lack of domestic technological capability or a greater dependency on foreign inventive output. Foreign patenting rates were lower in regions that were more innovative, even when the outlier of the United States was excluded from the analysis. In the case of Japan, indigenous Japanese technological capacity was more advanced than is generally assumed, and this condition at least partially accounted for the low rate of foreign penetration in their technology markets.

The specific design of patent institutions significantly influenced global markets in ideas. In particular, the statistical analysis reveals that effective examination systems promoted trade in patents. The "American system" of patent rules and standards was universally associated with prior examination for novelty, and this model was emulated by followers such as Canada and Germany. Objective examination by specialized employees of the Patent Office served to reduce uncertainty about the technical value of the patent. Unlike administered systems, patent examiners merely determined the novelty of the patent property, and it was up to the patentee to secure returns in the market. After surviving the filter of examination, the patentee could more easily use the certified grant to mobilize capital to commercially develop the patented technology or to sell or license the rights to those who were better positioned to directly exploit the patent. Private parties could always, as they did under the registration systems prevailing in much of the world, pay third parties to make the same determination as the patent examiners. However, a centralized examination system reduced barriers to entry for inventors who could not retain their own private examiner, generated economies of scale, and produced positive externalities. Trade in patented technologies was, as a result, much more extensive under examination regimes, holding other factors constant. Technologically creative people without the start-up capital to go into business and directly exploit their discoveries were major beneficiaries.

Some economists contend that international markets for technology will benefit society, even if the transfer occurs because of expropriation. Many developing countries supported compulsory licenses and working requirements to ensure that patent grants were consistent with their social and economic agendas. However, U.S. policy has always rejected proposals to impose constraints and conditions on patent rights, considering them a disincentive to inventive activity. In some cases, the constraints were redundant, because many foreigners obtained patents with the intention of profiting from working their inventions in the overseas market anyway. In others, such policies were not strongly enforced, or could be avoided by hiring well-connected local agents. According to Spanish legislation, patents had to be implemented within three years of granting or the patent right would be revoked, but just 23% of patents were indeed put into practice.[39] Policies like these invariably were associated with rent-seeking rather than with positive economic outcomes. Even if stipulations like the need to practice the invention did not significantly discourage foreign patentees, restrictions of this nature added to the implicit and explicit cost of patenting. Moreover, these requirements were most discouraging for individuals without a great deal of personal wealth, so they tended to increase inequality in the distribution of inventors.

As discussed before, the rationale for international treaties to coordinate intellectual property rules and standards was based on the assumption that harmonization would reduce the transaction costs of exchanges and transfers across borders. However, neither foreign patenting rates nor assignments were enhanced by adherence to such treaties. Instead, international markets for patents were more active in countries that did not participate in patent conventions. These results may have occurred because the provisions of multilateral treaties were not well enforced. The political economy of international agreements was contentious, as with Trade-Related Intellectual Property Rights and negotiations with China today. Fundamentally divergent interests created a divide between consumers and suppliers of innovations, so the terms that were ratified in intellectual property treaties had to satisfy the lowest common denominator. The United States, in particular, frequently achieved its aims in the realm of global technology markets through bilateral treaties and trade sanctions and negotiations rather than in multilateral patent conventions.

Foreign Patenting and Markets for Inventions in the United States

Any discussion of global markets in invention requires a closer scrutiny of the American experience. The United States stood out in its strong enforcement of a patent system that favored inventive rights and in the proliferation of patents and patented output in deep and extensive markets for technology. American patents accounted for two-thirds of the total granted in all of the sample countries during the nineteenth century. This was true even though patent examiners rejected a significant number of U.S. patent applications, whereas patents were merely registered in countries like England, Spain, and New South Wales. Today, in marked contrast to the nineteenth century, foreign residents obtain the majority of patents filed in the United States (Figure 11.3). An analysis of the historical process that got underway during the second Industrial Revolution promises

---

[39] Sáiz González (1996, 1999).

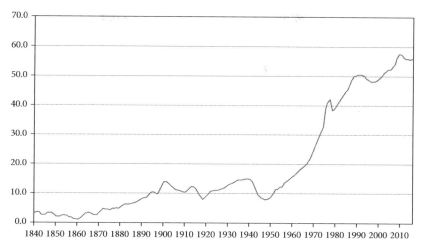

Figure 11.3 Foreign Patenting in the United States, 1840–2015 (Percentage)

Notes and Source: U.S. Patent Office. The graph shows the patents granted to foreigners as a percentage of total patents issued, three-year moving average.

to offer insights to better understand the factors that influenced changes over time in national comparative advantage in innovation.

Naomi Lamoreaux and Kenneth Sokoloff conducted an extensive survey of U.S. markets in invention during the second Industrial Revolution.[40] They examined patent assignments that occurred at the time the patent was granted, as well as a sample of assignments that were completed after the patent was issued. During the 1870s, inventors tended to be personally involved in the commercialization of their patented innovations, granting licenses to manufacturers in outlying regions. Over time a division of labor occurred, whereby invention and commercialization became separate pursuits, and specialized inventors sold off or licensed their rights to others. Intermediaries such as patent agents and patent attorneys played an important and productive role in facilitating transactions. Overall, their findings illustrate the depth of these markets in ideas and show its rapid expansion throughout the United States. Their project is exceedingly informative about markets in inventions by domestic American residents but does not take into account the experience of foreign patentees.

My own analysis sheds further light on long-term changes in the market for ideas by highlighting the patterns for foreign inventors who were granted patent protection in United States between 1870 and 1930. The random sample included

---

[40] Lamoreaux et al. (2011, 2013).

over nine thousand patents that were granted in 1870, 1900, and 1930, allocated to the sector of final use. These records included assignments at the time the patent was issued, the number of discoveries claimed in the patent specification, characteristics of domestic and foreign inventors and coinventors, whether an attorney signed the patent document, and the number of citations that other inventors made to the patent from the time of its issue through to the present. Of the sample, 36% of patents were assigned at the time the patent was issued, and 27% were assigned to corporations. However, patents can be transferred to other owners at any time during their term, so the information on assignments at issue underestimates the extent of markets in invention. Just over 10% of all patents were granted to foreign inventors. The majority of patents were for machine inventions (25%), whereas consumer products accounted for 13%, the technology-intensive electrical inventions accounted for 7%, and 4% of patents covered chemical discoveries.

These patterns show that a rapid change in the organization of invention occurred between 1900 and 1930. The probability that a patent would be assigned to a corporation markedly increased over this period, as did the role of coinvention and team production. Corporate assignments featured larger numbers of patent claims, perhaps indicating attempts to secure protection over a greater scope for their discoveries. Citations to these inventions by other patentees offer a proxy for the technical value of the patent, whereas the sale of the right was correlated with market value. Corporate assignments, however, were less related to commercial value and increasingly reflected procedural transfers from employees to their employers.[41] Foreign patentees who filed in the United States exhibited a lower propensity to employ attorneys, supporting the argument that the American institutions exhibited greater transparency, ease of processing, and straightforward administrative procedures. International patents tended to be of higher average value than domestic patents and therefore were positively related with assignments. At the same time, relative to resident inventors, foreign patentees were significantly less likely to assign their rights at the time the patent was issued, and they were also not as likely to assign them to corporations. Foreign patentees were often principals in their own companies or entrepreneurial independent inventors who were attempting to tap into the extensive American product markets.

Assignments and foreign patenting in the sample were higher in the electrical and chemical industries, in both of which Germans were at the forefront of advances in technology. The chemical industry in particular is interesting, for it provided an early sign of the shift in global comparative advantage in leading-edge technological innovations that would evolve over the twentieth century.

---

[41] For the legal aspects of employee-inventors, see Fisk (1998).

These patterns mirrored the experience of American innovators in the nineteenth century. The introduction of German national patent laws in 1877 bolstered innovations in their chemical industry, and German firms began to expand internationally, acquiring large portfolios of foreign patents.[42] Corporations like Bayer (Farbenfabriken), Badische Anilin und Soda–Fabrik (BASF), and Hoechst used patent rights to foreclose on potential rivals in the German market and overseas as well.[43]

The prominent role of intellectual property in Bayer's American business strategy can be discerned from its appointment of a patent attorney, Anthony Gref, as the president of its U.S. subsidiary. These enterprises combined intellectual property rights with such alternative methods of appropriation as trade secrecy, trademarks, and cartelization as key elements of their strategy to secure a competitive edge. Gref was active in using the courts to put an end to cheaper parallel imports of products into the United States.[44] In Germany, patents were offered for the protection of chemical processes alone but did not protect the final products, whereas in the United States, German patentees were able to exclude rivals from both the processes and the product itself. Thus, in part because of the differences in patent institutions, in Germany the market structure of this particular industry was more competitive than in the United States.

The overall patterns for Germans obtaining U.S. patents were quite distinct from the experience in German markets for technology, and the differences provide more specific insights into the influence of favorable patent rules and standards on markets for innovation. In the first decade of the twentieth century, over four thousand patents were granted to protect chemical and allied inventions, two-thirds of which were issued to foreign inventors. As Table 11.4 illustrates, in this industry German patentees dominated the ranks of patents as well as assignments in the United States. For instance, 16% of French chemical patents issued in the United States were assigned, as were 21% of British patents and 34% of American patents, whereas the assignment rates for German and Swiss patents were 75% and 87%, respectively. These remarkably high propensities to assign property rights for patented inventions can be compared to an average rate in Germany itself of 8%. Thus, 68% of assignments went to four German companies, which operated as a loose cartel or a "community of interest."[45] Germany supported a liberal work-for-hire patent policy, whereby

---

[42] Murmann (2003) provides an extensive study of the German chemical industry that compares the German innovation system to the experience of other countries.

[43] Marsch (1994).

[44] *Merck Report*, vol. 6 (1897).

[45] These included Aktiengesellschaft fur Farben, Badische Anilin Fabrik, Bayer/Farbenfabrik Elberfeld, and Meister Lucius & Bruening (Hoechst). See *United States Congressional Report on Schedule A: Chemicals, Oils, and Paints* (1912), p. 361.

Table 11.4 Domestic and Foreign Patenting and Assignments in the U.S. Chemical Industry, 1900–1910

All Chemical Patents	Total Patents	Total Assignments	% Assigned
Electrochemistry	256	117	45.7
Bleaching and dyeing	1,187	939	79.1
Chemicals	1,517	728	48.0
Explosives	156	61	39.1
Pharmaceuticals	649	155	23.9
Plastics	116	45	38.8
Glue	23	6	26.1
Liquid coating compositions	121	25	20.7
Ammonia and turpentine	43	11	25.6

All Foreign	Foreign patents	Foreign Assignments	Assignments as % Patents
Electrochemistry	89	25	21.4
Bleaching and dyeing	1,049	901	96.0
Chemicals	980	536	73.6
Explosives	59	6	9.8
Pharmaceuticals	212	67	43.2
Plastics	67	23	51.1
Glue	11	1	16.7
Liquid coating compositions	41	4	16.0
Ammonia and turpentine	8	0	0.0

Domestic U.S.	U.S. Patents as % Total	U.S. Assignments as % U.S. Patents	U.S. Assignments as % Total Assignments
Electrochemistry	65.2	55.1	78.6
Bleaching and dyeing	11.6	27.5	4.0
Chemicals	35.4	35.8	26.4
Explosives	62.2	56.7	90.2
Pharmaceuticals	67.3	20.1	56.8
Plastics	42.2	44.9	48.9
Glue	52.2	41.7	83.3
Liquid coating compositions	66.1	26.3	84.0
Ammonia and turpentine	81.4	31.4	100.0

Table 11.4 *Continued*

German	German Patents as % Total Patents	German Assignments as % German Patents	German Assignments as % Total Assignments
Electrochemistry	7.8	45.0	7.7
Bleaching and dyeing	69.9	92.5	81.8
Chemicals	45.2	68.5	64.6
Explosives	17.9	17.9	8.2
Pharmaceuticals	18.0	47.9	36.1
Plastics	32.8	31.6	26.7
Glue	34.8	12.5	16.7
Liquid coating compositions	16.5	15.0	12.0
Ammonia and turpentine	16.3	0.0	0.0

Notes and Sources: United States Congressional Report: H.R. No. 326, *Report on Schedule A: Chemicals, Oils and Paints* (1912).

corporations could file for patents that their employees had created, implying that German assignments primarily reflected economic transfers. However, assignment rates for German patents in the United States varied significantly across different industrial categories, suggesting that higher assignment rates also reflected the greater commercial viability of German discoveries.[46]

German enterprises virtually monopolized the market for dyes and chemicals, in particular, taking full advantage of their patent portfolios. Americans obtained just 12% and 35%, respectively, of patents granted in the United States in these fields. U.S. concerns about the German monopoly over this area of innovation peaked during the outbreak of hostilities in World War I.[47] An amendment of the Trading with the Enemy Act of 1917 authorized the confiscation of German intellectual property. The Chemical Foundation was formed two years later to manage several thousand expropriated patents, trademarks, and copyrights on behalf of the American chemical industry. Access to this windfall stock of intellectual property likely served as a subsidy that temporarily boosted U.S. capabilities and innovations. However, after the end of the war, despite the loss of their patents, the German firms were once again able to leverage their expertise and know-how to retain their competitive edge in dyes and chemicals

---

[46] Burhop (2010) estimated that 85% of assignments in Germany were economic transactions rather than procedural transfers.

[47] Steen (2001).

relative to American competitors. This event revealed that effective transfer of technology also requires tacit and explicit knowledge and experience, which can only be acquired through consensual negotiations and direct involvement in research and production.

The case of phenacetin, an analgesic that Bayer patented in the United States, exemplifies the conflicts that foreign patenting created for intellectual property policy. The German corporation priced phenacetin significantly lower in other countries where product patents were not granted for pharmaceuticals. For instance, the price in the United States was $1, whereas Canadians paid 15 cents, creating an arbitrage opportunity that would benefit American consumers. Bayer issued explicit instructions on its foreign packages that purchasers of their goods overseas were prohibited from resale in the United States. Edward Dickerson, a U.S. assignee of the Bayer patent, obtained a legal injunction against the sale of phenacetin in the United States, which the defendant had purchased outside the country. In keeping with the absolute rights conferred by the U.S. patent system during the term of the grant, the court ruled that the parallel importation of phenacetin, even if legally purchased from Bayer overseas, constituted an infringement. American patents guaranteed the right to make, use, or vend and to exclude, and thus "the letters patent allowed the foreign corporation to place restrictions barring resale in the United States by purchasers of phenacetine."[48]

Some policymakers attributed the underdeveloped state of the U.S. chemical industry to the irony of the strong protection for foreigners under its uniquely favorable patent laws:

> The American market is the most valuable in the world, and the foreign inventor or his foreign assignees naturally take all the advantage that the law gives them to exploit this market as profitably as they can. This very largely accounts for the tardiness with which the chemical industry develops in the United States.[49]

At the same time, the German patent office may have administered their own patent rules in a discriminatory fashion that was biased against foreign inventors, including those from the United States.[50] Thus, German enterprises were able to successfully exploit the differences across countries in patent institutions to dominate both the domestic and foreign markets.

In Britain, lobbyists for their domestic chemical industry succeeded in getting protectionist patent legislation passed that provided for working requirements.

---

[48] *Dickerson v. Tinling*, 84 F. 192, 195 (1897).
[49] *Report on Schedule A* (1912), p. 362.
[50] See Richter and Streb (2011).

Some American firms were sufficiently alarmed by developments in the chemicals market to petition Congress to revise the patent laws so that

> no patent shall be granted to a citizen of any foreign country which does not grant a corresponding patent to a citizen of the United States: And provided further, That no patent shall be granted upon any drug, medicine, or medicinal chemical except in so far as the same relates to a definite process for the preparation.[51]

These legislative measures for protectionist intellectual property rules in the chemical industry were defeated in Congress. The anomaly of wartime policies was just that—a temporary aberration. Numerous other similar proposals over the past century were also rejected, because they were not in keeping with the fundamentally market-oriented principles of the American patent system.

Conclusions

Enterprise and innovation have long spanned national and international borders and have led to persistent debates about markets in patented ideas that still have not been resolved. The historical experience indicates that technological capabilities and trade in patented ideas and innovations were not exogenous. Innovation markets responded to the incentives that specific institutional and organizational rules and standards provided. Salient features of technology markets today emerged during the course of the nineteenth century and crystallized during the second Industrial Revolution.

Corporations and individual patentees used a wide array of business strategies that were adapted to the circumstances they encountered in different environments. Thus, patterns of patenting and assignments differed significantly to accommodate and take advantage of country-specific rules and institutions. Innovative enterprises employed transfers of patent rights to acquire inventions from employees as well as to reward them, to collude with rivals in the same industry, to monopolize output markets and block potential competitors, to specialize in invention or commercialization, and to increase technical capabilities and productivity. Patentees' ability to follow select strategies depended on the nature of legal and market institutions, highlighting the need to understand how the design of specific mechanisms affected the extent to which desired social objectives could be attained.

---

[51] Hearings before the Committee on Patents, H.R. 13679 (1904), p. 3.

The study of markets in the later era and of the experience of "follower economies" raises other dimensions of the relevant tradeoffs. The U.S. patent system was open to all first and true inventors who created discoveries that were new to the world. This policy soon placed foreign inventors on an equal footing with domestic inventors, a position that was not a cause for concern as long as Americans retained their position as the world's leaders in technological innovations. However, the very openness of the system and its emphasis on the diffusion of information offered advantages that foreign competitors in the chemical industry and in machine-tool innovations were able to use to compete against domestic U.S. enterprise in this sector. These were just the grounds that other nations, and in particular the developing countries, were citing to support their less generous patent institutions and their employment of such liability rules as compulsory licensing and working requirements. For many developing economies, strong patents would primarily protect the rights of foreigners and would hinder their ability to imitate the technologies of the advanced countries.

The American experience in the chemical industry, however, suggests that dynamic comparative advantage was an outgrowth of endogenous factors and could not be achieved merely by expropriating property rights. Successful technological innovation also required inherent domestic capabilities and tacit knowledge acquired through learning by doing. Interest groups in the nascent U.S. chemical industry lobbied to change the market orientation of American patent rules to provide narrow benefits to their own constituents through compulsory licensing and working requirements. The costs to these domestic groups at the time were evident, but their efforts to retreat from competitive markets in ideas were repudiated. Property rights in inventions in the United States were not designed to enable protectionism and the political interests of special groups. Instead, policymakers acknowledged that open markets in ideas and innovation generated positive net benefits to society in general.

Intellectual property rights, like all other institutions, involve costs and benefits for all stakeholders. In the American context, these tradeoffs have been most evident in the realm of copyrights, which featured continual and continuing controversies about oligopsony buyers, international piracy, and cartelization among sellers, which had the potential to limit access to knowledge and learning.[52] The democratic American system of patents, by contrast, promoted dynamic competition in vibrant markets for patented ideas and innovations that dramatically expanded the choice set for consumers at ever-falling prices over time. This real world of literally millions of new ideas that were promptly alchemized into a society of material plenty was far removed from the abstract theories of "patent monopoly" and contrived scarcity that are still enshrined in the economics literature.

---

[52] Khan (2005).

12

Innovations in Law

The great inventions . . . have built up new customs and new law.
—Benjamin Cardozo (1921)

Technological disruption has been a defining feature of the American experience since the start of the nineteenth century. Moreover, as such prominent
commentators as Thomas Paine and Alexis de Tocqueville have pointed out,
U.S. policy has always been distinguished by the central role of law and the judiciary. Accordingly, the relationship between law and technology is critical for understanding the evolution of the knowledge economy. The standing of the United
States as a "republic of technology" was matched by the readiness of the judiciary
to accommodate the radical transformations caused by innovations. Legal rules
functioned as effective enabling institutions that simultaneously facilitated technological change and adapted to the disruptions that such innovations created.

Courts in the seventeenth and early eighteenth centuries essentially functioned as administered systems, engaging in pervasive social and economic regulation that encompassed both the private and public realms.[1] They monitored
and enforced dominant moral and religious codes and imposed restrictions on
commerce through price controls, licensing, enforcement of contracts, and property rights. Soon after the first decade of the eighteenth century, as the scale of
market activity increased, a division of labor across institutions led to caseloads
in civil courts that primarily involved economic transactions to enforce debt
contracts. Their mandate shifted from market regulation to facilitating exchange,
through secure property rights, liability rules that placed responsibility on the
least-cost avoider, and decisions that tended to allocate resources to their most
highly valued use. At the outset of industrialization, therefore, the legal system
was well prepared to accommodate the new economic challenges of the nineteenth century.

The unprecedented technical progress of the early industrial era brought
about discrete and measurable changes in the lives, lifestyles, and livelihoods

---

[1] For a quantitative analysis of the evolution of colonial courts that employs an extensive dataset of
district court cases, see Khan (2008a). The empirical analysis of civil lawsuits in Khan (2000) shows
how the expansion of markets promoted cooperative solutions.

Inventing Ideas. B. Zorina Khan, Oxford University Press (2020). © Oxford University Press.
DOI: 10.1093/oso/9780190936075.001.0001

of Americans that, arguably, exceed those of our own time. Less dramatic advances in knowledge and their applications also significantly promoted social welfare. The diffusion of information about hygiene and medical discoveries among households extended life expectancies and improved the standard of living. Technological innovations also affected the scope and nature of the law. Competition policy, medical malpractice, nuisance, trespass and torts, the allocation of riparian rights, and admiralty law all reflected turmoil wrought by technical changes. Advances in forensic science and technology transformed the enforcement and adjudication of criminal law. Organizational innovations influenced the nature of property rights, employment contracts, and liability rules.

Technological change was not limited to domestic issues, for it also facilitated more numerous and more rapid transactions with other nations during peace and war. Indeed, the very boundaries of maritime sovereignty were set by existing technology—the three-mile territorial limit was determined by the maximum distance of a cannon shot. Innovations like submarines, underwater international cables, and manned airplane flights created jurisdictional and third-party effects among nations that the legal system had to address. The legal implications of naval blockades and sanctions changed as newer ships and submarines developed, and the law of agency and bottomry incorporated developments in communications that meant ships at sea were no longer completely cut off from their owners on land.

Clearly, technological change was not unknown before this time, but the innovations of the nineteenth century were significantly different from those of previous centuries because their sphere of influence was so much larger. New means of transportation made national and international transactions routine and extended the practical boundaries of markets and social interactions. Dominant corporations like Standard Oil raised issues of taxation, jurisdiction, the boundaries of the firm, and other far-ranging legal and economic dilemmas. Moreover, the expansion of communications networks introduced time as a central feature of such interactions and facilitated productivity changes through greater intensity of work and leisure. As a result of both factors, nineteenth-century technologies not only engendered conflicts between transactors but also created a world in which the pace, scale, and scope of third-party effects were potentially much larger. This in turn raised the policy question of how to ensure that technological progress would increase social welfare without imposing undue costs, especially in terms of disadvantaged groups without an economic voice.

Legal institutions were at the center of emerging questions about technology. Patents and copyrights, as the subject of federal law, exhibited greater uniformity than if under state jurisdiction and thus facilitated the development of a national market. The framers of the American Constitution had been certain that social welfare would be maximized through the "progress of science and useful arts," and that this would be best achieved through a complementary relationship between law and the market. The wish to further technological innovation through private initiative created a paradox: to promote diffusion and enhance social welfare, it would first be necessary to limit diffusion and to protect exclusive rights. Thus, part of the debate about law and technology has always centered on the boundaries of the private domain relative to the public domain. Technology was also shaped by other areas of property law, as well as by rules regarding contracts, torts, crime, and constitutional issues. The relationship between law and technology was reciprocal because, just as law shaped technology, technical innovations significantly influenced legal innovations.

As we currently grapple with the tradeoffs that accompany innovations such as search engines, the development of the right to privacy is especially interesting. This new legal concept was integrated into common law to compensate for the potential of new technologies to infringe on the rights of both users and third parties. Samuel Warren and Louis Brandeis, in one of the most effective law review articles ever published, argued that "modern enterprise and invention" subjected the ordinary individual to unwarranted suffering that could not be alleviated through existing laws of copyright, tort, trespass, slander, and libel. Instant photographs and "numerous mechanical devices" led to the "evil of invasion of privacy."[2] The concept of a legal right to privacy immediately entered into litigated arguments, and the New York Supreme Court, in *Schuyler v. Curtis et al.* (1891), quoted directly from the law review article but distinguished between private individuals and public figures who by implication ceded the right to privacy. In a Massachusetts case three years later the wife of the great inventor George H. Corliss tried to enjoin the publication of a photograph of her late husband. The court rejected the plea because her husband was "among the first of American inventors, and he sought recognition as such," permitting thousands of his photographs to be distributed at the Centennial Exposition in Philadelphia.[3]

How and why the common law changed constitutes a standard debate in political and legal histories. A classic source of dissension relates to the arguments of scholars who agree that American legal institutions were flexible but contend that the judiciary was captured by the interests of a small group in society. Morton Horwitz, in particular, admits that the antebellum legal system played a key role in the nascent industrialization of the United States but argues that judges were biased in favor of capitalists and industrialists, whom they regarded as key to the promotion of economic development. The judiciary reinterpreted existing legal rules in property, torts, and contracts in an instrumentalist fashion to place the

---

[2] S. D. Warren and L. Brandeis, "Right to Privacy," *Harvard Law Review* 4 (1890): 193.
[3] *Schuyler v. Curtis et al.*, 15 N.Y.S. 787 (1891); *Corliss v. Walker Co.*, 64 F. 280 (1894).

burdens of expansion on hapless workers and helpless farmers. In so doing, judicial decisions led to outcomes that subsidized the efforts of industrialists, regardless of the statutes and of legal precedent. Judges assumed the role of legislators to the extent that "judge-made law" should be viewed as a derogatory term. This "ruthless" transformation meant that the economically progressive classes were able to "dramatically . . . throw the burden of economic development on the weakest and least active elements of the population."[4]

Although the specifics of this subsidy hypothesis have been challenged, it has proven to be a resilient interpretation of the American experience. Its most recent incarnation is in research that hypothesizes that regulation in the Gilded Age was an optimal response to the failures of the legal system and makes the heroic assumption that courts were more susceptible to capture than were regulators. The authors argue that large-scale corporations wielded excessive power in the courts, "routinely bribed" judges and juries, and engaged in other legal and illegal tactics to ensure outcomes that were biased in their favor. Consequently, the legal system "broke down." This alleged "subversion of justice" proved to be inappropriate for the needs of the time and was replaced by regulatory agencies, which were not as open to the same corrupting influences.[5]

Critics of these different versions of the subsidy thesis regard the most effective rebuttal to be simply an objective and extensive reading of lawsuits and legal procedures. They highlight the complementary relationship between legislature, common law, the Constitution, and the judiciary.[6] Similarly, I find little empirical evidence to support claims of either overt corruption or bias. Effective policies toward furthering innovations, whether by statute or common law, required a balancing of costs and benefits that was far more subtle than a monolithic promotion of the interests of any one specific group in society.

The major arguments in this chapter are based on statistics computed from several thousand decisions at the state and federal levels. New technologies in the nineteenth century raised questions about the relevance of existing legal rules and ultimately caused changes in the law, albeit with a lag. Since the judiciary is by its nature conservative and technology is dynamic, the legal system potentially could have functioned as a significant bottleneck to innovation. Instead, the common law was sufficiently flexible to cope with new discoveries. This flexibility did not occur because of any preconceived bias toward any particular group in society. Indeed, the United States remained a largely agrarian society well into the nineteenth century, and industrialization depended on an efficient

---

[4] See Horwitz (1977: 101).
[5] Glaeser and Shleifer (2003).
[6] Karsten (1997) argues that court decisions toward contracts, torts, and property tended to protect workers and were not perceptibly biased toward defendants or capitalist developers.

agricultural sector. Instead, we can identify five different mechanisms through which technological change had an impact on the law: technical innovations affected existing analogies, altered transaction costs, increased the speed and scope of transactions, influenced norms and expectations at both the industrial and societal levels, and changed judicial and legislative conceptions of the most effective means to promote the public interest.

In the first instance, courts attempted to mediate between parties to disputes that related to the incursions of new technologies through a process that can be termed "adjudication by analogy."[7] Early on, the law was stretched to accommodate discrete changes by attempting to detect some degree of equivalence across technologies, either by form or by function. Second, inappropriate analogies tended to increase the frequency of legal conflicts or appeals, which served as a signal that revisions were insufficient. Under these circumstances, inappropriately reasoned rulings increased the cost of transacting and made it necessary for legal doctrines and legislation to change to encompass the new innovations. The third mechanism was activated by technologies, such as major advances in transportation and communications, that led to a more rapid pace of activity and thereby produced pressures for timely responses in the legal system. Fourth, judicial decisions attempted to enforce community standards and expectations, which were a function of the current state of technology. Finally, the judiciary recognized that, to increase overall social welfare, the law must evolve to allow citizens the most effective way to take advantage of new technological opportunities.

It is undoubtedly true that, as the proponents of the subsidy thesis pointed out, a number of changes in the common law during the nineteenth century benefited corporations, and some decisions were harsh toward frail widows and worthy workers. However, the tendency was not monolithic, and some scholars have even produced evidence in support of the notion that judges interpreted contract law to protect employees. Other doctrinal developments, such as the abolition of privity of contract, served to increase, rather than decrease, manufacturer liability. Procedural innovations that benefited low-income plaintiffs included the adoption of contingency fees and class action suits. Moreover, it was also true that overall social advantages could result from outcomes that might seem to be unduly favorable to one party. For instance, advantages to the general public accrued when federal statutes prohibited a few creditors from using state laws to bankrupt a national railroad that was undergoing temporary difficulties

---

[7] The court in *N.Y. Times Co. v. Tasini*, 533 U.S. 483, cautioned against rigid analogies that preclude dynamic standards: "But no definitive choice among competing analogies (broadcast, common carrier, bookstore) allows us to declare a rigid single standard, good for now and for all future media and purposes . . . aware as we are of the changes taking place in the law, the technology, and the industrial structure related to telecommunications."

during a recession. In the face of such varying outcomes, economic logic may allow us to understand better the general tenor of legal decisions, even though it is obvious that the motivation for legal doctrines or decisions was not limited to economic reasoning.

Innovations in Law and Technology

Technology extends into every facet of our lives, from reproduction to death. So does the legal system. My first book, *The Democratization of Invention*, examined the nature and impact of federal laws and litigation in the realm of patents and copyrights. Copyright laws, for instance, illustrated the difficulties and dilemmas that accompanied the introduction of mimeographs, flash photography, cinematography, piano rolls, phonographs, radio, and "information technology," including the stock ticker and the telegraph. Even the preliminary decision about whether these technologies fell under the subject matter to be protected by the law created deep conflicts that were complicated by constitutional questions about freedom of speech and the needs of a democratic society. This chapter considers the relationship between the common law and major new technologies—steamboats and canals, railroads, telegraphy, medical and public health innovations, and the automobile. Technological innovations led to legal innovations, changed the relative importance of state and federal policies, and ensured a continual debate about the boundaries of judicial oversight and bureaucratic regulation.

American society at the start of the nineteenth century was still overwhelmingly agrarian, but the new century created a new era of industrial leadership. The advent of industrialization and more extensive markets created conflicts between the rights of farmers and mill owners, mill owners and their workers, and enterprises and consumers, all of which required legal mediation. Technological advances and legal change had reciprocal and mutually reinforcing effects. Property laws and contracts attempted to define rights and allocate liability within a changing context. In particular, tort law developed as a distinct body of thought independently of property and contract law, because new technologies, urbanization, and more frequent exchanges among strangers were associated with more accidental injuries and higher transaction costs. At the same time, the costs of injuries created incentives for inventors to direct their attention to safety devices, such as steam gauges, safety elevators, and more effective railroad couplers, air brakes, and crossing signals.[8] The courts responded by quickly

---

[8] In the entire period before 1860, only 771 patents mentioned safety in the specification, but during the decade of the 1860s, some 1,940 patents did so, and in the following decade this number increased to more than 3,021 patented inventions.

altering the standards of due care to incorporate emerging technological options, but with the proviso that such options should be cost effective. We can gain a clearer perspective through a closer assessment of key technologies of the day.

Canals and Railroads

The development of cheap and efficient internal transportation was a prerequisite for economic development in a country as vast as the United States, so it is not surprising that transportation was a key element of state policy and private initiative. Before 1830, the major focus was on the financing and construction of turnpikes. State involvement was largely limited to the grant of charters, and private investors and entrepreneurs funded an extensive network of turnpikes in the Northeast. After the state of New York built the hugely successful Erie Canal in 1825, numerous other public and private canal ventures were undertaken throughout New England, the Middle Atlantic, and Midwest. The United States also possessed ready access to natural bodies of water, and advances in steamboat technologies increased their importance as a conduit for commerce. Between 1830 and 1860, national steamboat tonnage increased by a factor of ten, and shipping rates on upriver transport fell dramatically. As a result of these technical and price savings, the effective distance between towns was reduced significantly, and this led to a rapid expansion in markets and in inventive activity.

In the antebellum period some 650 lawsuits involved canals, and another 468 dealt with steamboats. Transportation along water routes raised many of the issues that the railroads later would confront, including the nature of state charters, the role and effectiveness of canal commissioners, compensation for injuries to passengers and workers, takings and just compensation, discriminatory prices, taxation, and the legitimacy of financing schemes. In the era of canal-building mania, the courts provided well-needed ballast to the airy bubbles of canal boosters. For instance, *Newell v. People* (1852) held that a New York State statute, permitting debt to be paid from hypothetical future canal revenue surpluses, was unconstitutional. Many states altered their constitutions to restrict debt financing at both the state and municipal levels because of their unhappy experience when financial panics adversely affected the creditors and shareholders in canals.

A significant number of the lawsuits involved conflicts between different cohorts of technologies: could canals and turnpikes block railroads because their charters were drawn up earlier and implicitly conferred exclusive rights that could not be eroded by later technologies? The famous Charles River Bridge decision in 1837 rejected this view since, if earlier charters ensured monopoly profits and rights of exclusion against future developers, the benefits from subsequent competition and new technological change would be reduced or eliminated. Progress also meant that already existing property rights might have to be defined more narrowly, to accommodate claims by newcomers and higher potential benefits to society. For instance, the old common law rule that property rights in land extended upward and downward without limit no longer applied, and courts allowed railroads and bridges the right to cross privately owned waterways and turnpikes.

New technologies required a balancing of the benefits to be derived from their applications against the harm that was associated with their use. They brought the possibility that economic and social advances could be blocked by holdouts or by individuals with conflicting interests who threatened to make the transaction costs associated with innovations prohibitively high. The use of eminent domain played an important part in the promotion of turnpikes, canals, railroads, and telegraphs by reducing or eliminating such costs. The U.S. Constitution advocated the right of eminent domain to ensure that private property could be taken for public use as long as just compensation was offered. This clause raised questions about the security of private property, what was considered public use, and how "just" compensation was to be determined in a nonconsensual, nonmarket exchange.

In the nineteenth-century transportation cases, just compensation for takings was ascertained through mutual agreement, by commissioners in an administrative process, or by a jury. Legislatures determined the extent and constraints of "public use." Their decisions were straightforward in the specific case of canals or railroads that, though privately owned, offered valuable common carrier services to the general public. In other instances, the benefits to the public were less direct, but this did not entirely rule out the application of the doctrine of eminent domain. In 1832, Jasper Scudder brought a case in equity against the Trenton Delaware Falls Company, which had been incorporated to create water power for some seventy manufacturing mills. Scudder's counsel argued that the corporation was created only for private purposes since the benefits of the water mills would derive solely to private individuals; thus, it was inappropriate to allow the use of eminent domain. The chancellor rejected this viewpoint because manufacturing enterprises, though admittedly privately owned, contributed to employment and general economic prosperity, and indeed promised to generate far larger communal benefits than some turnpikes actually produced.[9]

To an even greater extent than canals, railroads quickly gained public approval and became a symbol of American progress. Economic historians rightly caution against an inflated assessment of the role of locomotives in the

---

[9] *Scudder v. Trenton Delaware Falls Company*, 1 N.J. Eq. 694 (1832).

nineteenth-century economy, given the existence of viable alternatives, but it is undoubtedly true that the significance of railways increased over this period in terms of use, employment, and social impact. Justice Caruthers of the Tennessee Supreme Court lyrically wrote in 1854 that

> the common dirt road for wagons is superseded by turnpikes, and these again by the railroad. . . . Blessings innumerable, prosperity unexampled, have marked the progress of this master improvement of the age. Activity, industry, enterprise and wealth seem to spring up as if by enchantment, wherever the iron track has been laid, or the locomotive moved.[10]

Other courts demonstrated a similar eagerness to ensure that the common law kept up with innovations in transportation and other technologies.

Approval of any new technology is never universal, however, and many baulked at the railroad's expanding influence. One such controversy related to the policy of the railroads to rationalize the norms for reckoning time. The measurement of time varied widely by townships, which created transaction costs for train schedules. Accordingly, more than 188 railroads decided to adopt a standard time on November 18, 1883, and a large number of cities did likewise. However, even though Congress approved standard time for the District of Columbia in 1884, this innovation was not formally recognized by the federal government until 1918. A significant number of lawsuits arose to settle these different interpretations of time. Southern courts in particular evinced some hostility to the railroad interests and felt that, according to one Georgia judge, "to allow the railroads to fix the standard of time would be to allow them at pleasure to violate or defeat the law." Similarly, a Texas court declared that "the only standard of time recognized by the courts is the meridian of the sun, and an arbitrary standard set up by persons in business will not be recognized."[11]

An enduring and grim legacy of new modes of transportation was the number of accidents and injuries, which grew rapidly after the Civil War. Legal historians have attributed the development of tort law in the nineteenth century to disputes regarding the injuries and negative externalities that the railroads generated. In 1890, more than 29,000 individuals were injured in railroad accidents and 6,335 persons were killed; in 1913, injuries attained the quite astonishing level of 200,308, with almost 11,000 fatalities in that one year alone. Still, both the harms and the legal issues were not entirely unprecedented. The benefits from all improvements in internal transportation came at a higher risk if only because of the growth in the number and scope of transactions. Steamboats proved to

---

[10] *Louisville & N. R. Co. v. County Court of Davidson*, 33 Tenn. 637 (1854).
[11] *Henderson v. Reynolds*, 84 Ga. 159 (1889); *Parker v. State*, 35 Tex. Crim. 12 (1898).

be especially hazardous because of fires from sparks and accidents when high-pressure boilers exploded. This led to the passage of federal statutes in 1838 and 1852 that regulated safety, and assigned the burden of proof in negligence cases to steamboat owners and captains.

Although regulatory policies succeeded in generating and funding useful research, improvements in safety were predominantly due to private initiatives that would have likely proceeded in the absence of federal regulation. Figure 12.1 shows the annual number of patents granted for railroad safety and for safety-related inventions in general, expressed as a percentage of all patents. The two series are pro-cyclical and behave very like each other until World War I. After this period, railroad traffic was reduced significantly, and patents for railroad safety fell relative to overall safety patents. Both series suggest that investments in safety-related innovations were primarily responding to the market rather than to regulation.

These data bear out the conclusions of researchers who find little impact from regulation on the adoption of such devices as air brakes and automatic couplers. Neither the oversight of the railroads by the Interstate Commerce Commission nor the introduction of federal railroad safety legislation in 1893 was associated with spurts in railroad safety patents relative to safety

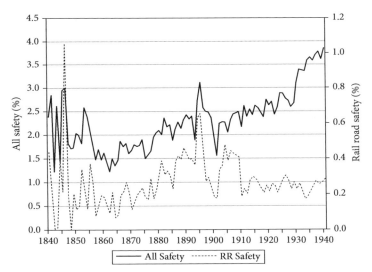

Figure 12.1 Safety-Related Inventions in Railroad and All Sectors, 1840–1940 (Percent of All Patents)

Notes and Sources: U.S. Patent Office Reports. Safety-related inventions are patent specifications that include multiple occurrences of variations of the word "safety."

patents in general. When government intervention favored the development of automatic train controls, the innovation proved to be ineffective in terms of both technical and cost factors. Railroads rejected provisions mandating specific devices that were incompatible with other forms of equipment and might become obsolete quickly, but they were not opposed to safety-related legislation.[12] In particular, the patent data suggest that we should not underestimate market incentives for enterprises to invest in safety and to self-regulate.

A number of scholars view legal tort doctrines as presumptively biased against workers and favorable toward employers and enterprises, but this claim is questionable. The common law for unintended torts adhered to four major rules in deciding liability: industry norms, the fellow servant rule, contributory negligence, and the assumption of risk. The judiciary held enterprises to a standard of care that aligned with industry norms, and only punished deviations away from the norm. This business rule, by relying on established community standards, economized on information gathering by the judiciary. The fellow servant rule was first upheld in a railroad case in 1842, which absolved the railroad from liability due to contributory negligence on the part of another employee.[13] Railroads that tried to introduce rules to alter hazardous but convenient habits encountered resistance from workers. A rule of contributory negligence created incentives for workers to monitor each other. This made sense in contexts such as railroad operations in which workers were mobile and had a great deal of discretion, implying high monitoring and enforcement costs for employers. Nevertheless, after the Civil War, several state legislatures limited the use of the fellow servant rule in railroad accidents, and in 1908 the Federal Employers' Liability Act abolished it entirely.

The assumption-of-risk doctrine involves the idea that rational individuals will weigh the costs and benefits of their actions, so employees will engage in a risky activity only if compensated for the expected harm either through insurance or through a higher wage premium. Thus, economic analysis supports

---

[12] Aldrich (1997).

[13] *Farwell v. Boston & W. R. R. Corp.*, 45 Mass. 49 (1842). Liability rules give incentives for precautionary behavior and also have implications for informational and administrative costs: negligence rules give both parties incentives for efficient precaution but have higher informational and administrative costs; whereas a rule of strict liability toward enterprises minimizes transaction costs but creates little incentive for victims to invest in precaution. If firms are held strictly liable and consumer demand is not very responsive to price changes, firms can increase prices, implying that the cost of injuries will be borne by consumers in general. If consumer demand is responsive to price changes, shareholders in the firm will bear the costs of injuries in the form of lower net earnings, and the firm will tend to overinvest in resources to reduce harm. In all cases, we would expect competitive wages to adjust to incorporate the relative riskiness of the tasks of the occupation.

the nineteenth-century policy that, as long as the employer was not negligent or deficient in safety standards, there was little need for judicial intervention when employees in risky jobs were injured in the normal course of employment.[14] However, it should be noted that this approach presumes that workers have many alternatives from which to choose and that wages will adjust to reflect a risk premium. The empirical evidence suggests that wages indeed incorporated a risk premium, although workers were not perfectly compensated for risk-bearing.

We can further examine the extent to which variation of standards comported with economic logic, in the case of passengers and freight. Although employees arguably assumed the risk inherent in railroad or other industrial occupations, this was not as true of passengers. Hence, the law held railroads to higher standards of care for passengers than for employees, and if a passenger was injured, the burden of proof was on the railroad to show why it should not be held liable. The argument has been made that judges protected passenger safety and the interests of the propertied class above those of the railroads, and it may be expected that, even if this were not so, juries would be more inclined to favor passenger plaintiffs over corporate defendants. In the case of goods to be transported, once the items were conveyed to the train, they were completely within the control of the shipper; hence, railroads were strictly liable for freight. Courts rejected the claim that slave passengers fell under the same standards as property, for the "carrier cannot, consistent with humanity and regard to the life and health of the slave, have the same absolute control over an intelligent being endowed with feelings and volition, that he has over property placed in his custody."[15] In short, the legal records do not support the notion that the judiciary was biased in favor of any single party and instead suggest a genuine attempt to generate outcomes that were equitable in every sense of the term.

Improvements in transportation and communications created a national market in which state laws were increasingly discordant and discriminatory. These questions were initially addressed in the case of waterways, when federal admiralty laws were applied to steamships engaged in interstate commerce, but railroad litigation provided a greater impetus toward federalization. Some states refused to honor charters of "foreign railroads" that were granted in other jurisdictions; others tried to add to their coffers by taxing interim transactions or imposing restrictions on rates and operations, even though the final destination was in another state. As Figure 12.2 indicates,

---

[14] A key guide to the impact of state legislation to offer insured benefits to workers is Fishback and Kantor (2000).

[15] *Wilson v. Hamilton*, 4 Ohio St. 722 (1855).

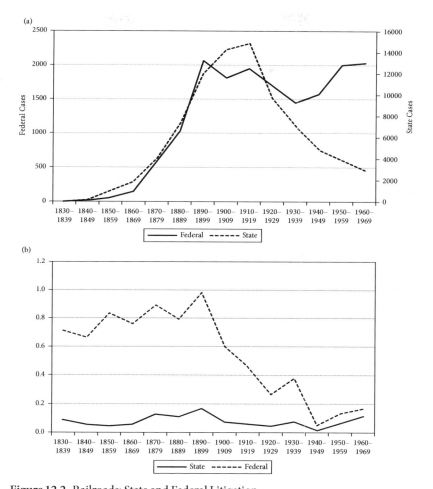

Figure 12.2 Railroads: State and Federal Litigation
(a) Railroads: State and federal litigation, 1830–1970. (b) Railroads: State and federal litigation relative to usage.

Notes and Sources: Usage reflects millions of passenger miles traveled, from the *Historical Statistics of the United States*. Reported state and federal cases.

the disproportionate appeal to federal courts relative to state courts was an integral part of the policies of the railroad companies well into the twentieth century. Their victories in the Supreme Court changed the interpretation of the Constitution: in particular, the commerce clause, the prohibition of lawsuits against state governments in the Eleventh Amendment, and the due process clause of the Fourteenth Amendment. Railroad companies ultimately succeeded in obtaining legal recognition that the public interest was not consistent with constraints on market expansion that benefited narrowly partisan local interests.

This recognition did not occur instantaneously, but through a long process of appeals, illustrating the role of the appellate system in achieving greater social efficiency. Railroads questioned state regulation of rates in the Granger cases of 1877 but were defeated. The judiciary hesitated to apply the due process clause of the Fourteenth Amendment and conceded the right of the states to regulate rates for undertakings that affected the public interest. However, in the California Railroad Tax Cases of 1882, the court agreed that a local tax violated the railroad's due process rights and, further, was inconsistent with the equal protection provision, because the railroad was being taxed differently from other enterprises.[16] In 1890, the U.S. Supreme Court ultimately upheld the view that state policy regarding rates was within the jurisdiction of the courts under the "substantive due process" clause of the Constitution. Forty-one federal cases in the 1890s involved questions of due process that were raised in connection with the railroads; the following decade there were 87, and by the 1920s the number had increased to 449 cases. These decisions enabled the federal judiciary to overrule state policies and allowed them to support private property rights that the state actions would have constrained.[17]

Several other significant legal doctrines were influenced by the public interest nature of the railroads, most noticeably in bankruptcy and reorganization. Federal bankruptcy legislation was intermittent and largely unenforced for much of the nineteenth century until the passage of the National Bankruptcy Law of 1898. State rulings initially followed the English bias toward the rights of creditors, who were generally allowed to levy against and sell distressed property on a firstcomer basis. This created perverse incentives for creditors to race to force the firm into bankruptcy even when the corporation might be viable in the long run. Clearly, sectional interests were not necessarily mutually consistent or appropriate for dealing with interstate enterprises like railroads. The result was a legislative vacuum that became especially problematic during the panic of 1873 when almost a fifth of railroad operations failed. Federal courts were reluctant to grant individual creditors the right to dissolve national corporations at the cost

---

[16] *Railroad Tax Cases*, 13 F. 722 (1882).

[17] *Ex parte Young*, 209 U.S. 123 (1908). Although the Supreme Court abandoned the use of substantive due process to protect private property in the 1930s, the concept endured in other contexts, especially in the struggle to promote civil liberties. In *Ex parte Young* (1908), the Supreme Court ruled that federal courts could prevent state officials from enforcing policies that conflicted with the Fourteenth Amendment, a decision that would have lasting implications for the movement to end racial segregation in schools.

of losing the public benefits of a functioning interstate railroad. Instead, court-appointed receivers kept the railway operating during bankruptcy while the firm was reorganized and financially restructured. Strikes were not tolerated during receivership, and lawsuits could not be brought against receivers during restructuring, although equity courts tried to ensure that existing management did not unduly skew outcomes in their own favor. This gradual shifting of bias toward the rights of debtors was consolidated in federal legislation that was enacted after the great depression of 1893. However, railroads themselves were not covered by federal bankruptcy statutes until 1933, when equity receiverships became redundant.

The process of railroad consolidation accelerated after the Civil War and, at the same time, exacerbated the tensions between state and federal oversight of commerce. As discussed earlier, railroads appealed to federal courts to mediate, but the major forces acting on railroad concerns remained at the state level until the end of the century. In 1887, the Federal Interstate Commerce Act superseded many elements of state policies, as did several other federal acts up to passage of the Transportation Act of 1920. At this point, federal regulation influenced content, access, ownership, safety, pricing, consolidations, and operations, not only in the railroad industry but also in other key enterprises, such as electric utilities and the telephone. Despite the rhetoric that accompanied the introduction of federal regulatory commissions, it is worth repeating that regulation had a long common law tradition vested in court rulings toward natural monopolies and other enterprises that involved the public interest. Moreover, judicial oversight was not made redundant by the advent of regulation; instead, regulatory enforcement depended heavily on court decisions. Although much of the focus has been on state and federal regulation, the historical evidence on technological innovations highlights the incentives for firms to self-regulate.

Telegraphy

The telegraph, although not quite a "Victorian Internet," emerged in the 1840s as the first commercially viable means of interstate electronic communication.[18] Telegraphy diffused so rapidly that by 1851 the Bureau of the Census reported that seventy-five companies with more than twenty thousand miles of wire were in operation. These small-scale enterprises proved to be inefficient, and a series of consolidations and exits ultimately resulted in the domination of Western Union. In 1870, Western Union alone operated almost 4,000 offices

[18] See Standage (1998).

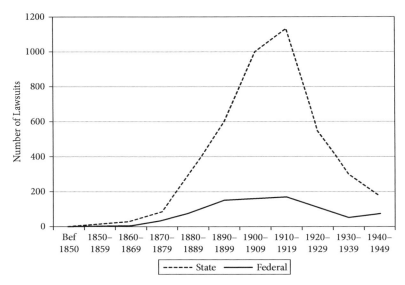

Figure 12.3 Telegraph: State and Federal Litigation, 1840–1950

Notes and Sources: Reported state and federal cases. Usage data (millions of messages sent) are from *Historical Statistics of the United States*.

and handled more than nine million messages. By 1890, its 19,382 offices were dealing with approximately fifty-six million messages. Diffusion of this form of communication was impressive, but like the twenty-first-century internet, the applications were predominantly among businesses rather than consumers. Perhaps as a result of this business orientation, the law did not draw an analogy to newspapers or other print media, nor did it raise First Amendment questions about freedom of speech. Instead, the courts and legislature stressed a comparison with postal roads, turnpikes, and railways. The Post Roads Act of 1866 designated telegraph companies as common carriers who were granted privileges including rights of way on public lands and waterways, access to free timber and resources, and recourse to eminent domain. In return, the telegraphs assumed the public interest duties of common carriers analogous to the transportation enterprises.[19] These perspectives and concerns have survived and re-emerged in today's policy debates about "net neutrality" and the internet.

As the pattern in Figure 12.3 suggests, several common legal issues affected transportation and communications technologies. The Supreme Judicial Court

---

[19] Cook (1920).

of Massachusetts argued that, while the telegraph was undoubtedly a valuable means of communication,

> its use is certainly similar to, if not identical with, that public use of transmitting information for which the highway was originally taken, even if the means adopted are quite different from the post-boy or the mail coach. It is a newly discovered method of exercising the old public easement, and all appropriate methods must have been deemed to have been paid for when the road was laid out.[20]

It was fortunate for telegraph companies that courts supported the idea that the previously granted rights of use also extended to the newer technology: "If this were not true . . . the advancement of commerce, and the increase in inventions for the aid of mankind would be required to adjust themselves to the conditions existing at the time of the dedication, and with reference to the uses then actually contemplated."[21] An atypical award of $2,500 in damages given for use of a narrow plot of land illustrates the high costs that would have resulted if owners of the telegraph lines had had to contract new bargains with holders of public easements. In states that rejected such analogies, including California, Illinois, Maryland, Mississippi, and Missouri, property owners were able to sustain costly injunctions and compensation for trespass or reductions in the value of their land.

A second consequence was that the most significant doctrines in telegraph cases related to the duties of common carriers. English legal decisions dating back to the Middle Ages raised questions of a duty to serve the public and to charge just rates in so doing, especially in the case of monopolies. According to the Supreme Court of California in 1859:

> The rules of law which govern the liability of telegraph companies are not new. They are old rules applied to new circumstances. Such companies hold themselves out to the public as engaged in a particular branch of business, in which the interests of the public are deeply concerned. They propose to do a certain service for a given price. There is no difference in the general nature of the legal obligation of the contract between carrying a message along a wire and carrying goods or a package along a route. The physical agency may be different, but the essential nature of the contract is the same.[22]

---

[20] *Pierce v. Drew*, 136 Mass. 75 (1883).
[21] *Magee v. Overshiner*, 150 Ind. 127 (1898).
[22] *Parks v. Alta California Tel. Co.*, 13 Cal. 422 (1859).

As common carriers, telegraph companies were not held vicariously liable for criminal transactions and in some cases were not permitted to refuse messages even if the sender was engaged in suspected illegal transactions.

Telegraph companies that accepted the designation of common carrier and its benefits were obligated to charge reasonable, nondiscriminatory rates. This stipulation allowed judicial oversight over competition policy well before the federal antitrust statutes were enacted. Courts adopted an economic definition of discrimination, rejecting charges of anticompetitive behavior if the differences in price were justified in terms of difference in costs. For instance, in *Western Union Tel. Co. v. Call Publishing Co.* (1895), the court held that the telegraph company had not engaged in "unjust discrimination" because it faced different circumstances and costs in meeting the needs of a morning newspaper relative to an evening newspaper, which explained the differential tariffs charged. However, courts varied in their support for quantity discounts, some arguing that this pricing policy suppressed competition and encouraged the creation of monopolies.

The established telegraph law for much of the nineteenth century accepted the common carrier analogy, but quite early on some noticed that the comparison was somewhat strained. The common carrier designation had an important implication for the telegraph company because it implied assumption of liability for the "goods carried." Railroads as common carriers were strictly liable for freight entrusted to their care and thus could be viewed as insurers of goods consignments. Under this doctrine, the liability of telegraph companies for their messages could be enormous, since an error in the transmission of a buy or sell order could amount to many thousands of dollars. At the same time, unlike the value of consignments on railroads or turnpikes, clearly the intrinsic value to the telegraph company of any message was significantly lower than its value to the sender and receiver of the message. To insure against mistakes, the telegraph company required that the message should be repeated at a cost of half the regular rate or else liability was limited to the cost of the transmission.

The courts were confronted with disputes that challenged the right of companies to limit their liability by discriminating in this way, since common carriers were supposed to assume that risk themselves. The stakes increased when businesses began to use abstruse codes or ciphers to protect their confidentiality and to reduce the cost of sending lengthy messages. Cotton exporters who wished to convey the message "We make firm bid two hundred bales of fully middling cotton at 43-4d twenty-eight millimeters, January and February delivery, shipment to Havre" instead required Western Union to send the words "Holminop, New Orleans, Galeistraf, dipnoi, Granzoso, Liebsesin Dipnoi liciatorum, diomus, grapholite, Gradatos and Texas." In another case, the telegraph operator transmitted the word "chatter" rather than the "charter" of the ciphered message, and the difference between the letter "r" and the letter "t" cost the sender about $1,000, leading to an action against the telegraph company for $1,054 in damages.

In response, the analogy to common carriers was ultimately rejected. The Supreme Court in the landmark decision *Primrose v. Western Union* (1894) ruled, "Telegraph companies resemble railroad companies and other common carriers. . . . *But they are not common carriers*; their duties are different, and are performed in different ways; and they are not subject to the same liabilities."[23] Instead of common carriers, some courts treated telegraph messages as bailments. Bailees were not expected to act as insurers, but only to hold to reasonable standards of diligence in completing their task, with damages generally limited to the price of their services. Certainly, in the case of coded messages, it was impossible for the telegraph company to determine the relative importance of the communication and to regulate the amount of care it took accordingly.

Western Union was justified in charging higher rates for important messages by requiring that they should be repeated, since

> it does not exempt the company from responsibility, but only fixes the price of that responsibility, and allows the person who sends the message either to transmit it at his own risk at the usual price, or by paying in addition thereto half the usual price to have it repeated, and thus render the company liable for any mistake that may occur.[24]

This was simply the liability standard that had been set in the classic English case of *Hadley v. Baxendale* (1854), but its application to the telegraph industry was delayed because of the faulty common carrier analogy.

The advent of the telegraph raised other interesting questions in the area of contract law. Previous methods of communication had depended on physical delivery through the postal service, whereas telegraph transmissions could be received within minutes. Time was therefore introduced as an important part of a contract conveyed by telegraph, and charges of negligence were related to slight delays or errors in transmission. Other cases determined that a telegraph message could be regarded as a valid form of contract even if it were not signed in handwriting by both parties. As the California Supreme Court expressed it in 1900, "Any other conclusion than the one here reached would certainly impair the usefulness of modern appliances to modern business, tend to hamper trade, and increase the expense thereof."[25] The development of international cable

---

[23] *Primrose v. Western Union*, 154 U.S. (1894) (my emphasis).
[24] *Camp v. Western Union Tel. Co.*, 58 Ky. 164 (1858).
[25] *Brewer v. Horst & Lachmund Co.*, 127 Cal. 643 (1900).

services further increased market efficiency and the ability to monitor agents engaged in distant transactions. At least one outcome of this standard was to reduce the autonomy of agents at sea, for the first time constraining their ability to enter into contracts that would bind the owners of the ship without the owners' previous consent.

As with other technologies, conflicts arose because of nuisance and trespass, including claims that electrolysis destroyed water pipes and that the high-voltage electric lines of urban tramcars interfered with telegraph and telephone transmissions. Again, courts avoided taking sides or assigning fault and instead tried to determine the lowest cost avoider, given the existing state of the art. The opinion in an 1890 lawsuit between a telephone company and an electric railway effectively described the role of technological advances in determining the standards of liability:

> In solving these questions, we are compelled to bear in mind the fact that the science of electricity is still in its experimental stage; that a device which today may be the best, cheapest, and most practicable, may, in another year, be superseded by something incomparably better fitted for the purpose. It is quite possible, too, that the legal obligations of the parties may change with the progress of invention, and the duty of surmounting the difficulty be thrown upon one party or the other, as a cheaper or more effectual remedy is discovered. . . . [T]he question of his liability will depend upon the fact whether he has made use of the means which, in the progress of science and improvement, have been shown by experience to be the best; but he is not bound to experiment with recent inventions, not generally known, or to adopt expensive devices, when it lies in the power of the person injured to make use himself of an effective and inexpensive method of prevention.[26]

Public Health and Medical Technologies

Legal doctrines about public health and medicine drew on metaphors that echoed policies toward transportation and communications technologies.[27] Advances in steamboats, railroads, and the telegraph and telephone were presented as the natural object of public policy because they were integral to broad-based economic and social growth. Numerous other innovations such as the water closet or faucets were extolled with less rhetorical flair but could be interpreted as no less significant to social welfare and thus fell within the proper scope for state law

---

[26] *Cumberland Telephone and Telegraph Co. v. United Electric R'y Co.*, 42 F. 273 (1890).

[27] Reiser (1981) provides an excellent general introduction to the history of medical technology.

and judicial intervention. Innovations that affected the quality and length of life fell into this category, including those that improved hygiene, sanitation, pollution, and medical techniques and devices. Medical and health issues in particular were at the forefront of contentious legal decisions that related to private disputes and public laws.

In the early nineteenth century, it is likely that cures were regarded, as one judge put it, as "in the hands of Him who giveth life, and not within the physical control of the most skillful of the profession."[28] Doctors tended to be trained informally and were unattached to medical networks or hospitals. By the 1890s, however, doctors had acquired significant authority, and even general practitioners appealed to current findings in both science and technology. Health care had become specialized and organized within institutions, and the laboratory was an important unit in hospitals as well as for doctors in private practice. The industrialization of medicine occurred partly because of technological advances that provided doctors with a formidable array of new diagnostic tools. Toward the end of the nineteenth century these included the stethoscope, ophthalmoscope, laryngoscope, microscope, X-ray machine, spirometer, neurocalometer, blood pressure gauge, and electrocardiograph. Medical instruments facilitated tests and treatment for notorious diseases like tuberculosis, typhoid, and cholera and encouraged specialization within the profession.

Technological innovation affected medical malpractice through its impact on both the demand side and the supply side. To observers from other countries, American medicine had ironically lost sight of the patient in its obsession with technological advances. The demand for legal redress was partly related to social expectations that were raised by the achievements attained in medical technology and by the diffusion of such knowledge among laypersons. The supply of disputes likely increased because more doctors were available to offer second (and different) opinions and alternative services, as well as because of the rapid adoption and more extensive usage of medical devices. Impersonal mechanical diagnoses and laboratory tests quickly became the gauge of effective treatment, even if there was little systematic evidence to demonstrate their actual efficacy. This assessment was complicated by the desire of patients themselves for more technological inputs in their medical care, so that the battery of tests that made up the physical checkup became an annual routine early in the twentieth century.

Technological innovations in the field of medicine had varying effects on the propensity to litigate. It was true that they could facilitate more accurate diagnoses and improve the treatment of patients, but innovations also led to greater uniformity in treatment that made defective practices more measurable and

---

[28] *Grindle v. Rush*, 7 Ohio 123 (1836).

manifest. Some doctors were accused of malpractice because they were less pro-
ficient with new devices or less up-to-date, but new discoveries also tended to
foster unrealistic expectations among patients. The application of X-rays in medical litigation illustrates the role of new technologies in such disputes. Wilhelm
Conrad Roentgen first published his discovery of "a new kind of ray" at the end
of 1895 in the German-language *Proceedings of the Würzburg Phisico-Medical
Society*. Only a few months later the use of X-rays was introduced in the United
States, and ordinary citizens were captivated by the discovery. Doctors who
failed to use the machines, despite the dangers of burns to patients, risked being
accused of incompetence and a violation of their fiduciary duty. Less than two
years after its U.S. introduction, a midwestern jury was instructed in a trial to
draw conclusions from X-ray photographs. Patients retained the services of expert witnesses who used X-ray evidence to prove their case, and doctors countered with their own technically backed proofs.

As with other technologies, the law adjusted the accepted legal standard
for proper medical care to incorporate current innovations. The courts considered malpractice as a physician's breach of the fiduciary duty to offer competent services through negligence, ignorance, or lack of due care. Physicians
were initially held to a standard of competence that took into consideration
the type of community in which they practiced. In 1824, a dispute in the remote village of Lubec, Maine, involved a patient whose local doctor had allegedly botched treatment of a dislocated joint. The judge ruled that it was
not to be expected that a doctor in a small rural town would possess the
same degree of skill as a European-trained specialist in Boston. Later courts
argued that doctors should be held to a nationally accepted standard because
improvements in transportation and communications had created a national
market, with equality of access to information.

Public health had long been considered a legitimate concern of the state. From
the earliest years of settlement, local governments regulated the provision of
food and sanitation, enacted laws to prevent nuisances, and called on formidable
police powers to deal with perceived dangers to community welfare. Measures
to counter infectious diseases elicited especially draconian measures, including
lengthy quarantines, forcible entry and the seizure or destruction of private property, criminal prosecution, and imprisonment. Public health policy in the nineteenth century was closely aligned with sanitation technology and engineering.
The police power of the state to ensure the health and safety of the public was
used to enforce the provision of running water and the use of water closets in
private properties. These actions led to protests that such regulation was unconstitutional. The City of New York, for health and safety reasons, required tenement houses in the 1880s to provide running water on all floors. The owners of
one such tenement (oddly enough, a church) claimed that the costs of installing

the necessary facilities were so high as to constitute a taking of private property. Indeed, estimates suggested that the cost of improved sanitation and fittings in homes increased the cost of house construction by $15,000 in the period between 1850 and 1900. The takings argument was rejected by the appellate court, which pointed out that

> hand rails to stairs, hoisting shafts to be inclosed, automatic doors to elevators, automatic shifters for throwing off belts or pulleys, and fire escapes on the outside of certain factories. . . . Under the police power persons and property are subjected to all kinds of restraints and burdens in order to secure the general comfort and health of the public.[29]

The U.S. Supreme Court tended to support state health officials acting in the public interest, and states did not have to provide evidence to justify its public health policies as long as they were in accordance with "common beliefs." The dangers of such unfettered powers were illustrated in the eugenics movement that developed toward the end of the nineteenth century, appealing to allegedly scientific ideas. Scholars in genetic science, evolutionary biology, biostatistics, and sociology together reached the conclusion that the genetic composition of the population should be regulated by statute. Their supposedly scientific rationales provided an impetus for policies that ranged from restrictive immigration laws to the forced sterilization of individuals with allegedly undesirable genetic characteristics. The U.S. Supreme Court affirmed these policies on the grounds of public interest, in part by appealing to the advent of new innovations. Advances in medical technology, for example, meant that sterilization could be effected readily and safely, rather than by the former invasive and risky measures. The court's approval of compulsory sterilization drew on the public health analogy of compulsory vaccination, which served the public interest as well as the interest of the parties directly involved irrespective of their individual wishes.[30]

Automobiles

The automobile for some is the most evocative icon of the American way of life. In 1920, only 1% of American homes had central heating, but 26% owned automobiles; only a decade later, car ownership had increased to 60%. The automobile, to an even greater extent than the railroad or other transportation

---

[29] *Health Department v. Trinity Church*, 145 N.Y. 32 (1895).
[30] Only Justice Butler dissented from the egregious decision in *Buck v. Bell*, 274 U.S. 200 (1927).

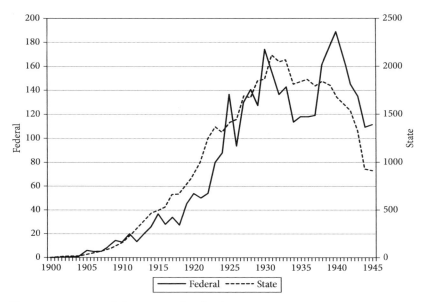

Figure 12.4 Automobiles: State and Federal Litigation, 1900–1945
Source: Reported state and federal cases.

innovations, changed patterns of work, leisure, residence, and crime. As early as 1906, the author of a standard legal treatise pointed out that

> many branches of the law are being affected by the horseless carriage figuring in litigation. Where the automobile's permeating influence will stop is beyond prophesy. It is certain, however, that the motor car, including everything connected with it, is bound to be the subject of a vast amount of litigation in the future.[31]

By 1931, the updated edition of the same treatise ran to twenty volumes, reflecting the rapid increase in both state and federal litigation.

Although litigation increased markedly, federal courts did not play a major role in the public policies that developed toward motor vehicles (Figure 12.4). We may speculate whether the decentralized nature of motor vehicle ownership necessarily encouraged state governance or if changes at the federal level would have occurred if the interstate highways had been constructed more rapidly.

---

[31] Huddy (1906), and subsequent editions.

The common carrier concept was applied to commercial motor vehicles, but analogies from the era of the railroads proved to be of limited relevance and the doctrine was modified almost beyond recognition. Rate regulation of common carrier motor vehicles was viewed as redundant, because the number of alternative modes of transportation ensured that competition protected the public from exorbitant prices. States established commissions to issue licenses or "certificates of public convenience and necessity" that regulated the numbers of carriers and their routes, modes of operation, and ownership issues, such as whether railroads should be allowed to offer vehicular common carrier service. As with all licensing, despite the stated objectives, the end result was to limit competition rather than uphold standards that benefited public safety or convenience.

The case of the automobile illustrates the ambiguities of attitudes toward overt constraints on individual behavior as opposed to regulations that affected enterprises in the name of the public. The majority of automobile accidents were caused by human error rather than mechanical flaws in the technology, and terms such as "speed maniac" or "road hog" had already entered the public lexicon at the turn of the century. The dual standard toward regulation was evident in responses to measures to deal with automobile torts, which were enormously more costly than those associated with railroads or mining. The increased use of motor vehicles was accompanied by a disproportionate growth in harm: in 1920, automobiles caused some eleven thousand deaths (half of whom were children); in 1924, this number more than doubled, with over seven hundred thousand injuries, and substantial property damage. The fatality rate for automobile accidents rose from fewer than five deaths per million persons in 1906 to seventy-two deaths per million a decade later.

Public policy was again required to mediate among competing claims. Efforts included the passage of legislation to provide rules and regulate behavior, and third-party means of compensating those who were harmed. Safety measures that regulated behavior—drivers' tests and licenses, vehicle registration, age limits, and traffic regulations—were introduced in a slow and haphazard fashion. In the 1920s and 1930s, states imposed an inconsistent jumble of regulations on driver behavior, but enforcement was lax and such legislation was not at the forefront of policies toward automobiles. Instead, the primary approach was through decentralized private dispute resolution in state courts, which rapidly became clogged with lawsuits brought by victims of "jitneys," taxicabs, trucks, and privately operated vehicles.

As in all tort cases, the issues centered on liability for harms and on compensation. When conflicts appeared between existing and former technologies, judges refused to assign unilateral blame and instead ensured that the lowest-cost outcome prevailed. For instance, more than nine hundred lawsuits dealt with problems caused when cars startled horses. In *Macomber v. Nichols* (1876), the judge declared:

> Persons making use of horses as the means of travel or traffic by the highways have no rights therein superior to those who make use of the ways in other modes. . . . Horses may be, and often are, frightened by locomotives in both town and country, but it would be as reasonable to treat the horse as a public nuisance from his tendency to shy and be frightened by unaccustomed objects, as to regard the locomotive as a public nuisance from its tendency to frighten the horse.[32]

The earliest standards required the driver of the car to defer to horses, since the latter were more common. When automobiles became the norm, however, the standard reversed to reflect that new development.

A landmark legal innovation occurred when courts overturned the privity of contract doctrine to take into account the circumstances of automobile manufacture and the complexity of the vehicle's technology. Before 1906, there were no cases involving manufacturers' liability except when the item was held to be inherently dangerous: "The general rule is that a contractor, manufacturer, vendor or furnisher of an article is not liable to third parties who have no contractual relations with him for negligence in the construction, manufacture or sale of such article."[33] In *Johnson v. Cadillac Motor Co.* (1919), the plaintiff was seriously injured by a defective tire on his automobile, which had been sold by a retail dealer. The court held that no contractual relationship existed between the driver and the manufacturer and dismissed the complaint. Judge Coxe, in his dissent from this decision, implied that the buyer of complicated new mechanisms of new technologies could not readily judge their safety as well as the manufacturer:

> The principles of law invoked by the defendant had their origin many years ago, when such a delicately organized machine as the modern automobile was unknown. Rules applicable to stagecoaches and farm implements become archaic, when applied to a machine which is capable of running with safety at the rate of 50 miles an hour.

Coxe's argument was similar to the landmark decision in *MacPherson v. Buick Motor Co.* (1916), which stated that a manufacturer had a duty of care even to third parties who were not directly involved in contractual relations with the

---

[32] *Macomber v. Nichols*, 34 Mich. 212 (1876).
[33] *MacPherson v. Buick Motor Co.*, 217 N.Y. 382 (1916).

firm. Cardozo rejected the privity of contract defense because the standard approach had to change with the times:

> Precedents drawn from the days of travel by stagecoach do not fit the conditions of travel to-day. The principle that the danger must be imminent does not change, but the things subject to the principle do change. They are whatever the needs of life in a developing civilization require them to be.

The point was affirmed by the appellate court in *Johnson*. Drawing on a shaky analogy to a principle that had always been accepted by the common law, the court likened the automobile manufacturer to a producer of poisonous drugs or "imminently dangerous articles" who had a duty of care to the public. However, Cardozo correctly highlighted the extent to which harm could be foreseen, since "foresight of the consequences involves the creation of a duty."

Predictability of outcome was also emphasized in *Chittenden v. Columbus* (1904). When the court imposed a fine of $25 on a motorist who was exceeding the town speed limit of seven miles per hour, the plaintiff protested that the law illegally discriminated against automobiles, since street cars were allowed to go faster. The court disagreed because, unlike automobiles, streetcars ran on set tracks and could thus be anticipated and avoided more easily by others. If injury could be foreseen, efficiency required that the law offer incentives to avoid such harm by placing liability on those who could avoid it at lowest cost. The producer of a complex technology, rather than the user, was better able to control whether one of its components malfunctioned. The automobile was such a complicated mechanism it was unlikely that the ordinary driver could detect a structural deficiency, whereas it was readily within the capability of manufacturers to test each part and ensure that it was safe. A corollary of this doctrine was that the federal courts later upheld General Motors' right to stipulate that their dealers should use only General Motors' replacement parts: exclusive contracts of this sort did not lessen competition but ensured quality control, since any defects would have adverse effects on the company's reputation and liability.

Automobiles influenced the rise of enterprise liability, a legal doctrine that absolved users from responsibility for their actions on the grounds that technology had outpaced their understanding. However, the majority of automobile accidents did not occur because of tortious actions by enterprises but involved harms caused by negligence on the part of drivers or pedestrians. Several legal innovations were a response to the falling prices for the new technology, which encouraged its diffusion throughout the population. The first automobile owners were wealthy individuals who were likely to hire chauffeurs, which led to legal questions of agency that could be subsumed in the existing law of master and servant. The law of agency had to be modified when the price of cars fell to the point at which ordinary families could afford to purchase vehicles that they drove themselves. The family agency doctrine took into account the likelihood that other family members would be just as likely to drive the car as the owner, and courts held the owner (generally the father) vicariously liable for the actions of the rest of the family. This holding encouraged the owner of the vehicle to monitor and regulate the actions of family members to ensure that their behavior was consistent with safe use.

Conclusions: Innovations in Law and Regulation

We live in interesting times; but so did the population of the nineteenth and twentieth centuries. The rapid diffusion of technological discoveries elevated standards of living and transformed the daily lives of ordinary citizens. Technological change was not uniformly benevolent, and it is appalling to modern observers to assess the costs in terms of injuries, mortality, morbidity, and environmental damage that accompanied these economic advances. Innovations also had redistributive effects, interfering with existing water rights, reducing returns to railroad stockholders when automotive vehicles substituted for passenger and freight transportation, or even enhancing the wage premium to personal beauty in new service-oriented occupations. The incentives to invent and innovate were influenced by the rules and standards of social and economic exchange, and those rules had to innovate in turn, to effectively accommodate the new technologies.

This book suggests that one of the reasons for the relative success of the United States during the long nineteenth century was its dependence on a network of adjacent institutions that proved to be sufficiently flexible to provide incentives to promote technological innovations, and to create the means to moderate their effects to protect the public interest. The discussion in this chapter highlighted the market for ideas and innovations and its relationship to enabling rules and standards that were implemented by a prescient judiciary. President Theodore Roosevelt did likewise in his 1908 address to Congress, noting that "for the peaceful progress of our people during the twentieth century we shall owe most to those judges who hold to a twentieth century economic and social philosophy and not to a long outgrown philosophy, which was itself the product of primitive economic conditions." In short, the democratic market orientation of the American legal system played a key role in the advances of this era.

Courts confronted a continuous stream of disputes that arose as humankind went about the commonplace business of life and from these unpropitious materials created decisions that were based on analogies drawn from historical experience, logic, and the attempt to serve the community in general. An analysis of law reports supports the notion that the judiciary objectively weighed costs and benefits, and ultimately the decisions that prevailed promoted social welfare rather than the interests of any single group. American judges understood that one of the best means to protect the rights of customers and to constrain the power of corporations was through market competition. The legal system formed a decentralized method of dispute resolution that was continuously calibrated to the changes that affected society, technological or otherwise. This is not to say that every judge was of the caliber of Joseph Story or Benjamin Cardozo, but a system of appeals ensured that "the tide rises and falls, but the sands of error crumble."[34]

Regulation through administration, on the other hand, was too often a function of a unique cataclysmic event—a stock market crash, a single epidemic or terrorist attack, the sinking of a ship, a fire or train collision that resulted in much loss of life—that gripped the public imagination and provided the political impetus for policies that might have been appropriate for that event but later proved to be ineffective guides for future actions or outcomes. Regulation and "protective" legislation typically came about as a result of political interests, rather than economic understanding, and often constituted a veiled attempt at raising barriers to entry or increasing the costs of competitors and of disdained social groups. Regulatory provisions were most effective when they simply codified the historical tendencies of the common law and ultimately depended on enforcement from the federal legal system. Administrative bodies such as the Interstate Commerce Commission (ICC) and the Federal Trade Commission (FTC) at times were headed by legal practitioners: Brandeis is credited (or blamed) for the establishment of the FTC and Securities and Exchange Commission (SEC), and Cooley was the first ICC commissioner. Rather than substitutes, the legal system was a valuable and necessary monitor for state and federal regulatory systems, but their relative importance varied with time and circumstance.

Although the nineteenth century is frequently characterized as the heyday of untethered competition, one is impressed with the extent to which new technologies were both enabled and constrained by common law holdings to conform to prevailing conceptions of social welfare. The major innovations considered here—the railroad, the telegraph, medical technologies and public health strategies, and the automobile—were regarded as integral to social progress. Because they were vested with a public purpose, dominant private enterprises were conscripted to serve the needs of the community. It is therefore not surprising that judges such as Cardozo saw the ultimate objective of law to be the promotion of "social utility." From this perspective, neither is it surprising that courts

[34] Cardozo (1921: 177).

ensured the protection of railroad passengers, consumers, children, debtors, and other classes of society at the same time as they were attempting to provide incentives for the growth of innovation and private enterprise.

The advent of each new technology created uncertainty about how the law would be interpreted, which analogies would be applied, and what the prevailing standard would be. This uncertainty likely accounts, at least in part, for the increase in the number of lawsuits that initially occurred, even after adjusting for the scale of use. The courts were consistently at the forefront of policies toward technology in the nineteenth century and provided a gauge of legislative needs. Legislation encountered the technologies of the day with a lag and tended to follow signals emanating from the conflicts before the courts. Thus, legal decisions, although statute bound and based on historical experience, were typically forward looking. We can only speculate about the subsequent fall in litigation rates that all of the figures exhibit, but the decline in part reflected learning by all parties involved, greater certainty about standards, and the introduction of new legislation that resolved outstanding issues, or in some instances resulted from a shifting of oversight from the courts to other institutions.

In the context of technological innovations, market integration ran up against the constraints of individual state policies that inhibited standardization and increased the costs of transacting. The first national enterprises—the railroads and the telegraph companies—appealed to the federal courts to apply provisions of the Constitution. Had they failed, the consequences would have been harmful not just for big business and market integration but also for the attempts of social reformers who wished to override the political biases of state legislatures. While federalism was a prerequisite for market integration, the converse did not necessarily hold, since general market integration did not preclude state oversight, especially for technologies whose use was predominantly local. During the period under review, roads were largely intrastate and unconnected, making long-distance travel prohibitively costly for most purposes. This was at least one reason that the law toward automobile users was predominantly state oriented and relatively few federal questions arose in the courts. Instead, federal policies were mainly directed toward resolving free-rider problems among states by matching state funding to construct interstate highways.

The automobile does not fit readily into a conceptually coherent model of legal and technological change. The railroad facilitated the development of big business and confronted the accompanying growth of federal oversight and administrative regulation. In contrast, even with growing market integration, the automobile was associated with decentralized consumer use, extensive harms to ordinary citizens by other ordinary citizens, few interstate issues, and increased oversight by states and municipalities. The decentralization of activities that occurred with widespread automobile ownership meant that individuals would have had to bear the consequences of pervasive regulation. Instead of legal or regulatory measures to significantly limit private use, the scale of harms afflicted by automobile users motivated an institutional shift toward private insurance markets. Policymakers were reluctant to follow the vaccination analogy that allowed incursions into the private sphere of consumer activities in the name of the public interest.

Effective policies toward innovations required a social calculus that was far more complex than the monolithic promotion of the interests of any one specific group in society. Technological advances altered the costs and benefits of transacting within a particular network of rules and standards, and institutions proved to be sufficiently flexible to encompass these changes. We can gain some insights into the effectiveness of American legal institutions from the experience of developing countries today. Institutional scleroses, the prevalence of inefficient regulatory bureaucracies, corruption, and inadequate legal systems have resulted in widespread poverty and the absence of incentives for increased productivity. If the subsidy thesis had been correct, and the legal system early on was captured to promote the interests of a favored few, it is quite unlikely that the United States would have experienced more than a century of relatively democratic economic growth and technological progress.

In short, since the founding of the Republic, innovation institutions have altered as the scale and scope of market and society have evolved, but the central policy objective of promoting the public interest has remained the same. *Salus populi suprema lex est*. Or, as Benjamin Cardozo expressed it, "the final cause of law is the welfare of society." That is, after all, one of the chief virtues of a society that is bound and enabled by prescient constitutional principles.

13

National Innovation Systems and Innovation in Nations

> Factitious reward is superfluous . . ., no sovereign can find another measure so exact as is thus afforded by the free operations of trade.
>
> —Jeremy Bentham (1825)[1]

The analysis in this book identified a spectrum that ranged from market-oriented policies to nonmarket administered systems in which key economic decisions about the allocation of rewards and resources are made by the state and privileged interest groups. In recent years, there has been a resurgence of claims that direct government involvement in technological innovation has led to, and is even necessary for, economic and technical progress. According to these authors, the historical evidence demonstrates the effectiveness of these interventions by an "entrepreneurial state." Ha-Joon Chang, for instance, appeals to a selection of the secondary literature to support the contention that institutions like private property and free markets were less important than state initiatives in funding, direct investment, and regulation.[2] Follower enterprises have depended on the foresight and leadership of the dominant state to attenuate risk, to act as a pioneer in providing funding and research and other forms of support, and to identify the paths that the private sector should pursue. If the venturesome state did not pick the winners, it was very likely that technological innovation would languish, reduced to the status of Cinderella in a scenario where the prince did not find the glass slipper. Studies in this genre even claim that the "courageous State" has led a timid private sector and has "been behind most technological revolutions and periods of long-run growth."[3]

Numerous works on technological change similarly propose the advantages of "national innovation systems" (NIS).[4] Like the advocates of the "entrepreneurial

---

[1] "Factitious reward is superfluous, whenever natural reward is adequate to produce the desired effect. Under this head may be classed all inventions in the arts which are useful to individuals, and whose products may become articles of commerce. In the ordinary course of commerce the inventor will meet with a natural reward exactly proportioned to the utility of his discovery, and which will unite within itself all the qualities which can be desired in a factitious reward. After the most mature consideration, no sovereign can find another measure so exact as is thus afforded by the free operations of trade." Bentham (1825: 67).

[2] Chang (2003).

[3] Mazzucato (2015: 22–23).

[4] Freeman (1995); Lundvall (1992).

Inventing Ideas. B. Zorina Khan, Oxford University Press (2020) © Oxford University Press.
DOI: 10.1093/oso/9780190936075.001.0001

state," NIS proponents highlight the benefits of enlightened government policies that substitute for the market, in the form of indirect and direct statist participation in entrepreneurship and innovation. These authors are persuaded that history reveals the "vast innovation potential that can be unleashed with adequate government policies."[5] They identify explicit structures and purposeful linkages of federal government organizations and agencies, corporations, universities, and state-funded research. The general assumption is that markets fail in the realm of knowledge and technology, so technical progress and success in commercialization can best be achieved through social engineering by visionary coordinated government actions.

Empirically, studies about the efficacy of the "entrepreneurial state" and NIS tend to be limited to generalizations from the experience of the twentieth century. Their methodology is not based on testable hypotheses but on verification, where authors cite case studies showing successful examples of government support for innovation, especially during and after World War II. As such, it is useful to consider these claims "out of sample" in a longer historical period. At the state level, it is virtually impossible to control for all of the variables and relevant activities that are simultaneously changing. However, centralized and decentralized innovation institutions share similar characteristics and fall into the same analytical class of administered systems in their attempts to assign values and allocate resources for inventive activity and technological change. Thus, we can draw on the empirical results in this book and its quantitative analyses of large samples of panel data that provide detailed and specific information on different institutions in Europe and the United States. The combination of these "hyperlinked" results about administered systems, when matched with the qualitative case studies, provides more representative insights into the accuracy of claims about NIS.

NIS models propose state-forged linkages across key innovation systems. Instead, this chapter points to internally generated associations across "adjacent institutions." Adjacent or related institutions affect relative prices/incentives that necessarily (given the "relative" in relative prices) exert an influence beyond the boundaries of any particular system. For example, a subsidy for any favored enterprise or activity is an indirect tax on related enterprises or activities. Rule changes in any institution not only will bring about responses in that specific area but also are likely to create secondary and spillover effects in adjacent institutions. Adjacent institutions can operate as complements, or substitutes such as when administered systems replace market operations or crowd out private initiatives. Institutional change is most productive when adjustments quickly occur as

[5] Perez (2013).

spontaneous responses to alterations in costs and benefits. If rules and standards are not adaptable to new circumstances, stasis or inertia will bring about inefficient adjustments in adjacent institutions or will induce individuals to alter their preferred strategies to find second-best solutions at higher cost.

Innovation Policy in Britain

Scholars of European economic development often contend that inequality, elites, and rare scientific knowledge played a central and favorable role in the process of technological innovation. By other accounts, English elites administered institutions and patronage in a manner that was dismissive of practical pursuits and practitioners, family firms pursued policies to protect their narrow rents, and a colonial bureaucracy sponsored a mercantilist agenda.[6] Chapter 5 showed that, in the Royal Society of Arts (RSA), mercantilism and protectionism persisted in the decisions of committee members, well after their alleged demise in the open market. Studies that offer plaudits for elites and top-down administered systems typically fail to address additional historical facts: subsequent economic growth was unbalanced, productivity gains were largely concentrated in a few capital-intensive industries, and Britain's early industrial leadership was soon eroded and ultimately lost.

The experience of Britain throughout the first industrial era does not match well with the NIS narrative. The British state and other nonmarket institutions were involved in various pursuits that influenced inventors and inventions, but these initiatives were largely lacking in "connexity," and included few feedback mechanisms to ensure productive adjustments to changes. As discussed in Chapter 4, innovation policies featured uncoordinated elite administered systems in the realm of both decentralized and centralized institutions. Early antecedents included the Royal Society, which coalesced in the 1660s as an "invisible college" for the improvement of "natural knowledge" through observation and experimentation. Numerous societies for the promotion of science and useful knowledge were founded after the middle of the eighteenth century throughout Britain and other European countries.

The RSA typified such efforts to influence innovation, as Chapter 5 showed. Like other groups whose existence depend on the kindness of strangers, the RSA was not modest in proclaiming its own merits: "nor has any nation received more

---

[6] Davis and Huttenback (1986), for instance, show how suboptimal outcomes were sustained because of skewed political economic power. Colonial ventures created a net social loss but nevertheless survived, because they redistributed income from consumers and domestic enterprise to the influential financiers and gentry who were disproportionately represented in Parliament. Reform efforts were stymied by the privileged groups who benefited from the inefficient rules and institutions.

real advantage from any public body whatever than has been derived to this country from the rewards bestowed by this Society."[7] Awards reflected the views of what judges considered to be a valuable or worthy contribution, which often diverged from the factors that would prove to be successful in the marketplace. The elite judges of the RSA considered one of its missions to decry the "vulgar and gaudy" tastes of the masses, and to educate consumers by example so that "no manufacturer will have to complain that his best productions are left on his hands, and his worst preferred."[8] The RSA itself ultimately became disillusioned with their own innovation policies and prize system, which they acknowledged had done little to promote technological progress and industrialization.

These findings suggest that some skepticism is warranted about claims regarding the causal link between directed measures in NIS and long-term economic development. As Adam Smith had cautioned, administrative decisions about who should be rewarded and how much should be given to them are often arbitrary and idiosyncratic:

> For if the legislature should appoint pecuniary rewards for the inventors of new machines, etc., they would hardly ever be so precisely proportional to the merit of the invention as this is. For here, if the invention be good and such as is profitable to mankind, he will probably make a fortune by it; but if it be of no value he will also reap no benefit.[9]

Britain also invested in more centralized state funding for technology, but in an idiosyncratic and unsystematic manner that was far removed from the NIS thesis. Their elite bias was all the more evident in state payouts and prizes, which tended to be related to the inventor's social status and the influence of patrons, rather than to the inherent economic or technical value of the contribution. As William Kenrick warned in 1774:

> There is indeed no little danger that both the quantum and the facility of obtaining of parliamentary premiums, may depend as well on personal interest as on particular ingenuity, or public utility. . . . [T]his method, of giving public encouragement to the authors of new inventions, is so liable to be perverted by partiality or prejudice, that it can, by no means, be consistent with sound policy to permit the indiscriminate application of individuals to be indulged in the use of it.[10]

---

[7] Cited in *Gentleman's Magazine* 83 (1798): 333.
[8] The International Exhibition of 1862, vol. 1, p. 10 (no author).
[9] Adam Smith, *Lectures on Jurisprudence* (1982 ed.), p. 103.
[10] Kenrick (1774: 27).

David Hartley, an Oxonian and member of Parliament, obtained patent protection for a fireproofing invention in 1773, which he claimed would have prevented the Great Fire of London, and a special act of the legislature extended this patent for a full term of thirty-one years. The following year, Hartley's parliamentary associates in the House of Commons voted to allocate him the sum of £2,500 to engage in tests and experiments, in an early example of a state subsidy for research and development.[11] The rationale for the grant was that Hartley had "employed great sums of money out of his own private fortune, and must necessarily advance still larger sums before the said invention can be completed, and rendered to general public utility." The method of fireproofing provided some entertainment to the gentry, as Hartley's demonstrations involved setting structures on fire, but it proved to be costly and impracticable and before too long had "sunk into obscurity."

Decisions made by the state and by similar administered systems could not be appealed, increasing the potential for misallocation of resources. Numerous examples indicate that awards did not have the force of contracts that could be prosecuted if the authorities failed to deliver on their promises. George Murray, the telegraph inventor, whose innovations contributed in part to the development of the internet, was promised £16,500 but only received £2,000, and as a result died deeply in debt. The ammunitions inventor Alexander Forsyth was enjoined from taking out a patent for his invention, and the master-general of the ordnance assured him that he would be compensated for his improvement. However, in 1807, a new appointee to the position put an end to Forsyth's operations. The inventor spent years fruitlessly communicating with officials and pursuing a return for his percussion lock, which was already in general use in the military. Forsyth received a small sum in 1842, but he died just before officials finally acknowledged that he deserved greater compensation.

Even eminent inventors like Marc Isambard Brunel and Sir Francis Smith were not exempt from such adverse occurrences. Brunel demonstrated his plan for steam-propelled tugs to the navy, which approved of his planned procedures in 1814. After he had gone on to make investments and experiments, however, the navy board reneged on its earlier holding, declaring that his proposal was "too chimerical to be seriously entertained," leaving him to bear the expenditures he had already made. Similarly, Francis Smith, the inventor of a significant improvement in propellers, made an agreement with the navy to build a ship that led to the outlay of £10,500. The Admiralty denied that they had entered into any

---

[11] 14 Geo. III. C. 85, sec. 24., "Any sum or sums of money not exceeding 2500*l.* to be paid to David Hartley, Esq., towards enabling him to defray the charge of experiments, in order to ascertain the Practicability and Utility of his Discovery of a method to secure Buildings and Ships from Fire." To put this into perspective, an agricultural worker at this time would have earned about 12 pence per day.

such arrangement and, as a result, his company went bankrupt. However, Smith's many influential supporters ensured that he obtained a pension of £200, a private subscription of £2,678, a new job, and, several years later, a knighthood. Charles Lancaster, the celebrated inventor and gunmaker of elliptical bore rifles, aired his tribulations with the War Office in a pamphlet, which finally led to recompense that was significantly less than the amount owed.

John Palmer had introduced innovations in the management of the postal service in the face of determined opposition from superiors and parliamentary representatives, who little expected him to succeed. Palmer, an outsider with a theatrical background, had negotiated compensation that included a percentage of the profits from his reorganization. His efforts were enormously successful and led to a large increase in the profitability of the service. William Pitt's government granted him a pension but overturned his claim to a share in the large profits. Palmer's son continued to lobby for justice on his elderly father's behalf, and after prosecuting their cause over two decades at a cost of over £13,000, Parliament made the full payment of £50,000 to the Palmer family.

Similar difficulties were evident in Charles Babbage's dealings with the government over a project that has been identified as a precursor to the modern computer. Babbage had engaged in a verbal agreement in 1823 with Lord Goderich that the government would underwrite the construction of his Difference Engine, beginning with an advance of £1,500. However, Goderich reported a different sense of what the terms had been and would not own to any further liability. Babbage was forced to appeal to the prime minister, who took a personal interest in the matter. With the prime minister's backing, Babbage obtained a formal acknowledgment that the government had procured the Difference Engine, and all the work was being completed on their behalf. As a result, large sums were made available for this project over time, totaling more than £17,000. The government then refused to provide any more capital to underwrite the construction. Subsequent assessments of this example of government involvement in innovation have been curiously divergent, including supporters who fault the government for declining to fully finance the project and those who conclude the Difference Machine was flawed in conception and should never have been funded.

In general, one protester noted, the government "should remember how often it had been led away by the fashionable rumour of the day, or other circumstances, to bestow sums in this way, which they might now wish to be recalled."[12] For instance, Parliament had given out the enormous sum of £5,000 in June 1739 to Mrs. Johanna Stevens of Hammersmith, whose remedy for dissolving kidney and

---

[12]   W. Woodfall, *The Parliamentary Register*, vol. 3 (1802), p. 414.

bladder stones "has cured hardly any body since it was made public"—a fact that was scarcely surprising, since the major ingredients were ground eggshells and snails. Another princely award went to Edward Jenner for proposing a method of preventing smallpox that had been practiced (as he himself acknowledged) since "time immemorial" among dairymaids and farmers in England, France, Germany, and other countries. Parliament, whose members knew nothing about dairymaids and the background of the process, allocated £10,000 in 1802 and £20,000 in 1807 to compensate Jenner for not keeping the discovery secret.

In the case of the Fourdrinier brothers' claims for compensation, the recommendations in the parliamentary debates ranged from £20,000 to nothing, and Parliament finally settled on £7,000 as a compromise.[13] Some felt "surprised at the smallness" of the accorded sum, while others such as the chancellor of the exchequer thought this payout would be a "very serious evil" that would encourage rent-seeking, especially since the Fourdriniers had neither invented nor introduced paper-making machinery to England. Another member of parliament wished to increase the award to cover the £3,000 that Fourdrinier's son had spent on lobbying expenses. In a similarly arbitrary decision, Sir Humphry Davy received £2,000 for his invention of a safety lamp, whereas the uneducated artisan George Stephenson, who had resolved the same problem using more practical methods, was given the "paltry sum of 100 guineas." Stephenson's supporters were so outraged at this blatant unfairness on the part of the government authorities that they raised a private subscription of £1,000, which they presented to him at a celebratory dinner.

The safety lamp case was not an isolated example of public awards that were explicitly and demonstrably influenced by questions of social status.[14] Parliament discussed at the same sitting the awards to Jenner, and to Henry Greathead for his improvement in lifeboats. Greathead was a boatbuilder and thus belonged to a lower class than either Jenner or the members of Parliament who debated his merits. "Mr. Freere thought that in fixing rewards, the rank of the persons to whom they were to be given ought to be considered, and he could not but think that the sum of £1000 a proper remuneration to one in Mr. Greathead's circumstances." The chancellor of the exchequer agreed that "reference should be had to the condition in life of the person to be rewarded, and it would probably be felt, that in £1000 was a larger sum to Mr. Greathead, than £10,000 to

---

[13] Great Britain, *Hansard's Parliamentary Debates*, vol. 80 (1840), pp. 1328–1330.

[14] Bowden (1919: 12): "It is obvious that rewards of this nature were unequally distributed, and were apt to be the result not of merit but of influence. An inventor without merit might secure recognition through political agencies, and a man deserving recognition but lacking connection with parliamentary and ministerial forces was likely to be neglected. Minor improvements and devices or processes of dubious merit were at times the subjects of prolonged discussion, while many of the most important inventions were entirely unnoticed."

Dr. Jenner."[15] Nevertheless, although Jenner was deemed superior to a boat-builder, he was still not of the highest standing, and parliamentarians objected that it would "pollute and desecrate the ground" if a statue to honor him were placed in Trafalgar Square.[16] The discussions in these instances were remarkably frank about the variation in rewards to inventors from different social classes, but such views were implicit in most British innovation policies.

The public support of inventors and scientific research in Britain therefore is longstanding, and certainly predates the period before the world wars. Moreover, the lessons from this history are somewhat different from the claims of statists, and are instead consistent with the administered innovation model. They illustrate the frequent lack of specialized knowledge among decision makers, incorrect prices and unreliable promises, cognitive dissonance and outright corruption, high costs of lobbying, and incentives for rent-seeking. And, just as in the case of prizes, we might expect a selection effect, where well-connected researchers who were unlikely to succeed in the market would pursue government patronage rather than trying to commercialize their ideas themselves. By contrast, the majority of my sample of notable inventors who achieved financial success did so through the marketplace, either by directly commercializing products or through their intellectual property rights.[17]

British Patents and Government Oversight

As discussed in previous chapters, the British patent system was an outgrowth of a classical regime of privileges. Members of the royal court and petty officers were not interested in offering incentives for riskier new inventions; they were primarily attracted by the more secure returns from monopoly rights to existing goods and markets. As a result, "the system of monopolies, designed originally to foster new arts, became degraded into a system of plunder."[18] The Crown itself benefited from the revenues that accrued from payments, and its agents made up an interest group who had a strong incentive to block disruptive ideas and any policy changes that would reduce their own profit stream.

---

[15] Mr. Grey and Sir M. W. Ridley "denied that Mr. Greathead was a man at all apt to be injured by £2000 or a much larger sum. He was a very intelligent and ingenious man, and had been long a respectable boat-builder." However, Greathead was awarded £1,000, and £200 to reimburse his stay in London, since the chancellor had long delayed bringing the question of his compensation before Parliament. Woodfall, *The Parliamentary Register*: 421–422.

[16] *British Medical Journal* (1858): 398.

[17] According to MacLeod (2012), a market-based innovation approach did not persist in the United Kingdom because "enterprise could be time consuming, financially risky, and demeaning." However, private enterprise has always been time consuming and risky, and the conviction that a market orientation was "demeaning" is telling.

[18] Hyde (1920: 17).

Administrators continued to view patent grants as de facto monopolies rather than as incentives for technological creativity. As such, judges construed patent rights narrowly and limited the options that patentees could exercise. Patent rules were enforced in the context of English common laws that prohibited contracts in restraint of trade, general agreements to refrain from competition, collusion between rivals to fix prices or to restrict output, and other anticompetitive practices that were likely to result in public harm. These limits to property were later formalized as working requirements and licenses of right or compulsory licenses. The practice of using patents and associated joint-stock companies to engross existing industries continued, with the approbation of a Parliament that wished to ensure the continuity of the old order and the protection of businesses with connections to influential individuals and families. British industrial policy generally followed the principle of favoring specific businesses and interest groups, rather than promoting "creative destruction" for the benefit of the public.

British patent rules deliberately limited the sorts of inventors that would be granted monopoly rights. Patent fees were set high to deter working-class inventors from obtaining property rights in invention, since the assumption was that only elites were capable of making useful contributions. Moreover, the number of outside investors in patent rights was restricted, which limited the ability of impecunious inventors to mobilize funding. As a result, patented inventions in Britain tended to be highly capital intensive, and many patentees belonged to the class of wealthy or well-connected inventors. Chapter 10, for instance, showed that 35% of female British patentees were drawn from the professional and elite classes.

As a royally bestowed privilege, "Crown use" enabled the British government to expropriate or use any patented invention without making payments or even acknowledging the rights of the inventor. In 1872, *Dixon v. The London Small Arms* raised the question of whether the Crown could delegate to third parties the right to infringe without legal repercussions. The War Department had been acting on the assumption that, as the Queen's agents, they could authorize or enter into agreements with rifle manufacturers who would also be indemnified against patentees' claims and could infringe on patented inventions as freely as the Crown. The War Department issued a memorandum noting that "the companies should be protected by the department against the patentees in the manufacture of the arms to be contracted for." The judicial ruling stipulated that employees of the Crown did have the right to expropriate patented inventions.[19]

The statutory reforms of 1883 required the Crown to offer compensation for patentees whose rights had been seized by the state. Thus, in 1919 the Royal

---

[19] *The Justice of the Peace*, vol. 39 (1875), pp. 86–87.

Commission on Awards to Inventors (RCAI) was convened to consider remuneration to patentees and inventors for government usage of their inventions during wartime. The commissions included government officials and technical experts, as well as consultants, whose deliberations illustrate the difficulties facing monopsonistic administrators attempting to supplant the price system. The first commission paid out some £1.5 million for a few hundred cases from a total of over 1,800 inventors' claims that were submitted after World War I, in hearings that dragged on for years. Their deliberations about key inventions such as the development of the tank revealed the extent to which status and connections influenced administered decisions and outcomes in military technology.[20]

World War II surprisingly led to rather smaller total payments, but with greater variance in the individual awards, to patentees primarily in telecommunications and wireless technologies, armaments, and aeronautics. The work of this second committee was even slower and less effective, and after an entire decade they had paid out total compensation of just £600,000. Of this amount, Sir Frank Whittle, the engineer who helped to invent the turbojet engine and gas turbines, received £100,000, in part because the Ministry of Supply lobbied the committee on his behalf.[21] The RCAI also allocated £50,000 to Sir Watson-Watt, one of a large team of contributors to the radar. In short, fully 25% of the payments over a period of ten years went to just two prominent inventors.

The Earl of Denbigh highlighted the deficiencies and conflicts of interest arising from public rewards for inventors, especially in the context of inventions that the War Office had administered.[22] Denbigh pointed to the enormous waste in resources, noting that "where one invention had succeeded and been adopted into the service, many had failed and been found wanting." These government bodies frequently made mistakes and inconsistent decisions, such as when the Admiralty offered £15,000 for the rights to an untested fish torpedo, while another such device by a different inventor, which had been successfully commercialized, was rejected. Some officials exploited their positions to profit from the ideas submitted by inventors, who were "brought into collision with the officials

---

[20] For instance, in 1912 the British War Office received a design for a tank, which the RCAI admitted was a "very brilliant invention which anticipated and in some respects surpassed that actually put into use in the year 1916." This invention was submitted (twice) by an unknown Australian Lancelot de Mole, but the War Office completely ignored his proposals, so he received no compensation from the RCAI. On the other hand, a British colonel who merely declared that a large share of the credit for the tank belonged to him was awarded £1,000.

[21] Giffard (2016). Whittle accumulated numerous prizes and honors, including the Draper Prize award of $185,000, and his estate was valued at £673,000.

[22] Hansard's Parliamentary Papers, "War Office, Rewards to Inventors," July 10, 1871, pp. 1321–1332. Lord Northbrook bridled at the suggestion that any impropriety had occurred, since "on that Council there were the Surveyor General of Ordnance, the Financial Secretary, the Adjutant General, the Inspector General of Artillery, the Inspector General of Fortifications, and other high officials," and their elite status indicated that there was "no ground for the imputation of prejudice."

of the Government, who from interested reasons or professional jealousy might be disposed to throw obstacles in the way of a fair estimate of the inventor's claims to recompense."

Representatives of the artisanal working class similarly challenged the inefficiencies of the administered innovation systems that prevailed in Britain. They protested that nonmarket institutions of this nature

> give more power to Government. . . . It would tax the whole nation for the benefit of a few. Only a small portion of the nation derives any immediate advantage from an invention. No competent judge or tribunal could be found for carrying such a scheme into effect. No plan upon this basis would work satisfactorily, and the whole odium of maladministration would be cast upon the men who directed the machinery, instead of, as at present, upon a system or upon the laws of human progress. It is not the business of Government or any of its agents to bestow rewards, or to stimulate invention.[23]

The National Innovation System in France

France provides the closest historical analog to an NIS that has continuously operated in dirigiste mode for more than three centuries through to the modern period. In many key areas of industry and innovation, "private planning was never considered in France."[24] As Figure 13.1 illustrates, France was an early leader in scientific achievements and technological discoveries but rapidly lost its initial advantage. This decline in comparative advantage in part can be attributed to the actions of bureaucratic state administration that inhibited and supplanted markets. The French monarchy and Republic alike present a prime example of rent-seeking and redistribution, with arbitrary policies that failed to offer incentives for the creation of useful knowledge, individual entrepreneurship, and innovation.[25]

Careful studies of "bureaucrats in business" have cautioned about the inefficiencies that can arise when markets are replaced by decisions by government officials, and many have proposed an inverse relationship between state involvement and the potential for long-run economic growth.[26] French policies toward industry and innovation were based on a strong central government, and manifested in an administrative technocracy that was motivated by

[23] *Mechanics' Magazine* (1861), p. 163.
[24] Dobbin (1994: 6, 25).
[25] North and Thomas (1973).
[26] Shirley et al. (1995).

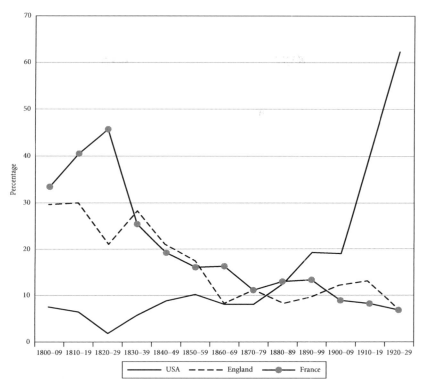

Figure 13.1 Science in England, France, and the United States, 1800–1930

Notes and Sources: The percentages in the graph do not sum to one hundred because the data include information from other European countries that are not shown in the figure. The final decade is computed by extrapolation. The calculations are based on counts of medical and scientific discoveries reported in Ben-David (1960).

the unflinching conviction of their capacity to improve on market outcomes in matters of science, education, and technological discoveries. Economic initiatives in France were typically formulated as a fearful mercantilist reaction to British industrial and political advances, sought by parties who risked losses in open competition.[27]

Jean-Pierre Hirsch characterizes the contradictions of a society that indulged in "deux rêves du commerce" (two dreams of commerce), which featured "a contradictory and often regrettably unfortunate relationship between French entrepreneurs and their national institutions."[28] French entrepreneurs vacillated

[27] Keyder (1985).
[28] Hirsch (1991: 10).

between a desire for regulation when it furthered their own interests and a quest for entrepreneurial freedom from vexatious constraints that hampered their particular pursuits. These twin motivations transformed the loose connexity in Britain into a tendency for "concertation" or directed cooperation between business and the state.

The ability of individual groups with innovative ideas to influence actual outcomes often turned out to be tenuous when confronted by the power of a centralized administration that wielded the authority of technical and engineering expertise. A detailed study of the railroad sector in France shows how the statist bureaucracy and its engineers worked according to a blueprint that "precluded competition."[29] This group of technocrats and bureaucrats dismissed the input of other constituencies as a useless distraction from the realization of their own conception of a national railroad network. These officials were intent on micromanaging the entire process from the provision of land, capital, and technology through to establishing the prices and managerial principles of the actual operations. Their efforts failed, and the French railroads were noted for large operating deficits and having one of the highest rates of injuries and accidents in Europe in the early twentieth century. Far from imposing sanctions on monopolies, the authorities forced the consolidation of the industry into an oligopoly consisting of six regional companies.

The chapter on France discussed how its technology policies were based on a complex array of publicly administered rewards and incentives that were designed to increase the nation's standing relative to England and other industrial competitors. Inventors and importers or introducers of inventions could profit from appointment to the nobility, lifetime pensions, assistance to spouses and offspring, interest-free loans, lump-sum grants, bounties or subsidies, tax exemptions, gifts of land and other assets, royal employment, and a host of other pecuniary and nonmonetary benefits. Large numbers of exclusive privileges were allocated to applicants, especially those who were well connected and could find favor with members of the court or influential statesmen and patrons. Numerous panels of administrators were marshaled in Paris and around the country to assess thousands of petitions for awards from hopeful parties, in an ever-changing institutional context. Members of these boards deliberated about the submitted inventions and recommended whether or not rewards should be bestowed on the petitioners, the amount that should be given, and the terms of the grant. These procedures created a class of professional supplicants, many of whom had no intention of commercializing their products and instead directed

---

[29] Dobbin (1994).

their efforts to arbitrage among the many potential administrative channels for state compensation.

French innovation institutions, despite the democratic rhetoric, functioned in a manner that reflected the elitist biases in Britain and similarly rejected diversity and perpetuated inequality of access and outcomes. Jury members on administered innovation panels were often appointed as a means of honoring the individual in question, rather than because they were technically qualified to make such determinations. Committees made awards based on questionable judgments about the marketability of the inventions that were presented. They selected uneconomical devices because they were substitutes for foreign imports or were overly optimistic about the extent to which the submissions for prizes were likely to succeed as commercial products. Just as in the case of the RSA, public accounts of French societies and state bureaucracies typically emphasized successes but omitted consideration of failures or nonresponses.

Patents were granted through a registration system, where the sole filter was the ability to pay costly fees. As a result, my analysis of patent records showed that members of the nobility and manufacturers obtained a disproportionate number of patents earlier in the nineteenth century. Key contributory factors for the bias against the poor included the high price of patent protection, the ability to obtain property rights without necessarily being the original creator, the lack of government assurance regarding the validity of the grant, and the uncertainty of enforcement at law. Working requirements in the patent system further necessitated setting up a manufacturing establishment to make the invention; this stricture could be avoided with the exercise of legal ingenuity, but the need to justify a "nonpracticing" strategy was an added transaction and monetary cost. The underlying uncertainty of the property right in patents increased the difficulties for impecunious inventors who wished to mobilize venture capital through the marketplace.

The French patent laws included further provisions that encouraged rent-seeking rather than commercialization through individual initiative. According to the statute of 1790, "when the inventor prefers to deal directly with the government, he is free to petition either the administrative assemblies or the legislature, if appropriate, to turn over his discovery, after demonstrating its merits and soliciting a reward." Through this policy, the award of assistance and pensions to inventors and their families continued well into the nineteenth century. Instead of efforts to engage in private enterprise, patentees and inventors lobbied for the state to pay upfront for patent fees, to fund extensions of their property rights, and to give out lump-sum payments for their discoveries, which (they assured) were guaranteed to revolutionize the industry and assure the French of world leadership in that particular field.

Adjacent Institutions in France

The French experience thus offers insight into the operation of an extensive NIS that spanned the entire portfolio of government incentives and institutions that could be directed to influence industrial change and innovation. Protectionist agendas on the part of the state melded well with the interests of domestic innovators who were not necessarily competitive in the marketplace. The French entrepreneurial state unsuccessfully attempted to force "hothouse growth," and thus transformed individual innovators into dependent petitioners of the state.[30] French innovation policies transmuted a potential market for inventions into a political market for special interests.

Chapter 6 discussed the many adjacent institutions that affected the prospects of inventors and enterprise in France. An important part of the maintenance of privilege was created through symbiotic relationships between the state and education, which were reflected in all levels of schooling. Tocqueville deplored the permanent bonds in French society between the political sphere, the powerful state bureaucracies, and the way in which knowledge was controlled and managed by a select group of technocrats.[31] Scholars of mobility in France were also struck by the strong degree of continuity in socioeconomic status across generations and by the extent to which class and power were replicated through the educational hierarchy.[32] The overall philosophy of the French educational system was based on "an ingrained belief that manual work was undignified, the province of the lower classes, whereas intellectual work was more noble, and suited uniquely for the upper class."[33]

These elite biases were replicated in the pedagogical approach to science, engineering, and technology. The prestigious state-run professional schools such as the École Polytechnique, the École des Mines, and the École des Ponts et Chaussées ("the grandest of the grandes écoles") gave preferment to the upper classes who could satisfy the preparation, admissions process, and expenses that were required for entry. Most of the students at the École Polytechnique in the first half of the nineteenth century were the sons of prominent military men, government administrators, and wealthy professionals, and, by design, few were from the business or manufacturing sector, and almost none from the working class.[34] The Écoles des arts et métiers primarily offered manual training in jobs with little prospects of socioeconomic advancement. It might be argued that the curriculum of the top schools provided valuable human capital that explains their close correlation with higher income and employment. However, this was

[30] Landes (1949).
[31] Shinn (1992).
[32] Anderson (1982).
[33] Kranakis (1997).
[34] See Daumard (1958).

hardly the case, since the classes emphasized rote learning in pure theory, classical studies in Greek and Latin, and abstract mathematics, with little attention to originality, problem solving, or applied research.

Engineers and graduates of the grandes écoles obtained favored positions through the interlocking relationship of these institutions with the state bureaucracy. The state reserved its most powerful and highly paid positions for elite graduates of the Ponts et Chaussées, Mines, Génie Maritime, Génie Militaire, Artilleries, Manufactures de l'État, Hydrographie, Poudres et Saltpètres, and Télégraphes. Civil engineering jobs were regarded as less important and those employees typically belonged to the middle classes, whereas the practical jobs for machinists and other skilled artisans were designated for the lower classes. The elitist structure of education was replicated in the hierarchical nature of employment, with resulting negative implications for the allocation of talent and for technological progress. French engineers made notable contributions to abstract theory but fell short in applied areas and in empirical research and development, which were more relevant to technological advances.

Specific technical fields such as cartography and mining provide more insight into the ways in which routinized privilege limited private sector enterprise and innovation. The usual state support was available for French scientists and engineers in these specialties.[35] As in many other fields and pursuits, French mapmaking was dominated by generations of the same family, who benefited from exclusive state patronage. César-François Cassini de Thury, Jean-Dominque Cassini, and their subsequent descendants were cartographers, who produced the first geometrical maps that encompassed the entire kingdom of France. Centralized state support for innovations in cartography was motivated by the objective of maintaining political control rather than by the stated goal of promoting transportation and advances in private industry. These publicly sponsored works created knowledge that was valuable for the state's purposes, such as for engaging in military strategies, and for bureaucratic administration. They also helped expand the resources and employment prospects for the elite engineers and military corps who were involved in the mapmaking process. However, state-sponsored maps were not as useful for private enterprise.

French achievements in mineralogical mapmaking in the nineteenth century generally lagged well behind the private initiatives in England. Again, in France geological cartography and surveys became increasingly centralized and controlled by the state bureaucracy. Such maps were the province of bureaucratic mining administrators, primarily graduates from the national École des mines.[36] Despite their attempts to control and micromanage the production of mining

[35] Konvitz and Barraclough (1987).
[36] Savaton (2007).

maps, it was impossible for these administrators to collect all the detailed local information that was required for accurate output. The engineers from the grand mining school in Paris depended on the cooperation of provincial mapmakers but at the same time regarded them as amateurs and refused to accord credit to their contributions, reducing their incentives to participate. In both mapmaking and mining, elite civil servants justified their costly expenditures by appealing to their utility for economic activities, even though their efforts were not as efficient as private enterprise and of limited value to industrial progress.

In short, the welter of administered policies toward innovation in France provides an excellent model of an NIS in historical perspective and also illustrates the deficiencies of this model. Conscious linkages between the state, industry, and higher education still resulted in uncoordinated and often conflicting bureaucratic initiatives, which encouraged inventors to engage in rent-seeking and to arbitrage multiple awards across disparate agencies. When combined with a bias toward elites, both in the centers of decision making and in the recipients of favors, this "top-down" dominance of relevant institutions contributed to an ossified economic and social structure. In an era of industrialization that required the capacity to respond to rapid changes in the marketplace, and a diversity of ideas, the French NIS and its adjacent institutions created inhibitions for private entrepreneurship and initiative whose repercussions are still evident today.

Innovation Policies in the Early American Republic

From the distance of more than two hundred years, "the founding" of American institutions conveys the impression of a discrete moment in time, the outcome of an epiphany experienced by a cadre of extraordinary individuals. The intellectual property clause of the Constitution especially might project this aura of inevitability because it was passed unanimously and without debate, with the intent to "promote the Progress of Science and useful Arts, by securing for limited Times to Authors and Inventors the exclusive Right to their respective Writings and Discoveries." Instead, it is worth noting that the founding was not a moment but a process, and the founders' choices were initially expansive and fluid, before crystallizing into policies that were unique in their objective and structure relative to any other in the world.

The early American colonies recognized the importance of technological innovation and implemented a wide range of policy instruments to further manufactures and inventions.[37] Strategies included monopoly privileges in

---

[37] See Khan (2010).

the form of patents of introduction, as well as premiums (innovation prizes), bounties, grants, and other encouragements for infant enterprises and imported discoveries. Typically, patent grants were conditioned on compliance with strict conditions, such as maximum prices, minimum quantities produced and marketed, compulsory licensing, and working requirements. However, colonial legislators did not slavishly replicate European institutions and practices but moderated inherited rules to accommodate the perceived needs of a new society. The Dutch colonies, in particular, resolved to ensure that support was available for all innovative individuals in the population and not just for the wealthy.

The Massachusetts Bay Colony granted Samuel Winslow a 1641 patent for the monopoly right to produce salt using a new method for ten years, but it is unclear whether he had devised the invention or merely imported it. One of their first patents, in the modern sense of protecting new ideas, was given in 1646 to Joseph Jenks for his improvements in water mills and the manufacture of scythes. Some inventors were even allowed to retain in perpetuity the monopoly right for their discovery. These early measures frequently advocated the use of premiums (innovation prizes) at the government level. In 1775 the Continental Congress "recommended to the several Provincial Conventions, to grant such premiums, for the refining of Sulphur in their respective Provinces, as may be judged proper." The influential Alexander Hamilton was also a strong supporter of the use of premiums as an integral element of a national innovation policy.[38]

The delegates who gathered in Philadelphia in the summer of 1787 to draw up a blueprint to "promote the general Welfare" therefore had ample suggestions that they could extract from history, in Europe and in the American colonies themselves. The debates record a list of proposals, submitted on August 18, 1787: "to encourage, by proper premiums and provisions, the advancement of useful knowledge and discoveries," and "to establish public institutions, rewards and immunities, for the promotion of agriculture, commerce, trades, and manufactures." However, the convention rejected this bundle of incentives for invention and innovation, because such powers were "deemed too broad and sweeping" and allowed overly expansive discretion to the government.[39] The

[38] The 1791 *Report on Manufactures* recommended a fund "to induce the prosecution and introduction of useful discoveries, inventions and improvements, by proportionate rewards, judiciously held out and applied—to encourage by premiums both honorable and lucrative the exertions of individuals. . . . It may confidently be affirmed that there is scarcely any thing, which has been devised, better calculated to excite a general spirit of improvement than the institutions of this nature. They are truly invaluable."

[39] According to Joseph Story, *Commentaries on the Constitution*, vol. 2 (1833): "In regard to the rejection of the proposition in the convention to establish institutions, rewards, and immunities for the promotion of agriculture, commerce, trades, and manufactures . . . [i]t is notorious, that, in the convention, an attempt was made to introduce into the constitution a power to encourage manufactures; but it was withheld. . . . [I]t involved a direct power to establish institutions, rewards, and immunities for all the great interests of society, and was, on that account, deemed too broad and sweeping. It would establish a general, and not a limited power of government."

unique preamble to the intellectual property clause ("to promote the progress of science and useful arts") instead implied that private monopolies to benefit privileged individuals or special groups were not to be permitted. Instead, the primary objective was to encourage social welfare through advances in knowledge and technology, and the means to achieve this end was through the protection of private property rights to the first and true inventors of novel ideas.

The legislature's creation of a uniquely American system was a deliberate and conscious process that can be detected in the amendments to the initial bill that was laid before Congress. The draft of this early patent bill echoed British practices, but the copy that Washington later approved differed significantly from historical precedent, in ways that favored the rights of inventors. The most minor of these changes is suggestive: rather than in the name of the executive, patents were to be granted in the name of the people of the United States. The House deleted a clause mimicking the English policy of granting patents for imported inventions. The Senate extended the initial definition of novelty: U.S. patents would be granted for inventions that were new and original to the world. A section regarding interferences (or conflicting applications) was replaced by a stipulation that information about prior patent grants should be readily available. The Senate suggested forcing patentees to work the patent or else license others to do so, but the House rejected this as an unwarranted infringement of the patentee's rights. Moreover, reductions were made to the fee schedule to ensure accessibility.

The innovative U.S. policy toward innovation provided a marked contrast to historical precedent and attitudes in the American colonies and in other countries. This approach was evident in early patent disputes. Stearns and Barrett both owned patents granted in 1809 for silk textile machines, and they decided to resolve their differences by setting up exclusive territories.[40] Barrett would have the exclusive right to sell his machines in Massachusetts and Rhode Island, whereas Stearns would have the right to produce and sell in the rest of the United States. If the deal was broken, the nonbreaching party would obtain a penalty payment of $1,000 for each machine used or sold. This collusive behavior was held to be reasonable, rather than an illegal restraint of trade. Even if they had not entered into an overt restraint, the court found, the inventors would still have been able to earn excess returns by virtue of their superior inventive skills. The courts' tolerance for restrictions of this nature illustrated that patent rights tended to be interpreted as liberally as possible, despite their potential to increase market power.[41]

---

[40] *Stearns v. Barrett*, 22 F. Cas. 1175 (1816).
[41] See also Mossoff (2011), who provides an excellent analysis of patenting in the sewing machine industry.

The Patent Office fulfilled the Coasian mandate for market efficiency by securing property rights for the first and true inventor, facilitating trade in ideas, and ensuring the dissemination of information to potential patentees and to the public. Once the patent was granted, it was up to inventors to secure returns from their ideas, through commercialization of ideas and innovations that were of value in the marketplace. Efficient markets in patent rights and inventions were facilitated by specialized intermediaries, who helped to minimize transaction costs for buyers and sellers.[42] Both the transparency of the patent application process and the effective national and international market in ideas disproportionately benefited inventors from relatively disadvantaged backgrounds. These individuals were able to use their patent rights to secure venture capital and to obtain advance funding for potential research and development. Some chose to completely specialize in inventive activity, appropriating returns by transferring their rights to others who were more adept at commercialization. As a result, the distribution of both inventions and inventors in the United States was more diverse and "democratic" than in Europe.[43]

This is not to say that the early patent rules were entirely bereft of nonmarket features, and some might consider patent extensions to be somewhat subject to discretion or political connections. Patents in the antebellum era were granted for fourteen years with the prospect of an increase in the term, to allow the inventors of important discoveries to extract higher potential income.[44] In the period through to 1865, terms were extended in some 1,150 cases (under 2% of total grants), and these extensions generated a great deal of public controversy precisely because the inventions were socially valuable. The extension process was systematic and transparent, however, and the procedures were established at law.[45] Unlike the initial grant of the property right, the presumption was against the petition to extend, and the patentee was required to provide under oath

---

[42] Lamoreaux and Sokoloff (2001).

[43] "In the courts of the United States, a more just view had been taken of the rights of inventors. . . . [T]he construction of the British statute had been exceedingly straight and narrow, and different from the more liberal interpretation of our laws." *Pennock v. Dialogue*, 27 U.S. 1 (1829), 10.

[44] The Patent Act of 1836 noted that the public interest should be considered before granting extensions, but "it is just and proper that the term of the patent should be extended, by reason of the patentee, without neglect or fault on his part, having failed to obtain, from the use and sale of his invention, a reasonable remuneration for the time, ingenuity and expense bestowed upon the same, and the introduction thereof into use." At present, analogous measures include extensions in the patent term for new chemical entities that have been subjected to regulatory delays in the U.S. Food and Drug Administration approval process.

[45] Some inventors submitted petitions to Congress, but these authorities deferred to the Patent Office. See, for instance, the Senate Committee on Patents response of June 1854, regarding Cyrus McCormick's claims: "Every inventor of a valuable article adds so much to the wealth of the world, and it is but just that the law should secure to him a fair reward. The committee, therefore, recommend a reference of the question to the Commissioner of Patents, to be by him tried and determined upon its merits, and according to the settled principles of the patent laws."

documented proof of the estimated value of the invention, receipts of expenses, and proof of due diligence in commercialization. The Commissioner of Patents gave notice to the public of the application to extend and moderated formal hearings that included the depositions of all interested parties, with full evidence entered into the legal record. The transaction costs of these proceedings were high, so the 1861 revision of the statutes increased all patent terms to seventeen years without the possibility of further extension.

Government and the Business of Innovation

The commerce clause of the U.S. Constitution authorized federal oversight of interstate economic activity.[46] Since transactions across state lines were strongly affected by technologies that facilitated connections between places and people, it is not surprising that federal policies were typically directed toward innovations in transportation and communications. Many of these technologies were associated with economies of scale and industrial concentration, which raised questions about how to supervise and order business conduct to best promote efficient outcomes. These debates often addressed whether it was advisable for the government to acquire controlling interests in businesses, with advocates of nationalization invoking European precedents.

According to Acemoglu and Robinson, "state capacity" was a primary factor in explaining the progress of American technology, and they test this hypothesis by using the extent of postal services as a proxy for state capacity.[47] The post office was an anomalous institution, however. Direct employment in the U.S. federal government in the early nineteenth century was primarily in the postal and military services.[48] That pattern changed dramatically over the twentieth century, but the expansion in scale did not result in a fundamental change in scope until after the "defining moment" of the Great Depression.[49] The U.S. Postal Service monopoly is a rare and unrepresentative example where the advocates of nationalization prevailed, resulting in the oldest government-owned enterprise in the United States. During the colonial period, the government held a monopoly for the provision of postal service, and the Constitution gave Congress the right to

---

[46] U.S. Const. art I., § 8, cl. 3. The landmark Supreme Court decision in *Gibbons v. Ogden*, 22 U.S. 1 (1824) decided the scope of monopoly rights over a new technology, in this instance, the steamboat. Gibbons provided the legal foundation for federal regulation of American enterprise through the regulation of natural monopolies and the Sherman Act. Khan (2011a).

[47] Acemoglu et al. (2016).

[48] In 1900, government expenditures accounted for approximately 7%, and its purchases consisted of just 5% of gross national output.

[49] Sunstein (1987) discusses the way in which the regulatory administration of the New Deal failed to incorporate the checks and balances embodied in the Constitution.

establish postal roads and post offices.[50] This clause was interpreted to mean that the federal government should retain a monopoly over the industry, with the right to use criminal penalties to enforce barriers to entry. No other competitors were allowed to intrude on the government's exclusive right to transport letters and packages along its designated routes.

Joseph Nock's dealings with the post office provide an early example indicating that government affiliates would be subject to the same laws as other participants in the marketplace and held especially accountable in their interactions with inventors and "meritorious patentees." Nock was an award-winning lock and key maker from Philadelphia, who had obtained two patents in 1838 and 1839 for a new means of manufacturing locks, which together were valued at $80,000. He entered into an agreement whereby his patent rights were partially assigned to the post office, and to fulfill the contract he moved his business and family to Washington, DC to manufacture locks for the Postal Service. The post office reneged on the contract, leading to his bankruptcy and loss of patent rights.[51] He appealed to the Senate, which repudiated the post office's allegation that his work was shoddy, and awarded him damages of approximately $22,000 plus interest.

Complaints against the Postal Service were continually voiced about poor service, oppressive prices, lack of innovation, and even corruption. Private providers such as Lysander Spooner's American Letter Mail Company began service in contravention of the ban on private delivery, and the emergence of such private competition led to steep declines in postal rates and revenues.[52] In response, postal officials harassed private carriers with lawsuits, and many were imprisoned. Transportation firms were held vicariously liable for the conveyance of private letters in violation of the Postal Service exclusive franchise. Congress enacted legislation in 1845 to reinforce government control of the industry, and significant fines were levied against private firms that attempted to make incursions into the monopoly. Regardless of the attempts to shore up its market power, the Postal Service provided a cautionary tale that ultimately *reduced* public support for government entry into business and innovation.

The Louisville and Portland Canal provides another perspective on federal policies toward monopoly and the public interest, as it was possibly the first private enterprise to be transformed into a U.S. government–owned corporation.[53]

---

[50] U.S. Const. art. I, § 8, cl. 7.

[51] The case was prolonged on technical issues, and Nock was finally awarded approximately $27,500 (see *Nock v. the United States*, Court of Claims, 1866).

[52] Lysander Spooner deliberately set out to break the Postal Service monopoly, offering competing services at prices significantly below the official rates. Many newspapers reported on his conflict with the post office, observing that "the persons engaged in this enterprise contend that the laws of Congress prohibiting private mails are unconstitutional, and they are anxious to have them tested on this point as speedily as possible." *Philadelphia Inquirer*, January 18, 1844, p. 2.

[53] See Trescott (1958). The waterway was critical to Western commerce; it bypassed the Ohio Falls, the only significant obstacle along the well-traveled Ohio River.

The government wished to avoid the responsibilities of outright ownership, foreseeing an unprofitable diversion of public revenues, but the canal's private investors were equally anxious to divest themselves of a losing proposition and engineered a gradual buyout by withholding dividend payments to the government shares. However, the post office and the Louisville and Portland Canal proved to be anomalies; unlike most other countries, in the United States the response to monopoly concerns was not national ownership of enterprise, but regulation by adjacent legal institutions.

Congress occasionally made concessions to aid enterprises that were deemed to be in the national interest. Members pointed to the example of the French state, and that of other seafaring European nations, which offered large sums to support new investments in transatlantic shipping services. Despite strong opposition, and a very narrow majority vote in the Senate on the measure, Congress likewise appropriated annual subsidies for the operation of ocean-going steam liners. The rationale was that the subsidy was necessary to match the French and British policies and to ensure American competitiveness in the international market. As a result, the Edward K. Collins steamship line was established to transport mail between New York and Liverpool twenty times each year.[54] The initial contract in 1847 promised government outlays of $19,250 for each roundtrip, but the venture proved unprofitable and Collins requested further aid, leading to a net government expenditure of approximately $800,000 each year between 1853 and 1855.

Cornelius Vanderbilt noted that "it is utterly impossible for a private individual to stand in competition with a line drawing nearly one million dollars per annum from the national treasury, without serious sacrifice."[55] Vanderbilt was probably hoping to receive matching government funding, but he nevertheless launched his own steamship line in 1855 as a wholly private enterprise. Other competitors such as the Inman line and the American line also plied the transatlantic trade without any help from the government. Despite the federal payout, the Collins corporation struggled to survive in the international market, and its shareholders never received any dividends. The federal subsidy was withdrawn, and bankruptcy was declared in 1858. Ultimately, attempts to revive large grants for the transatlantic trade achieved little success, meeting with the dry rejoinder that the example of France and its national imitators could "hardly be appealed to as successful."[56]

U.S. government support for new technologies tended to be transient, as the aeronautical industry further illustrates.[57] In 1898, President McKinley

[54] Fowler (2017).
[55] William Barney, *The Ocean Monopoly and Commercial Suicide* (private publication, 1856), p. 5.
[56] John J. Lalor, *Cyclopaedia of Political Science* (1884), p. 821.
[57] Parkinson (1963).

authorized an appropriation to aid scientist Samuel Langley in developing aircraft, as part of national military strategy. Langley, secretary of the Smithsonian, quickly spent down some $50,000 in government funding, as well as a further sum of $20,000 from the Smithsonian Institution. The Board of Ordnance and Fortification, which administered the support to Langley, rejected competing designs from other aircraft inventors, which they judged were less applicable for the military. Langley's scientific approach to manned flight failed and led to widespread censure in Congress (one member scathingly remarked that "the only thing [Langley] made fly was Government money"). As a result, the board policy in 1904 stipulated that aeronautic devices "must have been brought to the stage of practical operation without expense to the government." That was the response they offered when rejecting the application of the Wright brothers the following year. France, by contrast, had a longstanding interest in military aeronautics, dating back to its employment of hot-air balloons and dirigibles early in the nineteenth century and, on the eve of World War I, led the world in government support for the aviation industry.

The greatest test of the American belief in decentralized enterprise occurred in markets for information technology and telecommunications that have since been deemed "natural monopolies." Technological innovations such as the telegraph and more efficient transatlantic shipping expanded the size and complexity of national and international markets. Many of the "great inventions" of the era were associated with enormous economies of scale, and industrial concentration raised questions about how to supervise and order business conduct to ensure socially efficient outcomes. These debates often addressed whether it was advisable for the government to acquire controlling interests in businesses, with advocates of nationalization invoking European precedents favoring government ownership and administered systems.

The telegraph emerged in the 1840s as the first commercially viable means of interstate electronic communication. In most European countries, this technology was regarded as essential for the military and national security, and was either owned or operated by the state. The French state initially prohibited the private development of telegraphic systems. The government constructed the early telegraph system and monopolized its use until 1850, arguing that the telegraph was a political, rather than a commercial, innovation. In England, private enterprise introduced the telegraph, but the government nationalized the industry in 1870 and turned its control over to the post office.

Similar arguments were put before the U.S. Congress, but lobbyists for the Postal Service, who wished to consolidate with the telegraph operations, were soundly defeated. Although Congress funded the first telegraph line between Baltimore and Washington, government oversight of the developing telecommunications sector was minimal. The industry was soon dominated by the

Western Union Corporation.[58] Western Union was the object of extensive legislative efforts to restrain its "monopoly of knowledge," but despite widespread concerns, the telegraph remained a private enterprise in the United States. The decision not to nationalize the telegraph was due to a realization that the buyout and operation would be an unprofitable drain on the exchequer and to the unpopularity of such measures among the American electorate.

The telephone industry, like the telegraph, reflected a distinctly American approach to addressing natural monopolies in new technologies. The telephone industry raised similar issues regarding the limits of the legitimate exercise of monopoly power in an emerging technology. Alexander Graham Bell received the key patents for the electric speaking telephone and assigned the patent rights to the American Bell Telephone Company, a Massachusetts corporation that was ultimately reorganized as American Telephone & Telegraph, one of the most dominant firms in U.S. history.[59] After Congress rejected yet another bill seeking to regulate the prices charged for telephony, Bell executives observed that the measure was defeated largely because legislators were persuaded by the firm's claim that rapid innovation in the industry required constant updates and investment costs, whereas in Britain, the telephone system was nationalized in 1912 as yet another extension of the state's post office monopoly.

Public aversion to government control over key innovations was temporarily defeated during public crises such as the Great War, but (apart from the government monopoly on the Postal Service) the United States generally avoided public ownership and instead opted for regulation of varying degrees. In particular, judicial intervention had important implications for the oversight of railroads and telegraph and telephone enterprises. American legal traditions distinguished between dominance resulting from patented innovation and unlawful practices that led to monopoly power. Courts applied a rule of reason, even concluding that Western Union was justified in price discrimination, because this allowed the firm to reduce the problem of asymmetric information.[60]

---

[58] See Postmaster General, Government Ownership of Electrical Means of Communication, S. Doc. No. 63-399 (2nd Sess. 1914). Telegraphy diffused so rapidly that, by 1851, seventy-five companies with over twenty thousand miles of wire were in operation. Western Union was the result from a consolidation of regional telegraph companies that occurred in 1851, and by 1866 it accounted for more than 90% of the market. The company was the target of almost a hundred legislative initiatives that proposed to limit its reach.

[59] "The Telephone Monopoly: Annual Meeting of the American Bell Company," *New York Times*, March 28, 1888, p. 3. In 1887, American Bell reported total revenues of $3.45 million relative to expenditures of $1.24 million and had six thousand employees on its roster.

[60] *Camp v. W. Union Tel. Co.*, 58 Ky. 164 (1858): "it does not exempt the company from responsibility, but only fixes the price of that responsibility, and allows the person who sends the message either to transmit it at his own risk at the usual price, or by paying in addition thereto half the usual price to have it repeated, and thus render the company liable for any mistake that may occur." This was simply the standard of limiting liability to the level of foreseeable reliance, as in the classic 1854 case of *Hadley v. Baxendale*, 156 Eng. Rep. 145, but its application to the telegraph industry was delayed because of the inaccurate common carrier analogy inherited from the railroads.

Patentees were able to establish exclusive territories, include noncompete clauses, participate in patent pools, and enforce vertical restraints; and courts held that state antitrust laws were not applicable to the federal property rights vested in patents. At the same time, populist protesters throughout the nation lobbied against monopolistic practices of patentees, and the 1884 platform of the Greenback and Antimonopoly parties declared their intention to regulate patent-based monopolies. Still, legislators were aware that patents incentivized substitutes that could actually serve to promote competition: "But for the patent laws there would, probably, be but one printing-press company, but one type-writer company, but one electric company, but one adding-machine company, but one of many now listed in the thousands."[61] Even on the eve of the passage of the federal antitrust statute in 1890, patentees were given wide latitude in the strategies they adopted. Indeed, antitrust authorities would not achieve significant success in prosecuting claims about patent-based business practices until well into the twentieth century.[62]

Adjacent Institutions in the United States

The proponents of NIS emphasize the importance of explicit linkages between innovation and educational institutions. From the founding of the early Republic, Americans recognized that, as the Northwest Ordinance of 1787 expressed it, "Knowledge, being necessary to good government and the happiness of mankind, schools and the means of education shall forever be encouraged." Copyrights were protected primarily as a means to promote learning and education. By the end of the nineteenth century, the number of colleges and universities in the United States exceeded those in Europe. The states adopted various and disparate efforts to promote specialized knowledge in science and engineering in higher education. Rensselaer Polytechnic Institute was established in 1824 and was the precursor of numerous other specialized institutions that were founded after the Civil War. The pragmatic orientation of the U.S. Military Academy at West Point, as well as the Army Corps of Engineering, increased investments in applied knowledge and physical infrastructure.

The federal government occasionally bestowed land for schools in the antebellum period, including institutions with special purposes, such as education for the disabled. Justin Butterfield, the Land Office commissioner, further proposed in his 1849 report:

---

[61]   Hearing before the House Committee on Patents, 62nd Cong. 10 (1912).
[62]   Khan (1999a, 1999b).

With an industrious population possessing extraordinary ingenuity our country, it is believed, would soon stand foremost among the nations of the earth, if suitable rewards were held out by the government for important improvement in agriculture and the arts and sciences. This could be done by the appropriation, for the purpose, of a small portion of the proceeds of the public lands.

The Morrill Act of 1862 was the first federal initiative to underwrite higher education throughout the United States, through the allotment of over eleven million acres in land grants to the states. Within the space of a decade, this policy had led to the endowment of some thirty-two industrial colleges and universities, with a special emphasis on agriculture and mechanical training.[63] Many of the top universities in the nation today, such as the University of California, the University of Michigan, the University of Minnesota, and Cornell University, were the beneficiaries of this transfer from the federal government.

At the centennial celebrations of the Morrill Act, John F. Kennedy characterized this policy as the "most ambitious and fruitful system of higher education in the history of the world." However, scholars in this area warn against an overly optimistic assessment of the act.[64] The number of private institutions and their students vastly outweighed the land-grant institutions, and the course of higher education was influenced by many other factors besides the legislation. The impact of the measure was uneven and questionable in scope, as its aims were rejected by populists in the South and in the West, and the policy was largely ineffective in some states like Texas. Many of the most successful initiatives were not in agriculture but in engineering studies, which became more prominent toward the end of the nineteenth century. Still, land-grant institutions and agricultural research and extension services enhanced the ability of disadvantaged individuals ("the sons of toil") to invest in human capital and to achieve higher incomes and social mobility.

The strength of the American university network owed in part to such government investments. However, it benefited even more from the diversity of decentralized institutions that competed to meet the needs of particular professions, interests, and populations. Most notably, unlike British and French

---

[63] Subsequent laws in 1890 and the Nelson Amendment of 1908 allocated annual endowments of $25,000 and $50,000, respectively, to these institutions. Federal appropriations (in nominal dollars) increased over time, from $404,000 in 1875 to $1,303,000 in 1890, $3,462,000 in 1920, and $3,677,000 in 1930.

[64] According to the Office of Education, in 1915–1917, there were sixty-eight land-grant colleges, seventeen of which were "historically black" institutions, with student enrollments of approximately 121,000 white individuals and just under 11,000 black scholars. During the same period, 662 institutions of higher learning existed in the United States, with total enrollments of approximately 330,000 students and over $110 million in expenditures.

institutions, elite universities in the United States like Yale and Columbia rapidly responded to changing demands of industry, introducing innovative courses and new departments in applied science and engineering. As such, any linkages between university and industry in the United States emerged spontaneously through a market process, long before the advent of sustained government initiatives. In the 1930s, federal funding barely covered a quarter of academic research spending, and this appropriation overwhelmingly financed work that was directly related to the procurement needs of national defense and the military.[65] In sum, as the great inventors demonstrated, centralized linkages between higher education, industry, and innovation were neither necessary nor typical of the sorts of creativity that created the second Industrial Revolution.

Government of Inventions

The United States attained global leadership in technological change and innovation mainly through its market-oriented innovation polices. The notion of an NIS draws heavily on the experience of the period after the outbreak of World War II, which was obviously skewed owing to the military need to mobilize resources for national security and defense. Such patterns were hardly typical of the development of American technology during peacetime, nor were they representative of prior conflicts such as the Civil War era and World War I. The federal government in the nineteenth century hesitated to substitute its powers of making awards for compensation that could be allocated through the market mechanism. In the United States, although William T. G. Morton repeatedly appealed to Congress for a similar reward as Jenner's in England, he failed to obtain any payment.[66] When the National Academy of Sciences was founded, its objective was not to lobby the state to fund the sciences, but rather for scientists to offer the government the benefits of its specialized knowledge.[67]

The most common suspension in the historical belief of a limited role for government in the realm of innovative activities occurred in the context of the military and during wartime.[68] Vernon Ruttan, for example, contends that military conflict has generated crucial technological advances, general

---

[65] Mowery et al. (2015).

[66] Report No. 114, 30 Cong. 2nd Sess. (1849).

[67] *Proceedings of the National Academy of Sciences* (1863–1894, 1895).

[68] The overall share of government revenues and expenditures in the nineteenth-century economy was minimal; federal and state revenues together accounted for approximately 4% of gross domestic product in 1840, and this figure changed to just over 7% by 1900. In 1935, under a quarter of academic research and development received federal support, and this figure jumped to two-thirds by 1960. The majority of federally supported academic support has been skewed toward the defense and health sectors.

purpose technologies that have revolutionized entire industries, and dramatically transformed economic prospects.[69] Like many others, he cites the Springfield Armory and the development of interchangeable gun parts, which have been touted as a pioneering example of an active role for the government in technologies that had larger consequences and spillover benefits beyond the initial investments.[70] The conventional accounts trace the dissemination of these techniques through the establishments of government contractors like Simeon North and Asa Waters, which created efficiency gains that spread through time and place to the automobile industry and the modern economy.

These Panglossian narratives have been challenged after closer examination of the historical evidence. The French had introduced the method of interchangeable parts at least by 1785, but the process floundered owing, ironically, to its character as a failed "engineering project driven by state bureaucrats following their own operational logic."[71] Many American patentees had invented devices capable of uniform production, which were applied in sectors independently of the armories, ranging from axes, clocks, and watches to woodwork.[72] Industries such as harvesters and agricultural machines advanced without reference to interchangeability. The Singer Sewing Machine Company and McCormick's Harvesting Machine enterprise (later International Harvester Corporation) emerged as global multinational companies, not because of engineering best practice, but because of their innovative marketing and selling techniques. As such, it is not at all clear whether U.S. manufacturing would have been retarded had the armories never existed. Government-sponsored efforts sporadically occurred during wartime and waned in the aftermath, whereas the private sector independently and continuously developed and commercialized key inventions throughout the past three centuries.

Case studies for statist successes range from innovations in weaponry to the atomic bomb, the space program, and the contributions of the defense agencies to the development of the computer and Internet. Other lessons, however, can be drawn from less well-examined facets of such administered innovation systems. For instance, government efforts during wars were often directed toward the expropriation of patent rights rather than to promoting inventive activity and innovation. The secretary of war in 1869 was so incensed by the need to negotiate with patentees and their "improper claims" that he proposed a statute that would,

---

[69] Ruttan (2006).
[70] Smith (1985).
[71] Alder (2010: 6).
[72] Hoke (1990: 12) concluded that "the American System is primarily a private sector phenomenon," independent of any public sector initiatives. He notes that technological change stagnated in the federal armories, where market prices and costs were frequently ignored.

as in England, allow for the use of eminent domain against patents.[73] His proposal failed to pass Congress, but similar measures were approved during World War I. The government also allowed patented inventions to be held secret during wartime, if deemed to pose a risk to safety or to the war effort.[74] However, against these actions by U.S. war departments, both foreign and domestic patentees had the right of appeal to the Court of Claims, the Supreme Court, and Congress, and the government could not avoid liability by seeking to undermine the validity of the patent right or by delegating responsibility to its contractors.

Even enemy aliens who owned U.S. patents were compensated by the federal government for property that had been seized during the world wars. After the Great War, reparations were made for 1,069 claims by inventors from formerly hostile nations, and over $13 million was paid to inventors from Germany, Austria, and Hungary. American concern about the German monopoly in chemicals and dyes peaked during the outbreak of hostilities in World War I, and an amendment of the Trading with the Enemy Act of 1917 authorized the confiscation of German intellectual property.[75] The Chemical Foundation Inc. was formed two years later to manage several thousand expropriated patents, trademarks, and copyrights on behalf of the American chemical industry. This windfall stock of intellectual property revealed the extent to which effective transfer of technology also requires tacit and explicit knowledge and experience since, after the end of the war, the German firms were still able to leverage their expertise and know-how to retain their competitive edge in dyes and chemicals.

It should be noted that, apart from wartime, compulsory licenses and other nonmarket measures have always been strongly rejected in American patent policies. In general, when the U.S. government became involved in the market for inventions, it was typically as a consumer of patented innovations that paid inventors the competitive price or a fair and reasonable royalty rate. This form of participation involved different considerations from monopsonistic rewards or prize systems, since the government was simply one demander among many others in the deep and efficient market for patented inventions. The famous inventor Thomas Blanchard received almost $19,000 in government royalties for the right to use his patent for turning irregular lathes to fashion gunstocks. J. H. Hall's patent rights and machinery to make breech-loading rifles and carbines

---

[73] "These [patent] difficulties have continued to embarrass this Department, and to affect injuriously the interests of the Government; and it is respectfully suggested whether a law may not be devised, which, while affording protection to all inventors in the rights secured to them by patents, will enable the Government to use unrestrictedly any improvement which it may be desirable for it to use. . . . Such a law would relieve this Department of much annoyance and embarrassment, and would tend, in my opinion, to increase to a considerable degree the efficiency of the public service." *Annual Reports of the Secretary of War* (1871), p. 251.

[74] Act, October 6, 1917, c. 95.

[75] Steen (2001).

earned him over $37,500. The navy similarly expended millions of dollars on royalties and patent rights for inventions, such as George Taylor's "marine camel," Frederick Sickel's cut-off engines, and Worthington and Baker's steam pumps and percussion water-gauges. The Department of War and the Navy accounted for 90% of the federal government usage of patented inventions during World War I and received a congressional appropriation of $1 million to acquire basic patents relating to aircraft manufacturing.[76]

The development of the computer is often cited as an example of government incubation of an important technology. However, as in the case of the military, the initial role of the government was as an overly officious customer, rather than as a necessary promoter of novel inventive activities. This was certainly the case with Herman Hollerith's tabulating system that created the data processing industry and facilitated significant practical steps toward the electronic computer. The director of the census wished to speed up the processing of the 1890 decennial census, and Hollerith was selected owing to his ingenious ideas, for which patent applications had been submitted in 1884.[77] Clearly, the business of the decennial census could hardly sustain a profitable ongoing venture, and Hollerith's start-up (the Tabulating Machine Company of 1896) did not attain a stable financial basis until after the firm entered into deals with private corporations like the railroads.

On the expiration of Hollerith's original patents in 1906, the government bureau decided to develop its own tabulating system to "emancipate the Census Office from outside dictation."[78] Hollerith's company had already received almost $750,000, and the Census Office was loath to continue making payments based on his other unexpired patents that covered improvements on the original machine. The Bureau of Standards appropriated $40,000 in federal funds to experiment in its own machine shop, employing former workers of Hollerith's in an attempt to circumvent his existing patents. According to Hollerith's counsel, "this purpose is simply to put the Government with all its power and resources in competition with this sole inventor in respect of this matter of tabulating machines," which would allow "the greatest competitor in the world, the United States government, [to] undertake, if successful, to destroy the inventor's property." Although Hollerith obtained a temporary injunction, his legal dispute with the federal government was unsuccessful; he opted not to pursue the matter before the Court of Claims and instead negotiated a buyout of his company. The

---

[76] Select Committee on Expenditures in the War Department (1919).

[77] Hollerith's patent applications included an "Apparatus for Compiling Statistics" and the "Art of Compiling Statistics," filed on September 23, 1884.

[78] U.S. Congress, Hearings before subcommittee of House Committee on Appropriations, G.P.O. (1906). The quotes in this paragraph are all taken from this report.

Figure 13.2 Counting Heads: Hollerith Tabulating Machine
Herman Hollerith, a former statistician at the Census Bureau, was employed at
the Patent Office and obtained a landmark 1884 patent for his improvement on
automatic tabulating machines. This discovery was a key step in the evolution of
discoveries that would culminate in the mainframe computer. The U.S. Census
Bureau unsuccessfully attempted to invent around Hollerith's patents. Hollerith's
firm was a precursor to IBM Corporation.
Source: Scientific American 63, no. 9 (1890).

bureau's project to build its own tabulators ultimately failed, and they instead retained the services of IBM, the successor to Hollerith's firm.[79]

Innovation Policies in Nations

Alexis de Tocqueville, with his usual acuity, highlighted the multitude of decentralized efforts that characterized entrepreneurial behavior in America. He contrasted this democratic orientation of enterprise to the inherited privileges and state-directed policies that influenced outcomes in France and Britain, noting that "at the head of any new venture, in France you will see the government, and in England a member of the elite."[80] Unlike other nations in Europe, the United States succeeded in revising its inherited institutions toward more inclusive political and economic arrangements. Market-oriented rules and principles and an accompanying network of adjacent institutions proved sufficiently flexible to accommodate needed adjustments. As Thomas Jefferson pointed out, "laws and institutions must go hand in hand with the progress of the human mind."[81]

France, Britain, and the United States have sequentially dominated the records of technological achievements over the past three centuries. In Europe, administered systems were prevalent during industrialization, in the selection of favored parties who would benefit from subsidies and in mercantilist policies to influence the course of technology and commerce. Such top-down direction also affected the selection of winners and the determination of financial returns for inventive ideas by parliaments, bureaucrats, elites, and influential members of private and public committees. Administered policies suppressed disruptive ideas and diversity, served to perpetuate inequality and fostered rent-seeking, suboptimal productivity, and patterns of unbalanced growth. By contrast, Americans deliberately rejected administered systems as a means of allocating inventive talent and resources, in favor of market-oriented incentives and institutions. Rather than depending on the rents that could be gained from a diverse array of administered schemes, creative individuals were encouraged to appeal to the market and to bear the consequences of success or failure themselves.

Unlike innovation prizes, patents fulfilled the economic function of securing property rights but delegated the prospect of returns to the market. As the *Westminster Review* noted:

---

[79] Heide (2009).
[80] Alexis de Tocqueville, *De la démocratie en Amérique* (1864), p. 176.
[81] In a letter to Samuel Kercheval, July 12, 1810.

Give a man a sum of money for his invention, and you run the risk of paying him either too much or too little. Give him a patent, and you secure the invention for the public, while his remuneration in money is absolutely determined according to its value. If the invention enrich him, it must also have benefited the nation. If the invention be a delusion, the public suffers no loss and the patentee reaps no gain.[82]

These sentiments were echoed by the federal U.S. judiciary: "But if the invention . . . be more or less useful is a circumstance very material to the interest of the patentee, but of no importance to the public. If it be not extensively useful, it will silently sink into contempt and disregard."[83] As such, market-oriented institutions, rather than an entrepreneurial state or NIS, propelled the rise and global dominance of American industry and innovation. These institutions were sufficiently flexible to accommodate the rapid transformations that characterize the knowledge economy then and now.

Innovations and commercialization in the development of the digital economy succeeded because a lack of centralized authority enabled a diversity of viewpoints "from the edges" and permitted risk-taking that generated both useful contributions and useful failures. A detailed study of current information technology came to the "surprising conclusion" that the ability of governments to significantly shape outcomes was limited and that technological change occurred through the combined—often unpredicted and sporadic—effects of numerous uncoordinated institutions.[84] The evidence from two centuries of technological history suggests that such a conclusion is hardly surprising. As Friedrich Hayek noted, "this raises for a competitive society the question, not how we can 'find' the people who know best, but rather what institutional arrangements are necessary in order that the unknown persons who have knowledge specially suited to a particular task are most likely to be attracted to that task."[85]

[82] *Westminster Review*, vol. 91–92 (1869), p. 64.
[83] *Lowell v. Lewis*, 15 F. Cas. 1018 (1817).
[84] Greenstein (2017).
[85] Hayek (1948: 95).

14

Conclusion

Now and Then

> The age of invention has just begun to dawn. . . . [T]he promise is that
> our children will live in a world that we would not recognize.
> —E. B. Moore (1912)[1]

Technological change helped to transform the United States from an undistinguished colony into the global leader in culture and industry, now making investments in orbital architecture to commercialize resources on distant planets. As I write these words, in the spring of 2020, the U.S. Patent Office has recorded a cumulative total of more than ten million patent grants. This rapid and sustained pace of technical advance creates a curious compression of time and perception that makes it difficult to fully appreciate the achievements of the past. Each throng of novel discoveries becomes the necessity of the present, and we regard the breakthroughs of even a decade ago with amused disdain.

The Bowdoin College Yearbook of 1876 noted that "some of our class at times expressed the opinion that it would be a great improvement if a system of water works could be introduced and the buildings piped, so that the students need not have to go out to the well in stormy weather for a pail of water." But, the authors added philosophically, it was probably the case "had they had all of these comforts and conveniences, they would only have wanted more, and would have become so enervated that they would have disliked to do the slightest work themselves." What, one wonders, would they have thought of the experience of current cohorts of Bowdoin students, who are daily served a vast array of gourmet dishes in the most highly rated college dining hall in the country, and who cannot imagine existence without laptops, Wi-Fi access, and their ubiquitous smartphones?

Rapid technological progress creates a certain hubris, where each generation is convinced that their own era is markedly different from all others, and this is particularly true of the age of the internet and information technologies. This

---

[1] E. B. Moore, "Next Few Years Will Eclipse All Ages in Invention," *Electrician and Mechanic* 24 (1912): 316.

Inventing Ideas. B. Zorina Khan, Oxford University Press (2020). © Oxford University Press.
DOI: 10.1093/oso/9780190936075.001.0001

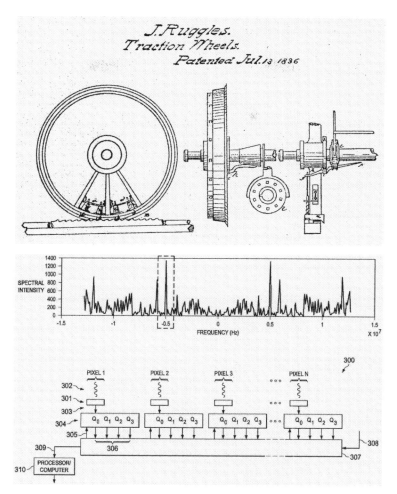

Figure 14.1 Two Centuries of Patented Progress

The first U.S. patent, issued in 1790, was signed by George Washington, Thomas Jefferson, and Edmund Randolph. The official numbering of patents began in 1836. The ten million patents recorded since then provide a valuable index of the progress that resulted from market-oriented innovation institutions.

Source: U.S. Patent Office.

book, however, has emphasized continuities rather than disjuncture. Debates about knowledge, ideas, and growth have been central to economic and political thinking in all cultures. The Pennsylvania Frame of Government in 1683 emphasized the link between universal access to schooling and innovation in its intent to "erect and order all public schools, and encourage and reward the authors of useful sciences and laudable inventions." George Washington, who gave the first and shortest State of the Union address to Congress in January 1790, was unlikely to encounter any disagreement—even in European parliaments—when he stated that "Knowledge is in every country the surest basis of public happiness." Similarly, writers through the ages from the classical political economists to new growth theorists have speculated about the sorts of ideas, inventions, and inventors, broadly defined, that would best contribute to the wealth or failure of nations.

Nevertheless, controversies have always surrounded specific proposals for the best ways to generate new ideas, and these divergences in opinion have increased in the digital economy. Over the past two centuries, vastly different approaches have been adopted and abandoned among private and public institutions. Early European perspectives—ambivalence or hostility toward accessible property rights in ideas and an enthusiasm for elite administered innovations—are currently experiencing a renaissance. The number, scope, and magnitude of private and state-sponsored prizes have all increased remarkably over the past few decades, motivated by "invented ideas" or mythical historical evidence. European and American governments alike have proposed innovation prize competitions for a vast array of projects including robotics, defense technologies, and environmental research. Developing countries with prohibitively high unemployment and limited fulfillment of basic needs have offered million-dollar bounties for esoteric moonshot inventions and lobbied international organizations to support prize systems as substitutes for patent systems.

Silicon Valley elites have likewise proposed a plethora of grand innovation prizes for dramatic schemes. The Google Lunar X-Prize was typically flamboyant, promising a payout of $30 million for the first successful private effort to land a spacecraft on the moon. "A successful Google Lunar XPRIZE would result in cost-effective and reliable access to the Moon, allowing for the development of new methods of discovering and using space resources, and in the long-term, helping to expand human civilization into space."[2] The competition continued for over a decade (2007–2018) and has been applauded, cited, and studied as a classic example of a successful innovation incentive—but it ultimately failed to achieve the stated objectives and the prize money was withdrawn in 2018 without much fanfare or public notice. Interestingly, a few teams decided to carry on even in the absence of the promised prize, because "the real opportunity is in opening the lunar frontier and the multibillion dollar industry that follows"—that is, in the marketplace.

---

[2] https://lunar.xprize.org/about/why-the-moon.

Technological prizes make for captivating narratives, but their implementation remains opaque and little is known about their efficacy. Policymakers that investigate the advisability of offering innovation prizes as inducements for technological progress invariably confront a dearth of reliable empirical evidence. They nevertheless invariably conclude that inducement prizes would serve as an effective strategy for ensuring competitiveness in innovation. When one points to cautionary historical outcomes, as I did in a workshop at the National Academies of Sciences, the usual rejoinder is that "this time is different." In the absence of representative data and systematic analysis, the authors of these grand (and often grandiose) schemes, whether at the level of private or national institutions, risk echoing the experiences—and errors—of their elite counterparts in administered systems across time and place.

Part of the reason for deficiencies in our current understanding of the economics of technological change and economic growth owes to a "nirvana approach," where an imperfect institution is deemed inefficient relative to an unexamined ideal.[3] The myopic focus on "optimal" systems has continually failed to penetrate the "black box" of real firms, technological change, and prevailing economic growth processes. This book, by contrast, offers an assessment of real institutional arrangements, including property rights and markets in patented ideas, as well as systematic empirical evidence on how administered innovation institutions have actually functioned in different contexts. The detailed comparisons at the individual level across institutions, place, and time provide novel insights into the sources of long-run innovation and economic development.

This research draws on the experiences of over one hundred thousand creative men and women in the United States and Europe, during the first and second Industrial Revolutions. The records document their creative breakthroughs, as well as their participation in mechanics institutes, membership in technical societies, interactions with intermediaries like attorneys and agents, and appearances in bitter court disputes. These inventive pioneers are the ancestors of today's software coders, the teenage entrepreneur who is certain that his patent for an improved coffee cup holder will make his fortune, the scientist whose start-up to produce a new biotech product fails spectacularly in the knowledge economy. They are not all heroic figures, and some are even scoundrels, claiming other people's innovations as their own, and exploiting their political connections

---

[3] Demsetz (1969). "The view that now pervades much public policy economics implicitly presents the relevant choice as between an ideal norm and an existing 'imperfect' institutional arrangement. This nirvana approach differs considerably from a comparative institutional approach in which the relevant choice is between alternative real institutional arrangements." According to Merrill and Smith (2011), a world of positive transaction costs requires a comparative institutional analysis to make the Coasian approach "more Coasian."

to corner the market. Information about all these extraordinary ordinary innovators allows us to appreciate the incrementalism and individualism of all useful economic activity. This approach establishes a reliable microfoundation for general macroeconomic theories about the role of endogenous innovation in long-run growth processes.

The quest for a consensus regarding the central question of the sources of economic progress has proven to be elusive. Academic economists, pundits, and policymakers alike have reported and circulated numerous competing claims that bear on the relationship between institutions, technology, and growth. When equally qualified commentators differ, how is the interested but nonspecialized observer to differentiate among opposing conclusions? Historical variation across both time and place offers vital clues regarding the validity of conflicting claims. Moreover, the study of the past allows us to identify and orient the discussion around "historical parameters," consisting of fixed events and outcomes that are not subject to individual interpretation. Economic analysis should, at the very least, be consistent with the actual historical facts.

"What Did We Learn?"

Stanley Engerman, an iconic economic historian whose path-breaking empirical research has shed light on the economics of institutions, has a habit of asking at the end of a conference, "Well, what did you learn?" Ventures to countless archives in basements and attics and literal bunkers surrounded by chain link fences, from San Francisco to Kew Gardens in England and uncharted regions outside the Péripherique in Paris, yielded a rich store of detailed original information. These primary sources were then photographed, digitized, and subjected to exhaustive (and exhausting) statistical scrutiny. These extensive datasets together reveal how different institutional arrangements actually worked and the consequences for the global economic and technology leaders in the two centuries of modern economic growth leading up to World War II.

This study shows that the scope of comparative history matters. The usual frame of reference for long-run growth is directed toward the question of why Britain was the first industrial nation. However, scholarship whose standard for comparison or "historical parameter" is limited to the British Industrial Revolution risks arriving at faulty conclusions about the sources of economic growth. A broader time span allows for the analysis of historical parameters that capture the loss of comparative advantage in Europe and the ascendancy of the U.S. economy since the nineteenth century. This wider perspective reveals that technological success or failure did not owe to the European focus on scarce scientific knowledge, the special insights of special social classes, or the heroic efforts of entrepreneurial government officials to compensate for deficiencies of the "timid private sector." Rather, the capacity for sustained economic progress depended on the degree to which institutions constrained or enabled the ability of ordinary individuals to take advantage of their innovative ideas and creativity.

The political revolution of 1776 paralleled an equally significant American revolution in economic thinking about institutions and useful ideas, and conventional economic theory still needs updating to reflect those insights. Modern macroeconomics has deployed impressive mathematical models and intellectual capital in the quest to improve on Adam Smith. Yet, the data freedom of mathematical modeling and empirical studies of aggregate data both seem to have descended into conclusion anarchy, and mainstream studies still cannot adequately explain why the United States became the wealthiest economy in the world. The research in this book, by contrast, is grounded in the notion that outcomes occurred because individuals responded to specific incentives. The empirical analysis shows how differential institutional rules and incentives actually worked and their consequences for individual behavior and broader aggregate patterns.

Conventional macroeconomic theories mesh very well with early European attitudes and assumptions. The neoclassical school models economic growth as a function of additions to exogenous or inelastic supply factors in the "upper-tails of the distribution," including the knowledge of elites, great inventions, and "general purpose technologies," along with large-scale investments in physical and scarce human capital. This is a good analog of the policies and institutional orientation in Europe, but further analysis is needed to penetrate beyond correlations to determine causal relationships with productivity and long-run growth. Closer inspection of the actual historical details suggests that elites and elite institutions entailed a misallocation of resources, which served to inhibit technological progress and sustained growth. As economists put it, such top-down efforts ran into diminishing returns. Even when it was recognized that existing policies had failed (as in the case of the British patent system and the Royal Society of Arts), the overall governance structure and adjacent institutions proved to be too inflexible to permit effective reforms.

Endogenous growth theorists like Paul Romer emphasize that "the key step in understanding economic growth is to think carefully about ideas," which can be reproduced at low cost, generate spillover benefits, and lead to increasing returns.[4] Innovation growth theorists have further hypothesized about links between institutions and technology and "economic life."[5] This perspective has deep intellectual roots in economic thinking. Adam Smith proposed a virtuous

---

[4] Romer (1990, 1992).
[5] Aghion et al. (1998).

cycle in which market expansion leads to specialization among individuals, the division of labor, and inventive activity that fueled further expansion, resulting in balanced growth that was evenly distributed throughout the economy. Smith's own commentary on the events in the former British colony (pronounced, according to an indignant American contemporary, "as phlegmatically as he would appraise a bale of cotton") demonstrated his acute understanding of the political economy of the day: "From shopkeepers, tradesmen, and attorneys, [Americans] . . . are employed in contriving a new form of government for an extensive empire, which they flatter themselves, will become, and which, indeed, seems very likely to become, one of the greatest and most formidable that ever was in the world."[6]

Adam Smith's *Wealth of Nations* was first published in 1776 and quickly accorded "bestseller" status in the American colonies.[7] U.S. delegates to Congress, who were drawing up a blueprint for an unprecedented political-economic system, eagerly obtained copies of the book, exchanged reviews, and debated about how Smith's ideas applied to the American context. Thomas Jefferson owned a personal copy in his library and declared, "in political economy I think that it is the best book extant." In 1783, James Madison put Smith on a list of volumes for the proposed congressional library, and his own writings echoed Smithian analysis, including economic faith in ordinary individuals and their divergent ideas, and reservations about elite factions and their qualifications for "instructing the people." The famous American jurist James Kent wrote in 1787 to Nathaniel Lawrence, a delegate at the New York ratifying convention, "I have just been reading Smith on the Wealth of Nations & he has taught me to look with an unfavorable eye on monopolies—But a monopoly of the mental kind I take to be laudable and an exception to the rule."[8]

This book has considered the costs and benefits of markets in ideas relative to administered innovation systems, and the specific mechanisms and incentives that Smithian and non-Smithian institutions created for individual behavior. Mathematical speculations about growth are typically matched with aggregate data, so it is hardly surprising if endogenous growth is found to be inconsistent with calibrations involving variables like "world research output." The complexity of decentralized knowledge and individual responses to incentives can only be detected within such aggregates. Micro-level comparisons of different countries over time helped to shed light on the accumulated effects of incremental adjustments and responses that generated shifts in overall comparative

---

[6] Smith (1902: 148).
[7] The most popular books in American libraries between 1777 and 1790 were *The Wealth of Nations*, Locke's *Treatises*, and Rousseau's *Emile*. See Lundberg and May (1978).
[8] Kaminski et al. (2003: 247).

advantage. In Britain, France, and the United States, the different rules and standards vested in institutions affected the scale of the population *of inventors*, specialization and the division of labor within and across firms and markets, the presence of spillovers, and the diversity of useful ideas and innovations available in the market.

In the United States, when access to markets improved, the increase in expected profits (which Abraham Lincoln termed the "fuel of interest") created an incentive for rapid technological change ("the fire of genius"). Expansions in market demand induced "shopkeepers, tradesmen, and attorneys" to increase the population of both ordinary and great inventors and encouraged specialization and the division of labor among them. Scale effects were endogenous, not exogenous, and related to the proportion of the population whose responses to incentives increased inventive activity and innovation. The discussion in Chapter 9 on knowledge spillovers further shows that positive external effects depended on the specific institutional mechanisms in place to facilitate the diffusion of ideas. The spread and adoption of inventions then fueled additional market expansion, productivity gains, and higher expected profits in a complex self-sustaining process that would likely defy mathematical modeling. It cannot be overemphasized that the most crucial part of this process related to the diversity of individuals, firms, and ideas that led to a richer and more variable choice set from which the market selected the most highly valued solutions.

The standard textbook analysis of patents as monopolies is also a good match to the European approach, but it fails to comprehend the American model. Patents in Europe were subject to very high fees, which were a good source of revenues for debt-ridden monarchs and for rent-seeking administrators. That the high costs would favor elites and deter the ordinary inventor was counted as an additional benefit. These grants were made in a registration system without any examination for novelty, enabling wealthy patentees to acquire rights to an invention that could have belonged to someone else. The state reserved the arbitrary right to modify this monopoly grant, through expropriation or by stipulating that the patent should be "worked." As a result, European patents were not far removed from the earlier world of arbitrary privileges. These ex post monopoly grants took something away from the public and made it into a pricier private good—or created a deadweight loss, in economic terms—which led to ambivalence about the social value of patent institutions. The emphasis on the higher worth of elite contributions was even more evident in the embrace of prizes and other administered innovation systems, which were regarded as superior to undirected decentralized markets for the ideas of "ordinary" individuals.

The economic model of innovation revealed in U.S. policy choices was instead based on four precepts that differed significantly from this patent-as-monopoly trope. First, the primary principle of the American innovation system was that it placed property rights in useful knowledge at the center of its strategy for promoting progress. According to the American approach, "An invention is property of the highest order." Note that the intellectual property declaration in the U.S. Constitution was the only clause to pass unanimously and without any debate in an otherwise contentious Constitutional Convention. Inventors had a legal and economic right to their own inventive ideas—and this is the only occurrence of the word "right" in the document—which the Constitution "secured." In short,

> the inventor has a property in his invention; a property which is often of very great value, and of which the law intended to give him the absolute enjoyment and possession . . . involving some of the dearest and most valuable rights which society acknowledges, and the constitution itself means to favor.[9]

The second precept relates to U.S. enforcement of these property rights, which was recognized as the strongest in the world. As a nineteenth-century writer wryly noted, U.S. patents constituted a "right to sue." Society was not bestowing property rights for inventions, it was defending them, and federal protection in the Constitution and Supreme Court reduced the scope for individual discretion and arbitrary decisions that prevailed in Europe. The rationale for the defense (as opposed to the grant) was based on the recognition of market failure, where "the most difficult thing in the world is to prove an invasion of property of this character—property protected by patents."[10] Since useful ideas were more readily "assailed" or stolen, enforcement needed to be correspondingly stronger for patent property than for tangible property.

The third principle was that patents were not monopolies. American patents were granted solely for novel ideas that inventors had demonstrably created themselves. As nineteenth-century jurists noted, "a patent is that which brings out from the realm of mind something that never existed before, and gives it to the country."[11] This was a public good—in the sense of a good to the

---

[9] 15 Fed. Cas. 1018 (D. Mass 1817). The first quote is from the *Annual Report of the Commissioner of Patents* (1871), p. 7.

[10] *Singer v. Walmsley*, 1 Fish. 558 (Md. 1859). A theory of market failure seems irrelevant for explaining why U.S. property rights in ideas existed in the first place, since there is no market failure in land or in houses or most other goods to which property protection attaches. As explained in the first chapter, in standard economic analysis, markets in knowledge are often held to fail because ideas can be replicated at zero cost, and it is impossible to exclude others from obtaining access. The failure of knowledge markets seems somewhat exaggerated on both grounds. For instance, Crawford (1990), who researched archival papers on the Nobel Prize grants, identifies a natural exclusion mechanism to such knowledge: "practically all the materials are in Swedish, which make them as inaccessible to those unfamiliar with this language as if they were encrypted by the National Security Agency." I suspect that the majority of articles in the *American Economic Review* enjoy a comparable natural right of exclusion against the general public.

[11] "When we consider the priceless blessings which have accrued to our land, by the intellect and ingenuity of the country in this department, we feel almost lost in wonder at the vastness of the

public—because patents often opened up new markets or lowered production costs and induced falling prices in the long run. A key analytical question is always, what is the relevant counterfactual, or assumed alternative? The "ex ante perspective" offered a comparison relative to the world *before* the inventor was induced to come up with the idea. Economic models today still fail to appreciate this insight: they are instead based on the European assumption that the invention has already been created, and the alternative is that the idea is in the public domain; as such, the patent "monopoly" to a private entity reduces net social benefits. According to the early U.S. perspective, by contrast, patents were associated with both static and dynamic increases in social welfare over time. Unlike the standard economic view of positive spillover effects as a source of "market failure," early policies celebrated the fact that benefits to the inventor created even greater benefits for society.

In summary, the underlying economic model that informed U.S. technology policies in the nineteenth century highlighted the role of patents as property rights that facilitated markets in ideas.[12] The European monopoly model initially treated patentees with suspicious resentment and hostility but at the same time directed fewer initiatives to curb their excesses in innovation markets through antitrust measures. As I have shown elsewhere, antitrust policies at the state level had been implemented in U.S. courts long before the Sherman Act of 1890. Federal antitrust was adopted as part of an inherently protectionist agenda to shelter firms that were losing out in the competitive process, and after the 1970s antitrust policies became increasingly at odds with patent policies.[13] Today, these continuing protectionist conflicts between antitrust and innovation are becoming all the more manifest and problematic for successful technology-oriented enterprises.

Administered Innovation Systems

Harold Demsetz has long highlighted the need to explicitly gauge the relative costs of market and nonmarket alternatives.[14] This book has empirically tested the assumption in economic theory that innovation prizes were

interests which have been created by the ingenuity of the country and the immense amount now invested, in this department of property." *Singer v. Walmsley*, 1 Fish. 558 (Md. 1859).

[12] Additional implications of this property-based analysis include Hayek's emphasis on access to decentralized knowledge, and Henry Smith's (2008) reminder that property economizes on information costs.

[13] Khan (2011a).

[14] Demsetz (1964).

superior to alternative mechanisms owing to their nice mathematical properties. Administered innovation systems depended on top-down arrangements where elites or bureaucrats made central decisions about prices, values, and the allocation of resources. They typically enshrined the conviction that elites were essential for economic and technical progress and could produce superior outcomes to decentralized knowledge and open markets. As a result, Europeans deliberately designed institutions and implemented strategies that served to reduce the potential population of inventors and the scale of both useful inventive ideas and commercial innovations.

French institutions have long exemplified this technocratic paternalism, in the course of which resources are diverted into wasteful rent-seeking and mercantilist measures to suppress outside competition and disruptive ideas. In England, the scope and depth of markets in patents and inventions was limited because of the conviction that elites and technocrats were best suited to identifying and contributing to important technological choices. Aspects of administered innovation were evident in British patent rules and manifested in many of its adjacent institutions, including the educational and legal systems. Britain was unable to retain its lead for a multitude of reasons that other scholars have identified such as changes in relative factor prices, but a primary contributory factor included institutional obstacles to creative nonelite inventors who were directing their attention to supposedly small incremental improvements in the market.

For mainstream economists, "there is little evidence to suggest that monopsony is important to our economy."[15] Administered innovation systems, by contrast, are best described as monopsonistic, since they consist of a single buyer who sets a fixed price/prize and makes the decisions about who is to benefit. As the empirical results in these pages show, this implies that the price will almost never be right. If the value of the invention is greater than the expected amount of the award (the amount times the probability of winning), then a process of adverse selection will lead to only lemons being submitted for prizes. If the expected award greatly exceeds the value of the invention, this creates a misallocation of resources in the affected market and through diversion from other markets. Moreover, these fixed prices cannot adjust to unanticipated future changes in the market, leading to greater disequilibria over time. When patents and prizes are complementary, returns to inventors can lead to overcompensation and (as the French example shows) create incentives for some applicants to pursue rents by "stacking" grants and other awards rather than through efforts to obtain benefits from the market through satisfying demanders.

[15] Manning (2003: 135).

Monopsony systems led to arbitrary decisions and unfair discrimination, where outcomes reflected the biases of the buyer. Even in the absence of corruption or incompetence, cognitive dissonance among judges resulted in a lack of appreciation for contributions from individuals of different backgrounds, however remarkable their creativity. In Britain, this lack of calibration of awards to the value of inventions was all the more evident in the case of working-class inventors. Wealthier individuals were universally more likely to get prizes, in all of these analyzed samples and in all of these countries, holding the merit of their invention constant. These biases were further distorted by a cascade effect: when judges were not able to objectively determine relative values, they tended to give out awards to those who had already been recognized. This leads to the phenomenon of very skewed distributions of awards, such as the Singer Company, which accumulated over two hundred prizes in the nineteenth century. Multiple awards often reflected the candidate's determination rather than merit.

Women inventors in particular were disadvantaged by the operation of administered institutions, despite official declarations of equality on the books. At the Franklin Institute, prizes were specifically designated for "ingenious men and women," but no women at all were recognized in the antebellum period and just five received any accolades over the entire nineteenth century. Men were universally offered higher amounts of cash and gold and silver medals. As inventors and exhibitors, women generally were granted lesser awards, lower financial sums, and inferior medals—in some instances, women were bestowed with butter knives, ladles, teaspoons, pencils, and thimbles. Even other women with feminist political agendas and higher social status were harsh in their judgments about the flurry of "feminine inventions" for powder puffs, corsets, and kitchen utensils and tried to exclude their inventors from exhibitions, despite the commercial value of these improvements.

Another central finding is that governance problems have been integral to all facets of such administered organizations, including the determination of eligibility, nominations, administration, and final decisions. "Nomination nepotism" has been a pervasive feature of science and technology awards, including the Nobel Prizes.[16] Administrators diverted resources away from the disbursement of funds toward expenditures on their own salaries or interests.[17] Despite rules to avoid impropriety, officers of the Franklin Institute were significantly more likely to obtain awards than outsiders, and this was true in several other institutions examined. Between 1731 and 1839, the vast majority of Copley Medals (90%)

---

[16]   Kantha (1991).

[17]   Crosland (1979). "Of the annual budget of the Académie des sciences, one finds that nearly all of it was devoted to the salaries, or, more strictly, the honoraria of members, and to general administrative expenses."

went to higher-status gentlemen and professionals, with only 10% given to artisans or tradesmen, owing in part to "internal favoritism" in the selection process.[18] Thus, even in the absence of outright incompetence or corruption, governance difficulties proliferated in administered innovation systems, whether private or state run. These political-economic concerns were compounded at the national level, where inventors had little recourse when states reneged on promises to distribute awards for inventive discoveries. As Jeremy Bentham succinctly observed about such measures, "the province of reward is the last asylum of arbitrary power."[19]

Of course, the prospect of error in decision making is present in all institutions. Effective outcomes over time depend on the operation of feedback mechanisms to censure or impose costs on incorrect choices. Incompetence in the marketplace leads to exit in the long run.[20] However, the norms of administered innovation systems typically tend toward secrecy and a lack of accountability for decisions and outcomes. The Nobel Prize charter explicitly dictates that "Against the decision of the adjudicators in making their award no protest can be lodged."[21] Innovation institutions in Europe and America similarly lacked third-party oversight, there was little or no transparency about processes and outcomes, and decision makers did not bear significant costs or consequences for poor or even disastrous choices. In the absence of effective feedback mechanisms, administered systems faced few or no incentives for change, and those who benefited from inefficiencies had an incentive to block any initiatives for reforms in existing arrangements. Thus, despite early evidence of the failure of its efforts, the practices of the Royal Society of Arts persisted for almost a century before meaningful reforms were implemented, and other prize-granting institutions in Europe were equally slow in adapting to failures and inefficient strategies.

Prizes and Incentives for Inventive Activity

Such research findings were not unknown to the few careful scholars who took the time to actually study the records rather than simply accepting the overblown self-promotion of these administered institutions. Samuel Sidney, an assistant

[18] Bektas and Crosland (1992).
[19] Bentham (1825: 93).
[20] In competitive markets, penalties are imposed for incompetence and rewards for productive outcomes, and profits and losses over time serve as a signal for the reallocation of resources toward their most highly valued use. Contestability (the potential for entry by competitors who are attracted by positive profits) helps to ensure that monopolists in the market cannot long act like textbook monopolists.
[21] Code of Statutes Given at the Royal Palace in Stockholm on the 29th June 1900 (1901), p. 6.

commissioner at the 1851 Crystal Palace Exhibition, spent ten years studying prize systems in exhibitions as well as the incentives that various societies administered.[22] The results of his meticulous researches made him deeply skeptical of these elitist winner-take-all arrangements. In general, outcomes were largely idiosyncratic, although risk-averse or unqualified panels tried to avoid controversy by making the award to the person or the firm with the most established reputation. Over time, the potential for disputed outcomes led to an inflation in the number of prizes and a corresponding fall in their value. His investigations led him to conclude that improvements in market demand and competition provided more successful incentives than prizes.

A central finding of my own extensive empirical analysis is that innovation prizes and other administered systems did not offer effective inducements for inventive activity at appropriate prices. The unmatched strength of a market is in finding the right price, which will reflect the "opportunity cost" or the value of the good or service in other alternative uses. For applicants, the expected value is equal to the probability of winning times the market value of the invention, so prizes are unlikely to serve as an effective incentive unless the stated payout far exceeds the market value of the induced good or service. Prize announcements will obviously have an effect if the promised expected price is excessively high: if you offer a reward of $200 million for breakthroughs in getting your toaster fixed, then it will surely attract a throng of toaster specialists to try to resolve your problem. At the same time, the disproportionate payment will have unforeseen consequences beyond your toaster dilemma, such as inducing oncologists to switch from finding cures for cancer to competing for your blockbuster payout. The problems would be compounded if, at the end of ten years, you were to announce that nobody had satisfied your conditions, and no payouts would be made. In any event, we cannot make inferences about the general efficacy of prize incentives from extreme outliers of this nature or from the usual case studies cited in the literature.

This book instead systematically analyzed large numbers of representative records in decentralized and centralized institutions in Britain, France, and the United States, amounting to over sixty thousand prizes. The samples were drawn from such prominent prize-granting institutions as the Royal Society of Arts, the Franklin Institute, and the Society for the Encouragement of National Industry, among others. A historical parameter that supports the conclusions from my empirical findings is that even these institutions ultimately acknowledged the failure of their attempts at inducing useful inventions. If prizes failed as incentive mechanisms, and administered institutions also acknowledged their own

---

[22] Sidney (1862).

failure to positively affect the path of technological innovation, why did they proliferate during the eighteenth and nineteenth centuries—and why are they so popular today?

Prize systems clearly provide private benefits to their funders, administrators, and applicants for awards. Many enthusiasts about prizes today still belong to "a large and increasing class in modern society, composed of gentlemen of wealth and position, with a slight knowledge of divers practical pursuits, some enthusiasm, a great love of patronage, and nothing to do."[23] Philanthropists have the satisfaction of an enhanced reputation and are able to draw attention to their own particular or peculiar concerns. Both the funding and award of prizes reflect the self-interest and biases of their administrators, as seen in the dockets of the institutions examined in this book.[24] Administrators and judges boost their status and potential income through their involvement on panels. Some increase their own prospects of gaining a future prize, while others are able to serve as influential patrons for their protégés, if only because they gain inside information about the norms and unwritten procedures. Committee members benefit from networking and opportunities to participate in the elite social circles of members of prize-granting institutions.[25]

In the modern era of teamwork and collective invention, "blockbuster" prizes like the Netflix award provide a focal point to organize and coalesce the attention of different groups, allowing the monopsonistic funder to benefit from all of their investments and the ideas expressed in interim reports, while paying out a fixed price for a single solution to a private problem. Participants in the Netflix contest were well aware of the miniscule probability of winning, but the expected prize payout was merely a windfall. Indeed, for most prize awards, the applicants' investments of time and resources exceed even the absolute value of the award, independently of the probabilities of winning. The Netflix Prize was not a true contest at all, because the contributors were interested in ancillary factors such as the potential to learn from others and the likelihood of securing better jobs. Similarly, the major benefit to Netflix itself was not the algorithm, which proved to be irrelevant in a changing market for its services, but the advertising notoriety and "buzz" that the competition created. In short, prize systems offer diffuse and

---

[23] Sidney (1862: 377).

[24] Access to historical Nobel Prize information reveals ample evidence of biases, including the research fields that were singled out for prizes relative to important areas that were ignored.

[25] Nonmonetary prizes are especially important as a signal of quality in cultural industries such as books and movies, because the value of these "experience goods" can only be determined by consuming the good. However, even here we observe "long-tailed distributions" where the majority of prizes accrue to a few recipients, and there is an exponential growth in the number of awards. Such prizes also help to validate literal and figurative "moonshots," or ventures based on largely ephemeral claims.

imprecise benefits to both grantors and recipients, largely through diffuse and imprecise means, to achieve equally diffuse and imprecise goals.

European elites were convinced that members of their own class were motivated by honor and eminence, whereas financial prizes merely attracted the lower classes. As Jeremy Bentham satirically expressed it, these institutions assumed "the mechanic or peasant pockets the money. The peer or gentleman ornaments his cabinet with a medal."[26] Peers and gentlemen might have been interested in medals as interior decoration, but honorary prizes also attracted large numbers of manufacturers who chose medals over cash and marked their products with images and tallies of the number of prizes they had obtained. International and national exhibitions mainly provided opportunities for manufacturers to promote and market their products, so it is not surprising that awards for exhibits were largely idiosyncratic and did not reflect inventive value. These "innovation prizes" were not about the technology; they were about the winners and sponsors.

Innovation prizes functioned as a means of signaling and product differentiation, offering winners a relative advantage in the market for customers and potential funding. Manufacturers and retailers accumulated numerous prizes as a useful marketing strategy, comparable to investments in advertisements and enhanced brand name capital. Participation in international exhibitions was especially worthwhile for export-oriented producers who wished to penetrate foreign markets. Since firms attended to obtain prizes in these literal star wars, it was in the interest of organizers to offer larger numbers of low-cost awards, which then reduced the signaling value. Predictably, these events declined in frequency and popularity, as more effective sources of advertisement, mass entertainment, and commercialization developed toward the end of the nineteenth century.

From the broader perspective of national technology policy, using prizes as inducements is the equivalent of pushing on a string, given the lack of predictable connection between the objectives of the grantors and the objectives of competitors. Prizes can be effective for private entities who are able to free-ride off the efforts of the entire cohort striving for the award, while only paying for one successful solution; however, social welfare is reduced by the lost resources and investments made by the many losers in the prize competitions. This is especially true if the objective of the competition is highly specific to the grantor and

---

[26] Bentham (1825: 85). The notion that honorary prizes are necessary because certain cultural norms are antithetical to monetization seems flawed. After all, courts and juries routinely assign dollar values for far more fraught intangibles such as injuries and emotional distress, and even compute and pay out compensation for loss of life. Rather, honorary prizes seem to be effective in situations where the award sidesteps informational problems, where the income elasticity of the recipient is low, or where the award enables parallel returns such as more consulting opportunities.

results cannot readily be transferred to other projects. Moreover, the secrecy involved in most prize systems tends to inhibit the diffusion of useful information, especially for outsiders. These net social losses suggest that prize competitions are inappropriate policy instruments for government agencies that should be promoting overall welfare. The prize-granting institutions in all three countries studied here uniformly abandoned attempts at inducing inventions by these means, and switched to other activities such as research grants to facilitate inventive activity and efforts to improve their patent systems.

By contrast, the deficiencies of administered systems highlighted the net advantages of markets in patented ideas. Patent incentives were aligned with productivity because financial rewards would accrue only for contributions that were valued in the marketplace. Jeremy Bentham pointed to the lower social cost of the market for patents, which "adapts itself with the utmost nicety to those rules of proportion to which it is most difficult for reward artificially instituted by the legislator to conform. . . . [I]t unites every property which can be wished for in a reward."[27] Moreover, as Friedrich Hayek pointed out, the market mechanism coordinates and taps into decentralized knowledge in a manner that cannot be readily replicated by even the most adept administrators, especially in the dynamic and rapidly changing environment for novel technologies.

Markets for Patented Ideas Redux

The greatest divergence in history was the rise of the United States and its continued leadership in the global economy from the nineteenth century onward. American achievements through the second Industrial Revolution owed little to specialized elites, the dictates and decisions of special committees to judge inventions, or ambitious measures by the government to simulate entrepreneurial functions. Instead, private property rights in inventive ideas and supportive adjacent institutions were at the core of American technological policy initiatives. Knowledge has been recognized as central to progress in all societies; the innovation of the American approach was to further designate knowledge as an economic good that would be best produced and exchanged through an open market in ideas, in a benign Smithian process. The ultimate arbiter of rewards and the allocation of resources would be the consumer, rather than the arbitrary decisions of groups with the power to bestow or withhold benefits. Some observers of patent laws pointed to "the extremely liberal propositions of the United States, which one could only recognize as approaching the ideal of the future."[28]

---

[27] Bentham (1825: 92).
[28] Cited in Penrose (1951: 81).

The chapters in this book show at a very granular level that inventors responded to, and benefited from, the ability to protect their ideas with patents. Skeptics point out, as an implied or explicit indictment of the benefits of patent systems, that many inventors do not obtain patents for their discoveries. The argument rests on a non sequitur: some firms are able to benefit from lead time, firstcomer advantages, private rights of exclusion, or trade secrecy; therefore, patents are unnecessary for all firms. The relevant concern, however, is not the truism that all inventions are not patented. Creative individuals have always pursued diverse means of benefiting from their ideas. Most educators do not copyright their lectures, because they obtain compensation from their colleges and from correlates with their reputation; this does not imply that copyrights for professors are irrelevant or unimportant. The American model was based on the right of all creative individuals to freely choose among alternatives means of benefiting from their discoveries, including whether or not to patent, or whether or not to "work" their patented idea.

What is decidedly beyond debate is that the framers, the U.S. Constitution, and the Supreme Court put property rights in ideas at the center of American economic growth strategy. The nineteenth century was the age of patented invention in the United States, which had the world's largest population of productive inventors. The U.S. Patent Office was deluged with applications from across the country and from inventors of every social and economic background. Americans obtained the largest number of patents in the entire world, both before and after adjusting for population and the size of the economy. As shown elsewhere in this book, prior to 1870, U.S. patents totaled almost half of all the patents filed in the rest of the world, and that numerical gap increased during the second half of the nineteenth century. American patentees were so eager to protect their ideas that they filed caveats with the Patent Office to give advance notice of their intention to obtain property rights. Patents continue to matter greatly to certain inventors and industries, as the ten millionth patent filing in 2018 demonstrates (Table 14.1). In accordance with endogenous growth models, networks of patented ideas accumulated and contributed to increasing returns in the knowledge economy.

Indeed, one of the constant complaints about the patent system has always been that *too many* patents were being claimed and commercialized.[29] One of the authors of these sentiments acknowledged the "insuperable difficulties" of

---

[29] "Every lady is enveloped in patents, from the crown of her head to the soles of her feet, each of which is of as much importance in itself as the patent for a tooth-pick, or a toy popgun. . . . And such is also the fact with respect to the numerous or rather the innumerable host of patents for trivial inventions in kitchen utensils and those used in dwelling-houses in the ordinary course of domestic uses and economy." *United States Congressional Record: Proceedings and Debates of the 45th Congress* (1879), p. 308. The other cited quotes in the paragraph are from the same source.

Table 14.1 Progress of Useful Knowledge in the United States

Patent Number	Date	Inventors	Subject Matter
First ("1X")	July 1790	Samuel Hopkins	Method of making potash
No. 1	July 1836	John Ruggles	Cog for locomotive wheels
No. 1,000,000	August 1911	Francis H. Holton	Vehicle tire durability
No. 2,000,000	April 1935	Joseph Ledwinka	Pneumatic tires for railways
No. 3,000,000	September 1961	Kenneth Eldredge	Automatic reading system for data processors
No. 4,000,000	December 1976	Robert Mendenhall	Process to recycle asphalt compositions
No. 5,000,000	March 1991	L. Ingram et al.	Method of using bacteria to produce ethanol
No. 6,000,000	December 1999	Jeffrey C. Hawkins and Michael Albanese	Synchronization of data across devices
No. 7,000,000	February 2006	John P. O'Brien	Improvement in polysaccharide fibers
No. 8,000,000	August 2011	Robert J. Greenberg et al.	Visual prosthesis for retinal degeneration
No. 9,000,000	March 2012	Matthew Carroll	Windshield wiper fuel reservoir
No. 10,000,000	June 2018	Joseph Marron	Laser detection

Source: U.S. Patent Office.

determining which inventions were of low worth but expressed an admirable faith in the "judgment and discretion" of Congress to establish itself as the final arbiter of economic value. Congress, of course, declined to take up this mandate, to the great relief of cooks everywhere whose necessities include four different types of patented lemon zesters. However, even this critic "freely admitted" that, by creating incentives for everyone in the population,

> our patent laws have operated to stimulate the inventive faculties of our people, and . . . placed us in the front rank of nations, if not in advance of all. . . . Such inventors and discoverers are the great benefactors, not only of our own people,

but of mankind. Their inventions and discoveries have revolutionized the world and advanced the progress of the human race.

Patentees pursued their claims all the way to the U.S. Supreme Court, secure in the knowledge that the rights to property in new ideas were enshrined in the Constitution itself. Litigation about every aspect of business has always been central to the economy, involving firms, their competitors, consumers and other stakeholders, and the state and federal governments. Disruptive technologies by definition would engender disputes about torts, contracts, real property, and crime. Hostility against "patent sharks" (the nineteenth-century version of today's troll) was part of a broader populism directed to large corporations and their wealthy owners, a populism that was leveraged by other competitors who would benefit from free access to patented ideas. Their orchestrated outrage about patent litigation led to continual demands for congressional action, but these bills failed to persuade and were never translated into legislative measures during the second Industrial Revolution.

A final incontrovertible historical parameter is that countries that wished to emulate American economic achievements openly recognized and voluntarily began to adopt the distinctive U.S. rules and standards toward property rights in patents. The central role of patents and the market for technology in American policy was acknowledged by prominent and influential foreign observers and policymakers. Sir William Thomson (Lord Kelvin), a renowned British inventor and scientist, was a judge at the 1876 Centennial Exhibition in Philadelphia, which featured displays of Bell's telephone, the Westinghouse air brake, Edison's improved telegraph, sewing machines, refrigerator cars, and numerous other patented discoveries. He observed that, "judged by its results in benefiting the public, . . . the American patent law must be admitted to be most successful. . . . [I]t seemed that every good thing deserving a patent was patented."[30] Switzerland may have been able to make excellent artisanal chocolate and music boxes in the absence of patent laws, but when they wished to become competitive in global innovation markets, they voluntarily introduced a patent system. Countries like Switzerland, Britain, and Germany reformed their intellectual property laws in direct response to the American experience.

At this point, we might indulge ourselves by speculating about a largely unanswerable question. If all technological achievements over the past two centuries of American history were obliterated except for the universe of patented inventions, how close would we be to today's standard of living? My own view is that we would not be far from the current frontier, given a substitution effect

---

[30] Great Britain, *Parliamentary Papers*, House of Commons, vol. 34 (1877), p. 271.

where markets for ideas responded to perceived needs and shortfalls in supply and demand. But, with greater certainty, another historical parameter is that the lives of ordinary people were transformed by the creativity of a *populous* army of equally ordinary peers in pursuit of returns in the marketplace—from the patentees of paper clips (one of the truly great inventions, in my view) and paper bags to windshield wiper reservoirs. In the race for prizes, there could be only one first-place winner, whereas in the democratic open market for ideas, all participants with useful inventions could be winners.

Now and Then

The mark of a successful project in economics—as opposed to one in engineering—is that it excites (provokes) further questions. In the case of economic history, this "whataboutism" inevitably prompts inquiries about the relevance to the present. The twentieth century introduced changes in the organization of technology, research and development, markets for finance and venture capital, and the role of the government. I have stressed that this book adheres to a sort of academic Smithian principle, where the scope of objective observations is limited by the extent of the original datasets. Although the caveat does not limit my liability, this brief section will venture beyond those data to speculate about the relevance of my results to modern developments in human capital and education, centralized administered systems and government support for technology, and markets in invention. Finally, I return to the specific questions about institutions and growth with which this book started, now phrased as "Why not China?"

Several chapters in this book considered how human capital was related to the production of new ideas and inventions and the population of inventors. The timing of educational investments and the cross-country patterns suggest that "upper tail knowledge" and costly specialized human capital was neither necessary nor sufficient for sustained economic growth. The effectiveness of such factors depended, as always, on the details, including the quality and appropriateness of science and technology training (rote learning vs. problem solving; pure signaling vs. a rigorous curriculum; theoretical vs. pragmatic orientations). Engineers in the United States benefited society enormously by facilitating access to markets through improvements in infrastructure. However, they were significantly less likely to appear in the rosters of "great" and "ordinary" inventors than their counterparts in the lower ends of the distribution of technical knowledge.

Commercially successful inventions were not necessarily the most scientifically or technically advanced technologies.

French technocratic paternalism, in particular, illustrated how an emphasis on the special insights and contributions of technical elites could actually divert a society from technological and economic advance. The French model enshrined the conviction that the graduates of elite universities possessed the most appropriate knowledge and insights into the optimal course for technology and industry. Narrow technocratic training in exclusive programs largely served as a filter that guaranteed an influential position on graduation and encouraged the perspective that certified elites should direct outcomes rather than respond to the shifting, unpredictable needs of the mass market. The potentially arbitrary nature of "exclusive" (in the dual sense of elite and closed) systems is still evident in France today, in both minor and significant dimensions, ranging from archives where access depends on the patronage of an insider to "flagrant example[s] of government incompetence in promoting innovative activities" that have resulted in "unmitigated disaster."[31]

More broadly, the results of administered systems lead to doubts about government policies to support or substitute for the efforts of private entrepreneurs and to "nudge" market outcomes. Among economists, the French approach to economic development has re-emerged in the guise of Richard Thaler's "libertarian paternalism," now dressed in elegant outfits of mathematical formulae, dedicated to the "attempt to steer people's choices in welfare-promoting directions without eliminating freedom of choice."[32] Case studies that focus on successes tend to overlook countervailing evidence. Government research and development initiatives in the major industrial countries still tend to be highly concentrated in the military and defense industries and a handful of high-technology sectors. Josh Lerner offers a balanced and perceptive survey of the role of the government in promoting technological innovation through direct interventions and indirect support for venture capital and entrepreneurship. In the United States, he identifies effective contributions from such public sector initiatives as the Small Business Investment Company and the American research development programs, as well as a modicum of public subsidies and funding for venture capital. However, Lerner's overall evaluation is far more mixed, as the title of his

---

[31] Lerner (2009); Cohen and Noll (1991).

[32] Thaler and Sunstein (2008). Thaler, winner of the Nobel Prize in 2017 for his formative contributions to the field of behavioral economics, suggests that ordinary individuals systematically make choices that they themselves often identify as suboptimal. This implies the need for "choice architects," who not only provide accurate information but also help to shape choices toward outcomes that individuals themselves would have chosen. The empirical evidence in these chapters shows that enlightened administered innovation systems generally fail in the attempt to "nudge" or direct those whom elites perceive to be misguided and uninformed.

book suggests, because of the many caveats and counterexamples that can also be drawn from other case studies.[33]

Numerous studies have shown that firms' responses to government measures to remedy market failure can lead to further unanticipated social costs. The French example (Chapter 6) similarly indicated how benefits can be outmatched by the potential for overcompensation, distortions, and a misallocation of resources, especially when little attention is paid to the alternatives that are sacrificed. In the biopharmaceutical field today, one observes similar efforts to accumulate returns from multiple sources, such as viral gene therapy treatments that received federal research grants, tax credits for half of research and development expenditures, exclusive rights accorded to biologic therapies, and patent protection and other benefits, along with costly market prices for the final product. Government regulations at times reflect the bias that "known lives" are typically valued more highly than "unknown lives."[34] The Orphan Drug Acts in the United States and in Europe, in particular, succeeded in their objectives, in part by shifting spending by pharmaceutical companies from broader classes of diseases toward discoveries for diseases affecting small numbers of patients in the population, including "ultra-orphan" problems (affecting fewer than a thousand individuals). Medical researchers have questioned the resulting increased burden on health care budgets as well as the costs in terms of other treatments sacrificed.

The discussion of national innovation systems in Chapter 13 highlighted the importance of adjacent institutions that interact with any given institution in a manner that can reinforce or undermine desired objectives. Patentees were unlikely to flourish if the legal system persistently overturned property rights in ideas. Negative interaction effects of "crony capitalism," according to some political economic studies, reduce or eliminate the benefits from state and corporate expenditures and efforts to promote financial ventures and innovation.[35] In modern Russia, China, and parts of Latin America, for example, collusion among elites in privileged positions in the state and business sectors allow the diversion of large sums to enrich a few, under the guise of investments to improve infrastructure and innovative capacity.[36]

---

[33] A book review of "The Entrepreneurial State," in *The Economist*, August 13, 2013, notes that committed advocates of public sector entrepreneurship typically fail to concede "how often would-be entrepreneurial states end up pouring money down ratholes. The world is littered with imitation Silicon Valleys that produce nothing but debt. Yes, private-sector ventures also frequently fail, but their investors know when to stop: their own money runs out."

[34] Such issues are discussed in McCabe et al. (2005).

[35] Haber (2013); Pei (2016).

[36] By contrast, more positive outcomes for state policies have been recorded in smaller economies such as Singapore, Taiwan, and Ireland. Hobday (1995) highlights incentives from expansions in export markets that initially generated incremental improvements and minor product innovations.

A growing amount of research in transition economies as well as in developed countries reports the tendency for politically connected enterprises to exhibit inefficiencies and significantly underperform their peers.[37] A further concern is the degree to which government efforts to aid innovation and technology "crowd out" private sector activity. Crowding out by government funding provides a windfall for favored businesses but also creates distortions because tax revenues are diverted to subsidize ventures that would still have occurred in the absence of the transfer. Several research surveys remain ambivalent about the overall net effects, but a number of studies have found severe crowding out in such examples as the U.S. Small Business program.[38]

The scope and depth of markets in ideas and inventions in the nineteenth relative to the twenty-first century have also been raised in discussions of the applicability of insights from the historical record. Property rights in ideas through the patent system helped to promote deep and active markets in inventions. Flourishing markets for both patented and unpatented ideas still serve to allocate resources today toward higher-valued uses, through a division of labor and specialization among "outside" and "inside" inventors, intermediaries, and firms. Licensing of patents in secondary and tertiary markets and cross-licensing (the mutual exchange of related patent rights) have always been a significant aspect of such transactions, as shown by business records, litigation, and archival assignment documents, although more research is needed to estimate the scope and scale of private contracts. During the 1980s, American universities responded to legal rules by significantly increasing their efforts to extract returns from their research through higher patenting and licensing. A large-scale survey of American companies showed that almost half of innovative firms had acquired technological innovations from the market, including customers, suppliers, independent inventors, and other outsiders.[39] The authors concluded that "external sources of invention make a significant contribution to the overall rate of innovation in the economy."[40]

In modern markets for invention, as in the past, the distinction between "insiders" and "outsiders" is frequently blurred. "Independent" inventors often include an employee acting as a principal on his or her own behalf (such as a corporate software engineer who has come up with an idea on his own time), rather than one who is unattached to a firm. A fascinating series of case studies show how firms treat outside submission of ideas, including internal submissions that are outside the inventor's regular job description.[41] In corporations like Yamaha,

---

[37] Shirley et al. (1995).
[38] Wallsten (2000); David et al. (2000).
[39] Arora et al. (2016).
[40] Arora et al. (2004).
[41] Holte (2016).

National Geographic, Nexon, eBay, Hershey, and General Electric, the stated policies toward the submission of unsolicited ideas range from complete openness, to invitations to submit that are limited to patented inventions, to the refusal to consider any submissions.[42] Many firms echo Under Armor, which describes itself as "an idea house" based on an "open platform of innovation," since "we are entrepreneurs and innovators and understand that great innovation can come from both inside and outside our company."[43] As discussed in Chapter 3, innovative crowdsourcing platforms like Innocentive act as brokers for idea submissions from networks of hundreds of thousands of solvers.[44] Technological innovations such as blockchain ledgers are likely to facilitate decentralized exchanges of ideas and inventive solutions. In short, the market in both patented and unpatented ideas has expanded in scale and scope in the current incarnation of the knowledge economy but retains its central characteristics.

Follow the Leader

Today's developing countries encounter very different circumstances and concerns than Britain, France, or the United States in the nineteenth century. Nevertheless, an approach that highlights distinctions between markets in ideas and administered systems still holds crucial lessons for interpreting current patterns. As the first chapter discussed, studies of early British economic achievements directed attention to other possible candidates for early industrial leadership, including debates about "Why not China?" Now, attention has again been drawn to this region, and to the remarkable transformation of the Chinese economy that accelerated toward the end of the twentieth century. Economic development in China over the very long run has followed a complex pattern perhaps best described by a (sino?) sine-curve. Historically unprecedented economic growth rates have raised the possibility that China might surpass all other nations and attain its declared ambitions to overtake global competitors in Europe and the United States.

Over the first two decades of the twenty-first century, growth rates in China surged to the extent that the total size of its economy surpassed that of the United States, adjusted for purchasing power or relative prices in the two countries. The

---

[42] Yamaha, for instance, only considers patented submissions: "if you send us any Idea that is not granted as a patent, Yamaha shall return your Idea without any review or evaluation. If an Idea you sent is officially registered as a patent, Intellectual Property Division will review and give you a feedback." Atlas Copco encourages "ideas that are product- or service related, of a technical or marketing nature, that relate to Atlas Copco's technologies or the way we do business. Atlas Copco welcomes them all." These quotes are from the companies' websites.

[43] https://uaideas.force.com/.

[44] https://www.innocentive.com/.

current steep drive to convergence in China dates from the market reforms in the 1980s ("it doesn't matter whether a cat is black or white, as long as it catches mice") that partially liberalized the nonstate sector.[45] Some economists credit this growth to a reduction in inefficiencies, which might imply that the observed changes reflect a movement toward the efficient frontier rather than an expansion in production possibilities.[46] Despite the historically high growth rates, Chinese total factor productivity and the level of output per person are still significantly below the corresponding U.S. rates, and it is not clear when or even whether China might achieve convergence in these key measures of economic welfare.

China offers a fascinating case study of a centralized administered system that is attempting to create a top-down market in ideas, and also illustrates how individual responses to incentives can lead to unintended consequences. State bureaucrats have drawn up a list of correlates with technological change and directed significant resources to boosting each category, from investments in scarce human capital, science and technology, and university infrastructure to intellectual property institutions.[47] As a result, China is now among the global leaders in almost every measure of science and technology inputs. The number of scientists and engineers jumped from 1.2 million in 1982 to 3.2 million in 2010, and some 1.1 million undergraduate degrees in these subjects were granted in 2010. Chinese citizens make up the largest group of foreign students in U.S. doctoral programs, and the quantity of scientific publications by Chinese scholars is second only to the United States. Wealthy businessmen and elite scientists have even founded the Future Science Awards, a domestic version of the Nobel Prize.

The Chinese experience in intellectual property rights aptly illustrates some of the complexities behind generalities about innovation and institutions. One of the most memorable experiences in my professional life was in Wuzhen, China, a historic town crisscrossed with canals, which is the permanent site for the World Internet Conference. I was invited there to lead an intensive workshop on the evolution of the U.S. patent and copyright system, and numerous members of the Chinese media listened intently to live translation of the lengthy presentation, and later asked detailed questions about the graphs and tables illustrating

---

[45] Deng Xiaoping's statement is often stated as a rationale for the shift away from planning toward the mixed "socialist market economy."

[46] Zhu (2012).

[47] Xie et al. (2014). The film industry in China similarly illustrates how their intellectual property policies have endogenously responded to changing economic realities. During the period when the market for domestic films was not well developed in China, there was little incentive to offer protection for movies. In recent years, however, Chinese-made films have become more profitable, leading to a significant increase in concern about reducing piracy. The 2017 Film Industry Promotion Law allows for stiff penalties for infringement. The government has also committed to supporting the industry through measures such as fiscal policies, and state funding of 1 billion yuan each year.

the costs and benefits of intellectual property policies. Some economists suppose that this sort of enlightened interest in intellectual property rights by such "follower countries" as China and India helps to explain their rapid convergence toward the growth paths of the early industrializers.

Quantitative measures, however, need to be adjusted to incorporate an assessment of the institutional details associated with the aggregate patterns. The World Intellectual Property Organization notes that the Chinese corporations Huawei and ZTE have risen to the top of the list for international patent applications. There was also a corresponding increase in total patent applications for China (Figure 14.2).[48] However, the rapid run-up in patent statistics does not entirely reflect market-oriented processes. Rather, the patterns owe in large part to administered efforts by the state to boost the numbers through an extensive array of incentives that may be termed "prizes for patents." Patentees can increase their chances of academic tenure, obtain coveted residence permits in attractive locations, or get cash payments and other types of bonuses. Firms leverage inflated patent portfolios to acquire windfall benefits from the authorities that range from large credits and subsidies to profitable state contracts.

Domestic patenting in China seems to be of lower (but increasing) quality relative to comparable foreign patents. Information about the quality of technological capabilities is revealed, for instance, in the percentage of applications that are actually granted, evidence from patent renewals, and other indicators of patent quality.[49] Similar questions have been raised about the quality of scientific output and about questionable practices to manipulate citations and other quality indices in a black-market "publication bazaar."[50] The Chinese example therefore mirrors the historical experience of countries like France and highlights the potential costs of a centralized administered innovation system that fosters unintended consequences including incentives for corruption and unethical conduct. Empirical studies in the political economy of China point to the need for efficiency gains in the form of a decentralized approach to governance, and the evidence in this book suggests that such benefits would also apply to technology markets.[51] Economic progress in a country of over one billion residents is necessarily contingent on private initiative and incentives for productivity, entrepreneurship, and innovation across the entire population. To

---

[48] The first modern patent law of 1984 has been amended several times, in the direction of enhancing the value of property rights and the functioning of markets in those rights. Statutory enforcement is relatively stringent, including criminal sanctions for infringement, but intellectual property piracy is still pervasive.

[49] Hu and Jefferson (2009). Patent protection may have had a stronger effect through the incentives for foreign investment. According to the World Economic Forum, China's technological standing largely owed to the efforts of foreign direct investors (http://reports.weforum.org/).

[50] Hvistendahl (2013).

[51] Stromseth et al. (2017).

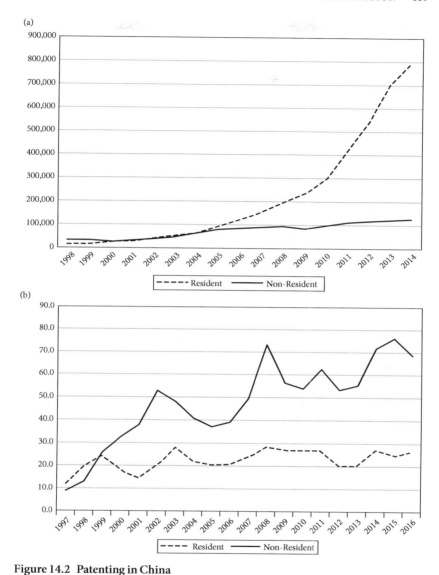

Figure 14.2 Patenting in China
(a) Patent applications in China, by residency. (b) Percentage of patent applications granted in China, by residency.
Source: World Intellectual Property Organization.

date, China has experienced the benefits of removing constraints on markets, but until its administrators acknowledge that decentralization and "spontaneous coordination" are an essential prerequisite for self-sustaining growth,

China is likely to fall short of its goal to overtake the United States as the global economic leader.

Future Perfect?

Popular and academic perspectives on technology have always ranged along a spectrum from fulsome wonder at an age of "infinite progress" to despair about the potential to revert to "a new dark age."[52] According to some dismal economists, we have entered an age of diminishing returns because of the end of the era of great inventions, or because of the inherent nature of science and technological change.[53] Their pessimism implicitly owes to the conviction that inventive activity arises from rare supply factors such as genius, and exogenous general purpose technologies that do not respond elastically to expansions in market demand. Or perhaps, like Edward Bellamy's hero in the futurist 1888 novel *Looking Backward*, pessimists feel that "if we could have devised an arrangement for providing everybody with music in their homes, perfect in quality, unlimited in quantity, suited to every mood, and beginning and ceasing at will, we should have considered the limit of human felicity already attained, and ceased to strive for further improvements."[54]

By contrast, observers who have documented the propensity of market-oriented incentives to induce relatively ordinary inventors to solve emerging problems have tended to be notably more optimistic about society's ability to elicit the sort of creativity that would exceed our best expectations. This link between markets and optimism about the future was evident in the reports of the Commissioners of Patents, especially at the end of the nineteenth century, when American residents contemplated a world that patented innovations had dramatically transformed over the course of their own lifetime. The head of the Patent Office, John S. Seymour, observed that "the relation which exists between industrial demand and inventive activity is very close. . . . [S]hould any change or advance in industrial conditions cause a sudden increased demand for some article, means for producing that article or its equivalent will be created very rapidly in the brains of ambitious inventors."[55] This elastic response was evident in inventions involving simple innovations through to complex technologies. The introduction of home delivery of mail induced hundreds of patents for letter boxes. The beginning of "big digs" for new canal projects

---

[52] Bridle (2018); Reese (2013).
[53] Gordon (2017); Cowen and Dutton (2011); Jones (2009).
[54] Bellamy (1888: 157–158).
[55] *Annual Report of Commissioner of Patents* (1895), p. xiii.

promptly stimulated numerous patents for excavators, newspaper articles about the need for a specific kind of bottle led to a thousand patent applications to meet the demand, and new systems of voting resulted in spikes in voting machine inventions.

Charles H. Duell, the son of a former Commissioner of Patents, was head of the U.S. Patent Office at the start of the twentieth century, by which time inventors were filing applications for some fifty thousand inventions, and over twenty thousand assignments were being recorded each year. Duell is often falsely identified as a technological pessimist who thought everything had already been invented, but he was adamant in his belief that the patent system would ensure the continuity of progress.[56] His successor, Edward B. Moore, was equally hyperbolic in his expectations about the ability of market incentives to generate unimaginable future advances, which he attributed to the favorable American patent institutions: "The accomplishments of the last half-century, while marvelous almost beyond conception, will not begin to compare with what will be done in the next half-century."[57]

In the twenty-first century, the sources of inventive activity include more scientific training and technical human capital, and greater investments in research and development by large corporations, relative to the early industrial era. At the same time, these supply factors reflect differences in scale and degree for specific industries, rather than in the underlying fundamentals for productive technological discovery.[58] After all, many of the most transformative features of the digital economy were devised by college dropouts or by liberal arts graduates whose training mimics the wholistic and flexible creativity of great thinkers and inventors of the nineteenth century.[59] Just as in the second Industrial Revolution, an apprenticeship in a high-technology startup can in some instances offer more valuable and relevant training than an advanced degree in science and

---

[56] He wrote in the *Annual Report of the Commissioner of Patents* (1900), p. xii: "The world owes as much to inventors as to statesmen or warriors. To them the United States is the greatest debtor. . . . [I]n this century the debt will be piled still higher, for inventors never rest."

[57] E. B. Moore, "Next Few Years Will Eclipse All Ages in Invention," *Electrician and Mechanic* 24 (1912): 316. "The patent laws of this country have been a greater protection to the inventor than have those of any of the other nations and are being widely adopted."

[58] Capital market imperfections helped to induce "in house" innovation within firms, so we might expect that technological change that reduces such transactions costs will lead to a shift back to innovations in the market. Today, science accelerators like Indiebio.com provide lab equipment and other fixed assets that enable independent scientists to become entrepreneurs.

[59] Entrepreneurs who never went beyond high school or dropped out of undergraduate colleges include Bill Gates and Paul Allen (Microsoft), Larry Ellison (Oracle), Steve Jobs (Apple), Mark Zuckerberg (Facebook), David Karp (Tumblr), Peter Cashmore (Mashable), Michael Lazaridis (Research in Motion), Jack Dorsey and Evan Williams (Twitter), Shawn Fanning and Sean Parker (Napster), Michael Dell (Dell Computers), Travis Kalanick (Uber), Jan Koum (WhatsApp), and Daniel Elk (Spotify). The legendary Chinese entrepreneur Jack Ma never wrote a line of code and merely obtained an undistinguished undergraduate degree in English. Bureaucrats are unlikely to identify or elicit such radically disruptive contributions from seemingly unqualified individuals.

engineering.[60] As Thomas Edison showed, deficiencies in technical education can be resolved by tapping into labor markets or collaborations in teams. Indeed, the promise of blockchains and "decentralized autonomous organizations" lie in a reversion to the nineteenth-century world of independent market interactions, in which this alchemy of diverse ideas and individual creativity resulted in discoveries that generated enormous value for all of society.[61]

The twentieth century has been characterized as "the American century," but at this critical juncture, new global competitors are adopting economic policies and institutions that have the potential to outpace U.S. achievements. Whether the twenty-first century will remain the American century will largely depend on the extent to which the lessons of the past are kept to the forefront. American technological and industrial progress owed to democratic open-access markets in ideas where entrepreneurial innovators succeeded, not by decree of administrators, but because their creations satisfied the ultimate judges—consumers in the marketplace. The evolution of administered innovation systems over the past three centuries largely serves as a cautionary tale rather than as a success story. The economic history of innovations instead suggests that the best incentive for necessary changes is failure in the marketplace; while the best prize for creative contributions to the knowledge economy is success in the marketplace.

[60] Marc Benioff, the CEO of Salesforce, calls for "a moonshot goal to create five million apprenticeships in the next five years." One of these tech billionaires offers thirty fellowships of $100,000 every year to induce young people to drop out of college. Switzerland is a leader in global competitiveness, in part because of its apprenticeship system, where the majority of high school graduates enter apprenticeships, many attached to jobs in innovative industries.

[61] Buterin (2014).

Patents and Prizes: Primary Sources of Data

Dataset	Location	Period	Sample	Women
			Number	*Number*
UNITED STATES				
PATENTS	Federal	1790–1930	67,214	4,200
PRIZES				
American Institute	New York	1847–1870	5,705	38
Centennial Exhibition	Pennsylvania	1876	641	641
Exhibition of Industry of All Nations	New York	1853	3,160	104
Franklin Institute	Pennsylvania	1840–1897	5,068	106
Mechanics' Institute	Massachusetts	1837–1874	4,617	596
Mechanics' Institute	Ohio	1850–1881	3,772	356
Mechanics' Institute	California	1858–1897	4,855	787
Mechanics' Institute	Missouri	1858–1870	2,272	296
World's Columbian Fair	Illinois	1893	102	102
TOTAL U.S. PRIZES			30,192	3,026
FRANCE				
PATENTS	National	1791–1855	5,000	1,211
PRIZES				
Exhibitions of National Industry	National	1798–1850	21,833	382
Paris Exposition	International	1855	10,731	263
Society for Encouragement of National Industry	National	1802–1914	1766, plus monetary values	
BRITAIN				
PATENTS	National	1750–1930	20,700	3,091
PRIZES				
Royal Society of Arts	National	1750–1850	2,600	263

Notes: For details on each of the sources, see the relevant chapters. These counts do not include additional datasets that were analyzed such as the membership of the Franklin Institute, industry-level information on the Crystal Palace exhibition and other world's fairs, the sample of great inventors and their inventions in Britain and the United States, design patents, patents extensions, patent assignments, antitrust cases, patent litigation, and several thousand civil litigation cases about major technologies, among others.

Industrial Exhibits as Measures
of Inventive Activity

A number of researchers have used counts of exhibits to make broad claims about patents and patent systems, and this section considers the validity of this procedure. The general reader can skip this technical coda, which concludes that, both conceptually and in practice, unthinking counts of exhibits have little or nothing to tell us about the economics of patents. The point might seem obvious: after all, a single printing press on display at an exhibition can include hundreds of unidentifiable patents. However, such authors typically do not identify the limitations of these data, so it seems worthwhile to spell out the details here.

It is useful to reiterate at this point a few salient points about the American approach, which influenced patent laws around the world. The U.S. patent system was internationally recognized as the most favorable toward inventors, because of the predictable procedures, low fees, strong enforcement, quality of the examination system, and systematic mechanisms for the diffusion of information. Technically trained employees of the Patent Office conducted an examination of patent applications to ensure that inventive ideas were novel, and questions of utility or usefulness were left for the market to determine. Patents were granted only to the first and true inventor, and neither employers nor the government could obtain property rights for the work that their employees created, except by means of a legal transfer or assignment. Patentees were required to fully disclose their incremental contribution to the technology and to distinguish between their own efforts and those of prior inventors. The inventor could be barred from rights of exclusion for undue delay in applying for property rights protection or if it was ruled that the idea had been ceded to the public domain. Patentees were not only prompt in applying for protection for ideas they had reduced to practical use but also even filed caveats notifying the Patent Office of the progress of their invention before formal application. Consequently, it was unlikely that intended patentees would display their invention at a public exhibition prior to filing the patent.

Exhibitions offer valuable insights into the efficiency of prize systems and about efforts to commercialize and advertise innovations. What do these exhibits tell us about the population of patents or novel inventions? The answer is, very little. Some economists claim that exhibitions shed light on inefficiencies in patent institutions, alleging that such data prove that the propensity to patent inventive ideas was low, and American inventors were actively avoiding the patent system. The concept of the "propensity to patent" compares the number of patented items to some precisely specified total population of inventions. In exhibitions data, both the numerator and denominator of this indicator are measured with significant error. Consider the denominator of "total inventions." International and local exhibitions alike featured fine art paintings, manufactured goods, sculpted busts, minerals and horticultural and botanical specimens, displays of published books, knitting and needlework, confectionery and simple baked goods, abnormally small or monstrously large specimens, and an array of items that could not remotely be regarded as technological inventions. As such, a blind count of exhibits—even those in a particular industry—is quite irrelevant as a measurement of actual inventive activity.

As a first step in any study of technological innovations at exhibitions, it is necessary to exclude such peripheral items. Table A.1 presents the descriptive statistics for the resulting dataset of over 5,100 technological inventions and innovations at the Massachusetts Mechanics' Association (MMA) exhibitions. These technical exhibits received 298 gold medals, 1,739 silver medals, and 1,200 bronze medals. Bronze medals were cheap and plentiful, given for exhibits that were relatively undistinguished, and almost never mentioned in subsequent records when itemizing accolades that an inventor or invention had earned. Although some of the participants traveled from New York, Philadelphia, and as far away as Michigan and Ohio, the exhibition was primarily a display of technologies that were created in Massachusetts and, to a lesser extent, New England. Thus, the population of goods exhibited at these localized fairs is largely unaffected by the disparate transportation costs that create a distance bias in data from international exhibitions.

The numerator of "propensity to patent" calculations is the number of patented exhibits. This procedure requires checking the name of the exhibitor and then trying to find that specific name in the patent records over several decades. If no match is made, then economists who follow this procedure conclude that the item was not patented. Such a process will significantly underestimate the extent of patenting, for a number of reasons. Clearly, ordinary names present a problem, as do inconsistencies such as the exhibitor "Johnny B. Goode" who is also "John Goode" the patentee. Equally important, many exhibitors were manufacturing firms and their agents. Since entries were listed under the names of their exhibitors and not the name of the inventor, even if that item were patented, the lack of a match to the patent records would still be counted as unpatented. Also, one exhibit does not necessarily equal one patent, since a displayed steam engine might be covered by dozens of patents. Such errors in matching will necessarily generate a low "propensity to patent."

If one were to follow this procedure, only 845 or 16.4% of total MMA exhibits can be traced in the patent records, which is similar to other estimates that have been made of alleged "propensities to patent." In the United States, firms cannot obtain patent rights on their own accord, so even if a firm at the exhibition owned an enormous portfolio of patents, it would be impossible to detect this. Firms were more likely to own larger amounts of patents than individual exhibitors, so the inability to include firms in the calculations of the propensity to patent biases estimates downward. Thus, the denominator should be adjusted to take into account the number of exhibits attributed to firms. If firms are omitted from the base, then at least 24% of the exhibits were patented, and this figure increases over time. The "exhibitor is patentee" variable in Figure A.1 further identifies the number of exhibits whose exhibitors obtained at least one patent at some point in their career, even if the specific item at the fair was not patented. Again, the representation of patentees is higher in the second period, and now at least 43.4% of exhibits were patented, if adjustments are made for firms. The point is not that this is a low or high "propensity," but rather that this calculation is inherently flawed, and does not provide reliable insights into patenting or the effectiveness of the patent system. We might certainly be able to trace 11% of patented exhibits; however, it would be incorrect to further claim that this implied "89% of innovations at this exhibition were not patented."

At the same time, it is true that a considerable and diverse amount of creativity at invention was indeed occurring outside the formal patent system, and it is interesting to

Table A.1 Awards at the Massachusetts Mechanics Association Exhibition, 1837–1874

	Before 1855		After 1855		Total	
	N	%	N	%	N	%
Awards						
Gold medal	146	6.4	152	5.3	298	5.8
Silver medal	940	41.4	799	27.7	1,739	33.8
Bronze medal	213	9.4	986	34.2	1,200	23.3
Other	973	42.8	943	32.7	1,916	33.2
Total	2,272	100	2,880	100	5,153	100
Location						
Massachusetts	1,950	85.8	2,592	89.8	4,542	88.0
Other New England	157	6.9	154	5.3	311	6.0
Mid-Atlantic	150	6.6	124	4.3	274	5.3
Other	16	0.7	16	0.6	32	0.5
Prize Winners						
Women	281	12.4	214	7.4	495	9.6
Companies	572	25.1	1,082	37.5	1,654	32.1
Age, mean and (SD)	37.1	(10.3)	42.7	(11.3)	40.5	(11.3)
Participation in fairs, mean and (SD)	2.0	(2.1)	1.9	(2.2)	2.0	(2.1)
Occupation of Prize Winners						
Artisan	156	24.1	183	18.5	339	20.7
Machinist/engineer/inventor	42	6.5	139	14.1	181	11.1
Manufacturer	200	30.9	301	30.5	501	30.6
Merchant/professional/white collar	197	30.4	295	29.9	492	30.1
Other	53	8.2	69	7.0	122	7.5
Patenting						
Patentable subject matter	801	35.3	1,635	56.7	2,436	47.2
Prize winner is patentee	456	20.0	1,065	36.9	1,521	29.5
Patent obtained for exhibit	212	9.3	633	21.9	845	16.4
Career patents, mean and (SD)	1.4	(16.2)	3.1	(13.0)	2.4	(14.5)
Sectors						
Agriculture	62	2.7	117	4.1	179	3.5
Construction	115	5.1	214	7.4	329	6.4
Manufacturing	1,681	74.0	1,948	67.5	3,629	70.4
Transportation	187	8.2	404	14.0	591	11.5
Other	227	10.0	203	7.0	430	8.3

Notes and Sources: Reports of Exhibitions of MMA (1837–1874); U.S. Patent Records (1790–2009); Manuscript censuses (federal) (1850–1880). (SD): standard deviation. Patentable subject matter: exhibits that fall into classes that could be patented, as gauged from a subject search of all patent records. Patentable subject matter does not imply that the invention would have qualified for a patent, which would require additional scrutiny for novelty. "Prize winner is a patentee" refers to those who had ever attained a patent. Career patents: total patents that the patentee obtained over their lifetime.

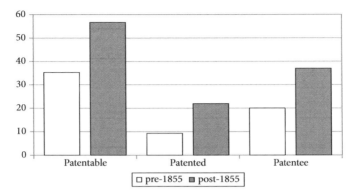

Figure A.1 Patenting and Patentability of Innovation Prizes (Percentages)

Notes and Sources: The MMA sample was matched with the patent records to determine whether the invention at the exhibition was patentable ("patentable"), whether the inventor had obtained a patent for the exhibited invention ("patented"), and whether the exhibitor had ever obtained a patent over the course of his or her entire life ("patentee"). See text for details.

speculate why such items were not patented. Consider the argument that such inventors had actively rejected the patent option and instead decided to appropriate returns through other means, such as trade secrets. Secrecy seems somewhat implausible as a general explanation of unpatented exhibits, for it is unlikely that secrecy would be promoted by participating in a public exhibition. Perhaps inventors compared the expected costs of getting and enforcing a patent relative to the expected benefits of patent protection and decided that the net present value of patenting was negative. If so, this suggests that many of these unpatented inventions were likely of minimal economic value.

Even if it were possible to identify patented exhibits with zero error, a straightforward explanation for not patenting an exhibit is that many exhibits were simply not patentable. Patent examiners award property rights based on novelty in technological areas that involve legally patentable subject matter. The item might have been ineligible for patent protection because it was not novel or because it fell outside the subject matter that could be patented. It is not feasible to determine the amount of novel inventive capital vested in unpatented exhibits, but we can categorize the patentability of each item in terms of subject matter. Patentability of exhibits can be confirmed through a knowledge of patent laws, careful reading of the jury reports, and searching the patent records to determine if any such patents had ever been granted. For instance, goods that just featured high-quality workmanship and mere changes in appearance or form (e.g., decorative flourishes, silver plating used in place of bronze) were not patentable, and neither were better ways of raising silkworms, unusually shaped ivory combs, hand-cut crystal, or exceptionally large church bells.

Application of this minimal filter of subject matter suggests that less than half, or a total of 47.2%, of the Massachusetts exhibits were patentable. This in turn indicates that at least 34.7% (845 patents out of 2,436 patentable exhibits) of eligible items were covered by patent protection, a figure that would be much higher if one could make similar adjustments for inventive novelty. Patentability statistics thus indicate that much of the creativity in national and international exhibitions was quite different from the creativity that resulted in patents or in enhanced capacity for economic growth.

Another consideration is the sorts of industries that were covered by exhibits. In the analysis in this book, the exhibits and patents were allocated to a sector and industry of final use. In the period between 1790 and 1850, 22.3% of national patents in the United States were in agriculture, 16.7% in construction, 40.1% in manufacturing, 12.8% in transportation, and 8% in the miscellaneous category. In contrast to the relatively more even sectoral dispersion of patents, the majority of the entries at the MMA fairs fell into the manufacturing category. Thus, patent protection extended to a wider range of technologies and industries than items at exhibitions. The exhibits were allocated to twelve more detailed industrial categories, and Table A.2 presents the industrial distribution of the exhibits, their patentability, and those that were actually patented. Heat and power-related innovations (ranges, furnaces, lamps, electrical goods, and the like) accounted for 9.7% of the entire sample, but 19.1% of the patentable and 18.6% of patented entries. In comparison, apparel made up 6.2% of all innovations, but only a miniscule share of those that were patented/patentable.

Statistical tests confirm that both the patentable and patented exhibits varied significantly across industrial category. However, the shares of the total number of awards were 5.8% gold medals, 33.8% silver medals, and 23.3% bronze medals, and there is little variation in these allocations across industries. Transportation accounted for 6% of all exhibits and garnered an equivalent proportion of each category of award. In other words, the medals in each industry were proportional across the different industrial lines, and these patterns are common to all exhibitions, whether domestic or international. This lack of variation of awards across such disparate technologies implies that prizes were apportioned on a quota basis to each technology class on display and were largely unrelated to the quality of inventive input. In short, exhibits can tell us a great deal about prizes and administered systems, but their ability to tell us anything valid about patents or patent systems is quite limited.

Table A.2 Industrial Distribution of Prizes at Massachusetts Exhibitions, 1837–1874

Industry	Total	Patentable	Patents	Gold Medal	Silver Medal	Bronze Medal
Agriculture (*n*)	358	200	73	20	129	81
Col %	6.9	8.2	8.6	6.7	7.4	6.8
Row %	—	55.6	20.4	5.6	36.1	22.7
Apparel (*n*)	319	33	6	18	95	66
Col %	6.2	1.4	0.7	6.0	5.5	7.3
Row %	—	10.3	1.9	5.7	29.9	20.8
Arts (*n*)	609	167	40	39	95	66
Col %	11.8	6.9	4.7	13.1	12.4	11.3
Row %	—	27.4	6.7	6.4	35.5	22.2
Construction (*n*)	329	185	79	19	113	79
Col %	6.4	7.6	9.4	6.4	6.5	6.6
Row %	—	56.2	23.9	5.8	34.2	23.9
Furniture (*n*)	305	75	38	11	95	73
Col %	5.9	3.1	4.5	3.7	5.5	6.1
Row %	—	24.6	12.5	3.6	31.2	23.9
Heat and power (*n*)	499	464	157	33	150	143
Col %	9.7	19.1	18.6	11.1	8.6	11.9
Row %	—	93.0	31.5	6.6	30.1	28.7
Manf. machines (*n*)	493	441	125	36	161	133
Col %	9.6	18.1	14.8	12.1	9.3	11.1
Row %	—	89.5	25.4	7.3	32.8	27.1
Manf. goods (*n*)	898	350	144	52	307	179
Col %	17.4	14.4	17.0	17.5	17.7	14.9
Row %	—	39.0	16.0	5.8	34.2	19.9
Printing and publish. (*n*)	295	71	22	12	100	69
Col %	5.7	2.9	2.6	4.0	5.8	5.8
Row %	—	24.1	7.5	4.1	33.9	23.4
Scientific (*n*)	132	51	17	9	41	26
Col %	2.6	2.1	2.0	3.0	2.4	2.2
Row %	—	38.6	12.9	6.9	31.3	19.9
Textiles (*n*)	620	185	71	31	226	140
Col %	12.0	7.6	8.4	10.4	13.0	11.7
Row %	—	29.8	11.5	5.0	36.5	22.6
Transportation (*n*)	300	214	73	18	106	76
Col %	5.8	8.8	8.6	6.0	6.1	6.3
Row %	—	71.3	24.3	6.0	35.3	25.3
Total (*n*)	5,157	2,436	1,521	298	1,739	1,200
%	100	47.2	29.5	5.8	33.8	23.3

Notes and Sources: See Table A.1. The percentages in the table include the undisplayed calculations for a total of 1,915 exhibits that were awarded diplomas.

Statistical Analysis of Knowledge Spillovers

Spatial Autocorrelation

The discussion in Chapter 9 is based on quantitative measurements of knowledge spillovers. The analysis considers whether patented inventions and prize-winning innovations differed in their spatial dependence. We employ two different measures of geographic adjacency. It is generally agreed that influence is inversely related to distance, and we measure distance from other counties using specific locations described in degrees of latitudes and longitudes. The second distance variable uses a contiguous counties approach that calculates the effects of patenting or prize innovations in the county in question on adjacent counties that share a common border ("queen contiguity"). According to the gravity model of technological knowledge, mechanisms that generate spillovers depend on spatial proximity, which is precisely defined in terms of a spatial matrix with dimensions ($N \times N$), where $N = 1,788$ counties.

Spatial autocorrelation exists when the values of a variable are a function of its location and spatial characteristics that are defined in terms of a specific measure of distance. If spatial autocorrelation is statistically significant, this is a result that is interesting in itself. This correlation also has further implications for the validity of conventional procedures, since significant correlation implies that the usual method of merely adding fixed effects for regions or states will involve bias owing to unobserved heterogeneity. The null hypothesis of zero spatial autocorrelation implies that the variable in question is a spatially independent and identically distributed draw from a standard normal distribution.

Moran's I statistic allows us to test for the existence of global spatial autocorrelation. An alternative test, Geary's C statistic, leads to similar conclusions.

Moran's I can be computed as

$$I = \frac{n}{S_0} \frac{\sum_i \sum_j w_{ij} (x_i - \overline{x})(x_j - \overline{x})}{\sum_i (x_i - \overline{x})^2}$$

where

n = number of locations, indexed by i and j
w_{ij} = spatial weight matrix
x = variable of interest
$\overline{x}$ = the mean of x
$S_0 = \sum_i \sum_j w_{ij}$

The analysis employs a weight matrix that is based on distance, where the distance between county i and county j is measured from centered values of longitude and latitude. Any off-diagonal entry in the matrix represents the inverse of the distance between point i and point j. Moran's I ranges from −1 to 1 and has an expected value of $-1/(n-1)$, which tends to zero as n increases. Thus, a value that exceeds zero indicates positive spatial autocorrelation (similar values are closely located), and a value that is less than zero implies negative autocorrelation (dissimilar values are closely located). The Z statistic normalizes the value and provides a standard t-test for statistical significance.

Table A.3 presents the results of testing the hypothesis of spatial correlation among the patents per capita at the county level. The results for total patents are highly significant, with a Z statistic of 14.3, implying that we can reject the null hypothesis of zero spatial autocorrelation in inventions that were patented. Per capita patenting over this period was affected by strong spatial localization, implying the existence of geographical spillover effects. For purposes of comparison with the data on prize-winning innovations, we note that New York displays a statistically significant pattern of correlation, both in the antebellum period and after. New England and the entrants into technological markets in the West and Midwest (the "other" regional category) also experienced high benefits from contiguous counties that were innovators. It is noticeable and plausible that in the postbellum period the degree of spatial autocorrelation falls somewhat in other areas (even becoming

Table A.3 Spatial Autocorrelation: Per Capita Patents, 1835–1870

	Moran's I Statistics (County Level)		
	Z Coefficient	*Pr > $|Z|$*	*N*
All patents	14.30	0.00	1,078
Regions			
New York	*3.45*	*0.00*	*109*
Mid-Atlantic	3.40	0.00	143
New England	12.57	0.00	113
Other	12.4	0.00	713
Antebellum Period			
New York	*2.75*	*0.00*	*54*
All patents	12.2	0.00	496
Mid-Atlantic	3.01	0.00	69
New England	6.80	0.00	60
Other	10.9	0.00	313
Postbellum Period			
New York	*2.73*	*0.00*	*54*
All patents	11.7	0.00	582
Mid-Atlantic	0.08	0.93	74
New England	4.82	0.00	53
Other	11.30	0.00	400

Notes and Sources: The Moran I statistics are based on an assumption of normality. The observations comprise counties, and the analysis is over county-level patents per capita. The spatial weights are derived from distance based on latitudes and longitudes. See text for discussion.

indistinguishable from zero in the Mid-Atlantic) but experiences a moderate increase in the frontier regions. As followers or latecomers, the frontier areas were likely beneficiaries from the investments that the Northeast had made in technological inputs.

Table A.4 relates to the prize innovations that were not identified as patented. The Z coefficient for the overall sample of the prizes is only marginally significant. The region of interest here is New York, which was the place of residence for most of the innovators, and it is striking that in each level of the table relating to New York, we cannot reject the null hypothesis. These prize innovations in New York were not spatially autocorrelated, which implies that such innovations did not generate much in the way of geographical spillovers. The differences in outcome across patents and prize-winning innovations within New York further suggests that state-specific factors were unlikely to account for the variation in geographical spillovers.

Estimation of Knowledge Spillovers

The spatial autocorrelation analysis revealed that patents were significantly influenced by location and by the degree of inventive activity in adjacent counties, but prizes were not. Prize innovations may not have led to significant spillovers, but another question is the extent to which patents were spatially associated with rates of innovation and

Table A.4 Spatial Autocorrelation: Per Capita Prizes, 1837–1870

	Moran's I Statistics (County Level)		
	Z Coefficient	Pr > |Z|	N
All prizes	1.91	0.05	233
Regions			
New York	−0.75	0.45	68
Mid-Atlantic	3.72	0.00	47
New England	2.42	0.02	67
Other	1.79	0.07	51
Antebellum Period			
New York	−0.83	0.41	45
All exhibits	2.16	0.03	159
Mid-Atlantic	3.05	0.00	30
New England	2.63	0.01	43
Other	1.67	0.09	41
Postbellum Period			
New York	0.38	0.71	23
All exhibits	3.87	0.00	74
Mid-Atlantic	2.21	0.03	17
New England	2.39	0.02	24
Other	1.46	0.15	10

Notes and Sources: The Moran I statistics are based on an assumption of normality. The observations comprise counties, and the analysis is over county-level innovations per capita. The spatial weights are derived from distance based on latitudes and longitudes. See text for discussion.

commercialization in general. We now address this question by estimating the impact of geographical clustering of patents in counties adjacent to the county of residence for the prize-winning innovator. The analysis takes advantage of spatial econometric techniques that can be used to model spatial lags. The estimation is over per capita innovations at the county level.

In particular, we estimate the following equation:

$$\text{Per Capita Prizes } (P) = \rho W \Lambda + X\beta + \varepsilon$$

where ρ is a spatial lag parameter

W is a weights matrix, which designates counties as neighbors if they are contiguous

Λ is a vector of per capita patents

X is a matrix of other exogenous variables

β indicates the relevant parameters for exogenous variables

ε is the vector of error terms

The dependent variable is the log of per capita prize innovations at the county level. The first term on the right-hand side is the product of the weights matrix and the vector Λ of per capita patents at the county level. It therefore represents the spatial lag of patents for the innovations in a county or a weighted measure of patents in all of the counties adjoining a given county (queen contiguity).

The ordinary least squares regressions are reported in Table A.5, but similar results were obtained using negative binomial specifications. The inclusion of spatial effects here increases our ability to explain variation in exhibited innovations, and in all specifications the spatial lag parameter is statistically significant. The analysis also tests the impact of location in terms of latitude and longitude on the dependent variable. The regression analysis supports the hypothesis that patents were associated with geographical spillovers that benefited both potential patentees and prize-winning innovations.

Table A.5 Regressions: Determinants of Innovation Prizes per Capita

Dependent Variable: **Prizes per Capita at County Level**

	(1)	(2)	(3)
Intercept	−2.25	−3.70	3.71
	(3.07)***	(3.75)***	(1.00)
Spatial lag of patents per capita	0.29	0.23	0.27
(Log)	(3.56)***	(2.69)***	(2.89)***
Postbellum period	0.50	0.38	0.40
	(3.32)***	(2.54)***	(2.68)***
Manufacturing employment	—	0.12	0.03
(Log)		(2.06)**	(0.45)
Urbanization	—	0.002	0.003
		(1.72)*	(2.26)**
Regions			
New England	—	—	0.47
			(1.87)*
New York	—	—	0.41
			(1.98)*
Other	—	—	−0.06
			(0.17)
Latitude	—	—	−0.11
			(2.72)***
Longitude	—	—	0.03
			(0.77)
R^2	0.11	0.16	0.22
F	13.6	10.6	6.5
N	267	267	267

Notes and Sources: See text in appendix. The dependent variable consists of prize innovations per capita at the county level. The spatial lag is computed in terms of "queen contiguity" as a measure of the patents per capita in counties adjacent to the specific county in which the prize-winning innovation originated.

Summary Judgment on Innovation Prizes

Administered Innovation Systems

Arrangements where economic decisions about values, rewards, and the allocation of resources are made by administrators or panels:

- Monopsony (single buyer confronting numerous sellers)
- Non–market oriented
- Top-down, bureaucratic decision making
- Lack feedback mechanisms/transparency

Who Gets Prizes?

- Idiosyncratic/random allocation
- Outcomes determined by identity of judges and of applicants
- Winners tend to be insiders, wealthier candidates, or those with connections
- Awards unrelated to productivity or value of invention/innovation
- Unfair discrimination can occur (e.g., women, candidates from nonelite backgrounds, nepotism)
- Cascade effect: prior winners more likely to receive further awards (especially likely when panels do not have the ability to accurately distinguish among competing claims)

Administration of Awards

- Panels often chosen based on connections and celebrity/reputation rather than relevant expertise
- Administrative costs generally outweigh award made
- Transparency: decision making is usually secret, without any external monitoring
- No penalties or incentives to acknowledge failures and make adjustments; absence of error-correcting mechanisms
- Impossible for administrators to find the "right price"
- Social capture when administrators have the potential to become award applicants, or when prior winners are appointed to judging panel
- "Grand innovation approach": views inventive process as a unitary discrete event, which ignores the numerous incremental contributions that make up any "great invention"; essentially expropriates the inventive capital of all prior contributors and gives the reward to a single "winner"; technological change is a process to which many have contributed rather than a single outcome created by a single winner

- Generally lacks any follow-up once the prize is awarded
- No investments in making the specifications of the invention accessible and useful to the general public

Benefits of Prize Competitions to Participants

A. Benefits to Members of Prize Panels/Grantors

- Enhanced reputation and celebrity
- Networking opportunities
- Increased likelihood of future award
- Access to privileged information
- Bypass labor market mechanisms
  Numerous prize contestants working on solution without compensation; reduces costs of monitoring and other transactions costs
- Redistribution of risk
  Prizes eliminate risk of innovation for the grantor by shifting the costs to outsiders: payment made only if successful outcome is achieved
- Transforms process of technological change ("trial and error and error") into a single event

B. Benefits to Prize Winners

- Monetary payout may be a windfall rather than an inducement
- "The prize is not the goal"
  Many contestants incur expenditures that exceed the award itself. They benefit from returns in adjacent markets, celebrity and advertising, product differentiation, information and learning gained from the projects of other participants, and the prospect of stacking awards (pursuing additional prizes/grants)
- Prize facilitates access to venture capital and other forms of funding

Assessment of Inducement Prize Systems

The assessment of prize systems tends to be biased, drawn from unrepresentative case studies rather than from systematic empirical analysis. A more objective evaluation needs to incorporate the following issues:

- Opportunity costs
  What are the next-best alternatives that are sacrificed when prizes are offered for a particular problem (such as "finding out whether we are alone in the universe")?
- Technology creation versus diversion
  Do inducement prizes create new inventions or merely divert resources toward the prize?

- Post hoc, ergo propter hoc fallacies
  The tendency to incorrectly attribute causality simply because an outcome (invention) occurs after a particular event (prize offer)
- Adverse selection and lemons problem
  If applicants must choose between prizes and returns in the market, the tendency is for those with commercially valuable ideas to bypass the prize system and those with "lemons" to lobby for administered awards
- Stacking of awards
  When applicants can obtain multiple forms of compensation, an initial prize winner has a greater tendency to pursue a series of administered payouts rather than to attempt to gain returns in the market through commercialization
- Prizes may serve as windfalls rather than incentives, if the benefits to the contestants are nonmonetary or obtained in adjacent markets
- The paradox of prizes
  The value of nonmonetary prizes depends on relative scarcity—if everyone gets a gold star, then the signal value is zero; if the signal value is significant, their allocation is likely to generate controversy, which creates an incentive for grantors to inflate the number of awards, which in turn diminishes their signal value
- Prize races: returns to losers?
  From the point of view of the monopsony buyer, specific targeted prizes are more effective, but this is more costly for the losing competitors, who are less likely to obtain returns from related markets
- Prize systems as lotteries
  Lotteries are essentially regressive; wealthier contestants are more likely to win, especially in challenges that require long-term commitments and expenditures
- Expected payouts
  Cannot be accurately estimated because of unpredictable factors such as perceptions of fairness, credibility of grantors, effort of other teams in competition, etc.
- Option value of innovations
  Prizes involve the upfront exercise of the option on an array of innovation choices; likely to foreclose prematurely on future potential prospects and outcomes
- Effectiveness as inducement mechanism
  If "the prize is not the goal" and motivations and objectives of contestants are unpredictable, uncertain, diffuse, and imprecise, this implies that such awards are unlikely to function effectively as mechanisms to induce a particular objective

When Are Prizes (Potentially) Effective?

- To achieve philanthropic or nonprofit objectives
  This might include circumstances where market failure occurs, although the ultimate goal should be to enable markets to work rather than to replace the market mechanism with monopsonies
- Social objectives
  Prizes can help to promote unique, qualitative, social, or technical goals that are not scalable or for which there is no market
- To publicize or draw attention to otherwise ignored issues

To focus attention, facilitate coordination, or signal quality: however, if the objective is publicity or opportunity to work with/learn from other competitors, then from a social perspective there are likely to be more effective means of marketing

- As signals of quality

  In markets for experience goods and instances where informational costs are high
- Design of prize system
  - Transparency and accountability in rules and decision-making
  - Projects with short completion times

    Since the revenue is fixed, a longer time period increases uncertainty and costs to participants, which reduces expected profits
  - Finance is staggered, with follow-up monitoring
  - Coordination among prize-granting agencies to prevent duplicative efforts
  - Specific mechanisms in place for scaling, commercialization to meet consumer needs
  - Rules to eliminate rent-seeking; overcompensation through multiple sources
  - Governance issues are explicitly recognized and addressed
- Government as prize sponsors

  For economic efficiency, the government should have broader objectives than that of a private monopsony, enable open and effective governance, and promote social welfare
  - Procurement should take place through the open market rather than through prize competitions
  - Redistributional effects and deadweight losses associated with funding prizes through taxation
  - Measures to reduce transaction costs and barriers to entry
  - Policies to reduce the negative impact on losers in the competition
  - Avoid crowding out (where state initiatives simply displace private efforts)
  - Measures to ensure that inventions are scalable, and reduced to practical use that will benefit the final user
  - Disclosure and public domain

  As in the case of the patent system, state-funded prize technologies should be disclosed in sufficient detail to be accessible and usable to a person who is skilled in the arts and deposited in the public domain

In sum, the distortions and deadweight loss of monopsony prizes and administered systems can lead to significant welfare costs. Prizes and prize systems are most effective when they mimic the rules and standards of the market mechanism and the flexibility of its adjacent institutions.

Select Bibliography

Acemoglu, Daron. 1995. "Reward Structures and the Allocation of Talent." *European Economic Review* 39 (1): 17–33.

Acemoglu, Daron, Jacob Moscona, and James A. Robinson. 2016. "State Capacity and American Technology: Evidence from the Nineteenth Century." *American Economic Review* 106 (5): 61–67.

Acemoglu, Daron, and James A. Robinson. 2013. *Why Nations Fail: The Origins of Power, Prosperity, and Poverty.* New York: Broadway Business.

Aghion, Philippe, L. Ljungqvist, Peter Howitt, Peter W. Howitt, Maxine Brant-Collett, and Cecilia García-Peñalosa. 1998. *Endogenous Growth Theory.* Cambridge, MA: MIT Press.

Ahn, JaeBin, Amit K. Khandelwal, and Shang-Jin Wei. 2011. "The Role of Intermediaries in Facilitating Trade." *Journal of International Economics* 84 (1): 73–85.

Alder, Ken. 2010. *Engineering the Revolution: Arms and Enlightenment in France, 1763–1815.* Chicago: University of Chicago Press.

Aldrich, Mark. 1997. *Safety First: Technology, Labor, and Business in the Building of American Work Safety 1870–1939.* Baltimore: Johns Hopkins University Press.

Allan, David G. C. 1979. "The Society for the Encouragement of Arts, Manufactures and Commerce: Organisation, Membership and Objectives in the First Three Decades (1755–84)." PhD dissertation, University of London.

Allen, Robert C. 1999. "Tracking the Agricultural Revolution in England." *Economic History Review* 52 (2): 209–235.

Allen, Robert C. 2009. *The British Industrial Revolution in Global Perspective.* Cambridge: Cambridge University Press.

Anderson, Robert D. 1982. "New Light on French Secondary Education in the Nineteenth Century." *Social History* 7 (2): 147–165.

Andrews, Edward Deming, and Faith Andrews. 1982. *Work and Worship among the Shakers: Their Craftsmanship and Economic Order.* New York: Dover Publications.

Arora, Ashish, Andrea Fosfuri, and Alfonso Gambardella. 2004. *Markets for Technology: The Economics of Innovation and Corporate Strategy.* Cambridge, MA: MIT Press.

Arora, Ashish, Wesley M. Cohen, and John P. Walsh. 2016. "The acquisition and commercialization of invention in American manufacturing: Incidence and impact." *Research Policy* 45 (6): 1113–1128.

Arrow, Kenneth. 1962. "Economic Welfare and the Allocation of Resources for Invention." In *The Rate and Direction of Inventive Activity: Economic and Social Factors,* 609–626. Cambridge, MA: National Bureau of Economic Research.

Babbage, Charles. 1830. *Reflections on the Decline of Science in England, and on Some of Its Causes.* London: B. Fellowes.

Bally, Edward, and Edward Dubied. 1878. *Industry and Manufactures in the United States: Look Out for Yourselves!* Boston: Beacon Press.

Barany, Michael J. 2015. "The Myth and the Medal." *Notices of the AMS* 62 (1).

Bardhan, Pranab, and John E. Roemer. 1992. "Market Socialism: A Case for Rejuvenation." *Journal of Economic Perspectives* 6 (3): 101–116.

Barker, Richard J. 1969. "The Conseil General des Manufactures under Napoleon (1810–1814)." *French Historical Studies* 6 (2): 185–213.

Barnes, Sarah V. 1996. "England's Civic Universities and the Triumph of the Oxbridge Ideal." *History of Education Quarterly* 36 (3): 271–305.

Baten, Joerg, and Jan Luiten Van Zanden. 2008. "Book Production and the Onset of Modern Economic Growth." *Journal of Economic Growth* 13 (3): 217–235.

Baumol, William J. 1990. "Entrepreneurship: Productive, Unproductive, and Destructive." *Journal of Political Economy* 98 (5): 893–921.

Beard, Charles A., and Mary Beard. 1927. *The Rise of American Civilization.* New York: Macmillan.

Beauchamp, Christopher. 2015. "The First Patent Litigation Explosion." *Yale Law Journal* 125: 848.

Bektas, M. Yakup, and Maurice Crosland. 1992. "The Copley Medal: The Establishment of a Reward System in the Royal Society, 1731–1839." *Notes and Records of the Royal Society* 46 (1): 43–76.

Bellamy, Edward. 1888. *Looking Backward, 2000–1887.* Boston: Ticknor.

Benabou, R., and J. Tirole. 2003. "Intrinsic and Extrinsic Motivation." *Review of Economic Studies* 70 (3): 489–520.

Ben-David, Joseph. 1960. "Scientific Productivity and Academic Organization in Nineteenth Century Medicine." *American Sociological Review* 25 (6): 828–843.

Benkler, Yochai. 2002. "Coase's Penguin, or, Linux and 'The Nature of the Firm.'" *Yale Law Journal* 1: 369–446.

Bentham, Jeremy. 1825. *The Rationale of Reward.* London: Hunt.

Berg, Maxine. 1982. *The Machinery Question and the Making of Political Economy 1815–1848.* Cambridge: Cambridge University Press.

Bergson, Abram. 1967. "Market Socialism Revisited." *Journal of Political Economy* 75 (5): 655–673.

Bessen, James, and Michael J. Meurer. 2008. *Patent Failure: How Judges, Bureaucrats, and Lawyers Put Innovators at Risk.* Princeton, NJ: Princeton University Press.

Bingham, Alpheus, and Dwayne Spradlin. 2011. *The Open Innovation Marketplace: Creating Value in the Challenge Driven Enterprise.* London: FT Press.

Boldrin, Michele, and David K. Levine. 2008. *Against Intellectual Monopoly.* New York: Cambridge University Press.

Bonassieux, Pierre, and Eugène Lelong. 1900. *Conseil de Commerce et Bureau du Commerce, 1700–1791, Inventaire analytique des procès-verbaux.* Paris: Imprimerie Nationale.

Borjas, George J., and Kirk B. Doran. 2015. "Prizes and Productivity How Winning the Fields Medal Affects Scientific Output." *Journal of Human Resources* 50 (3): 728–758.

Bourdieu, Pierre. 1998. *The State Nobility: Elite Schools in the Field of Power.* Palo Alto: Stanford University Press.

Bowden, Witt. 1919. *The Rise of the Great Manufacturers in England, 1760–1790.* London: H.R. Haas.

Bradley, Margaret. 1979. "The Financial Basis of French Scientific Education and Scientific Institutions in Paris, 1790–1815." *Annals of Science* 36 (5): 451–491.

Brandt, L., D. Ma, and T. G. Rawski. 2014. "From Divergence to Convergence: Reevaluating the History behind China's Economic Boom." *Journal of Economic Literature* 52 (1): 45–123.

Branstetter, Lee G., Raymond Fisman, and C. Fritz Foley. 2006. "Do Stronger Intellectual Property Rights Increase International Technology Transfer?" *Quarterly Journal of Economics* 121 (1): 321–349.

Bray, Francesca. 2007. "Gender and Technology." *Annual Review of Anthropology* 36: 37–53.

Bresnahan, Timothy F., and Robert J. Gordon. 2008. *The Economics of New Goods.* Vol. 58. Chicago: University of Chicago Press.

Bret, Patrice. 2002. "L'État, l'armée, la science. L'invention de la recherche publique en France (1763–1830)." *Annales historiques de la Révolution française* 328 (1): 278–278.

Bridle, James. 2018. *New Dark Age: Technology, and the End of the Future.* London and New York: Verso Books.

Broadberry, Stephen, Bruce Campbell, Alexander Klein, Mark Overton, and Bas van Leeuwen. 2015. *British Economic Growth 1270–1870.* Cambridge: Cambridge University Press.

Bruce, Robert V. 1989. *Lincoln and the Tools of War.* Urbana-Champaign: University of Illinois Press.

Bruegel, Martin. 1997. "Du temps annuel au temps quotidien: la conserve appertisée à la conquête du marché, 1810–1920." *Revue d'histoire moderne et contemporaine* 44 (1): 40–67.

Bruland, Kristine. 2004. "Industrialisation and Technological Change." *Cambridge Economic History of Modern Britain* 1: 1700–1860.

Brunt, Liam, Josh Lerner, and Tom Nicholas. 2012. "Inducement Prizes and Innovation." *Journal of Industrial Economics* 60 (4): 657–696.

Bulletin. Various years. Paris: La Société d'Encouragement pour l'Industrie Nationale.

Burhop, Carsten. 2010. "The Transfer of Patents in Imperial Germany." *Journal of Economic History* 70 (4): 921–939.

Burton, M. Diane, and Tom Nicholas. 2017. "Prizes, Patents and the Search for Longitude." *Explorations in Economic History* 64: 21–36.

Buterin, Vitalik. 2014. "A Next-Generation Smart Contract and Decentralized Application Platform." Ethereum White Paper.

Butrica, Andrew J. 1998. "Creating a Past: The Founding of the Société d'encouragement pour l'industrie nationale Yesterday and Today." *Public Historian* 20 (4): 21–42.

Cantor, Geoffrey, and Sally Shuttleworth, eds. 2004. *Science Serialized: Representation of the Sciences in Nineteenth-Century Periodicals.* Cambridge, MA: MIT Press.

Cardozo, Benjamin Nathan. 1921. *The Nature of the Judicial Process.* New Haven, CT: Yale University Press.

Cardwell, Donald, Stephen Lowell, and Richard Leslie Hills. 2003. *The Development of Science and Technology in Nineteenth-Century Britain: The Importance of Manchester.* Variorum collected studies series, CS765. Farnham: Ashgate.

Casanova, Jean-Claude, and Maurice Lévy-Leboyer. 1991. *Entre l'État et le marché. L'économie française des années 1880 à nos jours.* Paris: Gallimard.

Casson, Herbert N. 1909. *Cyrus Hall McCormick: His Life and Work.* Chicago: McClurg.

Cattell, James McKeen. 1906. *A Statistical Study of American Men of Science.* Vol. 24. Science New Series.

Chang, Ha-Joon. 2003. *Globalization, Economic Development and the Role of the State.* London: Zed Books.

Chesnais, François. 1993. "The French National System of Innovation." In *National Innovation Systems: A Comparative Analysis,* edited by Richard R. Nelson, 192–229. New York: Oxford University Press.

Clark, Gregory. 2008. *Farewell to Alms: A Brief Economic History of the World*. Vol. 27. Princeton, NJ: Princeton University Press.

Coase, Ronald H. 2012. *The Firm, the Market, and the Law*. Chicago: University of Chicago Press.

Cohen, Linda, and Roger Noll. 1991. *The Technology Pork Barrel*. Washington, DC: Brookings Institution.

Cohen, Wesley M., and Richard C. Levin.1989. "Empirical Studies of Innovation and Market Structure." In *Handbook of Industrial Organization*, 2, edited by Richard Schmalensee, and Robert D. Willig, 1059–1107. New York: Elsevier.

Cook, William W. 1920. *A Treatise on Telegraph Law*. New York: Wm. Siegrist.

Cooke, William F. 1857. *The Electrical Telegraph: Was it Invented by Professor Wheatstone?* London: W. H. Smith and Son.

Cordato, M. F. 1989. *Representing the Expansion of Woman's Sphere: Women's Work and Culture at the World's Fairs of 1876, 1893, and 1904*. New York: New York University.

Cowen, Tyler, and E. P. Dutton. 2011. *The Great Stagnation: How America Ate All the Low-Hanging Fruit of Modern History, Got Sick, and Will (Eventually) Feel Better*. New York: Dutton.

Crafts, Nicholas F. R., and C. Knick Harley. 1992. "Output Growth and the British Industrial Revolution: A Restatement of the Crafts-Harley View." *Economic History Review* 45 (4): 703–730.

Crawford, Elisabeth. 1990. "The Secrecy of Nobel Prize Selections in the Sciences and Its Effect on Documentation and Research." *Proceedings of the American Philosophical Society* 134 (4): 408–419.

Crawford, E., J. L. Heilbron, and R. Ullrich. 1987. *The Nobel Population 1901–1937: A Census of the Nominators and Nominees for the Prizes in Physics and Chemistry*. Berkeley: University of California.

Crosland, Maurice. 1979. "From Prizes to Grants in the Support of Scientific Research in France in the Nineteenth Century: The Montyon Legacy." *Minerva* 17 (3): 355–380.

Crouzet, François. 2003. "The Historiography of French Economic Growth in the Nineteenth Century." *Economic History Review* 56 (2): 215–242.

Daguerre, Louis Jacques Mandé. 1839. *Historique et description des procédés du daguerréotype et du diorama*. Paris: Lerebours/Susse.

Dardo, Mauro. 2004. *Nobel Laureates and Twentieth-Century Physics*. Cambridge: Cambridge University Press.

Darney, Virginia. 1982. *Women and World's Fairs: American International Expositions, 1876–1904*. PhD dissertation. Emory University.

Daumalin, Xavier, and Henri Tachoire. 2007. "Un couple d'innovateurs marseillais et la Société d'encouragement pour l'industrie nationale: les époux Degrand-Gurgey." In *Encourager l'innovation en France et en Europe*, 123–140. Paris: CTHS.

Daumard, Adeline. 1958. "Les élèves de l'École polytechnique de 1815 à 1848." *Revue d'histoire moderne et contemporaine* 5 (3): 226–234.

Davenport, Samuel Thomas. 1868. "A Glance at the Past and Present of the Society of Arts, with Some Suggestions as to the Future." *Journal of the Society of Arts* 17 (836): 1–28.

David, Paul A., Bronwyn H. Hall, and Andrew A. Toole. 2000. "Is Public R&D a Complement or Substitute for Private R&D? A Review of the Econometric Evidence." *Research Policy* 29 (4–5): 497–529.

Davies, Robert B. 1969. "'Peacefully Working to Conquer the World': The Singer Manufacturing Company in Foreign Markets, 1854–1889." *Business History Review* 43 (3): 299–325.

Davis, Lance Edwin, and Robert A. Huttenback. 1986. *Mammon and the Pursuit of Empire: The Political Economy of British Imperialism 1860–1912.* Cambridge: Cambridge University Press.

de Neuville, A. 1900. "Le génie de l'invention chez les femmes." *La Revue mondiale: ancienne Revue des revues* 32: 184–191.

De Ville, Kenneth Allen. 1990. *Medical Malpractice in Nineteenth-Century America: Origins and Legacy.* New York: New York University Press.

Demsetz, Harold. 1964. "The Exchange and Enforcement of Property Rights." *JLE* 7 (October): 11–26.

Demsetz, Harold. 1969. "Information and Efficiency: Another Viewpoint." *Journal of Law and Economics* 12 (1): 1–22.

Des Cilleuls, Alfred. 1898. *Histoire et régime de la grande industrie en France aux XVIIe et XVIIIe siècles.* Paris: Giard et Brière.

Desclosières, Gabriel. 1881. *Vie et inventions de Philippe de Girard, inventeur de la filature mécanique du lin.* 2e éd. Paris: A. Pigoreau.

Diamond, Jared M. 1998. *Guns, Germs and Steel: A Short History of Everybody for the Last 13,000 Years.* New York: Random House.

Dobbin, Frank. 1994. *Forging Industrial Policy: The United States, Britain, and France in the Railway Age.* New York: Cambridge University Press.

Döring, Thomas, and Jan Schnellenbach. 2006. "What Do We Know about Geographical Knowledge Spillovers and Regional Growth?: A Survey of the Literature." *Regional Studies* 40 (3): 375–395.

Dossie, Robert. 1768–1782. *Memoirs of agriculture, and other oeconomical arts.* Vol. 1–3. London: J. Nourse.

Dowey, James. 2017. "Mind over Matter: Access to Knowledge and the British Industrial Revolution." PhD dissertation, London School of Economics and Political Science.

Dubbey, John Michael. 2004. *The Mathematical Work of Charles Babbage.* Cambridge: Cambridge University Press.

Eamon, William. 2006. "Markets, piazzas, and villages." In *The Cambridge history of science,* edited by David Lindberg et al., vol. 3, 206–223. Cambridge: Cambridge University Press.

Easterly, William. 2001. *The Elusive Quest for Growth.* Cambridge, MA: MIT Press.

Eccles, R. G. 1899. "Do We Obey the Code of Ethics?" *Journal of the American Medical Association* 33 (27): 1646–1648.

Elliot, Jonathan, ed. 1891. *Debates in the Several State Conventions, on the Adoption of the Federal Constitution, as Recommended by the General Convention at Philadelphia, in 1787.* Philadelphia: J. B. Lippincott.

Engerman, Stanley L., and J. Matthew Gallman. 1997. "The Civil War Economy: A Modern View." In *On the Road to Total War: The American Civil War and the German Wars of Unification, 1861–1871,* edited by Jorg Nagler and Stig Förster, 217–248. Cambridge: Cambridge University Press.

Engerman, Stanley L., and Kenneth L. Sokoloff. 2005. "Institutional and Non-Institutional Explanations of Economic Differences." In *Handbook of New Institutional Economics,* edited by Claude Ménard and Mary Shirley, 639–665. Dordrecht: Springer.

Engerman, Stanley L., and Kenneth L. Sokoloff. 2012. *Economic Development in the Americas since 1500: Endowments and Institutions*. New York: Cambridge University Press.

English, James, F. 2005. *The Economy of Prestige: Prizes, Awards, and the Circulation of Cultural Value*. Cambridge, MA: Harvard University Press.

Epstein, Stephan R., and Maarten Prak, eds. 2008. *Guilds, Innovation and the European Economy, 1400–1800*. Cambridge: Cambridge University Press.

European Defense Industrial Base Forum. 2013. "State Ownership in the European Defense Industry: Change or Continuity?" Occasional Paper.

Fama, Eugene F. 1980. "Agency Problems and the Theory of the Firm." *Journal of Political Economy* 88 (2): 288–307.

Fehr, Ernst, and Armin Falk. 2002. "Psychological Foundations of Incentives." *European Economic Review* 46 (4–5): 687–724.

Feuerverger, Andrey, Yu He, and Shashi Khatri. 2012. "Statistical Significance of the Netflix Challenge." *Statistical Science* 27 (2): 202–231.

Field, Alexander J. 2003. "The Most Technologically Progressive Decade of the Century." *American Economic Review* 93 (4): 1399–1413.

Fishback, Price V., and Shawn E. Kantor. 2007. *A Prelude to the Welfare State: The Origins of Workers' Compensation*. Chicago: University of Chicago Press.

Fisk, Catherine L. 1998. "Removing the 'Fuel of Interest' from the 'Fire of Genius': Law and the Employee-Inventor, 1830–1930." *University of Chicago Law Review* 65 (4): 1127–1198.

Ford, Caroline C. 2016. *Natural Interests: The Contest over Environment in Modern France*. Cambridge, MA: Harvard University Press.

Fowler Jr., William M. 2017. *Steam Titans: Cunard, Collins, and the Epic Battle for Commerce on the North Atlantic*. New York: Bloomsbury Publishing.

Fox, Robert. 1968. "The John Scott Medal." *Proceedings of the American Philosophical Society* 112 (6): 416–430.

Fox, Robert. 1973. "Scientific Enterprise and the Patronage of Research in France 1800–70." *Minerva* 11 (4): 442–473.

Fox, Robert, and Anna Guagnini, eds. 1993. *Education, Technology and Industrial Performance in Europe, 1850–1939*. Cambridge: Cambridge University Press.

Freeman, Chris. 1995. "The 'National System of Innovation' in Historical Perspective." *Cambridge Journal of Economics* 19 (1): 5–24.

Freeman, John R., and Raymond D. Duvall. 1984. "International Economic Relations and the Entrepreneurial State." *Economic Development and Cultural Change* 32 (2): 373–400.

Fressoz, Jean-Baptiste. 2007. "The Gas Lighting Controversy: Technological Risk, Expertise, and Regulation in Nineteenth-Century Paris and London." *Journal of Urban History* 33 (5): 729–755.

Frey, B. 1997. *Not Just for the Money—An Economic Theory of Personal Motivation*. Cheltenham, UK: Edward Elgar.

Freyer, Tony A. 2006. *Antitrust and Global Capitalism, 1930–2004*. Cambridge: Cambridge University Press.

Friedman, Robert Marc. 2001. *The Politics of Excellence: Behind the Nobel Prize in Science*. New York: Times Books.

Fuller, Claud E., and Richard D. Steuart. 1944. *Firearms of the Confederacy*. Huntington, W.Va.: Standard Publications.

Furman, Jeffrey L., Markus Nagler, and Martin Watzinger. 2018. "Disclosure and Subsequent Innovation: Evidence from the Patent Depository Library Program." No. w24660. Cambridge, MA: National Bureau of Economic Research.

Furman, Jeffrey L., Michael E. Porter, and Scott Stern. 2002. "The Determinants of National Innovative Capacity." *Research Policy* 31 (6): 899–933.

Galasso A., M. Schankerman, and C. Serrano. 2013. "Trading and Enforcing Patent Rights." *RAND Journal of Economics* 44: 275–312.

Gallini, Nancy, and Suzanne Scotchmer. 2002. "Intellectual Property: When Is It the Best Incentive System?" *Innovation Policy and the Economy* 2: 51–77.

Galvez-Behar, G. 2008. *La République des inventeurs: Propriété et organisation de l'innovation en France (1791–1922)*. Rennes: Presses universitaires de Rennes.

Garrigos-Simon, Fernando J., Ignacio Gil-Pechuán, and Sofia Estelles-Miguel. 2015. *Advances in Crowdsourcing*. New York: Springer.

Geiger, Roger L., and Nathan M. Sorber. 2013. *The Land-Grant Colleges and the Reshaping of American Higher Education*. New York: Routledge.

Giffard, Hermione. 2016. *Making Jet Engines in World War II: Britain, Germany, and the United States*. Chicago: University of Chicago Press.

Gille, Bertrand. 1959. *Recherches sur la formation de la grande entreprise capitaliste: (1815–1848)*. Paris: S.E.V.P.E.N.

Gille, Bertrand. 1961. *Le Conseil général des manufactures (inventaire analytique des procès-verbaux, 1810–1829)*. Paris: EHESS.

Gillespie, Charles C., ed. 1980. *Dictionary of Scientific Biography*. New York: Charles Scribner and Sons.

Gillispie, Charles C. 2004. *Science and Polity in France: The End of the Old Regime*. Princeton, NJ: Princeton University Press.

Glaeser, Edward L., and Andrei Shleifer. 2003. "The Rise of the Regulatory State." *Journal of Economic Literature* 41 (2): 401–425.

Gneezy, Uri, Stephan Meier, and Pedro Rey-Biel. 2011. "When and Why Incentives (Don't) Work to Modify Behavior." *Journal of Economic Perspectives* 25 (4): 191–210.

Goldfarb, Brent, and Magnus Henrekson. 2003. "Bottom-Up versus Top-Down Policies towards the Commercialization of University Intellectual Property." *Research Policy* 32 (4): 639–658.

Goldin, Claudia. 2001. "The Human-Capital Century and American Leadership: Virtues of the Past." *Journal of Economic History* 61 (2): 263–292.

Goldin, Claudia, and Larry F. Katz. 2008. *The Race between Education and Technology*. Cambridge, MA: Harvard University Press.

Goldsmith, Oliver. 1834. *Miscellaneous Works*. London: Allan Bell & Co.

Golinski, Jan. 1999. *Science as public culture: Chemistry and enlightenment in Britain, 1760–1820*. Cambridge: Cambridge University Press.

Gompers, Paul, and Josh Lerner. 2001. "The venture capital revolution." *Journal of Economic Perspectives* 15 (2): 145–168.

González, J. Patricio Sáiz. 1996. *Legislación histórica sobre propiedad industrial: España (1759–1929)*. Madrid: Oficina Española Patentes.

González, J. Patricio Sáiz. 1999. *Invención, patentes e innovación en la España contemporánea*. Madrid: Oficina Española Patentes.

Goodwin, George. 2016. *Benjamin Franklin in London: The British Life of America's Founding Father*. New Haven, CT: Yale University Press.

Gordon, Robert J. 2016. *The Rise and Fall of American Growth: The US Standard of Living since the Civil War*. Princeton, NJ: Princeton University Press.

Gowing, Margaret. 1978. "Science, Technology and Education: England in 1870." *Oxford Review of Education* 4 (1): 3–17.

Great Britain Board of Trade. 1907. *Report of the Committee Appointed by the Board of Trade to Make Enquiries with Reference to the Participation of Great Britain in Great International Exhibitions*. London: HMSO.

Great Britain Committee on International Exhibitions. 1908. *Report of the Committee Appointed by the Board of Trade to Make Enquiries with Reference to the Participation of Great Britain in Great International Exhibitions*. London: HMSO.

Greenstein, Shane M. 2017. *How the Internet Became Commercial: Innovation, Privatization, and the Birth of a New Network*. Princeton, NJ: Princeton University Press.

Greif, Avner. 2006. *Institutions and the Path to the Modern Economy: Lessons from Medieval Trade*. New York: Cambridge University Press.

Griffiths, Trevor, Philip A. Hunt, and Patrick K. O'Brien. 1992. "Inventive Activity in the British Textile Industry, 1700–1800." *Journal of Economic History* 52 (4): 881–906.

Griliches, Zvi. 1998. "Patent Statistics as Economic Indicators: A Survey." In *R&D and Productivity: The Econometric Evidence*, 287–343. Chicago: University of Chicago Press.

Haber, Stephen. 2013. *Crony Capitalism and Economic Growth in Latin America: Theory and Evidence*. Palo Alto: Hoover Institution Press.

Hall, A. Rupert. 1974. "The Royal Society of Arts: Two Centuries of Progress in Science and Technology." *Journal of the Royal Society of Arts* 122 (5218): 641–658.

Hall, Bronwyn, Christian Helmers, Mark Rogers, and Vania Sena. 2014. "The Choice between Formal and Informal Intellectual Property: A Review." *Journal of Economic Literature* 52 (2): 375–423.

Hargittai, István. 2002. *The Road to Stockholm: Nobel Prizes, Science, and Scientists*. Oxford: Oxford University Press.

Hayek, Friedrich A. 1937. "Economics and Knowledge." *Economica* 4 (13): 33–54.

Hayek, Friedrich A. 1945. "The Use of Knowledge in Society." *American Economic Review* 35 (4): 519–530.

Hayek, Friedrich A. 1948. *Individualism and Economic Order*. Chicago: University of Chicago.

Hayek, Friedrich A. 2012. *Law, Legislation and Liberty: A New Statement of the Liberal Principles of Justice and Political Economy*. London: Routledge.

Heckscher, Eli F. 2013. *Mercantilism*. London: Routledge.

Hegde, Deepak, and Hong Luo. 2017. "Patent Publication and the Market for Ideas." *Management Science* 64 (2): 652–672.

Heide, Lars. 2009. *Punched-Card Systems and the Early Information Explosion, 1880–1945*. Baltimore, MD: Johns Hopkins University Press.

Hendrix, Michael. 2014. *The Power of Prizes: Incentivizing Radical Innovation*. U.S. Chamber of Commerce Foundation.

Herbertz, Claus, and Dirk Sliwka. 2013. "When Higher Prizes Lead to Lower Efforts—The Impact of Favoritism in Tournaments." *Economics Letters* 120 (2): 188–191.

Hilaire-Pérez, Liliane. 1991. "Invention and the State in 18th-Century France." *Technology and Culture* 32 (4): 911–931.

Hilaire-Pérez, Liliane. 2000. *L'invention technique au siècle des Lumières*. Paris: Albin Michel.

Hilaire-Pérez, Liliane, Christine MacLeod, and Alessandro Nuvolari. 2013. "Innovation without Patents." *Revue économique* 64 (1): 5–8.

Hirsch, Fred. 2005. *Social Limits to Growth*. London: Routledge.

Hirsch, Jean-Pierre. 1991. *Les deux rêves du commerce: entreprise et institutions dans la région lilloise (1780–1860)*. Paris: École des Hautes Études en Sciences Sociales.

Hobday, Mike. 1995. "East Asian Latecomer Firms: Learning the Technology of Electronics." *World Development* 23 (7): 1171–1193.

Hoffman, Philip T. 2015. *Why Did Europe Conquer the World?* Vol. 68. Princeton, NJ: Princeton University Press.

Hoke, Donald. 1990. *Ingenious Yankees: The Rise of the American System of Manufactures in the Private Sector*. New York: Columbia University Press.

Holte, Ryan T. 2016. "Patent Submission Policies." *Akron L. Rev.* 50: 637.

Horn, Jeff. 2015. *Economic Development in Early Modern France: The Privilege of Liberty, 1650–1820*. New York: Cambridge University Press.

Hornbeck, Richard, and Pinar Keskin. 2015. "Does Agriculture Generate Local Economic Spillovers? Short-Run and Long-Run Evidence from the Ogallala Aquifer." *American Economic Journal: Economic Policy* 7 (2): 192–213.

Horwitz, Morton J. 1977. *The Transformation of American Law, 1780–1860*. New York: Oxford University Press.

Howells, Jeremy. 2006. "Intermediation and the Role of Intermediaries in Innovation." *Research Policy* 35 (5): 715–728.

Howse, Derek. 1998. "Britain's Board of Longitude: The Finances, 1714–1828." *Mariner's Mirror* 84 (4): 400–417.

Hsieh, Chang-Tai, Erik Hurst, Charles I. Jones, and Peter J. Klenow. 2019. "The Allocation of Talent and Us Economic Growth." *Econometrica* 87 (5): 1439–1474.

Hu, Albert G. Z., and Gary H. Jefferson. 2009. "A Great Wall of Patents: What Is Behind China's Recent Patent Explosion?" *Journal of Development Economics* 90 (1): 57–68.

Huddy, Xenophon P. 1906. *The Law of Automobiles*. Albany, NY: M. Bender.

Hudson, Derek, and Kenneth W. Luckhurst. 1954. *The Royal Society of Arts, 1754–1954*. London: J. Murray.

Hunter, Michael. 1994. *The Royal Society and Its Fellows, 1669–1700, the Morphology of an Early Scientific Institution*. Oxford: British Society for the History of Science.

Hvistendahl, Mara. 2013. "China's Publication Bazaar." *Science* 342 (6162): 1035–1039.

Hyde, William. 1920. *The English Patents of Monopoly*. Vol. 1. Cambridge, MA: Harvard University Press.

Jacob, Margaret C. 1997. *Scientific Culture and the Making of the Industrial West*. New York: Oxford University Press.

Jaffe, Adam B., and Josh Lerner. 2011. *Innovation and Its Discontents: How Our Broken Patent System Is Endangering Innovation and Progress, and What to Do about It*. Princeton, NJ: Princeton University Press.

Jaffe, Adam B., and Manuel Trajtenberg. 2002. *Patents, Citations, and Innovations: A Window on the Knowledge Economy*. Cambridge, MA: MIT Press.

Janeway, William H. 2012. *Doing Capitalism in the Innovation Economy: Markets, Speculation and the State*. Cambridge: Cambridge University Press.

Jensen, Michael C., and William H. Meckling. 1976. "Theory of the Firm: Managerial Behavior, Agency Costs and Ownership Structure." *Journal of Financial Economics* 3 (4): 305–360.

Johnson, Benjamin Pierce. 1863. *Report on International Exhibition of Industry and Art.* London, 1862: C. Van Benthuysen.

Johnson, James, and John Henry Johnson. 1890. *The Patentee's Manual: A Treatise on the Law and Practice of Patents for Inventions.* London: Longmans.

Jones, Benjamin F. 2009. "The Burden of Knowledge and the "Death of the Renaissance Man": Is Innovation Getting Harder?" *Review of Economic Studies* 76 (1): 283–317.

Jones, Charles I., and Paul M. Romer. 2010. "The New Kaldor Facts: Ideas, Institutions, Population, and Human Capital." *American Economic Journal: Macroeconomics* 2 (1): 224–245.

Kaminski, John P., et al., eds. 2003. *Ratification of the Constitution by the States.* New York: Wisconsin Historical Society Press.

Kantha, S. Sri. 1991. "The Question of Nepotism in the Award of Nobel Prizes: A Critique of the View of Hans Krebs." *Medical Hypotheses* 34 (1): 28–32.

Karsten, Peter. 1997. *Heart Versus Head: Judge Made Law in Nineteenth Century America.* Chapel Hill: University of North Carolina Press.

Kay, Luciano. 2012. *Technological Innovation and Prize Incentives: The Google Lunar X Prize and Other Aerospace Competitions.* Cheltenham, UK: Edward Elgar Publishing.

Kealey, Terence, and Martin Ricketts. 2014. "Modelling Science as a Contribution Good." *Research Policy* 43 (6): 1014–1024.

Keller, Wolfgang. 2002. "Geographic Localization of International Technology Diffusion." *American Economic Review* 92 (1): 120–142.

Kenrick, W. 1774. *An Address to the Artists and Manufacturers of Great Britain; Respecting an Application to Parliament for the Farther Encouragement of New Discoveries and Inventions in the Useful Arts.* London: Domville.

Kent, Max Louis. 2007. "The British Enlightenment and the Spirit of the Industrial Revolution: The Society for the Encouragement of Arts, Manufactures and Commerce (1754–1815)." PhD dissertation, University of California, Los Angeles.

Keyder, Caglar. 1985. "State and Industry in France, 1750–1914." *American Economic Review* 75 (2): 308–314.

Khan, B. Zorina. 1995. "Property Rights and Patent Litigation in Early Nineteenth-Century America." *Journal of Economic History* 55 (1): 58–97.

Khan, B. Zorina. 1999a. "Federal Antitrust Agencies and Public Policy towards Patents and Innovation." *Cornell Journal of Law and Public Policy* 9 (Fall): 133–1699.

Khan, B. Zorina. 1999b. "The Calculus of Enforcement: Legal and Economic Issues in Antitrust and Innovation." *Advances in the Study of Entrepreneurship, Innovation, and Economic Growth* 12: 61–106.

Khan, B. Zorina. 2000. "Commerce and Cooperation: Litigation and Settlement of Civil Disputes." *Journal of Economic History* 60 (4): 1088–1119.

Khan, B. Zorina. 2005. *The Democratization of Invention: Patents and Copyrights in American Economic Development, 1790–1920.* New York: Cambridge University Press.

Khan, B. Zorina. 2008a. "'Justice of the Marketplace': Legal Disputes and Economic Activity on America's Northeastern Frontier, 1700–1860." *Journal of Interdisciplinary History* 39 (1): 1–35.

Khan, B. Zorina. 2008b. "Innovations in Law and Technology, 1790–1920." In *Cambridge History of Law in America*, vol. 2, 483–530, 796–801. New York: Cambridge University Press.

Khan, B. Zorina. 2009. "War and the Returns to Entrepreneurial Innovation among U.S. Patentees, 1790–1870." *Special Issue on the Cliometrics of Patents, Brussels Economic Review* 52 (3/4): 239–274.

Khan, B. Zorina. 2010. "Looking Backward: Founding Choices in Innovation and Intellectual Property Protection." In *Founding Choices: American Economic Policy in the 1790s,* edited by Douglas Irwin and Richard Sylla, 315–342. Chicago: University of Chicago Press.

Khan, B. Zorina. 2011a. "Antitrust and Innovation Before the Sherman Act." *Antitrust Law Journal* 77 (3): 757–786.

Khan, B. Zorina. 2011b. "Premium Inventions: Patents and Prizes as Incentive Mechanisms in Britain and the United States, 1750–1930." In *Understanding Long-Run Economic Growth: Geography, Institutions, and the Knowledge Economy,* edited by Dora L. Costa and Naomi R. Lamoreaux, 205–234. Chicago: University of Chicago Press.

Khan, B. Zorina. 2013a. "Selling Ideas: An International Perspective on Patenting and Markets for Technology, 1790–1930." *Business History Review* 87 (1): 39–68.

Khan, B. Zorina. 2013b. "Trolls and Other Patent Inventions: Economic History and the Patent Controversy in the Twenty-First Century." *George Mason Law Review* 21: 825.

Khan, B. Zorina. 2013c. "Going for Gold: Industrial Fairs and Innovation in the Nineteenth-Century United States." Special Issue on Innovation without Patents, *Revue Economique* 64 (1): 89–114.

Khan, B. Zorina. 2015a. "The Impact of War on Resource Allocation: 'Creative Destruction,' Patenting, and the American Civil War." *Journal of Interdisciplinary History* 46 (3): 315–353.

Khan, B. Zorina. 2015b. "Inventing Prizes: A Historical Perspective on Innovation Awards and Technology Policy." *Business History Review* 89 (4): 631–660.

Khan, B. Zorina. 2016. "Invisible Women: Entrepreneurship, Innovation, and Family Firms in Nineteenth-Century France." *Journal of Economic History* 76 (1): 163–195.

Khan, B. Zorina. 2017a. "Designing Women: Consumer Goods Innovations in Britain, France and the United States, 1750–1900." National Bureau of Economic Research Working Paper Series No. 23086.

Khan, B. Zorina. 2017b. "Prestige and Profit: The Royal Society of Arts and Incentives for Innovation, 1750–1850." National Bureau of Economic Research Working Paper Series No. 23042.

Khan, B. Zorina. 2018. "Human Capital, Knowledge and Economic Development: Evidence from the British Industrial Revolution, 1750–1930." *Cliometrica* 12 (2): 313–341.

Khan, B. Zorina. 2019a. "Intellectual Property and Economic Development: Lessons from American and European History." In *Intellectual Property and Economic Development,* edited by Carlos M. Correa. Cheltenham, UK: Edward Elgar.

Khan, B. Zorina. 2019b. "Related Investing: Corporate Ownership and Capital Mobilization during Early Industrialization." Working Paper.

Khan, B. Zorina, and Kenneth L. Sokoloff. 1998. "Patent Institutions, Industrial Organization and Early Technological Change: Britain and the United States, 1790–1850." In *Technological Revolutions in Europe,* edited by Maxine Berg and Kristine Bruland, 292–313. Cheltenham, UK: Edward Elgar.

Khan, B. Zorina, and Kenneth L. Sokoloff. 2001. "The Early Development of Intellectual Property Institutions in the United States." *Journal of Economic Perspectives* 15 (3): 233–246.

Khan, B. Zorina, and Kenneth L. Sokoloff. 2004. "Institutions and Democratic Invention in 19th-Century America: Evidence from 'Great Inventors,' 1790–1930." *American Economic Review* 94 (2): 395–401.

Khan, B. Zorina, and Kenneth Sokoloff. 2006. "Institutions and Technological Innovation during Early Economic Growth: Evidence from the Great Inventors of the United States, 1790–1930." In *Institutions, Development, and Economic Growth*, edited by Cecilia García-Peñalosa and Theo S. Eicher, 123–158. Cambridge, MA: MIT Press.

Khan, B. Zorina, and Kenneth L. Sokoloff. 2009. "A Tale of Two Countries: Innovation and Incentives among Great Inventors in Britain and the United States, 1750–1930." In *Macroeconomics in the Small and the Large*, edited by Roger Farmer, 140–156. New York: Edward Elgar.

Konvitz, Josef, and Henry Barraclough. 1987. *Cartography in France, 1660–1848: Science, Engineering, and Statecraft.* Chicago: University of Chicago Press.

Kotar, S. L., and J. E. Gessler. 2014. *Cholera: A Worldwide History.* Jefferson, NC: McFarland.

Kranakis, Eda. 1997. *Constructing a Bridge: An Exploration of Engineering Culture, Design, and Research in Nineteenth-Century France and America.* Cambridge, MA: MIT Press.

Kremer, Michael. 1998. "Patent Buyouts: A Mechanism for Encouraging Innovation." *Quarterly Journal of Economics* 113 (4): 1137–1167.

Kuegler, Alice. 2018. "The Responsiveness of Inventing: Evidence from a Patent Fee Reform." UCL Working Paper.

Lamoreaux, Naomi R., and Kenneth L. Sokoloff. 1996. "Long-Term Change in the Organization of Inventive Activity." *Proceedings of the National Academy of Sciences* 93 (23): 12686–12692.

Lamoreaux, Naomi R., and Kenneth L. Sokoloff. 2001. "Market Trade in Patents and the Rise of a Class of Specialized Inventors in the 19th-Century United States." *American Economic Review* 91 (2): 39–44.

Lamoreaux, Naomi R., and Kenneth Sokoloff. 2009. *Financing Innovation in the United States, 1870 to Present.* Vol. 1. Cambridge, MA: MIT Press.

Lamoreaux, Naomi R., Kenneth L. Sokoloff, and Dhanoos Sutthiphisal. 2011. "The Reorganization of Inventive Activity in the Early Twentieth Century US." In *Understanding Long-Run Economic Growth: Geography, Institutions, and the Knowledge Economy*, edited by Dora L. Costa and Naomi R. Lamoreaux, 235–274. Chicago: University of Chicago Press.

Lamoreaux, Naomi R., Kenneth L. Sokoloff, and Dhanoos Sutthiphisal. 2013. "Patent Alchemy: The Market for Technology in US History." *Business History Review* 87 (1): 3–38.

Landes, David S. 1949. "French Entrepreneurship and Industrial Growth in the Nineteenth Century." *Journal of Economic History* 9 (1): 45–61.

Landes, David S. 1969. *The Unbound Prometheus: Technological Change and Industrial Development in Western Europe from 1750 to the Present.* New York: Cambridge University Press.

Landes, David S. 1983. *Revolution in Time: Clocks and the Making of the Modern World.* Vol. 2000. Cambridge, MA: Belknap.

Lange, Oskar, Fred Taylor, and Benjamin Lippincott. 1938. *On the Economic Theory of Socialism.* Minneapolis: University of Minnesota Press.

Layton, Edwin T. 1990. "Newton Confronts the American Millwrights, or, Action and Reaction Are Not Always Equal." In *Beyond History of Science,* edited by Elizabeth Garber, 179–193. Bethlehem: Lehigh University Press.

Lemercier, Claire. 2003. "La chambre de commerce de Paris, acteur indispensable de la construction des normes economiques (premiere moitie du XIXE siècle)." *Genèses* 1: 50–70.

Lenoir, B. A. 1830. *Traité de la culture de la vigne et de la vinification.* Paris: Mme Ve Bouchard-Huzard.

Lerner, Joshua. 2009. *Boulevard of Broken Dreams: Why Public Efforts to Boost Entrepreneurship and Venture Capital Have Failed and What to Do about It.* Princeton, NJ: Princeton University Press.

Lévy-Leboyer, Maurice, and Jean-Claude Casanova. 1991. *Entre l'Etat et le marché: l'économie française des années 1880 à nos jours.* Paris: Gallimard.

Liu, Shimeng. 2015. "Spillovers from Universities: Evidence from the Land-Grant Program." *Journal of Urban Economics* 87: 25–41.

Lundberg, D., and H. May. 1978. "The Enlightened Reader in America." *American Quarterly* 28 (2): 262–293.

Lundvall, Bengt-Åke. 1992. *National Systems of Innovation: Towards a Theory of Innovation and Interactive Learning.* London: Pinter Publishers.

Machlup, Fritz. 2014. *Knowledge: Its Creation, Distribution and Economic Significance.* Vol. 1: *Knowledge and Knowledge Production.* Princeton, NJ: Princeton University Press.

Machlup, Fritz, and Edith Penrose. 1950. "The Patent Controversy in the Nineteenth Century." *Journal of Economic History* 10 (1): 1–29.

MacLeod, Christine. 2002. *Inventing the Industrial Revolution: The English Patent System, 1660–1800.* Cambridge: Cambridge University Press.

MacLeod, Christine. 2012. "Reluctant Entrepreneurs: Patents and State Patronage in New Technosciences." *Isis* 103 (2): 328–339.

MacLeod, Roy, and Russell Moseley. 1980. "The 'Naturals' and Victorian Cambridge: Reflections on the Anatomy of an Elite, 1851–1914." *Oxford Review of Education* 6 (2): 177–195.

Maine, Henry Sumner. 1885. *Popular Government: Four Essays.* London: Murray.

Manning, Alan. 2003. *Monopsony in Motion: Imperfect Competition in Labor Markets.* Princeton, NJ: Princeton University Press.

Marsch, Ulrich. 1994. "Strategies for Success: Research Organization in German Chemical Companies and IG Farben until 1936." *History and Technology, an International Journal* 12 (1): 23–77.

Massachusetts Charitable Mechanic Association. 1892. *Annals, 1795–1892.* Boston: Rockwell and Churchill.

Mazzucato, Mariana. 2015. *The Entrepreneurial State: Debunking Public vs. Private Sector Myths.* London: Anthem Press.

McCabe, Christopher, Karl Claxton, and Aki Tsuchiya. 2005. "Orphan Drugs and the NHS: Should We Value Rarity?" *BMJ: British Medical Journal* 331 (7523): 1016.

McCloskey, Deirdre N. 2016. *Bourgeois Equality: How Ideas, Not Capital or Institutions, Enriched the World.* Vol. 3. Chicago: University of Chicago Press.

McCloy, Shelby T. 2015. *French Inventions of the Eighteenth Century.* Lexington, KY: University Press of Kentucky.

McGaw, Judith A. 1997. "Inventors and Other Great Women: Toward a Feminist History of Technological Luminaries." *Technology and Culture* 38 (1): 214–231.

McNeill, William H. 2013. *The Pursuit of Power: Technology, Armed Force, and Society since AD 1000*. Chicago: University of Chicago Press.

Merges, Robert P. 1988. "Commercial Success and Patent Standards: Economic Perspectives on Innovation." *California Law Review* 76: 803.

Merges, Robert P. 2000. "One Hundred Years of Solicitude: Intellectual Property Law, 1900–2000." *California Law Review* 88: 2187.

Merrill, Thomas W., and Henry E. Smith. 2011. "Making Coasean Property More Coasean." *Journal of Law and Economics* 54 (4): S77–S104.

Meyer-Thurow, Georg. 1982. "The Industrialization of Invention: A Case Study from the German Chemical Industry." *Isis* 73 (3): 363–381.

Minard, Philippe. 1998. *La Fortune du colbertisme. État et industrie dans la France des Lumières*. Paris: Fayard.

Mitch, David. 2018. "The Role of Education and Skill in the British Industrial Revolution." In *The British Industrial Revolution*, edited by Joel Mokyr, 241–279. New York: Routledge.

Mohr, James C. 2002. *Doctors and the Law: Medical Jurisprudence in Nineteenth-Century America*. New York: Oxford University Press.

Mokyr, Joel. 1992. *The Lever of Riches: Technological Creativity and Economic Progress*. New York: Oxford University Press.

Mokyr, Joel. 2002. *The Gifts of Athena: Historical Origins of the Knowledge Economy*. Princeton, NJ: Princeton University Press.

Mokyr, Joel. 2016. *A Culture of Growth: The Origins of the Modern Economy*. Princeton, NJ: Princeton University Press.

Mokyr, Joel. 2018. *The British Industrial Revolution: An Economic Perspective*. London: Routledge.

Moser, Petra. 2005. "How Do Patent Laws Influence Innovation? Evidence from Nineteenth-Century World's Fairs." *American Economic Review* 95 (4): 1214–1236.

Moser, Petra. 2013. "Patents and Innovation: Evidence from Economic History." *Journal of Economic Perspectives* 27 (1): 23–44.

Mossoff, Adam. 2000. "Rethinking the Development of Patents: An Intellectual History, 1550–1800." *Hastings LJ* 52: 1255.

Mossoff, Adam. 2011. "The Rise and Fall of the First American Patent Thicket: The Sewing Machine War of the 1850s." *Arizona Law Review* 53: 165.

Mott, Frank Luther. 1930. *A History of American Magazines: 1741–1850*. Cambridge, MA: Harvard University Press.

Mougayar, William. 2016. *The Business Blockchain: Promise, Practice, and Application of the Next Internet Technology*. Hoboken, NJ: John Wiley & Sons.

Mowery, David C., Richard R. Nelson, Bhaven N. Sampat, and Arvids A. Ziedonis. 2015. *Ivory Tower and Industrial Innovation: University-Industry Technology Transfer before and after the Bayh-Dole Act*. Palo Alto, CA: Stanford University Press.

Mowery, David C., and Nathan Rosenberg. 1991. *Technology and the Pursuit of Economic Growth*. New York: Cambridge University Press.

Murmann, Johann Peter. 2003. *Knowledge and Competitive Advantage: The Coevolution of Firms, Technology, and National Institutions*. New York: Cambridge University Press.

Murphy, Kevin M., Andrei Shleifer, and Robert W. Vishny. 1991. "The Allocation of Talent: Implications for Growth." *Quarterly Journal of Economics* 106 (2): 503–530.

Murray, Fiona, et al. 2012. "Grand Innovation Prizes: A Theoretical, Normative, and Empirical Evaluation." *Research Policy* 41 (10): 1779–1792.

Musselin, Christine. 2013. *The Long March of French Universities*. London: Routledge.

Musson, A. E., and Eric Robinson. 1969. *Science and Technology in the Industrial Revolution*. Manchester: University Press.

Narayanan, Arvind, and Vitaly Shmatikov. 2008. "Robust De-Anonymization of Large Sparse Datasets." Security and Privacy, IEEE Symposium.

National Academy of Sciences. 1895. *Proceedings of the National Academy of Sciences: 1863–94*. Washington, DC: National Academies Press.

National Economic Council. 2009. "A Strategy for American Innovation." Washington, DC.

National Research Council. 2007. *Innovation Inducement Prizes at the National Science Foundation*. Washington DC: National Academies Press.

National Research Council, Committee on the Design of an NSF Innovation Prize. 2007. *Innovation Inducement Prizes at the National Science Foundation*. Washington, DC: National Academies Press.

Nef, John U. 1950. *War and Human Progress: An Essay on the Rise of Industrial Civilization*. London: Routledge and Kegan Paul.

Nicholas, Tom. 2010. "The Role of Independent Invention in US Technological Development, 1880–1930." *Journal of Economic History* 70 (1): 57–82.

Nicholas, Tom. 2011. "Did R&D Firms Used to Patent? Evidence from the First Innovation Surveys." *Journal of Economic History* 71 (4): 1032–1059.

Nicholas, Tom. 2013. "Hybrid Innovation in Meiji, Japan." *International Economic Review* 54 (2): 575–600.

Niépce, Isidore, and Joseph-Nicéphore Niépce. 1841. *Historique de la découverte improprement nommée daguerréotype: précédé d'une notice sur son véritable inventeur Joseph-Nicéphore Niépce, par son fils*. Paris: Astier Librairie.

Nishimura, Shigehiro. 2011. "International Patent Control and Transfer of Knowledge: The United States and Japan before World War II." *Business & Economic History* Online 9.

North, Douglass C., and Robert Paul Thomas. 1973. *The Rise of the Western World: A New Economic History*. New York: Cambridge University Press.

Nuvolari, Alessandro. 2002. "Collective Invention during the British Industrial Revolution: The Case of the Cornish Pumping Engine." *Cambridge Journal of Economics* 28 (3): 347–363.

Nuvolari, Alessandro. 2006. "The Making of Steam Power Technology: A Study of Technical Change during the British Industrial Revolution." *Journal of Economic History* 66 (2): 472–476.

Ó Gráda, Cormac. 2016. "Did Science Cause the Industrial Revolution?" *Journal of Economic Literature* 54 (1): 224–239.

Office of Science and Technology Policy. 2012. "Implementation of Federal Prize Authority." Washington, DC: GPO.

Olmstead, Alan L., and Paul W. Rhode. 2008. *Creating Abundance*. New York: Cambridge University Press.

O'Neill, John J. 1944. *Prodigal Genius: The Life of Nikola Tesla*. New York: Ives Washburn.

Owen, Nancy Elizabeth. 2001. *Rookwood and the Industry of Art: Women, Culture, and Commerce, 1880–1913*. Athens, OH: Ohio University Press.

Parente, Stephen L., and Edward C. Prescott. 2002. *Barriers to Riches*. Cambridge, MA: MIT Press.

Parker, Harold T. 1965. "Two Administrative Bureaus under the Directory and Napoleon." *French Historical Studies* 4 (2): 150–169.

Parker, Geoffrey. 1995. *The Military Revolution: Military Innovation and the Rise of the West, 1500–1800*. Cambridge: Cambridge University Press.

Parkinson, Russell J. 1963. "Politics, Patents and Planes: Military Aeronautics in the United States, 1863–1907." PhD dissertation, Duke University.

Paskins, Matthew. 2014. "Sentimental Industry: The Society of Arts and the Encouragement of Public Useful Knowledge, 1754–1848." PhD dissertation, University College London.

Pei, Minxin. 2016. *China's Crony Capitalism*. Cambridge, MA: Harvard University Press.

Penrose, Edith Tilton. 1951. *The Economics of the International Patent System*. Baltimore, MD: Johns Hopkins University Press.

Perpigna, A. 1852. *The French Law and Practice of Patents for Inventions, Improvements, and Importations*. Paris and London: Perpigna.

Persson, Karl Gunnar, and Paul Sharp. 2015. *An Economic History of Europe*. Cambridge: Cambridge University Press.

Plattes, Gabriel. 1744, reprint of 1641. "A Description of the Famous Kingdome of Macaria." In *The Harleian Miscellany*. London: Osborne.

Popper, Karl R. 2013. *The Open Society and Its Enemies*. Princeton, NJ: Princeton University Press.

Postrel, Virginia I. 2004. *The Substance of Style: How the Rise of Aesthetic Value Is Remaking Commerce, Culture, and Consciousness*. New York: Perennial.

Raj, Kapil. 2007. *Relocating Modern Science: Circulation and the Construction of Knowledge in South Asia and Europe, 1650–1900*. New York: Springer.

Reese, Byron. 2013. *Infinite Progress: How the Internet and Technology Will End Ignorance, Disease, Poverty, Hunger, and War*. Austin, TX: Greenleaf Book Group.

Reichard, Heinrich August Ottokar. 1827. *Guide classique du voyageur en France, dans les Pays-Bas et en Holland*. Paris: Chez Audin.

Reiser, Stanley Joel. 1981. *Medicine and the Reign of Technology*. Cambridge: Cambridge University Press.

Renouard, Augustin. 1843. *Examen du projet de loi relatif aux brevets d'invention*. Paris: Journal des Économistes.

Rice, Stephen P. 2004. *Minding the Machine: Languages of Class in Early Industrial America*. Berkeley: University of California Press.

Richardson, James. 1878. "Our Patent System and What We Owe to It." *Scribner's Monthly*, November.

Richter, Ralf, and Jochen Streb. 2011. "Catching-Up and Falling Behind: Knowledge Spillover from American to German Machine Toolmakers." *Journal of Economic History* 71 (4): 1006–1031.

Roberts, William H. 2003. *Civil War Ironclads: The US Navy and Industrial Mobilization*. Baltimore: JHU Press.

Romer, Paul M. 1990. "Endogenous Technological Change." *Journal of Political Economy* 98 (5): S71–S102.

Romer, Paul M. 1992. "Two Strategies for Economic Development: Using Ideas and Producing Ideas." *World Bank Economic Review* 6 (1): 63–91.

Romer, Paul M. 1994. "The Origins of Endogenous Growth." *Journal of Economic Perspectives* 8 (1): 3–22.

Rosanvallon, Pierre. 2004. *Le modèle politique français. La société civile contre le jacobinisme de 1789 à nos jours*. Paris: Seuil.

Rose-Ackerman, Susan, and Bonnie J. Palifka. 2016. *Corruption and Government: Causes, Consequences, and Reform*. New York: Cambridge University Press.

Rosenberg, Nathan. 1974. "Science, Invention and Economic Growth." *Economic Journal* 84 (333): 90–108.

Rosenthal, Jean-Laurent, and Roy Bin Wong. 2011. *Before and beyond Divergence*. Cambridge, MA: Harvard University Press.

Rostow, Walt W. 1960. *The Stages of Growth: A Non-Communist Manifesto*. Cambridge: Cambridge University Press.

Royal Society for the Encouragement of Arts, Manufactures, and Commerce. Various years. *Transactions of the Society*. London: RSA.

Ruttan, Vernon W. 2006. *Is War Necessary for Economic Growth?: Military Procurement and Technology Development*. New York: Oxford University Press.

Sampat, Bhaven N. 2006. "Patenting and US Academic Research in the 20th Century: The World before and after Bayh-Dole." *Research Policy* 35 (6): 772–789.

Sanderson, Michael. 1999. *Education and Economic Decline in Britain, 1870 to the 1990s*. Cambridge: Cambridge University Press.

Savaton, Pierre. 2007. "The First Detailed Geological Maps of France: Contributions of Local Scientists and Mining Engineers." *Earth Sciences History* 26 (1): 55–73.

Schumpeter, Joseph A. 2010. *Capitalism, Socialism and Democracy*. Routledge.

Scotchmer, Suzanne. 2004. *Innovation and Incentives*. Cambridge, MA: MIT Press.

Shinn, Terry. 1992. "Science, Tocqueville, and the State: The Organization of Knowledge in Modern France." *Social Research* 59 (2): 533–566.

Shirley, Mary M. et al. 1995. *Bureaucrats in Business: The Economics and Politics of Government Ownership*. Vol. 4. Washington, DC: World Bank Publications.

Sidney, Samuel. 1862. "On the Effect of Prizes on Manufacturers." *Journal of the Society of Arts* 10 (492): 369–384.

Sinclair, Bruce. 1974. *Philadelphia's Philosopher Mechanics: A History of the Franklin Institute 1824–1865*. Baltimore: Johns Hopkins University Press.

Smith, Adam. 1976. *An Inquiry into the Nature and Causes of the Wealth of Nations*. Chicago: University of Chicago Press.

Smith, Adam. 1982. *Lectures on Jurisprudence*. Indianapolis: Liberty Fund.

Smith, Adam. 1902. "Colonial Policy." Reprinted in *The Ideas That Have Influenced Civilization, in the Original Documents*, vol. 7, edited by Oliver Joseph Thatcher. Milwaukee, WI: Roberts-Manchester Publishing Company.

Smith, David Kammerling. 2002. "Structuring Politics in Early Eighteenth-Century France: The Political Innovations of the French Council of Commerce." *Journal of Modern History* 74 (3): 490–537.

Smith, Henry E. 2008. "Mind the Gap: The Indirect Relation between Ends and Means in American Property Law." *Cornell Law Review* 94: 959.

Smith, Merritt Roe. 1985. "Army Ordnance and the 'American System' of Manufacturing, 1815–1861." In *Military Enterprise and Technological Change*, edited by Merritt Roe Smith, 40–68. Cambridge, MA: MIT Press.

Sobel, Dava. 1995. *Longitude: The True Story of a Lone Genius Who Solved the Greatest Scientific Problem of His Time*. New York: Walker.

Sokoloff, Kenneth L. 1988. "Inventive Activity in Early Industrial America: Evidence from Patent Records, 1790–1846." *Journal of Economic History* 48 (4): 813–850.

Sokoloff, Kenneth L., and B. Zorina Khan. 1990. "The Democratization of Invention during Early Industrialization: Evidence from the United States, 1790–1846." *Journal of Economic History* 50 (2): 363–378.

Solow, Robert M. 1994. "Perspectives on Growth Theory." *Journal of Economic Perspectives* 8 (1): 45–54.

Soltow, Lee. 1975. *Men and Wealth in the United States, 1850–1870*. New Haven, CT: Yale University Press.

Southard, Frank Allen. 1931. *American Industry in Europe*. Boston: Houghton Mifflin.

Spulber, Daniel F. 1989. *Regulation and Markets*. Cambridge, MA: MIT Press.

Spulber, Daniel F. 2013. "How Do Competitive Pressures Affect Incentives to Innovate When There Is a Market for Inventions?" *Journal of Political Economy* 121 (6): 1007–1054.

Spulber, Daniel F. 2014. *The Innovative Entrepreneur*. New York: Cambridge University Press.

Squicciarini, Mara P., and Nico Voigtländer. 2015. "Human Capital and Industrialization: Evidence from the Age of Enlightenment." *Quarterly Journal of Economics* 130 (4): 1825–1883.

Standage, Tom. 1998. *The Victorian Internet: The Remarkable Story of the Telegraph and the Nineteenth Century's Online Pioneers*. London: Weidenfeld & Nicolson.

Steen, Kathryn. 2001. "Patents, Patriotism, and 'Skilled in the Art' USA v. The Chemical Foundation, Inc., 1923–1926." *Isis* 92 (1): 91–122.

Stigler, George Joseph. 1994. *Production and Distribution Theories*. Piscataway, NJ: Transaction Publishers.

Stimson, Dorothy. 1948. *Scientists and Amateurs: A History of the Royal Society*. New York: H. Schuman.

Stromseth, Jonathan R., Edmund J. Malesky, and Dimitar D. Gueorguiev. 2017. *China's Governance Puzzle: Enabling Transparency and Participation in a Single-Party State*. New York: Cambridge University Press.

Sunstein, Cass R. 1987. "Constitutionalism after the New Deal." *Harvard Law Review* 101: 421–510.

Swanson, Kara W. 2009. "The Emergence of the Professional Patent Practitioner." *Technology and Culture* 50 (3): 519–548.

Taylor, Etta. 1893. *A Practical Business Guide for American Women of All Conditions and Ages, Who Want to Make Money, but Do Not Know How*. Minneapolis: EM Taylor.

Terrell, Thomas, and William Peter Rylands. 1895. *The Law and Practice Relating to Letters Patent for Inventions*. London: Sweet & Maxwell.

Thaler, Richard H., and Cass R. Sunstein. 2008. *Nudge. The Politics of Libertarian Paternalism*. New Haven, CT: Yale University Press.

Thompson, W. P. 1920. *Handbook of Patent Law of All Countries*. London: Stevens & Sons.

Thurston, Robert Henry. 1876. *Reports of the Commissioners of the United States to the International Exhibition held at Vienna, 1873*. Vol. 1. Washington, DC: U.S. Government Printing Office.

Tirole, Jean. 2017. *Economics for the Common Good*. Princeton, NJ: Princeton University Press.

Tocqueville, Alexis. 1864. *De la démocratie en Amérique, tome II, Oeuvres completes*. Paris: Michel Lévy.

Trajtenberg, Manuel. 1990. "A Penny for Your Quotes: Patent Citations and the Value of Innovations." *Rand Journal of Economics* 21 (1): 172–187.

Trescott, Paul B. 1958. "The Louisville and Portland Canal Company, 1825–1874." *Mississippi Valley Historical Review* 44 (4): 686–708.

Trumbull, Gunnar. 2004. *Silicon and the State: French Innovation Policy in the Internet Age.* Washington, DC: Brookings Institution Press.

Tversky, Amos, and Eldar Shafir. 1992. "Choice under Conflict: The Dynamics of Deferred Decision." *Psychological Science* 3 (6): 358–361.

Twain, Mark. 1889. *A Connecticut Yankee in King Arthur's Court.* New York: Harper & Brothers.

United States. 1877. *Report of the United States Centennial Commission.* Philadelphia: J. B. Lippincott.

U.S. Bureau of the Census. 1975. *Historical Statistics of the United States, Colonial Times to 1970.* Washington, DC: U.S. Government Printing Office.

U.S. Congress. 1880. *Reports of Committees, Report No. 622 of the Committee of Patents,* 48th Congress, 2nd Session of the Senate, May 17. Washington, DC: U.S. Government Printing Office.

U.S. Congress. 1919. *War Expenditures: Aviation.* Pts. 1–44 in 4 vols. Washington, DC: U.S. Government Printing Office.

U.S. Congress. 1912. *Report on Schedule A: Chemicals, Oils, and Paints,* H.R. No. 326, 62nd Congress 2nd Session. Washington, DC: U.S. Government Printing Office.

U.S. Office of Education. 1921. *Statistics of Land Grant Colleges and Universities.* Issue 88. Washington, DC: U.S. Government Printing Office.

U.S. Patent Office. Various years. *Annual Report of the Commissioner of Patents.* Washington, DC: U.S. Government Printing Office.

Vanriest, Elise. 2015. *Verre et verriers à Paris dans la seconde moitié du XVIe siècle, 1547–1610.* Thesis, Sorbonne, Paris.

Vojáček, J. 1936. *A Survey of the Principal National Patent Systems.* New York: Prentice-Hall.

Wadsworth, Alfred P., and Julia de Lacy Mann. 1965. *The Cotton Trade and Industrial Lancashire, 1600–1780.* Manchester: Manchester University Press.

Wajcman, Judy. 2000. "Reflections on Gender and Technology Studies: In What State Is the Art?" *Social Studies of Science* 30 (3): 447–464.

Wallsten, Scott J. 2000. "The Effects of Government-Industry R&D Programs on Private R&D." *RAND Journal of Economics* 31 (1): 82–100.

Warner, Deborah J. 1979. "Women Inventors at the Centennial." In *Dynamos and Virgins Revisited: Women and Technological Change In History,* edited by Martha Moore Trescott, 102–119. Metuchen, NJ: Scarecrow Press.

Washington, H. A. 1853–1854. *The Writings of Thomas Jefferson, VI.* Washington, DC: Government Printing Office.

Weber, Max. 1978. *Max Weber on Law in Economy and Society (20th Century Legal Philosophy Series).* Berkeley: University of California Press.

Weimann, Jeanne Madeline. 1981. *The Fair Women.* Chicago: Academy Chicago.

Wilkins, Mira. 1974. "The Role of Private Business in the International Diffusion of Technology." *Journal of Economic History* 34 (1): 166–188.

Wilkins, Mira. 1988. "European and North American Multinationals, 1870–1914: Comparisons and Contrasts." *Business History* 30 (1): 8–45.

Wilson, Mark. 2006. *The Business of Civil War: Military Mobilization and the State, 1861–1865.* Baltimore: JHU Press.

Wood, Henry Trueman. 1912. "The Royal Society of Arts VI.—The Premiums. (1754–1851)." *Journal of the Royal Society of Arts* 60 (3088): 263–274.

Wood, Henry Trueman. 1913. *A History of the Royal Society of Arts*. London: J. Murray.

Wood, R. Derek. 1980. "The Daguerreotype Patent, the British Government, and the Royal Society." *History of Photography* 4 (1): 53–59.

Wright, Brian D. 1983. "The Economics of Invention Incentives: Patents, Prizes, and Research Contracts." *American Economic Review* 73 (4): 691–707.

Xie, Yu, Chunni Zhang, and Qing Lai. 2014. "China's Rise as a Major Contributor to Science and Technology." *PNAS* 111 (26): 9437–9442.

Zhu, X. 2012. "Understanding China's Growth: Past, Present, and Future." *Journal of Economic Perspectives* 26 (4): 103–124.

Zipf, Catherine W. 2007. *Professional Pursuits: Women and the American Arts and Crafts Movement*. Knoxville, TN: University of Tennessee Press.

Zuckerman, Harriet. 1967. "Nobel Laureates in Science: Patterns of Productivity, Collaboration, and Authorship." *American Sociological Review* 32 (3): 391–403.

No author identified

1853. "Récompense nationale accordée aux héritiers de Philippe de Girard, inventeur de la filature mécanique du lin." *Le Génie industriel* 5: 297–298.

1856. *Rapport sur l'exposition universelle de 1855 présenté à l'Empereur*. Paris: Imprimerie Impériale.

1861. "Medical Patents and Our National Code of Ethics." *Boston Medical and Surgical Journal* 63: 145–147.

1871. "War Office, Rewards to Inventors." *Hansard's Parliamentary Papers*, July 10: 1321–1332.

1885. "Awards at Exhibitions." *Electrical Review*, August 22, p. 172.

1886. "Women Inventors." *Woman's Journal*, December 4.

1887. "Report of the Exhibition." *The Repository* 51.

1897. "Maria E. Beasley." *North American*, February 13, p. 8.

1924. "Broadcasting Suit One of Patents: Battle of the Air Developing a Mass of Litigation Which May Bring Congressional Legislation." *Wall Street Journal*, March 12.

Index

Printed in Great Britain
by Amazon

59909454R00273